DevelopMentor Series Page

Servlets and JavaServer Pages™

The J2EE™ Technology Web Tier

Jayson Falkner
Kevin Jones

✦✦ Addison-Wesley

Boston • San Francisco • New York • Toronto • Montreal
London • Munich • Paris • Madrid
Capetown • Sydney • Tokyo • Singapore • Mexico City

Many of the designations used by manufacturers and sellers to distinguish their products are claimed as trademarks. Where those designations appear in this book, and Addison-Wesley was aware of a trademark claim, the designations have been printed with initial capital letters or in all capitals.

The authors and publisher have taken care in the preparation of this book, but make no expressed or implied warranty of any kind and assume no responsibility for errors or omissions. No liability is assumed for incidental or consequential damages in connection with or arising out of the use of the information or programs contained herein.

The publisher offers discounts on this book when ordered in quantity for bulk purchases and special sales. For more information, please contact:

U.S. Corporate and Government Sales
(800) 382-3419
corpsales@pearsontechgroup.com

For sales outside of the U.S., please contact:

International Sales
(317) 581-3793
international@pearsontechgroup.com

Visit Addison-Wesley on the Web: www.awprofessional.com

Library of Congress Cataloging-in-Publication Data
Falkner, Jayson.
    JAVA Servlets and JavaServer pages: the J2EE technology Web tier/Jason Falkner,
Kevin James
        p. cm.
    ISBN 0-321-13649-7 (alk. paper)
    1. Java (Computer program language) 2. Servlets. 3. JavaServer pages. I. Jones, Kevin.
II. Title.

QA76.73.J3F355   2003
005.13'3—dc21   2003052156

Pearson Education, Inc.
Rights and Contracts Department
75 Arlington Street, Suite 300
Boston, MA 02116
Fax: (617) 848-7047

ISBN 0-321-13649-7
Text printed on recycled paper
1 2 3 4 5 6 7 8 9 10—CRS—0706050403
First printing, September 2003

*Thanks to Teresa, Harry, Sam, and Alex. Without you
I couldn't do what I do.
—Kevin Jones*

*To James and Joleen Falkner. Your support has produced yet
another sizable piece of gibberish. Words fail to express
how thankful I am for your love.
—Jayson Falkner*

Contents

Preface

The goal of this preface is to briefly but accurately introduce this book and its content. The preface is broken into four main parts: about the authors, an overview of the book's content, a list of the conventions used throughout the book, and an explanation of the book's cover. All parts are relevant to the book; however, not all parts may be of personal interest to you. It is suggested at least the first two sections be read because they explain who wrote this book and what the book is about. The last two sections are not helpful unless you decide to read any portion of the book.

About the Authors

Two authors collaborated on this book: Jayson Falkner and Kevin Jones. Both Jayson and Kevin are well-known developers in the JavaServer Pages (JSP) and Servlets communities, and both authors have worked extensively with the technologies. *Servlets and JavaServer Pages*™: *The J2EE*™ *Technology Web Tier* originally started as Jayson's project; however, during the JavaOne 2002 conference the two authors met. It turns out Kevin was thinking of working on a similar title, and the two decided to collaborate.

Jayson Falkner

Jayson is a J2EE developer from the United States. He started developing with J2EE just before JSP 1.1 and Servlets 2.2 were released and has been focusing on the technologies since. Jayson is best known as the Webmaster of JSP Insider, `http://www.jspinsider.com`, and for asking far too many questions in the popular Servlet and JSP forums. Jayson has worked on numerous JSP titles and is constantly present at the popular Java conferences. Jayson participated on the JSR 152 expert group, JSP 2.0, and helped with the Tomcat 5 reference implementation.

Jayson prefers to think of himself as a tax-dodging student, who is currently working on a Ph.D. in bioinformatics at the University of Michigan; however, he also works professionally as a J2EE consult with Amberjack Software LLC. Open-source software and free Java development are Jayson's specialties. You can thank (or complain) to Jayson for dictating the use of Mozilla and Tomcat with this book.

You can get in touch with Jayson by sending an email to `jayson@jspinsider.com`.

Kevin Jones

Kevin is a longtime Java developer and educator, and has been involved in the training industry for the last twelve years. For the last eight years Kevin has been involved in writing and delivering Java training and consulting on various Java projects, and for the last four years has concentrated on J2EE and specifically Web technologies.

Kevin spoke at JavaOne in 2000 and was invited to become a member of JSR 53, the "Java Servlet 2.3 and JavaServer Pages 1.2 Specifications" and also JSR 52 "A Standard Tag Library for JavaServer Pages". Since then Kevin has successfully spoken at JavaOne in 2001 and 2002 as well as participating in JSR 154 (Servlets 2.4) and, like Jayson, in JSR 152.

Kevin is responsible for the Java curriculum at DevelopMentor, where he teaches the Essential Java Web Development class that covers much of the material in this book, as well as many other Java classes.

You can reach Kevin at `kevinj@develop.com` or through his Web site at `http://kevinj.develop.com`

How the Book Is Organized

In this book you will find a few, hopefully delightful, things. The book is a complete guide to Servlets and JavaServer Pages and their practical use for developers familiar with HTML and basic Java. If you are unfamiliar with the terms *Servlets* and *JavaServer Pages*, think of this book as a complete guide to building dynamic, Java-based Web sites. It is assumed you understand Java and HTML. Never does the book attempt to test these two skills; however, code examples in this book do not include explanations of fundamental Java concepts and HTML syntax.

Before introducing the book's content, there are a few points worth mentioning in relation to competing technologies, especially since you are likely standing next to several books about building Web sites using the plethora of other "superior" technologies. At all times this book follows the open-source mindset—that is, software you need is free and you get all the source-code. It will cost you or your development team absolutely nothing to get and use *all* the software demonstrated, both directly and indirectly. In comparison to the primary competitor of Servlets and JSP, Microsoft's .NET and Microsoft's ASP .NET, you will have no software costs, no licensing costs, and the freedom to choose any operating system that supports Java, such as Linux, Windows, OSX, and Solaris. Compared to other open-source solutions, namely PHP or Perl, this book offers a truly robust solution to developing Web applications. You will get everything you need, including built-in security, portability, and a Web server. A Servlet and JSP-based Web application does not need an additional Web server, such as IIS or Apache, installed to serve up Web pages and provide encryption for secure connections. Additionally, Servlet and JSP-based code, even code for multiple Web sites being run on the same server, can literally be packaged up into one big file and moved between a development environment and a production environment, even if the two places are using different operating systems—you can not do this with technologies such as PHP or Perl. Additionally, Servlets and JSP are an official part of J2EE, Java's solution to the hardest problems of application programming. If you plan on programming the largest and most complex of Web applications (including multi-server projects), this book still provides relevant code—surely a bonus compared to other popular, open-source technologies that are not meant for large Web applications.

The table of contents provides a complete list of the book's contents, but the titles of most chapters are meaningless to a new user of Servlets and JavaServer Pages. Here is a complete description of the book's content, divided by chapters, explaining why the chapter is in this book:

- **Setting Up a Servlet and JSP Environment (Chapter 1):** Before jumping straight to the technologies, you need to have two things: knowledge of why Servlets and JSP are important and a development environment (for Windows, Linux or OS X) for using Servlets and JSP. These two topics are covered completely in Chapter 1. While the content may not be something you will ever reference again in the future, it is a required introduction for new Servlet and JSP users.

- **Java Servlets (Chapters 2)** and **JavaServer Pages (Chapter 3):** Chapters 2 and 3 provide detailed coverage of Servlets and JavaServer Pages. The chapters are not the most exciting of the book, but the material is needed as groundwork for the later chapters.

- **Exception Handling (Chapter 4):** Web sites built using Servlets and JavaServer Pages provide specialized methods of handling exceptions. The mechanism is required in order to appropriately show a user-friendly error page when something goes wrong. Chapter 4 explains how Servlets and JSP extend the standard Java exception-handling scheme. Since error handling is not commonly a well-understood feature of Java, this chapter does not assume fluent use of Java's *try-catch-finally* statement.

- **JavaBeans and the JSP Expression Language (Chapter 5):** The term "JavaBean" is used to mean many things in the Java world. As applied to Servlets and JSP, JavaBeans are little more than a fancy name for a simple Java class; however, the ambiguity of the term combined with its popular use merits a complete discussion about JavaBeans. Complementing this discussion is an introduction to the JSP expression language (new in JSP 2.0). The JSP expression language can greatly simplify the task JavaBeans were previously used for. Chapter 5 provides a complete discussion of the new JSP EL, and a discussion on good programming practices using both the JSP EL and JavaBeans.

- **JavaServer Pages Standard Tag Library (Chapter 6)** and **Custom Tag Libraries (Chapter 7):** Custom Tags is a popular feature of JavaServer Pages that allow static text, such as HTML-like tags, to be linked with Java classes. The functionality is at the center of several popular JSP programming techniques, since it allows for a developer to easily abstract code from pages designed to display HTML. Understanding and using JSP custom tags is a skill every JSP developer should have. Chapter 6 covers the standard set of custom tags, and Chapter 7 is dedicated to explaining the mechanism of creating and using new custom tags.

- **Filters (Chapter 8):** A Filter is something that a developer can use to cleanly intercept and modify requests and responses. The functionality works well for caching and security reasons; however, it is also conceptually a key part to building a good Web application. Chapter 8 explains Filters and provides several examples of how Filters are popularly used.

- **Managing State in a Web Application (Chapter 9):** The vast majority of the World Wide Web relies on stateless protocols—that is, communicating with one user twice is by default indistinguishable from communicating with two users once. However, most every Web site relies on being able to keep track of who is receiving information. Chapter 9 details both the problem and common solutions. Servlets and JavaServer Pages provide a seamless solution to keeping state with a user, but it is very important as a Web developer that you understand how the problem is solved. Without such knowledge you may encounter unpredictable results from even a simple Web application.

- **Security (Chapter 10):** Security is an all-important topic for an obvious reason: if information communicated via the Internet needs to be confidential something needs to guarantee confidentiality. The task of providing security is always in check by the persistence of people trying to break security. Servlets and JSP provide a relatively simple method of using up-to-date security mechanisms. Chapter 10 details how security works, how Servlets and JSP implements security, and how to configure a secure Web site.

- **Design Patterns (Chapter 11), Internationalization (Chapter 12),** and **Multi-Client Support (Chapter 13):** Understanding how technology works does not mean one knows how to best use the technology. Complimenting the earlier chapters of the book, several popular tricks, techniques, and all-around good programming practices are explained in the last part of the book. This information is exactly the type of information a developer needs, assuming one understands the technology, and exactly the type of information omitted from books that only detail a technology. Chapter 11, Chapter 12, and Chapter 13 all explain popular approaches to using Servlets and JSP to solve real world problems.

- **Database Connectivity (Chapter 14):** A database is almost always at the center of a Web site, for good reason; however, the topic of databases merits a full book. As a developer you will benefit from understanding the basic theories of databases and how a database can be used with Servlets and JSP. Chapter 14 provides a crash course to basic use of a database and a detailed discussion of using a database with Servlets and JSP. In practice Chapter 14 is no replacement for a good book on your favorite database, but Chapter 14 will enable you to create and use a database from scratch.

- **Building a Complete Web Application (Chapter 15):** Ending the book is one grand look at everything covered and a discussion on how all the previous chapters are to be used in practice. How better to accomplish this then by building a real Web application?

Chapter 15 uses all of the previous chapters to construct a book support site for this book, the same Web application seen online http://www.jspbook.com. The task is not difficult because it is little more than a rehash of the concepts covered in this book and recycling snippets of code, but the chapter nicely concludes the book and really proves you can build a good Web application based on the content of this manuscript.

You can do much with Servlets and JSP, and this book attempts to cover it all. If you read through the whole text you will be fluent with the technologies and able to take full advantage of them. Every chapter does rely on previous chapters. Concepts and buzzwords are explained fully only once in the book, in what is thought the appropriate place, and you are expected to read completely from the start to the end.

The Book Support Web Site

Servlets and JavaServer™ Pages: The J2EE™ Technology Web Tier is not a perfect book, nor is everything the book covers best put in text. In a best attempt effort at ensuring the book is top quality, even after publication, a book support site is maintained at http://www.jspbook.com. At the book support site you will find numerous things including current updates, FAQ, news about the book, working code examples, references, and a method to reach the authors. This book support site is not the standard publisher-supported site (and Addison-Wesley's site is quite nice), but it is something created and supported completely by the authors. You are encouraged to use the book support site as a place to aid your reading of the book and communicate with the authors.

Conventions Used in the Book

For clarity, a few arbitrary conventions are followed by this book. As authors our goal is to try and convey our thoughts and experiences clearly. Where possible we attempt to follow standardized or de-facto coding methods and writing techniques. In cases where we have to make up a method of conveying information it needs to be clear that we are doing just that. Documented here are all of the arbitrarily official standards that are used in this book.

InTextCode Style

When dealing with technical information there are times when terms are ambiguous. One word in English might be spelled and pronounced exactly the same in code but refer to a completely different meaning. In cases where a literal name or value of a technical term is used, it will always appear in the `InTextCode` style. This style signifies that the word is a direct reference to a file, variable name, Object type, or any other specific code reference.

Foo

Throughout the book there are many examples of code. These examples are all thoroughly tested and are functional illustrations of a point at hand. For the most part code is always intended to be helpful. However, sometimes an example relies on having a particular situation or circumstance occur to be meaningful. In these cases a slightly contrived bit of code might be required to illustrate what the important example is doing. In these cases the contrived code is not meant to be helpful beyond educational purposes. In order to distinguish clearly between what code is slightly contrived and what code is actually helpful a convention is used to flag purely educational code. Whenever the `foo` keyword appears in code, you should be suspect of its practical use. Some examples of places where `foo` appears include `com.jspbook.foo` package and code that is named with `foo` appearing in the title. In the case of the `com.jspbook.foo` package the `foo` keyword means code in this package is not too helpful on its own. Instead, `com.jspbook.foo` classes are usually built to directly complement a helpful class appearing in the `com.jspbook` package. When the `foo` keyword appears in the title of code, perhaps a JSP named `Foo.jsp`, it signals the whole page is slightly contrived. Be conscious of occurrences of the `foo` keyword and do not focus on them but rather the point they illustrate.

Mozilla and Tomcat

For consistency two primary pieces of software, Mozilla and Tomcat, are used throughout the book and will be indirectly visual in examples. As further explained later, all JSP and Servlets rely on a main piece of software called a container. The reference container for JSP is Tomcat, `http://jakarta.apache.org/tomcat`. All code in this book is tested against Tomcat, and many screenshots show common behavior of the container. Be aware that Tomcat is the specific container in all of these cases, and different containers might have slightly different results. This warning does not imply that the code would not work in other containers; code should seamlessly work on any JSP 2.0 and Servlet 2.4 container. The mention is solely to prevent possible confusion that might arise from examples that give different styles of the same result when executed.

Mozilla is the very popular open-source Web browser that is built with an emphasis on compliance to Internet standards. The results of a JSP or Servlet are almost always intended for rendering by a Web browser. In almost every screenshot the Web browser is visible. This browser is Mozilla, http://www.mozilla.org, unless specifically mentioned otherwise. Mozilla was chosen because it is both a truly superb piece of software and because it behaves in a way that is to be expected by other Web browsers.

The Book's Cover

The cover of this book shows ¾ of a yard-gnome. A yard-gnome[1] is a ceramic gnome that is intended to decorate a yard. Gnomes themselves are fictitious creatures that have little if anything to do with yards. A question you might be asking is "What do yard-gnomes have to do with Servlets and JSP or the J2EE Web Tier?" The answer is absolutely nothing. The cover resulted from a style restriction we had to use for this book and a bad joke that has obviously eluded far too many people.

Yard-Gnomes on Holiday and Yard-Gnomes in France

Being that a yard-gnome does appear on the cover, two things are suggested of creative readers. Traditionally yard-gnomes are hidden in the background of pictures, particularly vacation pictures. Take a picture with this book hidden in the background and email it to the book support site. Your picture will be displayed unless it grossly violates the laws that govern common sense. Additionally, it is fun to note that in France there is a serious problem of gangs stealing yard-gnomes and returning them to "their natural habitat" or forested areas, particularly city parks. If you can think of some way to replicate this phenomena using the gnome on this book's cover, please send a picture via email to the book support site.

Special Thanks

There are a few people who helped directly with this book, and there are countless people who helped indirectly. To everyone who helped with this book: thanks!

---

1. Garden-gnome in the United Kingdom.

Special thanks to Ann Sellers and Shelley Kronzek, our editors at Addison-Wesley. You are both fantastic editors, and without you this book would never have been published. It was a pleasure working with you.

Also special thanks to Kenyon Brown, Patrick Cash-Peterson, and Tyrrell Albaugh, our production team at Addison-Wesley. Production sometimes seems to take forever; thanks to them, it didn't.

Special thanks to Eduardo Pelegri-Llopart and Mark Roth for leading the JSP 2.0 specification and for formalizing the ideas of the expert group and JSP community.

Special thanks to all of the members of the JSP and Servlet expert groups for all the hard work involved with Servlets 2.4 and JavaServer Pages 2.0.

Special thanks to all the Servlet and JSP developers who have helped the technologies grow and thrive. You are the inspiration for this book.

Special thanks to Casey Kochmer. Casey is a longtime friend of Jayson's, co-founder of JSP Insider, and one of the inspirations for this book. Without you, Casey, this book would never have been published.

Special thanks to the countless reviewers of this manuscript. We always had plenty of good advice from the reviewers. Thanks for helping make this a better book.

Special thanks to the instructors at DevelopMentor. This group of people constantly challenge the way I think about software and software development. Without them I would not be the person I am. In particular, thanks to Simon Horrell for constantly playing "devil's advocate" and forcing me to question all my assumptions.

Chapter 1

Setting Up a Servlet and JSP Environment

Before you start developing with Servlets and JavaServer Pages, you need to understand two very important things: Why is using the technology desirable, and what is needed in order to use the technology? This chapter answers these two questions, and in the process provides an introduction to the entire book. We start with an introduction to traditional Web development. The discussion describes why Servlets and JSP were initially created and why the technologies are currently popular. The end of the discussion segues to the software needed in order to run the book's examples.

It is preferred that you follow the instructions in this chapter to ensure your coding environment most closely matches the one all of the code examples of this book have been tested against. If you are using an already established Servlet/JSP environment, make sure it has support for JavaServer Pages 2.0, Servlets 2.4, and the Java 2 Standard Edition 1.4. Examples in this book require these technologies and some features covered are not backwards-compatible.

A Quick History of Web Development

The Servlet and JSP environment extends past the need for basic Java support. Any computer running JSP or Servlets needs to also have a *container*. A container is a piece of software responsible for loading, executing, and unloading the Servlets and JSP. The reasons for this are largely related to the history of server-side Web development. A quick overview of one of the earliest and most prominent server-side dynamic content solutions, CGI, and the differences between it and Servlets is very helpful in understanding why a JSP/Servlet container is required. The exact life cycle events that are managed by a container are discussed in Chapter 2.

CGI

The Common Gateway Interface, or CGI, is commonly referred to as one of the first practical technologies for creating dynamic server-side content. With CGI a server passes a client's request to an external program. This program executes, creates some content, and sends a response to the client. When first developed, this functionality was a vast improvement over static content and greatly expanded the functionality available to a Web developer. Needless to say CGI quickly grew in popularity and became a standard method for creating dynamic Web pages. However, CGI is not perfect.

CGI was originally designed to be a standard method for a Web server to communicate with external applications. An interesting point to note is that the functionality available for generating dynamic Web pages was really a side effect of this design goal. This largely explains why CGI has maybe the worst life cycle possible. As designed, each request to a CGI resource creates a new process on the server and passes information to the process via standard input and environment variables. Figure 1-1 provides a diagram of this single-phase CGI life cycle.

While it does work, the CGI life cycle is very taxing on server resources and greatly limits the number of concurrent CGI users a server can support. In case you are unfamiliar with operating systems and processes, a good analogy to use would be starting up and shutting down a Web server each time a user makes a request. As you probably know, this is almost never the case for a real Web server. It takes a noticeable amount of time to start and stop the entire process. A better solution is to start the server process once, handle all requests, and then

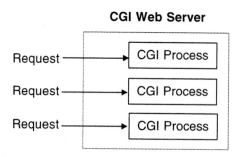

Figure 1-1 CGI Life Cycle

shut it down when there is no longer a need for a Web server. Starting and stopping a Web server is like the single-phase life cycle of CGI, and it was a very noticeable problem. CGI did not scale well and would often bring a Web server to a halt.

Even with poor performance by today's standards, CGI was a revolutionary step in the evolution of server-side programming. Developers had a cross platform method of creating dynamic content using most any of their favorite scripting and programming languages. This popularity sparked second-generation CGI implementations that attempted to counter the performance problems of original CGI, namely FastCGI. While the single phase life cycle still existed, CGI implementations improved efficiency by pooling resources for requests. This eliminated the need to create and destroy processes for every request and made CGI a much more practical solution. Figure 1-2 shows the improved implementation of CGI. Instead of one request per a process, a pool of processes is kept that continuously handle requests. If one process finishes handling a request, it is kept and used to manage the next incoming request rather than start a new process for each request.

This same pooling design can still be found in many of today's CGI implementations. Using pooling techniques, CGI is a viable solution for creating dynamic content with a Web server, but it is still not without problems. Most notable is the difficulty in sharing resources such as a common logging utility or server-side object between different requests. Solving these problems involves using creative fixes that work with the specific CGI and are custom-made for individual projects. For serious Web applications, a better solution, preferably one that addresses the problems of CGI, was required.

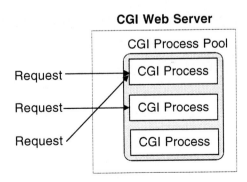

Figure 1-2 Pooled CGI Resources

Java Servlets

In the Java world, Servlets were designed to solve the problems of CGI and create robust server-side environments for Web developers. Similar to CGI, Servlets allow a request to be processed by a program and let the same program produce a dynamic response. Servlets additionally defined an efficient life cycle that included the possibility of using a single process for managing all requests. This eliminated the multi-process overhead of CGI and allowed for the main process to share resources between multiple Servlets and multiple requests. Figure 1-3 gives a diagram of a Web server with Servlet support.

The Servlet diagram is similar to that of second-generation CGI, but notice all the Servlets run from one main process, or a parent program. This is one of the keys to Servlet efficiency, and, as we will see later, the same efficiency is found with JSP. With an efficient design and Java's cross-platform support, Servlets solved the common complaints of CGI and quickly became a popular solution to dynamic server-side functionality. Servlets are still popular and are now also used as the foundation for other technologies such as JSP. Currently, Servlets and JSP combined make up the official "Web Tier" for the Java 2 Enterprise Edition, J2EE[1].

Containers

Servlet performance can be attributed directly to a Servlet *container*. A Servlet container, also called "container" or "JSP container", is the piece of software

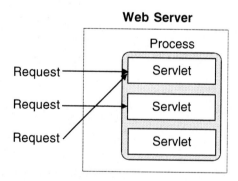

Figure 1-3 Servlet Web Server Diagram

---

1. This book's title, *The J2EE Technology Web Tier*, comes directly from the marketing jargon Sun uses. Logically, Web Tier means the code that interacts with the World Wide Web.

that manages the Servlet life cycle. Container software is responsible for interacting with a Web server to process a request and passing it to a Servlet for a response. The official definition of a container is described fully by both the JSP and Servlet specifications. Unlike most proprietary technologies, the JSP and Servlet specifications only define a standard for the functionality a container must implement. There is not one but many different implementations of Servlet and JSP containers from different vendors with different prices, performance, and features. This leaves a Servlet and JSP developer with many options for development software.

With containers in mind, the previous diagram of Servlets is better drawn using a container to represent the single process that creates, manages, and destroys threads running Servlets on a Web server. Note that this may or may not be a separate physical process. Figure 1-4 shows a Web server using a Servlet container.

Only Servlets are depicted in Figure 1-3, but in the next two chapters the Servlet and JSP life cycles are covered in detail, and it will be clear that a container manages JSP in exactly the same way as Servlets. For now it is safe to assume that Servlets and JSP are the same technology. What Figure 1-4 does not show is that in some cases a container also acts as the Web server rather than a module to an existing server. In these cases the Web server and container in Figure 1-3 are essentially the same thing.

Given you now know a little more about containers, it should be clear that a container must be installed to run Servlets and JSP. Examples in this book require a Servlet 2.4 and JSP 2.0-compatible container. If you do not have one, do not worry. A walk-through is provided later in this chapter, explaining how to obtain

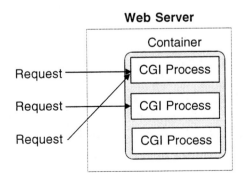

Figure 1-4 Container Process

the reference implementation JSP 2.0 and Servlet 2.4 container. If you have a previously installed container, make sure it supports the correct version of Servlets and JSP; older containers do not support some of the features of JSP 2.0 and Servlet 2.4 specifications. In this book specifically, all examples were created and tested using the reference implementation container, Tomcat. Version 5 of Tomcat is the reference implementation for both Servlets 2.4 and JSP 2.0. If you need to install a compatible container, take the time to now download and install Tomcat 5.

Getting Java Support

Servlets and JavaServer Pages, also meaning all containers, rely on the Java programming language. In the case of Servlets, the code is nothing more than a Java class that implements the appropriate interface(s). Compiling a Servlet is identical to compiling a Java class. JSP is slightly more abstract. JSP, is compiled and used exactly like a Servlet, but the process is almost always done automatically, without a JSP developer noticing. When authoring a JSP, a developer uses a combination of markup and code to make a page that usually resembles an HTML or XML document. This page is compiled into a class file by the Servlet container and automatically loaded.

The official Java platform is designed, owned, and managed by Sun Microsystems. Unlike most other programming languages, Java is not designed for you to compile to platform-specific instructions. Instead Java is compiled down to byte code that gets interpreted by the computer running your Java program. This means a Java program developed and compiled on one computer will run on any other computer with Java support; Servlets and JSP can be compiled and run on most any operating system. This includes most all the Windows, Linux, and Macintosh operating systems. This book assumes you are installing a JSP environment on one of these systems and instructions are provided for installation on each.

Downloading the Java 2 Standard Edition 1.4

Java 2 Standard Edition 1.4 (J2SE 1.4) support is required for code examples in this book. Sun Microsystems provides a free reference implementation of Java 1.4 online. Unless you are using Macintosh OS X, go to `http://java.sun.com/j2se/1.4/` and download the latest Java distribution for your computer. Macintosh OS X has proprietary support for Java 2. If you are running OS X, no additional downloads are needed.

Java only needs to be installed once on your computer and only for the specific operating system you are using. It is not required that you read all of the sections covering installation on all of the featured platforms. They exist only to give readers a guide to their specific operating system. Complete coverage of the Java 2 Standard Edition 1.4 is outside the scope of this book; however, later use of the J2SDK by this book will not require comprehensive knowledge of the tools provided by Sun. If you are looking for a detailed guide for this information, refer to *Thinking In Java, 3rd Edition*[2], by Bruce Eckel.

Installing J2SE 1.4 on Microsoft Windows

Microsoft Windows comes in many varieties, with early versions having a big distinction between a desktop computer and a computer designed to be a server. Practically speaking, a desktop computer running Windows 95 or Windows 98 is a not a good choice for installing a production environment for Servlets and JSP, but a Windows 95 or Windows 98 computer will suffice in order to try this book's examples. The Java distribution for Microsoft Windows will run on all versions of the operating system excluding Windows 3.x. In this book, the focus is on installing Java on a Windows NT, 2000, or XP computer. However, we realize that many readers have a desktop PC running Windows 95 or Windows 98 at home. An attempt will be made to help you if this is the case.

After downloading the J2SE 1.4, it must be installed on your system. The download should be an executable file that can be run by double-clicking it. Double-click on this file and follow the installation wizard through all the steps. It does not matter where you install the J2SE 1.4, but it is worth noting the location, as it is needed in a later part of this chapter.

Installation of the Java 2 Standard Development Kit 1.4 is now complete. Skip ahead to the section entitled, "Tomcat".

Installing J2SE 1.4 on Linux Distributions

Linux comes in far more varieties than Windows and operates on many more hardware architectures. A walk-through installation guide for all Linux distributions is not attempted, but this guide should work on the vast majority of distributions. Specifically this section gives a walk-through of installing the J2SE 1.4 on Red Hat Linux 7.3. It will greatly resemble installation on any Linux distribution for x86 processors, as an RPM is not used. If you downloaded the RPM or

---

2. A free copy of the book can be found online, http://www.mindview.net/Books/TIJ/.

equivalent for your distribution, feel free to install it, make note of the installation directory, and skip to the next section of this chapter.

At the introduction to this section, you should have downloaded the J2SE 1.4 Linux binary installation file. The file should be named something similar to `j2sdk-1_4_0_01-linux-i586.bin` with appropriate version numbers for the latest release. Any post-1.4 release should be adequate; this guide uses version 1.4.0_01. From the command prompt make sure the file has executable permissions and execute the program. These are what the commands would be to make the file executable and then execute it; assume the download is in the `/root/download` directory and you have proper permissions.

```
chmod +x /root/download/j2sdk-1_4_0_01-linux-i586.bin
/root/download/j2sdk-1_4_0_01-linux-i586.bin
```

When the file executes, Sun's licensing terms are displayed and you have the option of agreeing to continue the installation. Figure 1-5 shows an example display of the licensing terms.

If you agree to the terms, files will automatically be unpacked to a `j2sdk1.4.0` directory created by the installation program. You can move this directory to any location you prefer, but remember the location where the J2SDK 1.4 is because it will be needed later when the environment variables are set. Installation of the standard Java development kit is now complete.

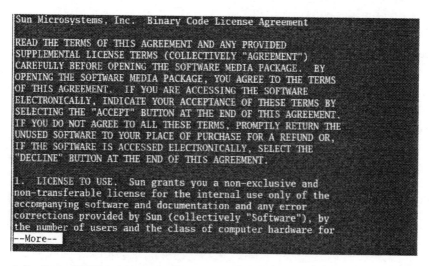

Figure 1-5 Sun's J2SDK 1.4 Licensing Terms

For Non-x86 Users: Compiling Java for Yourself

It is possible you are either an advanced user who dislikes non-optimized code or that you do not have an x86 microprocessor. Both of these cases are largely outside the scope of this book, but a quick pointer should get you well on your way if that is what you seek. The "official" Java Linux code is maintained at Blackdown Linux, `http://www.blackdown.org`. Visit Blackdown Linux if you need the source code to either optimize your Java distribution or compile it for a different architecture.

Tomcat

Tomcat, the reference implementation of Servlets and JSP, is part of the open source Apache Jakarta project and is freely available for download from `http://jakarta.apache.org/tomcat`[3]. Tomcat can be run on Windows, Linux, Macintosh, Solaris, and most any of the other Unix distributions. You can use Tomcat both commercially and non-commercially as specified by the Apache Software Foundation License.

The next few sections provide a walk-through for installing Tomcat on Windows, Linux distributions, and Macintosh OS X. If needed, follow the appropriate section to get Tomcat correctly set up for later examples.

Installing Jakarta Tomcat 5 on Windows

The Tomcat installation for Windows greatly resembles installing any other piece of Windows software. The process involves downloading the Tomcat installation executable file and running it to launch the Windows installation wizard. After a few simple clicks, the wizard will have set up Tomcat to work with your Windows distribution.

If you have not done so already, download the Windows executable file for the Tomcat installation. You can find it at the following URL, `http://jakarta.apache.org/builds/jakarta-tomcat/release/`. Simply follow the links to the latest Tomcat 5 Windows executable file—as of this writing, the 5.0.2 beta release of Tomcat is at `http://jakarta.apache.org/builds/jakarta-tomcat/release/v5.0.2-alpha/bin/jakarta-tomcat-5.0.2.exe`. After downloading the executable, double-click on it to start the installation wizard. A screen similar to

---

3. This part of the book is perhaps the most important. If for any reason you are having trouble installing Tomcat, please consult the book support site, http://www.jspbook.com, for a complete, up-to-date Tomcat 5 installation guide.

Figure 1-6 should appear notifying you that the Tomcat Installer located a J2SDK installation.

Click OK and continue on to the screen displaying the Apache Software Foundation license. Read through the terms and make sure you agree with Tomcat's licensing. If you accept the terms, the installation continues and you can choose what components you wish to install. The default ones should be fine, as shown in Figure 1-7.

Proceed with the installation wizard to the next screen, and you can choose a directory to install Tomcat. Figure 1-8 shows the corresponding installation wizard screen. Choose any directory you prefer.

After choosing an installation directory, the wizard will ask for some initial Tomcat configuration information, including a port number and administrative access information. The default options are fine, but later on in the chapter we will be changing the port Tomcat uses to be port 80 instead of 8080. You may change the port to 80 via the installation wizard now or later on in the chapter. Figure 1-9 displays the corresponding installation wizard screen.

The final piece of configuration information Tomcat requires is the location of your Java Virtual Machine, which should be wherever you installed it earlier in the chapter. By default Tomcat attempts to locate the most recent JVM for you, as shown in Figure 1-10.

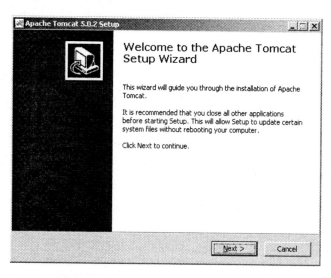

Figure 1-6 Windows Installation Wizard

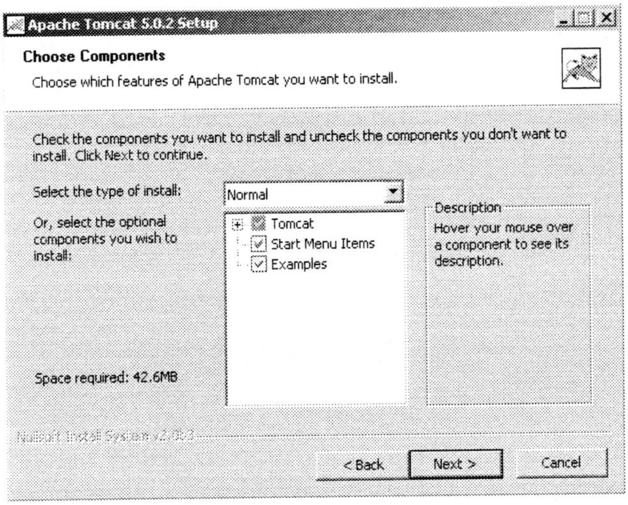

Figure 1-7 Installation Wizard Choosing Tomcat's Components

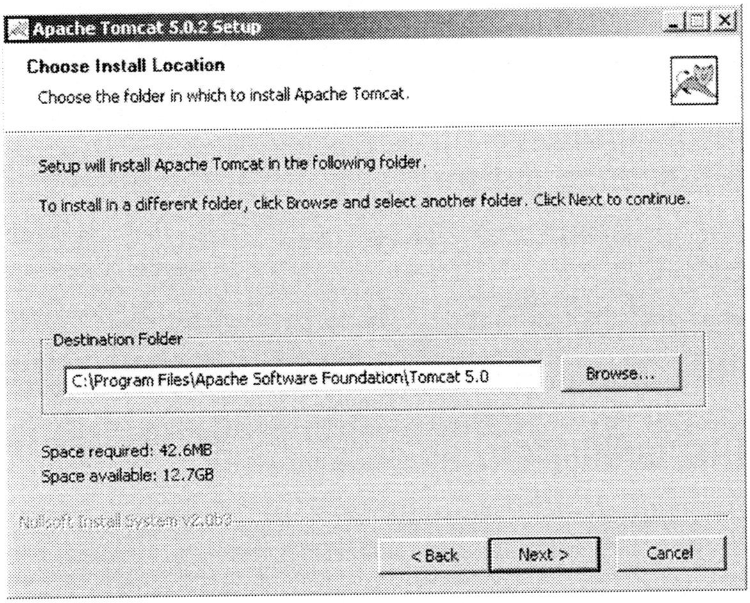

Figure 1-8 Installation Wizard for Installing Tomcat

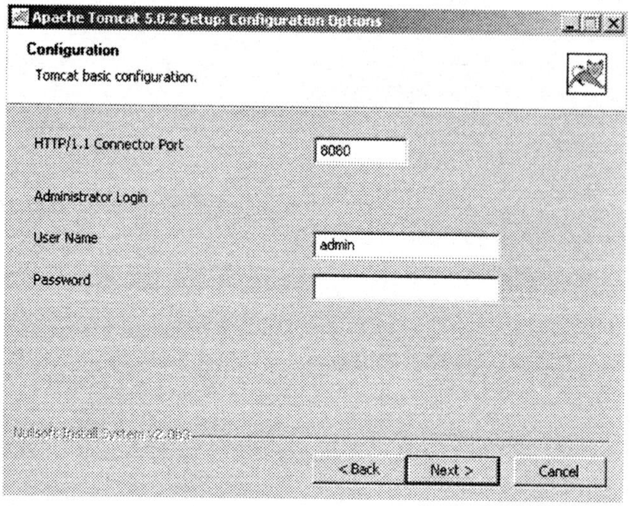

Figure 1-9   Installation Wizard for Configuring Tomcat

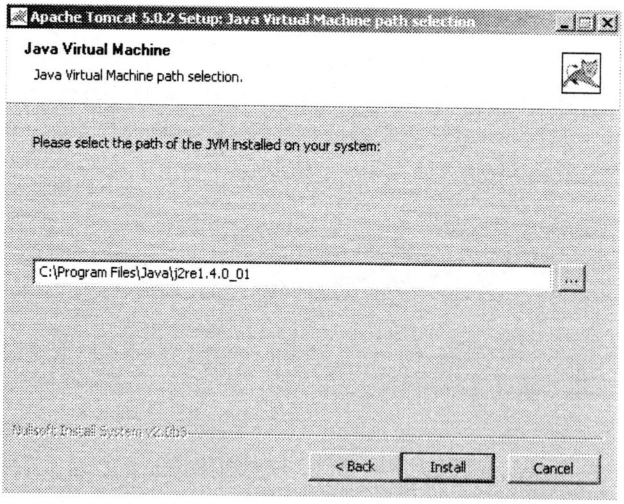

Figure 1-10   Installation Wizard Showing the Location of the Current JVM

The default JVM found by the installation wizard should be fine, but you can change the location to be any JVM you desire (note a Java 1.4-compatible JVM is required to execute this book's examples). Finally, the installation wizard will automatically install all the Tomcat files. Figure 1-11 shows the corresponding installation wizard screen.

To complete the installation and run Tomcat, start the server by double-clicking on the Tomcat icon or by executing the startup script `startup.bat` found in the `TOMCAT_HOME/bin` directory. Check the service is running by browsing to your local computer on port 8080 (or 80 if you changed Tomcat's port via the installation wizard), `http://127.0.0.1:8080`. A Tomcat welcome page should be displayed[4] as shown in Figure 1-12.

Installation of Tomcat is complete, and you are now ready to run book examples. Tomcat comes bundled with documentation and examples of both Servlets and JSP. Feel free to examine the bundled examples, but this book will not cover them further. Before continuing, there are two important scripts to be aware of.

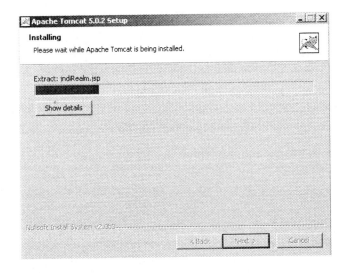

Figure 1-11 Installation Wizard for Installing Tomcat Files

---

4. Port 8080 should not be previously in use, but if it is, you will not be able to see the Tomcat welcome page. If you are sure you have correctly installed Tomcat and think a port bind is causing problems, consult the later section in this chapter which deals with changing the port Tomcat runs on.

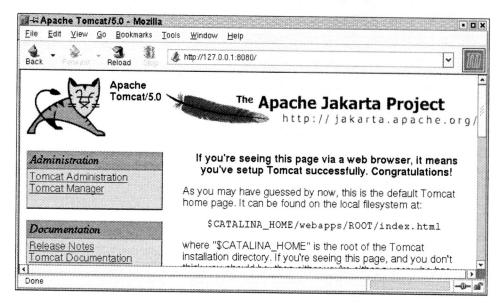

Figure 1-12 Tomcat Welcome Page after Completing the Installation

- **startup.bat:** The `startup.bat` script in the `TOMCAT_HOME/bin` directory is used to start the Tomcat container and Web server. Servlet and JSP code examples rely on Tomcat, and you must have Tomcat turned on before testing them.
- **shutdown.bat:** The `shutdown.bat` script in the `TOMCAT_HOME/bin` directory is used to terminate the Tomcat container and Web server.

It is important to be aware of these two scripts because from time to time an example will require that Tomcat be restarted. When this is asked, it is assumed Tomcat is currently running and implies that the `shutdown.bat` script and then `startup.bat` be executed to reload the server. Alternatively you can also use an automated utility like Ant, which is discussed later in this chapter, to manage reloading, compiling, and other repetitive aspects of developing Servlets and JSP.

Windows 9X/ME "out of environment space"

Just because you are using Windows 9x, or Millennium, does not mean you will have a problem, but be aware that a common problem does exist. If when executing `startup.bat` or `shutdown.bat`, an "out of environment space" error occurs, do the following. Right-click on the `startup.bat` and `shutdown.bat` files. Click on Properties then on the Memory tab. For the Initial environment field, enter 4096. After you click apply, Windows will create shortcuts in the directory which you can use to start and stop the container. Use these shortcuts to start and stop Tomcat.

What is happening is that the batch file is not allocating enough memory to execute its commands. The fix is to simply add more memory. The Tomcat developers are aware of this problem and are trying to incorporate fixes into `startup.bat` and `shutdown.bat`.

Installing Jakarta Tomcat 5 on Linux and Macintosh OS X

The Tomcat project is continuously expanding the different types of installation packages in which Tomcat releases are available. If you notice a Tomcat installation package that matches special installation software for your specific Linux distribution, feel free to download and use the appropriate file. For this walkthrough, installation will be of the compiled Java code packaged in a tarball[5]. Download the Tomcat tarball `jakarta-tomcat-5.0.tar.gz"` from `http://jakarta.apache.org/builds/jakarta-tomcat/release/`. Installation is as easy as decompressing the Tomcat binaries and setting two environment variables.

Decompress the tarball by using the tar and gzip compression utilities from the command prompt. Here is what the command would look like if you had placed the download in the `/usr` directory.

```
gunzip -c /usr/jakarta-tomcat-5.0.tar.gz | tar xvf -
```

The Tomcat binaries will be available in the `/usr/jakarta-tomcat-5.0` directory or a similarly named directory that matches the version of Tomcat you downloaded. For the rest of this walk-through, it is assumed this is the directory you are also using. If not, change the directory name in examples to match the location where you uncompressed Tomcat.

Before starting Tomcat, two environment variables need to be set: JAVA_HOME and TOMCAT_HOME. The JAVA_HOME variable corresponds to the directory of the J2SDK 1.4 installed earlier in this chapter. The TOMCAT_HOME variable corresponds to the directory into which you just uncompressed Tomcat. Set and export the

---

5. A tarball is a commonly used Unix term for a file compressed using gzip and tar compression. The de facto standard for distributing Unix and Linux programs is by means of a tarball because the compression is often significantly better than only ZIP.

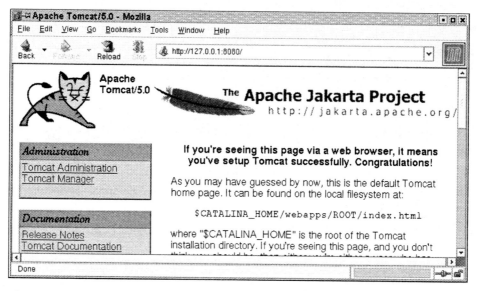

Figure 1-13 Tomcat Welcome Page Appears after Starting Tomcat

two environment variables. The commands would be similar to the following if the J2SDK is installed in the `/usr/java/jdk1.4` directory and Tomcat 5 is installed in the `/usr/jakarta-tomcat-5.0` directory; replace each variable accordingly to match your specific case:

```
JAVA_HOME=/usr/java/jdk1.4
TOMCAT_HOME=/usr/jakarta-tomcat-5.0
export JAVA_HOME TOMCAT_HOME
```

Tomcat is now ready to run. Start the server by executing the startup script `startup.sh` found in the `/usr/jakarta-tomcat-5.0/bin` directory. Check the service is running by browsing to your local computer on port 8080, `http://127.0.0.1:8080`. A Tomcat welcome page should be displayed[6] as shown in Figure 1-13.

Installation of Tomcat is complete, and you are now ready to run book examples. Tomcat comes bundled with documentation and examples of both Servlets and JSP. Feel free to examine the bundled examples, but this book will

---

6. Port 8080 should not be previously in use, but if it is, you will not be able to see the Tomcat welcome page. If you are sure you have correctly installed Tomcat and think a port bind is causing problems, consult the later section in this chapter, which deals with changing the port Tomcat runs on.

not cover them further. Before continuing on, there are two important scripts to be aware of.

- **startup.sh:** The `startup.sh` script in the `TOMCAT_HOME/bin` directory is used to start the Tomcat container and Web server. Servlet and JSP code examples rely on Tomcat, and you must have Tomcat turned on before testing them.
- **shutdown.sh:** The `shutdown.sh` script in the `TOMCAT_HOME/bin` directory is used to terminate the Tomcat container and Web server.

It is important to be aware of these two scripts because from time to time an example will require that Tomcat be restarted. When this is asked, it is assumed Tomcat is currently running and implies that the `shutdown.sh` script and then `startup.sh` be executed to reload the server. Also be aware that the environment variables previously set will not persist between different terminal sessions and need to either be included in a startup script or set for each session.

Alternatively, you can also automate the redundant process of compiling book examples and reloading Tomcat by using a build utility. Use of the Jakarta Ant build utility is strongly encouraged with this book and is covered later in this chapter.

Configuring Tomcat

Tomcat is a robust JSP and Servlet container. It not only provides complete support for the JSP and Servlet specifications, but it can also act as a standalone Web server. By default, this is exactly what Tomcat does, and the default configuration is all we need for this book's examples. Full instructions on configuring Tomcat are outside the scope of this book. There are many different Servlet and JSP containers available, and it is not very practical to devote a large part of this book to Tomcat-specific information. There is only one important aspect of configuring Tomcat that needs to be discussed. If you would like to learn more about using Tomcat to its full potential, some good resources are listed at the end of this section.

Switching Tomcat to Port 80, the Default HTTP Port

For all practical purposes it does not matter what port you run Tomcat on. Ports 8080, 80, 1234, and 9999 all work the same. However, any port besides 80, which is being used for HTTP, comes with some slight annoyances that it would be nice to avoid. Specifically, the default port for HTTP is port 80. Recall the previously used URL for Tomcat's welcome page, `http://127.0.0.1:8080/index.html`. The `localhost` address, `127.0.0.1`, is universal, but the `8080` is required because Tomcat's HTTP connector is not listening on port `80`; the default configuration for Tomcat is for it to listen on port `8080`. The `8080` is slightly annoying, especially when needing to add the `8080` to all local absolute links in your Web application.

In order to simplify the book examples and to avoid confusion, we will now configure Tomcat to use port 80, which is the default HTTP port. This is done by editing Tomcat's configuration file, `/conf/server.xml`. Open this file with your favorite text editor and do a search for '8080'; you should find the following entry:

```
<!-- Define a non-SSL Coyote HTTP/1.1 Connector on port 8080 -->
<Connector className="org.apache.coyote.tomcat5.CoyoteConnector"
        port="8080" minProcessors="5" maxProcessors="75"
        enableLookups="true" redirectPort="8443"
        acceptCount="10" debug="0"
        connectionTimeout="20000"
        useURIValidationHack="false" />
```

The entry is responsible for configuring Tomcat's HTTP connector and the port it listens on. Change the entry to use port 80 by replacing 8080 with 80:

```
<!-- Define a non-SSL Coyote HTTP/1.1 Connector on port 8080 -->
<Connector className="org.apache.coyote.tomcat5.CoyoteConnector"
        port="80" minProcessors="5" maxProcessors="75"
        enableLookups="true" redirectPort="8443"
        acceptCount="10" debug="0"
        connectionTimeout="20000"
        useURIValidationHack="false" />
```

Tomcat will then listen for HTTP requests on port 80, which is assumed when no port is specified. Shut down and restart Tomcat so that it uses the new port. Both `http://127.0.0.1` and `http://127.0.01:80` will now display the Tomcat welcome page. Likewise, all subsequent requests, which do not specify a port, will be directed to Tomcat. Make sure to restart Tomcat before testing out the changes[7].

---

7. If another service, such as Apache or IIS, is running on port 80, Tomcat will not be able to use the port. Either choose a different port, configure Tomcat to work with the service, terminate the conflicting service, or change the services default port. Additional help with configuring Tomcat to use an existing Web server is outside the scope of this book.

Tomcat User's Guide

The Tomcat's User's Guide is the official documentation for Tomcat. This should be the first place you look for help when configuring and using Tomcat. The Tomcat User's Guide can be found online at the Jakarta Tomcat Web site, `http://jakarta.apache.org/tomcat`.

Tomcat User Mailing List

The Tomcat user mailing list is the best place to find community support for configuring and using Tomcat. This mailing list consists of most all the Tomcat developers and many of the current users of Tomcat. By posting a question on this mailing list, you can try to solicit information from the current Tomcat experts. You can subscribe to this mailing list by following the instructions on the Jakarta Mailing List page, `http://jakarta.apache.org/site/mail.html`.

Be warned the Tomcat user mailing list generates a lot of traffic. A hundred or more emails a day is not uncommon; however, it is only an issue if you do not wish to deal with that volume of email. There are many benevolent people, which is obvious on the Tomcat user mailing list because of the unbelievable amount of questions they answer. An alternative to using the Tomcat user mailing list is to consult the online archives, which can be found using the same link.

Book Support Site

For the most current information and updates of this chapter's walk-through guides, use the book support site, `http://www.jspbook.com`. Along with the latest versions of the walk-through guides, this site also contains a Frequently Asked Question (FAQ) section for questions relating to this book. Many of these questions answer problems relating to Tomcat configuration issues for various software environments. Additionally, the book support site is intended to provide a place that can deal with any unexpected issues occurring after publication.

Web Applications

A "Web Application", not the commonly used "Web application" meaning any Web-savvy program, is the proper term for a complete Servlet and/or JSP project. Anytime you develop a JSP or Servlet, it is part of a larger Web Application. Each Web Application has its own unique configuration files and resources for use.

These files and resources are defined by the JSP specification and Servlet specification and managed by your container. In summary they consist of:

- **Configuration:** Each Web Application includes a configuration file, web.xml. This configuration file customizes the resources of a Web Application in an efficient and structured fashion. Web Applications keep web.xml private from outside visitors and also provide a place for privately storing other custom configuration information.

- **Static Files and JSP:** A Web Application's primary purpose is to serve content on the World Wide Web. This content includes dynamic resources such as Servlets and JSP, but it also includes static resources such as HTML pages. A Web Application automatically manages JSP and static resources deployed in it.

- **Class Files and Packages:** A Web Application also loads and manages custom Java code. For application-specific class files such as Servlets, a special location is designated from which a container can load and manage compiled code. Web Applications define a similar location for including Java Archive, JAR, files that contain packaged resources.

By the end of the chapter, most of these configuration files and resources will have been introduced and discussed, but an in-depth analysis of them cannot be attempted without understanding more about JSP and Servlets. As the book progresses, all of the preceding will be fully defined and explored. But before discussing any part of a Web Application, one must be created.

Making a Web Application from scratch requires two things. First, a directory to hold all of the files for the Web Application is needed. The directory can be located anywhere on your local computer. For simplicity, create a directory named jspbook under the /webapps directory of your Tomcat installation. The webapps folder is Tomcat's default location for storing Web Applications. To make this a Web Application, you also need to add a web.xml configuration file. To do this, go to the jspbook directory and create a subdirectory called WEB-INF. Inside the /WEB-INF directory create a file called web.xml. Save Listing 1-1 as the contents of web.xml.

Listing 1-1 web.xml Skeleton File

```
<web-app xmlns="http://java.sun.com/xml/ns/j2ee" version="2.4">
</web-app>
```

Do not worry about the details of this for now; this will all be explained later.

Next, the container needs to be informed that a new Web Application exists[8]. With Tomcat this can be done in one of two ways: by adding an entry in the `server.xml` file located in the `/conf` directory of a Tomcat installation, or by placing an XML file containing the configuration into Tomcat's `/webapps` directory. Placing the file in the `/webapps` directory is the preferred option; it makes upgrading Tomcat versions easier as changes to `server.xml` do not need to be transferred. To configure a Web application, Tomcat requires a `Context` tag. Create a file called `jspbook.xml` in TOMCAT_HOME/webapps directory with Listing 1-2 as its content.

Listing 1-2 Simple Web Application Deployment File for Tomcat

```
<Context path="/jspbook" docBase="jspbook" debug="0"/>
```

Restart Tomcat to reflect the changes made in the `server.xml` configuration file and to load the new Web Application. You can now browse to the newly created jspbook Web Application by using the following URL, `http://127.0.0.1/jspbook/`. Because nothing has been placed in this Web Application, an empty directory is displayed as shown in Figure 1-14.

The jspbook Web Application is used for examples throughout the rest of the book. Until you know a little more about JSP and Servlets, it will be difficult to create dynamic content using this Web Application; however, nothing stops you from using static resources such as an HTML file. Try creating a simple HTML page that welcomes a visitor. Copy and name the following HTML code Listing 1-3 as `index.html` and place it in the `/webapps/jspbook` directory of the Tomcat installation.

Listing 1-3 index.html

```
<html>
  <head>
    <title>Welcome!</title>
  </head>
  <body>
  Welcome to the example Web Application for
  <i>Servlets and JSP, the J2EE Web Tier</i>.
  </body>
</html>
```

---

8. The following step is not strictly necessary as Tomcat automatically treats directories within its /webapps directory as a webapp. This support does not include subdirectories of webapp.

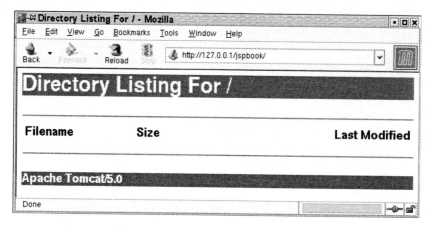

Figure 1-14 Empty Directory Listing for jspbook Web Application

Refresh the Web browser you used to previously view the empty Web Application directory. It now displays a little welcome message, as shown in Figure 1-15, instead of the empty directory listing, as shown in Figure 1-14.

Any static content placed in the Web Application will be made available for users to see. The index.html page happens to be the default page Tomcat displays for a Web Application, and that is why it appeared by default when the empty directory was refreshed. Notice that the URL automatically changed to `http://127.0.0.1/jspbook/index.html`[9]. This behavior is not standard among all JSP containers, but the behavior can always be configured on a per Web Application basis. Web Application configuration involves using the Web Application Deployment Descriptor file web.xml.

/WEB-INF and web.xml

The Servlet specification defines a configuration file called a deployment descriptor that contains meta-data for a Web Application and that is used by the container when loading a Web Application. This file is always located in the /WEB-INF directory of a Web Application and must be named web.xml. When a container loads a Web Application, it checks this file. As noted, web.xml contains application meta-data, such as default pages to show, Servlets to load, and

---

9. Microsoft's Internet Explorer is notorious for improperly handling this. If the URL does not change, do not worry. As long as the correct page is shown, everything is fine.

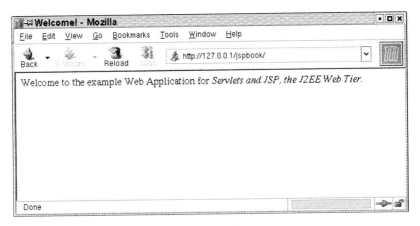

Figure 1-15   index.html Rendered by Web Browser

security restrictions to place on files. The Servlet specification also defines that the entire /WEB-INF directory of any Web Application must be kept hidden from users of the application. In other words, a user cannot browse to http:// 127.0.0.1/jspbook/WEB-INF. Try it—any configuration information for your Web Application is unattainable by a client unless you specifically create something to expose it.

You already have the skeleton of a Web Application configuration file. Further configuration information can be placed in between the starting and ending web-app tags. Try it out by adding Listing 1-4 to define the default page that your Web Application displays.

Listing 1-4   web.xml welcome File Configuration

```
<web-app xmlns="http://java.sun.com/xml/ns/j2ee" version="2.4">
  <welcome-file-list>
    <welcome-file>welcome.html</welcome-file>
  </welcome-file-list>
</web-app>
```

Save the changes and restart your container so the Web Application reflects them. Use a Web browser to visit http://127.0.0.1/jspbook again. This time the index.html page is not shown by default; a directory listing is shown instead (see Figure 1-16), which includes index.html.

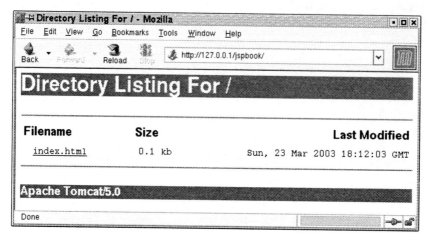

Figure 1-16 Directory Listing

The preceding outcome is the result of the new elements added to `web.xml`. The `welcome-file-list` element defines a list of welcome files in descending preference. The name of each welcome file is defined as the body of the `welcome-file` element. In the meta-data just added, one specific file was listed as default page: `welcome.html`. If file exists, the container would show it instead of the empty directory. If you would like to experiment, try changing the name of `index.html` to `weclome.html` and it will appear as the default page for the Web Application.

The rest of `web.xml` configuration is left for discussion in later sections of the book. Both JSP and Servlets have many configuration elements that can be added to `web.xml`. This book covers most all of them in examples, but a complete reference can always be found in the Servlet 2.4 schema.

Java Classes and Source Files

Throughout the book examples will be taking advantage of existing Java APIs as well as creating new Java classes. One of the most common mistakes new Servlet and JSP developers make is where they place Java source code and compiled Java classes. The intuitive approach is to place these files in the same directory as that in which static content is placed for the Web Application. While it may seem logical at first, this approach has two problems. The first is that any individual browsing to your Web site will, by default, be able to access any files not in the `/WEB-INF` directory. This means your code is freely available for people to download and use or possibly abuse. The second problem is that the container will ignore the code when it is loading the Web Application. The second issue is more problematic because the Web Application's Servlets and JSP will not be able to import and use the custom code.

The correct place to put custom code is in the `/WEB-INF/classes` directory of a Web Application. Code that is placed in this directory is loaded by the container when needed and can be imported for use by Servlets and JSP in the same Web Application. Should the code be part of a package, create a directory structure that matches the package names. An example of this would be if a class were created for the `com.foo.example` package. The appropriate place to put the compiled Java class is the `/WEB-INF/classes/com/foo/example` directory of a Web Application. For now, create the `/WEB-INF/classes` directory so that it is ready for later code examples.

Java Archive (JAR) Files

A Java Archive file is a convenient method for consolidating a set, usually a package, of Java class files into one compressed, portable file. The Java specifications define the exact rules of a JAR file, but an easy way to think of them is nothing more than a set of Java classes ZIP-compressed together. JAR files are a very popular method of distributing Java code and are commonly used by Web Applications. As defined in the Servlet specification, any JAR file placed in the `/WEB-INF/lib` directory of a Web Application is made available for use by code in the same Web Application. Later examples in this book will give some concrete examples of using this functionality. The complete specifications for creating and using a basic JAR are not in the scope of this book. You can find a complete guide to creating JAR files in the J2SE documentation included with your J2SE download. The task is not hard but is outside the scope of this text.

Web Application Resource (WAR) Files

Web Application Resource files are functionally similar to JAR files, but are used to consolidate an entire Web Application into one compressed and portable file. WAR files are officially defined by the Servlet specification. The compression used for a WAR file is also ZIP; using existing JAR utilities in the Standard Java Development Kit can easily make WAR files. WAR files are a great solution for packaging a Web Application and they are commonly used to bundle documentation with examples for JSP and Servlet-related software.

Most of the examples found in later chapters deal with expanding and enhancing existing Web Applications. WAR files are only helpful to either start a Web Application or to package a finished one. For this reason WAR files will not be appearing often in later chapters. WAR files are mentioned here for reasons of completeness and because the online book support site packages all of this book's examples into a WAR. If you would like to skip retyping code examples from the book, feel free to download the example WAR at `http://www.jspbook.com/jspbook.war`.

If you would ever like to make a WAR file, simply ZIP compress an entire working Web Application. For example, at any time you can create a WAR of your progress through this book by ZIP-compressing all of the contents in the `jspbook` directory. Using the ZIP utility on Linux, the following commands would be used:

```
zip -r jspbook.war jspbook
```

The `zip` utility would then compress the entire application into one file named `jspbook.war`. In order to deploy this file with Tomcat, simply place `jspbook.war` in the `/webapps` directory and restart Tomcat.

Note that WAR files are only as portable as you make them. Several times in upcoming chapters notes will be made about this point. For example, if you access a file using the file's absolute path name, there is no guarantee a similar file will be found on all servers with containers using your WAR. However, if a custom file is packaged in a WAR, the file can always be accessed using the Servlet API.

Ant

The Jakarta Ant project is popular with Java developers and for good reason. Ant is a cross-platform build utility that is easy to use and configure. Ant uses an XML configuration file typically called `build.xml`. If you are unfamiliar with build utilities, do not worry. This book does not rely on such knowledge. Ant is treated purely as a complimentary tool. If you have used Ant before, you should appreciate this, or if you have not used Ant, hopefully you will be glad we introduced the tool to you. At any time you can opt to completely ignore Ant and simply compile `.java` files by hand and reload Tomcat using the appropriate scripts. At no point will this book tell you to use Ant to do this. Instead, an example will dictate that Tomcat, the Web Application, or both need to be reloaded, or that code needs to be compiled. In these cases it is implied you can use Ant if you so desire.

What Does Ant Do?

Ant performs "tasks", any number of them, and in any order, possibly dependent on previously accomplished tasks. There are many default tasks that Ant defines; Ant also allows for Java developers to code custom tasks. In use, Ant takes a simple build file, which defines tasks to be done, and does them. For this book we will make a build file that turns off Tomcat, compiles code, then turns Tomcat back on. The tasks are all simple but after trying several of the code examples in this book, you might be glad Ant consolidates the redundant steps.

Installing Ant

Install Ant by downloading the latest distribution from `http://jakarta.apache.org/ant`. This book uses Ant 1.5, but any subsequent release should work fine. Binary distributions of Ant are available in either ZIP or tarball form. Download the format you are most familiar with and save the compressed file in a convenient location. Unpack the distribution and installation of Ant complete. Because the files are Java binaries, there is no need to run an installer or compile a platform-specific distribution.

Using Ant

Ant is designed to be simple to use. The `/bin` directory of the Ant distribution contains an executable file named `ant` that runs Ant. You can execute Ant at any time by running `$ANT_HOME/bin/ant`; replace `$ANT_HOME` with the appropriate directory of the Ant distribution. By default, Ant looks to the current directory and tries to use a file named `build.xml` as its build file. Listing 1-5, which is included in the example WAR, is a build file for use with this book.

Listing 1-5 Ant Build File for Use with This Book

```xml
<?xml version="1.0" ?>
<project name="jspbook" default="build" basedir=".">
  <target name="build">
    <echo>Starting Build [JSP Book - http://www.jspbook.com]</echo>
    <!-- Turn Tomcat Off -->
    <antcall target="tomcatOff"/>
    <!-- Compile Everything -->
    <antcall target="compile"/>
    <!-- Turn Tomcat On -->
    <antcall target="tomcatOn"/>
    <echo>Build Finished [JSP Book - http://www.jspbook.com]</echo>
  </target>

  <target name="tomcatOff">
    <echo>Turning Off Tomcat [http://www.jspbook.com]</echo>
    <exec executable="bash" os="Windows">
      <arg value="../../bin/shutdown.bat"/>
```

```
      </exec>
      <exec executable="bash" os="Linux">
        <arg value="../../bin/shutdown.sh"/>
      </exec>
    </target>

    <target name="tomcatOn">
      <echo>Starting Tomcat [http://www.jspbook.com]</echo
      <exec executable="bash" os="Windows">
        <arg value="../../bin/startup.bat"/>
      </exec>
      <exec executable="bash" os="Linux">
        <arg value="../../bin/startup.sh"/>
      </exec>
    </target>

    <target name="compile">
      <echo>Compiling Book's Examples [http://www.jspbook.com]</echo>
      <javac
        srcdir="WEB-INF/classes"
        extdirs="WEB-INF/lib:../../common/lib"
        classpath="../../common/lib/servlet.jar"
        deprecation="yes"
        verbose="no">
        <include name="com/jspbook/**"/>
      </javac>
    </target>
</project>
```

Save the preceding code as `build.xml` in the base directory of the jspbook Web Application. You do not need to care about the entries in the build file; however, they should be intuitive. If you are interested, you can find further documentation for the Ant tasks online at `http://jakarta.apache.org/ant/manual/index.html`.

Use of the build file is simple. From shell, or command prompt in Windows, switch to the directory of the jspbook Web Application. For instance, if Tomcat was installed in `/usr/jakarta-tomcat/`[10], then the desired directory would be `/usr/jakarta-tomcat/webapps/jspbook`. From there, execute Ant. Assuming

---

10. These are UNIX file systems. In Windows, the starting '/' is replaced by the drive, such as `C:\`, and subsequent '/' are replaced with '\'. For instance, `C:\jakarta-tomcat\webapps\jspbook`.

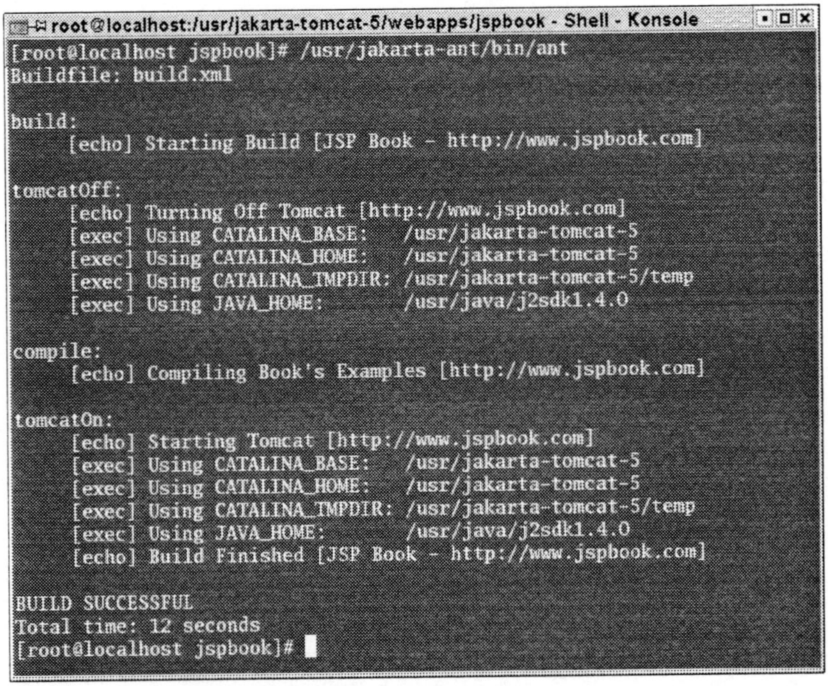

Figure 1-17 Ant Execution of the Book's Build File

Ant is in your classpath, you can simply type `ant`, or a full path can be used such as `/usr/jakarta-ant-1.5/bin/ant`. Ant automatically looks for `build.xml` and will execute the specified tasks. Execution should look similar to Figure 1-17.

Note the build file turns off Tomcat, compiles all the book's code, and turns Tomcat back on. Should an example request any of these tasks, simply run Ant and the job is finished.

Summary

The first and most important step to developing with Servlets and JSP is setting up the appropriate environment. This chapter focused on providing a detailed explanation of the requirements for a Servlet and JSP environment and provided a walk-through for installing one on a majority of the popular operating systems. By doing this, you will be ready for the code examples of later chapters and can better learn through hands-on experience developing Servlets and JSP.

A Web Application is the term given to a complete collection of static content, JSP, Servlets, custom code, and configuration information for all of the previously mentioned. This chapter also established a Web Application for use with examples to come. As you go through the book, the jspbook Web Application will be expanded and enhanced to demonstrate the many aspects of developing with Servlets and JSP.

Chapter 2 discusses Servlets and JSP at the lowest possible level by introducing and explaining the basics of the Servlet API.

Chapter 2

Java Servlets

In this chapter the concept of Servlets, not the entire Servlet specification, is explained; consider this an introduction to the Servlet specification starting strictly with Servlets. At times the content of this chapter may seem dry, even reminiscent of the actual specification. While an attempt is always made to liven the material up, however, there are several relevant but boring aspects of Servlet development that need to be presented now. Do attempt to read the whole chapter straight through, but also remember you can always reference this chapter when needed.

This chapter discusses the following topics:

- An explanation of what Servlets are and why you would want to use them.
- The Servlet life cycle—that is, how a container manages a Servlet.
- Building Servlets for use on the World Wide Web, which includes a review of the HTTP protocol.
- Configuring Servlets using `web.xml`.
- Coding both text-producing and non-text-producing Servlets.
- Handling HTML forms and file uploads.
- *Request dispatching*—Servlet to Servlet communication and including or forwarding to other resources in the Web Application.
- *Application context* and communicating with the container via a Servlet.
- Servlet event listeners.

What Servlets Are and Why You Would Want to Use Them

Java Servlets are an efficient and powerful solution for creating dynamic content for the Web. Over the past few years Servlets have become the fundamental building block of mainstream server-side Java. The power behind Servlets comes from the use of Java as a platform and from interaction with a Servlet container. The Java platform provides a Servlet developer with a robust API, object-orientated programming, platform neutrality, strict types, garbage collection, and all the security features of the JVM. Complimenting this, a Servlet container provides life cycle management, a single process to share and manage application-wide resources, and interaction with a Web server. Together this functionality makes Servlets a desirable technology for server-side Java developers.

Java Servlets is currently in version 2.4 and a part of the Java 2 Enterprise Edition (J2EE). Downloads of the J2SE do not include the Servlet API, but the official Servlet API can be found on Sun Microsystems' Servlet product page, `http://java.sun.com/products/servlets`, or bundled with the Java 2 Enterprise Edition. Servlet API development is done through the Java Community Process, `http://www.jcp.org`, but the official reference implementation of the Servlet API is open source and available for public access through the Tomcat project, `http://jakarta.apache.org/tomcat`.

The Servlet 2.4 API includes many features that are officially defined by the Servlet 2.4 specification, `http://java.sun.com/products/servlets`, and can be broken down as follows.

Web Applications

Servlets are always part of a larger project called a Web Application. A Web Application is a complete collection of resources for a Web site. Nothing stops a Web Application from consisting of zero, one, or multiple Servlets, but a Servlet container manages Servlets on a per Web Application basis. Web Applications and the configuration files for them are specified by the Servlet specification.

Servlets and HTTP Servlets

The primary purpose of the Servlet specification is to define a robust mechanism for sending content to a client as defined by the Client/Server model. Servlets are most popularly used for generating dynamic content on the Web and have native support for HTTP.

Filters

Filters were officially introduced in the Servlet 2.3 specification. A *filter* provides an abstracted method of manipulating a client's request and/or response before it actually reaches the endpoint of the request. Filters greatly complement Servlets and are commonly used for things such as authentication, content compression, and logging.

Security

Servlets already use the security features provided by the Java Virtual Machine, but the Servlet specification also defines a mechanism for controlling access to resources in a Web Application.

Internationalization

One of the best features of a Servlet is the ability to develop content for just about any language. A large part of this functionality comes directly from the Java platform's support for internationalization and localization. The Servlet API keeps this functionality and can be easily used to create content in most of the existing languages.

The focus of this chapter is to introduce Servlets and explain how to use HTTP Servlets for creating dynamic content on the Web. For simplicity, this chapter focuses on the basics of Servlets and leaves more complex but practical examples for discussion in pertinent, later chapters. Filters, security, and true internationalization issues are all discussed in later chapters as they pertain to both Servlets and JSP.

Servlet Life Cycle

The key to understanding the low-level functionality of Servlets is to understand the simple life cycle they follow. This life cycle governs the multi-threaded environment that Servlets run in and provides an insight to some of the mechanisms available to a developer for sharing server-side resources. Understanding the Servlet life cycle is also the start of this book's descent to a lower level of discussion, one the majority of this book follows. Functional code examples appear often to illustrate an idea or point. Compiling and running these examples is encouraged to fully understand concepts and to familiarize yourself with Servlets for the later chapters.

The Servlet life cycle (see Figure 2-1) is the primary reason Servlets and also JSP outperform traditional CGI. Opposed to the single-use CGI life cycle,

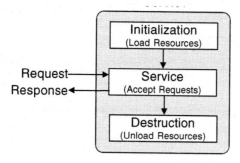

Figure 2-1   Diagram of the Servlet Life Cycle

Servlets follow a three-phase life: *initialization, service,* and *destruction,* with initialization and destruction typically performed once, and service performed many times.

Initialization is the first phase of the Servlet life cycle and represents the creation and initialization of resources the Servlet may need to service requests. All Servlets must implement the `javax.servlet.Servlet` interface. This interface defines the `init()` method to match the initialization phase of a Servlet life cycle. When a container loads a Servlet, it invokes the `init()` method before servicing any requests.

The service phase of the Servlet life cycle represents all interactions with requests until the Servlet is destroyed. The `Servlet` interface matches the service phase of the Servlet life cycle to the `service()` method. The `service()` method of a Servlet is invoked once per a request and is responsible for generating the response to that request. The Servlet specification defines the `service()` method to take two parameters: a `javax.servlet.ServletRequest` and a `javax.servlet.ServletResponse` object. These two objects represent a client's request for the dynamic resource and the Servlet's response to the client. By default a Servlet is multi-threaded, meaning that typically only one instance of a Servlet[1] is loaded by a JSP container at any given time. Initialization is done once, and each request after that is handled concurrently[2] by threads executing the Servlet's `service()` method.

---

1. This description of Servlets is slightly misleading. There are many complications to do with loading Servlets that will be touched upon throughout this chapter and the rest of the book.
2. Servlets require the same state synchronization required by all multi-threaded Java objects. For simplicity, state management–related issues, including proper synchronization, are not discussed until Chapter 9. Read Chapter 9 before assuming you know everything about Servlets.

The destruction phase of the Servlet life cycle represents when a Servlet is being removed from use by a container. The `Servlet` interface defines the `destroy()` method to correspond to the destruction life cycle phase. Each time a Servlet is about to be removed from use, a container calls the `destroy()` method, allowing the Servlet to gracefully terminate and tidy up any resources it might have created. By proper use of the initialization, service, and destruction phases of the Servlet life cycle, a Servlet can efficiently manage application resources. During initialization a Servlet loads everything it needs to use for servicing requests. The resources are then readily used during the service phase and can then be cleaned up in the destruction phase.

These three events form the Servlet life cycle, but in practice there are more methods a Web developer needs to worry about. Content on the Web is primarily accessed via the HyperText Transfer Protocol (HTTP). A basic Servlet knows nothing about HTTP, but there is a special implementation of Servlet, `javax.servlet.http.HttpServlet`, that is designed especially for it.

Servlets for the World Wide Web

When the term Servlet is mentioned, it is almost always implied that the Servlet is an instance of `HttpServlet`[3]. The explanation of this is simple. The HyperText Transfer Protocol (HTTP)[4] is used for the vast majority of transactions on the World Wide Web—every Web page you visit is transmitted using HTTP, hence the `http://` prefix. Not that HTTP is the best protocol to ever be made, but HTTP does work and HTTP is already widely used. Servlet support for HTTP transactions comes in the form of the `javax.servlet.http.HttpServlet` class.

Before showing an example of an `HttpServlet`, it is helpful to reiterate the basics of the HyperText Transfer Protocol. Many developers do not fully understand HTTP, which is critical in order to fully understand an `HttpServlet`. HTTP is a simple, stateless protocol. The protocol relies on a client, usually a Web browser, to make a request and a server to send a response. Connections only last long enough for one transaction. A transaction can be one or more request/response pairs. For example, a browser will send a request for an HTML page followed by multiple requests for each image on that page. All of these

---

3. Note that at the time of writing there is only one protocol-specific servlet and it is HTTP. However, at least one JSR is looking to add additional protocol-specific servlets. In this particular case, it is the SIP (Session Initiation Protocol).

4. Voracious readers are advised to read the current HTTP specification, `http://www.ietf.org/rfc/rfc2616.txt`. This book is not a substitute for the complete specification. However, this book does provide more than enough detail for the average Web developer.

requests and responses will be done over the same connection. The connection will then be closed at the end of the last response. The whole process is relatively simple and occurs each time a browser requests a resource from an HTTP server[5].

Requests, Responses, and Headers

The first part of an HTTP transaction is when an HTTP client creates and sends a *request* to a server. An HTTP request in its simplest form is nothing more than a line of text specifying what resource a client would like to retrieve. The line of text is broken into three parts: the type of action, or method, that the client would like to do; the resource the client would like to access; and the version of the HTTP protocol that is being used. For example:

```
GET /index.html HTTP/1.0
```

The preceding is a completely valid HTTP request. The first word, GET, is a method defined by HTTP to ask a server for a specific resource; /index.html is the resource being requested from the server; HTTP/1.0 is the version of HTTP that is being used. When any device using HTTP wants to get a resource from a server, it would use something similar to the above line. Go ahead and try this by hand against Tomcat. Open up a telnet session with your local computer on port 80. From the command prompt this is usually accomplished with:

```
telnet 127.0.0.1 80
```

Something similar to Figure 2-2 should appear.

The telnet program has just opened a connection to Tomcat's Web server. Tomcat understands HTTP, so type[6] in the example HTTP statement. This HTTP request can be terminated by a blank line, so hit Enter a second time to place an additional blank line and finish the request[7].

```
GET /jspbook/index.html HTTP/1.0
```

The content of index.html is returned from the Web Application mapped to /jspbook (the application we started last chapter), as shown in Figure 2-3.

---

5. HTTP 1.1 allows these "long-lived" connections automatically; in HTTP 1.0 you need to use the Connection: Keep-Alive header.

6. Microsoft's telnet input will not appear in the window as you type. To fix this, type LOCAL_ECHO and hit Return. Also note that if you are using Microsoft XP, then the telnet window is not cleared after it is connected.

7. If using Microsoft Window's default telnet program, be aware that the connection is *live*—that is, type in the full request correctly (even if it does not appear when you are typing it) and do not hit Backspace or Delete.

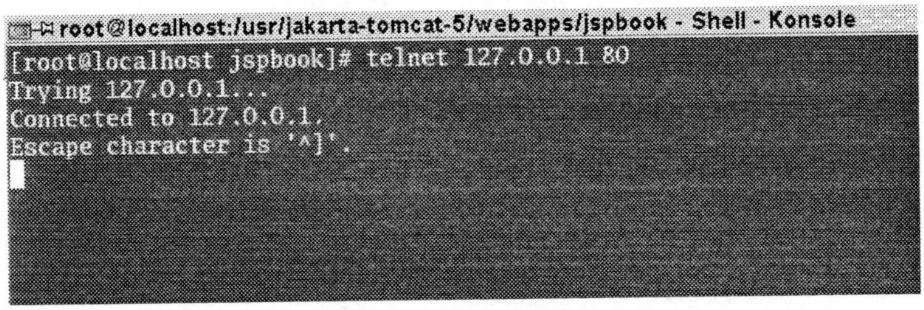

Figure 2-2 Telnet to localhost:80

You just sent a basic HTTP request, and Tomcat returned an HTTP response. While usually done behind the scenes, all HTTP requests resemble the preceding. There are a few more methods to accompany GET, but before discussing those, let's take a closer look at what Tomcat sent back.

The first thing Tomcat returned was a line of text:

```
HTTP/1.1 200 OK
```

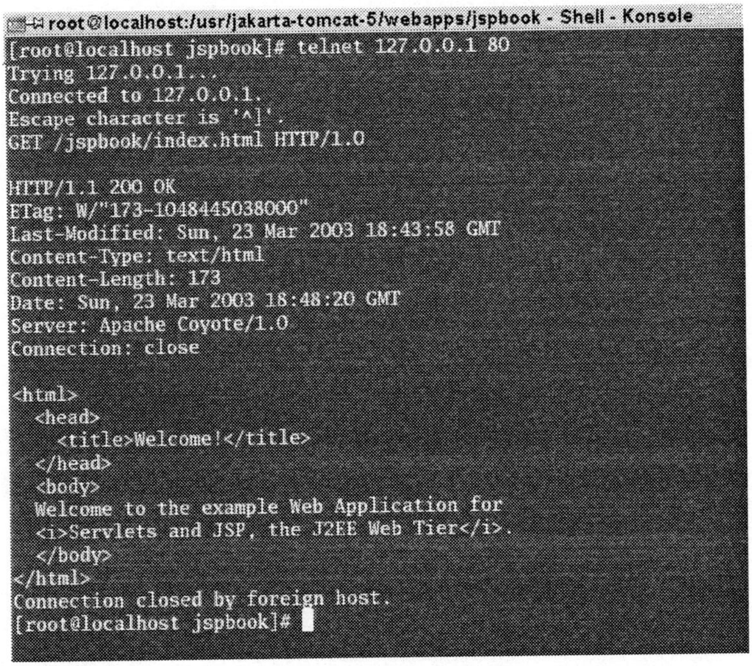

Figure 2-3 Manual HTTP Request and the Server's Response

This is an HTTP status line. Every HTTP response starts with a status line. The status line consists of the HTTP version, a status code, and a reason phrase. The HTTP response code 200 means everything was fine; that is why Tomcat included the requested content with the response. If there was some sort of issue with the request, a different response code would have been used. Another HTTP response code you are likely familiar with is the 404 "File Not Found" code. If you have ever followed a broken hyperlink, this is probably the code that was returned.

HTTP Response Codes

In practice, you usually do not need to understand all of the specific HTTP response codes. JSP, Servlets, and Web servers usually take care of these codes automatically, but nothing stops you from sending specific HTTP response codes. Later on we will see examples of doing this with both Servlets and JSP. A complete list of HTTP response codes along with other HTTP information is available in the current HTTP specification, `http://www.ietf.org/rfc/rfc2616.txt`.

Along with the HTTP response code, Tomcat also sent back a few lines of information before the contents of `index.html`, as shown in Figure 2-4.

All of these lines are HTTP headers. HTTP uses *headers* to send meta-information with a request or response. A header is a colon-delimited name:value pair—that is, it contains the header's name, delimited by a colon followed by the header's value. Typical response headers include content-type descriptions, content length, a time-stamp, server information, and the date the content was last changed. This information helps a client figure out what is being sent, how big it is, and if the data are newer than a previously seen response. An HTTP request will always contain a few headers[8]. Common request headers consist of the user-agent details and preferred formats, languages, and content encoding to receive. These headers help tell a server what the client is and how they would prefer to get back information. Understanding HTTP headers is important, but for now put the concept on hold until you learn a little more about Servlets. HTTP headers provide some very helpful functionality, but it is better to explain them further with some `HttpServlet` examples.

---

8. There are no mandatory headers in HTTP 1.0; in HTTP 1.1 the only mandatory header is the `Host` header.

```
HTTP/1.1 200 OK
ETag: W/"173-1048445038000"
Last-Modified: Sun, 23 Mar 2003 18:43:58 GMT
Content-Type: text/html
Content-Length: 173
Date: Sun, 23 Mar 2003 18:48:20 GMT
Server: Apache Coyote/1.0
Connection: close
```

Figure 2-4 Example HTTP Headers

GET and POST

The first relatively widely used version of HTTP was HTTP 0.9. This had support for only one HTTP method, or verb; that was GET. As part of its execution, a GET request can provide a limited amount of information in the form of a *query string*[9]. However, the GET method is not intended to send large amounts of information. Most Web servers restrict the length of complete URLs, including query strings, to 255 characters. Excess information is usually ignored. For this reason GET methods are great for sending small amounts of information that you do not mind having visible in a URL. There is another restriction on GET; the HTTP specification defines GET as a "safe" method which is also idempotent[10]. This means that GET must only be used to execute queries in a Web application. GET must not be used to perform updates, as this breaks the HTTP specification.

To overcome these limitations, the HTTP 1.0 specification introduced the POST method. POST is similar to GET in that it may also have a query string, but the POST method can use a completely different mechanism for sending information. A POST sends an unlimited amount of information over a socket connection as part of the HTTP request. The extra information does not appear as part of a URL and is only sent once. For these reasons the POST method is usually used for sending sensitive[11] or large amounts of information, or when uploading files. Note that POST methods do not have to be idempotent. This is very important, as it now means applications have a way of updating data in a Web application. If an application needs to modify data, or add new data and is

---

9. A query string is a list started by a question mark, ?, and followed by name-value pairs in the following format, paramName=paramValue, and with an ampersand, &, separating pairs, for example, /index.html?fname=bruce&lname=wayne&password=batman.

10. An idempotent operation is an operation that if run multiple times has no affect on state—that is, it is query only not update.

11. However, realize that the data are still visible to snoopers; it just doesn't appear in the URL.

sending a request over HTTP, then the application must not use GET but must instead use POST. Notice that POST requests may be idempotent; that is, there is nothing to stop an application using POST instead of GET, and this is often done when a retrieval requires sending large amounts of data[12]. However, note that GET can never be used in place of POST if the HTTP request is nonidempotent.

In the current HTTP version, 1.1, there are in total seven HTTP methods that exist: GET, PUT, POST, TRACE, DELETE, OPTIONS, and HEAD. In practice only two of these methods are used—the two we have already talked about: GET and POST.

The other five methods are not very helpful to a Web developer. The HEAD method requests only the headers of a response. PUT is used to place documents directly to a server, and DELETE does the exact opposite. The TRACE method is meant for debugging. It returns an exact copy of a request to a client. Lastly, the OPTIONS method is meant to ask a server what methods and other options the server supports for the requested resource.

As far as this book is concerned, the HTTP methods will not be explained further. As will soon be shown, it is not important for a Servlet developer to fully understand exactly how to construct and use all the HTTP methods manually. HttpServlet objects take care of low-level HTTP functionality and translate HTTP methods directly into invocations of Java methods.

HTTP Response Codes

An HTTP server takes a request from a client and generates a response. Responses, like requests, consist of a response line, headers, and a body. The response line contains the HTTP version of the server, a response code, and a *reason phrase*. The reason phrase is some text that describes the response, and could be anything, although a recommended set of reason phrases is given in the specification. *Response codes* themselves are three-digit numbers that are divided into groups. Each group has a meaning as shown here:

- 1xx: Informational: Request received, continuing process.
- 2xx: Success: The action was successfully received, understood, and accepted.
- 3xx: Redirection: Further action must be taken in order to complete the request.

---

12. The other issue is that GET sends data encoded using the application/x-www-urlen-coded MIME type. If the application needs to send data in some other format, say XML, then this cannot be done using GET; POST must be used. For example, SOAP mandates the use of POST for SOAP requests to cover this exact problem.

- 4xx: User-Agent Error: The request contains bad syntax or cannot be fulfilled.
- 5xx: Server Error: The server failed to fulfill an apparently valid request.
- Each Status: Code has an associated string (reason phrase).
- The status code you'll see most often is 200. This means that everything has succeeded and you have a valid response. The others you are likely to see are:
  - 401: you are not authorized to make this request
  - 404: cannot find the requested URI
  - 405: the HTTP method you have tried to execute is not supported by this URL (e.g., you have sent a POST and the URL will only accept GET)
  - 500: Internal Server Error. You are likely to see this if the resource to where you are browsing (such as a Servlet) throws an exception.

If you send a request to a Servlet and get a 500 code, then the chances are your Servlet has itself thrown an exception. To discover the root cause of this exception, you should check the application output logs. Tomcat's logs are stored in /logs[13] directory of the Tomcat installation.

Coding an HttpServlet

Previously, it has been shown that Servlets have a three-part life cycle: initialization, service, and destruction. An HttpServlet object shares this life cycle but makes a few modifications for the HTTP protocol. The HttpServlet object's implementation of the service() method, which is called during each service request, calls one of seven different helper methods. These seven methods correspond directly to the seven HTTP methods and are named as follows: doGet(), doPost(), doPut(), doHead(), doOptions(), doDelete(), and doTrace(). The appropriate helper method is invoked to match the type of method on a given HTTP request. The HttpServlet life cycle can be illustrated as shown in Figure 2-5.

While all seven methods are shown, remember that normally only one of them is called on a given request. More than one might be called if a developer

---

13. Note that you can configure Tomcat to log output to the console window. This is often done during development because it is easier to read the console than open a log file. See the Tomcat documentation if you would like to do this.

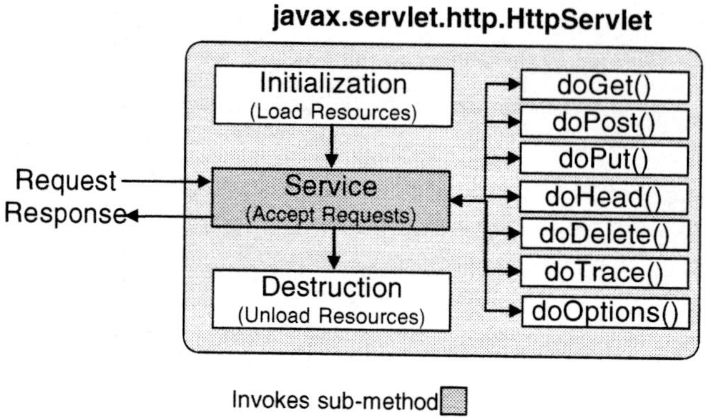

javax.servlet.http.HttpServlet

Figure 2-5 HttpServlet Life Cycle

overrides the methods and has them call each other. The initialization and destruction stages of the Servlet life cycle are the same as described before.

Coding an `HttpServlet` is straightforward. The `javax.servlet.http.HttpServlet` class takes care of handling the redundant parts of an HTTP request and response, and requires a developer only to override methods that need to be customized. Manipulation of a given request and response is done through two objects, `javax.servlet.http.HttpServletRequest` and `javax.servlet.http.HttpServletResponse`. Both of these objects are passed as parameters when invoking the HTTP service methods.

It is time to step through coding and using a basic Servlet. A basic "Hello World" Servlet is appropriate for getting started (see Listing 2-1). Take the following code and save it as `HelloWorld.java` in the `/WEB-INF/classes/com/jspbook` directory of the jspbook Web Application.

Listing 2-1 HelloWorld.java

```
package com.jspbook;

import java.io.*;
import javax.servlet.*;
import javax.servlet.http.*;

public class HelloWorld extends HttpServlet {

    public void doGet(HttpServletRequest request,
                      HttpServletResponse response)
```

```
        throws IOException, ServletException
{
        response.setContentType("text/html");
        PrintWriter out = response.getWriter();

        out.println("<html>");
        out.println("<head>");
        out.println("<title>Hello World!</title>");
        out.println("</head>");
        out.println("<body>");
        out.println("<h1>Hello World!</h1>");
        out.println("</body>");
        out.println("</html>");
    }
}
```

You can probably see exactly what the preceding code is doing. If not, do not worry about understanding everything just yet since we have not learned how to deploy a Servlet for use which has to come before dissecting the code. For now understand that the preceding is the complete code for an `HttpServlet`. Once deployed, this example Servlet will generate a simple HTML page that says "Hello World!".

Deploying a Servlet

By itself a Servlet is not a full Java application. Servlets rely on being part of a Web Application that a container manages. Using a Servlet to generate dynamic responses involves both creating the Servlet and deploying the Servlet for use in the Web Application.

Deploying a Servlet is not difficult, but it is not as intuitive as you might think. Unlike a static resource, a Servlet is not simply placed in the root directory of the Web Application. A Servlet class file goes in the `/WEB-INF/classes` directory of the application with all the other Java classes. For a client to access a Servlet, a unique URL, or set of URLs, needs to be declared in the Web Application Deployment Descriptor. The `web.xml` deployment description relies on new *elements*[14]: `servlet` and `servlet-mapping` need to be introduced for use in `web.xml`. The `servlet` element is used to define a Servlet that should be loaded by a Web Application. The `servlet-mapping` element is used to map a Servlet to a given URL or set of URLs. Multiple tags using either of these elements can appear to define as many Servlets and Servlet mappings as needed. Both of these elements

---

14. An element is the proper name for the unique word that comes immediately after the starting less than, "<", of an XML tag.

also have sub-elements used to further describe them. These sub-elements are self-descriptive, and they are introduced by use in an upcoming example.

Open up the /WEB-INF/web.xml file of the jspbook Web Application and edit it to match Listing 2-2.

Listing 2-2 Deploying HelloWorld Servlet

```xml
<web-app xmlns="http://java.sun.com/xml/ns/j2ee" version="2.4">

  <servlet>
    <servlet-name>HelloWorld</servlet-name>
    <servlet-class>com.jspbook.HelloWorld</servlet-class>
  </servlet>
  <servlet-mapping>
    <servlet-name>HelloWorld</servlet-name>
    <url-pattern>/HelloWorld</url-pattern>
  </servlet-mapping>

  <welcome-file-list>
    <welcome-file>welcome.html</welcome-file>
  </welcome-file-list>
</web-app>
```

Highlighted is the new addition to web.xml. In the highlight, notice that both an instance of the servlet and servlet-mapping element is used. In general this is how every Servlet is deployed. A Servlet is first declared by a servlet element that both names the Servlet and gives the location of the appropriate Java class. After declaration, the Servlet can be referenced by the previously given name and mapped to a URL path. The name and class values are assigned by a given string in the servlet-name and servlet-class tags, respectively. The Servlet's name is arbitrary, but it must be unique from any other Servlet name for that Web Application. In the body of the servlet-mapping tag, the name and URL path for a Servlet are given by a string value in the body of the servlet-name and url-pattern tags, respectively. The name must match a name previously defined by a servlet element. The URL path can be anything as defined by the Servlet specification:

- An exact pattern to match. The pattern must start with a /, but can contain anything afterwards. This type of pattern is used for a one-to-one mapping of a request to a specific Servlet.

- An extension match, *.extension. In this case all URLs ending with the given extension are forwarded to the specified Servlet. This is

Figure 2-6 HelloWorld Servlet

commonly used in Servlet frameworks and can force many requests to go to the same Servlet[15].

- A path mapping. Path mappings must start with a / and end with a /*. In between anything can appear. Path mappings are usually used for forwarding all requests that fall in a certain directory to a specific Servlet.
- Default Servlet, /. A default Servlet mapping is used to define a Servlet for forwarding requests when no path information is given. This is analogous to a directory listing[16].

With the HelloWorld Servlet, an exact pattern match was used that forwards any request for /HelloWorld directly to the Servlet (see Figure 2-6). Translating any of these URL patterns to a full URL involves prefixing the pattern with the URL to the Web Application. For the HelloWorld Servlet in the jspbook Web Application, this would be http://127.0.0.1/jspbook/HelloWorld. Restart Tomcat to update your changes and use this URL to browse to the HelloWorld Servlet[17]. A simple HTML page should be displayed that says "Hello World!". For non-English readers, our apologies; internationalizing this properly would require chapter precedence of 1, 12, then 2.

---

15. It is used, for example, by Tomcat to map all requests to .jsp to a Servlet that knows how to process JavaServer Pages.

16. The default Servlet was used when you sent the first request to http://localhost/jspbook.

17. Tomcat can be configured to automatically reload a Web Application when any part of that application changes. See the Tomcat documentation for more details.

Understand Servlet Deployment!

Deploying a Servlet is relatively simple but very important. Pay attention in the preceding example because for brevity further examples do not include the verbose deployment description. A single sentence such as "Deploy Servlet *x* to the URL mapping *y*". is used to mean the same thing. Only when it is exceptionally important to the example is the full deployment descriptor provided.

Web Application Deployment Descriptor Structure

Each and every Servlet needs to be deployed before it is available for a client to use. The HelloWorld Servlet example introduced the Web Application Deployment Descriptor elements that do this, but before you go on deploying more Servlets, there is some more information to be aware of. The schema for `web.xml` defines which elements can be used and in what order they must appear. In the previous example this is the reason that both the `servlet` and `servlet-mapping` elements appeared before the `welcome-file-list` element. This is also the reason that the `servlet` element was required to appear before the `servlet-mapping` element[18].

From the preceding three elements it might seem arrangement is of alphabetical precedence, but this is not the case. The arrangement of elements must match the given listing with the Web Application Deployment Descriptor schema. This rather long title should sound familiar—it is the same XML schema that defines what can appear in `web.xml`. The current complete schema can be found in the Servlet 2.4 specification. The element ordering is defined by the root `web-inf` element and is, in ascending order, as follows: `icon`, `display-name`, `description`, `distributable`, `context-param`, `filter`, `filter-mapping`, `listener`, `servlet`, `servlet-mapping`, `session-config`, `mime-mapping`, `welcome-file-list`, `error-page`, `jsp-config`, `resource-env-ref`, `message-destination-ref`, `resource-ref`, `security-constraint`, `login-config`, `security-role`, `env-entry`, `ejb-ref`, `ejb-local-ref.`, `message-destination`, and `locale-encoding-mapping-list`.

Understanding the order is not difficult, but it is a problem quite a few new Servlet developers ask about. It is well worth mentioning it now to avoid causing any confusion later. Keep in mind that this order also applies to multiple elements of the same name. If two Servlets are deployed, both of the `servlet` elements must be listed before any of the `servlet-mapping` elements. It does not

---

18. Not all Servlet containers enforce the schema, however. Consult your container's documentation for more information.

matter what order a group of the same elements are in, but it does matter that they are properly grouped.

Servlet Configuration

Sometimes it is necessary to provide initial configuration information for Servlets. Configuration information for a Servlet may consist of a string or a set of string values included in the Servlet's `web.xml` declaration. This functionality allows a Servlet to have initial parameters specified outside of the compiled code and changed without needing to recompile the Servlet. Each servlet has an object associated with it called the `ServletConfig`[19]. This object is created by the container and implements the `javax.servlet.ServletConfig` interface. It is the ServletConfig that contains the initialization parameters. A reference to this object can be retrieved by calling the `getServletConfig()` method. The `ServletConfig` object provides the following methods for accessing initial parameters:

`getInitParameter(String name)`

The `getInitParameter()` returns a `String` object that contains the value of the named initialization parameter or null if the parameter does not exist.

`getInitParameterNames()`

The `getInitParameterNames()` method returns the names of the Servlet's initialization parameters as an `Enumeration` of `String` objects or an empty `Enumeration` if the Servlet has no initialization parameters.

Defining initial parameters for a Servlet requires using the `init-param`, `param-name`, and `param-value` elements in `web.xml`. Each `init-param` element defines one initial parameter and must contain a parameter name and value specified by children `param-name` and `param-value` elements, respectively. A Servlet may have as many initial parameters as needed, and initial parameter information for a specific Servlet should be specified within the servlet element for that particular Servlet.

Using initial parameters, the HelloWorld Servlet can be modified to be more internationally correct. Instead of assuming the Servlet should say "Hello World!", it will be assumed the Servlet should say the equivalent for any given language. To accomplish this, an initial parameter will be used to configure the

---

19. In fact, in the standard Servlet library a Servlet and a ServletConfig are the same object—that is, GenericServlet implements both `javax.servlet.Servlet` and `javax.servlet.ServletConfig`.

proper international "Hello" message. While `HelloWorld.java` will still not be perfectly compliant for all languages, it does demonstrate initial parameters. Modify `HelloWorld.java` to match the code in Listing 2-3.

Listing 2-3 InternationalizedHelloWorld.java

```
package com.jspbook;

import java.io.*;
import javax.servlet.*;
import javax.servlet.http.*;

public class InternationalizedHelloWorld extends HttpServlet {

  public void doGet(HttpServletRequest request,
                    HttpServletResponse response)
    throws IOException, ServletException {
      response.setContentType("text/html");
      PrintWriter out = response.getWriter();
      out.println("<html>");
      out.println("<head>");
      String greeting;
      greeting =
       getServletConfig().getInitParameter("greeting");
      out.println("<title>" +greeting+"</title>");
      out.println("</head>");
      out.println("<body>");
      out.println("<h1>" +greeting+"</h1>");
      out.println("</body>");
      out.println("</html>");
  }
}
```

Save the preceding code as `InternationalizedHelloWorld.java` in the `/WEB-INF/classes/com/jspbook` directory of the jspbook Web Application. Since this is the second code example, a full walk-through is given for deploying the Servlet. In future examples it will be expected that you deploy Servlets on your own to a specified URL.

Open up `web.xml` in the `/WEB-INF` folder of the jspbook Web Application and add in a declaration and mapping to `/InternationalizedHelloWorld` for the InternationalizedHelloWorld Servlet. When finished, `web.xml` should match Listing 2-4.

Listing 2-4   Updated web.xml

```xml
<web-app xmlns="http://java.sun.com/xml/ns/j2ee" version="2.4">

  <servlet>
    <servlet-name>HelloWorld</servlet-name>
    <servlet-class>com.jspbook.HelloWorld</servlet-class>
  </servlet>
  <servlet>
    <servlet-name>InternationalizedHelloWorld</servlet-name>
    <servlet-class>
      com.jspbook.InternationalizedHelloWorld
    </servlet-class>
  </servlet>
  <servlet-mapping>
    <servlet-name>InternationalizedHelloWorld</servlet-name>
    <url-pattern>/InternationalizedHelloWorld</url-pattern>
  </servlet-mapping>
  <servlet-mapping>
    <servlet-name>HelloWorld</servlet-name>
    <url-pattern>/HelloWorld</url-pattern>
  </servlet-mapping>

  <welcome-file-list>
    <welcome-file>welcome.html</welcome-file>
  </welcome-file-list>
</web-app>
```

The InternationalizedHelloWorld Servlet relies on an initial parameter for the classic "Hello World" greeting. Specify this parameter by adding in the following entry to web.xml.

```xml
...
  <servlet>
    <servlet-name>InternationalizedHelloWorld</servlet-name>
    <servlet-class>
      com.jspbook.InternationalizedHelloWorld
    </servlet-class>
    <init-param>
      <param-name>greeting</param-name>
      <param-value>Bonjour!</param-value>
    </init-param>
  </servlet>
...
```

Leave the `param-name` element's body as `greeting`, but change the value specified in the body of the `param-value` tag to be a greeting of your choice. A candidate for a welcome message *en francais*[20] would be "Bonjour!" After saving any changes, reload the jspbook Web Application and visit the Internationalized-HelloWorld Servlet to see the new message. Figure 2-7 shows an example browser rendering of InternationalizedHelloWorld Servlet's output.

Instead of the basic "Hello World!", the Servlet now displays the initial parameter's value. This approach is nowhere near the best of solutions for internationalization issues, but it does work in some cases and is a good example to introduce initial Servlet configuration. In general, the initial parameter mechanism shown previously is used to provide simple configuration information for an entire Web Application. The HelloWorld Servlet example demonstrated initial parameters for one Servlet, but later on in the chapter it will be shown that the same method is used to provide initial parameters for an entire Web Application.

Limitations of Configuration: web.xml Additions

Initial parameters are a good method of providing simple one-string values that Servlets can use to configure themselves. This approach is simple and effective, but is a limited method of configuring a Servlet. For more complex Servlets it is not uncommon to see a completely separate configuration file created to accompany `web.xml`. When developing Servlets, keep in mind that nothing stops you from doing this. If the parameter name and parameter values mappings are

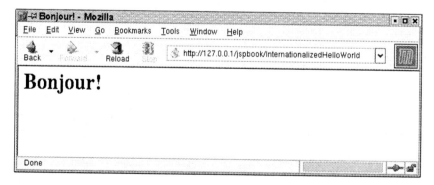

Figure 2-7 Browser Rendering of InternationalizedHelloWorld Servlet

---

20. In French.

not adequate, do not use them! It is perfectly OK to create a custom configuration file and package it in a WAR with the rest of a Web Application. A great example of doing this is shown by the Jakarta Struts framework appearing in Chapter 11. The Struts framework relies on a control Servlet that is configured via a custom and usually lengthy XML file.

Client/Server Servlet Programming

A Servlet request and response is represented by the `javax.servlet.Servlet Request` and `javax.servlet.ServletResponse` objects, or a corresponding subclass of them. For HTTP Servlets the corresponding classes are `HttpServlet Request` and `HttpServletResponse`. These two objects were quickly introduced with the HelloWorld Servlet example, but the example was primarily focused on showing how a Servlet is deployed for use. Coding and deploying are the fundamental parts of Servlet development. Deployment was explained first because it is the exact same process for any given Servlet. Once explained it is a fairly safe assumption that you can repeat the process or simply copy and edit what already exists. Servlet code varies greatly depending on what the Servlet are designed to do. Understanding and demonstrating some of the different uses of Servlets are a lot easier if time and space are not devoted to rehashing the mundane act of deployment. Servlet code is where discussion is best focused, and that is exactly what the rest of the chapter does.

Since this is a Servlet-focused book, very little time is going to be spent on discussing the normal techniques and tricks of coding with Java. Any good Java book will discuss these, and they all are valid for use with Servlets. Time is best spent focusing on the Servlet API. Understanding HTTP and the `HttpServlet` class is a good start, but knowledge of the `HttpServletRequest` and `HttpServlet Response` objects are needed before some useful Servlets can be built.

HttpServletRequest and HttpServletResponse

The Servlet API makes manipulating an HTTP request and response pair relatively simple through use of the `HttpServletRequest` and `HttpServletResponse` objects. Both of these objects encapsulate a lot of functionality. Do not worry if it seems like this section is skimming through these two objects. Detailing all of the methods and members would be both tedious and confusing without understanding the rest of the Servlet API, but API discussion has to start somewhere and these two objects are arguably the most important. In this section discussion will only focus on a few of the most commonly used methods of each object.

Later chapters of the book cover the other methods in full and in the context of which they are best used.

HttpServletResponse

The first and perhaps most important functionality to discuss is how to send information back to a client. As its name implies, the HttpServletResponse object is responsible for this functionality. By itself the HttpServletResponse object only produces an empty HTTP response. Sending back custom content requires using either the getWriter() or getOutputStream() method to obtain an output stream for writing content. These two methods return suitable objects for sending either text or binary content to a client, respectively. Only one of the two methods may be used with a given HttpServletResponse object. Attempting to call both methods causes an exception to be thrown.

With the HelloWorld Servlet example, Listing 2-1, the getWriter() method was used to get an output stream for sending the HTML markup. In the first few lines of HelloWorld.java, a getWriter() call obtained a java.io.PrintWriter object suitable for sending back the text.

```
PrintWriter out = response.getWriter();
out.println("<html>");
out.println("<head>");
out.println("<title>Hello World!</title>");
```

Using an instance of a PrintWriter object consists of providing a String object and calling either the print(), println(), or write() methods. The difference between the methods is that println appends a new line character, '\n', to each line of response text. In both the HelloServlet.java code and the generated HTML page, the println() method was used to make the lines of HTML easy to read. As Table 2-1 shows, the HTML markup matches each println() call used in HelloWorld.java. In practice the lines of HTML will not always match up so nicely to the code in a Servlet, but the same idea is the reason println() is usually preferred over solely using the print() method. When the HTML markup does not match what is expected, it is far easier to debug by matching calls to the println() method.

Using a PrintWriter is not meant to be complex, and it should now be clear how to use the PrintWriter object for sending text. Above and beyond what has previously been shown is sending custom encoded text. So far only one type of text has been sent, the default text encoding of HTTP, ISO-8895-1, but changing the character encoding is possible and is covered in full in Chapter 12.

Table 2-1 HTML Markup from HelloWorld Servlet

Generated Markup	HelloWorld.java
`<html>`	`out.println("<html>");`
`<head>`	`out.println("<head>");`
`<title>Hello World!</title>`	`out.println("<title>Hello World!</title>");`
`</head>`	`out.println("</head>");`
`<body>`	`out.println("</head>");`
`<h1>Hello World!</h1>`	`out.println("<h1>Hello World!</h1>");`
`</body>`	`out.println("</body>");`
`</html>`	`out.println("</html>");`

Compared to using the `getWriter()` method, the `getOutputStream()` method is used when more control is needed over what is sent to a client. The returned `OutputStream` can be used for sending text, but is usually used for sending non-text-related binary information such as images. The reason for this is because the `getOutputStream()` method returns an instance of a `javax.servlet.ServletOutputStream` object, not a `PrintWriter`. The `ServletOutputStream` object directly inherits from `java.io.OutputStream` and allows a developer to write raw bytes. The `PrintWriter` objects lack this functionality because it always assumes you are writing text.

In most practical situations it is rarely needed to send raw bytes rather than text to a client, but this functionality is something a good Servlet developer should be aware of[21]. Often the incorrect mindset is to think Servlets can only send dynamically created text. By sending raw bytes, a Servlet can dynamically provide any form of digital content. The primary restriction on this functionality is being able to create the needed bytes for a desired content. For commonly used formats, including images and audio, it is not uncommon to see a Java API built to simplify the task. Combining this API with the Servlet API, it is then relatively easy to send the custom format. A good example to use would be the Java API for

---

21. Note that for better efficiency you may want to use the `OutputStream` rather than the `PrintWriter` to send text. The `PrintWriter` accepts Unicode strings whereas the `OutputStream` accepts bytes. See *Java Performance and Scalability Volume 1* by Dov Bulka for more details.

Advanced Imaging (JAI). Using this API many of the popular image formats can be produced from the server-side, even on servers not supporting a GUI.

Full discussion of non-text-producing Servlets is outside the scope of this book. Producing custom images, audio, and other non-text formats via Java is not something specific to Servlets. The only thing a Servlet needs to do is appropriately set a MIME type and send a client some bytes, but that is not a good reason to completely avoid an example. For completeness, Listing 2-5 provides a Servlet that dynamically generates an image and sends the bytes using a `ServletOutputStream`.

Listing 2-5   DynamicImage.java

```java
package com.jspbook;

import javax.servlet.*;
import javax.servlet.http.*;
import java.io.*;
import java.awt.*;
import java.awt.image.*;
import com.sun.image.codec.jpeg.*;

public class DynamicImage extends HttpServlet {

  public void doGet(
    HttpServletRequest request,
    HttpServletResponse response)
    throws ServletException, IOException {

    response.setContentType("image/jpeg");

    // Create Image
    int width = 200;
    int height = 30;
    BufferedImage image = new BufferedImage(
      width, height, BufferedImage.TYPE_INT_RGB);

    // Get drawing context
    Graphics2D g = (Graphics2D)image.getGraphics();

    // Fill background
    g.setColor(Color.gray);
    g.fillRect(0, 0, width, height);
```

```
  // Draw a string
  g.setColor(Color.white);
  g.setFont(new Font("Dialog", Font.PLAIN, 14));
  g.drawString("http://www.jspbook.com",10,height/2+4);

  // Draw a border
  g.setColor(Color.black);
  g.drawRect(0,0,width-1,height-1);

  // Dispose context
  g.dispose();

  // Send back image
  ServletOutputStream sos = response.getOutputStream();
  JPEGImageEncoder encoder =
    JPEGCodec.createJPEGEncoder(sos);
  encoder.encode(image);
  }
}
```

Save the preceding code as `DynamicImage.java` in the `/WEB-INF/classes/com/jspbook` directory of the jspbook Web Application. Compile and deploy the DynamicImage Servlet with a mapping to the `/DynamicImage` URL extension of the jspbook Web Application. After reloading the Web Application, browse to `http://127.0.0.1/jspbook/DynamicImage`. A JPEG formatted image is dynamically generated on each request to the Servlet. Figure 2-8 shows an example of one of the dynamically generated images.

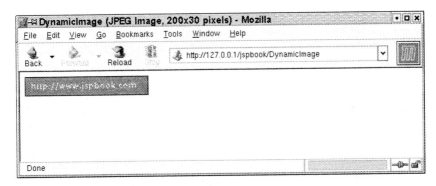

Figure 2-8 DynamicImage Servlet

Before going out and creating your own image-producing Servlet, a fair warning should be given regarding the preceding code. For simplicity the code uses an object from the `com.sun.image.codec.jpeg` package that is unofficially included in the J2SDK 1.4. Code from the `com.sun` package is not guaranteed to be around in future Java releases, nor is it meant for developers to use. A proper solution would be to use an instance of the `ImageEncoder` class from the Java Advanced Imaging API, but that would have required you download and install the JAI before running the example.

Response Headers

Along with sending content back to a client, the `HttpServletResponse` object is also used to manipulate the HTTP headers of a response. HTTP response headers are helpful for informing a client of information such as the type of content being sent back, how much content is being sent, and what type of server is sending the content. The `HttpServletResponse` object includes the following methods for manipulating HTTP response headers:

- **addHeader(java.lang.String name, java.lang.String value):** The `addHeader()` method adds a response header with the given name and value. This method allows response headers to have multiple values.

- **containsHeader(java.lang.String name):** The `containsHeader()` method returns a `boolean` indicating whether the named response header has already been set.

- **setHeader(java.lang.String name, java.lang.String value):** The `setHeader()` method sets a response header with the given name and value. If the header had already been set, the new value over-writes the previous one. The `containsHeader()` method can be used to test for the presence of a header before setting its value.

- **setIntHeader(java.lang.String name, int value):** The `setIntHeader()` sets a response header with the given name and integer value. If the header had already been set, the new value overwrites the previous one. The `containsHeader()` method can be used to test for the presence of a header before setting its value.

- **setDateHeader(java.lang.String name, long date):** The `setDateHeader()` sets a response header with the given name and date value. The date is specified in terms of milliseconds since the epoch. If the header had already been set, the new value overwrites the previous one. The `containsHeader()` method can be used to test for the presence of a header before setting its value.

- **addIntHeader(java.lang.String name, int value):** The `addIntHeader()` method adds a response header with the given name and integer value. This method allows response headers to have multiple values.

- **addDateHeader(java.lang.String name, long date):** The `addDateHeader()` method adds a response header with the given name and date value. The date is specified in terms of milliseconds since the epoch[22]. This method doesn't override previous response headers and allows response headers to have multiple values.

In the introduction to HTTP that appeared earlier in this chapter, a few HTTP response headers were seen, and in the HelloWorld Servlet the `Content-Type` response header was used. In both these cases, elaboration on the headers' semantics was conveniently skipped. This was done intentionally to simplify the examples, but it is time to clarify what these unexplained HTTP headers mean (see Table 2-2), along with introducing some of the other helpful headers that can be set by an `HttpServletResponse` object.

In most cases the most important header to worry about as a Servlet author is `Content-Type`. This header should always be set to 'text/html' when a Servlet is sending back HTML. For other formats the appropriate MIME type[23] should be set.

Response Redirection

Any HTTP response code can be sent to a client by using the `setStatus()` method of an `HttpServletResponse` object. If everything works OK, Servlet will send back a status code 200, OK. Another helpful status code to understand is 302, "Resource Temporarily Moved". This status code informs a client that the resource they were looking for is not at the requested URL, but is instead at the URL specified by the `Location` header in the HTTP response. The 302 response code is helpful because just about every Web browser automatically follows the new link without informing a user. This allows a Servlet to take a user's request and forward it any other resource on the Web.

Because of the common implementation of the 302 response code, there is an excellent use for it besides the intended purpose. Most Web sites track where vis-

22. A common reference in time; January 1, 1970 GMT.
23. Multipart Internet Mail Extensions defined in RFCs 2045, 2046, 2047, 2048, and 2049

Table 2-2 HTTP 1.1 Response Header Fields

Header Field	Header Value
Age	A positive integer representing the estimated amount of time since the response was generated from the server.
Location	Some HTTP response codes redirect a client to a new resource. The location of this resource is specified by the Location header as an absolute URI.
Retry-After	The Retry-After response header field can be used with a 503 (Service Unavailable) response to indicate how long the service is expected to be unavailable to the requesting client. The value of this field can be either a date or an integer number of seconds (in decimals) after the time of the response.
Server	The Server field is a string representing information about the server that generated this response.
Content-Length	The Content-Length entity header field indicates the size of the message body, in decimal number of octets (8-bit bytes), sent to the recipient or, in the case of the HEAD method, the size of the entity body that would have been sent had the request been a GET.
Content-Type	The MIME type that corresponds to the content of the HTTP response. This value is often used by a browser to determine if the content should be rendered internally or launched for rendering by an external application.
Date	The Date field represents the date and time at which the message was originated.
Pragma	The Pragma field is used to include implementation-specific directives that may apply to any recipient along the request-response chain. The most commonly used value is "no-cache", indicating a resource shouldn't be cached.

itors come from to get an idea of what other sites are sending traffic. The technique for accomplishing involves extracting the "`referer`" (note the slightly inaccurate spelling) header of an HTTP request. While this is simple, there is no equally easy way of tracking where a site sends traffic. The problem arises because any link on a site that leads to an external resource does send a request back to the site it was sent from. To solve the problem, a clever trick can be used that relies on the HTTP 302 response code. Instead of providing direct links to external resources, encode all links to go to the same Servlet on your site but include the real link as a parameter. Link tracking is then provided using the Servlet to log the intended link while sending the client back a 302 status code along with the real link to visit.

As you might imagine, using a Servlet to track links is very commonly done by sites with HTTP-aware developers. The HTTP 302 response code is used so often it has a convenience method, `sendRedirect()`, in the `HttpServlet` `Response` object. The `sendRedirect()` method takes one parameter, a string representing the new URL, and automatically sets the HTTP 302 status code with appropriate headers. Using the `sendRedirect()` method and a `java.util.` `Hashtable`, it is easy to create a Servlet for tracking link use. Save the code in Listing 2-6 as `LinkTracker.java` in the `/WEB-INF/classes/com/jspbook` directory of the jspbook Web Application. Deploy the Servlet to the `/LinkTracker` URL mapping.

Listing 2-6 LinkTracker.java

```
package com.jspbook;

import java.util.*;
import java.io.*;
import javax.servlet.*;
import javax.servlet.http.*;

public class LinkTracker extends HttpServlet {
  static private Hashtable links = new Hashtable();

  String tstamp;
  public LinkTracker() {
    tstamp = new Date().toString();
  }

  public void doGet(HttpServletRequest request,
                    HttpServletResponse response)
    throws IOException, ServletException {

    String link = request.getParameter("link");
    if (link != null && !link.equals("")) {
      synchronized (links){
        Integer count = (Integer) links.get(link);
        if (count == null) {
          links.put(link, new Integer(1));
        }
```

```
      else {
        links.put(link, new Integer(1+count.intValue()));
      }
    }
    response.sendRedirect(link);
  }
  else {
    response.setContentType("text/html");
    PrintWriter out = response.getWriter();
    request.getSession();
    out.println("<html>");
    out.println("<head>");
    out.println("<title>Links Tracker Servlet</title>");
    out.println("</head>");
    out.println("<body>");
    out.println("<p>Links Tracked Since");
    out.println(tstamp+":</p>");
    if (links.size() != 0) {
      Enumeration enum = links.keys();
      while (enum.hasMoreElements()) {
        String key = (String)enum.nextElement();
        int count = ((Integer)links.get(key)).intValue();
        out.println(key+" : "+count+" visits<br>");
      }
    }
    else {
      out.println("No links have been tracked!<br>");
    }
    out.println("</body>");
    out.println("</html>");
  }
}
public void doPost(HttpServletRequest request,
                   HttpServletResponse response)
  throws IOException, ServletException {
  doGet(request, response);
}
}
```

To complement the LinkTracker Servlet, some links are needed that use it. The links can be to any resource as long as they are encoded properly. Encoding the links is not difficult; it requires the real link be passed as the link parameter in a query string. Listing 2-7 is a simple HTML page that includes a few properly encoded links. Save the HTML as `links.html` in the base directory of the jspbook Web Application.

Listing 2-7 Some Links Encoded for the LinkTracker Servlet

```html
<html>
  <head>
    <title>Some Links Tracked by the LinkTracker Servlet</title>
  </head>
  <body>
Some good links for Servlets and JSP. Each link is directed
through the LinkTracker Servlet. Click on a few and visit
the <a href="LinkTracker">LinkTracker Servlet</a>.
<ul>
  <li><a href="LinkTracker?link=http://www.jspbook.com">
    Servlets and JSP Book Support Site</a></li>
  <li><a href="LinkTracker?link=http://www.jspinsider.com">
    JSP Insider</a></li>
  <li><a href="LinkTracker?link=http://java.sun.com">
    Sun Microsystems</a></li>
</ul>
  </body>
</html>
```

After reloading the Web Application, browse to `http://127.0.0.1/jspbook/` `links.html`. Figure 2-9 shows what the page looks like after rendered by a browser. Click a few times on any combination of the links.

Each link is directed through the LinkTracker Servlet, which in turn directs a browser to visit the correct link. Before each redirection the LinkTracker Servlet

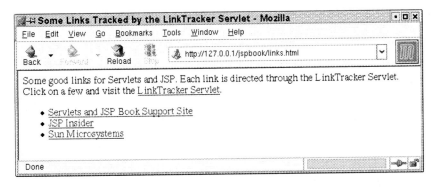

Figure 2-9 Browser Rendering of links.html

logs the use of the link by keying the link URL to an `Integer` object in a `Hashtable`. If you browse directly to the LinkTracker Servlet, `http://127.0.0.1/jspbook/LinkTracker`, it displays information about links visited. Figure 2-10 shows what the results look like after tracking a few links. Results are current as of the last reloading of the LinkTracker Servlet. This example does not log the information for long-term use, but nothing stops such a modification from being made.

Response Redirection Translation Issues

Response redirection is a good tool to be aware of and works with any implementation of the Servlet API. However, there is a specific bug that tends to arise when using relative response redirection. For instance:

```
response.sendRedirect("../foo/bar.html");
```

would work perfectly fine when used in some Servlets but would not in others. The trouble comes from using the relative back, "../", to traverse back a directory. A JSP can correctly use this (assuming the browser translates the URL correctly), but the JSP can use it only if the request URL combined with the redirection ends up at the appropriate resource. For instance, if `http://127.0.0.1/foo/bar.html` is a valid URL, then `http://127.0.0.1/foo/../foo/bar.html` should also be valid. However, `http://127.0.0.1/foo/foo/../foo/bar.html` will not reach the same resource.

This may seem like an irrelevant problem, but we will soon introduce request dispatching that will make it clear why this is an issue. Request dispatching allows for requests to be forwarded on the server-side—meaning the

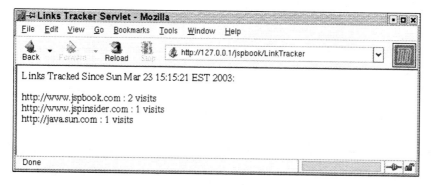

Figure 2-10 Browser Rendering of Link Statistics from the LinkTracker Servlet

requested URL does not change, but the server-side resource that handles it can. Relative redirections are not always safe; " ../" can be bad. The solution is to always use absolute redirections. Either use a complete URL such as:

```
response.sendRedirect("http://127.0.0.1/foo/bar.html");
```

Or use an absolute URL from the root, "/", of the Web Application.

```
response.sendRedirect("/for/bar.html")
```
[24];

In cases where the Web application can be deployed to a non-root URL, the `HttpServletRequest getContextPath()` method should be used in conjunction:

```
response.sendRedirect(request.getContextPath()+"/foo/bar.html");
```

Further information about the `HttpServletRequest` object and use of the `getContextPath()` method is provided later in this chapter.

Auto-Refresh/Wait Pages

Another response header technique that is uncommon but helpful is to send a wait page or a page that will auto-refresh to a new page after a given period of time. This tactic is helpful in any case where a response might take an uncontrollable time to generate, or for cases where you want to ensure a brief pause in a response. The entire mechanism revolves around setting the Refresh response header[25]. The header can be set using the following:

```
response.setHeader("Refresh", "time; URL=url" );
```

Where "time" is replaced with the amount of seconds, the page should wait, and "url" is replaced with the URL that the page should eventually load. For instance, if it was desired to load `http://127.0.0.1/foo.html` after 10 seconds of waiting, the header would be set as so:

```
response.setHeader("Refresh", "10; URL=http://127.0.0.1/foo.html");
```

Auto-refreshing pages are helpful because they allow for a normal "pull" model, waiting for a client's request, to "push" content. A good practical use case

---

24. Another option is to use the JavaServer Pages Standard Tag Libraries redirect tag. The JSTL is covered in Chapter 7.

25. The Refresh header is not part of the HTTP 1.0 or HTTP 1.1 standards. It is an extension supported by Microsoft Internet Explorer, Netscape Navigator 4.x, and Mozilla-based clients.

would be a simple your-request-is-being-processed-page that after a few seconds refreshes to show the results of the response. The alternative (also the most commonly used approach) is to wait until a request is officially finished before sending back any content. This results in a client's browser waiting for the response, sometimes appearing as if the request might time-out and resulting in the user making a time-consuming request twice[26].

Another practical use case for wait page would be slowing down a request, perhaps to better ensure pertinent information is seen by the user. For example, a wait page that showed either an advertisement or legal information before redirecting to the appropriately desired page.

It should be clear that there are several situations where the Refresh response header can come in handy. While it is not a standard HTTP 1.1 header, it is something that is considered a de facto standard[27].

HttpServletRequest

A client's HTTP request is represented by an `HttpServletRequest` object. The `HttpServletRequest` object is primarily used for getting request headers, parameters, and files or data sent by a client. However, the Servlet specification enhances this object to also interact with a Web Application. Some of the most helpful features include session management and forwarding of requests between Servlets.

Headers

HTTP headers set by a client are used to inform a server about what software the client is using and how the client would prefer a server send back requested information. From a Servlet, HTTP request headers can be accessed by calling the following methods:

- **getHeader(java.lang.String name):** The `getHeader()` method returns the value of the specified request header as a string. If the request did not include a header of the specified name, this method returns null. The header name is case insensitive. You can use this method with any request header.

---

26. Auto-refresh pages help tremendously reduce this problem, but you should also ensure the Web application accurately maintains state. Chapter 9 thoroughly covers state management.

27. Be aware, however, that the Refresh and Redirect solutions shown here do have a downside. They both involved extra roundtrips from the client to the server. Roundtrips are expensive in terms of time and resources used, and a Web application should seek to minimize them.

- **getHeaders(java.lang.String name):** The `getHeaders()` method returns all the values of the specified request header as an `Enumeration` of `String` objects. Some headers, such as `Accept-Language`, can be sent by clients as several headers, each with a different value rather than sending the header as a comma-separated list. If the request did not include any headers of the specified name, this method returns an empty `Enumeration` object. The header name is case insensitive. You can use this method with any request header.

- **getHeaderNames():** The `getHeaderNames()` method returns an `Enumeration` of all the names of headers sent by a request. In combination with the `getHeader()` and `getHeaders()` methods, `getHeaderNames()` can be used to retrieve names and values of all the headers sent with a request. Some containers do not allow access of HTTP headers. In this case `null` is returned.

- **getIntHeader(java.lang.String name):** The `getIntHeader()` method returns the value of the specified request header as an `int`. If the request does not have a header of the specified name, this method returns −1. If the header cannot be converted to an integer, this method throws a `NumberFormatException`.

- **getDateHeader(java.lang.String name):** The `getDateHeader()` method returns the value of the specified request header as a `long` value that represents a `Date` object. The date is returned as the number of milliseconds since the epoch. The header name is case insensitive. If the request did not have a header of the specified name, this method returns −1. If the header cannot be converted to a date, the method throws an `IllegalArgumentException`.

HTTP request headers are very helpful for determining all sorts of information. In the later chapters HTTP request headers are used as the primary resource for mining data about a client. This includes figuring out what language a client would prefer, what type of Web browser is being used, and if the client can support compressed content for efficiency. For now it is helpful to understand that these headers exist, and to get a general idea about what type of information the headers contain. Listing 2-8 is a Servlet designed to do just that. Save the following code as `ShowHeaders.java` in the `/WEB-INF/classes/com/jspbook` directory of the jspbook Web Application.

Listing 2-8   ShowHeaders.java

```java
package com.jspbook;

import java.util.*;
import java.io.*;
import javax.servlet.*;
import javax.servlet.http.*;

public class ShowHeaders extends HttpServlet {

  public void doGet(HttpServletRequest request,
                    HttpServletResponse response)
    throws IOException, ServletException {
      response.setContentType("text/html");
      PrintWriter out = response.getWriter();
      out.println("<html>");
      out.println("<head>");
      out.println("<title>Request's HTTP Headers</title>");
      out.println("</head>");
      out.println("<body>");
      out.println("<p>HTTP headers sent by your client:</p>");
      Enumeration enum = request.getHeaderNames();
      while (enum.hasMoreElements()) {
        String headerName = (String) enum.nextElement();
        String headerValue = request.getHeader(headerName);
        out.print("<b>"+headerName + "</b>: ");
        out.println(headerValue + "<br>");
      }
      out.println("</body>");
      out.println("</html>");
  }
}
```

Compile the Servlet and deploy it to the /ShowHeaders path of the jspbook
Web Application. After reloading the Web application, browse to http://
127.0.0.1/jspbook/ShowHeaders to see a listing of all the HTTP headers your
browser sends (see Figure 2-11).

The preceding is a good example of the headers normally sent by a Web
browser. They are fairly self-descriptive. You can probably imagine how these
headers can be used to infer browser and internationalization information. Later

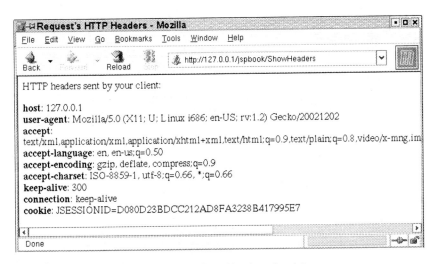

Figure 2-11 Browser Rendering of the ShowHeaders Servlet

on we will do just that[28], but for now we end our discussion of request headers with Table 2-3, which lists some of the most relevant and helpful ones.

Form Data and Parameters

Perhaps the most commonly used methods of the `HttpServletRequest` object are the ones that involve getting request parameters: `getParameter()` and `getParameters()`. Anytime an HTML form is filled out and sent to a server, the fields are passed as parameters. This includes any information sent via input fields, selection lists, combo boxes, check boxes, and hidden fields, but excludes file uploads. Any information passed as a query string is also available on the server-side as a request parameter. The `HttpServletRequest` object includes the following methods for accessing request parameters.

- **getParameter(java.lang.String parameterName):** The `getParameter()` method takes as a parameter a parameter name and returns a `String` object representing the corresponding value. A null is returned if there is no parameter of the given name.

---

28. In particular, the Referer header is perfect for tracking who sends traffic to your Web site; this is similar to the LinkTracker Servlet and very complementary. However, implementing referer tracking via a Servlet is cumbersome compared to using a filter. Therefore, a referer-tracking example is saved for the later chapter about filters.

Table 2-3   HTTP Request Headers

Name	Value
Host	The Host request header field specifies the Internet host and port number of the resource being requested, as obtained from the original URL given by the user or referring resource. Mandatory for HTTP 1.1.
User-Agent	The User-Agent request header field contains information about the user agent (or browser) originating the request. This is for statistical purposes, the tracing of protocol violations, and automated recognition of user agents for the sake of tailoring responses to avoid particular user-agent limitations.
Accept	The Accept request header field can be used to specify certain media types that are acceptable for the response. Accept headers can be used to indicate that the request is specifically limited to a small set of desired types.
Accept-Language	The Accept-Language request header field is similar to Accept, but restricts the set of natural languages that are preferred as a response to the request.
Accept-Charset	The Accept-Charset request header field can be used to indicate what character sets are acceptable for the response. This field allows clients capable of understanding more comprehensive or special-purpose character sets to signal that capability to a server that is capable of representing documents in those character sets. The ISO-8859-1 character set can be assumed to be acceptable to all user-agents. Referer (*sic*) The Referer request header field allows the client to specify, for the server's benefit, the address (URI) of the resource from which the Request URI was obtained.

- **getParameters(java.lang.String parameterName):** The getParameters() method is similar to the getParameter() method, but it should be used when there are multiple parameters with the same name. Often an HTML form check box or combo box sends multiple values for the same parameter name. The getParameter() method is a convenient method of getting all the parameter values for the same parameter name returned as an array of strings.

- **getParameterNames():** The `getParameterNames()` method returns a `java.util.Enumeration` of all the parameter names used in a request. In combination with the `getParameter()` and `getParameters()` method, it can be used to get a list of names and values of all the parameters included with a request.

Like the ShowHeaders Servlet, it is helpful to have a Servlet that reads and displays all the parameters sent with a request. You can use such a Servlet to get a little more familiar with parameters, and to debug HTML forms by seeing what information is being sent. Listing 2-9 is such a Servlet.

Listing 2-9 ShowParameters.java

```
package com.jspbook;

import java.util.*;
import java.io.*;
import javax.servlet.*;
import javax.servlet.http.*;

public class ShowParameters extends HttpServlet {

  public void doGet(HttpServletRequest request,
                    HttpServletResponse response)
    throws IOException, ServletException {

    response.setContentType("text/html");
    PrintWriter out = response.getWriter();
    out.println("<html>");
    out.println("<head>");
    out.println("<title>Request HTTP Parameters Sent</title>");
    out.println("</head>");
    out.println("<body>");
    out.println("<p>Parameters sent with request:</p>");
    Enumeration enum = request.getParameterNames();
    while (enum.hasMoreElements()) {
      String pName = (String) enum.nextElement();
      String[] pValues = request.getParameterValues(pName);
      out.print("<b>"+pName + "</b>: ");
      for (int i=0;i<pValues.length;i++) {
        out.print(pValues[i]);
      }
      out.print("<br>");
    }
```

```
    out.println("</body>");
    out.println("</html>");
  }
  public void doPost(HttpServletRequest request,
                     HttpServletResponse response)
    throws IOException, ServletException {
    doGet(request, response);
  }
}
```

Compile and deploy the ShowParameters Servlet in the jspbook Web Application with a mapping to /ShowParameters path. After reloading the jspbook Web Application, create a few simple HTML forms and use the Servlet to see what parameters are sent. If your HTML is out of practice, do not worry. Listing 2-10 provides a sample HTML form along with a link to a great online HTML reference, http://www.jspinsider.com/reference/html.jsp.

Listing 2-10 exampleform.html

```
<html>
  <head>
    <title>Example HTML Form</title>
  </head>
  <body>
  <p>To debug a HTML form set its 'action' attribute
     to reference the ShowParameters Servlet.</p>
  <form action="http://127.0.0.1/jspbook/ShowParameters"
    method="post">
    Name: <input type="text" name="name"><br>
    Password: <input type="password" name="password"><br>
    Select Box:
    <select name="selectbox">
     <option value="option1">Option 1</option>
     <option value="option2">Option 2</option>
     <option value="option3">Option 3</option>
    </select><br>
    Importance:
    <input type="radio" name="importance" value="very">Very,
    <input type="radio"
      name="importance" value="normal">Normal,
    <input type="radio" name="importance" value="not">Not<br>
```

```
  Comment: <br>
  <textarea name="textarea"
    cols="40" rows="5"></textarea><br>
  <input value="Submit" type="submit">
  </form>
  </body>
</html>
```

Either save the preceding HTML, or create any other HTML form and set the action attribute to `http://127.0.0.1/jspbook/ShowParameters`, and browse to the page. Save the preceding HTML as `exampleform.html` in the base directory of jspbook Web Application and browse to `http://127.0.0.1/jspbook/exampleform.html`. Figure 2-12 shows what the page looks like rendered by a Web browser.

Fill out the form and click on the button labeled Submit to send the information to the ShowParameters Servlet. Something resembling Figure 2-13 will appear.

On the server-side each piece of information sent by a form is referenced by the same name as defined in your HTML form and is linked to a value that a user entered. The ShowParameters Servlet shows this by using `getParameterNames()` for a list of all parameter names and subsequently calling `getParameters()` for the matching value or set of values for each name. The core of the Servlet is a simple loop.

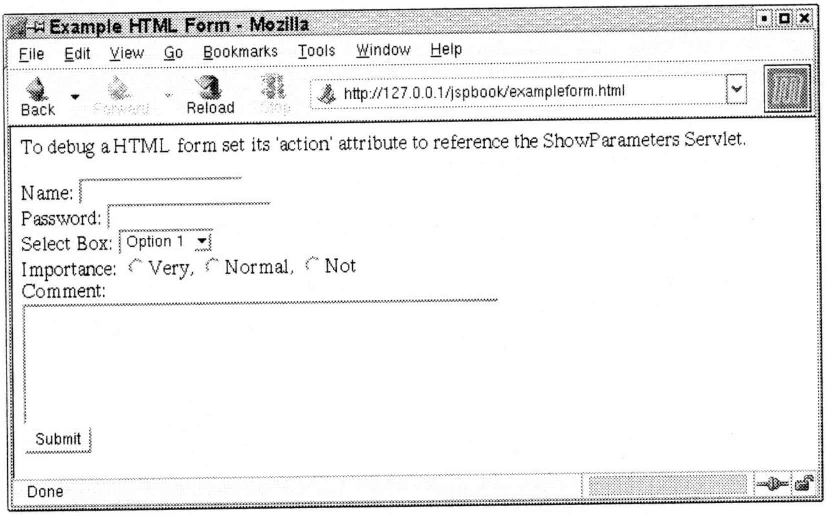

Figure 2-12 Browser Rendering of exampleform.html

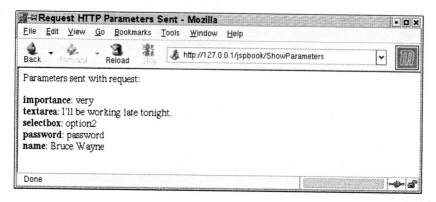

Figure 2-13 Browser Rendering of the ShowParameters Servlet

```
Enumeration enum = request.getParameterNames();
while (enum.hasMoreElements()) {
  String pName = (String) enum.nextElement();
  String[] pValues = request.getParameterValues(pName);
  out.print("<b>"+pName + "</b>: ");
  for (int i=0;i<pValues.length;i++) {
    out.print(pValues[i]);
  }
  out.print("<br>");
}
```

Using parameters, information can be solicited from HTML clients for use by a Servlet. While the ShowParameters Servlet only takes parameters and echoes them back to a client, normally those parameter values are used with other code to generate responses. Later on in the book this functionality will commonly be used with Servlets and JSP for further interacting with clients, including sending email and user authentication.

File Uploads

File uploads[29] are simple for HTML developers but difficult for server-side developers. Sadly, this often results in discussion of Servlets and HTML forms that conveniently skip the topic of file uploads, but understanding HTML form file uploads is a needed skill for any good Servlet developer. Consider any situation

---

29. Be aware that it is possible to execute a Web Application directly from a WAR file, in which case the application may not have access to the file system, so the file upload code may fail.

where a client needs to upload something besides a simple string of text, perhaps when a picture needs to be uploaded. Using the `getParameter()` method will not work because it produces unpredictable results—usually mangling the file being sent or failing to find the content of the file at all.

The reason file uploads are usually considered difficult is because of how the Servlet API handles them. There are two primary MIME types for form information: `application/x-www-form-urlencoded` and `multipart/form-data`. The first MIME type, `application/x-www-form-urlencoded`, is the MIME type most everyone is familiar with and results in the Servlet API automatically parsing out name and value pairs. The information is then available by invoking `HttpServletRequest getParameter()` or any of the other related methods as previously described. The second MIME type, `multipart/form-data`, is the one that is usually considered difficult. The reason why is because the Servlet API does nothing to help you with it[30]. Instead the information is left as is and you are responsible for parsing the request body via either `HttpServletRequest getInputStream()` or `getReader()`.

The complete `multipart/form-data` MIME type and the format of the associated HTTP request are explained in RFC 1867, `http://www.ietf.org/rfc/rfc1867.txt`. You can use this RFC to determine how to appropriately handle information posted to a Servlet. The task is not very difficult, but, as will be explained later, this is usually not needed because other developers have created complementary APIs to handle file uploads.

To best understand what you are dealing with when `multipart/form-data` information is sent, it is valuable to actually look at the contents of such a request. This can be accomplished by making a file-uploading form and a Servlet that regurgitates the information obtained from the `ServletInputStream` provided. Listing 2-11 provides the code for such a Servlet. This Servlet accepts a `multipart/form-data` request and displays the contents of it as plain text.

Listing 2-11 ShowForm.java

```
package com.jspbook;

import java.util.*;
import java.io.*;
```

---

30. In practice, most implementations of the Servlet API try to be merciful on developers who attempt to invoke `getParameter()` functionality on forms that post information as `multipart/form-data`. However, this almost always results in parsing the name-value pairs and missing the uploaded file.

```
import javax.servlet.*;
import javax.servlet.http.*;

public class ShowForm extends HttpServlet {

  public void doPost(HttpServletRequest request,
                     HttpServletResponse response)
    throws IOException, ServletException {

    response.setContentType("text/plain");
    PrintWriter out = response.getWriter();

    ServletInputStream sis = request.getInputStream();
    for (int i = sis.read(); i != -1; i = sis.read()) {
        out.print((char)i);
    }
  }
  public void doGet(HttpServletRequest request,
                    HttpServletResponse response)
    throws IOException, ServletException {
    doPost(request, response);
  }
}
```

Save the preceding code as `ShowForm.java` in the `/WEB-INF/classes/com/jspbook` directory of the jspbook Web Application. Deploy the Servlet to `/ShowForm`. From now on information posted by any form can be viewed by directing the request to `http://127.0.0.1/jspbook/ShowForm`. Try the Servlet out by creating an HTML form that uploads a file (Listing 2-12).

Listing 2-12   multipartform.html

```
<html>
  <head>
    <title>Example HTML Form</title>
  </head>
  <body>
  <p>The ShowForm Servlet will display the content
  posted by an HTML form. Try it out by choosing a
  file (smaller size is preferred) to reference the
  ShowParameters Servlet.</p>
  <form action="http://127.0.0.1/jspbook/ShowForm"
    method="post" enctype="multipart/form-data">
    Name: <input type="text" name="name"><br>
```

```
        File: <input type="file" name="file"><br>
        <input value="Submit" type="submit">
    </form>
    </body>
</html>
```

Save the preceding code as `multipartform.html` in the base directory of the jspbook Web Application and browse to it. Displayed is a small HTML form with two inputs, a name and a file to upload. Figure 2-14 provides a browser rendering of the page.

Fill in the form with any value for the Name field and any file for the File field. A smaller file is preferred because its contents are going to be displayed by the ShowForm Servlet and a large file will take up a lot of space. A good candidate for a file is `multipartform.html` itself. After completing the form, click on the Submit button. The ShowForm Servlet will then show the content that was posted. For example, using `multipartform.html` as the file would result in something similar to the following:

```
---------------------------19675139261365180540154 0383426
Content-Disposition: form-data; name="name"

blah blah
---------------------------19675139261365180540154 0383426
Content-Disposition: form-data; name="file";
filename="multipartform.html"
Content-Type: text/html
```

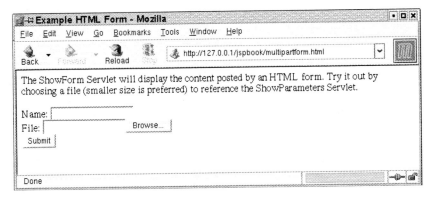

Figure 2-14 Browser Rendering of multipartform.html

```
<html>
  <head>
    <title>Example HTML Form</title>
  </head>
  <body>
  <p>The ShowForm Servlet will display the content
  posted by an HTML form. Try it out by choosing a
  file (smaller size is preferred) to reference the
  ShowParameters Servlet.</p>
  <form action="http://127.0.0.1/jspbook/ShowForm"
    method="post" enctype="multipart/form-data">
    Name: <input type="text" name="name"><br>
    File: <input type="file" name="file"><br>
    <input value="Submit" type="submit">
  </form>
  </body>

</html>
```

```
---------------------------19675139261365180540154 0383426--
```

This would be the type of information you have to parse through when handling a `multipart/form-data` request. If the file posted is not text, it will not be as pretty as the preceding, but there will always be a similar format. Each multipart has a unique token declaring its start. In the preceding the following was used:

```
---------------------------19675139261365180540154 0383426
```

This declares the start of the multipart section and concluded at the ending token, which is identical to the start but with '--' appended. Between the starting and ending tokens are sections of data (possibly nested multiparts) with headers used to describe the content. For example, in the preceding code the first part described a form parameter:

```
Content-Disposition: form-data; name="name"
```

```
blah blah
```

The `Content-Disposition` header defines the information as being part of the form and identified by the name "name". The value of "name" is the content following; by default its MIME type is `text/plain`. The second part describes the uploaded file:

```
Content-Disposition: form-data; name="file";
filename="multipartform.html"
```

```
Content-Type: text/html

<html>
  <head>
    <title>Example HTML Form</title>
  </head>
  <body>
...
```

This time the `Content-Disposition` header defines the name of the form field to be "file", which matches what was in the HTML form, and describes the content-type as `text/html`, since it is not `text/plain`. Following the headers is the uploaded content, the code for `multipartform.html`.

You should be able to easily imagine how to go about creating a custom class that parses this information and saves the uploaded file to the correct location. In cases where the uploaded file is not using a special encoding, the task is as easy as parsing the file's name from the provided headers and saving the content as is. Listing 2-13 provides the code for doing exactly that, and accommodates a file of any size. The Servlet acts as a file upload Servlet, which places files in the `/files` directory of the jspbook Web Application and lets users browse through, optionally downloading previously uploaded files.

Listing 2-13   FileUpload.java

```java
package com.jspbook;

import java.io.*;
import javax.servlet.*;
import javax.servlet.http.*;

public class FileUpload extends HttpServlet {
  public void doPost(HttpServletRequest request,
                     HttpServletResponse response)
  throws IOException, ServletException {

    response.setContentType("text/html");
    PrintWriter out = response.getWriter();

    out.println("<html>");
    out.print("File upload success. <a href=\"/jspbook/files/");
    out.print("\">Click here to browse through all uploaded ");
    out.println("files.</a><br>");
```

```
ServletInputStream sis = request.getInputStream();
StringWriter sw = new StringWriter();
int i = sis.read();
for (;i!=-1&&i!='\r';i=sis.read()) {
  sw.write(i);
}
sis.read(); // ditch '\n'
String delimiter = sw.toString();

int count = 0;
while(true) {
  StringWriter h = new StringWriter();
  int[] temp = new int[4];
  temp[0] = (byte)sis.read();
  temp[1] = (byte)sis.read();
  temp[2] = (byte)sis.read();
  h.write(temp[0]);
  h.write(temp[1]);
  h.write(temp[2]);
  // read header
  for (temp[3]=sis.read();temp[3]!=-1;temp[3]=sis.read()) {
    if (temp[0] == '\r' &&
        temp[1] == '\n' &&
        temp[2] == '\r' &&
        temp[3] == '\n') {
      break;
    }
    h.write(temp[3]);
    temp[0] = temp[1];
    temp[1] = temp[2];
    temp[2] = temp[3];
  }
  String header = h.toString();

  int startName = header.indexOf("name=\"");
  int endName = header.indexOf("\"",startName+6);
  if (startName == -1 || endName == -1) {
    break;
  }
  String name = header.substring(startName+6, endName);
  if (name.equals("file")) {
    startName = header.indexOf("filename=\"");
    endName = header.indexOf("\"",startName+10);
    String filename =
```

```
      header.substring(startName+10,endName);
  ServletContext sc =
    request.getSession().getServletContext();

  File file = new File(sc.getRealPath("/files"));
  file.mkdirs();
  FileOutputStream fos =
    new FileOutputStream(
      sc.getRealPath("/files")+"/"+filename);

  // write whole file to disk
  int length = 0;
  delimiter = "\r\n"+delimiter;
  byte[] body = new byte[delimiter.length()];
  for (int j=0;j<body.length;j++) {
    body[j] = (byte)sis.read();
  }
  // check it wasn't a 0 length file
  if (!delimiter.equals(new String(body))) {
    int e = body.length-1;
    i=sis.read();
    for (;i!=-1;i=sis.read()) {
      fos.write(body[0]);
      for (int l=0;l<body.length-1;l++) {
        body[l]=body[l+1];
      }
      body[e] = (byte)i;
      if (delimiter.equals(new String(body))) {
        break;
      }
      length++;
    }
  }

  fos.flush();
  fos.close();
}
if (sis.read() == '-' && sis.read() == '-') {
  break;
}
}
}
out.println("</html>");
}
public void doGet(HttpServletRequest request,
```

```
                    HttpServletResponse response)
  throws IOException, ServletException {
    doPost(request, response);
  }
}
```

Save the preceding code as `FileUpload.java` in the `/WEB-INF/classes/com/jspbook` directory of the jspbook Web Application. The code parses through each part of the form data—that is, each parameter or file—and saves all files in the `/files` directory of the jspbook Web Application.

The code is purposely left as one large Servlet because it is initially easier to digest the information if it is all in one place; nothing stops you from reimplementing the preceding code in a more object-oriented fashion, perhaps modeling an enhanced version of the `getParameter()` method. Two important points should be noted about the code for the FileUpload Servlet. At all times information is read directly from the `ServletInputStream` object—that is, directly from the client and minimally buffered. This allows for very large files to be handled equally well as files of a small size. Additionally, this parses completely through the information in the HTTP post—that is, it determines the delimiter and keeps parsing until the end of the request, when the delimiter with '--' appended is found.

```
ServletInputStream sis = request.getInputStream();
StringWriter sw = new StringWriter();
int i = sis.read();
for (;i!=-1 && i!='\r'; i=sis.read()) {
  sw.write(i);
}
sis.read(); // ditch '\n'
String delimiter = sw.toString();

int count = 0;
while(true) {
  ...
  if (sis.read() == '-' && sis.read() == '-') {
    break;
  }
}
```

The while loop loops indefinitely, reading through each part of the form data. Recall form information is posted with a delimiter such as:

```
-----------------------------1967513926136518054015403834263\r\n
```

Used to separate each section, ended with the same delimiter with '--' appended:

```
---------------------------------19675139261365180540154038342 6--
```

The code for FileUpload.java automatically reads a section using the delimiter, but the code conditionally continues based on what is found immediately after the delimiter. Should the character sequence '\r\n' be found then the loop continues, with the characters discarded. However, should the character '—' be found, the loop is terminated because the end of the form information has been found.

The body of the indefinite while loop is responsible for parsing out the header and the content of the form-data part. Header information is found by parsing, starting from the delimiter, until the appropriate character sequence, '\r\n\r\n', is found.

```java
StringWriter h = new StringWriter();
int[] temp = new int[4];
temp[0] = (byte)sis.read();
temp[1] = (byte)sis.read();
temp[2] = (byte)sis.read();
h.write(temp[0]);
h.write(temp[1]);
h.write(temp[2]);
// read header
for (temp[3]=sis.read();temp[3]!=-1;temp[3]=sis.read())
{
  if (temp[0] == '\r' &&
      temp[1] == '\n' &&
      temp[2] == '\r' &&
      temp[3] == '\n') {
    break;
  }
  h.write(temp[3]);
  temp[0] = temp[1];
  temp[1] = temp[2];
  temp[2] = temp[3];
}
String header = h.toString();
```

Recall that form-part header information is separated from content by a blank line, '\r\n'—meaning the end of a line followed by a blank line; '\r\n\r\n', signifies the division between header and content information, which is why

'\r\n\r\n' is being searched for. The actual search is trivial; a temporary array, `temp`, that holds four characters is used to check the last four characters parsed. After the entire header is parsed, it is echoed in the response, and the name of the form-part is determined.

```
int startName = header.indexOf("name=\"");
int endName = header.indexOf("\"",startName+6);
if (startName == -1 || endName == -1) {
  break;
}
String name = header.substring(startName+6, endName);
```

The form-part's name is specified, if it was provided, using the following format, `name="name"`, where `name` is the name as specified in the HTML form using the name attribute. The preceding code does nothing more than use the string manipulation functions of the String class to determine the value of `name`.

After the name of the form-part is determined, the matching content is selectively handled: if the name is "file", the contents are saved as a file; any other name is treated as a form parameter and echoed back in the response. There is nothing special about the name "file"; it is an arbitrary name chosen so that FileUpload.java knows to save the content as a file. The code used to save the file is similar to the code used to parse header information, except this time the delimiter is the form-part delimiter, not '\r\n\r\n'.

```
if (name.equals("file")) {
  startName = header.indexOf("filename=\"");
  endName = header.indexOf("\"",startName+10);
  String filename =
    header.substring(startName+10,endName);

ServletConfig config = getServletConfig();
ServletContext sc = config.getServletContext();
FileOutputStream fos =
  new FileOutputStream(sc.getRealPath("/")+filename);

// write whole file to disk
int length = delimiter.length();
byte[] body = new byte[delimiter.length()];
for (int j=0;j<body.length-1;j++) {
  body[j] = (byte)sis.read();
  fos.write(body[j]);
}
int e = body.length-1;
```

```
      i = sis.read();
      for (;i!=-1;i=sis.read()) {
        body[e] = (byte)i;
        if (delimiter.equals(new String(body))) {
          break;
        }
        fos.write(body[e]);
        for(int k=0;k<body.length-1;k++) {
          body[k] = body[k+1];
        }
        length++;
      }

      fos.flush();
      fos.close();
      out.println("<p><b>Saved File:</b> "+filename+"</p>");
      out.println("<p><b>Length:</b> "+ length+"</p>");
    }
```

The code first determines the name of the file being uploaded by searching for a special string, `filename="name"`, where `name` is the file's name, in the header. Next, a file is created in the `/files` directory of the Web Application[31] with the same name, and the content is saved.

In order to use the FileUpload Servlet, an HTML form, similar to `multi-partform.html`, needs to be created. The form may include any number of input elements of any type and in any order, but one file input must be present and the input must be named "file". Listing 2-14 is a simple example. Save the following code as `fileupload.html` in the root directory of the jspbook Web Application.

Listing 2-14 fileupload.html

```
<html>
  <head>
    <title>Example HTML Form</title>
  </head>
  <body>
  <p>Select a file to upload or
  <a href="/jspbook/files/">browse
```

---

31. The `ServletContext` and `ServletConfig` objects, both discussed later in this chapter, are required in order to save a file relative to the Web Application. Discussion of this is skipped right now in favor of the proper explanation provided later.

```
  currently uploaded files.</a></p>
  <form action="http://127.0.0.1/jspbook/FileUpload"
    method="post" enctype="multipart/form-data">
    File: <input type="file" name="file"><br>
    <input value="Upload File" type="submit">
  </form>
  </body>
</html>
```

The HTML form posts information to `/FileUpload`, the deployment of the FileUpload Servlet. Browse to `http://127.0.0.1/jspbook/fileupload.html` to try out the newly created HTML form. Figure 2-15 provides a browser rendering of the form.

Fill in the form fields. The file field should be a file you wish to have on the server; try something such as a picture. Upon clicking on the Submit button, the form's information, including the file, is uploaded to the FileUpload Servlet. The FileUpload Servlet saves the file and displays a summary page, as shown in Figure 2-16.

Verify the file has been successfully uploaded by clicking on the link provided to browse the `/files` directory of the jspbook Web Application. Tomcat displays the default directory listing that includes the file just uploaded. To download the file or any other file in the directory, simply click on the file's listing.

In general, the UploadFile Servlet is demonstrating how a Servlet can parse multi-part form data and save uploaded files. The code can be adapted for other situations where files need to be uploaded, perhaps an online photo album or a more robust file sharing service. It should be noted that no restriction exists on what may

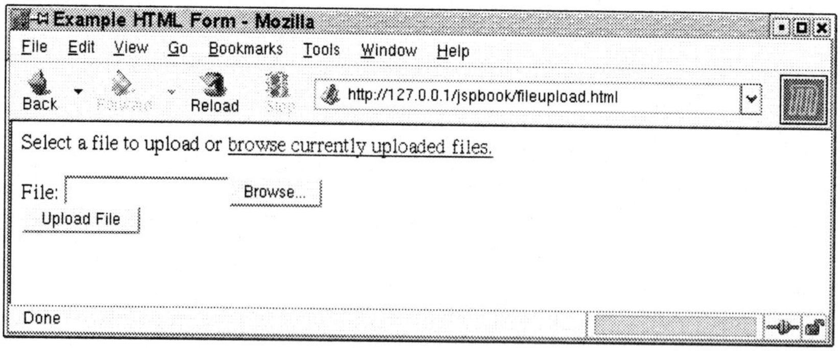

Figure 2-15 Browser Rendering of fileupload.html

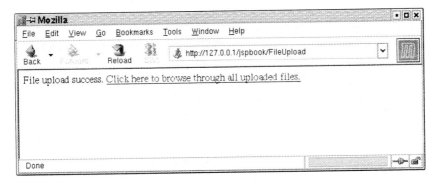

Figure 2-16 Browser Rendering of the FileUpload Servlet's Response

be done with a file uploaded by an HTML form. In the FileUpload.java example, the file is saved in the `/files` directory of the Web Application, but the file could just as easily been saved elsewhere in the Web Application or not saved at all.

Using a File Upload API

As a good developer, it is helpful to understand exactly how the Servlet API handles file uploads; however, in most every practical case you can do away with manually parsing and handling a file upload. File uploads are nothing new, and several implementations of file upload API exist. A good, free, open source file upload API is the Jakarta Commons File Upload API, `http://jakarta.apache.org/commons/fileupload/`. Download the latest release of the code (it is a very small JAR) and put the JAR file in the `/WEB-INF/lib` directory of the jspbook Web Application.

There are several reasons a file upload API can be helpful. A great reason is it can greatly simplify your code. Consider the FileUpload Servlet in the previous section. Using the Jakarta Commons File Upload API, the code can be reduced to Listing 2-15.

Listing 2-15 FileUploadCommons.java

```
package com.jspbook;

import java.io.*;
import javax.servlet.*;
import javax.servlet.http.*;
import org.apache.commons.fileupload.*;
import java.util.*;
```

```
public class FileUploadCommons extends HttpServlet {
  public void doPost(HttpServletRequest request,
                     HttpServletResponse response)
  throws IOException, ServletException {

    response.setContentType("text/html");
    PrintWriter out = response.getWriter();

    out.println("<html>");
    out.print("File upload success. <a href=\"/jspbook/files/");
    out.print("\">Click here to browse through all uploaded ");
    out.println("files.</a><br>");

    ServletContext sc = getServletContext();
    String path = sc.getRealPath("/files");
    org.apache.commons.fileupload.FileUpload fu = new
      org.apache.commons.fileupload.FileUpload();
    fu.setSizeMax(-1);
    fu.setRepositoryPath(path);
    try {
      List l = fu.parseRequest(request);
      Iterator i = l.iterator();
      while (i.hasNext()) {
        FileItem fi = (FileItem)i.next();
        fi.write(path+"/"+fi.getName());
      }
    }
    catch (Exception e) {
      throw new ServletException(e);
    }

    out.println("</html>");
  }
  public void doGet(HttpServletRequest request,
                    HttpServletResponse response)
  throws IOException, ServletException {
    doPost(request, response);
  }
}
```

The code more closely follows good object-oriented programming by abstracting request parsing logic. Instead of implementing RFC 1867 by hand, as we did in `FileUpload.java`, the Jakarta Commons File Upload API handles all the work.

```
ServletContext sc = getServletContext();
String path = sc.getRealPath("/files");
FileUpload fu = new FileUpload();
fu.setSizeMax(-1);
fu.setRepositoryPath("/root/todelete");
try {
  List l = fu.parseRequest(request);
  Iterator i = l.iterator();
  while (i.hasNext()) {
    FileItem fi = (FileItem)i.next();
    fi.write(path+"/"+fi.getName());
  }
}
catch (Exception e) {
  throw new ServletException(e);
}
```

We will not discuss the file upload API in depth, but it should be easy to follow what is going on. The `FileUpload` object abstracts all of the code responsible for parsing `multipart/form-data` information. The only thing we need to care about is limiting the size of file uploads and specifying a temporary directory for the API to work with. The `parseRequest()` method takes a `HttpServlet Request` and returns an array of files parsed from the input—what more could you ask for?

In addition to simplifying code, there are a few other reasons that justify using an existing file upload API. There are several nuances of file uploads that need to be dealt with; multiple files can be uploaded, different encodings can be used, and excessively large files might be uploaded. In short, the less code you have to manage the better, and a good file upload API can easily take care of handling `multipart/form-data` information. Certainly consider using an existing file upload API when working with Servlets and file uploads. If anything, the Jakarta Commons File Upload API provides an excellent starting point for handling file uploads or creating a custom file upload API.

Request Delegation and Request Scope

Request delegation is a powerful feature of the Servlet API. A single client's request can pass through many Servlets and/or to any other resource in the Web Application. The entire process is done completely on the server-side and, unlike response redirection, does not require any action from a client or extra information sent between the client and server. Request delegation is available through the `javax.servlet.RequestDispatcher` object. An appropriate instance of a

`RequestDispatcher` object is available by calling either of the following methods of a `ServletRequest` object:

- **getRequestDispatcher(java.lang.String path):** The `getRequestDispatcher()` method returns the `RequestDispatcher` object for a given path. The path value may lead to any resource in the Web Application and must start from the base directory, "/".
- **getNamedDispatcher(java.lang.String name):** The `getNamedDispatcher()` method returns the `RequestDispatcher` object for the named Servlet. Valid names are defined by the `servlet-name` elements of `web.xml`.

  A `RequestDispatcher` object provides two methods for including different resources and for forwarding a request to a different resource.
- **forward(javax.servlet.ServletRequest, javax.servlet.ServletResponse):** The `forward()` method delegates a request and response to the resource of the `RequestDispatcher` object. A call to the `forward()` method may be used only if no content has been previously sent to a client. No further data can be sent to the client after the forward has completed.
- **include(javax.servlet.ServletRequest, javax.servlet.ServletResponse):** The `include()` method works similarly to `forward()` but has some restrictions. A Servlet can `include()` any number of resources that can each generate responses, but the resource is not allowed to set headers or commit a response.

Request delegation is often used to break up a large Servlet into smaller, more relevant parts. A simple case would include separating out a common HTML header that all pages on a site share. The `RequestDispatcher` object's `include()` method then provides a convenient method of including the header with the Servlet it was separated from and in any other Servlet needing the header. Any future changes to the header, and all the Servlets automatically reflect the change. For now, an example of simple Servlet server-side includes will be held in abeyance. JavaServer Pages[32] provide a much more elegant solution to this problem, and in practice Servlet request delegation is usually used for an entirely different purpose.

---

32. JSP is based directly off Servlets and is covered in full in Chapter 3.

In addition to simple server-side includes, request delegation is a key part of server-side Java implementations of popular design patterns. With respect to Servlet and JSP, design patterns are commonly agreed-upon methods for building Web Applications that are robust in functionality and easily maintainable. The topic of design is given a whole chapter to itself, Chapter 11, so no direct attempt will be given to demonstrate it now. Instead, discussion will focus on laying the foundation for Chapter 11 by explaining the new object scope that request delegation introduces.

With Java there are well-defined scopes for variables that you should already be familiar with. Local variables declared inside methods are by default only available inside the scope of that method. Instance variables, declared in a class but outside a method or constructor, are available to all methods in the Java class. There are many other scopes too, but the point is that these scopes are helpful to keep track of objects and help the JVM accurately garbage-collect memory. In Servlets, all of the previous Java variable scopes still exist, but there are some new scopes to be aware of. Request delegation introduces the *request scope*.

Request scope and the other scopes mentioned in this chapter are not something officially labeled by the Servlet specification[33]. The Servlet specification only defines a set of methods that allow objects to be bound to and retrieved from various containers (that are themselves objects) in the `javax.servlet` package. Since an object bound in this manner is referenced by the container it was bound to, the bound object is not destroyed until the reference is removed. Hence, bound objects are in the same "scope" as the container they are bound to. The `HttpServletRequest` object is such a container and includes such methods. These methods can be used to bind, access, and remove objects to and from the request scope that is shared by all Servlets to which a request is delegated. This concept is important to understand and can easily be shown with an example.

An easy way to think of request scope is as a method of passing any object between two or more Servlets and being assured the object goes out of scope (i.e., will be garbage-collected) after the last Servlet is done with it. More powerful examples of this are provided in later chapters, but to help clarify the point now, here are two Servlets that pass an object. Save the code in Listing 2-16 as `Servlet2Servlet.java` in the `/WEB-INF/classes/com/jspbook` directory of the jspbook Web Application.

---

33. Request scope and other scopes are officially recognized in the JSP specification

Listing 2-16 Servlet2Servlet.java

```java
package com.jspbook;

import java.io.*;
import javax.servlet.*;
import javax.servlet.http.*;

public class Servlet2Servlet extends HttpServlet {

  public void doGet(HttpServletRequest request,
                    HttpServletResponse response)
    throws IOException, ServletException {
      response.setContentType("text/html");

      String param = request.getParameter("value");
      if(param != null && !param.equals("")) {
        request.setAttribute("value", param);
        RequestDispatcher rd =
request.getRequestDispatcher("/Servlet2Servlet2");
        rd.forward(request, response);
        return;
      }

      PrintWriter out = response.getWriter();
      out.println("<html>");
      out.println("<head>");
      out.println("<title>Servlet #1</title>");
      out.println("</head>");
      out.println("<body>");
      out.println("<h1>A form from Servlet #1</h1>");
      out.println("<form>");
      out.println("Enter a value to send to Servlet #2.");
      out.println("<input name=\"value\"><br>");
      out.print("<input type=\"submit\" ");
      out.println("value=\"Send to Servlet #2\">");
      out.println("</form>");
      out.println("</body>");
      out.println("</html>");
  }
}
```

Deploy the preceding Servlet and map it to the `/Servlet2Servlet` URL extension. Next, save the code in Listing 2-17 as `Servlet2Servlet2.java` in the `/WEB-INF/classes/com/jspbook` directory of the jspbook Web Application.

Listing 2-17   Servlet2Servlet2.java

```
package com.jspbook;

import java.io.*;
import javax.servlet.*;
import javax.servlet.http.*;

public class Servlet2Servlet2 extends HttpServlet {

  public void doGet(HttpServletRequest request,
                    HttpServletResponse response)
    throws IOException, ServletException {
      response.setContentType("text/html");

      PrintWriter out = response.getWriter();
      out.println("<html>");
      out.println("<head>");
      out.println("<title>Servlet #2</title>");
      out.println("</head>");
      out.println("<body>");
      out.println("<h1>Servlet #2</h1>");
      String value = (String)request.getAttribute("value");
      if(value != null && !value.equals("")) {
        out.print("Servlet #1 passed a String object via ");
        out.print("request scope. The value of the String is: ");
        out.println("<b>"+value+"</b>.");
      }
      else {
        out.println("No value passed!");
      }
      out.println("</body>");
      out.println("</html>");
  }
}
```

Deploy the second Servlet and map it to the `/Servlet2Servlet2` URL extension. Reload the jspbook Web Application and the example is ready for use. Browse to `http://127.0.0.1/jspbook/Servlet2Servlet`. Figure 2-17 shows what the Servlet response looks like after being rendered by a Web browser. A

Figure 2-17 Browser Rendering of Servlet2Servlet

simple HTML form is displayed asking for a value to pass to the second Servlet. Type in a value and click on the button labeled Send to Servlet #2.

Information sent from the HTML form is sent straight back to the same Servlet that made the form, Servlet2Servlet. The Servlet verifies a value was sent; creates a new String object; places the String in request scope; and forwards the request to the second Servlet, Servlet2Servlet2. Figure 2-18 shows what a browser rendering of the second Servlet's output looks like. The content on the page shows the request was delegated to the second Servlet, but you can verify the request was delegated by the first Servlet by looking at the URL. This technique is extremely useful and discussed further in the design pattern chapter.

ServletContext

The `javax.servlet.ServletContext` interface represents a Servlet's view of the Web Application it belongs to. Through the `ServletContext` interface, a Servlet can access raw input streams to Web Application resources, virtual directory translation, a common mechanism for logging information, and an *application scope* for binding objects. Individual container vendors provide specific implementations of `ServletContext` objects, but they all provide the same functionality defined by the `ServletContext` interface.

Initial Web Application Parameters

Previously in this chapter initial parameters for use with individual Servlets were demonstrated. The same functionality can be used on an application-wide basis to provide initial configuration that all Servlets have access to. Each Servlet has a

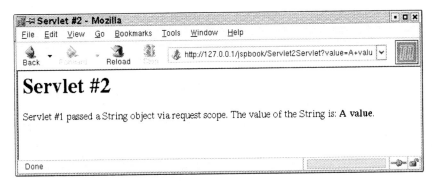

Figure 2-18 Browser Rendering of Request Delegated to Servlet2Servlet2

`ServletConfig` object accessible by the `getServletConfig()` method of the Servlet. A `ServletConfig` object includes methods for getting initial parameters for the particular Servlet, but it also includes the `getServletContext()` method for accessing the appropriate `ServletContext` instance. A `ServletContext` object implements similar `getInitParam()` and `getInitParamNames()` methods demonstrated for `ServletConfig`. The difference is that these methods do not access initial parameters for a particular Servlet, but rather parameters specified for the entire Web Application.

Specifying application-wide initial parameters is done in a similar method as with individual Servlets, but requires replacement of the `init-param` element with the `context-param` element of `Web.xml`, and requires the tag be placed outside any specific `servlet` tag. Occurrences of `context-param` tags should appear before any Servlet tags. A helpful use of application context parameters is specifying contact information for an application's administration. Using the current jspbook `web.xml`, an entry for this would be placed as follows.

```
...
<web-app>
    <context-param>
      <param-name>admin email</param-name>
      <param-value>admin@jspbook.com</param-value>
    </context-param>
    <servlet>
      <servlet-name>helloworld</servlet-name>
      <servlet-class>com.jspbook.HelloWorld</servlet-class>
...
```

We have yet to see how to properly handle errors and exceptions thrown from Servlets, but this initial parameter is ideal for error handling Servlets. For now, create a Servlet that assumes it will be responsible for handling errors that might arise with the Web Application. In Chapter 4 we will show how to enhance this Servlet to properly handle thrown exceptions, but for now pretend a mock error was thrown. Save the code in Listing 2-18 as `MockError.java` in the `/WEB-INF/classes/com/jspbook` directory of the jspbook Web Application.

Listing 2-18 MockError.java

```
package com.jspbook;

import java.io.*;
import javax.servlet.*;
import javax.servlet.http.*;

public class MockError extends HttpServlet {

  public void doGet(HttpServletRequest request,
                    HttpServletResponse response)
    throws IOException, ServletException {

    response.setContentType("text/html");
    PrintWriter out = response.getWriter();
    out.println("<html>");
    out.println("<head>");
    out.println("<title>An Error Has Occurred!</title>");
    out.println("</head>");
    out.println("<body>");
    ServletContext sc =
      getServletConfig().getServletContext();
    String adminEmail = sc.getInitParameter("admin email");
    out.println("<h1>Error Page</h1>");
    out.print("Sorry! An unexpected error has occurred.");
    out.print("Please send an error report to "+adminEmail+".");
    out.println("</body>");
    out.println("</html>");
  }
}
```

Reload the jspbook Web Application and browse to `http://127.0.0.1/jspbook/MockError` to see the page with the context parameter information

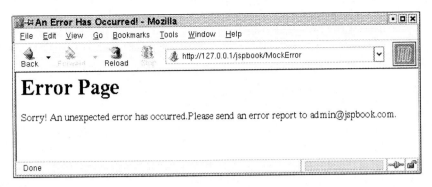

Figure 2-19 Browser Rendering of the MockError Servlet

included. Figure 2-19 shows what the MockError Servlet looks like when rendered by a Web browser.

Notice the correct context parameter value was inserted in the error message. This same parameter might also be used in other various Servlets as part of a header or footer information. The point to understand is that this parameter can be used throughout the entire Web Application while still being easily changed when needed.

Application Scope

Complementing the request scope, a `ServletContext` instance allows for server-side objects to be placed in an application-wide scope[34]. This type of scope is ideal for placing resources that need to be used by many different parts of a Web Application during any given time. The functionality is identical to that as described for the `HttpRequest` object and relies on binding objects to a `ServletContext` instance. For brevity this functionality will not be iterated over again, but will be left for demonstration in later examples of the book.

It is important to note that an application scope should be used sparingly. Objects bound to a `ServletContext` object will not be garbage collected until the `ServletContext` is removed from use, usually when the Web Application is turned off or restarted. Placing large amounts of unused objects in application scope does tax a server's resources and is not good practice. Another issue (that will be gone into in more detail later) is that the `ServletContext` is not truly

---

34. There is also a session scope that will be covered in detail in Chapter 9.

application-wide. If the Web Application is running on multiple servers (say, a Web farm), then there will be multiple `ServletContext` objects; any updates to one `ServletContext` on one server in the farmer will not be replicated to the other `ServletContext` instances.

Virtual Directory Translation

All the resources of a Web Application are abstracted to a virtual directory. This directory starts with a root, "/", and continues on with a virtual path to sub-directories and resources. A client on the World Wide Web can access resources of a Web Application by appending a specific path onto the end of the HTTP address for the server the Web Application runs on. The address for reaching the jspbook Web Application on your local computer is `http://127.0.0.1`. Combining this address with any virtual path to a Web Application resource provides a valid URL for accessing the resource via HTTP.

A Web Application's virtual directory is helpful because it allows fictitious paths to link to real resources located in the Web Application. The only downside to the functionality is that Web Application developers cannot directly use virtual paths to obtain the location of a physical resource. To solve this problem, the `ServletContext` object provides the following method:

`getRealPath(java.lang.String path)`[35]

The `getRealPath()` method returns a `String` containing the real path for a given virtual path. The real path represents the location of the resource on the computer running the Web Application.

To compliment the `getRealPath()` method, the `ServletContext` object also defines methods for obtaining a listing of resources in a Web Application or for an `InputStream` or URL connection to a particular resource:

- **getResourcePaths(java.lang.String path):** The `getResourcePaths()` method returns a `java.util.Set` of all the resources in the directory specified by the path. The path must start from the root of the Web Application, "/".
- **getResourceAsStream(java.lang.String path):** The `getResourceAsStream()` method returns an instance of an

---

35. Again, be aware that a Servlet container is free to load Web Applications from places other than the file system (for example, directly from WAR files or from a database); in that case this method may return null.

`InputStream` to the physical resource of a Web Application. This method should be used when a resource needs to be read verbatim rather than processed by a Web Application.

- **getResource(java.lang.String path):** The `getResource()` method returns a URL to the resource that is mapped to a specified path. This method should be used when a resource needs to be read as it would be displayed to a client.

It is important to remember that a Web Application is designed to be portable. Hard coding file locations in Servlet code is not good practice because it usually causes the Servlet not to work when deployed on a different server or if the Web Application is run directly from a compressed WAR file. The correct method for reading a resource from a Web Application is by using either the `getResource()` or `getResourceAsStream()` methods. These two methods ensure the Servlet will always obtain access to the desired resource even if the Web Application is deployed on multiple servers or as a compressed WAR.

The most common and practical use for virtual directory translation is for accessing important flat files packaged with a Web Application. This primarily includes configuration files but is also used for miscellaneous purposes such as simple flat file databases. An ideal example would be one involving a complex Servlet using a custom configuration file; however, a complex Servlet like this has yet to appear in this book. For a demonstration, a simple Servlet will be created that reads raw files and resources from a Web Application (Listing 2-19). While not necessary for most real-world uses, this Servlet is ideal for learning as it effectively shows the source code of an entire Web Application.

Listing 2-19 ShowSource.java

```
package com.jspbook;

import java.io.*;
import javax.servlet.*;
import javax.servlet.http.*;
import java.util.*;

public class ShowSource extends HttpServlet {

    public void doGet(HttpServletRequest request,
                      HttpServletResponse response)
        throws IOException, ServletException {
```

```java
    PrintWriter out = response.getWriter();

    // Get the ServletContext
    ServletConfig config = getServletConfig();
    ServletContext sc = config.getServletContext();

    // Check to see if a resource was requested
    String resource = request.getParameter("resource");
    if (resource != null && !resource.equals("")) {

        // Use getResourceAsStream() to properly get the file.
        InputStream is = sc.getResourceAsStream(resource);
        if (is !=  null) {
            response.setContentType("text/plain");
            StringWriter sw = new StringWriter();
            for (int c = is.read(); c != -1; c = is.read()) {
                sw.write(c);
            }
            out.print(sw.toString());
        }
    }
    // Show the HTML form.
    else {
        response.setContentType("text/html");
        out.println("<html>");
        out.println("<head>");
        out.println("<title>Source-Code Servlet</title>");
        out.println("</head>");
        out.println("<body>");
        out.println("<form>");
        out.println("Choose a resource to see the source.<br>");
        out.println("<select name=\"resource\">");
        // List all the resources in this Web Application
        listFiles(sc, out, "/");
        out.println("</select><br>");
        out.print("<input type=\"submit\" ");
        out.println("value=\"Show Source\">");
        out.println("</body>");
        out.println("</html>");
    }
}

// Recursively list all resources in Web App
void listFiles(ServletContext sc, PrintWriter out,
```

```
      String base){
    Set set = sc.getResourcePaths(base);
    Iterator i = set.iterator();
    while (i.hasNext()) {
      String s = (String)i.next();
      if (s.endsWith("/")) {
        listFiles(sc, out, s);
      }
      else {
        out.print("<option value=\""+s);
        out.println("\">"+s+"</option>");
      }
    }
  }
}
```

Save Listing 2-15 as `ShowSource.java` in the `/WEB-INF/classes/` `com/jspbook` directory of the jspbook Web Application. Compile the code and deploy the Servlet to the `/ShowSource` path extension of the jspbook Web Application, and after reloading the Web Application, browse to `http://127.` `0.0.1/jspbook/ShowSource`. Figure 2-20 shows what a browser rendering of the Servlet's output looks like.

The Servlet uses the `getResourcePaths()` method to obtain a listing of all the files in the Web Application. After selecting a file, the Servlet uses the `get` `ResourceAsStream()` method to obtain an `InputStream` object for reading and displaying the source code of the resource.

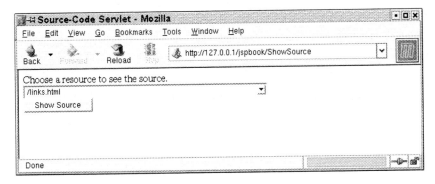

Figure 2-20   Browser Rendering of the ShowSource Servlet

Application-Wide Logging

A nice but not commonly used feature of Servlets is Web Application-wide logging. A `ServletContext` object provides a common place all Servlets in a Web Application can use to log arbitrary information and stack traces for thrown exceptions. The advantage of this functionality is that it consolidates the often odd mix of custom code that gets used for logging errors and debugging information. The following two methods are available for logging information via a Web Application's `ServletContext`:

- **log(java.lang.String msg):** The `log()` method writes the specified string to a Servlet log file or log repository. The Servlet API only specifies a `ServletContext` object implement these methods. No specific direction is given as to where the logging information is to be saved and or displayed. Logged information is sent to `System.out` or to a log file for the container.

- **log(java.lang.String message, java.lang.Throwable throwable):** This method writes both the given message and the stack trace for the `Throwable` exception passed in as parameters. The message is intended to be a short explanation of the exception.

With J2SDK 1.4 the Servlet logging feature is not as helpful as it has previously been. The main advantage of the two `log()` methods is that they provided a common place to send information regarding the Web Application. Most often, as is with Tomcat, a container also allowed for a Servlet developer to write a custom class to handle information logged by a Web Application. This functionality makes it easy to customize how and where Servlet logging information goes. The downside to using the `ServletContext log()` methods is that only code that has access to a `ServletContext` object can easily log information. Non-Servlet classes require a creative hack to log information in the same manner. A better and more commonly used solution for Web Application logging is to create a custom set of API that any class can access and use. The idea is nothing new and can be found in popularized projects such as Log4j, `http://jakarta.apache.org/log4j` or with the J2SDK 1.4 standard logging API, the `java.util.logging` package. Both of these solutions should be preferred versus the Servlet API logging mechanism when robust logging is required.

In lieu of demonstrating the two `ServletContext log()` methods, a brief explanation and example of the `java.util.logging` package is given in Chapter 4. A flexible and consolidated mechanism for logging information is needed in any serious project. The Servlet API logging mechanism does work for simple cases, but this book encourages the use of a more robust logging API.

Distributed Environments

In most cases a `ServletContext` object can be considered as a reference to the entire Web Application. This holds true for single machine servers running one JVM for the Web Application. However, J2EE is not designed to be restricted for use on a single server. A full J2EE server, not just a container supporting Servlets and JSP, allows for multiple servers to manage and share the burden of a large-scale Web Application. These types of applications are largely outside the scope of this book, but it should be noted that application scope and initial parameters will not be the same in a distributed environment. Different servers and JVM instances usually do not share direct access to each other's information. If developing for a group of servers, do not assume that the `ServletContext` object will be the same for every request. This topic is discussed further in later chapters of the book.

Temporary Directory

One subtle but incredibly helpful feature of the Servlet specification is the requirement of a temporary work directory that Servlets and other classes in a Web Application can use to store information. The exact location of the temporary directory is not specified, but all containers are responsible for creating a temporary directory and setting a `java.io.File` object, which describes that directory as the `javax.servlet.context.tempdir` `ServletContext` attribute. Information stored in this directory is only required to persist while the Web Application is running, and information stored in the temporary directory will always be hidden from other Web Applications running on the same server.

The container-defined temporary directory is helpful for one really important reason: Web Applications can be run directly from a WAR; there is no guarantee that you can rely on using `ServletContext getRealPath()` to always work. To solve the problem, all Web Applications have access to at least one convenient place where temporary information can be stored, and that place is provided using the `javax.servlet.context.tempdir` attribute. There are a few good use cases where the `javax.servlet.context.tempdir` attribute is needed. In any situation where a Web Application is caching content locally (not in memory), the `javax.servlet.context.tempdir` attribute temporary directory is the ideal place to store the cache. Additionally, the temporary directory provides a place to temporarily store file uploads or any other information a Web Application is working with.

In practice, it is usually safe to assume your Web Application will be deployed outside of a WAR, especially when you have control over the deployment; however, in cases where a Web Application is intended for general use, the provided temporary directory should always be used to ensure maximum portability of your code. Later on in the book some use cases that deal with the temporary directory are provided; if you took a look at either of the previously mentioned file-upload API, you would have noticed they both take advantage of the temporary directory.

Servlet Event Listeners

The final topic to discuss in this chapter is Servlet event listeners. In many situations it is desirable to be notified of container-managed life cycle events. An easy example to think of is knowing when the container initializes a Web Application and when a Web Application is removed from use. Knowing this information is helpful because you may have code that relies on it, perhaps a database that needs to be loaded at startup and saved at shutdown. Another good example is keeping track of the number of concurrent clients using a Web Application. This functionality can be done with what you currently know of Servlets; however, it can much more easily be done using a listener that waits for a client to start a new session. The greater point being presented here is that a container can be used to notify a Web Application of important events, and Servlet event listeners are the mechanism.

All of the Servlet event listeners are defined by interfaces. There are event listener interfaces for all of the important events related to a Web Application and Servlets. In order to be notified of events, a custom class, which implements the correct listener interface, needs to be coded and the listener class needs to be deployed via web.xml. All of the Servlet event listeners will be mentioned now; however, a few of the event listeners will not make complete sense until the later chapters of the book. In general, all of the event listeners work the same way so this fact is fine as long as at least one good example is provided here.

The interfaces for event listeners correspond to request life cycle events, request attribute binding, Web Application life cycle events, Web Application attribute binding, session[36] life cycle events, session attribute binding, and session serialization, and appear, respectively, as follows:

---

36. As described by this chapter, HTTP is a stateless protocol. However, it is often necessary to maintain state for the duration of all of a particular client's requests. A mechanism exists for this, and the mechanism is commonly called session management. See Chapter 9 for a detailed discussion on the topic.

- javax.servlet.ServletRequestListener
- javax.servlet.ServletRequestAttributeListener
- javax.servlet.ServletContextListener
- javax.servlet.ServletContextAttributeListener
- javax.servlet.http.HttpSessionListener
- javax.servlet.http.HttpSessionAttributeListener
- javax.servlet.http.HttpSessionAttributeListener

Use of each listener is intuitive given an implementation of one and an example deployment descriptor. All of the listener interfaces define events for either the creation and destruction of an object or for notification of the binding or unbinding of an object to a particular scope.

As an example, let us create a listener that tracks the number of concurrent users. We could create a simple hit counter, by tracking how many requests are created; however, the previous hit counter examples in this chapter do a fine job providing the same functionality. Tracking the number of concurrent users is something that we have yet to see, and allows the introduction of *session scope*. For now, think of sessions as being created only once per unique client—regardless if the same person visits the site more than once. This is different from requests, which are created every time a client requests a resource. The listener interface we are going to implement is `HttpSessionListener`. It provides notification of two events: session creation and session destruction. In order to keep track of concurrent users, we will keep a static count variable that will increase incrementally when a session is created and decrease when a session is destroyed.

The physical methods required by the HttpSessionListener interface are as follows:

- **void sessionCreated(HttpSessionEvent evt):** The method invoked when a session is created by the container. This method will almost always be invoked only once per a unique client.
- **void sessionDestroyed(HttpSessionEvent evt):** The method invoked when a session is destroyed by the container. This method will be invoked when a unique client's session times out—that is, after they fail to revisit the Web site for a given period of time, usually 15 minutes.

Listing 2-20 provides our listener class's code, implementing the preceding two methods. Save the code as `ConcurrentUserTracker.java` in the `/WEB-INF/classes/com/jspbook` directory of the jspbook Web Application.

Listing 2-20 ConcurrentUserTracker.java

```java
package com.jspbook;

import javax.servlet.*;
import javax.servlet.http.*;

public class ConcurrentUserTracker implements HttpSessionListener {
  static int users = 0;

  public void sessionCreated(HttpSessionEvent e) {
    users++;
  }
  public void sessionDestroyed(HttpSessionEvent e) {
    users--;
  }
  public static int getConcurrentUsers() {
    return users;
  }
}
```

The listener's methods are intuitive and the logic is simple. The class is trivial to create because the container is managing all the hard parts: handling HTTP requests, trying to keep a session, and keeping a timer in order to successfully time-out unused sessions.

Deploy the listener by adding the entry in Listing 2-21 to web.xml. Add the entry after the starting webapp element but before any Servlet deployments.

Listing 2-21 Deployment of the Concurrent User Listener

```xml
<listener>
  <listener-class>
   com.jspbook.ConcurrentUserTracker
  </listener-class>
</listener>
```

Notice that the deployment does not specify what type of listener interface is being used. This type of information is not needed because the container can figure it out; therefore, deployment of all the different listeners is similar to the above code. Create a listener element with a child listener-class element that has the name of the listener class.

One more addition is required before the concurrent user example can be tested. The concurrent user tracker currently doesn't output information about concurrent users! Let us create a Servlet that uses the static `getConcurrent Users()` method to display the number of concurrent users. Save the code in Listing 2-22 as `DisplayUsers.java` in the `/WEB-INF/com/jspbook` directory of the jspbook Web Application.

Listing 2-22 DisplayUsers.java

```
package com.jspbook;

import java.io.*;
import javax.servlet.*;
import javax.servlet.http.*;

public class DisplayUsers extends HttpServlet {
  public void doGet(HttpServletRequest request,
                    HttpServletResponse response)
  throws IOException, ServletException {

    request.getSession();

    response.setContentType("text/html");
    PrintWriter out = response.getWriter();
    out.println("<html>");
    out.print("Users:");
    out.print(ConcurrentUserTracker.getConcurrentUsers());
    out.println("</html>");
  }
}
```

Deploy the Servlet to the `/DisplayUsers` URL mapping. Compile both `ConcurrentUserTracker.java` and `DisplayUser.java` and reload the jspbook Web Application for the changes to take effect. Test the new functionality out by browsing to `http://127.0.0.1/jspbook/DisplayUsers`. An HTML page appears describing how many users are currently using the Web Application. A browser rendering would be provided; however, the page literally displays nothing more than the text "Users:" followed by the number of current users.

When browsing to the Servlet, it should say one user is currently using the Web Application. If you refresh the page, it will still say only one user is using the Web Application. Try opening a second Web browser and you should see that the page states two people are using the Web Application[37]. Upon closing your Web browser, the counter will not go down, but after not visiting the Web Application for 15 minutes, it will. You can test this out by opening two browsers (to create two concurrent users) and only using one of the browsers for the next 15 minutes. Eventually, the unused browser's session will time-out and the Web Application will report only one concurrent user. In real-world use, odds are that several independent people will be using a Web Application at any given time. In this situation you don't need to do anything but visit the DisplayUsers Servlet to see the current amount of concurrent users.

The concurrent user tracker is a handy piece of code; however, the greater point to realize is how Servlet event listeners can be coded and deployed for use. Event listeners in general are intuitive to use; the hard part is figuring out when and how they are best used, which is hard to fully explain in this chapter. In later chapters of the book, event listeners will be used to solve various problems and complement code. Keep an eye out for them.

Summary

In this chapter the Servlet API was introduced, and focus was placed specifically on Servlets. Servlets are the fundamental building block of server-side Java. A Servlet is highly scalable and easily outperforms traditional CGI by means of a simple three-phase life cycle: initialization, service, and destruction. Commonly, the term Servlets actually refers to HTTP Servlets used on the World Wide Web. The `HttpServlet` class is designed especially for this user and greatly simplifies server-side Java support for HTTP.

The basics of the Servlet API consist of objects that represent a client's request, `HttpServletRequest`, the server's response, `HttpServletResponse`, a session for connecting separate requests, `HttpSession`, and an entire Web Application, `ServletContext`. Each of these objects provides a complete set of methods for accessing and manipulating related information. These objects also introduce two new scopes for Servlet developers to use: request and application. Binding an object to these various scopes allows a Servlet developer to share an object between multiple Servlets and requests for extended periods of time. What

---

37. This won't always appear to work on some browsers, namely Internet Explorer, due to browser tricks designed to be user-friendly. If you can open two complete different browsers, such as Mozilla and Internet Explorer, the Web Application will always report two concurrent users. If you are using Internet Explorer, make sure you open a new copy of the browser and not simply a new browser window.

was only briefly mentioned is that a third, commonly used scope, `session`, is also available. Session scope introduces several issues which merit a complete chapter's worth of information. Chapter 9 fully explains session scope and the issues relating to it.

Overall, this chapter is a reference to creating and using Servlets. Chapter 3 continues discussion of Servlets by introducing a complementary technology: JavaServer Pages.

Chapter 3

JavaServer Pages

JavaServer Pages (JSP) and Servlets are complementary technologies for producing dynamic Web pages via Java. While Servlets are the foundation for server-side Java, they are not always the most efficient solution with respect to development time. Coding, deploying, and debugging a Servlet can be a tedious task. Fixing a simple grammar or markup mistake requires wading through `print()` and `println()` calls, recompiling the Servlet, and reloading a Web Application. Making a grammar or markup mistake is not hard, and the problem is compounded in complex Servlets. JSP complements Servlets by helping solve this problem and simplifying Servlet development.

This chapter discusses the following topics:

- An explanation of JSP and why you would want to use the technology.
- The JSP life cycle—that is, how a container manages a JSP.
- Examination of the similarities and differences between JSP and Servlets.
- An introduction to JSP syntax and semantics.
- Configuring JSP via the Web Application Deployment Descriptor, web.xml.
- An explanation of the JSP implicit objects and why implicit objects are helpful.
- How to use the alternative JSP XML syntax.

As with Chapter 2, do read this chapter straight through. Chapters 2 and 3 describe the basic functionality on which all of the other chapters depend. Chapter 2 introduced Servlets and demonstrated several practical uses of them. This chapter complements Chapter 2 by providing a similar discussion on JavaServer Pages.

JSP 2.0 Specification

The first JavaServer Pages specification was released in 1999. Originally JSP was modeled after other server-side template technologies to provide a simple method of embedding dynamic code with static markup. When a request is made for the content of a JSP, a container interprets the JSP, executes any embedded code, and sends the results in a response. At the time this type of functionality was nothing terribly new, but it was and still is a helpful enhancement to Servlets.

JSP has been revised several times since the original release, each adding functionality, and is currently in version 2.0. The JSP specifications are developed alongside the Servlet specifications and can be found on Sun Microsystems' JavaServer Pages product information page, `http://java.sun.com/products/jsp`.

The functionality defined by the JSP 2.0 specifications can be broken down as follows:

JSP

The JSP specifications define the basic syntax and semantics of a JavaServer Page. A basic JavaServer Page consists of plain text and markup and can optionally take advantage of embedded scripts and other functionality for creating dynamic content.

JavaBeans

JavaBeans are not defined by the JSP specifications, but JSP does provide support for easily using and manipulating them. Often objects used on the server-side of a Web Application are in the form of what is commonly called a JavaBean.

Custom Tags and JSP Fragments

JSP provides a mechanism for linking what would normally be static markup to custom Java code. This mechanism is arguably one of the strong points of JSP and can be used in place of or to complement embedded scripts of Java code.

Expression Language

JSP includes a mechanism for defining dynamic attributes for custom tags. Any scripting language can be used for this purpose; usually Java is implemented, but the JSP specification defines a custom expression language designed specifically for the task. Often the JSP EL is a much simpler and more flexible solution, especially when combined with JSP design patterns that do not use embedded scripts.

Discussing the basics of JSP is the focus of this chapter. JavaBeans, Custom Tags, and the JSP Expression Language are all fully discussed in later chapters after a proper foundation of JSP is established.

JSP Life Cycle

Much like Servlets, understanding JSP requires understanding the simple life cycle that JSP follows. JSP follows a three-phase life cycle: initialization, service, and destruction, as shown in Figure 3-1. This life cycle should seem familiar and is identical to the one described for Servlets in Chapter 2.

While a JSP does follow the Servlet life cycle, the methods have different names. Initialization corresponds to the `jspInit()` method, service corresponds to the `_jspService()` method, and destruction corresponds to the `jspDestroy()` method. The three phases are all used the same as a Servlet and allow a JSP to load resources, provide service to multiple client requests, and destroy loaded resources when the JSP is taken out of service.

JSP is designed specifically to simplify the task of creating text producing `HttpServlet` objects and does so by eliminating all the redundant parts of coding a Servlet. Unlike with Servlets there is no distinction between a normal JSP and one meant for use with HTTP. All JSP are designed to be used with HTTP and to generate dynamic content for the World Wide Web. The single JSP `_jspService()` method is also responsible for generating responses to all seven of the HTTP methods. For most practical purposes a JSP developer does not

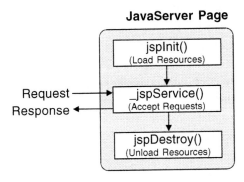

Figure 3-1 JSP Life Cycle

need to know anything about HTTP, nor anything more than basic Java to code a dynamic JSP.

The Difference Between Servlets and JSP

A clear and important distinction to make about JSP is that coding one is nothing like coding a Servlet. From what this chapter has explained, it might appear that JSP is just a simple version of Servlets. In many respects JSP is in fact a simple method of creating a text-producing Servlet; however, do not be fooled into thinking this mindset is always true. As the chapter progresses, it will be clear that JSP and Servlets are two very distinct technologies. Later, after custom tags are introduced, the degree of separation between the two will seem even larger. The use of JSP for easily making a Servlet really only applies in the simplest of cases.

To show how vastly different the code for a JSP can be from a Servlet, Listing 3-1 displays the code for the JSP equivalent of the HelloWorld Servlet (Listing 2-1 that appeared in Chapter 2).

Listing 3-1   HelloWorld.jsp

```
<html>
<head>
<title>Hello World!</title>
</head>
<body>
<h1>Hello World!</h1>
</body>
</html>
```

They are quite different! You'll recall the code for `HelloWorld.java` and notice the two look nothing alike. The code for the JSP is actually identical to the text generated by the HelloWorld Servlet, not the source code. Authoring an HTML-generating JSP is as easy as just authoring the HTML. Compared to using `print()` and `println()` methods in Servlets, the JSP approach is obviously easier. This is why simple JSP are usually considered a quick method of creating text-producing Servlets.

Deploying a JSP is also simpler; a Web Application automatically deploys any JSP to a URL extension that matches the name of the JSP. Test out `HelloWorld.jsp` by saving it in the base directory of the jspbook Web Application then browsing to `http://127.0.0.1/jspbook/HelloWorld.jsp`. Figure 3-2 shows the output of `HelloWorld.jsp` as rendered by a Web browser, identical to the HTML generated by the HelloWorld Servlet, Figure 2-6.

Figure 3-2 Browser Rendering of HelloWorld.jsp

From looking at the results of the example, it certainly does appear `Hello World.jsp` is a simple form of `HelloWorld.java`. What is not shown, but is very important to understand, is that `HelloWorld.jsp` is also actually compiled into equivalent Servlet code. This is done in what is called the *translation phase* of JSP deployment and is done automatically by a container. JSP translation both is and is not something of critical importance for a JSP developer to be aware of. JSP translation to Servlet source code is important because it explains exactly how a JSP becomes Java code. While it varies slightly from container to container, all containers must implement the same JSP life cycle events. Understanding these life cycle methods helps a JSP developer keep code efficient and thread-safe. However, JSP translation is not of critical importance because it is always done automatically by a container. Understanding what a container will do during the translation phase is good enough to code JSP. Keeping track of the generated Servlet source code is not a task a JSP developer ever has to do.

JSP translated to Servlet code can be found by looking in the right place for a particular container. Tomcat stores this code in the `/work` directory of the Tomcat installation. Generated code is never pretty, nor does it always have the same name. Listing 3-2 was taken from `HelloWorld$jsp.java` in the `/work/localhost/jspbook` directory. It is the Servlet code generated for `HelloWorld.jsp` that Tomcat automatically compiled and deployed.

Listing 3-2 Tomcat-Generated Servlet Code for HelloWorld.jsp

```
package org.apache.jsp;

import javax.servlet.*;
import javax.servlet.http.*;
```

```
import javax.servlet.jsp.*;
import org.apache.jasper.runtime.*;


public class HelloWorld$jsp extends HttpJspBase {


    static {
    }
    public HelloWorld$jsp( ) {
    }

    private static boolean _jspx_inited = false;

    public final void _jspx_init() throws
org.apache.jasper.runtime.JspException {
    }

    public void _jspService(HttpServletRequest request,
HttpServletResponse  response)
        throws java.io.IOException, ServletException {

        JspFactory _jspxFactory = null;
        PageContext pageContext = null;
        HttpSession session = null;
        ServletContext application = null;
        ServletConfig config = null;
        JspWriter out = null;
        Object page = this;
        String  _value = null;
        try {

            if (_jspx_inited == false) {
                synchronized (this) {
                    if (_jspx_inited == false) {
                        _jspx_init();
                        _jspx_inited = true;
                    }
                }
            }
            _jspxFactory = JspFactory.getDefaultFactory();
```

```
            response.setContentType("text/html;charset=ISO-
8859-1");
            pageContext = _jspxFactory.getPageContext(this, request,
response,
                "", true, 8192, true);

            application = pageContext.getServletContext();
            config = pageContext.getServletConfig();
            session = pageContext.getSession();
            out = pageContext.getOut();

            // HTML // begin
[file="/HelloWorld.jsp";from=(0,0);to=(8,0)]
                out.write("<html>\r\n<head>\r\n<title>Hello
World!</title>\r\n</head>\r\n<body>\r\n<h1>Hello
World!</h1>\r\n</body>\r\n</html>\r\n");

            // end

        } catch (Throwable t) {
            if (out != null && out.getBufferSize() != 0)
                out.clearBuffer();
            if (pageContext != null)
pageContext.handlePageException(t);
        } finally {
            if (_jspxFactory != null)
_jspxFactory.releasePageContext(pageContext);
        }
    }
}
```

Do not bother trying to read through and understand the generated code. The important point to understand is that a container handles a JSP as a Servlet but does so behind the scenes. This ties directly back to the greater point that JSP are really just Servlets. The difference between the two technologies is not in the life cycles or how a container manages them at runtime. The difference between Servlets and JSP is the syntax they offer for creating the same functionality. With JSP it is almost always simpler to create text-producing Servlets, but normal Servlets are still best suited for sending raw bytes to a client or when complete control is needed over Java source code.

JSP Syntax and Semantics

JSP is not governed by the syntax and semantics defined by the Java 2 specifications. Translated JSP source code is just Java, but when you author a JSP, you abide instead by the rules laid out in the JSP specification. With each release of the JSP specification, these rules grow, and they cannot be easily summed by a few sentences. The majority of this chapter focuses on explaining the current syntax and semantics of JSP. Much of the functionality found in JSP is taken directly from the underlying Servlet API which was already covered in Chapter 2. Expect to see lots of code examples demonstrating syntax, while repetitious semantics are only skimmed with a reference to the full explanation previously given in Chapter 2.

Elements and Template Data

Everything in a JSP is broken down into two generic categories called *elements* and *template data*. Elements are dynamic portions of a JSP. Template data are the static bits of text between. Template data are easily categorized as they are all the text arbitrarily placed on a JSP and meant to be directly sent to a client. Elements are easily categorized as custom actions, tags, and the content allowed to be in between as defined by the JSP specifications.

The concept of elements and template data is important to understand as it dictates when, where, and what text will do when placed in a JSP. This chapter has yet to introduce any elements, but it has shown a use of template text. The `HelloWorld.jsp` example was entirely template text. The corresponding Servlet generated from `HelloWorld.jsp` treated this text as static content and sent it as the content of a response. While `HelloWorld.jsp` only had one big chunk of template text, more complex JSP follow the same rule. Any chunk of template text is taken and sent directly to a client as it appears on the JSP. Elements on the other hand are not sent directly to a client. An element is interpreted by a JSP container and defines special actions that should be taken when generating a response.

Template text does not change, and this little section defines it in total. Elements are what make JSP dynamic, and elements are further explained throughout the rest of the chapter. Elements can be broken down into three different categories: scripting elements, directives, and actions. The following self-named sections explain these elements.

Two Types of Syntax

JSP containers are required to support two different formats of JSP syntax: normal and XML-compatible. The normal JSP syntax is a syntax designed to be easy to author. The XML-compatible JSP syntax takes the normal JSP syntax and modifies it to be XML-compliant[1]. Both syntaxes provide the same functionality, but the XML-compatible syntax is intended to be more easily used by development tools. In the examples of this book the normal JSP syntax is preferred as it is easily read, understood, and will be familiar if you have used older versions of JSP.

Just because the XML syntax will not be appearing much in this book's examples does not mean it is the lesser of the two syntaxes. The JSP XML syntax introduced in the JSP 1.2 specification, from a developer's perspective, is certainly a hassle to use compared to the regular syntax. This is largely due to the complexity and strict enforcement of syntax the JSP 1.2 XML syntax had. JSP 2.0 remedies the problem by providing a much more flexible XML syntax. Later on in the chapter this new, more flexible XML syntax is further explained.

Scripting Elements

The simplest method of making a JSP dynamic is by directly embedding bits of Java code between blocks of template text by use of scripting elements. In theory JSP does not limit scripting elements to only those containing Java code, but the specification only talks about Java as the scripting language, and every container by default has to support Java. Examples in this book use Java as a scripting language. There are three different types of scripting elements available for use in JSP: *scriptlets*, *expressions*, and *declarations*.

Scriptlets

Scriptlets provide a method for directly inserting bits of Java code between chunks of template text. A scriptlet is defined with a start ,<%, an end, %>, with code between. Using Java, the script is identical to normal Java code but without needing a class declaration or any methods. Scriptlets are great for providing low-level functionality such as iteration, loops, and conditional statements, but they also provide a method for embedding complex chunks of code within a JSP.

For many reasons complex scriptlets should be avoided. This is mainly due to the fact that the more scriptlets are used the harder it is to understand and maintain a JSP. In this chapter most of the scriptlet examples are purposely kept simple. This aids in directly demonstrating the core functionality of JSP, but it is also done so that examples do not appear to encourage heavy use of scriptlets. As

---

1. eXtensible Markup Language, http://www.w3.org/XML

an introduction, Listing 3-3 provides a simple JSP that loops to produce multiple lines of text. Looping is accomplished the same as in Java but by placing the equivalent Java code inside scriptlet elements.

Listing 3-3 Loop.jsp

```
<html>
<head>
<title>Loop Example</title>
</head>
<body>
<% for (int i=0; i<5;i++) { %>
 Repeated 5 Times.<br>
<% } %>
</body>
</html>
```

Save `Loop.jsp` in the base directory of the jspbook Web Application and browse to `http://127.0.0.1/jspbook/Loop.jsp`. The page shows up with the statement, "Repeated 5 Times.", repeated five times. Figure 3-3 shows what a browser rendering of the output looks like.

It is important to note that the contents of the scriptlet did not get sent to a client. Only the results of the scriptlet did. This is important because it shows that scriptlets are interpreted by a container and that code inside a scriptlet is not by default shared with visitors of the JSP.

A JSP may contain as many scriptlets as are needed, but caution should be taken not to overuse scriptlets. Scriptlets make a JSP very hard to maintain and are not easily documented; for example, tools like `javadoc` do not work with JSP.

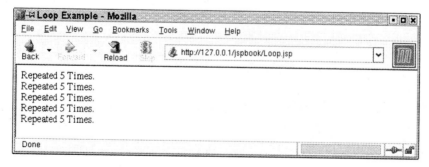

Figure 3-3 Browser Rendering of Loop.jsp

Expressions

Expressions provide an easy method of sending out dynamic strings to a client. An expression must have a start, `<%=`, end, `%>`, and an expression between. An expression element differs in syntax from a scriptlet by an equal sign that must appear immediately after the start. Expressions always send a string of text to a client, but the object produced as a result of an expression does not have to always end up as an instance of a `String` object. Any object left as the result of an expression automatically has its `toString()` method called to determine the value of the expression. If the result of the expression is a primitive, the primitive's value represented as a string is used.

Combined with scriptlets, expressions are useful for many different purposes. A good example is using a scriptlet that is combined with an expression to provide a method of iterating over a collection of values. The scriptlet provides a loop, while expressions and static content are used to send information in a response. `Iteration.jsp` (Listing 3-4) provides an example of this along with a demonstration of passing a non-`string` object as the result of an expression.

Listing 3-4 Iteration.jsp

```
<html>
<head>
<title>Iteration Example</title>
</head>
<body>
<%
 String[] strings = new String[4];
 strings[0] = "Alpha";
 strings[1] = "in";
 strings[2] = "between";
 strings[3] = "Omega";
 for (int i=0; i<strings.length;i++) { %>
 String[<%= i %>] = <%= strings[i] %><br>
<% } %>
</body>
</html>
```

Save `Iteration.jsp` in the base directory of the jspbook Web Application and browse to `http://127.0.0.1/jspbook/Iteration.jsp`. The page displays a list of an iteration through all of the values of the array. Figure 3-4 shows a browser rendering of the output sent by `Iteration.jsp`.

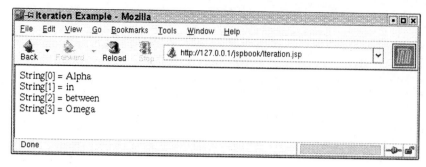

Figure 3-4   Iteration.jsp

Declarations

Declarations are the third and final scripting element available for use in JSP. A declaration is used like a scriptlet to embed code in a JSP, but code embedded by a declaration appears outside of the _jspService() method. For this reason code embedded in a declaration can be used to declare new methods and global class variables, but caution should be taken because code in a declaration is not thread-safe, unless made so by the writer of that code.

Listing 3-5 is a JSP designed to keep a page counter of how many times it has been visited. The JSP accomplishes this by declaring a class-wide variable in a declaration, using a scriptlet to increment the variable on page visits, and an expression to show the variable's value.

Listing 3-5   PageCounter.jsp

```
<%! int pageCount = 0;
 void addCount() {
    pageCount++;
 }
%>
<html>
<head>
<title>PageCounter.jsp</title>
</head>
<body>
<% addCount(); %>
This page has been visited <%= pageCount %> times.
</body>
</html>
```

Save `PageCounter.jsp` in the base directory of the jspbook Web Application and browse to `http://127.0.0.1/jspbook/PageCounter.jsp`. Refresh the browser a few times to watch the JSP count how many times it has been visited. Figure 3-5 shows a browser rendering of the output after visiting the JSP 6 times.

Using scriptlets, expressions, and declarations most anything can be created using JSP. An analogy to Servlets would be: *scriptlets* are code placed inside a service method, *expressions* are `print()` method calls, and *declarations* are code placed globally for a class to use. After the brief explanation above it should be fairly straightforward to start coding using sciptlets, expressions, and declarations, but it is still helpful to understand what the three different scripting elements translate to in a Java code.

Listing 3-6 is the code Tomcat generated from `PageCounter.jsp`. It contains the translation of all three of the scripting elements. The lines of importance are highlighted with an asterisk.

Listing 3-6 PageCounter$jsp.java

```
package org.apache.jsp;

import javax.servlet.*;
import javax.servlet.http.*;
import javax.servlet.jsp.*;
import org.apache.jasper.runtime.*;


public class PageCounter$jsp extends HttpJspBase {

    // begin [file="/PageCounter.jsp";from=(0,3);to=(4,0)]
```

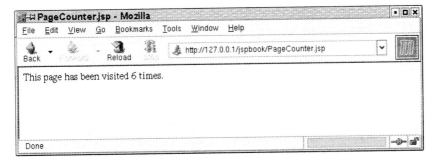

Figure 3-5 Browser Rendering of PageCounter.jsp

```
      int pageCount = 0;
      void addCount() {
        pageCount++;
      }
  // end

  static {
  }
  public PageCounter$jsp( ) {
  }

  private static boolean _jspx_inited = false;

  public final void _jspx_init() throws
org.apache.jasper.runtime.JspException {
  }

  public void _jspService(HttpServletRequest request,
HttpServletResponse  response)
      throws java.io.IOException, ServletException {

      JspFactory _jspxFactory = null;
      PageContext pageContext = null;
      HttpSession session = null;
      ServletContext application = null;
      ServletConfig config = null;
      JspWriter out = null;
      Object page = this;
      String  _value = null;
      try {

          if (_jspx_inited == false) {
              synchronized (this) {
                  if (_jspx_inited == false) {
                      _jspx_init();
                      _jspx_inited = true;
                  }
              }
          }
          _jspxFactory = JspFactory.getDefaultFactory();
          response.setContentType("text/html;charset=ISO-
8859-1");
```

```
                pageContext = _jspxFactory.getPageContext(this, request,
response,
                    "", true, 8192, true);

                application = pageContext.getServletContext();
                config = pageContext.getServletConfig();
                session = pageContext.getSession();
                out = pageContext.getOut();

                // HTML // begin
[file="/PageCounter.jsp";from=(4,2);to=(10,0)]

out.write("\r\n<html>\r\n<head>\r\n<title>PageCounter.jsp</title>\r\
n</head>\r\n<body>\r\n");

                // end
                // begin
[file="/PageCounter.jsp";from=(10,2);to=(10,15)]
                    addCount();
                // end
                // HTML // begin
[file="/PageCounter.jsp";from=(10,17);to=(11,27)]
                    out.write("\r\nThis page has been visited ");

                // end
                // begin
[file="/PageCounter.jsp";from=(11,30);to=(11,41)]
                    out.print( pageCount );
                // end
                // HTML // begin
[file="/PageCounter.jsp";from=(11,43);to=(14,0)]
                    out.write(" times.\r\n</body>\r\n</html>\r\n");

                // end

            } catch (Throwable t) {
                if (out != null && out.getBufferSize() != 0)
                    out.clearBuffer();
                if (pageContext != null)
pageContext.handlePageException(t);
            } finally {
                if (_jspxFactory != null)
```

```
_jspxFactory.releasePageContext(pageContext);
      }
    }
}
```

Thankfully this is the last bit of generated code that appears in this book. Reading through translated JSP is rarely required nor is it usually helpful[2], but it is certainly needed to understand what a container does when a JSP is translated to a Servlet. Taking the highlighted lines from `PageCounter$jsp.java`, each can be linked back to scripting elements from `PageCounter.jsp`.

In `PageCounter.jsp` a declaration is used to define a class-wide variable for counting the number of page visits and a method for incrementing it.

```
<%! int pageCount = 0;
 void addCount() {
    pageCount++;
 }
%>
```

Translated into `PageCounter$jsp.java`, the code of the declaration appears outside of the `_jspService()` method and is class-wide. This allows for the `addCount()` method to be coded as a real method of the Servlet and the `pageCount` variable to be accessible by all calls to the `_jspService()` method. The methods are **not thread-safe**, but for this particular example, it does not matter if the `pageCount` variable changes halfway through generating a response.

```
public class PageCounter$jsp extends HttpJspBase {

    // begin [file="/PageCounter.jsp";from=(0,3);to=(4,0)]
        int pageCount = 0;
        void addCount() {
           pageCount++;
        }
    // end
```

In `PageCounter.jsp` a scriptlet and expression are used to increase and send the value of the `pageCount` variable to client.

```
<% addCount(); %>
This page has been visited <%= pageCount %> times.
```

---

2. Except in the case of debugging, where it is often useful to see the JSP and the generated Servlet side-by-side.

Translated in `PageCounter$jsp.java`, the scriptlet is used verbatim, but the expression is turned into a call to the `print()` method of a `PrintWriter` object obtained from the corresponding `HttpServletResponse`. Both scripting elements are located in the `_jspService()` method, are thread-safe, and local to a specific client request.

```
public void _jspService(HttpServletRequest request,
HttpServletResponse  response)
        throws java.io.IOException, ServletException {
. . .
            // begin
[file="/PageCounter.jsp";from=(10,2);to=(10,15)]
                addCount();
            // end
            // HTML // begin
[file="/PageCounter.jsp";from=(10,17);to=(11,27)]
                out.write("\r\nThis page has been visited ");

            // end
            // begin
[file="/PageCounter.jsp";from=(11,30);to=(11,41)]
                out.print( pageCount );
            // end
. . .
    }
```

The point of the preceding code is to illustrate exactly where scriptlets, expressions, and declarations appear in Java source code generated from a JSP. It is important to understand that both scriptlets and expressions appear inside the `_jspService()` method and are by default thread-safe to a particular request. Declarations are not thread-safe. Code inside a declaration appears outside the `_jspService()` method and is accessible by a requests being processed by the JSP. Declarations, unlike scriptlets, can also declare functions for use by scriptlets.

Good Coding Practice with Scripting Elements

Before going out and recklessly coding JSP with scripting elements, there are a few important points to be made. Most prominent is the issue of thread safety[3].

---

3. "Thread safety" is not a Servlet-specific or JSP-specific issue. Whenever Java code is using multiple threads, state concurrency issues arise. Thread safety is a common term when describing these issues as it is important to ensure code is *thread-safe*—that is, able to work properly if multiple threads are running it. Chapter 9 provides a complete discussion on thread-safety and state management as the topics apply to Servlets and JSP.

Expressions can be considered harmless. Unless purposely used to cause a conflict, an expression is always going to be thread-safe. Declarations and scriptlets are more problematic. Using a scriptlet is analogous to declaring and using variables locally in the appropriate service method of a Servlet. Variables declared by a scriptlet are initialized, used, and destroyed once per a call to the `_jsp Service()` method. By default this makes scriptlets thread-safe, but they do not ensure the objects they access are thread-safe. If a scriptlet accesses an object in a scope outside of the `_jspService()` method, then a synchronized block should be used to ensure thread safety. Declarations are not thread-safe! A declaration appears outside the `_jspService()` method. Far too often declarations are completely misunderstood as an enhanced form of a scriptlet. They are not!

A common debate is whether scriptlets and declarations are needed at all with JSP. The power of JSP comes from easily creating text-producing Servlets. A JSP is maintainable if it is primarily markup, which is easily edited by page authors. Many developers take the stance that scripting elements destroy this feature of JSP and should be completely replaced by custom actions and the JSP expression language (new as of JSP 2.0, and covered in a later chapter). This viewpoint is valid, is endorsed by the authors ,and is further covered in later chapters, but custom actions are relatively heavyweight components compared to a simple embedded script. Scriptlets, declarations, and particularly expressions certainly have a place with JSP, but they should not be overused. If a page is littered with countless scripting elements, they are likely to do more harm than good. Always be conscious of how scripting elements are being used and if the code might be better encapsulated in other objects that can be used by a few scripting elements.

Directives

Directives are messages to a JSP container. They do not send output to a client, but are used to define page attributes, which custom tag libraries use and which other pages include. All directives use the following syntax.

```
<%@ directive {attribute="value"}* %>
```

Directives may optionally have extra whitespace after the `<%@` and before the `%>`. There are three different JSP directives for use on a page[4]: `page`, `taglib`, and `include`.

---

4. There are other directives that can only be used in tag files: `tag`, `attribute`, and `variable`.

<%@ page %>

The `page` directive provides page-specific information to a JSP container. This information includes settings such as the type of content the JSP is to produce, the default scripting language of the page, and code libraries to import for use. Multiple page directives may be used on a single JSP or pages included via JSP as long as no specific attribute, except `import`, occurs more than once. Attributes for the `page` directive are as follows.

language The `language` attribute defines the scripting language to be used by scriptlets, expressions, and declarations occurring in the JSP. The only defined and required scripting language value for this attribute is `java`. Different containers may provide additional language support; however, it is uncommon to see a JSP use a language other than Java for scripting elements.

In this book it is always assumed that the language appearing in scripting elements is Java (as that is currently the only defined language). Translation of a scripting element using Java code fragments into real Java code is easily done by any developer with previous Java experience. Understanding how and why a scriptlet example works is assumed to be intuitive because it is identical to understanding the Java equivalent.

extends The `extends` attribute value is a fully qualified Java programming language class name that names the superclass of the class to which this JSP is transformed. The `extends` attribute is analogous to the extends keyword used when authoring a Java class. This attribute should be used sparingly as it prevents a container from using a pre-built optimized class.

import The `import` attribute describes the types that are available for use in scripting elements. The value is the same as in an import declaration in the Java programming language, with multiple packages listed with either a fully qualified Java programming language-type names or a package name followed by `.*`, denoting all the public types declared in that package.

The default import list is `java.lang.*`, `javax.servlet.*`, `javax.servlet.jsp.*`, and `javax.servlet.http.*`. These packages can be assumed to be available by default with every JSP. The `import` attribute is currently only defined for use when the value of the language directive is `java`.

session The `session` attribute indicates that the page requires participation in an HTTP session. If `true`, then the implicit scripting variable `session` references the current/new session for the page. If `false`, then the page does not participate in a session and the `session` implicit scripting variable is unavailable, and any reference to it within the body of the JSP page is illegal and results in a fatal translation error. The default value of the `session` attribute is `true`.

buffer   The `buffer` attribute specifies the buffering model for the initial `out` implicit scripting variable to handle content output from the page. If the attribute's value is `none`, then there is no buffering and output is written directly through to the appropriate `ServletResponse` `PrintWriter`. Valid values for the attribute are sizes specified in kilobytes, with the `kb` suffix being mandatory. If a buffer size is specified, then output is buffered with a buffer size of at least the specified, value. Depending upon the value of the `autoFlush` attribute, the contents of this buffer are either automatically flushed or an exception is thrown when overflow would occur. The default value of the `buffer` attribute is 8kb.

autoFlush   The `autoFlush` attribute specifies whether buffered output should be flushed automatically when the buffer is filled, or whether an exception should be raised to indicate buffer overflow. A value of `true` indicates automatic buffer flushing and a value of `false` throws an exception. The default value of the `autoFlush` attribute is `true`. It is illegal to set the `autoFlush` attribute to `false` when the value of the buffer attribute is `none`.

isThreadSafe   The `isThreadSafe` attribute indicates the level of thread safety implemented in the page. If the value is `false`, then the JSP container shall dispatch multiple outstanding client requests, one at a time, in the order they were received, to the page implementation for processing by having the generated Servlet implement `SingleThreadModel`. If the attribute's value is `true`, then the JSP container may choose to dispatch multiple client requests to the page simultaneously. The default value of the `isThreadSafe` attribute is `true`.

isErrorPage   The `isErrorPage` attribute indicates if the current JSP page is intended to be an error page for other JSP. If `true`, then the implicit scripting variable `exception` is defined, and its value is a reference to the offending `Throwable` object. If the `isErrorPage` attribute value is `false`, then the `exception` implicit variable is unavailable, and any reference to it within the body of the JSP page is illegal and will result in a fatal translation error. The default value of the `isErrorPage` attribute is `false`.

errorPage   The `errorPage` attribute defines a relative URL to a resource in the Web Application to which any Java programming language `Throwable` object thrown but not caught by the page implementation is forwarded for error processing. The `Throwable` object is transferred to the error page by binding the object reference to request scope with the name `javax.servlet.jsp.jspException`.

If the value of the `autoFlush` attribute is `true`, and if the contents of the initial `JspWriter` have been flushed to the `ServletResponse` output stream, then any subsequent attempt to dispatch an uncaught exception from the offending page to an `errorPage` may fail.

contentType The `contentType` attribute defines the character encoding for the JSP page, and for the response of the JSP page and the MIME type for the response of the JSP page. The default value of the `contentType` attribute is `text/html` with `ISO-8859-1` character encoding for regular JSP syntax and `UTF-8` encoding for JSP in XML syntax.

pageEncoding The `pageEncoding` attribute defines the character encoding for the JSP. The default value of the `pageEncoding` attribute is `ISO-8859-1` for regular JSP and `UTF-8` for JSP in XML syntax.

isScriptingEnabled The `isScriptingEnabled` attribute determines if scripting elements are allowed for use. The default value (true) enables scriptlets, expressions, and declarations. If the attribute's value is set to false, a translation-time error will be raised if the JSP uses any scriptlets, expressions (non-EL), or declarations. This attribute is helpful for creating 'scriptless' JSP and can also be set using the `web.xml` `scripting-enabled` element.

isELEnabled The `isELEnabled` attribute determines if JSP EL expressions used in the JSP are to be evaluated. The default value of the attribute is `true`, meaning that expressions, `${...}`, are evaluated as dictated by the JSP specification. If the attribute is set to `false`, then expressions are not evaluated but rather treated as static text.

The page directive is by default set to accommodate the most common use of JSP: to make dynamic HTML pages. When creating a simple JSP, it is rarely needed to specify any of the page directive attributes except in cases where extra code libraries are needed for scripting elements or when producing XML content, which is happening more and more.

<%@ include %> and <jsp:include />

The include directive is used to include text and/or code at *translation time* of a JSP. The include directive always follows the same syntax, `<%@ include file="relativeURL" %>`, where the value of `relativeURL` is replaced with the file to be inserted. Files included must be part of a Web Application. Since include directives take place at translation time, they are the equivalent of directly including the source code in the JSP before compilation and do not result in performance loss at runtime.

Server-side includes are a commonly used feature of JSP. Includes allow the same repetitious bit of code to be broken out of multiple pages and have one instance of it included with them all. A good example to use is including a common header and footer with multiple pages of content. Usually this technique is used to keep a site's navigation and copyright information correct and maintainable for all individual pages on the site. As an example take the following two files, `header.jsp` and `footer.jsp`.

The `header.jsp` file (Listing 3-7) includes information that is to appear at the top of a page. It includes site navigation and other miscellaneous information. This header also tracks how many people have visited the site since the last time the Web Application was reloaded by reusing code from `PageCounter.jsp`.

Listing 3-7 header.jsp

```
<%! int pageCount = 0;
 void addCount() {
    pageCount++;
 }
%>
<% addCount(); %>
<html>
<head>
<title>Header/Footer Example</title>
</head>
<body>
<center>
<h2>Servlets and JSP the J2EE Web Tier</h2>
<a href="http://www.jspbook.com">Book Support Site</a> -
<a href="ShowSource">Sites Source code</a><br>
This site has been visited <%= pageCount %> times.
</center>
<br><br>
```

The `footer.jsp` file (Listing 3-8) includes information that is to appear at the very bottom of a page. It includes copyright information, disclaimers, and any other miscellaneous information.

Listing 3-8 footer.jsp

```
<br><br>
<center>
```

```
Copyright &copy; 2003
</center>
</body>
</html>
```

By themselves `header.jsp` and `footer.jsp` do not do much, but when combined with some content, a full page can be generated. For this example the content does not matter. Arbitrarily make up a JSP, but be sure to include `header.jsp` at the top of the page and `footer.jsp` at the bottom. Listing 3-9 provides an example of such a page.

Listing 3-9 content.jsp

```
<%@ include file="header.jsp" %>
Only the content of a page is unique. The same header and footer
are reused from header.jsp and footer.jsp by means of the include
directive
<%@ include file="footer.jsp" %>
```

Save all three files, `header.jsp`, `footer.jsp`, and `content.jsp`, in the base directory of the jspbook Web Application and browse to `http://127.0.0.1/jspbook/content.jsp`. All three files are mashed together at translation time to produce a Servlet that includes the contents of `header.jsp`, `content.jsp`, and `footer.jsp` in the appropriate order. Figure 3-6 shows a browser rendering of the output.

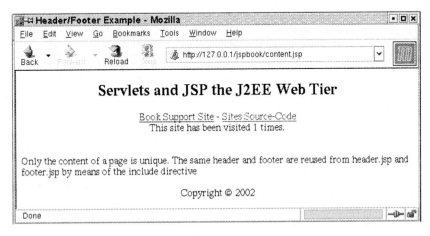

Figure 3-6 Browser Rendering of content.jsp

So what is the advantage of this approach over combining `header.jsp`, `content.jsp`, and `footer.jsp` all in one file in the first place? As the files are set up now, many more content pages can be created that reuse the header and footer. The header and footer can also be changed at any given time, and the changes are easily reflected across all of the JSP.

Translation-Time Includes

Translation time occurs when a JSP is being translated into a Servlet. The resulting Servlet does not know or care about what files were used to generate it. As a result the Servlet is unable to tell when a change has occurred in included files. The JSP specifications do not specify a mechanism for solving this problem, but JSP container vendors are free to implement solutions to the problem.

In cases where an entire site relies on translation-time includes for efficiency, a simple solution does exist for having changes in translation-time includes reflected on the entire site. A container relies on having the translated code of a JSP to compile and deploy a corresponding Servlet. When lacking the code, a container must re-translate a JSP and compile and deploy the corresponding Servlet. By forcing a container to re-translate all JSP, it can be ensured that translation-time includes are properly reflected by JSP that use them.

With Tomcat, JSP translated to Servlet source code can be found in the `TOMCAT_HOME/work` directory. Simply delete the contents of this directory to have Tomcat re-translate all JSP.

For non-translation-time includes JSP also defines the include action. Like the include directive, this action is used to include resources with the output of a JSP, but the include action takes place at runtime. While not as efficient, the include action automatically ensures that the most recent output of the included file is used. See the `<jsp:include />` section of this chapter for more information about the include action.

<%@ taglib %>

Custom actions were previously mentioned in this chapter, but are not fully covered until Chapter 7. Custom actions, also called custom tag libraries, allow a JSP developer to link bits of markup to customized Java code. The `taglib` directive informs a container what bits of markup on the page should be considered custom code and what code the markup links to. The `taglib` directive always follows the same syntax, `<%@ taglib uri="uri" prefix="prefixOfTag" %>`, where the `uri` attribute value resolves to a location the container understands and the prefix attribute informs a container what bits of markup are custom actions.

Further explanation and examples of using the `taglib` directive can be found in Chapter 7.

JSP Configuration

Directives are in the simplest sense configuration information for a JSP. The only problem with using directives for configuration is that they must be specified on a per-JSP basis. If you have 20 pages, then you will have to edit at least 20 directives. To simplify the task of doing mass JSP configuration, the `jsp-config` element is available for use in `web.xml`. There are two sub-elements of `jsp-config`: `taglib` and `jsp-property-group`. The taglib element can be used to configure a custom JSP tag library for use with a JSP. The `jsp-property-group` element allows for configuration that is similar to the directives but can be applied to a group of JSP.

For completeness the taglib element will be covered here and referenced in the later pertinent chapter about custom JSP tag libraries. Use of the `taglib` element is straightforward; first specify a taglib-uri child element, which defines the prefix custom tags are to use; next specify a `taglib-location` element, which defines the location of the custom tag library. For example:

```
...
<jsp-config>
  <taglib>
    <taglib-uri>foo</taglib-uri>
    <taglib-location>WEB-INF/foo.tld</taglib-location>
  </taglib>
</jsp-config>
...
```

For more on tag libraries see Chapter 7.

The `jsp-property-group` element is currently of much more relevance because it is an alternative for much of the functionality offered by the JSP directives. Basic use of the `jsp-property-group` element is always the same; first use a child url-pattern element to define the JSP to apply the properties to:

```
<jsp-config>
  <jsp-property-group>
```

```
    <url-pattern>*.jsp</url-pattern>
    ...
  </jsp-property-group>
</jsp-config>
```

In the preceding code the configuration will be applied to all files ending in
.jsp which would likely be all of the JSP in the Web Application. In general the
url-pattern element can have any of the values that are valid for use when
deploying Servlets or JSP via web.xml. By itself the url-pattern element does
nothing but match a set of properties to a specific set of JSP. The properties themselves must next be specified using more child elements of jsp-property-group.
The jsp-property-group element has the following children elements, which are
all fairly self-descriptive.

el-enabled   The el-enabled element configures if the JSP EL is available for
use on the specified JSP. A value of true enables EL use. A value of false disables
it. The functionality is analogous to the page directive's isELEnabled attribute.

scripting-enabled   The scripting-enabled element is analogous to the page
directive's isScriptingEnabled attribute. A value of false will cause a JSP to
raise a translation error if any scriptlets, expressions (non-EL), or directives are
used. A value of true will enable scripting elements for use.

page-encoding   The page-encoding element is analogous to the page
directive's pageEncoding attribute. An error will be raised if an encoding is set
using the page-encoding attribute and a different encoding is specified using the
pageEncoding attribute of a JSP's page directive.

include-prelude   The include-prelude element can be used to include the
contents of another resource in the Web Application before the contents generated by a JSP. Effectively the include-prelude element provides a method of
automatically including a header for all JSP that the jsp-property-group is configured for.

include-coda   The include-coda element can be used to include the contents
of another resource in the Web Application after the contents generated by a JSP.
Effectively the include-coda element provides a method that automatically
includes a footer for all JSP that the jsp-property-group is configured for.

is-xml   The is-xml element can be used to denote if the JSP are XML documents. JSP authored in XML syntax need not always be explicitly declared as
XML; however, declaring so is helpful for both validating the document and
taking advantage of JSP-XML features such as UTF-8 encoding.

Overall, the `jsp-property-group` element should be very intuitive to use. The only new functionality that has been introduced is due to the `include-prelude`, `include-coda`, and `is-xml` elements. Both `include-prelude` and `include-coda` are also very straightforward to use. In use, the two elements replace the need for header and footer includes using the JSP include directive or custom action. The `is-xml` element is new, but do not worry if it is unclear as to what the element is doing. Later on in this chapter JSP in XML syntax is addressed properly.

Application-Wide Headers and Footers

It is very common to build a Web Application that includes the same header and footer on every page. In these cases there are many methods that you can use to go about achieving the functionality, but arguably the easiest is to use the `include-prelude` and `include-coda` elements. Compared to manually including the header and footer on each page, as in Listing 3-9, little is gained, but it is slightly helpful to use the `include-prelude` and `include-coda` elements for two reasons. First, inclusion of the header and footer pages are consolidated to one single point, `web.xml`. The names or locations of the header and footer resources can easily be changed for any given reason. When using the include directive or action, this will not be the case. A change will be a slight bit more of a hassle, but it can still be done. The second benefit to using the `include-prelude` and `include-coda` elements is that pages of a Web Application only have to focus on content, nothing else. Granted, remembering to include a header and footer is not a difficult task, but it is a task all the same.

Using the `include-prelude` and `include-coda` elements for application-wide headers and footers is easy, and always done in a similar fashion as illustrated in Listing 3-10.

Listing 3-10   Application-Wide Header and Footer Files

```
<jsp-config>
  <jsp-property-group>
    <url-pattern>*.jsp</url-pattern>
    <include-prelude>/header.jsp</include-prelude>
    <include-coda>/footer.jsp</include-coda>
  </jsp-property-group>
</jsp-config>
```

As shown, the `jsp-property-group` is configured to apply to all JSP files; however, the configuration could be extended to include other resources if needed. The important point to see is that the configuration is being applied to everything of importance. Next, the `include-prelude` element and `include-coda` element are used to include a header and footer, respectively. The locations given are `/header.jsp` and `/footer.jsp`, but any other resource can be used.

Standard JSP Actions

Actions provide a convenient method of linking dynamic code to simple markup that appears in a JSP. The functionality is identical to the scripting elements but has the advantage of completely abstracting any code that would normally have to be intermixed with a JSP. Actions that are designed to be simple to use and work well help keep a JSP efficient and maintainable.

There are two types of actions available for use with JSP: standard and custom. All actions follow the same syntax, `<prefix:element {attribute= "value"}* />`, where the complete action is an XML-compatible tag and includes a given `prefix`, `element`, and a set of `attributes` and `values` that customize the action. Standard actions are completely specified by the JSP specification and are, by default, available for use with any JSP container. Custom actions are a mechanism defined by the JSP specification to enhance JSP by allowing JSP developers to create their own actions. The functionality of custom actions is not defined by the JSP specifications, and custom actions must be installed with a Web Application before being used.

Standard actions are summarized in this section. The standard actions include functionality that is commonly used with JSP and allow for: easily using Java Applets, including files at runtime; manipulating JavaBeans; and forwarding requests between Web Application resources.

<jsp:include/>

JSP complements the include directive by providing a standard action for including resources during runtime. The syntax of the include action is similar to an include directive and is as follows: `<jsp:include page="page" />`, where the page attribute value is the relative location in the Web Application of the page to include.

The include action can be used in a JSP the same as the include directive. Reusing the `header.jsp` and `footer.jsp` files from the include directive example in Listing 3-11 is a JSP that includes a header and footer at runtime.

Listing 3-11   runtimeInclude.jsp

```
<jsp:include page="header.jsp" />
Only the content of a page is unique. The same header and footer are
reused from header.jsp and footer.jsp by means of the include
directive.
<jsp:include page="footer.jsp" />
```

Save the code as `runtimeInclude.jsp` in the base directory of the jspbook Web Application and browse to `http://127.0.0.1/jspbook/runtimeInclude.jsp`. The same page is shown as with `content.jsp`. Figure 3-7 shows a browser rendering of `runtimeInclude.jsp`.

The end result looks the same, but it is important to distinguish the difference between the include directive and the include action. An include that occurs at runtime is always current with the resource it is including. An include done at translation time is only current with the resource as it was at the time of translation. A simple example (Listing 3-12) illustrates the point. Edit `footer.jsp` to include a small change, a disclaimer.

Listing 3-12   Edited footer.jsp

```
<br><br>
<center>
Copyright &copy; 2003<br>
<small>Disclaimer: all information on this page is covered by
this disclaimer.</small>
```

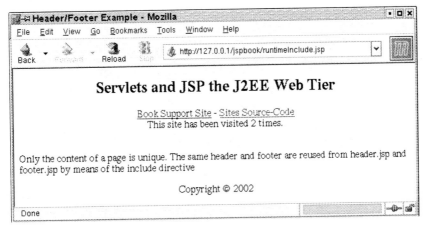

Figure 3-7   Browser Rendering of runtimeInclude.jsp

```
</center>
</body>
</html>
```

Now look at both content.jsp and runtimeInclude.jsp again to see the change. Figure 3-8 shows a browser rendering of runtimeInclude.jsp (http://127.0.0.1/jspbook/runtimeInclude.jsp). The page reflects the updates to footer.jsp automatically. This holds true for any update done to a resource that is included via the include action. However, content.jsp (http://127.0.0.1/jspbook/content.jsp) does not appear to reflect the change. It still looks identical to the pages that appeared in both Figure 3-6 and Figure 3-7 previously.

Runtime versus translation-time includes is the reason for the inconsistency. The content.jsp file was translated into a Servlet that included the exact contents of both header.jsp and footer.jsp before the edit was made to footer.jsp. To have the changes reflected, content.jsp must be re-translated to use the new footer.jsp. The runtimeInclude.jsp Servlet does not need to be re-translated because it relies on an include footer.jsp at runtime. The analogy to the Servlet API is that runtimeInclude.jsp uses RequestDispatcher include() method calls to access both header.jsp and footer.jsp, but content.jsp does not. The code for content.jsp was generated by directly including the code for header.jsp and footer.jsp before compiling the Servlet.

The difference between the include directive and include action is important to understand because it affects performance and consistency. A JSP that uses

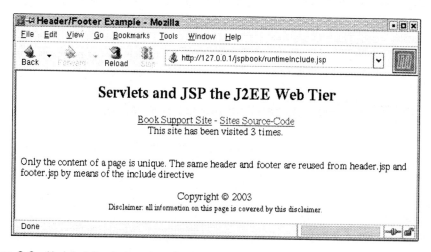

Figure 3-8 Updated Rendering of runtimeInclude.jsp

include directives has the same performance as if an include was never used, but the drawback is that this JSP will not automatically reflect updates to the included file. A JSP that uses include actions will always reflect the current content of an included page, but it suffers a slight performance loss for doing so.

<jsp:plugin/>, <jsp:fallback/>, <jsp:params/>, and <jsp:param/>

JSP has very strong Java ties. JSP was originally designed as a technology Java developers would easily be able to use. For this reason it is common to see JSP being used in conjunction with the many other Java technologies that currently exist. One of the prominent uses of Java is still Java Applets. A Java Applet is a Java application, run with many restrictions, that executes in a client's Web browser through a Java-supporting plug-in. Java Applets are not heavily tied with the JSP and Servlet specifications and will not be covered in this book.

The JSP specifications define custom actions for easily generating the proper custom code needed to embed a Java Applet in an HTML page. The Applet-related actions are: `plugin`, `fallback`, and `params`. The `plugin` action represents one Applet that should be embedded in an HTML page. The `plugin` action allows for the following attributes:

type   The `type` attribute identifies the type of the component: a Bean or an Applet. A *bean* is a component built to match the original intentions of the JavaBean specifications. An *Applet* is the commonly seen client-side Java functionality browsers implement via the Java plug-in.

code   The `code` attribute specifies either the name of the class file that contains the Applet's compiled subclass or the path to get the class, including the class file itself. It is interpreted with respect to the `codebase` attribute.

codebase   The `codebase` attribute specifies the base URI for the Applet. If this attribute is not specified, then it defaults the same base URI as for the current JSP. Values for this attribute may only refer to subdirectories of the directory containing the current document.

align   The `align` attribute determines the location of the Applet relative to where it is being displayed. Valid values are `bottom`, `middle`, and `top`.

archive   The `archive` attribute specifies a comma-separated list of URIs for JAR files containing classes and other resources that are to be loaded before the Applet is initialized. The classes are loaded using an instance of an `AppletClass Loader` with the given `codebase`. Relative URIs for archives are interpreted with respect to the Applet's `codebase`. Preloading resources can significantly improve the performance of Applets.

height   The `height` attribute defines the height in either pixels or percent that the window displaying the Applet should use. This value can be set at runtime via an expression if needed.

hspace   The `hspace` attribute determines the amount of whitespace to be inserted horizontally around the Applet.

jreversion   The `jreversion` attribute identifies the spec version number of the JRE the component requires in order to operate; the default is 1.2.

name   The `name` attribute specifies a name for the Applet instance, which makes it possible for Applets on the same page to find and communicate with each other.

vspace   The `vspace` attribute determines the amount of whitespace to be inserted vertically around the Applet.

width   The `width` attribute defines the width in either pixels or percent that the window displaying the Applet should use. This value can be set at runtime via an expression if needed.

The `fallback` action is used to provide notification to a client should the client's browser not be able to use the Java plug-in. The `fallback` action allows for an arbitrary text message to be included as its body, and must be a sub-tag to the `plugin` action. Text included in the `fallback` action is presented to a client should their browser fail to support the Java plug-in.

The `params` action is used to set parameters for the code being embedded by the `plugin` action. The `params` action requires one-to-many sub `param` actions. A `param` action has two attributes, `name` and `value`, that define a name and value, respectively, for a parameter. When using a `params` action with a `plugin` action, the `param` action must be a sub-tag of the `plugin` action.

Combining the `plugin`, `fallback`, `params`, and `param` actions, a fully customized Java Applet can easily be embedded in an HTML page. Using all the actions together is best shown through an example. Listing 3-13 embeds an Applet, `FooApplet.class`, in an HTML page that is generated by a JSP.

Listing 3-13   AppletExample.jsp

```
<html>
  <head>
    <title>Applet Example</title>
```

```
  </head>
  <body>
  <jsp:plugin
    type="applet"
    code="FooApplet.class"
    height="100"
    width="100"
    jreversion="1.2">
      <jsp:fallback>
      Applet support not found, can't run example.</jsp:fallback>
  </jsp:plugin>
  </body>
</html>
```

It is important to remember where everything takes place when using Applets and JSP. JSP executes on the server-side; Applets execute on the client-side. The result of `AppletExample.jsp` is going to be a plain HTML document with a reference to `FooApplet.class`. The actual code for `FooApplet.class` is downloaded by a Web browser by issuing a second request to the Web server from which the HTML came. A JSP does not send the Applet code inside the HTML page it generates, nor does the Applet code get executed on the Web server it came from. To further demonstrate this point, Listing 3-14 provides the code for `FooApplet.java`.

Listing 3-14 FooApplet.java

```
import javax.swing.*;
import java.awt.*;

public class FooApplet extends JApplet {
  public void init() {
    JLabel label = new JLabel("I'm an Applet.");
    label.setHorizontalAlignment(JLabel.CENTER);
    getContentPane().add(label, BorderLayout.CENTER);
  }
}
```

Compile the preceding code and place both `FooApplet.class` and `Applet Example.jsp` in the base directory of the jspbook Web Application. (Do not place `FooApplet.class` in the `/WEB-INF/classes/com/jspbook` folder. To use the Applet, a client must be able to download it. Placing the code in the `/WEB-INF` directory prevents any client from doing so.) After placing the two files, browse to `http://127.0.0.1/jspbook/AppletExample.jsp`. If your browser supports the Java plug-in version 1.2, it will load the example Applet. Figure 3-9 shows what the Applet looks like when run by a Web browser.

Should your browser not support the Java plug-in, the `fallback` message is displayed. Depending on the specific browser, it may also try to automatically download and install the Java plug-in.

The `plugin` action is designed to be easy to use, but it brings up several important points. The key point of this section is that the `plugin` action makes it easy to embed an existing Java Applet in an HTML document generated by a JSP. The `plugin` can optionally also include the `fallback`, `params`, and `param` actions as subtags to customize the Applet. Additional points brought up from this functionality were where Applets execute versus JSP and where to place Applet code in a Web Application. The two points are worth further explanation and are discussed in the remainder of this section.

To best clarify what the `plugin` action does, it is helpful to show the HTML source code generated by the action. The source code generated by `Applet Example.jsp` is listed in Listing 3-15 with the lines generated by the `plugin` action highlighted.

Listing 3-15 Output of AppletExample.jsp

```
<html>
  <head>
    <title>Applet Example</title>
  </head>
  <body>
    <object classid="clsid:8AD9C840-044E-11D1-B3E9-00805F499D93"
width="100"  height="100"
```

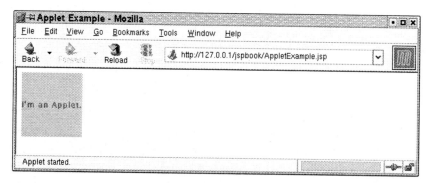

Figure 3-9 Browser Running FooApplet.class

```
codebase="http://java.sun.com/products/plugin/1.2.2/jinstall-1_2_2-
win.cab#Version=1,2,2,0">
<param name="java_code" value="FooApplet.class">
<param name="type" value="application/x-java-applet">
<COMMENT>
<embed type="application/x-java-applet;"  width="100"  height="100"
pluginspage="http://java.sun.com/products/plugin/"
java_code="FooApplet.class" >
<noembed>
```

```
</COMMENT>
Applet support not found, can't run example.
</noembed></embed>
</object>
```

```
   </body>
</html>
```

The code is a little cryptic but is certainly not the binary of `FooApplet.class`. What is highlighted is just a perfectly valid use of the HTML `object` element as defined by the HTML 4.0 specification[5]. The HTML `object` element is a more generic form of the now deprecated `applet` element that was designed to allow Applets to be referenced from HTML. The `object` element defines all the necessary information a browser needs to download the `FooApplet.class` file along with loading the appropriate browser plug-in to execute it. After reading the `object` element, the browser generates a completely new HTTP request for the `Foo Applet.class`. The URL is a combination of information specified by the object tag, but ends up being `http://127.0.0.1/jspbook/FooApplet.class`.

The URL a Web browser uses to download an Applet is the reason that Applet code should not be placed under the `/WEB-INF/classes` directory. Code in these directories is meant solely for use on the server-side and is not accessible by outside clients. By placing the Applet's code in the base directory alongside `AppletExample.jsp`, a Web browser is free to download and use it.

<jsp:forward/>

JSP provide an equivalent to the `RequestDispather.forward()` method by use of the forward action. The forward action forwards a request to a new resource and clears any content that might have previously been sent to the output buffer by

---

5. http://www.w3.org/TR/html4/

the current JSP. Should the current JSP not be buffered, or the contents of the buffer already be sent to a client, an `IllegalStateException` is thrown. The `forward` action uses the following syntax: `<jsp:forward url="relativeURL"/>`, where the value of `relativeURL` is the relative location in the current Web Application of the resource to forward the request to. Optionally the forward action may have `param` actions used as subelements to define request parameters. Where applicable, the `param` action values override existing request parameters.

`<jsp:forward/>` and `<jsp:include/>` parameters

Both the JSP forward and includes actions can optionally include parameters. The mechanism for doing this is the JSP `param` action. The `param` action may only appear in the body of either the `forward` or `include` actions and is used to define parameters. The syntax of the `param` action is as follows:

```
<jsp:param name="parameter's name" value="parameter's value"/>
```

The parameter is a key/value pair with the `name` attribute specifying the name and `value` attribute specifying the value. The values are made available to the forwarded or included resource via the `HttpServletRequest getParameter()` method, for instance, if the `forward` action was authored as the following:

```
<jsp:forward page="examplePage.jsp">
  <jsp:param name="foo1" value="bar"/>
  <jsp:param name="foo2" value="<%= foo %>"/>
</jsp:forward>
```

The fictitious page `examplePage.jsp` would have two additional request parameters set for it: `foo1` and `foo2`. The value of `foo1` would be 'bar' and the value of `foo2` would be the string representation of whatever the `foo` variable was. In the case where a parameter specified by the `param` action conflicts with an existing parameter, the existing parameter is replaced.

JavaBean Actions

As with Applets, JavaBeans are commonly used Java objects, and JSP provides default support for easily using them. The `<jsp:useBean />`, `<jsp:getProperty />`, and `<jsp:setProperty />` actions all relate to JavaBeans, but will not be fully covered in this chapter. Unlike Applets, JavaBeans are much more commonly used with Servlet and JSP projects. Later chapters rely on JavaBean knowledge, and JavaBeans are explained in depth in this book. Chapter 5 introduces, explains, and shows examples of JavaBeans and the custom JSP actions for using them.

Tag File Actions

A set of JSP standard actions exist for use with custom tags. These actions are `<jsp:attribute/>`, `<jsp:body/>`, `<jsp:doBody/>`, and `<jsp:invoke/>`. Chapter 7 covers these actions in depth.

Whitespace Preservation

Servlets provide direct control over calls to the `PrintWriter` object responsible for sending text in a response. JSP do not. JSP abstracts calls to the `PrintWriter` object and allows for template text to be authored as it should be presented to a client. Whitespace, while usually not important, is preserved as it appears in a JSP. This preservation can be seen by looking at the HTML source code generated by a JSP in any of this chapter's examples.

Whitespace preservation is also the reason some seemingly unaccountable formatting is included with JSP output. Take, for example, the following JSP (Listing 3-16) that is a slight modification of `HelloWorld.jsp`.

Listing 3-16 HelloDate.jsp

```
<%@ page import="java.util.Date"%>
<html>
<head>
<title>Hello World!</title>
</head>
<body>
<h1>Hello World!</h1>
The current date/time is: <%= new Date() %>.
</body>
</html>
```

Save `HelloDate.jsp` in the base directory of the jspbook Web Application and browse to `http://127.0.0.1/jspbook/HelloDate.jsp`. The page looks very similar to `HelloWorld.jsp` but now includes a date. In order to import the `java.util.Date` class, the `page` directive is used. Figure 3-10 shows a browser rendering of the results.

The code is a perfectly valid HTML document and looks fine when rendered as HTML. However, you'll notice that the formatting that surrounds the `page` directive was retained. There is an unneeded new line where the `page` directive

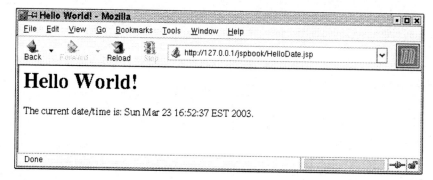

Figure 3-10   Browser Rendering of HelloDate.jsp

was used. This can be verified by looking at the HTML source code that was generated as highlighted in Listing 3-17.

Listing 3-17   HelloDate.jsp HTML Source Code Sent to a Browser

```
<html>
<head>
<title>Hello World!</title>
</head>
<body>
<h1>Hello World!</h1>
The current date/time is: Sun Apr 07 19:33:11 EDT 2002.
</body>
</html>
```

It is important to understand that formatting is retained by the JSP. In most cases, especially HTML, extra whitespace formatting does not matter. However, there are situations where whitespace and other extra formatting are of significance, particularly if using XML. In these cases there is an easy fix. Do not use extra formatting around JSP elements. Besides making things a little prettier, there is no need for it. For example, HelloDate.jsp can remove the unneeded whitespace if written as shown in Listing 3-18.

Listing 3-18   HelloDate.jsp Removing Unneeded Whitespace

```
<%@ page import="java.util.Date"%><html>
<head>
<title>Hello World!</title>
</head>
```

```
<body>
<h1>Hello World!</h1>
The current date/time is: <%= new Date() %>.
</body>
</html>
```

Attributes

There are two methods for specifying attributes in JSP elements: runtime values and translation time or static values. A *static value* is a hard-coded value that is typed into a JSP before translation time. There have been countless examples of static values; take for instance the `include` action `<jsp:include page="header.jsp"/>`. In this example the `page` attribute has a static value of `header.jsp`. Every time the JSP is visited, the `include` action tries to include this file. However, not all attribute values are required to be static. Some attributes can have a *runtime value*. A runtime value means an expression can be used to dynamically create the value of the attribute. In the preceding example of the *include* action, the following might appear:

```
<jsp:include page="<%= request.getParameter('file')%>"/>
```

In this case the value is dynamic and determined at runtime. This would be useful if there was a need to customize which page was included each time the JSP was visited.

Most basic uses of JSP do not rely on runtime values for attributes. Runtime values are much more helpful when used with JSP custom actions and will be further covered in Chapter 7 with custom tags and in Chapter 6 with the JTSL.

Comments

JSP allows for a developer to include server-side comments that are completely ignored when generating a response to send to a client. The functionality is very similar to HTML comments; however, the JSP comments are only available for viewing on the server-side. A JSP comment must have a start, `<%--`, an end, `--%>`, and comment information between. These comments are useful for providing server-side information or for "commenting out" sections of JSP code. Listing 3-19 shows an example of two comments: one to provide some information and another to comment out a bit of code.

Listing 3-19 JSPComment.jsp

```
<%@ page import="java.util.Date" %>
<html>
```

```
<title>Server-side JSP Comments</title>
  <body>
<%-- A simple example of a JSP comment --%>
<%--
  Code commented out on <%= new Date() %>.
--%>
  </body>
</html>
```

Save JSPComment.jsp in the base directory of the jspbook Web Application and browse to http://127.0.0.1/jspbook/JSPCcomment.jsp. A blank page is displayed because all the code on the JSP is commented out. Upon further examination of the source code that was generated by the JSP, it can be shown that none of the commented information was sent in the content of the response (Listing 3-20).

Listing 3-20 Output of JSPComment.jsp

```
<html>
<title>Server-side JSP Comments</title>
<body>


</body>
</html>
```

In addition to server-side JSP comments, more types of comments are available for use. With scriptlets and declarations, both of the Java comments are available for use. A line of embedded code can be commented out using //, or a chunk of code may be commented out by use of a block comment with a starting /* and end*/.

HTML/XML comments <!-- --> do not prevent text from being sent by a JSP. HTML/XML comments usually do not get rendered by a Web browser, but the information is passed on to the client-side. By changing JSPComment.jsp to use HTML/XML comments, the JSP output clearly illustrates the difference (Listing 3-21).

Listing 3-21 XMLComment.jsp

```
<%@ page import="java.util.Date" %>
<html>
  <title>Server-side JSP Comments</title>
  <body>
```

```
<!-- A simple example of a JSP comment -->
<!--
  Code commented out on <%= new Date() %>.
-->
  </body>
</html>
```

Save `XMLComment.jsp` in the base directory of the jspbook Web Application and browse to `http://127.0.0.1/jspbook/XMLComment.jsp`. A Web browser still displays a blank page, but only because the HTML/XML comments are ignored on the client-side. Listing 3-22 shows the output of `xmlcomment.jsp`.

Listing 3-22 Output of xmlcomment.jsp

```
<html>
<title>Server-side JSP Comments</title>
<body>
<!-- A simple example of a JSP comment -->
<!--
  Code commented out on Sun Mar 10 20:23:01 EST 2002.
-->
</body>
</html>
```

Unlike with `JSPComment.jsp`, `XMLComment.jsp` does send the comments to the client to deal with. Additionally JSP elements included inside the XML/HTML comments are still evaluated on the server-side. This example shows that when a chunk of code is to be commented out, it should be done with a JSP comment. However, should a comment be sent to a client, then the HTML-style comment can be used.

Quoting and Escape Characters

When authoring a JSP, it might be desirable to send text to a client that is equal in part or whole to a JSP element. This results in a conflict with the code's intended purpose and how the container will interpret code. To represent the literal value of JSP elements, in part or whole, escape characters must be used. JSP uses the following escape characters:

- A single-quote literal, `'`, is escaped as `\'`. This is only required should the literal be needed inside a single-quote delimited attribute value.

- A double-quote literal, ", is escaped as \". This is only required should the literal be needed inside a single-quote delimited attribute value.
- A back-slash literal, \, is escaped as \\.
- A %> is escaped as %\>.
- A <% is escaped as <\%.

The entities ' and " are available to represent single and double quotes, respectively.

The preceding examples should be fairly straightforward, but the following brief example is given for completeness. The code in Listing 3-23 shows how JSP identifies escape values that the JSP container normally interprets as elements.

Listing 3-23 EscapeCharacters.jsp

```
<% String copy="2000-2003"; %>
<html>
  <title>Server-side JSP Comments</title>
  <body>
  Scriptlets: <\% <i>script</i> %><br>
  Expressions: <\%= <i>script</i> %><br>
  Declarations: <\%! <i>script</i> %><br>
  <center>
  <small>Copyright &copy;
  <%= copy + " Single-Quote/Double-Quote Ltd,  \'/\"" %>
  </small>
  </center>
  </body>
</html>
```

Save EscapeCharacters.jsp in the base directory of the jspbook Web Application and browse to http://127.0.0.1/jspbook/EscapeCharacters.jsp. A small page appears with a brief explanation of some of the JSP elements. Figure 3-11 shows a browser rendering of the output from the JSP. The literal values are properly shown to a client instead of being misinterpreted by the JSP container.

Implicit Objects

JSP uses scripting elements as an easy method of embedding code within template text, but we have yet to show how to directly manipulate a request, response, session, or any of the other objects used with Servlets in Chapter 2. These objects all still exist with JSP and are available as *implicit objects*. The JSP implicit objects are automatically declared by a JSP container and are always available for use by scripting elements. The following is a list of the JSP implicit objects that are recognizable from Chapter 2.

config　The `config` implicit object is an instance of a `javax.servlet.` `ServletConfig` object. Same as with Servlets, JSP can take advantage of initial parameters provided in a Web Application Deployment Descriptor.

request　The `request` implicit object is an instance of a `javax.servlet.http.` `HttpServletRequest` object. The `request` implicit object represents a client's request and is a reference to the `HttpServletRequest` object passed into a `HttpServlet`'s appropriate service method.

response　The `response` implicit object is an instance of a `javax.servlet.` `http.HttpServletRequest` object. The `response` implicit object represents a response to a client's response and is a reference to the `HttpServlet` `Response` object passed into a `HttpServlet`'s appropriate service method.

session　The `session` implicit object is an instance of a `javax.servlet.http.` `HttpSession` object. By default JSP creates a keep session context with all clients. The session implicit object is a convenience object for use in scripting elements and is the equivalent of calling the `HttpServletRequest` `getSession()` object.

application　The `application` implicit object is an instance of a `javax.` `servlet.ServletContext` object. The application implicit object represents a Servlet's view of a Web Application and is equivalent to calling the `Servlet` `Config` `getServletContext()` method.

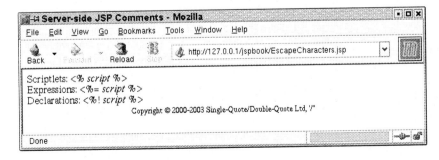

Figure 3-11　Browser Rendering of EscapeCharacters.jsp

Using any of the JSP implicit objects is as easy as assuming they already exist within a scripting element. With the objects listed previously, all of the Servlet examples in previous chapters can be replicated in JSP. Take, for example, the ShowHeaders Servlet (Listing 2-8 in Chapter 2). The ShowHeaders Servlet displayed a small HTML page listing all the HTTP request headers sent by a client. The Servlet relied on the `HttpServletRequest getHeaderNames()` and `get Header()` methods. After translating this Servlet into a JSP, the code appears as Listing 3-24.

Listing 3-24 ShowHeaders.jsp

```
<%@ page import="java.util.*"%>
<html>
  <head>
    <title>Request's HTTP Headers</title>
  </head>
  <body>
    <p>HTTP headers sent by your client:</p>
<%
    Enumeration enum = request.getHeaderNames();
    while (enum.hasMoreElements()) {
      String headerName = (String) enum.nextElement();
      String headerValue = request.getHeader(headerName);
%>
    <b><%= headerName %></b>: <%= headerValue %><br>
<% } %>
  </body>
</html>
```

Save the preceding code as `ShowHeaders.jsp` in the base directory of the jspbook Web Application and browse to `http://127.0.0.1/jspbook/Show Headers.jsp`. The results are identical to the previous Servlet at `http://127.0.0.1/jspbook/ShowHeaders`. Figure 3-12 shows what the output of `ShowHeaders.jsp` looks like when rendered by a Web browser.

Repeating Servlet code examples and translating them into JSP isn't the goal of this chapter. The preceding example is intended to clearly show how to use the implicit objects and how they can be used to achieve all the functionality of a Servlet. The scriptlets in the preceding JSP show this by using the `request` implicit object as if it had previously been declared by the JSP.

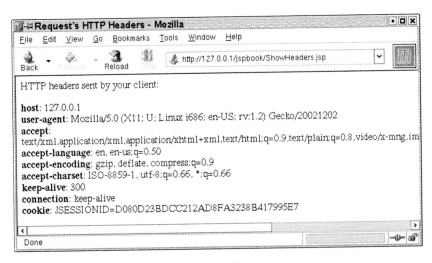

Figure 3-12   Browser Rendering of ShowHeaders.jsp

```
<%
   Enumeration enum = request.getHeaderNames();
   while (enum.hasMoreElements()) {
      String headerName = (String) enum.nextElement();
      String headerValue = request.getHeader(headerName);
%>
```

It is important to note that in no place was an object named `request` declared for use by the JSP. It was just used. The JSP container automatically and appropriately declares the implicit objects when translating the JSP into a Servlet.

JSP defines a few more implicit objects to accompany the aforementioned. The ones not listed do not directly map to Servlet equivalents. The additional implicit objects are `pageContext`, `page`, `out`, and `exception`, which are all explained in the following sections.

pageContext

The `pageContext` implicit scripting variable is an instance of a `javax.servlet.jsp.PageContext` object. A `PageContext` object represents the context of a single JavaServer Page including all the other implicit objects, methods for forwarding to and including Web Application resources, and a scope for binding objects to the page. The `PageContext` object is not always helpful when used by itself because the other implicit objects are already available for use. A `PageContext` object is primarily used as a single object that can easily be passed to other objects such as custom actions. This is useful since the page context holds references to the other implicit objects.

Request Delegation

The `pageContext` implicit object provides the equivalent of the `include` and `forward` directives for providing JSP request delegation. Scriptlets can use the following `PageContext` methods to provide JSP request delegation:

```
forward(java.lang.String relativeUrlPath)
```

The `forward()` method is used to redirect, or 'forward', the current `ServletRequest` and `ServletResponse` to another resource in the Web Application. The *relativeUrlPath* value is the relative path to a resource in the Web Application:

```
include(java.lang.String relativeUrlPath)
```

The `include()` method causes the resource specified to be processed as part of the current `ServletRequest` and `ServletResponse` being processed.

The `forward()` and `include()` methods can be used to include or forward a `ServletRequest` and `ServletResponse` to any resource in a Web Application. The resource can be a Servlet, JSP, or a static resource. The functionality is identical to that previously mentioned for Servlet request delegation.

Page Scope

In addition to the request, session, and application scopes, JSP introduces the *page scope*. The `PageContext` object provides the `getAttribute()`, `setAttribute()`, and `removeAttribute()` methods for binding objects to the current page. Objects bound in page scope only exist for the duration of the current page. Page scope objects are not shared across multiple JSP, and page scope is intended only for passing objects between custom actions and scripting elements. When using JSP to JSP communication, the request scope is still the appropriate scope to use.

out

The `out` implicit object is an instance of a `javax.servlet.jsp.JspWriter` object and is used to send content in a response. The `JspWriter` object emulates some of the functionality found in the `java.io.PrintWriter` and `java.io.Buffered Writer` objects to provide a convenient method of writing text in a buffered fashion. The out implicit object can be configured on a per JSP basis by the page directive.

Buffering

The initial JspWriter object is associated with the PrintWriter object of the ServletResponse in a way that depends on whether the page is or is not buffered. If the page is not buffered, output written to this JspWriter object will be written through to the PrintWriter directly. But if the page is buffered, the PrintWriter object will not be created until the buffer is flushed, meaning operations like setContentType() are legal until the buffer gets flushed. Since this flexibility simplifies programming substantially, buffering is the default for JSP pages.

By using buffering, the issue is raised about what happens when the buffer is exceeded. Two possibilities exist:

Flush the Buffer   One straightforward option is to simply flush the buffer once it is full. Content that would normally overflow the buffer now would not because the buffer writes extra content to a client. The drawback to this approach is that HTTP headers cannot be changed once content has been sent to a client. Headers always appear at the beginning of a HTTP response so they must be finalized before any content is flushed by the buffer.

Throw an Exception   Flushing the buffer is not a good approach when strict control needs to be kept over when content is sent to a client. In cases like this, exceeding the buffer is a fatal error. Doing so causes an exception to be thrown.

Both approaches are valid, and thus both are supported by JSP. The behavior of a page is controlled by the autoFlush attribute, which defaults to true. In general, JSP that need to be sure correct and complete data has been sent to their client may want to set autoFlush to false. On the other hand, JSP that do not need strict control can leave the autoFlush attribute as true, which is commonly the case when sending HTML to a browser. The two types of buffer uses are best suited for different needs and should be considered on a per use basis.

JspWriter and Response Committed Exceptions

A far too common and misunderstood error when using JSP is the IllegalStateException exception with "response already committed" given as the exception's message. This error arises after a JspWriter has sent some information to a client and a JSP tries to do something assuming no content has been sent. Avoiding this exception is easily done but requires that when a developer programs, he or she is conscious of how the `JspWriter` object works. The following are the two primary culprits of the aforementioned exception.

Manipulating Headers   With JSP, manipulation of the HTTP response headers is only allowed before the actual content of the response is sent. When phrased like this, it should seem quite intuitive, but far too often a JSP developer will ask why an `IllegalStateException` is thrown when they are changing header information. An easy fix for this problem is to either increase the buffer size by increasing the value of the `page` directive `buffer` attribute or simply moving problematic code to the top of the JSP. Moving header-changing code before content-generating code usually ensures there are no buffer conflicts when editing HTTP header information.

Forwarding   When forwarding between JSP, complete control of the `Servlet Request` and `ServletResponse` objects is given to the forwarded JSP. This allows for the forwarded page to have complete control over generating the appropriate response. Unlike Servlets, JSP automatically calls the `HttpServletRequest getWriter()` method to get a suitable object for writing information to a client. Forwarding between two JSP ensures calling this method twice, which in a normal Servlet would throw an exception. However, JSP bends this rule slightly by taking advantage of the `JspWriter` buffer. Should a JSP forward a request to another JSP after content has been sent to the buffer but before the response has been committed to a client, then everything is fine. The buffered data is simply discarded and the new JSP can freely create a response to a client. Should a JSP commit a response to a client and then forward the request to a different JSP, an exception occurs.

Committing a response and then forwarding a request always throws an `IllegalStateException`. The problem can be solved by either including all information in one JSP, not committing the response, or including the desired JSP rather than forwarding to it. An inclusion reuses the `JspWriter` object of the page doing the include.

Understand and avoid the above two problems. The cryptic error commonly plagues new JSP developers. Solving the problem is easy if the `JspWriter` object and associated buffer are properly understood.

config

The normal JSP deployment scheme automatically done by a container works, but nothing stops a JSP developer from declaring and mapping a JSP via the Web

Application Deployment Descriptor, `web.xml`. A JSP can be manually deployed in the same fashion as a Servlet by creating a Servlet declaration in `web.xml` and replacing the `servlet-class` element with the `jsp-page` element. After being declared, the JSP can be mapped to a single or set of URLs same as a Servlet.

As an example, if it was necessary to remove the ShowHeaders Servlet and map `ShowHeaders.jsp` to the `/ShowHeaders` path in addition to the automatically defined `/ShowHeaders.jsp` path, the task could be accomplished with the following entries in `web.xml`.

```
<servlet>
  <servlet-name>ShowHeaders</servlet-name>
  <jsp-file>/ShowHeaders.jsp</jsp-file>
</servlet>
<servlet-mapping>
  <servlet-name>ShowHeaders</servlet-name>
  <url-pattern>/ShowHeaders</url-pattern>
</servlet-mapping>
```

The only change was replacing the previous line, `<servlet-class>com.jspbook.ShowHeaders</servlet-class>`, with the `jsp-file` element and the location of the JSP.

Initial Configuration Parameters

Through use of the `jsp-file` element, a JSP can be mapped using a custom entry in `web.xml`. All of the child elements of the `servlet` element are still valid, and initial parameters can be defined. In Chapter 2 the InternationalizedHelloWorld Servlet, Listing 2-3, was used to demonstrate the functionality of initial parameters. Listing 3-25 is a quick rehash of the example, but in JSP form.

Listing 3-25 InternationalizedHelloWorld.jsp

```
<html>
<head>
<title>Hello World!</title>
</head>
<body>
<h1><%=config.getInitParameter("greeting")%></h1>
</body>
</html>
```

The code is nothing spectacular. What is important to notice is the JSP relies on an initial parameter named "greeting". Without the initial parameter, the JSP would not function correctly, but a container will automatically deploy the page anyhow. Save the code as `InternationalizedHelloWorld.jsp` in the base directory of the jspbook Web Application and browse to `http://127.0.0.1/jspbook/InternationalizedHelloWorld.jsp`. A page appears that says "null". Figure 3-13 shows a browser rendering of the output. By default a JSP has no initial parameters, and a JSP container doesn't validate that initial parameters are properly defined before deploying a JSP. The result is a HelloWorld example that says nothing.

To fix the JSP, an entry in `web.xml` needs to be made so the "greeting" initial parameter can be defined. Add the following elements to `web.xml`.

```
<servlet>
  <servlet-name>InternationalizedHelloWorldJSP</servlet-name>
  <jsp-file>/InternationalizedHelloWorld.jsp</jsp-file>
  <init-param>
    <param-name>greeting</param-name>
    <param-value>Bonjour!</param-value>
  </init-param>
</servlet>
<servlet-mapping>
  <servlet-name>InternationalizedHelloWorldJSP</servlet-name>
  <url-pattern>/InternationalizedHelloWorld.jsp</url-pattern>
</servlet-mapping>
```

The `servlet` element defines a Servlet deployment for the Servlet generated from `InternationalizedHelloWorld.jsp`, and the `servlet-mapping` element maps the URL pattern `/InternationalizedHelloWorld.jsp` to the JSP. Inside the servlet element, the needed "greeting" initial parameter is given to make the JSP display a "Hello World" message. Reload the jspbook Web Application and

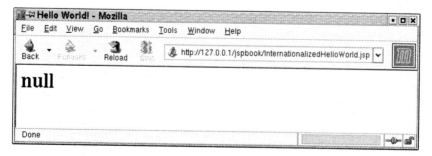

Figure 3-13 InternationalizedHelloWorld.jsp without Initial Parameters

Figure 3-14 InternationalizedHelloWorld.jsp with Parameters

browse back to `http://127.0.0.1/jspbook/InternationalizedHelloWorld.`
`jsp`. This time the JSP displays the appropriate hello message. Figure 3-14 shows
a browser rendering of the output.

page

The `page` implicit object represents the current class implementation of the page
being evaluated. If the scripting language of the page is `java`, which by default it
is, the page object is equivalent to the `this` keyword of a Java class.

JSP in XML Syntax

JSP comes in two different varieties of syntax. The original, or classic, JSP uses a
free-form syntax. With JSP 1.2, another XML-compliant form of JSP syntax, JSP
Documents, was introduced. Both syntaxes provide the same functionality and
take advantage of all the features of JSP. The reason the second syntax was introduced was to keep JSP current with the widespread adoption of XML. XML-
compliant JSP can be created and manipulated using any existing XML tool.
Classic JSP requires a specialized parser built to specifically understand the
unique syntax of JSP.

Since the introduction of XML-compliant JSP, there have been no significant
moves in the JSP community toward supporting the new syntax. The majority of
JSP developers, books, and tools still largely use the classic JSP. Reasons for this
are partly due to the fact that JSP documents are new, but are largely related to
the fact that JSP XML syntax is not easy to use. In some senses the first release of
the JSP XML syntax was very half-baked in an odd way. It is too strict. The syntax

does not lack compliance to XML rules, nor does it lack functionality. It is just too restrictive and cryptic for the average JSP developer to use.

The best way to illustrate the original flaw in JSP XML syntax is by showing a small example. This page is a simple version of what can be expected to be seen in most JSP. Listing 3-26 is the version of the page in the classic JSP syntax.

Listing 3-26 ClassicJSP.jsp

```
<html>
<head>
<title>A Simple Page in Classic JSP</title>
</head>
<body>
<h1>A Title</h1>
<% String text = "<b>bold text</b>";
   String link = "http://www.jspbook.com";
  if (true) { %>
  Here is bold text: <%= text %><br>
<% } %>
A link to a <a href="<%= link %>">website</a>.
</body>
</html>
```

Everything above should be recognizable. It is a page that uses a few scriptlets and expressions. Listing 3-27 shows the same code in a JSP Document.

Listing 3-27 JSPDocument.jsp

```
<?xml version="1.0"?>
<jsp:root xmlns:jsp="http://java.sun.com/JSP/Page">
  <html>
    <head>
      <title>A Simple Page in XML Compatible JSP</title>
    </head>
    <body>
    <h1>A Title</h1>
    <jsp:scriptlet>
    String text = "<b>bold text</b>";
    String link = "http://www.jspbook.com";
      if (true) {
    </jsp:scriptlet>
      Here is bold text:
        <jsp:expression>text</jsp:expression><![CDATA[<br>]]>
    <jsp:scriptlet>}</jsp:scriptlet>
    <![CDATA[A link to a <a href="]]>
```

```
      <jsp:expression>link</jsp:expression>
      <![CDATA[">website</a>.]]>
      </body>
    </html>
  </jsp:root>
```

The first point to notice is that the page gets bigger. This is always a minor drawback to using any form of XML. A little bit of space inefficiency is paid for compliance to XML document structuring rules. The space itself is not of concern in this case, but what should be a concern is that the JSP can no longer use free-form text. The JSP scripting elements must be expanded into full tags, and noncompliant HTML must be surrounded by a special XML syntax, `<![CDATA[ ]]>`. This is tedious to author and makes a page hard to maintain without a special XML reading and writing tool.

JSP Documents are not all bad. The idea behind them is a good one. XML, when used as intended, can be a very helpful thing. Custom XML documents can be incredibly easy to understand and are easily manipulated by countless XML tools that currently exist. The only drawback is that HTML is not XML. JSP is largely promoted as a tool that makes dynamic HTML generation easy. This is not a restriction of JSP, but it is arguably the most common use of the technology. The question to answer is, "To what extent is XML compatibility needed in your code?" If JSP need to be manipulated easily by other code, then XML is a good choice. The other question to ask is, "Are you only using JSP to simplify creating dynamic HTML?" If so, then it is a better choice to use the original JSP syntax.

In previous versions of JSP, the majority of users were geared toward using JSP for creating dynamic HTML. This is largely due to the fact that HTML has been the dominant technology on the Web, and this explains very much why JSP was originally created to simplify the task of creating it. However, HTML is no longer the most popular technology to use. XML, while not perfect, adequately fills the deficiencies of many technologies, including HTML, and has gained huge momentum, which is shown by industry-wide use. Currently, one of the best approaches to managing content is to either store it or communicate it via XML. Using XML for these purposes allows information to easily be shared and maintained in a meaningful manner. Because of this great flexibility, the trend has been to move away from more limited technologies, such as HTML, and toward XML. JSP reflects these changes as it too has changed to better incorporate XML for use in the J2EE Web Tier.

Understanding JSP documents is important. XML use will only continue to grow in the future, and it is important to understand what flexibility JSP has for interacting with it. Understanding how to author JSP documents is also easy as long as you understand a few simple conversion rules between classic JSP and JSP in XML syntax.

XML Rules

XML rules is quite the pun. XML does rule as a technology for authoring and sharing information on the Internet, but XML does have some important rules one must follow when using it. JSP Documents automatically inherit these rules. It does little good to directly explain JSP in XML syntax if regular XML syntax is not understood. However, this book is not about XML. It is about JSP and Servlets. A full tutorial on XML is not given in this book. Only the basics are explained to help get through the majority of the JSP in XML syntax use cases. If you are planning on extensively using XML with JSP and do not yet know much about XML, this book is not a substitute for an XML guide. To accompany this text, either read through the XML specifications, `http://www.w3.org/ XML`, or pick up a good book on XML.

JSP Documents

Aside from understanding the XML rules needed to author JSP in XML syntax, there are only a few simple conversions between regular JSP and JSP Documents. Not all pieces of regular JSP syntax are in an XML-incompatible form. JSP actions and custom actions are already in XML-compatible syntax. They are used identically in a JSP Document as used in regular JSP. The rest of JSP, namely scripting elements and directives, need to be converted to an XML form.

JSP Document Declaration

The JSP Document must be completely encapsulated by a root XML element, `root`. This element needs to also have the JSP namespace, `jsp`, pre-appended along with a declaration for the namespace. In general, a JSP Document always resembles Listing 3-28.

Listing 3-28 Declaration of a JSP Document

```
<?xml version="1.0"?>
<jsp:root xmlns:jsp="http://java.sun.com/JSP/Page">
  // JSP Document contents
</jsp:root>
```

The content encapsulated by the JSP Document is the content of the JSP.

Scripting Elements

All scripting elements must be converted for use in a JSP Document. The scripting element syntax classic JSP uses directly conflicts with XML syntax. Instead of using `<% %>`, `<%= %>`, and `<%! %>`, for scriptlets, expressions, and declarations, use `<jsp:scriptlet></jsp:scriptlet>`, `<jsp:expression></jsp:expression>`, and `<jsp:declaration></jsp:declaration>`, respectively.

This conversion in most cases is quite simple. Refer back to the first classic JSP versus JSP Document example, Listing 3-25 and Listing 3-26. Here is a section of the code from the classic JSP example that uses scriptlets and expressions.

```
<% String text = "<b>bold text</b>";
   String link = "http://www.jspbook.com";
  if (true) { %>
  Here is bold text: <%= text %> <br>
<% } %>

A link to a <a href="<%= link %>">website</a>.
```

Highlighted are the scriptlets and expressions. The conversion to JSP in XML syntax is the following:

```
<jsp:scriptlet>
String text = "<b>bold text</b>";
String link = "http://www.jspbook.com";
if (true) {
</jsp:scriptlet>
  Here is bold text:
  <jsp:expression>text</jsp:expression><![CDATA[<br>]]>
<jsp:scriptlet>}</jsp:scriptlet>
<![CDATA[A link to a <a href="]]>
<jsp:expression>link</jsp:expression>
<![CDATA[">website</a>.]]>
```

The straight change from classic scripting elements to JSP Document equivalents should be easily seen. Any text search and replace tool can easily accomplish the job. The more difficult part is checking to make sure the conversion results in a valid XML document. In the preceding case, it didn't. The example specifically included one of the most common errors that occurs when using JSP Documents. In a classic JSP, it is perfectly valid to use an expression or scriptlet right in the middle of template text: A link to a `<a href="<%= link %>">website</a>`.

In the trivial conversion to a JSP Document, this initially becomes the following:

```
A link to a <a href="
<jsp:expression>link</jsp:expression>
">website</a>.
```

However, the above code is not XML because the document is no longer well formed. The template text was being treated as XML. Embedding an expression tag for an attribute value is not allowed. To solve this problem, the conversion has to also include a specific encapsulation of the template text with XML CDATA sections or represent the problematic content with entities.

```
<![CDATA[A link to a <a href="]]>
<jsp:expression>link</jsp:expression>
<![CDATA[">website</a>.]]>
```

CDATA sections were used in the preceding snippet. It is a choice of personal preference choosing to use CDATA sections or entities when handling offending code. The point is, that converting straight between `<% %>` and `<jsp:scriptlet></jsp:scriptlet>` is trivial. What matters most is making sure a well-formed XML document is created. If not, replace offending code with entities or CDATA sections.

Directives

Recall that JSP directives always follow the format `<%@directive {attribute="value"}* %>`, where *directive* is the directive's name and *attributes* is a set of attributes with specified values. Like the scripting elements, this syntax does not comply with XML and needs to be converted. Unlike scripting elements the conversion is always trivial. JSP Documents use directives same as classic JSP but with the following syntax: `<jsp:directive.directive {attribute="value"} */>`. The conversion is just a straight swap and includes the same directive and attribute values.

For clarity, Listing 3-29 shows a brief example of a JSP in classic syntax, which uses a page and include directive.

Listing 3-29 JSPDocumentDirectives.jsp

```
<%@page errorPage="ErrorPage.jsp"%>
<%@include file="header.jsp"%>
```

```
  <h1>A Title</h1>
  <p>Some text.</p>
<%@include file="footer.jsp"%>
```

Converting the preceding code to XML syntax is as easy as doing a direct replacement of the directives. In general, this will always be the case with directives (Listing 3-30).

Listing 3-30   JSPDirectives.jsp

```
<?xml version="1.0"?>
<jsp:root xmlns:jsp="http://java.sun.com/JSP/Page">
  <jsp:directive.page errorPage="ErrorPage.jsp"/>
  <jsp:directive.include file="header.jsp"/>
    <h1>A Title</h1>
    <p>Some text.</p>
  <jsp:directive.include file="footer.jsp"/>
</jsp:root>
```

Encapsulating Template Text

One of the unaccountably ridiculous requirements of the original JSP in XML syntax is to require JSP Documents to surround template text with `<jsp:text>` elements. There are no XML requirements mandating this. This requirement was intended to be a feature for aiding JSP parsers but greatly complicates authoring template text in JSP Documents.

Summary

This chapter is an introduction to JavaServer Pages (JSP). JSP is a complementary technology to Servlets that provides an incredibly efficient way of developing a text-producing Servlet. Unlike Servlets, JSP is not authored in a Java 2-compliant syntax, but JSP is translated to and managed by a container same as a Servlet. After authoring a JSP, there is no need to manually deploy the JSP to a URL extension via `web.xml`. A container automatically deploys a JSP, but a `web.xml` entry can still be used to provide initial parameters or arbitrary URL extensions for a JSP.

A JSP is divided into two main parts: template text and dynamic elements. Template text consists of everything that would normally appear in `print()` or `println()` calls of a Servlet. Dynamic elements are special bits of syntax defined by the JSP specifications. A dynamic element is not treated directly as text but is instead evaluated by a container to perform some custom functionality.

JSP elements are broken down into three main categories: scripting elements, directives, and actions. Scripting elements are a method of directly embedding code between template text. Directives are a method of giving a JSP container configuration information at translation time. Actions are used to link XML-compatible tags to custom code that is not included in the JSP. The JSP specifications define a few default actions, but there also exists a method for binding custom code to custom actions. Custom actions are one of the more powerful features of JSP and are left for full coverage in Chapter 7.

There are two different syntax styles available for authoring JSP. The first is the classic JSP syntax and has been available since the original release of JSP. This classic syntax is what the majority of this book uses and is what is commonly considered the easiest syntax to author JSP. The alternative JSP syntax is available for situations where it is helpful to have a JSP be authored as an XML-compliant document. Both syntax styles provide the same functionality. Converting between the two types of JSP syntax is usually a trivial task.

Chapter 4

Exception Handling

Exceptions are an integral part of the Java programming language. When a program violates the rules of Java, the Java Virtual Machine halts execution of the program and generates an exception. Managing exceptions is something every Java program must do. Servlets and JSP are no different. Until now, the topic of programming errors has largely been ignored in favor of introducing JSP and Servlets. While necessary for the start of this book, errors are inevitable and need to be understood so they can be dealt with appropriately. It is the goal of this chapter to clearly explain what exceptions are and how to deal with them in Servlets and JSP.

This chapter discusses the following topics:

- A general review of Java's support for exceptions and how Java exception handling works.
- How to handle Servlet and JSP exceptions using Java's built-in exception handling mechanism.
- How to handle exceptions using the Servlet-specific Web Application Deployment Descriptor called `web.xml`.
- An introduction to the `java.util.logging` package for appropriately handling information that needs to be recorded, including a focus on logging exception information.
- A general philosophy for a Web Application's exception handling and logging.

The preceding points imply this chapter assumes little to nothing about previous knowledge of Java exception handling. This implication is true; the chapter is designed to be suited for both Java developers and "Java" developers who never bothered to truly learn exception handling, who are surprisingly abundant. The chapter is designed to be read straight through, but if you already have a firm grasp on Java exception handling, you may skip the first section and start in on the discussion of Servlet and JSP exception handling.

Errors and Exceptions

All Java errors are subclasses of the `java.lang.Throwable` class. When an error occurs within a running program, an appropriate instance of this class is created and said to be *thrown*. The same code can then *catch* the exception and handle it or let the JVM handle the problem, which usually results in terminating the current program. In some cases Java enforces code to try and handle exceptions, and in others the exceptions are left to freely pass to a JVM.

There are three main subclasses of the `Throwable` class that divide all errors into three main categories. As shown in Figure 4-1, errors in Java are grouped as either instances of the `Error`, `Exception`, or `RuntimeException` class.

Of the three primary `Throwable` subclasses, the most well-known branch is instances of `Exception`. The `Exception` object represents a problem that a program must be able to catch. If code neglects to properly catch all instances of `Exception` objects, a Java compiler will refuse to compile the delinquent code. Complementing `Exception` classes, instances of the `RuntimeException` class represent a runtime error that does not need to be caught by code. However, just because the error does not need to be caught does not mean it is not a serious problem. Instances of `RuntimeException` objects are used when an error should not be handled by local code and would only clutter things up if declared as an `Exception`. While helpful, `RuntimeException`s are inherently dangerous since they do not require code to account for them. `RuntimeException` objects are not as commonly used as `Exception` objects because of this risk. The third branch of

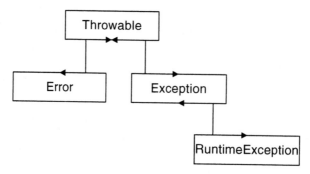

Figure 4-1   Throwable Subclass Tree

`Throwable` objects is subclasses of `Error`. An instance of the Error class represents something abnormally wrong that applications should not try to catch. If an instance of an `Error` object is thrown, it is almost always catastrophic to the executing program.

When programming a Web Application, it is common to use code that throws `Exception` objects, and in many cases, it is also helpful to design code for throwing and catching `RuntimeException` objects. Both `Exception` and `RuntimeException` objects are further covered by this chapter. Instances of the `Error` class are assumed to never occur and are considered outside the scope of this book.

Throwing Exceptions

Exceptions are *thrown* by use of the `throw` keyword followed by the `Throwable` object to be thrown. An exception may be thrown at any time, but the intended purpose of the `throw` keyword is to allow an exception to be thrown when a problem is detected at runtime. There are many good uses for throwing exceptions. One of the most common uses of exceptions is to verify correct parameters are passed into a function call. An exception can be thrown with a good explanation of what went wrong instead of using a convoluted system of return values. Listing 4-1 resembles code that accomplishes this.

Listing 4-1   Use of the throw Keyword

```
public void fooMethod(String value1, String value2) {
  if (value1 == null)
    throw new Exception("Value 1 can't be null!");
  if (value2 == null)
    throw new Exception("Value 2 can't be null!");
  // method's code...
}
```

Accompanying the `throw` keyword is the `throws` clause. The `throws` clause extends the signature of a method to reflect the fact that an exception might be thrown. Each method that uses the `throw` keyword and does not catch the exception must use the `throws` clause to declare `Exception` objects that are uncaught. To apply the throws clause to the preceding code, you would need to change the code to resemble Listing 4-2.

Listing 4-2   Proper Use of the throw Keyword

```
public void fooMethod(String value1, String value2)
  throws Exception {
  if (value1 == null)
```

```
    throw new Exception("Value 1 can't be null!");
  if (value2 == null)
    throw new Exception("Value 2 can't be null!");
  // method's code...
}
```

Subclassing Exception

It is always good to code with exceptions in mind. The Java exception handling mechanism is incredibly helpful for keeping code running smoothly and debugging a problem when something goes wrong. While valid, the previously given examples of exception throwing are skewed for the purposes of illustrating how the functionality works. In real use exceptions are almost never thrown as a direct instance of the Exception class. Exceptions are best thrown as a specific subclass of Exception that better relates to the nature of the exception.

A custom exception can easily be made by subclassing Exception. In general, code for a custom error is usually nothing more than a class that extends Exception with a call to the Exception constructor in its own, as shown in Listing 4-3.

Listing 4-3 CustomException.java

```
package com.jspbook.foo;

public class CustomException extends Exception {

  public CustomException(String message) {
    super(message);
  }
}
```

The CustomException code is to appear in an upcoming example, so it is placed in the com.jspbook.foo package. Save and compile CustomException.java in the /WEB-INF/classes/com/jspbook/foo directory of the jspbook Web Application.

Consolidation of Throwable Classes

In most cases it is impractical to throw every single type of exception that occurs. Cluttering up a method declaration only to include countless types of Throwable classes is not good practice in Java programming. A better solution is to consolidate types of Throwable classes by wrapping them with custom-categorized Throwable classes. If two or more types of exceptions really mean the same thing and are meant to be handled identically by catching code, then there is reason to consolidate them.

A good method of consolidating `Throwable` classes with a Web Application is to break exceptions into two categories, user-related exceptions and critical application exceptions. These two exceptions represent the general type of problems that might occur during runtime: either a user makes a mistake or the application fails to work as expected. In the case of a user mistake it is helpful to catch the problem and inform the user what they did wrong. In the case of an application mistake there is little a user can do. Instead an application mistake should display a polite error page to a user while simultaneously notifying the administrators.

The user and application types of exceptions are encouraged for use and followed throughout this book. For future examples save the following two classes. Listing 4-4 displays the custom `Throwable` class representing a user exception. The exception should immediately raise an alarm and so is made a "checked" exception by subclassing `Exception`.

Listing 4-4 UserException.java

```
package com.jspbook;

public class UserException extends Exception {

  // A constructor to set the description of the exception
  public UserException(String description) {
    super(description);
  }
}
```

The second class represents unforeseen application exceptions, as displayed in Listing 4-5. Any exception of this type is completely unexpected and represents a potentially serious problem with the Web Application. This exception is not made "checked", but assumed to be caught by one consolidated mechanism that appropriately logs the problem and notifies administrators. By extending the `RuntimeException` class, the code is not cluttered needlessly handling the problem since it should never occur.

Listing 4-5 AdminException.java

```
package com.jspbook;

public class AdminException extends RuntimeException {

  // A constructor to set the description of the exception
```

```
  public AdminException(String description) {
    super(description);
  }
}
```

Save and compile both of the preceding classes in the /WEB-INF/classes/ com/jspbook directory of the jspbook Web Application. Appropriately handling the preceding two exceptions is something that is developed throughout this chapter. There are many good methods, some with advantages compared to others, but before introducing anything complex, let's start the discussion at the basic level.

Try, Catch, Finally

Throwing exceptions is good, but catching them is just as important. Throwing an exception straight to the JVM is never good practice because it can result in stopping your application. When possible it is best to keep exception handling local. The Java specification uses the try statement with a catch clause to respectively attempt to execute possible exception throwing code and to handle any exceptions that might be thrown. The general format is to surround exception throwing code with a try statement and follow with one or more catch clauses to handle the different types of Throwable objects that might arise.

Before giving an example of the try-catch functionality, some code is needed that throws exceptions. Because this code is purely educational, it will accompany CustomException.java in the foo package. Save and compile Listing 4-6 in the /WEB-INF/classes/com/jspbook/foo directory of the jspbook Web Application.

Listing 4-6 ExceptionThrower.java

```
package com.jspbook.foo;

public class ExceptionThrower {

  public static void throwException(String message) throws
Exception{
    throw new Exception(message);
  }

  public static void throwCustomException(String message)
      throws CustomException{
    throw new CustomException(message);
  }
}
```

The `ExceptionThrower.java` only exists to throw `Exception` and `Custom Exception` objects. Its purpose is to provide a mock setup in which differing exceptions are thrown so the try-catch statement can be demonstrated. The JSP in Listing 4-7 uses the `ExceptionThrower` class to randomly throw an instance of either a `CustomException` or `Exception` object. A try statement surrounds the code with catch clauses to handle both types of exceptions.

Listing 4-7 ExceptionThrower.jsp

```
<%@ page import="com.jspbook.foo.*" %>
<html>
 <head>
   <title>ExceptionThrower</title>
 </head>
 <body>
<%
try {
   double rand = Math.random();
   if (rand <.5) {
       ExceptionThrower.throwException("foo");
   }
   ExceptionThrower.throwCustomException("foo");
}
catch (CustomException e) {
   out.println("Caught a CustomException: " + e.getMessage());
}
catch (Exception e) {
   out.println("Caught a Exception: " + e.getMessage());
}
%>
 </body>
</html>
```

Save `ExceptionThrower.jsp` in the base directory of the jspbook Web Application and browse to `http://127.0.0.1/jspbook/ExceptionThrower.jsp`. Each visit to the page causes either an `Exception` or `CustomException` to be thrown. Instead of seeing an error page (as shown later in Figure 4-3), the JSP catches the error and displays a little information about it. Figure 4-2 shows a browser rendering of the output.

In many situations code is going to be throwing various types of exceptions. Some exceptions might be caused from a user error, while others could be a critical bug in an application. Being able to catch, distinguish, and appropriately handle these exceptions is a necessity in keeping a Web Application running

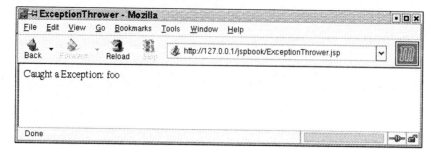

Figure 4-2 Browser Rendering of ExceptionThrower.jsp

smoothly. The try-catch mechanism appears quite often throughout this book, and it is important to be familiar with it.

Finally

When an exception is thrown, the offending code is stopped and control is passed to the code responsible for catching the exception. Stopping executing code in this manner is not always safe. Resources initially declared by the offending code are ignored, and there is no guarantee that they are properly cleaned up. With local variables and object references, the garbage collector still works, but in cases where non-local objects are in use, then a fall-back mechanism is needed to ensure the resource is properly terminated.

The `finally` clause complements the try-catch statement to provide this form of functionality. Whenever a block of code needs to be executed, regardless if an exception is thrown or not, then it should be included in a `finally` clause. Blocks of code appearing in a `finally` clause are always executed even if an executing of code in the `try` block is halted due to an exception.

JSP and Servlet Exceptions

With JSP and Servlets it is imperative to always catch exceptions. Should an exception be thrown from either a JSP or Servlet, it is passed to the container. What a container does with an exception differs, depending on the container vendor and the container's configuration, but by default a container usually tries to help by sending an error message followed by a stack trace to the client. Leaving a visitor with this type of page is not recommended if the client is valued.

Tomcat provides a good example of what type of page a user of a Web Application should never be allowed to see. If an exception happens to be thrown from either a JSP or Servlet, Tomcat automatically generates a simple error page. In case you don't know what this error page looks like, it can easily be found by throwing an unaccounted-for exception intentionally, as displayed in Listing 4-8.

Listing 4-8 ThrowException.jsp

```
<%
if (true)
 throw new Exception("An Exception foo!");
%>
```

Save `ThrowException.jsp` in the base directory of the jspbook Web Application and browse to `http://127.0.0.1/jspbook/ThrowException.jsp`. `ThrowException.jsp` throws an exception and lets Tomcat figure out what to do with it. Figure 4-3 shows a browser rendering of the Tomcat-generated debugging message.

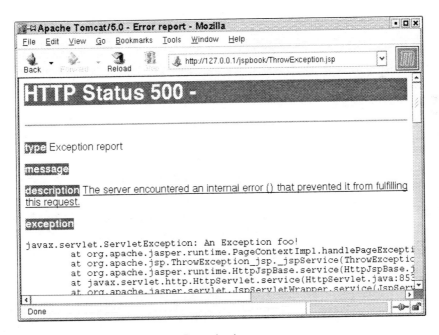

Figure 4-3 Browser Rendering of ThrowException.jsp

Figure 4-3 is hideous! There are easy ways to make sure a Web Application never lets a client see a generated exception page. In addition to using try-catch-finally statements, JSP and Servlets define specific methods for effectively managing exceptions. There is no excuse not to use them, and they ensure a visitor is never left with a cryptic error page.

Web Application Exception Handling

Exceptions thrown from a Servlet or JSP can be handled on an individual basis or on an application-wide basis. There are advantages to each of these approaches, and both deserve a full explanation. Handling exceptions on an individual basis slightly differs between Servlets and JSP, but primarily involves directly using try-catch-finally statements. The macro approach to Web Application error handling is through using `web.xml` to direct exceptions to custom-defined error pages.

Micro-Managing Exceptions

As with the previous examples in this chapter exceptions can easily be micro-managed through use of try-catch-finally statements. Both JSP and Servlets allow for directly embedding try-catch-finally statements. The functionality should be used liberally.

Error Handling JSP

In addition to the try-catch-finally statement, JavaServer Pages can use the `page` directive to specify a page that uncaught exceptions are passed to. The page directive's `errorPage` attribute can be assigned a relative URL value representing a JSP or Servlet especially designed to be an error page. A JSP designed to be an error page can set the `page` directive `isErrorPage` attribute to `true`; this makes the `exception` implicit scripting variable automatically available to represent a passed exception.

JSP error pages are a good way to ensure that raw exception messages with stack traces never reach a user. A JSP designed to be an error page can be styled to match the rest of a Web Application and show a polite message explaining a problem has occurred. Listing 4-9 displays the code for a simple custom JSP error page.

Listing 4-9 ErrorPage.jsp

```
<%@ page isErrorPage="true" %>
<html>
  <head>
```

```
    <title>An Error Has Occurred!</title>
  </head>
  <body>
  <h3>An Error Has Occurred</h3>
  Sorry, but this site is unavailable to render the service you
  requested. A bug in the system has caused an error to occur.
  Please send a description of the problem to
  <%= application.getInitParameter("admin email") %>.
  </body>
</html>
```

Save `ErrorPage.jsp` in the base directory of the jspbook Web Application. Because an error page is never intended for direct viewing, save the code in Listing 4-10 so that `ErrorPage.jsp` can be demonstrated.

Listing 4-10 ThrowExceptionToErrorPage.jsp

```
<%@ page errorPage="ErrorPage.jsp" %>
<%
    if (true)
       throw new Exception("An Exception!");
%>
```

The preceding code does a good job of representing a problematic JSP that uses `ErrorPage.jsp` as its error page. Save `ThrowExceptionToErrorPage.jsp` in the base directory of the jspbook Web Application and browse to `http://127.0.0.1/jspbook/ThrowExceptionToErrorPage.jsp`. Instead of displaying Figure 4-3 that you saw previously as a result of `ThrowException.jsp`, a friendly page is displayed. A brief explanation is given and a contact is provided for complaints. Figure 4-4 shows a browser rendering of the output from `ErrorPage.jsp`.

`ErrorPage.jsp` is only a simple example of a JSP error page. It is the equivalent of forwarding a request to a different resource after an exception is caught. More complex JSP error pages can be built that take advantage of the `exception` implicit object. When an exception is thrown by a page using the `errorPage` attribute of the page directive, the exception's information is not lost. An instance of the `Throwable` object is saved in request scope under the name `javax.servlet.jsp.jspException`. A Servlet or JSP being used as an error page can access this object in an attempt to find out what caused the problem. JSP provides a convenient mechanism for this purpose. The page directive `isErrorPage` attribute specifies if a JSP should automatically try to initialize the `exception` implicit scripting variable as a reference to the request scope attribute named

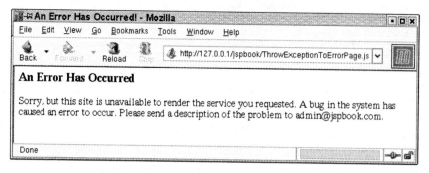

Figure 4-4 Browser Rendering of ErrorPage.jsp

javax.servlet.jsp.jspException. By setting the isErrorPage attribute to true, a JSP automatically has access to a passed exception.

A more helpful version of a JSP error page can be created by modifying ErrorPage.jsp. Relying on users to accurately describe what caused a problem is not a good idea. A better solution is to provide them with an error code description for inclusion with their feedback. The code in Listing 4-11 modifies ErrorPage.jsp to provide this functionality.

Listing 4-11 EnhancedErrorPage.jsp

```
<%@ page isErrorPage="true" %>
<html>
  <head>
    <title>An Error Has Occurred!</title>
  </head>
  <body>
  <h3>An Error Has Occurred</h3>
  Sorry, but this site is unavailable to render the service you
  requested. A bug in the system has caused an error to occur.
  Please send a description of the problem to
  <%= application.getInitParameter("admin email") %> with,
  "<%=exception.getMessage()%>", listed as the cause of the error.
  </body>
</html>
```

EnhancedErrorPage.jsp provides a user with both a contact email and an exception message that appear optionally along with feedback. By modifying ThrowExceptionToErrorPage.jsp, an error message can be passed for Enhanced ErrorPage.jsp to use, as shown in Listing 4-12.

Listing 4-12 ThrowExceptionToEnhancedErrorPage.jsp

```
<%@ page errorPage="EnhancedErrorPage.jsp" %>
<%
   if (true)
     throw new Exception("Generated by contrived code.");
%>
```

Save both `EnhancedErrorPage.jsp` and `ThrowExceptionToEnhancedError`
`Page.jsp` in the base directory of the jspbook Web Application and browse to
`http://127.0.0.1/jspbook/ThrowExceptionToEnhancedErrorPage.jsp`. This
time, in addition to the polite error page an exception message is provided for the
user to send as feedback. The exception message is the same one used in the constructor of the exception. Figure 4-5 shows a browser rendering of the output.

Error Handling Servlets

JSP is generally the easiest method of providing custom HTML error pages, but
Servlets work equally as well. In Servlets there is no equivalent of the `page`
directive's convenient `isErrorPage` attribute. To achieve the same functionality, a
Servlet acting as an error page has to explicitly retrieve the `Throwable` object from
request scope. This is not a difficult task, and it can be done by any Servlet.

The Servlet equivalent of `ErrorPage.jsp` has already been demonstrated in
Listing 2-17 in Chapter 2. To modify this example to be a real error page that
mimics `EnhancedErrorPage.jsp` is actually a trivial task. The code equivalent of
`isErrorPage="true"` is a few lines of code that access request scope for the
needed attribute. Listing 4-13 creates an EnhancedErrorPage Servlet designed to
act as an error page for JSP.

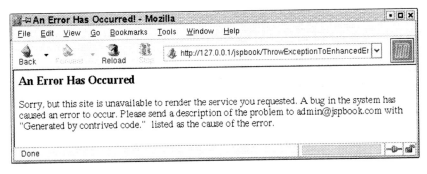

Figure 4-5 Browser Rendering of EnhancedErrorPage.jsp

Listing 4-13 EnhancedErrorPage.java

```java
package com.jspbook;

import java.io.*;
import javax.servlet.*;
import javax.servlet.http.*;

public class EnhancedErrorPage extends HttpServlet {

  public void doGet(HttpServletRequest request,
                    HttpServletResponse response)
    throws IOException, ServletException {

    response.setContentType("text/html");
    PrintWriter out = response.getWriter();

    // Load contact email from application initial parameters
    ServletContext sc = getServletConfig().getServletContext();
    String adminEmail = sc.getInitParameter("admin email");

    // Get the exception passed by JSP
    Exception e =

(Exception)request.getAttribute("javax.servlet.jsp.jspException");

    out.println("<html>");
    out.println("<head>");
    out.println("<title>An Error Has Occurred!</title>");
    out.println("</head>");
    out.println("<body>");
    out.println("<h3>An Error Has Occurred</h3>");
    out.println("Sorry, but this site is unavailable to render");
    out.println(" the service you requested. A bug in the");
    out.println("system has caused an error to occur. Please ");
    out.println("send a description of the problem to ");
    out.println(adminEmail +" with, \"" + e.getMessage() + "\", ");
    out.println(" listed as the cause of the error.");
    out.println("</body>");
    out.println("</html>");
    }
}
```

Save `EnhancedErrorPage.java` in the `/WEB-INF/classes/com/jspbook` directory of the jspbook Web Application. Deploy the Servlet to the `/Enhanced ErrorPage` URL extension and reload the Web Application. The EnhancedErrror Page Servlet now acts as an error page same as `EnhancedErrorPage.jsp`. The JSP in Listing 4-14 throws an `Exception` to test out the Servlet.

Listing 4-14 EnhancedErrorPageTest.jsp

```
<%@ page errorPage="EnhancedErrorPage" %>
<%
    if (true)
        throw new Exception("An Exception!");
%>
```

Save `EnhancedErrorPageTest.jsp` in the base directory of the jspbook Web Application and browse to `http://127.0.0.1/jspbook/EnhancedErrorPage Test.jsp`. The same results appear in Figure 4-5 that you saw previously, but with the Servlet mapped to `/EnhancedErrorPage` handling the results.

Macro-Managing Exceptions

Handling exceptions on an individual basis is not the only way to deal with errors. Through use of some exception handling techniques and `web.xml`, there are methods of allowing exceptions to be caught and dealt with on an application-wide basis. This macro style of exception handling consolidates Web Application error handling and complements individual exception handling techniques by catching unaccounted for problems.

There are a few good methods for handling exceptions on an application-wide basis. The most commonly used method is to modify a Web Application's default exception handling behavior via `web.xml`. The process involves letting JSP and Servlets throw exceptions and having the Web Application direct exceptions to predefined custom error pages. This mechanism is simple to implement and does a good job of handling most exceptions. More complicated methods of providing application-wide exception handling involve strategically designing the application for the purpose. Often a primary class, usually a Servlet, is used to handle all requests while dually ensuring proper error handling.

In this chapter only the Web Application configuration is discussed as a method of application-wide error handling. Other methods involving a predetermined application design are kept for discussion with JSP and Servlet design patterns, Chapter 11.

Web Application Error Pages

Error pages can be defined on a per Web Application basis by a Web Application Deployment Descriptor, web.xml. The error-page element is used to define error handling based on either the type of exception thrown or the HTTP status code set for a response. The error-page element must contain sub-elements that specify both a relative URL to an error page and either the HTTP response code or Throwable type to associate with it.

Exception-Based Error Pages

Based on the type of the Throwable object thrown, a Web Application can direct an exception to a specified error page. This functionality is configured in web.xml by using the error-page element with the exception-class and location sub-elements. The value specified in the exception-class element's body needs to be a fully qualified Java class, and the location element specifies a relative URL for the appropriate error page in the Web Application. The entry in web.xml always resembles Listing 4-15.

Listing 4-15   web.xml error-page Element

```
<error-page>
  <exception-type>Throwable</exception-type>
  <location>Relative URL</location>
</error-page>
```

There are three generic types of Throwable objects thrown by Servlets and JSP: IOException, ServletException, and JspException. When a Servlet is processing a call to the service() method, it has the option of throwing either an instance of an IOException or ServletException. Any JSP processing a request has the option of throwing an instance of a JspException object. Catching all three of these exceptions ensures that all checked exceptions thrown by a Servlet or JSP result in a custom error page. This sort of error catch is quite useful and can easily be done by adding a single entry to web.xml. Since IOException, ServletException, and JspException all share the same superclass, Exception, catching occurrences of the Exception class covers all three, as shown in Listing 4-16.

Listing 4-16   web.xml Error Page for All Checked Exceptions

```
<error-page>
  <exception-type>java.lang.Exception</exception-type>
  <location>/ErrorPage.jsp</location>
</error-page>
```

Add the preceding entry into `web.xml` after the ending `welcome-file-list` tag but before the closing `webapp` tag. Reload the jspbook Web Application to reflect the changes. With the new `error-page` entry, all exceptions are directed to `ErrorPage.jsp`. Try browsing back to the `ThrowException.jsp`, `http://127.0.0.1/jspbook/ThrowException.jsp`. Instead of seeing the undesired stack trace, as shown in Figure 4-3 previously, the content of `ErrorPage.jsp` is displayed. Figure 4-6 shows a browser rendering of the results.

Every Web Application should contain at least one generic error page as just demonstrated. Ensuring a user never has to see a cryptic stack-trace page is a top priority of a good Web site. More graceful solutions exist, but a simple, friendly error page should always be implemented as a starting point.

A Web Application Deployment Descriptor can be used to catch more than one type of `Throwable` object. In many cases different Servlets and JSP will throw different types of exceptions. In these cases it sometimes makes sense to have two or more different error pages that handle the different types of exceptions. Multiple `error-page` entries can be used to solve this problem. However, individual entries must have a unique value for the `exception-type` element. In cases where both a super- and subclass exist, for instance `Exception` and `Servlet Exception`, the superclass's error page takes priority.

HTTP Status Code–Based Error Pages

The same error page mechanism available for catching thrown exceptions can be applied to responses with undesired HTTP headers. This functionality is configured via `web.xml` by using the `error-page` element with the `error-code` and `location` sub-elements. The value in the body of the `error-code` element needs to be a valid HTTP response code and represents the specific code that results in a response being redirected to the error page. The location element provides the relative URL of the appropriate error handling resource located in the Web Application. The entry in `web.xml` always resembles Listing 4-17.

Listing 4-17 web.xml error-page Element

```
<error-page>
  <error-code>HTTP Code</error-code>
  <location>Relative URL</location>
</error-page>
```

It is always a good idea to provide a custom error page for all the HTTP error response codes. As an example, here is the error-page element being used to provide a custom page for the commonly seen code 404, "File Not Found", HTTP

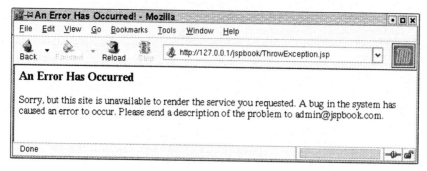

Figure 4-6 Browser Rendering of the web.xml Error Page

status code. By default Tomcat sends a server-generated page to describe a 404, "File Not Found", error. This page is a little prettier than the generated debugging page shown for exceptions, but it is nothing special. Figure 4-7 shows an example of a 404 page that has been generated by Tomcat. This page can be replicated by trying to browse to any resource that does not exist in the Web Application.

The page is simple and informative but usually does not complement a site's style. Additionally, most server-generated pages display some information about the server sending the page. In cases where it is imperative to keep a secure site, this has to be removed along with any HTTP headers containing the same information.

A `web.xml` entry for the error code solves the need for a custom page, as illustrated in Listing 4-18.

Listing 4-18 web.xml Error Page Entry for HTTP 404 Response Code

```
<error-page>
  <error-code>404</error-code>
  <location>/FileNotFound.jsp</location>
</error-page>
```

The preceding entry for `web.xml` defines an error page, `/FileNotFound.jsp`, to handle all requests to the Web Application that result in an HTTP 404 exception code. Add the example code into `web.xml` and reload the Web Application. However, before testing out the error page, save the code in Listing 4-19 as `FileNotFound.jsp` in the base directory of the jspbook Web Application.

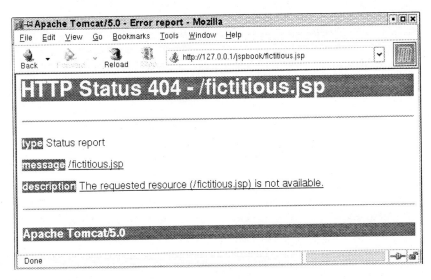

Figure 4-7 A Tomcat-Generated 404 Page

Listing 4-19 FileNotFound.jsp

```
<html>
 <head>
  <title>Bad URL</title>
 </head>
 <body>
 <h3>Bad URL</h3>
 The resource you are trying to reach,
 <%=request.getRequestURL()%>, does not exist on this server.
 </body>
</html>
```

Test out the new 404 error page by browsing to any resource in the jspbook Web Application that does not exist. A good choice would be `fictitious.jsp`. Browsing to `http://127.0.0.1/jspbook/fictitious.jsp` normally would result in a Tomcat-generated error page. Now the custom page, `FileNotFound.jsp`, is displayed. Figure 4-8 shows a browser rendering of the results.

Using `web.xml`, an error page can be specified for any of the HTTP error response codes. Each response code must have an individual `error-page` element with appropriate subelements in `web.xml`.

Customizing Web Application Exception Pages

Web Application error pages are passed extra information in a similar method as JSP error pages. When `web.xml` is used to handle an error, in addition to forwarding a request to the specified error page, a few objects are bound in request scope that describe the error. These objects are usually of little help to a user, but they can provide valuable information to developers. The Servlet specification defines the following attributes to be set by a Web Application in request scope when an error page is used:

- **javax.servlet.error.status_code:** The attribute bound in request scope with the name `javax.servlet.error.status_code` is an instance of a `java.lang.Integer` that represents the HTTP error status code. This attribute is only set when the error page is used as a result of an HTTP error status code.

- **javax.servlet.error.exception_type:** The attribute bound in request with the name is an instance of a `java.lang.Class` representing the type of the `Throwable` class bound to request scope with the name `javax.servlet.error.exception`.

- **javax.servlet.error.message:** The attribute bound in request with the name `javax.servlet.error.message` is a `String` object with a description of the error.

- **javax.servlet.error.exception:** The attribute bound in request scope with the name `javax.servlet.error.exception` is an instance of the `java.lang.Throwable` object thrown as the exception.

- **javax.servlet.error.request_uri:** The attribute bound in request scope with the name `javax.servlet.error.request_uri` is a

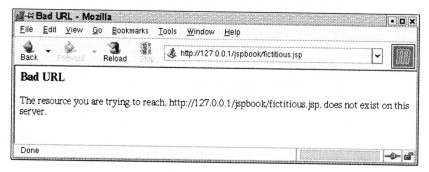

Figure 4-8 Browser Rendering of FileNotFound.jsp

`String` object representing the path to the Web Application resource that resulted in the error.

- **javax.servlet.error.servlet_name:** The attribute bound in request scope with the name `javax.servlet.error.servlet name` is a `String` object representing the name of the Servlet that caused the error.

A JSP or Servlet error page can take advantage of these attributes by using the `getAttribute()` method of the `HttpServletRequest` object forwarded to the error page. In the previous JSP error page example, Listing 4-11, a custom error page, was presented to a user informing them the appropriate error message to include with feedback. Taking the example one step further, a custom error page can be created that includes all of the available attributes sent to an error page. It usually does little good to directly present this information to a user. Instead, automatically including debugging with an email message is a better option for getting the feedback sent.

Sending email is not a trivial task. There are many existing API that implement popular email protocols, and it is usually easiest to use one of these API. The official J2EE API for manipulating email is the JavaMail API, `http://java.sun.com/products/javamail/index.html`. Unfortunately, it is outside the scope of this book to provide a tutorial on the JavaMail API; however, it is a good point to understand that you can send email from a JSP or Servlet. The JSP in Listing 4-20 works much like the `EnhancedErrorPage.jsp` but uses the JavaMail API to send an email to the application's administration whenever an exception arises. Please note that this example will not work unless you have installed the JavaMail API[1] and edited the email server configuration information.

Listing 4-20 EmailErrorPage.jsp

```
<%@ page
  isErrorPage="true"
  import="
    java.util.*,
    javax.mail.*,
    javax.mail.internet.*" %>kj
<%
  Properties props = new Properties();
  props.put("mail.smtp.server","your smtp server");
```

---

1. Installation of the JavaMail API is not difficult. It involves adding the JAR files from the JavaBean Activation Framework and the JavaMail API to the `/WEB-INF/lib` directory of a Web Application. However, configuring an email server can be quirky and is not a tangent we wish to cover in this book.

```
  Session msession = Session.getInstance(props,null);
  // email address from Chapter 2
  String email = application.getInitParameter("admin email");

  MimeMessage message= new MimeMessage(msession);
  message.setSubject("[Application Error]");
  message.setFrom(new InternetAddress(email));
  message.addRecipient(Message.RecipientType.TO, new
InternetAddress(email));
  String debug = "";

  Integer status_code

=(Integer)request.getAttribute("javax.servlet.error.status_code");
  if (status_code != null) {
    debug += "status_code: "+status_code.toString() + "\n";
  }
  Class exception_type=

(Class)request.getAttribute("javax.servlet.error.exception_type");
  if (exception_type != null) {
    debug += "exception_type: "+exception_type.getName() + "\n";
  }
  String m=
    (String)request.getAttribute("javax.servlet.error.message");
  if (m != null) {
    debug += "message: "+m + "\n";
  }
  Throwable e =
    (Throwable)
request.getAttribute("javax.servlet.error.exception");
  if (e != null) {
    debug += "exception: "+ e.toString() + "\n";
  }
  String request_uri =
    (String)request.getAttribute("javax.servlet.error.request_uri");
  if (request_uri != null) {
    debug += "request_uri: "+request_uri + "\n";
  }
  String servlet_name=

(String)request.getAttribute("javax.servlet.error.servlet_name");
  if (servlet_name != null) {
```

```
      debug += "servlet_name: "+servlet_name;
   }

   //set message, send email
   message.setText(debug);
   Transport.send(message);
%>
<html>
 <head>
  <title>EmailErrorPage</title>
 </head>
 <body>
  <h3>An Error Has Occurred</h3>
  Sorry, but this site is unavailable to render the service you
  requested. A bug in the system has caused an error to occur.
  Please send a description of the problem to
  <a href="mailto:<%=email%>"><%=email%></a>.
 </body>
</html>
```

Save the preceding code as `EmailErrorPage.jsp` in the base directory of the jspbook Web Application. Note, if you want the example to actually send an email, you must edit the highlighted section of code to be a valid IP address of an SMTP email server. Additionally, the administrative email address set in `Web.xml` must be a valid address for use with that server. Edit `web.xml` to use the new error page instead of `ErrorPage.jsp`. The entry in `web.xml` should now resemble Listing 4-21.

Listing 4-21 EmailErrorPage.jsp web.xml Entry

```
<error-page>
  <exception-type>java.lang.Exception</exception-type>
  <location>/EmailErrorPage.jsp</location>
</error-page>
```

After reloading the Web Application, the error page is ready for use. The next time an error is generated, an email is automatically sent to the site's administrators. The JavaMail code handles sending the email, while the information in the email is mined from the scoped exception information:

```
Integer status_code
```

```
=(Integer)request.getAttribute("javax.servlet.error.status_code");
   if (status_code != null) {
```

```
        debug += "status_code: "+status_code.toString() + "\n";
    }
    Class exception_type=

(Class)request.getAttribute("javax.servlet.error.exception_type");
    if (exception_type != null) {
        debug += "exception_type: "+exception_type.getName() + "\n";
    }
    String m=
        (String)request.getAttribute("javax.servlet.error.message");
    if (m != null) {
        debug += "message: "+m + "\n";
    }
...
```

The end result is that a user sees an error page, similar to all the other error pages shown in this chapter, and an email is sent to the site's administrators. Even if the user decides not to send feedback about the problem, the site still does. Figure 4-9 shows a browser rendering for the error page.

However, the preceding error page is not what is important. The important point in this example is that an email is automatically sent to the site's administrators via the JavaMail API. For example, assuming the page was used on www.jspinsider.com and administrative email was set to be jayson@jspinsider.com, Figure 4-10 shows the email that is sent.

A truly robust error page would not rely on a user to have to send any form of feedback. Leaving the option open is a good idea, but it is best to leave it open only for arbitrary user feedback. Keeping information about errors and other potentially sensitive data on the server-side should be preferred over routing it

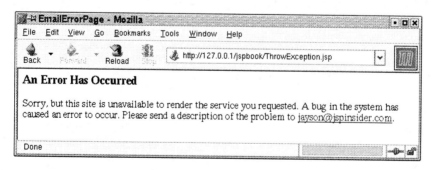

Figure 4-9 Browser Rendering of EmailErrorPage.jsp

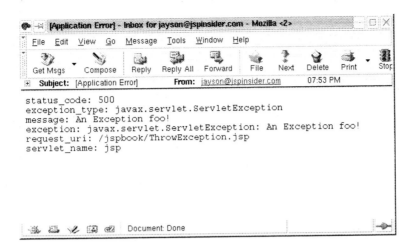

Figure 4-10 Email Generated by Code 4-20, Rendered by MozillaMail

through a client. In these cases it is best to use a form of server-side logging, such as Listing 4-20, to keep the important information recorded without ever routing it through a user. The `ServletContext log()` methods are also a candidate for doing this; however, as explained later in this chapter, a full logging API makes a better choice.

Exception Handling Priorities

Another important aspect of exception handling is to understand the priority in which exception pages are shown to a user. Try-catch statements are direct. The appropriate catch clause always has priority over any secondary exception mechanism such as the JSP `errorPage` attribute or `web.xml error-page` definitions. However, an ambiguity is present as to which takes priority, JSP error pages or Web Application-defined error pages. In this case the more local error page wins. A JSP error page defined by the page directive's `errorPage` attribute is always shown before an error page defined by `web.xml`.

Logging

Logging is the act of keeping a record of important information in some serialized form. Some simple examples of logs include a text file with lines of error messages or information printed to `System.err` or `System.out`. Sometimes logged information is designed to be kept for long periods of time. Other times logged information is meant for short-term use to quickly debug a running application. How long to persist, where information is sent, and what information is sent are all important issues to logging. Planning ahead and utilizing a robust logging mechanism helps solve these issues and keeps a project, especially a Web Application, running smoothly.

The Servlet API by default provides a limited and ambiguous method of logging information. The `ServletContext` object provides two `log()` methods that log information in a method left implemented by individual container vendors. For application-wide logging, this device is inadequate. With the two log methods, either a `String` or `String` with a `Throwable` object's stack trace can be logged. No attempt is given at distinguishing between different types of information to log, and all logging relies on access to a `ServletContext` object.

For the purpose of building a practical Web Application, a full-blown logging API is introduced and demonstrated in this section. The logging API is not specifically defined by Servlets or JSP; however, it is a valuable tool for any project including a Web Application.

The Problem with System.out.println()

The far too common mindset is to build a Java application and get by with a rudimentary set of debugging calls. Most commonly, this set of calls consists of using the `PrintStream` objects `System.out` or `System.err` to send temporary information to a terminal. This method of application debugging is simple and works for small projects, but it quickly falls apart in most any real-world situation.

`System.out.println()` debugging, which is analogous to `System.err.println()` debugging, is instant gratification. If code does not work, most every Java developer knows inserting a few simple `System.out.println()` method calls makes something appear somewhere obvious. Given enough `System.out.println()` calls, it is easy to find a code flaw and get a program in working shape. For this purpose, `System.out.println()` works perfectly fine; however, a problem occurs when an application needs to constantly log information and will need to log information for the foreseeable future. This information might be trivial statements, such as "made it here", or important information such as runtime listings of system workloads. Far too many times, calls to `System.out.println()` are used in these cases when they really should not.

The issue to think about is, What will the debugging code do in the future? Inserting `System.out.println()` calls only works until the calls are no longer needed. Going back and commenting the calls out for performance is not terribly helpful, especially when a bug arises. What happens when more than one developer starts working on the project? If two different developers use completely arbitrary calls to `System.out.println()`, or equivalents, then each is likely to hinder the other. Without a common logging mechanism it is hard to collaborate. Another very important issue is, What happens when the logging information needs to be piped to a different location? Instead of to a terminal screen, what about a log file, email, or a common repository? Manually fixing countless `System.out.println()` calls is a complete waste of time, especially if the fix is going to need even more changes later on.

A good and commonly agreed-upon solution to saving debugging information is by means of a simple, yet robust logging API. A dedicated API can abstract the logging process, provide a common interface for multiple developers, enable and disable levels of logged information for performance, and allow easy changes to be made to the logging code in the future. When done properly, the whole logging package can also be as easily implemented same as a few simple `System.out.println()` statements.

JDK 1.4 Logging Versus Log4j

The idea of logging and a dedicated logging API is not a new one. Robust methods of logging have been around for quite awhile and some mature API exist. The most notable of the logging API would have to be Log4j, the logging API for Java. Log4j is currently supported by the Apache community, `http://jakarta.apache.org/log4j`, and is at version 1.2. Log4j has some fantastic developers working behind it and is a true and tested logging API. In addition to Log4j, the standard Java development kit version 1.4 introduced a new logging API, the `java.util.logging` package. This J2SDK addition is positioned as the standard Java logging API and provides very similar functionality to Log4j.

In writing this book the choice had to be made between which of these logging API to use and push as a preferred choice. After some careful consideration and thorough use of both APIs the choice was made to use the `java.util.logging` package. The truth of the matter is that both packages do a more than sufficient job as a logging API. Log4j does have a slight advantage in terms of previous testing and widespread community use, but the `java.util.logging` package is already included in the default Java 1.4 download and will be around in future distributions.

Using the java.util.logging Package

The `java.util.logging` package is included with every Java SDK 1.4 distribution. No extra installation is required to use the API with this book's examples.

If the code does not work, you probably did not follow the installation steps in Chapter 1. Make sure you are using the Java 2 Standard Development Kit 1.4 release or a later version.

The `java.util.logging` package can be generalized into two parts, `Logger` and `Handler` objects. A `logger` object is responsible for logging information to one or more `Handler` objects. `Handler` objects are responsible for customizing where and how information is logged. Using the `java.util.logging` package is as simple as creating a instance of a `Logger` object, registering one or more `Handler` objects, and logging information as needed.

For common logging, such as to terminals or files, the `java.util.logging` package includes everything that is needed to implement a simple logging system. In more complex cases the same functionality is used; however, custom subclasses of `Logger` and `Handler` objects might be required. Overall, the process of logging is always the same. As a quick introduction to the simplicity of the API, it is helpful to see a concrete code example. Listing 4-22 provides an example of implementing a `Logger` object that sends information to `System.err`.

Listing 4-22 Logger.jsp

```
<%@ page import="java.util.logging.*"%>
<%
Logger logger = Logger.getLogger("example");
logger.addHandler(new ConsoleHandler());

String info = request.getParameter("info");
if (info != null && !info.equals("")) {
  logger.info(info);
}
%>
<html>
  <head>
    <title>A Simple Logger</title>
  </head>
  <body>
  <form>
  Information to log:<input name="info"><br>
  <input type="submit">
  </form>
  </body>
</html>
```

Save `Logger.jsp` in the base directory of the jspbook Web Application and browse to `http://127.0.0.1/jspbook/Logger.jsp`. A small form is displayed with one input box. Anything typed in the box is logged upon submission of the form. Figure 4-11 shows a browser rendering of the HTML form.

Information posted by the form is logged by the server to `System.err`. This can be verified by checking the location of `System.err`. By default, Tomcat saves all information sent to `System.err` in the `catalina.out` file located in the `/logs` directory of installation. Open up this file to see the logged information. For example, if "log test" was submitted via the HTML form, then the following line would be appended to `catalina.out`.

```
Mar 18, 2002 8:30:11 PM org.apache.jsp.Logger$jsp _jspService
INFO: log test
```

For the time being, disregard the extra information included with the entry. The point of this example is to illustrate a quick and easy use of the `java.util.logging` package. Achieving a simple default-formatted log entry requires a few lines of code. `Logger.jsp` demonstrates this with the following two lines.

```
Logger logger = Logger.getLogger("example");
logger.addHandler(new ConsoleHandler());
```

After the `Logger` object was created and a `Handler` added, the system was ready to log information. There are many ways to log information, but in the example, the convenient `info()` method was used.

```
logger.info(info);
```

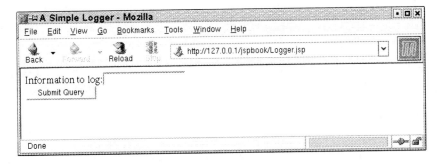

Figure 4-11 Browser Rendering of Logger.jsp

Subsequent calls to log information could also be included as desired; however, in this example, none were needed. The main purpose of the example was to introduce the general use of `Logger` and `Handler` objects. The `java.util.logging` package is easy to use and can be implemented with just a few lines of code. Discussion now expands to using the individual parts of the `java.util.logging` package for custom logging.

Handlers

`Handlers` are responsible for handling information that needs to be logged. Should the information go to a terminal screen, flat file, or any other resource, it is the responsibility of a `Handler` to make sure it gets there. Information published to a `Handler` is represented by a `java.util.logging.LogRecord` object. A `LogRecord` object includes information to log, where the information came from, how important the information is, and a time-stamp. How to appropriately style and present this information is the responsibility of a `java.util.logging.Formatter` object. Each `Handler` object has a `Formatter` object associated with it to appropriately style published `LogRecords`.

A few `Handler` objects are included with the `java.util.logging` package:

- **StreamHandler:** A `StreamHandler` object represents a `Handler` designed to export logged information to a `java.io.OutputStream`. The `StreamHandler` object includes a constructor that takes an `OutputStream` and `Formatter` object as parameters and uses them to format and stream logged information.

- **MemoryHandler:** The `MemoryHandler` object provides a cheap way to keep a set of `LogRecord` objects in memory. After established amounts of LogRecords are buffered, they are all published to an `Handler` object for appropriate handling. The `MemoryHandler` object is best used when it is expensive to constantly publish individual records, perhaps if a connection needs to be opened and closed during the logging of each record. Consolidating a set of logs during one connection can be much more efficient.

    The `MemoryHandler` object provides a constructor that takes as arguments a `Handler`, int value for a buffer size, and a push level. The `Handler` object is the `Handler` buffered `LogRecord` objects are published to, the int represents how many `LogRecord` objects to buffer, and the push level allows for important messages to cause the buffer to automatically flush.

- **SocketHandler:** A `SocketHandler` is a convenient method for logging information using a network socket. By default the `SocketHandler` formats logged information in an XML-compatible format. The `SocketHandler` object provides a constructor that takes as an argument a `String` representing a host URL and an `int` representing the port to use. The `Handler` automatically opens a `java.net.Socket` to the given URL on the specified port for logging information.

- **FileHandler:** A `FileHandler` object is a convenient `Handler` for logging information to a local file. The easiest use of the `FileHandler` object is to call the constructor providing a `String` that represents the file to use for logging information. More complex uses also exist for using the `FileHandler` object to automatically rotate logs between multiple files after a certain space limit has been reached.

The existing handlers in the J2SDK represent some of the most commonly used resources for saving logged information. Building an appropriate `Handler` object for most cases is nothing more than using one that already exists. Using all the aforementioned convenience `Handler` objects is not fully demonstrated by this book. The code is intuitive to use and is mentioned only to give an idea of what comes bundled with the `java.util.logging` package.

Formatting

The style in which a `Handler` object exports information is completely configurable. Every `Handler` object relies on a `Formatter` object to convert a `LogRecord` into an appropriate `String` of information to log. The `Formatter` object being used to style a specific `Handler` instance can be obtained or set using the `getFormatter()` or `setFormatter()` methods.

To code a custom `Formatter` object, extend the `Formatter` class and override the relevant methods. There are four possible methods of interest:

- **format(LogRecord record):** The `format()` method is invoked by a `Logger` class when publishing information to be logged. Passed as a parameter is the `LogRecord` object describing the information to log. The `format()` method returns a `String` representing the final format of the information to log.

- **formatMessage(LogRecord):** The `formatMessage()` method is a convenience method that can be invoked by the `format()` method to localize a message using a resource bundle. Resource bundles are further explained in Chapter 12.

- **getHeader(Handler handler):** The `getHeader()` method returns a header that should be used to surround a set of formatted log records. This method returns an empty `String` by default. In cases where a header must be included, such as the start of a parent XML element, this method can be overridden to produce the correct `String`.

- **getTail(Handler handler):** The `getTail()` method works much like the `getHeader()` method but is used to return a tail to be placed at the end of a set of log records. This method returns an empty `String` by default. In cases where a tail must be included, this method can be overridden to produce the correct text.

There are two Formatting objects included with the `java.util.logging` package: `SimpleFormatter` and `XMLFormatter`. The `SimpleFormatter` object takes an instance of a `LogRecord` and converts it into a human-readable string. The string is usually one or two lines long and resembles the entries seen with the `Logger.jsp` example, Listing 4-22. The `XMLFormatter` object takes a `LogRecord` and formats it into an XML format.

For most purposes the `SimpleFormatter` object does an adequate job of logging information. Text returned by the `SimpleFormatter` object's `format()` method includes a time-stamp, the class sending the information to log, and the information to log. However, for the jspbook Web Application, a simple custom `Formatter` object will be created for both example purposes and use throughout the book. Save the code in Listing 4-23 as `CustomLogger.java` in the `/WEB-INF/classes/com/jspbook` directory of the jspbook Web Application.

Listing 4-23 CustomFormatter.java

```
package com.jspbook;

import java.io.*;
import java.util.*;
import java.util.logging.*;

public class CustomFormatter extends Formatter {

  public String format(LogRecord log) {
    Date date = new Date(log.getMillis());
    String level = log.getLevel().getName();
```

```
    String string = "[" + level + " " +date.toString() + "]\n";
    string += log.getMessage() + "\n\n";
    Throwable thrown = log.getThrown();
    if (thrown != null) {
      string += thrown.toString();
    }
    return string;
  }
}
```

The preceding custom `formatter` is designed to work similar to the `SimpleFormatter` object but makes the styled result a little easier to read. The `String` returned by invoking the `format()` method includes a bracketed time-stamp followed by the logged message and an optional exception stack-trace. The general format is the following:

```
[time-stamp]
message
stack-trace
```

The brackets are used to easily distinguish separate log entries while the message and stack-trace provide information about what went wrong with the Web Application. Before actually using the `CustomFormatter` class, a custom `Logger` class needs to also be created for use with the jspbook Web Application.

Loggers

A `Logger` object is used to log messages for a specific system of application components. Loggers are designed to be flexible and include features such as local-specific logging and logging information according to levels of importance. `Logger` objects are managed by a `LogManager` object that is responsible for keeping and configuring a collection of loggers.

Not all of the features of `Logger` and `LogManager` classes are covered in this book. The flexibility of these classes is extensive and not commonly needed. What is covered in this section is the basic use of the `Logger` class with JSP and Servlets. This includes customizing a logger for use in a Web Application and taking advantage of the various levels of logged information. International use of the `Logger` class for local-specific logs is covered in Chapter 12. Topics outside this scope are left for publications that focus more deeply on the `java.util.logging` package.

Levels of Logged Information

All information logged through an instance of a `Logger` object is associated with a specific level. Levels are used to efficiently manage different types of logged information. A level may be arbitrarily assigned but is intended to give some information about the nature of the information to log. `Handler` and `Logger` objects can selectively log only certain levels of information, making it practical to channel different types of information to desired locations.

The level scheme the `java.util.logging` package uses is defined by the `java.util.logging.Level` object. The levels are listed, in descending order of importance, as follows:

- **SEVERE:** The `SEVERE` level is the highest level of importance. A `SEVERE` level represents a severe, or critical, message that is to be logged. Often the `SEVERE` Level is associated with a thrown exception.

- **WARNING:** The `WARNING` level is the second highest level of importance. A `WARNING` level association represents a message to be logged that includes a warning. Warnings are important to signal a future possibility of a severe problem but are not severe problems themselves.

- **INFO:** The `INFO` level represents an informative message to be logged. The message is less important than a warning or severe level message and is most helpful when debugging an application. The `INFO` level is commonly associated with the casual use of `System.out.println()` statements.

- **CONFIG:** The `CONFIG` level represents configuration information being echoed back by an application. Messages at the `CONFIG` level are less important than informative messages and are meant for helping debug an application.

- **FINE:** The `FINE` level represents a message that falls in none of the previous categories but is more important than a `FINER` or `FINEST` level message.

- **FINER:** The `FINER` level represents a message less important than a `FINE` message but more important than a `FINEST` message.

- **FINEST:** The `FINEST` level represents a message that is less important than all the other messages.

- **OFF:** A level of `OFF` has the effect of turning off logging on either a `Handler` or `Logger` object. This level can be used when no logging is desired and absolute performance is the goal. A `Logger` or `Handler` object set to the `OFF` level immediately returns when information logging is attempted.

- **ALL:** The `ALL` level setting logs all levels of messages.

Complementing these levels, the `Logger` object defines the following methods:

- **getLevel():** The `getLevel()` method returns a level object representing the current level the `Logger` is set to log messages. Messages of higher or equal priority to the level are logged.
- **setLevel(Level level):** The `setLevel()` method sets the current level a `Logger` object should log messages at. Messages below the level are discarded. When the `OFF` level is specified, all messages are ignored.
- **log(Level level, String message):** The `log()` method logs a given message at a given level. Should the message be below the current `Logger` object's level setting, it is discarded. For all of the allowed levels, self-named convenience methods also exist: `severe()`, `warning()`, `info()`, `config()`, `fine()`, `finer()`, and `finest()`. All of the convenience methods take as a parameter a `String` representing the message to log. Levels are implied.
- **log(Level level, String message, Throwable throwable):** The `log()` method logs a given message at a given level. The `LogRecord` object published by this method also includes the `Throwable` object specified as the throwable parameter.

Using the preceding methods a `Logger` object can effectively log information based on arbitrary levels. The common use of these levels is to safely log critical information at all times while keeping warning and debugging information around only when developers need it. The performance difference between logging all information versus only the important information can be noticeable and it often makes sense to distinguish between the two.

Fine, Finer, Finest, and All

One of the most criticized features of the `java.util.logging` package is the inclusion of the fine, finer, finest and all levels. These levels are commonly regarded as redundant versions of the info level. If a situation requires use of fine, finer, and finest logging, there is nothing wrong with these methods, but do not feel obliged to use them.

Custom Web Application Logging

A nice feature of the `java.util.logging` package is that it can be used to log information by any class. Compared to the `ServletContext log()` methods, this functionality is quite nice, but it does not mean it is beneficial to completely abstract logging away from Servlets and JSP. A logging mechanism designed to work with a Web Application should take full advantage of that Web Application. Remember the reasons leading to the introduction of the `java.util.logging` package. Normal logging schemes are usually inadequate; using `System.out.println()` method calls becomes inefficient as a project grows and is not easily maintained in the future. Using `ServletContext` object's `log()` methods is very limiting and ambiguous. A robust logging API such as the `java.util.logging` package solves these problems. However, the `java.util.logging` package is not designed to be the final solution to an application's logging needs. The framework is extensible and much can be gained from using the package to most effectively suit individual needs.

In the case of a Web Application the `java.util.logging` package can be combined with the functionality of JSP and Servlets. From this combination a site can have a robust logging mechanism that easily ports and is configurable by the same methods as the rest of the Web Application. A great use of combining these two APIs is a custom logging ServletContextListener that can initialize with the Web Application and a JSP that can configure the logging mechanism as well as provide a Web interface for administrative use. Listing 4-24 is the ServletContextListener class.

Listing 4-24 SiteLogger.java

```java
package com.jspbook;

import java.io.*;
import java.util.logging.*;
import javax.servlet.*;
import javax.servlet.http.*;

public class SiteLogger implements ServletContextListener {

  // Site Logger
  private static Logger logger;

  public static Logger getLogger() throws IOException {
    return logger;
  }
}
```

```
public void contextInitialized(ServletContextEvent e) {
  ServletContext sc = e.getServletContext();

  // Get an instance of a Logger
  logger = Logger.getLogger("global");
  logger.setLevel(Level.INFO);

  try {
    FileHandler fh = null;
    String root = sc.getRealPath("/");
    fh = new FileHandler(root+"WEB-INF/log.txt");
    fh.setFormatter(new CustomFormatter());
    logger.addHandler(fh);
  } catch (IOException ee) {
    System.err.println("Can't load logger: " +ee.getMessage());
  }

  sc.setAttribute("com.jspbook.SiteLogger", logger);
}

public void contextDestroyed(ServletContextEvent e) {
  ServletContext sc = e.getServletContext();
  sc.removeAttribute("com.jspbook.SiteLogger");
  logger = null;
}
}
```

Save `SiteLogger.java` in the `/WEB-INF/classes/com/jspbook` directory of the jspbook Web Application. Deploy the listener by adding an entry in `web.xml`, as shown in Listing 4-25.

Listing 4-25 SiteLogger web.xml Listener Deployment

```
...
  <listener>
    <listener-class>com.jspbook.SiteLogger</listener-class>
  </listener>
...
```

Compile `SiteLogger.java` and reload the Web Application. The SiteLogger class now functions as a general-purpose logging class. Any other class in the Web Application may invoke the static `getLogger()` method to obtain an instance of the Web Application's new logging mechanism.

For the listener to be of much help it must be used by other code in the Web application. First, let us create an administrative JSP for modifying the logger during runtime, as shown in Listing 4-26. The page will provide a method of setting the logger's current level and viewing the current log.

Listing 4-26 SiteLoggerAdmin.jsp

```
<%@ page import="java.util.logging.*, java.io.*"%>
<%
  // get logger
  Logger logger = com.jspbook.SiteLogger.getLogger();

  // get request parameters
  String level = request.getParameter("level");
  if (level != null && !level.equals("")) {
    logger.setLevel(Level.parse(level));
  }

  // set current level
  request.setAttribute("l", logger.getLevel());

  // set current log
  StringWriter sw = new StringWriter();
  request.setAttribute("log", sw);

  // parse in current log
  InputStream is  =
    application.getResourceAsStream("/WEB-INF/log.txt");
  if (is != null) {
    for (int i = is.read();i!=-1;i=is.read()) {
      sw.write((char)i);
    }
  } else {
    sw.write("Can't load log file!");
  }
%>
<html>
<head>
<title>Site Logging Configuration</title>
</head>
<body>
<h3>Set the site's logging level:</h3>
<b>Current level:</b> ${l}<br><br>
<form>
```

```
<select name="level">
  <option value="SEVERE">Severe</option>
  <option value="WARNING">Warning</option>
  <option value="INFO">Info</option>
  <option value="CONFIG">Config</option>
</select><br>
<input type="submit" value="Update Level"><br>
</form>

<h3>Current Log:</h3>
<pre>${log}</pre>
</body>
</html>
```

Save the preceding code as SiteLoggerAdmin.jsp in the root directory of the jspbook Web Application. The code provides an HTML form for changing the current level of the logger (only between severe, warning, info, and config), and the page displays the current log. You can test the page by browsing to `http://127.0.0.1/jspbook/SiteLoggerAdmin.jsp`; however, there is currently little to see. Nothing currently logs information via the SiteLogger class.

Save the following JSP as SiteLogger.jsp in the root directory of the jspbook Web Application. The code provides example code for how the SiteLogger class can be used to log information. An HTML form passes information to be logged and the level of the information. The JSP then takes this information, obtains a reference to the Logger class, and logs the information using the appropriate level.

Listing 4-27 SiteLogger.jsp

```
<%@ page import="java.util.logging.*"%>
<%
// get logger
Logger logger = com.jspbook.SiteLogger.getLogger();

// get required request parameters
String info = request.getParameter("info");
String level = request.getParameter("level");

// log information appropriately
if (info != null && !info.equals("") &&
    level != null && !level.equals("")) {
  logger.log(Level.parse(level), info);
}
```

```
%>
<html>
  <head>
    <title>A Simple Logger</title>
  </head>
  <body>
  <form>
  <table>
    <tr>
      <td>Level:</td>
      <td>
        <select name="level">
          <option value="SEVERE">Severe</option>
          <option value="WARNING">Warning</option>
          <option value="INFO">Information</option>
          <option value="CONFIG">Configuration</option>
        </select>
      </td>
    </tr>
    <tr>
      <td>Information to log:</td>
      <td><input name="info"><br></td>
    </tr>
  </table>
  <input type="submit">
  </form>
  <a href="SiteLogger">View/Configure Log</a>
  </body>
</html>
```

The HTML form is of little interest, it simply queries a string to log and a level. Of interest is the general code for using the SiteLogger class's `getLogger()` method and logging information.

```
<%
// get logger
Logger logger = com.jspbook.SiteLogger.getLogger();

// get required request parameters
String info = request.getParameter("info");
String level = request.getParameter("level");

// log information appropriately
if (info != null && !info.equals("") &&
```

```
level != null && !level.equals("")) {
logger.log(Level.parse(level), info);
}
%>
```

Highlighted are the relevant lines, and the code is unsurprisingly straight-forward. First, the `getLogger()` method is invoked to obtain an instance of the previously initialized Logger class. Next the Logger class is used same as any other java.util.logging.Logger class.

Test out the new functionality by browsing to `http://127.0.0.1/jspbook/SiteLogger.jsp`. An HTML form appears, allowing you to log information at arbitrary levels. Figure 4-12 provides a browser rendering of the form.

Try submitting several different messages using various levels. Next, view the information by browsing to `http://127.0.0.1/jspbook/SiteLoggerAdmin.jsp`. If you like, use SiteLoggerAdmin.jsp to set the level of the application-wide Logger class and notice how messages logged below this level are ignored. By default the SiteLogger class is set at info level.

All-around, the use of the SiteLogger class should be intuitive—even trivial—and that is exactly the point. Instead of relying on the default Servlet logging mechanism, a more robust solution can easily be implemented using a simple ServletContextListener class. At Web Application initialization, your favorite logging API, in this case `java.util.logging`, can be initialized for use. During runtime, a static method provides easy access to the logging functionality for all of your other classes. Using a true logging API to handle Web Application logging is not difficult, and it is something you should use in most every Web Application.

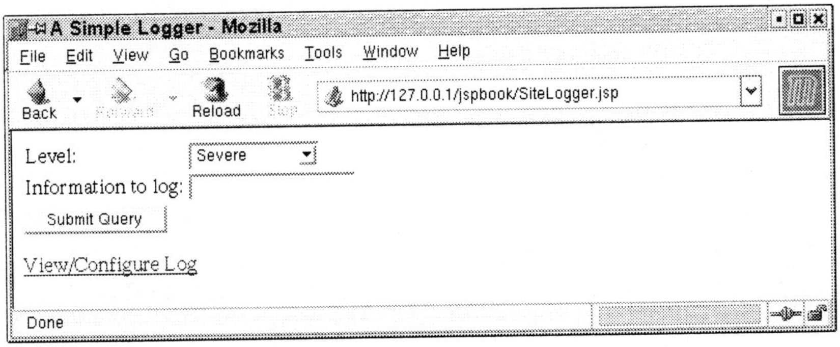

Figure 4-12 Browser Rendering of SiteLogger.jsp

Logging and Performance

With all this chapter's discussion of error handling and logging, the question is surely to be asked, "How does this affect a Web Application's performance?" Performance questions are never easily answered and are always tied to the specific use at hand. In this section there is no attempt at providing statistics or an allegedly credible benchmark. Instead, a brief discussion is provided about use of the `java.util.logging` package and how it affects performance of a Web Application.

Logging should be classified the same as error handling. Both of these techniques are critical to making a project work and continue to work. The only notable downside to logging is that it will always perform a little slower at runtime than the same code without logging calls. This is not an issue if the logged information must be kept, but it could become a problem if the logging information is not critical and should be ignored. The `java.util.logging` package solves this problem by allowing levels of logged information. Use levels to ensure that only important information is kept around during runtime in a production system. `Logger` and `Handler` objects return immediately if information sent to them is not above the level currently being logged. This behavior optimizes the inefficiency of using a logging API and in most practical cases makes the performance loss due to logging insignificant. The time it takes to immediately return from a hundred ignored log calls is easily dwarfed by the time it takes to send the ones and zeros of a Web page over a wire.

A General Philosophy for Exception Handling and Logging

Throughout the chapter several techniques have been introduced for handling exceptions and logging relevant information. Now it is time to introduce a general philosophy to use when handling a Web Application's exceptions and logging information. By no means is this a master philosophy; no formal proof of its effectiveness is present, but the philosophy will properly address all of the issues regarding Web Application error handling and logging. Having all this information in one place is helpful, especially when collaborating with other developers, because having a common, effective standard reduces the amount of development time you need to spend reinventing the same functionality.

The following list identifies the major issues that you must address when you're dealing with exceptions and logging. Each issue includes a solution, and the solution is based directly on material covered previously in this chapter:

- **Handle All Exceptions:** At all times handle all exceptions. Do not ever encourage coding practices that ignore exception handling—never put all-encompassing try-catch blocks around code and have the catch block do nothing. Always handle, throw, or re-throw an exception until it reaches the proper, predesignated place to be handled.

- **Consolidate Thrown Exceptions:** Reduce exceptions down to what is cared about and only what is cared about. For Web Applications it is suggested that the UserException and AdminException classes, as described previously, are used; in a Web Application you should care about two types of exceptions: something a user has done wrong—for example, sent the wrong information—and administrative exceptions—for example, your code, the Web Application, is broken. Note, by extending the Exception class and the RuntimeException class, as UserException and AdminException, respectively, do, you have easily consolidated exception handling. Should code throw a UserException, the exception is checked, and a developer should use a local try-catch block to handle the problem and inform the user. Should code throw an AdminException, the exception is unchecked, and a developer is not expected to do anything about it—rather, some previously defined mechanism, such as a `web.xml`-defined exception handling JSP or Servlet, is expected to handle the problem.

  Most all Java API have custom types of exceptions, and it is a pain to try and catch all of the different types of exceptions that exist. Consolidation makes Java exception handling practical.

- **Always Abstract Logging Functionality:** Always put a layer of abstraction around the actual code that logs information; preferably use the `java.util.logging` package that was explained by this chapter. Without a proper layer of abstraction you will always be stuck using whatever logging method was hard coded. Should you need to log information differently, perhaps to a different location such as a file or special computer on a network, it will take time to go back and fix all of the logging code. Compared to changing one implementation of an abstract logging interface, such as a `Handler` object, there is little argument for hard coding logging functionality. Additionally, when collaborating with multiple developers, a well-defined logging interface is a must. It can both ensure information is logged to the right place and that the information is correctly logged.

- **Consolidate Logging Functionality:** Create one easy-to-use class for all of a project's logging. Use the `java.util.logging` package to create one custom `Logger` object that is accessible to every class in the Web Application. The SiteLogger Servlet is a great example of this functionality. Developers should not need to worry about reimplementing logging API or about understanding a complex logging system. Also, reducing a Web Application's logging mechanism to one logging class provides a direct method of changing where information is logged. It is clearly desirable to have one logging class versus changing countless `System.out.println()` method calls (or other equivalents).

- **Always Create a Web Application-Wide Error Page:** Use `web.xml` to define at least one user-friendly error page to catch any thrown exception. Several examples of such error pages were provided in this chapter. Use at least one of them to ensure a user never sees a cryptic message generated by a container.

The five points represent a complete philosophy for handling a Web Application's exceptions and logging needs. After reading through this chapter, the points should come as no surprise. Take the philosophy and use or adapt it to handle exceptions.

Summary

Exceptions are a fundamental part of Java. When a program has a problem, an instance of a `Throwable` object is *thrown*. Java accounts for thrown exceptions by allowing bits of code to *catch* the offending object. Throwing and catching `Throwable` objects is a fundamental part of Java and is not specific to JSP and Servlets. In the first half of this chapter the basic exception handling mechanisms of Java were rehashed. Following this discussion the JSP and Servlet specific exception handling mechanisms were introduced.

Like all Java objects, JSP and Servlets can throw exceptions. Exceptions thrown to a Web Application are either caught and forwarded to an appropriate error page or handled by the container. This sort of application-wide exception handling is a very handy feature of JSP and Servlets. Preventing a user from seeing a cryptic Java debugging message is always a high priority. Web Application error handling easily provides a solution.

Web Applications can manage two distinct types of errors that might occur. The first type of error is a `Throwable` object thrown from a Servlet or JSP. Using the `web.xml` error-page, exception-type, and location elements, any type of thrown object can be caught and passed to an error. The second type of error is when a Servlet or JSP sends an HTTP response error code back with a response. Instead of showing the undesired content of the original page, the contents of an error page can be displayed by specifying the `error-page`, `error-code`, and `location` elements in `web.xml`.

When handling exceptions with JSP and Servlets, there is no great way of keeping track of information that pertains to the problem. The `ServletContext` `log()` methods are usually inadequate, and often a robust logging API is preferred as a solution. The second half of this chapter introduced using the `java.util.logging` package as a good solution for logging Web Application information. The `java.util.logging` package is a highly flexible and efficient solution for keeping track of all sorts of information during runtime. The SiteLogger Servlet (Listing 4-24) was introduced to help illustrate this point.

Exception handling and logging are critical parts of Servlets and JSP development. Problematic code is always a nuisance when programming so it helps to properly plan for the worst. This chapter rounded out a basic JSP and Servlet skill-set with good methods of keeping track of possibly problematic code. With these skills it is now safe to start introducing some of the more complex features and uses of the J2EE Web Tier. The next chapter introduces JavaBeans, how they interact with Servlets and JSP, and explains why they are commonly used in Web Applications.

Chapter 5

JavaBeans and the JSP Expression Language

In this chapter, we are going to take a look at JavaBeans and the JSP expression language (EL). The first half of the chapter is devoted solely to JavaBeans. JavaBeans have been around for a long time, and the term means many different things to Java developers. It is well worth understanding JavaBeans so that you can use them if desired, but most importantly understand what other developers mean when the topic is discussed. The second half of this chapter explains the JSP expression language (new as of JSP 2.0). The JSP EL provides a simple, elegant solution to embedding expressions in JSP and provides a method to avoid using the traditional JSP expression, `<%= %>`, and some of the JavaBean actions. In some cases the JSP EL is required in order to provide a practical solution to a problem, for instance, expression in JSP authored in XML syntax; in many other cases the JSP EL provides an arguably better solution to what JSP has traditionally offered.

Why introduce JavaBeans and the JSP EL now? There are several reasons, but put simply, JavaBeans are something you should know about, although the functionality is not as helpful as it used to be. However, the JSP EL is arguably a superior method of doing tasks commonly done by traditional JSP expressions or the JSP JavaBean actions. Therefore, it is helpful to introduce the functionality so the rest of the book can encourage its use; finally, when dealing with custom actions, namely Chapter 6 and Chapter 7, the JSP EL is required. In general, this chapter is taking care of some required housekeeping before we delve into the more complex aspects of Servlets and JSP; however, you can certainly expect to find several tips and techniques in this chapter that will apply to Servlet and JSP development on the whole.

This chapter discusses the following topics:

- What a JavaBean is and what constitutes a JavaBean.
- Servlet and JSP support for JavaBeans.
- Good uses of JavaBeans.
- What the JSP Expression Language (JSP EL) is.
- JSP EL syntax.
- JSP EL function: binding static Java methods to the JSP EL.
- Good uses of the JSP EL (relative to JSP Expression Language and JavaBeans).

Compared to the other chapters this one is small, but it is still meant to be read straight through. Discussion of JavaBeans and the JSP EL is kept almost completely separate until the very last section of the chapter.

JavaBeans

The term *JavaBean* commonly appears when using Servlets and JSP. In practice, JavaBean is really just a fancy name for a Java class that follows a few coding conventions. Technically, a JavaBean is any class that implements the `java.io.Serializable` interface and provides a default, no-argument constructor. A JavaBean conventionally also provides a few "getter" and "setter" methods, but technically, these are not necessary for a class to be considered a JavaBean. JavaBeans are never required for use with JSP and Servlets, but they commonly appear because they are helpful for passing scoped information. One of the goals of this chapter is to officially introduce JavaBeans and explain why they are helpful and why they are commonly used with JSP and Servlets.

Get and Set Methods

JavaBeans are usually very simple to create and use. Like anything, a JavaBean can be made complex, but the most common use of a JavaBean is as an object that stores data on the server-side. As a data-storage object, a JavaBean is just a simple class that typically has private data, called properties. These properties are typically made available through public accessors and mutators (i.e., getters and setters). The convention is to take the member name of the property and create two methods by adding "get" and "set" to the property's name with the first letter always capitalized. If, for example, a JavaBean had a variable named `value`, the appropriate get and set methods would be `getValue()` and `setValue()`. Listing

5-1 is an example of how a Java class might properly implement these methods to be considered a JavaBean.

Listing 5-1   ExampleBean.java

```
public class ExampleBean implements java.io.Serializable
{
String value;

    public ExampleBean() {
    }
    public String getValue(){
        return value;
    }
    public void setValue(String value){
        this.value = value;
    }
}
```

Note that the get and set methods in Listing 5-1 are not mandated by an interface. Get and set methods are completely dependent on the name of the variable they reference. An interface could not be used to adequately describe this, nor could an interface correctly guess the return value or parameters required for the methods. In the specific case of Listing 5-1 the property type was a `String`, and it returned a `String` object from `getValue()` and required a `string` parameter for `setValue()`. These requirements were completely arbitrary and can change depending on the particular JavaBean. The only important convention to keep consistent is the "get" and "set" added before the variable's name. In cases where there are many different variables, use many different get and set methods.

Why Get and Set Methods?

So why are get and set methods required by a JavaBean? In a word, encapsulation. From `ExampleBean.java` it might appear using a get and set method is a more tedious way of declaring a variable public. However, get and set methods do have some very helpful and practical uses. The variable being used by the get and set methods does not have to be known outside the class. Any bit of code can be included with the get and set methods. The value returned by the method does not have to be an actual variable located in the class. Instead, it might be derived from other variables or even created on the fly from something completely unrelated to the JavaBean. This level of abstraction is the most helpful feature of get and set methods.

Another helpful feature of JavaBeans is that other software can be built to take advantage of them. The use of methods to abstract member access is nothing new in the world of programming, but it can be done in many different ways. Get and set methods are a de facto method of supplying the functionality. This is very apparent in Servlets and JSP, as JSP provides a set of standard actions designed to manipulate JavaBeans. These standard actions can be very helpful and are com-

JavaBeans in More Detail

JavaBeans are defined in the JavaBeans specification that you can download from Sun's Java Web site (`http://java.sun.com/products/javabeans/`). The specification here talks about the full scope and use of JavaBeans. JavaBeans were originally designed for use in UI development and as such come with a great deal of support for Swing UI design tools. This support includes property listeners and event handling, none of which is needed for JSP and Servlet development.

The JavaBeans specification also appeared after Java itself was released. This meant that originally there were many classes in the JDK that wanted to be considered as JavaBeans but did not follow the naming conventions mentioned previously. To allow these classes to be "brought into the fold", the JavaBeans specification defines a set of helper classes in the java.beans package that allow a bean developer to define the properties the class wanted exposed as bean properties. These are classes such as `java.beans.BeanInfo`, and `java.beans.PropertyDescriptor`. Again, these classes will not be discussed further in this book as most, if not all, beans do not follow the get and set naming conventions.

The `java.beans` package also defines an "introspector" class (`java.beans.Introspector`). This class is used to discover the names of the accessors and mutators associated with a given bean property. The introspector will use Java reflection and the helper classes mentioned previously to discover the correct method names to be used. This is mentioned because when a JSP uses the tags we are about to discuss to manage JavaBeans, the generated Servlet will use this introspector class to ensure the bean access is done correctly. You will see code that uses this class when debugging JSP, so we do not want you to be surprised.

monly used in popular design patterns such as MVC. Chapter 11 of this book covers MVC along with how JavaBeans are used as part of that design idiom. Right now it is only important to have a good understanding of what JavaBeans are in relation to JSP and Servlets.

Servlets, JSP, and JavaBeans

JavaBeans would not have been mentioned if they were not commonly used with JSP and Servlets. There is no requirement mandating JavaBeans be used with JSP and Servlets, but the JSP standard actions and the JSP EL are a convenient way of using the beans for all levels of JSP developers. This is the primary reason JavaBeans are used as commonly as they are. Before looking at why this is the case, we need to see what exactly JSP provides as JavaBean standard actions.

The JSP standard actions, excluding the ones that relate to JavaBeans, were covered with JSP in Chapter 3. The JavaBean custom actions follow the same XML-compatible syntax and are also available for use with any JSP-compliant container. The actions are as described in the following sections.

<jsp:useBean/>

The `useBean` action declares a JavaBean for use in a JSP. Once declared, the bean becomes a scripting variable that can be accessed by both scripting elements and other custom tags used in the JSP. The full syntax for the `useBean` tag is as follows:

```
<jsp:useBean id="bean's name" scope="bean's scope" typeSpec/>
```

The `useBean` action must always have two things specified: the bean's name and information about what class should be used. Optionally, the `useBean` action may also specify a particular scope for the declared JavaBean. The value of the `id` attribute may be any value as a long as it is a unique name among other `useBean` declarations in the same JSP. If the name is not unique, an exception is thrown by the JSP container at translation time of the JSP.

Valid values for the scope attribute are as follow:

- **page:** The `page` value places the JavaBean as an attribute to the `javax.servlet.jsp.PageContext` for the current page. The bean is discarded upon completion of the current request.

- **request:** The `request` value places the JavaBean in request scope. The JavaBean is available from the current page's `ServletRequest` object via the `getAttribute()` method. The JavaBean is discarded upon completion of the current request.

- **session:** The `session` value places the JavaBean in session scope. The JavaBean can be accessed via the `getAttribute()` method of the `HttpSession` object associated with a client. The JavaBean automatically persists until the session is invalidated. A translation time error is raised if the `session` value is used on a JSP that has declared it is not participating in a session.

- **application:** The application value places the JavaBean in application scope. The JavaBean persists as long as the application does and can be accessed via the `getAttribute()` method of the Web Application's `ServletContext` object.

Along with the `id` attribute and `scope` attribute, the `useBean` action needs to know what Java class should be initialized as the JavaBean. In most cases this is done by simply using the `class` or `type` attribute and specifying as a value the fully qualified Java class name. However, the `useBean` action also allows for any of the following combinations to be used when declaring what type of JavaBean is to be initialized.

```
class= className
type= typeName   class= className
type= typeName   beanName= beanName
type= typeName
```

The attributes have the following meanings:

- **class:** The `class` attribute must declare the fully qualified name of the class that defines the JavaBean. The class name is case sensitive. If the `class` and `beanName` attributes are not specified, an instance of the JavaBean must be present in the given scope.

- **beanName:** The `beanName` attribute defines the name of a JavaBean, as expected by the `instantiate()` method of the `java.beans.Beans` class. The `beanName` attribute can be a runtime value specified by an expression.

- **type:** The `type` attribute, if specified, defines the type of the scripting variable defined. This allows the type of the scripting variable to be distinct from, but related to, the type of the implementation class specified. The type is required to be either the class itself, a superclass of the class, or an interface implemented by the class specified. The object referenced is required to be of this type; otherwise, a `java.lang.ClassCastException` shall occur at request time. If the `type` attribute is unspecified, the value is the same as the value of the class attribute.

Using <jsp:useBean/>

In the simplest of cases, a `useBean` action is equivalent to a scriptlet that declares a new instance of a variable as shown in Listing 5-2.

Consider the following use of the `useBean` action:

Listing 5-2   useBean Action

```
<html>
  <head>
    <title>useBean Example</title>
  </head>
  <body>
<jsp:useBean id="date" class="java.util.Date" />
The date/time is <%= date %>
  </body>
</html>
```

Listing 5-3 could have easily been authored as the following code. The only difference between the two is that the preceding code does not require the use of a scriptlet.

Listing 5-3   useBean Action When Declaring and Using Variables

```
<html>
  <head>
    <title>useBean Example</title>
  </head>
  <body>
<% java.util.Date date = new java.util.Date(); %>
```

```
The date/time is <%= date %>
  </body>
</html>
```

This translation should help clarify what the `useBean` action is doing when declaring and using variables in the page scope of a JSP. By using the `useBean` action, no scriptlets are required on the JSP. The functionality is the same as if a scriptlet was used, but it is important to see that by using the `useBean` action, some scriptlets can be eliminated from the JSP. This concept is more important in the upcoming section where the `getProperty` and `setProperty` actions are introduced. With these actions it is possible to fully remove the need for scripting elements.

The `useBean` action actually does more than simply create a bean, which is what the previous code showed. The `useBean` action first checks if the bean already exists in this scope and if so reuses the existing bean. Scope checking makes the `useBean` action a convenient method of passing beans via request, session, or application scope and accessing them in a JSP. This is important functionality to be aware of, and it is what makes the `useBean` action a helpful standard action.

By applying the scope check to Listing 5-3, the scriptlet would really resemble something similar to Listing 5-4. In page scope it is redundant, but in request, session, and application scopes, the check is helpful.

Listing 5-4   useBeanScriptletCheck.jsp

```
<html>
  <head>
    <title>useBean Example</title>
  </head>
  <body>
<%
  Object temp = pageContext.findAttribute("date");
  java.util.Date tdate = null;
  if (temp != null && temp instanceof java.util.Date) {
     tdate = (java.util.Date) temp;
  }
  else {
     tdate = new java.util.Date();
  }
%>
```

```
The date/time is <%= tdate %>
  </body>
</html>
```

It is important to note that the JavaBean is created only if the class attribute is used. If the type attribute alone is used, the JavaBean must already exist in the specified scope. Why is this considered necessary? In the design chapter, Chapter 11, the MVC pattern will be introduced. Using this design model a JSP and Servlet typically communicate by passing data in JavaBeans. A Servlet will typically create a JavaBean, store the bean in a particular scope, and then forward to the JSP. The JSP should only be called from the Servlet and should never have to create the JavaBean itself. To facilitate this, the type property should be used rather than class.

<jsp:getProperty/> and <jsp:setProperty/>

Complementing the useBean action are the getProperty and setProperty actions. The getProperty action provides a convenient way of invoking a get method, and the setProperty action provides a convenient way of invoking a set method. With all three of the bean-manipulating actions, it is now possible to remove the majority of scripting elements.

<jsp:getProperty/>

The getProperty action provides a way of removing many scriptlets and expressions. The action can be used to invoke a get method of a JavaBean and uses the following syntax.

```
<jsp:getProperty name="name" property="method" />
```

The name attribute references the name of a JavaBean previously introduced to the JSP by the useBean action. The property attribute is the name of the get method that should be invoked. The results of the get method are placed in the implicit out object after being converted to a string either by calling the toString() method or straight conversion in the case of primitives.

JavaBeans used by the getProperty action are found by invoking the PageContext findAttribute() method. A JavaBean previously set in a scope, such as request, session, or application, is not found unless useBean action has been used to make the bean visible to the JSP.

Consider the Java Bean in Listing 5-5. It is used as a simple data storage bean designed to hold information about a user.

Listing 5-5 User.java

```
package com.jspbook;

public class User {
  protected String name = null;
  protected String password = null;

  public String getName() {
    return name;
  }
  public void setName(String name) {
    this.name = name;
  }

  public String getPassword() {
    return password;
  }
  public void setPassword(String password) {
    this.password = password;
  }
}
```

Save the preceding code as User.java in the /WEB-INF/classes/com/jsp book directory of the jspbook Web Application. The JavaBean is nothing special. It has a get and set method for the name and password variables. Combining the useBean and getProperty actions, the User bean is used on the following JSP. Save Listing 5-6 as getProperty.jsp in the root directory of the jspbook Web Application.

Listing 5-6 getProperty.jsp

```
<html>
  <head>
    <title>useBean Example</title>
  </head>
  <body>
  <jsp:useBean id="user" class="com.jspbook.User" />
  <%
```

```
user.setName("Bob");
user.setPassword("password");
%>
Hello <jsp:getProperty name="user" property="name"/>, welcome to
this web page!
</body>
</html>
```

Notice the name attribute of the `getProperty` action matches up with the `id` of the `useBean` action and the `property` attribute is `name`, not `getName()`. The results of the `getProperty` action can be seen by then browsing to `http://127.0.0.1/jspbook/getProperty.jsp`. Figure 5-1 shows a browser rendering of the output.

<jsp:setProperty/>

The `setProperty` action is used to set values of a bean. The `setProperty` action uses similar attributes as the `getProperty` action but with the addition of a few new attributes. The syntax for the `setProperty` action is as follows.

```
<jsp:setProperty name="name" property="method" valueAttribute />
```

The `name` and `property` attributes are required and provide the name of the JavaBean and set method to be invoked on the bean. In addition to the `name` and `property` attributes, a value needs to be provided for a set method of the property's value. The value can be specified in one of two ways:

```
value="value"
```

Figure 5-1 Browser Rendering of getProperty.jsp

The `value` attribute is used to set a given value as the parameter for the set method. The value of the `value` attribute may be a runtime value specified by a expression.

`param="value"`

A value can be retrieved from a request parameter. If the `param` attribute is used, the value of this attribute is used as the name of a request parameter. The value of the request parameter is used as the value for the bean's set method.

In the case where there are multiple parameters needing to be set as values of a JavaBean, the convenient * value may be specified. When * is used as the value of the `param` attribute, a one-to-one mapping is attempted between each request parameter to a set method of the same name.

Either one of the above methods may be used to provide a value for a set method. If both methods are used, a translation time error is raised.

With the `useBean`, `getProperty`, and `setProperty` actions, many scriptlets and expressions can be eliminated from a JSP. The only functionality the three actions cannot accomplish is iteration, or conditional evaluation, but in Chapter 6, the JSTL fills this deficiency. Listing 5-7 can be rewritten using the `set Property` action as follows.

Listing 5-7   setProperty.jsp

```
<html>
  <head>
    <title>useBean Example</title>
  </head>
  <body>
  <jsp:useBean id="user" class="com.jspbook.User" />
  <jsp:setProperty name="user" property="name" value="Bob"/>
  <jsp:setProperty name="user" property="password"
value="password"/>
  Hello <jsp:getProperty name="user" property="name"/>, welcome to
this web page!
  </body>
</html>
```

The use of the `setProperty` action is straightforward. The scriptlet previously used in Listing 5-5 is replaced with two `setProperty` actions. In both uses of the `setProperty` action, the `value` attribute is used to specify a set, a `String` value. The JSP produces the same output shown in Figure 5-1 previously.

Bean Initialization

Typically, a JSP will not create JavaBeans. Many applications will be written using an MVC, or Model II, approach, in which case a Servlet will create the JavaBeans and JSP will reference them. However, for applications that use only a few JSP, beans are still useful. In these cases, in addition to creating beans, a JSP may need to initialize those beans.

Beans are Java objects with default constructors, which means that typically a bean will be created in a vanilla state. The bean may need to be initialized before use by calling the necessary set methods. To ensure a bean is properly initialized before use in a JSP, the JSP uses the `jsp:useBean` tag's body. Any code in the body of the tag is only executed when the bean is first created. So, for example, if a request comes into a JSP and that JSP has a `useBean` tag with request scope, that JSP will create the bean. If the `useBean` has a "body", that body will "execute". If the JSP then forwards to another JSP, and that JSP has a `useBean` tag for the same bean also with request scope, that bean will not be created. Just a reference will be retrieved from the request object. Even if that second `useBean` tag has a body, the body will not be executed. The body of the `useBean` tag is (morally) its constructor. An example is shown here

```
<jsp:useBean id="user" class="com.jspbook.User">
  <jsp:setProperty name="user" property="name" value="Bob"/>
  <jsp:setProperty name="user"
                   property="password"
                   value="password"/>
</jsp:useBean>
```

In this example, the `user` bean is in page scope. This means that whenever the page is executed, the bean will be created (remember that page scope means private to this page). Whenever a bean is created, its body is executed; that means the two `setProperty` calls will run and initialize the bean.

Good Use of JavaBeans

JavaBeans are not something meant to blow a developer away. The functionality provided by a JavaBean can be helpful but is not grandiose. What JavaBeans and the associated custom actions provide a developer with are two things: a simple, clean syntax and elimination of scripting elements. The simple, clean syntax is helpful because of its inherent properties. Keeping a JSP legible is a key factor to making it easy to maintain. The simple syntax is also helpful when cooperating with a mixed group of developers because it is easy to teach any level of programmer the `useBean`, `getProperty`, and `setProperty` actions. The equivalent scripting elements are also easy to use, but a few simple tags are always much more familiar to an HTML savvy developer. JavaBeans are also helpful because they help remove the need for scripting elements. By enforcing the use of the useBean, getProperty, and setProperty actions, a code stays clean and is done in a more object-orientated approach. There is never a need to embed lengthy bits of code in a scripting element. The better approach is to encapsulate the code in a Java object such as a bean.

Design Patterns and JavaBeans

The concept of what the useBean, getProperty, and setProperty actions are doing is helpful to understand. If an alternative to the standard actions is being used, it is usually a custom action mimicking the functionality of the standard actions but with a special enhancement for a particular framework or project.

The important thing to remember is the elimination of scripting element logic in a JSP. Logic encapsulated by scripting elements is almost always best placed elsewhere, usually in a Java class. JSP is powerful because it is as simple as authoring a static HTML or XML document. JSP can provide all of the functionality other dynamic server-side technologies can, but JSP is also easy to use for any, non-Java included, server-side developer. Building around this strong point is one of the best design patterns you can use, and it is one that JavaBeans happen to fit in nicely.

One thing to take into account when writing JavaBeans for use in JSP is that JavaBeans should be "environment agnostic". Good design will often separate the application into layers such as the business logic layer and the user interface layer. JavaBeans will be used for two things: executing business logic and/or carrying data between these layers. Beans that carry data are used to communicate between the business logic and the user interface layer. These beans typically have simple properties that are set in the business logic layer and accessed in the UI layer. Beans also execute business logic. The business logic is often independent of the environment in which it is executed—that is, the same business logic could be executed in a Servlet, JSP, or any other Java class.

To ensure that all beans are maximally reusable, a bean's functionality should not rely on data types from a particular environment. What this means in practice is that, for example, if a Servlet uses a bean, that bean should never be passed Servlet types, such as HttpServletRequest or HttpServletResponse references, as these objects are not available in other non-Servlet environments.

JSP. 2.0 Expression Language

One of the main features of JSP 2.0 is a JSP-specific expression language, commonly called the JSP EL. The JSP EL is superior to the JSP expressions described in Chapter 3 because it provides a cleaner syntax and a language designed specially for JSP. Additionally, the JSP EL works well with JSP in XML syntax. As is soon explained, the JSP EL does not require the use of characters that are part of XML markup—this means JSP EL can inherently work with JSP in XML syntax; regular JSP expressions do not.

The benefits of the JSP EL are easy to illustrate. A JSP author can use an expression, such as `<%= ... %>`, to access a runtime value. The syntax works, but it is awkward when embedded as a tag's attribute value, and the expression directly embeds Java syntax. For example, a custom tag with a dynamic attribute value previously had to be authored as the following:

```
<ex:tag attribute="<%= pageContext.getAttribute("value") %>">
```

The syntax is awkward because it complicates the simple custom tag syntax with markup inside a tag. Additionally, the expression must use complete Java syntax which further damages the simplicity of the markup. If the preceding was authored using the JSP EL, it would look like this:

```
<ex:tag attribute="${value}">
```

The functionality is the same, but the code is much simpler. Another feature of the JSP EL is that it can be used anywhere in a JSP, not just in a custom tag attribute. This makes the JSP EL a simple, powerful alternative to scripting elements.

Disabling the EL

Before JSP 2.0 the expression syntax, `${...}`, used by the JSP EL was not reserved. Because of this the EL might cause backwards compatibility issues with JSP 1.2 and earlier code. To prevent the new EL from causing troubles with old code, by default the JSP EL is disabled for Web Applications that use a `web.xml` file as defined by Servlets 2.3 or the following. For applications that use the Servlet 2.4 defined `web.xml`, the JSP EL is automatically enabled. Any individual JSP may enable or disable the JSP EL through use of the `isScripting Enabled` page directive as described in Chapter 2. The JSP EL may also be configured application-wide using the `scripting-enabled` element of the `web.xml` JSP configuration.

JSP EL Syntax

The JSP Expression Language is designed to be simple, robust, and minimally impact backwards compatibility issues. The expression language handles both expressions and literals. Expressions are always enclosed by the `${ }` characters. For example:

```
<c:if test="${value < 10}" />
```

Values that do not begin with `${` are still treated as a literal. The value of the literal is parsed to the expected type depending on the tag's TLD (Tag Library Descriptor) entry:

```
<c:if test="true" />
```

In cases where a literal value contains the `${` characters, it must be escaped with the `$\{` characters.

Attributes

Attributes in the EL are accessed by name, with an optional scope. Members, getter methods, and array items are all treated in the same fashion and replaced with a " . ". Properties accessed using this method may be nested arbitrarily deep. For example, an object `a` with a member `b` would be accessed as `${a.b}`. Likewise an array `a` could have the `b` member accessed with the same expression—in other words, `a[b]` could be written as `${a.b}` using the EL. Additionally, a JavaBean `a` with a getter method for `b` would use the same expression—in other words, `a.getB()` could also be written as `${a.b}`. Note that the two syntaxes are interchangeable, that is, `${a.b}` is the equivalent of `${a["b"]}`.

Objects do not have to be in page scope for the EL to use them. The EL evaluates an identifier by looking up its value as an attribute according to the behavior of `PageContext findAttribute()` method. For example, `${value}` will look for the attribute named `value` by searching the `page`, `request`, `session`, and `application` scopes in that order. If the attribute is not found, `null` is returned.

The EL defines a set of implicit objects with `pageContext`, `page`, `request`, `session`, and `application` matching the JSP equivalents. The EL additionally defines the following implicit objects:

- **Implicit Scoped-Attribute Objects:** The EL defines the implicit `pageScope`, `requestScope`, `sessionScope`, and `applicationScope` objects that each represent a `map` of the objects set in the respective scope.

- **param:** The `param` implicit object is a `Map` that maps parameter names to a single `String` parameter value. The value is obtained by calling the `ServletRequest getParameter()` method for individual names. In practice the `param` implicit object provides a convenient way of accessing request values.

- **paramValues:** The `paramValues` implicit object is a `Map` that maps parameter names to an array of `String` objects. Objects in the array are the values for that parameter name. The `paramValues` implicit object does not represent an array of all the request parameters, only all parameters with the same name. The `paramValues` implicit object returns values by invoking the `ServletRequest` `getParameterValues()` method.

- **header:** The `header` implicit object is a `Map` that maps all of the header values, which are available via `ServletRequest` `getHeaders()`.

- **headerValues:** The `headerValues` implicit object is a `Map` that maps all of the head values, which are available via `ServletRequest` `getHeaders()`. For completeness the `headerValues` object should be used when reading header values from a request, but in practice usually only one value is sent per header name, and using the header object is perfectly fine.

- **cookie:** A `Map` that maps the single cookie objects that are available by invoking `HttpServletRequest getCookies()`. If there are multiple cookies with the same name, only the first one encountered is placed in the `Map`.

When an expression references one of the implicit objects by name, the appropriate object is returned instead of the corresponding attribute. For example, `${request}` returns the `HttpServletRequest` object, even if there is an existing `request` attribute in some scope.

Literals

The JSTL EL defines the following literals:

- **Boolean:** The `true` and `false` boolean values have identical literal values as used in Java.
- **Long:** Long values are preserved as defined by Java.
- **Float:** Floating point values are preserved as defined by Java.

- **String:** String literal values are treated identically as in Java. Double quotes, ", are escaped as \ ", and single quotes, ', are escaped as \ ', and \ is escaped as \ \.
- **Null:** The `null` literal is as defined by Java.

Operators

The EL provides the basic arithmetic operators: +, -, *, and /, along with the modulus operator %. The EL also provides logic operators `and`, `or`, and `not`, which correspond to the Java operators &&, ||, and !, respectively. EL support for comparison operations is identical to Java: ==, !=, <, >, <=, >=. Comparisons may be made against other values or against boolean, string, integer, or floating point literals. The abbreviations `lt`, `gt`, `lte`, or `gte` may also be used as replacements for <, >, <=, and >=, respectively.

The EL operators use the following order of preference from top to bottom, left to right:

- []
- ()
- -
- *, /, div, %, mod
- +, -
- <, >, <=, >=, lt, gt, le, ge
- &&, and
- ||, or

Reserved Words

The EL defined a few reserved words that should not be used within EL expressions: `and`, `eq`, `gt`, `true`, `instanceof`, `or`, `ne`, `le`, `false`, `empty`, `not`, `lt`, `ge`, `null`, `div`, and `mod`. Some of the words currently do not do anything but may be used in future versions of the JSP specification.

EL Functions

A feature of the EL is *function binding*. An EL function borrows the idea of qualified namespaces, as used, to allow EL syntax to be linked to static Java functions. Functions that are available to be used by the EL must be specified by a TLD by using the `function` element. For example:

```
<taglib>
...
  <function>
  <name>foo</name>
  <function-class>com.jspbook.FooFunctions</function-class>
  <function-signature>
    String bar(String)
  </function-signature>
 </function>
</taglib>
```

The preceding code defines a function that named `foo` and maps to the `bar()` static function that must be defined by the `com.jspbook.FooFunctions` class. The signature of the method is additionally defined by the `function-signature` element in the TLD so that the EL can appropriately validate input and return the correct type of object. In general, each function is defined using one `function` element, and a TLD may define as many functions as needed.

EL functions are used by specifying the function name followed by `()`, with parameter values defined as needed. If the preceding function was being used, with the default namespace, it would be: `${bar('a string')}`. The expression would return a `String` object and could be used in either template text or a custom tag's attribute. Should functions from non-default namespaces be necessary, they must be declared explicitly by placing the appropriate namespace before the function call. For example, assuming the bar function was in a tag library declared with the prefix `f`, then it would be explicitly declared using: `${f:bar('a string')}`.

In theory, EL functions can do all sorts of things and JSTL 1.1 introduced a number of them, in particular string manipulation functions. Chapter 6 details the JSTL and associated functionality.

Good Uses of the JSP EL

There are several use cases where you can accomplish the same task using either traditional JSP expressions, the JSP EL, the JavaBean actions, or a combination of the three. In the one obvious case, putting XML-friendly expression in a JSP authored in XML syntax, always use the JSP EL; there is no reason not to. In most of the other cases, also consider using the JSP EL as a preferred choice. Compared to regular JSP expressions, the JSP EL provides a simpler, non-Java method of accomplishing the same job. Additionally, with JSP EL functions you can literally do anything that a regular JSP expression can do.

The most common use case of JSP expressions, JSP EL expressions, and JavaBeans is to access a scoped Java object and display it as a string. In this case the JSP EL does a great job, and for many practical purposes is all you will ever need the JSP EL to do. A simple `${foo}` and a scoped variable, in any scope, will be displayed as a string. The syntax is natural, simple, and most importantly adequate. For these reasons you will notice that almost every single example in the later chapters uses the JSP EL. In general, this book suggests you always prefer the JSP EL over the JavaBean actions and regular JSP expressions for this type of functionality.

Besides the more obvious good uses, the ones that you will find scattered throughout the book, an excellent use of the JSP EL is to not abuse its functionality. The JSP EL is nothing more than an expression language. Yes, the JSP EL can do arithmetic operations, boolean operations, and bind static Java methods; however, do not go out of the way to use this functionality. Keep in mind JSP provides several methods of accomplishing the same goal. If you want to take a stab at what most developers consider "good practice", read through the later chapters of this book. You should note that custom tags and Servlet-related functionality are commonly used to encapsulate a lot of code, and JSP is usually used as a simple presentation layer that only requires the basic `${foo}` use of the JSP EL.

The JSP EL Doesn't Require JavaBeans

A handy technique to speed up Web Application development is to use the JSP EL and `java.util.Properties` objects (or any map object) to replace JavaBeans. A good traditional design practice is to divide up a dynamic page into pure Java code and a simple JSP with as few scripting elements as possible. In order to communicate between the two parts, a JavaBean with the appropriate getter and setter methods would be used. Coding the JavaBean is straightforward; however, it does take a little bit of effort and time—possibly more than a little if you are unfamiliar with Java or don't have a nice build system set up for the Web Application. Take, for example, Listing 5-5 and a JSP logically similar to Listing 5-6, both that were shown previously. Listing 5-6 was an example of the JavaBean actions used to access a scoped JavaBean. We will reuse the JSP but change the code to use the JSP EL and then take the setter methods out of the JSP as shown in Listing 5-8.

Listing 5-8 NoJavaBean.jsp

```
<html>
  <head>
    <title>useBean Example</title>
```

```
  </head>
  <body>
  Hello ${user.name}, welcome to this web page!
  </body>
</html>
```

Note the page is simplified (as a result of good coding practice suggested in the last section), but we accomplished the same as before. A scoped JavaBean is expected to be available so that the appropriate name value is displayed. Assume the JavaBean is Listing 5-5 that you saw previously, a simple Java class with a few getter and setter methods. Finally assume the code that sets the bean's values is executed sometime before the JSP is invoked (it doesn't matter when or how; later chapters show that Filters are usually used for this). Listing 5-9 shows the changes.

Listing 5-9   NoJavaBean.jsp Bean Setting Logic

```
...// start of the class or scriptlet
String name = request.getParameter("name");
String password = request.getParameter("password");
// perform an validation required...
User user = new User();
user.setName(name);
user.setPassword(password);
request.setAttribute("user", user);
... // rest of class or scriptlet
```

The code does nothing surprising; a new instance of the JavaBean is created, populated, and put in request scope. Because the JSP EL expression matches the field "name" to the getName() method of Listing 5-5, the JSP will display the appropriate value.

However, there is no reason a JavaBean needs to be used. We could have just as easily used a java.util.Properties object and completely skipped whatever time and effort are associated with the JavaBean. Listing 5-10 shows what the code might contain.

Listing 5-10   NoJavaBean.jsp Bean Setting Logic, Using a Properties Object

```
...// start of the class or scriptlet
String name = request.getParameter("name");
String password = request.getParameter("password");
// perform an validation required...
Properties user = new Properties();
user.setProperty("name", name);
user.setProperty("password", password);
```

```
request.setAttribute("user", user);
... // rest of class or scriptlet
```

And now Listing 5-5 would not be needed for the JSP, Listing 5-7, to function properly. What we save is the time and effort required to code and deploy the JavaBean. What is lost is control over what happens during the getter and setter methods, which may or may not be an issue, and we also have the possibility of losing a little performance—the JavaBean is likely going to consume less memory than the Properties object.

However you look at it, the JSP EL does eliminate the need for JavaBeans in most practical situations. Not only do the scoped objects work the same, but it also tends to be easier to default to using `java.util.Properties` objects instead of JavaBeans. There is less work required to get the project going and less code to worry about maintaining; however, this is a moot point. Properties objects really only work well as a data storage JavaBean, as illustrated in Listing 5-5, and not much else. If you are doing some clever tricks with getter and setter methods, it is likely you will be stuck coding JavaBeans to complement your Web Application, whether you are using the JSP EL or not.

Summary

JavaBeans are a simple but helpful addition to JSP. As used by JSP, a JavaBean is really nothing more than a fancy name for a way to code a Java class. By following certain design restrictions, it is easy to create a set of JSP actions that can manipulate and use any of those classes. JavaBeans are an example of a set of design restrictions, primarily get and set methods, and the JavaBean standard actions are available for use with JSP.

The JSP EL is another helpful feature of JSP. The JSP EL provides an intuitive, non-Java method of writing expressions that do simple logic and access scoped variables. By itself there is little the JSP EL does, but the JSP EL is commonly used with custom tags and popular design patterns. Throughout the rest of the book the JSP EL will be appearing often; note how the JSP EL is used in examples and think about how it complements the JSP.

The final point presented in this chapter is that there are several good uses for the JSP EL. Simplifying JSP—removing classic JSP expressions and JavaBean actions—is a good example, and using JSP EL expression with JSP in XML syntax is almost required. However, the JSP EL in some respects eliminates the need for coding JavaBeans. Understand the technique, as it can simplify Web Application development.

Chapter 6

JavaServer Pages Standard Tag Library

Custom tag libraries are one of the most helpful tools available to a JSP developer; however, the set of tags defined by the JSP specification, known as "standard actions", does leave something to be desired. The JavaServer Pages Standard Tag Library (JSTL) is a complementary specification to J2EE that defines an extended set of standard JSP tags. The tags are based upon common uses of custom actions and include tags commonly found with popular frameworks and containers.

This chapter discusses the following topics:

- An introduction to the current official JSTL specification.
- Why you should consider using the JSTL.
- How to install the JSTL 1.0 reference implementation API.
- Detailed coverage of the various JSTL tags.
- Discussion on practical uses of the JSTL.

The greater point of this chapter is to introduce JSP custom tags by showing some examples of some arguably good implementations. In addition to learning about some helpful tags, this should help the next chapter's discussion when we discuss how to build your own custom tags.

JSTL 1.0 Specification

The JSTL 1.0 specification is an official Java Specification Request (JSR) done through Sun's Java Community Process (JCP), `http://www.jcp.org`. A copy of the JSTL specifications can be downloaded from the official JSTL Web page, `http://java.sun.com/products/jsp/jstl`. The idea of an extended set of JSP standard actions has been around since the early JSP specifications, but it only officially appeared just before the release of JSP 2.0. The JSTL 1.0 release includes the following tags:

- **Iteration and conditional:** Iteration and conditional logic are commonly needed by a JSP; however, the only standard method of achieving this functionality is by using scripting elements. Sometimes the use of scripting elements is not desired, so custom tags are built as replacements. The JSTL provides a standard set of custom tags for iterating through a collection or providing conditional logic.

- **Expression Language:** One of the much-anticipated features of the JSTL is the new JSP expression language it provides. The JSTL EL is a JSP-focused expression language designed to replace embedding Java code via JSP expression elements. The JSTL provides a few tags for evaluating arbitrary JSTL expressions. The JSTL expression language has been superseded by the expression language in JSP 2.0

- **URL manipulation:** JSP has a very limited support for URL manipulation. Resources outside a JSP application cannot be forwarded to or included using the standard JSP actions, nor does JSP provide a method of ensuring a URL is properly encoded with parameters and session information. The JSTL solves all of these problems with a set of URL manipulating tags.

- **i18n-capable text formatting:** Internationalization support is a difficult task and JSP provides no default support for it. The most common solutions to supporting i18N issues via JSP are standardized by the JSTL in a set of custom tags.

- **XML manipulation:** XML is widely used with Java, so the JSTL provides a set of custom tags designed particularly for manipulating XML.

- **Database access:** Databases are a standard solution to storing the information complex, dynamic Web sites rely on. The JSTL provides a set of SQL tags that allow for SQL queries to be performed on an existing database.

One of the much anticipated features of the JSTL is the new JSP expression language it provides. The JSTL EL is a JSP-focused expression language designed to replace scriptlets. Not all of the tags included in the JSTL are widely regarded as a good idea, but many of the tags are very beneficial to JSP developers. Each of the previous sets of tags are covered individually in this chapter. For each set an introduction to the tags is given along with examples of use and an objective view of how helpful the tags are and for what purposes they should be used.

Why You Should Use the JSTL

The JSTL is fairly new, but the functionality it replaces is not new. Everything the JSTL provides can be done, and usually is done, with existing sets of custom tags matched to a particular framework or JSP container. It is pointless to pretend that the JSTL should always be used versus previous existing solutions, but there are a few good reasons the JSTL should be adopted as the preferred solution. The JSTL is a standard, so it was built collectively by the members of the JSP community and it reflects a good, helpful implementation of many useful functions. Embracing the JSTL saves a developer from having to build equivalent tags or learn the equivalent set of tags being used by a particular project. The JSTL is also implemented under a liberal open source license and is hosted by the Apache Jakarta community[1]. The code can be used with no strings attached, and a strong development community continuously works to improve it.

Another great reason to use the JSTL is if you are either not a Java programmer or if you could care less about using the widely pushed MVC design pattern (explained in Chapter 7) that involves using Servlets, Filters, JavaBeans, and JSP. There are many JSTL tags whose use conflicts with the use JSP is primarily intended for: creating user interfaces. However, these tags are helpful in certain situations. In an attempt to promote good practice[2] within this book, we do not promote the use of some of the JSTL tags; the reasons are given in the respective sections. However, if you are building prototypes or small applications, then all of the JSTL tags can be useful (even the "evil" SQL tag library).

Installing the JSTL

For the examples in this chapter, an implementation of the JSTL needs to be installed. The source code and binary distributions of the JSTL can be found at `http://jakarta.apache.org/builds/jakarta-taglibs/releases/standard/`. Download the binary distribution and unpack the compressed file. With the JSTL 1.0 release are the following files:

---

1. The JSTL reference implementation—that is, container vendors are free to implement the JSTL and optimize it for use with their container.
2. In the authors' joint opinion, of course.

- **README:** The README file contains a brief summary of everything included in the JSTL 1.0 binary release.

- **/lib folder:** The /lib folder contains all of the JAR files required by the JSTL. The JAR files including the JSTL tag handlers also contain the required TLD files. For a simple installation of the JSTL, all of the files in the `/lib` directory can be copied into the `/WEB-INF/lib` directory of the jspbook Web Application. In practice this may not always be the best way to install the JSTL. There are many libraries that may conflict with files in the JDK or other JAR files previously installed in the application, such as the XML libraries, for example.

- **/tld folder:** The TLD folder contains a copy of each of the TLD files required for the individual JSTL sets of tags. Each set of tags includes two TLD files: one with the JSTL expression language enabled and one without.

- **standard-docs.war:** The `standard-docs.war` file is a WAR that contains the basic JSTL documentation. Deploying this WAR provides a convenient method of keeping a local copy of the JSTL documentation.

- **standard-examples.war:** The `standard-examples.war` file is a WAR that contains examples of the JSTL.

For the purposes of this book, the specific JSTL TLDs, `standard-docs.war` and `standard-examples.war` files, are not covered.

To install the JSTL for use with the jspbook Web Application, copy the `standard.jar` and `jstl.jar` files from the `/lib` directory of the JSTL binary release to the `/WEB-INF/lib` directory of the jspbook Web Application. Reload Tomcat and the installation is complete.

JSTL Expression Language

One of the main features of JSTL 1.0 was the addition of a new JSP-specific expression language, commonly called the JSTL EL; however, the JSTL 1.0 was released before the JSP 2.0 specification. JSP 2.0 standardized and extended the JSTL EL as the JSP expression language, as was covered in Chapter 5. The JSP 2.0 EL is a superset of the JSTL EL, and all examples in this book use the JSP 2.0 expression language. In the special case where you are developing with JSP 1.2 and the JSTL, consult the JSTL documentation for available JSTL functionality.

Twin Libraries

There are two libraries of each set of tags in the JSTL. One set of tags provides support for the EL; the other relies on only regular JSP expressions. The non-EL tags exist because the JSTL was standardized before JSP 2.0. There is no reason for this book to spend time discussing the JSTL tag libraries that implement support for the JSTL EL. The only reason the point is brought up is so that no confusion is had at the expense of the two similar libraries.

Core Tags

The core set of JSTL tags includes tags that are helpful in most every JSP project. These tags leverage the EL and seek to consolidate equivalent tags implemented by JSP frameworks, container vendors, and individual authors. Core JSTL tags all share the same URI, `http://java.sun.com/jstl/core`, and can further be segmented based on specific functionality.

General-Purpose Tags

Included with the core JSTL tags are a set of general-purpose tags. These tags along with the EL are used for common simple tasks, but the tasks themselves are not built to accomplish a specific larger goal. The tags consist of the `out`, `set`, `remove`, and `catch` actions.

<c:out>

The `out` tag takes a JSTL expression and evaluates the result, sending output to the page's current `JspWriter` object. The tag is helpful as an alternative to the commonly used `getProperty` action. In cases where a JavaBean is not present, or a developer prefers not to use the bean, the `out` action provides equivalent functionality. However, in JSP 2.0 `out` is largely irrelevant; simply putting the equivalent expression directly on the page has exactly the same effect.

The `out` action has three attributes:

- **value:** The value of the `value` attribute is the expression to evaluate. The results of the expression are sent to a client using the current page's `JspWriter` object. The value of the `value` attribute may be specified at runtime.
- **escapeXml:** The `escapeXml` attribute specifies if the output of the resulting string should be converted to character entity codes. By default the value is `true` and the characters `<`, `>`, `&`, `'`, and `"` result in

<, >, and &, ', and ". The value of the escapeXml attribute may be specified at runtime.

- **default:** The default attribute defines the default value to be used in case the expression fails or results in null.

The out action is very straightforward. Listing 6-1 illustrates the out action being used on a literal.

Listing 6-1   JSTLout.jsp

```
<%@ taglib uri="http://java.sun.com/jstl/core_rt" prefix="c" %>
<html>
<head>
<title>&lt;c:out&gt; Action Example</title>
</head>
<body>
<c:out value="${'<tag> , &'}"/>
</body>
</html>
```

The resulting page is illustrated in Figure 6-1. The literal value is properly escaped so it displays correctly in a browser. Should this not be what is required, the escapeXml attribute could be set to false, such as escapeXml="false".

A good question to ask is why the JSTL out tag is better than simply embedding the expression directly where it is needed. For most practical purposes there is no reason unless you are escaping markup syntax—namely < and > symbols as < and >. Using only an EL expression in Listing 6-1 would have resulted in <tag> literally appearing in the output instead of &lttag> tag, and in the browser rendering, the text would not have appeared.

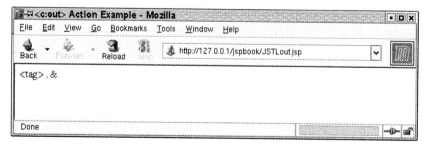

Figure 6-1   Browser Rendering of JSTLout.jsp

\<c:set\>

The `set` action is a JSTL-friendly version of the `setProperty` action. The tag is helpful because it evaluates an expression and uses the results to set a value of a JavaBean or a `java.util.Map` object.

The `set` action has the following attributes:

- **value:** The `value` attribute is the expression to be evaluated. This attribute may be a runtime value.
- **var:** The value of the `var` attribute is the name of an exported variable that is the result of the expression. The type of the variable is whatever the expression evaluates to. This attribute is used when the set action is evaluating a variable to be used by its body content or other components of the JSP.
- **scope:** The `scope` attribute defines the scope of the object named by the `var` attribute. Valid values are `page`, `request`, `session`, and `application`, with page being the default.
- **target:** The `target` attribute is the name of the target object whose property will be set. The object resulting must be either a JavaBean object with an appropriate setter method or a `java.util.Map` object. This attribute may be a runtime value.
- **property:** The `property` attribute is the name of the property to be set of the object specified by the `target` attribute. This attribute may be a runtime value.

There are two primary ways in which the `set` action is intended for use. The first use is to set a property of a JavaBean or `Map` object. In this case the set action uses the `value`, `target` and `property` attributes:

```
<c:set value="expression" target="target object"
  property="name of property" />
```

The second use is to set a scoped variable for use later in the JSP or another resource of the Web Application. In this case the `set` action would use the `value` and `var` attributes, optionally the `scope` attribute.

```
<c:set value="value" var="varName"/>
```

In both cases the `value` attribute can be omitted in favor of using the tag's body content to replace the expression. In general it is not recommended you design using the `set` action. As with the `setProperty` action, the `set` action embeds code in a JSP that is not desirable. The logic is better abstracted completely out of the JSP as done in the Model 2 design pattern, Chapter 11.

<c:remove>

The `remove` action provides a method of removing a scoped variable. This action is not normally particularly helpful, but it can aid in ensuring that a JSP cleans up any scoped resources it is responsible for. Scoped variables left in session or application scope can be a nuisance and should not be used unless needed.

The `remove` action has two attributes:

- **scope:** The `scope` attribute defines the scope to search when removing a variable. If the `scope` attribute is not defined, the variable is removed by calling the `PageContext` `removeAttribute(varName)` method. If the `scope` attribute is defined, the variable is removed by calling the `PageContext` `removeAttribute(varName, scope)` method.

- **var:** The `var` attribute defines the name of the variable to remove.

Use of the `remove` action is straightforward; however, it is not recommended you design using the `remove` action. With a good design and proper use of scoped variables, there should never be a need for a JSP to clean up a scoped resource. This type of logic is not something that is best suited for a JSP, and it should be abstracted completely out of the JSP as done in the Model 2 design pattern, Chapter 11.

<c:catch>

The `catch` action provides a method of error handling for specific parts of a JSP. The feature is helpful as it can prevent a non-critical exception from terminating the execution of a JSP. The `catch` action works by encapsulating its body content in a try-catch statement.

The `catch` action only has one attribute, `var`. The `var` attribute is the name of the variable in which a caught exception is stored. The type of the variable is the same type as the thrown exception. Should the `var` attribute not be specified, then the exception is caught and not saved.

Use of the `catch` action is straightforward. Simply surround problematic code with a `catch` action to prevent the exception from reaching the page's error handling mechanism. As with the `remove` and `set` actions, the `catch` action should not normally be used. The functionality it provides is much better placed outside of a JSP as dictated by the Model 2 design pattern, Chapter 11. Later on in the chapter a further explanation of the merits of avoiding the `remove`, `set`, and `catch` actions is provided with the JSTL SQL and XML tags.

Iteration

The core JSTL iteration tags exist to iterate over collections of objects. The tags exist as a good alternative to embedding a Java `for`, `while`, or `do-while` loop via a scriptlet. There are two core iteration tags: `forEach` and `forTokens`. The `forEach` tag is the more commonly used tag because it iterates over a collection of objects. The `forTokens` tag is used to break a string into tokens and iterate through each of the tokens.

There are good reasons why it would be better to eliminate iterating scriptlets in favor of the JSTL iteration tags. The first and obvious reason is to make it easier to understand what a JSP is doing. Eliminating scriptlets in favor of custom tags increases the amount of markup on a page and reduces the amount of Java code. The end result is a JSP that is easier to read. Consider the JSP in Listing 6-2, which uses an `Iterator` object and a `while` loop.

Listing 6-2   ScriptletIteration.jsp

```
<html>
<head>
<title>Iteration Example</title>
</head>
<body>
<%
  Iterator set = (Iterator)request.getAttribute("set");
  while (set.hasNext()) { %>
  The value is <%= set.next() %>
<% } %>
</body>
</html>
```

The code is purposely made about as simple as it can get; however, it is still difficult to see what is going on, especially if you are unfamiliar with Java as you would expect of many page-development authors. This is almost always the case, because code appearing in a scripting element is not markup. It is Java. Mixing Java with markup makes it difficult to read either. By using a set of JSP custom tags to replace iteration scriptlets, it is easier to read the page as a whole. Listing 6-3 illustrates what the equivalent page would look like using the JSTL `forEach` tag.

Listing 6-3 JSTLIteration.jsp

```
<%@ taglib uri="http://java.sun.com/jstl/core_rt" prefix="c" %>
<html>
<head>
<title>Iteration Example</title>
</head>
<body>
<c:forEach var="item" begin="0" items="${set}">
 The value is <c:out value="${item}"/>
</c:forEach>
</body>
</html>
```

The difference is minor, but it does result in a cleaner page. The markup of a custom tag matches the markup of the surrounding text. The result is that a JSP developer seeing this page for the first time should easily be able to figure out what is going on. The same logic holds true for more realistic and complex examples where there is much more markup and complex code being used in the iteration. In the case of scriptlets the more complex the JSP gets, the harder it is to understand what is going on and the harder it becomes to maintain code.

Another much more important benefit to using the JSTL iteration tags is to enforce clean development of JSP. Certain design patterns, such as Model 2, are built around removing unneeded code from a JSP, usually all the scripting elements. The reason is not to prevent a JSP developer from using iteration, but to prevent a JSP developer from having the freedom to embed arbitrary Java code in scriptlets. Allowing for any type of code can be detrimental to the design of a Web Application. By completely disabling scripting elements and only allowing JSTL iteration tags, it can be ensured a JSP does not have bad code embedded via scripting elements.

<forEach>

The forEach tag provides for iteration over a collection of objects. Currently, the forEach tag supports iteration over an array, java.util.Collection, java. util.Iterator, java.util.Enumeration, or a java.util.Map. In all cases the forEach tag iterates over each primitive, or object, in the collection and exposes it for use by the tag's body.

The forEach tag allows for the following attributes:

- **var:** The `var` attribute defines the name of the current object, or primitive, exposed to the body of the tag during iteration. Its type depends on the underlying collection. The `var` attribute must be a static String value.

- **items:** The `items` attribute defines the collection of items to iterate over. The value may be specified at runtime.

- **varStatus:** The `varStatus` attribute defines the name of the exported scoped variable that provides the status of the iteration. The object exported is of type `javax.servlet.jsp.jstl.LoopTag Status`. The attribute's value must be a static String value and it has nested scope.

- **begin:** The `begin` attribute is an `int` value that sets where the iteration should begin. If no value is specified, the iteration index begins at 0, or the first item of the collection. The value of the `begin` attribute may be a runtime value.

- **end:** The `end` attribute is an `int` value that determines inclusively where the iteration is to stop. If no value is specified, the iteration stops after going through the entire collection. The value of the `end` attribute may be a runtime value.

- **step:** The `step` attribute is an `int` value that determines the "step" to use when iterating. Only step items are iterated through—that is, if `step` is 2, then every other item is skipped during the iteration. The `step` value may be a runtime value.

The typical use of the `forEach` tag is to iterate through a collection passed via the request object. Listing 6-4 illustrates the tag used in a JSP. For more complex uses the iteration may begin, end, or selectively iterate over particular objects. Listing 6-4 illustrates an iteration starting at the second item of the collection and only using the first out of every three items in the collection.

Listing 6-4   JSTLIterationComplex.jsp

```
<%@ taglib uri="http://java.sun.com/jstl/core_rt" prefix="c" %>
<html>
<head>
<title>Iteration Example</title>
</head>
<body>
```

```
<c:forEach var="item" begin="0" items="${set}"
          begin="2" step="3">
 The value is <%= item %>
</c:forEach>
</body>
</html>
```

While the iteration tag is helpful in many cases, there is one well-known case that can be problematic. The common task of iterating over a JDBC ResultSet, showing a select number of results at a time, can cause trouble because of caching. Notably many iterations are generated by doing a query on a database, as covered in Chapter 14. When only showing a few select entries from a result, such as items 1 through 20 or 21 through 40, and so on, it is very reasonable to cache the complete query and only show chunks of it as requested. Compared to doing the query each time, this can save a lot of time, memory, and processing power. The problem arises because there are many logical places for caching the information. One would be the JSTL forEach tag, and another would be the database connection that is generating the results. Caching information in more than one place is not desirable, especially if it is a very large result set.

Avoiding the problem is simple. Choose where to cache information and then make sure it is only cached there. Be wary of JSTL forEach tag implementations that attempt to auto-cache for you[3]. Also be wary of any other code which "simplifies" this sort of task for you. While making it easier to develop, you are trading the amount of control you have over optimizations such as caches.

<forTokens>

The forTokens tag parses a String into tokens based on a given delimiter. All of the tokens are then iterated over, the same as the forEach tag. All of the attributes of the forEach tag are shared by the forTokens tag. One new attribute is additionally allowed: delims. The delims attribute defines the value used to delimit tokens in the source String. Any String value may be used as a delimiter. The delims attribute value may also be a runtime value.

Additionally the items attribute takes on a new meaning with the forTokens tag. Instead of defining a collection to iterate through, the items attribute is the String to parse.

---

3. The JSTL reference implementation "featured" auto-caching with the forEach tag. This caused problems, especially when used with the JSTL SQL tags and a JDBC driver that also auto-caches results. Large results would take up twice as much memory.

In use the `forTokens` tag is identical to the `forEach` tag but with the `delims` attribute specifying a token delimiter. Listing 6-5 provides an example of the `forTokens` tag iterating through a literal String value.

Listing 6-5 JSTLforTokens.jsp

```
<%@ taglib uri="http://java.sun.com/jstl/core_rt" prefix="c" %>
<html>
<head>
<title>Iteration Example</title>
</head>
<body>
<c:forTokens var="item" delims="~" items="token1~token2~token3">
 The value is <c:out value="${item}" />
</c:forTokens>
</body>
</html>
```

Conditionals

JSTL core conditional tags support simple statements such as a Java `if` and `switch`. The tags are a replacement for scriptlets commonly needed to accomplish the same functionality. Like the iteration tags, by using the conditional tags a cleaner markup-orientated syntax can be maintained in favor of scripting elements. There are two main groups of conditional tags: `if` and `choose`. The `if` tag mimics a simple Java `if` statement, while the `choose` tag mimics a Java `switch` or `if/else` statement.

<c:if>

The `if` tag allows the conditional execution of its body depending on the value of a test attribute. Should the test result in true, the contents of the tag's body are evaluated. Should the test result in false, the contents of the tag's body are skipped.

The `if` action has the following attributes:

- **test:** The `test` attribute is the condition for `if` the body content should be shown or not. A literal `true` or `false` value may be used, but an expression is most helpful.
- **var:** The `var` attribute is an optional attribute that defines the name of a scoped variable. A scoped variable defined by the `var` attribute contains the results of the `test` attribute and can be further used by the JSP.

- **scope:** The `scope` attribute defines the scope of the `var` attribute. Valid values for the `scope` attribute are `page`, `request`, `session`, and `application`.

Sometimes the `if` tag's functionality is best abstracted using a good design pattern, but there are cases where the `if` tag can be very convenient. A good example is reminding a user he or she needs to log in. A site's main page may be freely available to the public, but the rest of the site requires a user to have logged on. To remind a user they need to log on, a simple conditional can be used on the main page. Listing 6-6 illustrates how this could be done, assuming after logging in a session-scoped object, `user`, is set.

Listing 6-6 JSTLif.jsp

```
<%@ taglib uri="http://java.sun.com/jstl/core_rt" prefix="c" %>
<html>
<head>
  <title>&lt;c:if&gt; Action Example</title>
</head>
<body>
<c:if test="${user == null}">
<form>
  Name: <input name="name">
  Pass: <input name="pass">
</form>
</c:if>
<c:if test="${user != null}">
  Welcome ${user.name}
</c:if>

 <!--
   Rest of main page here...
   -->

</body>
</html>
```

The page has two simple checks: one for if the user is logged on and one for if he or she is not. Should the user be logged on, a welcome message is displayed.

```
<c:if test="${user != null}">
  Welcome ${user.name}
</c:if>
```

Should a user not be logged on, a log-on form is displayed.

```
<c:if test="${user == null}">
<form>
  Name: <input name="name">
  Pass: <input name="pass">
</form>
</c:if>
```

In both cases the full contents of the page will be shown. If the contents were restricted, then the `if` action would not be the best of choices. Instead two completely separate JSP should be shown, depending on if the user needs to log in or not.

<choose>, <when>, and <otherwise>

The `choose` tag performs conditional block execution of sub `when` tags. It renders the body of the first `when` tag whose test condition evaluates to true. If none of the test conditions evaluate to true, then the body of an `otherwise` tag is evaluated. If no `otherwise` tag is present, nothing happens.

The `choose` and `otherwise` tags have no attributes. The `when` tag has one attribute, `test`. The `test` attribute is an expression that determines if the condition of a `when` tag is true. If true, the body content of the `when` tag is evaluated.

Use of the `choose` tag is straightforward and the tag is as helpful as the `if` tag. In some situations it makes sense to move the functionality completely out of the JSP, but there are circumstances where the `choose` tag is a convenient solution. For example, you can author the equivalent of Listing 6-6 by using the `choose`, `when`, and `otherwise` tags that are shown in Listing 6-7.

Listing 6-7 JSTLchoose.jsp

```
<%@ taglib uri="http://java.sun.com/jstl/core_rt" prefix="c" %>
<html>
<head>
  <title>&lt;c:choose&gt; Action Example</title>
</head>
<body>
<c:choose>
  <c:when test="${user == null}">
  <form>
  Name: <input name="name">
  Pass: <input name="pass">
  </form>
```

```
      </c:when>
      <c:otherwise>
      Welcome ${user.name}"
      </c:otherwise>
   </c:choose>

   <!--
      Rest of main page here...
   -->

</body>
</html>
```

URL Manipulation

JSP provide weak support for URL manipulation. The JSP `include` action only allows for inclusion of resources in the Web Application. External pages or resources can only be included via a custom solution. JSP also manage state via cookies with a fall-back mechanism of URL rewriting. If a client does not support cookies, URL rewriting must be used, but there is no way to automatically rewrite all URLs. The JSTL provides a solution to both of these problems with a few custom tags.

<c:import> and <c:param>

The `import` tag provides all of the functionality of the `include` action but also allows for inclusion of absolute URLs. For example, using the `import` tag allows for inclusion of content from a different Web site or an FTP server. Content retrieved by the `import` tag can also be made available in a few different ways. By default the included information is directly sent to the page's current `JspWriter` object, but optional attributes may be used to specify a scoped variable or a `Reader` object where the content should be made available.

The `import` tag has the following attributes:

- **url:** The value of the `url` attribute is the URL to import. Valid values include both relative and absolute URLs. The value may be specified by a runtime value.

- **context:** The `context` attribute can be used to provide the name of a context when accessing a relative URL resource that belongs to a foreign context. The value may be specified by a runtime value. A foreign context is another Web Application that is executing on the same Web server. This value should be used if the URL is relative to that named foreign context. Note that this is the equivalent of a request dispatch across Web Application boundaries and may not work on particular containers due to security or other restrictions.

- **var:** The `var` attribute can be used to name a scoped variable to contain the resource's content. The type of the variable is String.
- **scope:** The `scope` attribute defines the scope of a variable named by the `var` attribute. Valid values are `page`, `request`, `session`, and `application`.
- **charEncoding:** The `charEncoding` attribute can be used to specify the character encoding of the content at the input resource. By default it is assumed the standard, `ISO-8859-1`, encoding is used.
- **varReader:** The `varReader` attribute is available to create a `Reader` object for use by content in the import tag's body. The value of the `varReader` attribute is the name of the scoped variable; the type of the variable is `java.io.Reader`.

There are two ways to use the `import` tag. The first is to import local or remote content and send it directly to the client. In this case the `url` attribute is required to specify the URL to include, optionally with the `context` and `charEncoding` attributes.

```
<c:import url="url" />
```

The results of such an include depend on the resource being included. If, for example, the following JSP was used:

```
<%@ taglib uri="http://java.sun.com/jstl/core" prefix="c" %>
<c:import url="http://www.jspbook.com" />
```

The result would be identical to the code generated by browsing to `http://www.jspbook.com`: relative style sheets and images wouldn't work, but the code would be the same.

The second method of using the `import` action is to import the contents of the URL to a scoped variable or to a `Reader` object. In this case the `import` action would be used with the `url` attribute and either the `varReader` or `var` attributes, optionally the `context`, `scope`, and `charEncoding` attributes. For instance, to show the source code of a local or remote Web page, you could combine the `import` and `out` actions as shown in Listing 6-8.

Listing 6-8 JSTLimport.jsp

```
<%@ taglib uri="http://java.sun.com/jstl/core_rt" prefix="c" %>

<html>
<head>
  <title>&lt;c:import&gt; Action Example</title>
</head>
<body>
Here is the source code of the main page:
<pre>
<c:import url="welcome.html" var="value"/>
<c:out value="${value}"/>
</pre>
</body>
</html>
```

The result of Listing 6-8 is a page that shows the code sent back from a response to `http://127.0.0.1/jspbook/welcome.html`. Note the code in the case of HTML; the source code is the same as the result. However, if Listing 6-8 is used to request a JSP, it shows the response, not the source code. Figure 6-2 shows a browser rendering of the results.

<c:param>

The `param` tag complements the `import` tag by allowing proper URL request parameters to be specified with a URL. Commonly, a URL request parameter is

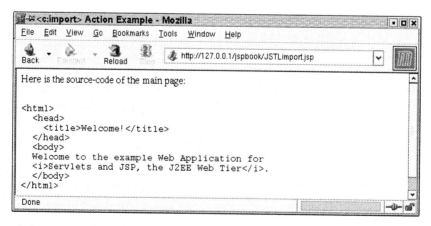

Figure 6-2 Browser Rendering of JSTLimport.jsp

hard coded to the end of a URL—for example, `test.jsp?name=value`. However, this practice does not always work because a URL must be encoded as defined in RFC 2396, `http://www.ietf.org/rfc/rfc2396.txt`. Without proper encoding, the URL parameters may not be correctly sent with a request. To ensure proper encoding, the JSTL provides the `param` tag.

The `param` tag has two attributes:

- **name:** The `name` attribute specifies the name of the URL parameter.
- **value:** The `value` attribute specifies the value of the URL parameter.

The `param` tag is used as a child of the `import` tag to set URL parameters.

<c:url>

The `url` tag is a method the JSTL provides to automatically encode URLs with session information and parameters. As a container is required to try and keep a session associated with a client, cookies[4] are used and work perfectly fine unless a client purposely disables them or does not support them. In the case where a client does not support cookies, session information needs to be directly encoded with a URL. A JSP developer can do this manually by replacing all URLs with a call to the `HttpServletResponse encodeURL()` method. For instance, the following anchor tag:

```
<a href="index.jsp">Book Site</a>
```

would be changed to:

```
<a href='<%= response.encodeURL("index.jsp")%>'>
Book Site</a>
```

The practice works; the JSTL `url` action is just an alternative method of writing the call to the `encodeURL()` method. The only real advantage the `url` tag provides is proper URL encoding, including any parameters specified by children `param` tags.

The `url` tag has the following attributes:

- **value:** The `value` attribute is used to provide the URL to be processed.

---

4. Cookies are formally covered in Chapter 9.

- **context:** The `context` attribute defines the name of the context when specifying a relative URL resource of a foreign context.
- **var:** The `var` attribute can be used to export the rewritten URL to a scoped variable. The value of the `var` variable is the processed URL. The type of the variable is String. The variable's scope depends on the `scope` attribute.
- **scope:** The `scope` attribute determines the scope of the object named by the `var` attribute. Valid values are `page`, `request`, `session`, and `application`.

The `url` tag only changes relative URLs to avoid accidentally exposing session information—that is, `/index.jsp` would be encoded, but `http://www.jspbook.com` would not.

For most practical purposes the `url` tag works but is just plain awkward. It does provide a method of encoding a URL with parameters, but do not think you always need to properly encode URLs. Preserving session information in case a client does not use cookies is helpful, but can be safely ignored unless a Web Application relies on always keeping session state. Should keeping session be mandated, then use the `encodeURL()` method or the `url` tag as needed. Alternatively, another cleaner solution to providing URL encoding support is to abstract the formatting via a multi-client design as covered in Chapter 13.

<redirect>

The `redirect` tag complements the URL manipulating tags by providing a tag that properly encodes a client-side redirection. The functionality of the `redirect` tag is equivalent to calling the `HttpServletResponse sendRedirect()` method. The tag may have child `param` tags used to define parameters.

The `redirect` tag allows the following parameters:

- **url:** The `url` attribute specifies the relative or absolute URL the client should be redirected to.
- **context:** The `context` attribute specifies the name of the context to use when the `url` attribute refers to a foreign context.

Using the `redirect` tag is straightforward; however, you are not encouraged to design around using it. The functionality provided by the `redirect` tag is best abstracted out of a JSP as shown in Chapter 11.

i18n-Capable Text Formatting

The JSTL i18n tags are a collection of text-formatting tags designed for internationalized Web sites. The tags are a good implementation to one of the most commonly used i18n solutions. The JSTL i18n text-formatting tags are covered along with other internationalization issues in Chapter 12.

XML Manipulation

XML today is used for many things. In the past it was mostly used as a data description format, but today, for example, one of the primary uses of XML is as a Web format for Web Services[5]. Because XML is so widely used, there are many situations where XML documents need to be created and manipulated. The JSTL XML tags provide a JSP-centric way of doing this. The XML tags are a well-done set of JSP custom tags that provide a flexible way of manipulating XML. As a good Servlet and JSP developer, you should understand Java and be able to take advantage of the functionality it provides. By implementing a Java-centric design pattern such as Model 2 via a Servlet or Filter, as defined in Chapter 11, it may be unnecessary to use the JSTL XML tags at all.

However, JSP can be used as a way of managing and creating XML for technologies such as Web Services. The JSTL XML tags are a good adjunct to the standard JSTL tags if you are mostly processing XML rather than plain HTML. However, this book assumes that you are writing Web Applications and not Web Services. It also assumes that you have no or limited XML knowledge. To get full value from the JSTL XML tags, you need to understand other XML-related technologies: XPath and XSLT. For these reasons only cursory coverage will be given to the XML tags.

What the XML tags provide are a few XML manipulation functions and the XML equivalent of the JSTL core and conditional tags. The specific tags are further explained:

- **Core XML Tags:** The JSTL XML tags provide equivalents to the core JSTL tags, but with support for both the EL and XPath. XPath allows queries to be done on XML documents to return subsets of the information. XPath is fairly analogous to using an SQL query on a relational database. By using XPath and the JSTL XML tags, it

---

5. Web Services is a technology for describing services and providing information online using XML. Due to the platform-neutral nature of XML, Web Services are growing as a popular solution for this need.

is easy to use an object representation of an XML document in a similar fashion as a JavaBean.

- **Flow Control Tags:** The JSTL XML flow tags consist of an XPath implementation of the `choose`, `when`, `otherwise`, `if`, and `forEach` tags.
- **Transformation Tags:** The JSTL XML transformation tags provide a method of applying XSLT transformations to XML content.

The only new set of functionality is found in the transformation tags. If you are familiar with XSLT, these tags provide an easy way to apply XSLT to XML documents—easy, assuming you are using JSP and the JSTL. The JSTL XML transformation tags do not offer any outstanding benefit besides working with JSP.

SQL Tags

The common use of SQL and Database Management Systems (DBMSs) merited the creation of a set of SQL tags. The JSTL SQL tags provide a simple interface for executing SQL queries on a database via JSP. How helpful these tags are is commonly questioned because they directly violate the idea of only placing presentation logic in a JSP. The functionality the SQL tags provide is best placed elsewhere in a Web Application as dictated by the Model 2 design pattern. Admittedly, the JSTL creators understood this, but the tags were still created as a simple way for a JSP developer, not necessarily a Java developer, to work with a database.

The view of the JSTL SQL tags taken in this book is that they are a poor substitute for understanding Java, JDBC, and a good design pattern. Understand this view is not always true, but it is one that applies to the majority of JSP projects you are likely to work on. As the book progresses, the alternative to using the SQL tags, JDBC, and Model 2 design are covered in full.

Justification for Skipping the SQL Tags

In this book there are many programming practices that are promoted but have a good chance of being misinterpreted. It is clearly stated in countless places, including the introduction and back of the book, that this book takes a Java skill set and applies it to Servlets and JSP to create good Web Applications. By "good", potentially complex is meant. You bought a book because you wanted direction and advice on doing things with Servlets and JSP—not just simple, figure-it-out-in-five-minute things, but also the hardest of tasks. Purposely discouraging use of select JSTL tags might appear to go against this, but it is the goal of this book that justifies skipping these tags.

All of the JSTL tags are designed to be simple to learn. They provide the same functionality an experienced Java developer has available but through a non-programming interface. In other words, Java allows a developer to do anything but requires learning a lot more before being able to start doing a little. The JSTL requires someone to learn very little but be able to do a lot, not as much as pure Java, but enough for building simple Web Applications. The JSTL SQL tags are intended for the cases where understanding or using as little Java as possible is desired. These types of cases do not merit a full book! You can figure this out in a matter of minutes, do an adequate job of building a Web Application, and save yourself $50 and some shelf space. You are encouraged to do this should the situation arise. However, in cases where you need to build something complex and build it right, a solid understanding of Java, Servlets, and JSP are what you need. That is what merits buying this book, and that is what this book is about.

Any Java developer will agree the larger a project gets, the more critical a good design pattern is to ensure the project is successful. Good design patterns do not pop into your head after five minutes of wishing you did not have to learn Java. Good design patterns evolve from the use of a technology and experience of other developers who previously did the same type of project. Should it be obvious or not, this book is preparing you for a sound understanding of good, proved JSP and Servlet design patterns, specifically the Model 2, or MVC design pattern, with an emphasis on how this allows for good internationalization support, multi-client support, and future project maintenance. The JSTL SQL tags do not fit into this overall goal. They promote a limited Model 2-conflicting use of the functionality JSP and Servlets provide and that is why they are skipped. The authors would say to never use these tags, so why are they in the JSTL? There are two arguments given for their inclusion: first, prototyping. If you are proto-typing, you often need a "quick and dirty" solution; the JSTL SQL tags are a quick and dirty SQL solution. Second, if you are writing a small Web Application (maybe a page or two), in which case you may feel that using MVC is overkill. However, you should remember that small applications quickly grow to be large applications, and using these tags may lead to all sorts of maintenance headaches.

On a slight tangent, if you truly desire to be a J2EE expert, it is wise to understand all of the options available to a Java, JSP, and Servlet developer. This allows you to make an informed and appropriate decision on a case-by-case basis when developing Web Applications. Understanding when JSP and Servlets are an overkill is helpful to save time and effort. A good understanding of the full JSTL is helpful in this regard as it nicely complements simple applications. If you are interested in a good, comprehensive discussion of the JSTL, we suggest the following book, *JSTL in Action* (ISBN 1930110529), by Shawn Bayern. He is the JSTL implementation leader, and explains all of the intricate uses of the JSTL.

Summary

The JSTL is a helpful tool for a JSP developer; it provides a standard set of custom tags that extend the standard JSP actions to incorporate the most commonly needed custom tags. Additionally, the JSTL expression language is a powerful new feature available to custom tag authors.

The JSTL is most helpful because it defines a standard set of iteration tags and conditional tags and because it inspired the JSP EL. These features of the JSTL aid a JSP developer in rapidly creating JSP without requiring the use of scripting elements. The expression language is particularly helpful because it is designed specifically for JSP. Compared to embedding Java syntax in a regular expression, the JSP EL is much more convenient.

Not all parts of the JSTL are intended for use by all JSP developers. Tags such as the SQL tags work, but are not suggested for use by readers of this book. A solid understanding of Java provides a finer, more flexible, and native solution to achieving the same functionality.

Chapter 7

Custom Tag Libraries

In Chapter 3, we introduced JavaServer Pages. The introduction focused on the core concepts of JSP and explained how JSP complements Servlets in the J2EE Web tier; however, a very important set of JSP functionality was completely ignored—custom tags. In Chapter 3 the topic of custom tags, also called custom actions, was avoided in favor of establishing the more fundamental concepts of JSP. Custom tag use is not a topic that can be fully covered by a few pages of discussion. A proper explanation of custom tags easily fills a chapter itself, while full coverage of custom tag uses can easily fill a few more.

In this chapter a complete introduction is given for custom tags. The topics of focus are how to build custom tags and why custom tags are helpful. These two subjects are important to understand before we get too far into the possible use cases for the technology. Being able to design and implement your own set of custom tags is an invaluable skill for a JSP developer to have. This skill can be applied to many different situations as was shown in Chapter 6 and will be shown in the later chapters covering security, internationalization, and multi-client design. Compared to a simple scriptlet, building a custom tag requires a notable amount more effort. If you are to be a good JSP developer, a full understanding of JSP custom tags is needed. This chapter is the foundation of such an understanding.

We discuss the following topics in this chapter:

- Why you should use custom tags.
- The basics of tag libraries (all types).
- How custom tags are used currently.
- New JSP 2.0 custom tags versus old custom tags.
- Tag library descriptors; the web.xml for a custom tag library.
- Simple JSP 2.0 custom tags.

- JSP 2.0 `.tag` files; JSP-like authoring of custom tags.
- Classic custom tags, pre-JSP 2.0.
- Mixing new and old custom tags.
- Tag scripting variables; setting and using scoped objects via custom tags.
- Tag library listeners; registering Servlet listeners via tag library descriptors.
- Tag library validation; compile-time checking of custom tag use.

This is one of the longer chapters; however, you are not expected to read the whole thing straight through. Only the first half of the chapter, all the way through the discussion of "simple" tags and `.tag` files, and the last few topics, tag library listeners and tag library validation are required; the complete discussion about classic custom tags is provided only for completeness. If you only care to know what is needed for the later chapters of the book (i.e., what you will likely need when developing new Web Applications), feel free to skip the discussion on pre-JSP 2.0 custom tags, but be aware almost all existing custom tag libraries are implemented via classic custom tags. If you want to be a well-informed JSP developer, you will certainly benefit from reading the whole chapter straight through.

Why Custom Tags?

A few points about custom tags have been touched on, but there are many good reasons as to why custom tags are helpful. Before we get to how one goes about building a custom tag, it is helpful to understand why exactly you would want to build one. In summary, here is a formal list of the primary reasons:

- **Custom tags provide a method to cleanly separate logic from content:** Custom tags and the scripting elements provide the same functionality. A JSP custom tag can do everything that can be done with a scriptlet. The difference is in how the two technologies are authored. Scriptlets directly embed code with chunks of static markup. Custom tags abstract code behind markup that resembles HTML. Scriptlets are not a good method for abstracting logic from formatting. A scriptlet often mixes both data-manipulating code and the code that is responsible for presenting data. This results in the JSP being overly complicated and requiring a competent Java developer to even create it. Custom tags move all of the logic into separate Java classes that are bound to simple tags. The logic can easily be manipulated without touching the JSP, and the simple tags can easily be used for authoring content.

- **Ease of use:** Custom tags are easy to use. Both programmers and non-programmers can intuitively use custom tags. They are an ideal mechanism to enhance the Web tier of an application, especially when collaborating with a mixed group of developers. An HTML-savvy developer with no Java experience can easily pick up and successfully use a custom tag library. For this reason custom tags are a great way to interface complex logic into a simple presentation layer authored in languages such as HTML or XML.
- **Portability:** Custom tags are portable. A complete set of custom tags can be packaged into a single JAR file and deployed across many Web Applications. Compared to scriptlets, this is a huge advantage, both when developing the code and when using existing custom tag libraries.

A good way to think of a custom tag is as a component, written in either Java or JSP, that encapsulates some behavior. To the page author, custom tags look like HTML, or at the very least XML. To a tag developer, a custom tag can either be a Java class or a fragment of a JSP. In all cases the syntax is very familiar and follows with the strong points of the respective language.

Tag Library Basics

A *Tag Library* is a collection of custom tags typically designed to complement each other and accomplish a common goal. The Tags within the library are written either in Java or as JSP fragments and can be used by a JSP as described by a *Tag Library Descriptor (TLD)* file. Most sets of custom tags come packaged as one JAR file which can be easily deployed with any Web Application.

An easy way to think of a custom tag is as an abstracted scriptlet. Similar to a scriptlet, the tag consists of code completely authored by a JSP developer or development tool. However, unlike a scriptlet the code itself is not present directly on the JSP. Instead of directly embedding code within a JSP, the code is abstractly bound to the JSP by means of a TLD. Figure 7-1 illustrates the concept.

Notice in Figure 7-1 that the abstracted code is referred to as either a "tag handler" or a "tag file". Both tag files and tag handler classes can be used to power a custom tag. Tag files are covered later in the chapter but function as easy ways

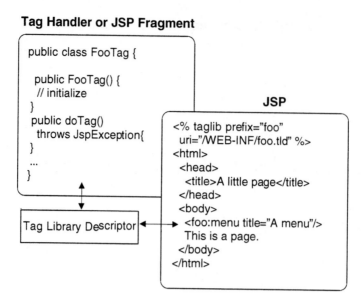

Tag Handler or JSP Fragment

```
public class FooTag {

  public FooTag() {
    // initialize
  }
  public doTag()
    throws JspException{
  }
  ...
}
```

JSP

```
<% taglib prefix="foo"
  uri="/WEB-INF/foo.tld" %>
<html>
  <head>
    <title>A little page</title>
  </head>
  <body>
    <foo:menu title="A menu"/>
    This is a page.
  </body>
</html>
```

Tag Library Descriptor

Figure 7-1 Overview of Custom Tags

to make tag handlers. Tag handlers are the official name for the Java class that encapsulates the code that makes a custom tag work.

Tag handlers, tag library descriptors, and the markup involved in using them are the focus of this chapter. The topics nicely fill a chapter and comprise everything you need to start building JSP custom tags.

How Are Tags Being Used?

Custom tags are commonly used for all the dynamic aspects of JSP. Tag libraries are not the best solution for everything, but they are the preferred method for embedding dynamic functionality in a JSP. Many simple and illustrative uses of custom tags appear throughout this chapter. Do not let this fool you into thinking this is a limitation of the technology. Custom tags have many practical uses that are covered in depth by the later chapters. As both a preview of the later chapters and as background information, here are some of the more helpful uses of custom tags.

MVC

Model View Control, also called Model 2, is currently the most commonly used design pattern for developing Web Applications. The MVC design pattern is popular because it focuses on breaking down a Web Application into logical partitions and encourages developers to abide by the divisions. The View partition corresponds to the part of the Web Application that is responsible for rendering data into a format the client is expecting. This division is commonly left to a JSP that can easily display information via the standard JSP actions or custom ones.

Internationalization

Internationalization is a very important issue with Web site development. Creating a multilingual site can be a daunting task. One very practical method of providing this sort of functionality via JSP is to encapsulate all text-producing elements as custom tags. Each tag would be responsible for determining the correct text to produce based on the locality of the client. This might be done as the following:

```
<%@taglib prefix="in" uri="/WEB-INF/i18n.tld" %>
<html>
<head>
<in:title id="groups"/>
</head>
...
```

The preceding is an example of a custom tag named title in an i18n tag library. The tag is passed an ID attribute that it will typically use as an index into a resource bundle, extracting the correct text based on the locale of the client. It is this extracted text that is displayed as the result of the tag and that appears as the page title.

Internationalization tags are popular because they solve i18n issues with a very clean approach. The internationalization chapter includes further information regarding internationalization issues and using custom tags to solve them.

Multi-Client Support

There are many more client types today than in the past. For example, Web browsers have different capabilities; there are clients that expect XML and handheld clients, such as phones and Personal Digital Assistants (PDAs), expect their data in WML format. A single Web site can support this multitude of clients. The issue is very similar to that of internationalization; however, it is a problem with appropriately formatting content rather than producing the same content in different languages. As with internationalization issues, custom tags provide a good solution to supporting various types of content format. The following is an example of how these tags might be used:

```
<%@taglib prefix="mct" uri="/WEB-INF/mct.tld" %>
<mct:page>
<mct:p>Some text</mct:p>
</mct:page>
```

The preceding is a similar illustration to that of the internationalization tag, but notice that both custom tags are used for the formatting, not the text. In these examples, the custom tags are responsible for generating the appropriate format for the client requesting the content. This is a helpful design feature for a Web site that might need to send the same content in HTML, XHTML, XML, PDF, or WML depending on the particular client.

The topic of multi-client support is further covered in Chapter 13.

Conditionals, Iterations, and Simple, Needed Tasks

There are countless cases that always seem to appear on a JSP. Some good examples of these cases are conditionals and iterations. A simple scriptlet suffices as does a simple custom tag, but the tag is almost always preferred to keep the code clean. Currently, JSP does not provide a set of standard actions that solve the most common cases, but there has been a move to integrate such tags into the set of standard actions. As you read in the previous chapter, the current version of the JavaServer Pages Standard Tag Library (JSTL) provides a few of these simple tags.

Countless Illogical Ways

Despite conventional wisdom, and in the author's opinion, there are countless custom tags being used in a manner that they should not be. These tags always seem to have a semi-plausible reason for existing but are frowned upon by many of the JSP community. Such tags are often used to place business logic onto a JSP. The authors have argued throughout the book that this is not good practice. As tags were originally designed to avoid this very practice, it seems perverse to use tags to do this. Why is this done? The answer is usually ease of use, but for all practical purposes, this excuse is not a good one.

In both the last chapter and this chapter there are some clear illustrations and commentary on these "bad" tags and why we believe you should not use them. It is not the intention of this book to illustrate bad practices, but without bringing up the bad uses, it is difficult to clearly illustrate what types of custom tags you should think hard about before using. Additionally, the issue of unhelpful tags is of significance or else it would not have even received a mention. There are many existing sets of tags, even standardized tags, that are, or at least should be, of little practical purpose.

New and Old Custom Tags

The JSP 2.0 specification was originally named the JSP 1.3 specification, but enough significant changes were introduced that it made sense to promote the new specification to JSP 2.0. Some of the most significant changes that pushed the title change are related directly to JSP custom tags. In previous versions of JSP, custom tags were something that were complex and suited only for Java developers. However, what custom tags did was so helpful that non-Java developers complained that JSP should extend its flexibility to make custom tags easy to use for all JSP authors. Additionally, JSP has been under scrutiny for a long time because many of its features (namely custom tags) can be used well outside the context of HTTP Servlets. JSP 2.0 introduces additions that solve these issues.

Claiming that all of the custom tag functionality introduced in JSP 2.0 is complementary to what already existed is simply not true. Many of the additions are a superior form of building custom tags. The better way to look at JSP 2.0 custom tags is to divide them into two categories: new "simple" custom tags and old custom tags. Both types of tags work and provide identical functionality. The difference between the two types of tags is that the new custom tags provide a more simple and intuitive solution. All custom tags can be used in any combination on the same JSP.

In this book the basic functionality of custom tags is completely covered by this chapter. First, the newer approach of building custom tags is introduced and explained. We would strongly encourage you to use the new simple approach; however, the older approach for implementing custom tags is also covered. It can be left as optional reading, but it is very helpful to understand because almost every existing custom tag was built following the strategy.

Tag Library Descriptors (TLDs)

Deciding how to approach the task of explaining custom tags is difficult because it is hard to know where to start. Tag handlers, JSP Fragments, and `.tag` files are by far the most important aspects of custom tags to explain; however, TLD files are needed before the majority of custom tags are able to do anything. A problem arises because it makes sense to try and explain TLD files first, but there many parts of the TLD that just do not make sense until tag handlers have been explained. To solve this problem, TLD files are explained via many little parts that appear throughout this chapter.

In this section the basics of TLD files are introduced, and discussion covers everything needed to start using simple tag handlers. TLD files are not covered completely by this part of the chapter. Slightly more complex parts of the TLD file, such as declaring attributes and initial parameters, are covered in the relevant later parts of this chapter. At the end of the chapter a brief recap of TLD files is given to summarize everything.

What Is a Tag Library Descriptor?

In the abstract sense a Tag Library Descriptor is the mechanism that binds custom tag code to the simple markup that appears in a JSP. The concrete form of a TLD is an XML file that usually appears in the /WEB-INF directory of a Web Application. You can also bundle a TLD with a packaged tag library JAR, but assume for now all TLD files appear as a simple XML file with the "tld" extension.

For this chapter you will need to have a TLD file that describes the custom tag examples. Start that file now by saving Listing 7-1 as example.tld in the /WEB-INF directory of the jspbook Web Application.

Listing 7-1 A Simple TLD File

```
<taglib
  xmlns="http://java.sun.com/xml/ns/j2ee"
  xmlns:xsi="http://www.w3.org/2001/XMLSchema-instance"
  xsi:schemaLocation="http://java.sun.com/xml/ns/j2ee
    http://java.sun.com/xml/ns/j2ee/web-jsptaglibrary_2_0.xsd"
  version="2.0">
  <tlib-version>1.0</tlib-version>
  <jsp-version>2.0</jsp-version>
  <short-name>Example TLD</short-name>
  <uri>http://www.jspbook.com/example.tld</uri>
  <tag>
    <name>foo</name>
    <tag-class>com.jspbook.FooTag</tag-class>
    <body-content>empty</body-content>
  </tag>
</taglib>
```

In the code you can see that a TLD file is nothing more than a collection of tag elements. All of the elements are important and inform a JSP container about the tag library. Listing 7-1 uses one `tag` element, but multiple `tag` elements can be used as needed to describe the complete tag library. This will be illustrated as the chapter progresses. In Listing 7-1 the very basic child elements of `tag` are used: `name`, `tag-class`, and `body-content`. `Name` defines the unique element name of the custom tag. The value specified in the body of the `name` element must be unique among all the other tags defined in the same TLD. The `tag-class` element specifies the Java class that should be loaded as the tag handler class. The value of the `tag-class` element does not have to be unique for the TLD, but it does have to be a fully qualified name of an existing Java class. The `body-content` element defines what type of code, if any, is allowed to be inserted inside the body of the custom tag when used by a JSP. Valid values for the `body-content` element are `empty`, `JSP`, `scriptless`, and `tagdependent` and indicate if the tag body should be empty; contain nested JSP syntax (including scripting elements); only contain template text, EL expressions, and JSP action elements (no scripting elements are allowed); or left as is for interpretation by the custom tag, respectively.

Other important points to note about Listing 7-1 are in the first few lines of code. After the XML declaration is the root node of the TLD, the `taglib` element. All of the other TLD elements must appear between the starting and ending `taglib` tags. Following the starting `taglib` tag are the following elements:

```
<tlib-version>1.0</tlib-version>
<jsp-version>2.0</jsp-version>
<short-name>Example TLD</short-name>
```

These elements are mandatory; however, unlike the `tag` element, they must only appear once. The `tlib-version` specifies the version number of the tag library. The `jsp-version` element defines the required version of JSP the tag library relies on. This value should be set according to your specific release of custom tags and the JSP functionality relied upon. The `short-name` element is used to give a short title to the set of custom tags. It is intended to aid JSP development tools.

Listing 7-1 is not a complete reference to the TLD elements. It is only the minimum requirement for a TLD file. The `example.tld` file will be filled out further as the chapter progresses, but it will never include all of the possible TLD elements. A complete reference for the JSP 2.0 TLD is available at `http://java.sun.com/xml/ns/j2ee/web-jsptaglibrary_2_0.xsd`.

Using a Tag Library Descriptor

After building both a TLD and the code the TLD links to, a tag library is ready for use in a JSP. There are currently a number of different methods of referencing a custom tag library. Each method is helpful in different situations, and it is good to understand all of them. The following sections cover some of the different methods.

Relative URI

A *relative URI* is defined by the JSP specification as a URI without a protocol and host and is the most direct method of informing a Web Application about the location of a TLD. Relative URIs are further divided into two. A root-relative URI is one that starts with a "/", while a non-root-relative URI has no leading "/." Using a relative URI is as easy as specifying the relative path to a TLD file as the value of the `taglib` directive's `uri` attribute.

Take, for example, a simple JSP that uses `example.tld` to define some custom tags. Listing 7-2 is an example of what this code might look like. The example also assumes the JSP is saved in the root directory of the jspbook Web Application.

Listing 7-2   Relative URI Definitions

```
<%@ taglib uri="/WEB-INF/example.tld" prefix="foo" %>
<html>
  <body>
    <foo:bar/>
  </body>
</html>
```

Both the HTML code and the `foo` tag serve no practical purpose and are used only to illustrate a tag. The important point of the example is how the `taglib` directive knows where to find the TLD file for the tag library. The TLD is identified by the actual path to the file, `/WEB-INF/example.tld`[1].

A relative URI is the easiest method for learning because it is direct and usually intuitive; however, there are a few major flaws that make this approach less desirable for practical use. If a non-root-relative URI is used, such as `<%@ taglib uri="example.tld" prefix="foo" %>`, then the URI for a specific JSP is different depending on where the actual JSP file is located relative to the TLD file. Should a JSP be moved to a different part of a Web Application, the URI value would need to be changed. Should the TLD file be moved, all JSP referencing it via a relative URI would need to be updated. In situations where either of these

---

1. Note a relative URI should always use forward slashes, /, never backward slashes, \, regardless of the operating system being used on the server.

cases happen frequently, using a relative URI becomes inconvenient. A relative URI can also be overly complex, depending on the location of files within a Web Application. A JSP in three subdirectories from the root directory would have a relative URI similar to "../../../WEB-INF/example.tld", which is slightly annoying to keep track of.

A root-relative URI does not have this problem; however, it has other issues. Suppose the tag developer decides to package his or her tags into a JAR file—this relative URI is now useless as the TLD will not be at the specified location. What is needed is "an extra level of indirection"[2].

Web Application-Defined URI

Compared to a relative URI a more practical approach is to define an application-wide abstract URI corresponding to the real location of the TLD file. JSP wishing to use the corresponding tag library would then use the abstract URI and let the Web Application resolve the actual location of the TLD file. This approach is beneficial because it allows for a simple fictional URI to be used by all JSP, taking advantage of the tags.

The only drawback to Web Application-defined URIs is they are slightly more complex to set up than a relative URI. An application-wide URI is defined by an entry in the `web.xml` file of a Web Application. Add Listing 7-3 into `/WEB-INF/web.xml` of the jspbook Web Application. Insert the entry after any instances of the `error-page` element.

Listing 7-3   web.xml TLD URI Definition

```
<taglib>
  <taglib-uri>http://www.jspbook.com/example</taglib-uri>
  <taglib-location>/WEB-INF/example.tld</taglib-location>
</taglib>
```

The `taglib` element defines an abstract URI that corresponds to a given location of a TLD file. The two child elements, `taglib-uri` and `taglib-location`, are used to create a unique, fictitious URI and reference the location of the actual TLD, respectively. The `taglib` element may only have one of each of these child elements, but a TLD file may have many `taglib` elements. This collection of `taglib` elements is called the `taglib` map.

---

2. "There is no problem in computer science that cannot be solved by adding an extra level of indirection".

Setting up a set of `taglib` entries in the `web.xml` file is a manual and possibly error-prone process. To get around this problem, the JSP specification offers an easy solution: it will build the map for you. To do this you simply do two things: to the TLD file add a `<uri></uri>` entry that contains the URI you want the developer to use, and place the TLD file in the Web Application's `WEB-INF` directory or a subdirectory of `WEB-INF`. Given the preceding URI, adding the following

```
<uri>http://www.jspbook.com/example</uri>
```

to the TLD file and placing the TLD file in `WEB-INF` would have exactly the same affect as adding the `taglib` map to the `web.xml` file.

As another convenience, a developer can package a tag library as a JAR file. In this case the developer should place any TLD files into the JAR's `META-INF` directory (or a subdirectory). Any JAR files placed in the Web Application are read by the container, and any TLDs found in the JAR's `META-INF` directory have their URIs added to the map automatically[3,4].

After a new `taglib` element has been added to `web.xml`, the Web Application must be restarted for the changes to take effect. Reload the jspbook Web Application so that the new application-wide URI is available for future examples in this chapter. Listing 7-4 illustrates a JSP that uses the newly defined URI.

Listing 7-4 Use of Abstract Custom Tag URI

```
<%@ taglib uri="http://www.jspbook.com/example" prefix="foo" %>
<html>
  <body>
    <foo:bar />
  </body>
</html>
```

Highlighted is the new URI, which is the same for all JSP using these tags. Notice also this URI does not resolve to any real TLD file, but it could be used to reference a real location. In many cases collections of tag libraries use the tag library's homepage as the relative URI. This practice inserts a subtle reminder of the tag's origin as well as a place to find out more information about the tags.

---

3. Note that even if you use a relative URI, the `taglib` map is always searched first before the container tries to resolve the URI to a file name.
4. The container may also add "well-known" URIs to the `taglib` map.

XML Namespaces and JSP in XML Syntax

With JSP 2.0 one of the original approaches of specifying custom tag libraries has been outdated with a much more flexible approach. In JSP 1.2 the "JSP in XML" syntax was introduced. Since the `taglib` directive is not XML-compatible, an alternative XML namespace-like approach was allowed for "JSP in XML" syntax. This approach works, but is now superseded by full XML namespace support for declaring a set of custom tags for a JSP in any syntax.

XML namespaces are an alternative method to declaring a set of custom tags in a JSP. The namespace support is XML-compatible and uses the syntax in Listing 7-5.

Listing 7-5 Use of XML Custom Tag Library Declaration

```
<prefix:name xmlns:prefix="URI"/>
```

In the preceding code `prefix` and URI are equivalent to the respective `taglib` directive attributes, and `name` is the name of a tag defined by the TLD. Note, in order to use this form of tag library declaration, the JSP must be declared as in XML format, such as a `.jspx` file.

Simple JSP 2.0 Custom Tags

JSP 2.0 gives a new meaning to what JSP developers have previously considered custom tags. JSP 2.0 introduces custom tags that have a simple life cycle and that can optionally be authored using JSP rather than Java code. The tags are referenced as "Simple" for two reasons. First is because they are arguably much simpler to write and use than the classic custom tag handlers. The second reason is because the functionality is based around the `javax.servlet.jsp.SimpleTag` interface.

Understanding how a Simple custom tag works starts with understanding the life cycle of the tag. This life cycle applies to Simple tags coded via Java or JSP tag files as shown in Figure 7-2.

The life cycle has two parts: initialization and `doTag()`. The initialization sets the tag's parent and body. Both the parent and body are important; the parent allows for tag collaboration and the body allows the tag to optionally process its body. The second part of the simple tag life cycle is the `doTag()` method. This method is invoked when the tag should do its action. Once the `doTag()` method returns, the custom tag has finished doing its job.

As a custom tag developer, typically only the `doTag()` part of the `SimpleTag` life cycle is of interest. A JSP container will appropriately set both the parent and body. It should be clear that only worrying about one thing, the `doTag()` method,

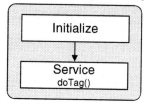

javax.servlet.jsp.tagext.SimpleTag

Initialize

Service
doTag()

Figure 7-2 SimpleTag Life Cycle

makes simple tags straightforward to code. If you want a custom tag to do anything, you simply provide a doTag() method. Ensuring proper synchronization and state management lies completely within the code of the doTag() method[5].

SimpleTag Interface

The `javax.servlet.jsp.tagext.SimpleTag` interface is the interface all `SimpleTag` classes must implement. The `SimpleTag` interface does not extend the `javax.servlet.jsp.tagext.Tag` interface and does not work like a classic JSP custom tag. The `SimpleTag` interface defines the following methods:

- **doTag():** The doTag() method is invoked by a JSP container during execution of the custom tag. A custom tag developer should override the doTag() method to execute any custom logic the tag is responsible for. Before execution of the doTag() method the setParent(), setJspBody(), and setJspContext() methods are all invoked by the JSP container. This allows the doTag() method to have full access to the JspFragment object representing its body and to the current JspContext. The doTag() method can return EVAL_PAGE or SKIP_PAGE to either continue evaluating the page after the tag or to skip evaluation of the rest of the JSP, respectively.

- **getParent():** The getParent() method returns the custom tag surrounding this tag, if it exists. The method returns java.lang.Object as the custom tag which may either be an instance of SimpleTag or Tag.

---

5. Relative to classic tag handlers—that is, pre-JSP 2.0, custom tags did not have this luxury. A few coding tricks were required to accomplish even simple things such as iteration and state management. If they are of interest, the latter half of this chapter discusses these outdated issues.

- **setJspBody(javax.servlets.jsp.JspFragment):** The `setJspBody()` method sets the current `JspFragment` object during runtime. This method is guaranteed to be properly invoked by a JSP container during runtime before the `doTag()` method.

- **setJspContext(javax.servlets.jsp.JspContext):** The `setJspContext()` method sets the current `JspContext` object during runtime. This method is guaranteed to be properly invoked by a JSP container during runtime before invoking the `doTag()` method.

- **setParent(javax.servlets.jsp.JspTag):** The JSP container invokes the `setParent()` method to set the current parent tag, if it exists. The method takes an argument of `javax.servlets.jsp.JspTag` as the parent that can be an instance of either `Tag` or `SimpleTag`. `JspTag` serves as a base class for `Tag` and `SimpleTag` for safety-type purposes.

Use of the `SimpleTag` interface is designed to be straightforward. The `javax.servlet.jsp.tagext.SimpleTagSupport` class exists as a base implementation of the interface. The only thing a custom tag author needs to do is extend `SimpleTagSupport` and override the `doTag()` method. For instance, a simple and unoriginal `"Hello World!"` tag would be coded as shown in Listing 7-6.

Listing 7-6 HelloSimpleTag.java

```
package com.jspbook;

import javax.servlet.jsp.tagext.SimpleTagSupport;
import javax.servlet.jsp.*;
import java.io.IOException;

public class HelloSimpleTag extends SimpleTagSupport {

  public void doTag() throws JspException, IOException {
    JspWriter out = jspContext.getOut();
    out.println("Hello World!");
  }
}
```

The code is simple. The `doTag()` method takes the current `JspContext` object, `jspContext`, and uses it to send "Hello World!" to the current `JspWriter` object. When the tag is used on a JSP, it will replace the custom tag syntax with "Hello World!". Try the tag out by deploying it in `/WEB-INF/example.tld`.

```
<tag>
  <name>hello</name>
  <tag-class>com.jspbook.HelloSimpleTag</tag-class>
  <body-content>empty</body-content>
</tag>
```

Save `HelloSimpleTag.java` in the `/WEB-INF/classes/com/jspbook` directory of the jspbook Web Application, compile the code, and reload the application for the change to take effect. Once the application has been reloaded, the tag is ready for use. Listing 7-7 is a simple JSP that uses the tag.

Listing 7-7 HelloSimpleTagTest.jsp

```
<%@ taglib prefix="ex" uri="WEB-INF/example.tld"%>
<html>
  <head>
    <title>A test of HelloSimpleTag.java</title>
  </head>
  <body>
    <ex:hello/>
  </body>
</html>
```

The preceding code is a simple HTML page that has the `hello` tag used in its body. Save Listing 7-7 in the base directory of the jspbook Web Application and browse to `http://127.0.0.1/jspbook/HelloSimpleTagTest.jsp`. The resulting page replaces the `hello` tag with "Hello World!" Figure 7-3 shows a browser rendering of the results.

All simple uses of the `SimpleTag` interface are similar to Listing 7-7. The important concept to see is that any code can be placed in the `doTag()` method. In the preceding example we saw how the code can access the current `JspContext` object of the page. This is important because the `JspContext` provides access to the current `JspWriter` for the page and because it can be cast to a `PageContext` object in order to access the `HttpServletRequest` and `HttpServletResponse`.

The simplicity of the `doTag()` method does a good job of hiding all of the complex things it can be used for. More complex tags can use the `doTag()` method in combination with attribute values, to evaluate the tag's body content, or to iterate over the body content multiple times. All of these uses are explained shortly. First, we start with how to add static and dynamic attributes to custom tags.

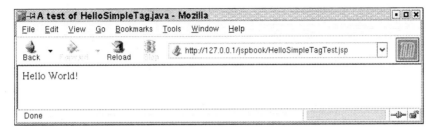

Figure 7-3 Browser Rendering of HelloSimpleTagTest.jsp

Attributes

In just about every SGML[6]-based language, attributes are relied upon to expand and customize the functionality of a tag. The markup linked to custom tags is no different. Attributes can be used with custom tags, and they are very helpful for expanding the functionality provided by a tag handler.

Attributes for a custom tag can either be *static* or *dynamic*. Static attributes are formally declared in the TLD. Dynamic attributes are freely declared during a specific use of the tag. The two different types of attributes are helpful for different reasons. Static attributes can be fully described in a TLD and have a limited but automatic set of validation logic associated with them. For instance, a static attribute can be declared in a TLD to have the name "value" and be required whenever the tag is used. This is helpful because it means a JSP developer will always be forced to use the "value" attribute when using the tag. In contrast, dynamic attributes need not be declared in the TLD. Dynamic attributes are more flexible because any attribute can be defined during a given use of the tag; however, the drawback is that validation of the attribute is slightly more complex.

Static Attributes and TLD Declaration

Static attributes require a JSP developer to do two things. First, a custom tag class needs to implement setter methods, identical to JavaBean setter methods, for all of the attributes of the tag. For example, assume a custom tag is needed to show the current date. Additionally, the format of the date needs to be flexible enough so that different uses of the tag can display different formats. The task is easy to

---

6. Standard Generalized Markup Language (SGML) is a standard that describes what markup languages, such as HTML, should use as syntax in order to be more easily understood.

complete using a simple tag, the `java.text.SimpleDateFormat` object, and an attribute. Listing 7-8 includes the complete code.

Listing 7-8 FormatDateTag.java

```
package com.jspbook;

import javax.servlet.jsp.tagext.*;
import javax.servlet.jsp.*;
import java.util.Date;
import java.text.SimpleDateFormat;
import java.io.IOException;

public class FormatDateTag extends SimpleTagSupport {
  private String format;

  public void setFormat(String format) {
    this.format = format;
  }

  public void doTag() throws JspException, IOException {
    JspWriter out = jspContext.getOut();
    if (format != null) {
      SimpleDateFormat sdf = new SimpleDateFormat(format);
      out.println(sdf.format(new Date()));
    }
    else {
      out.println(new Date().toString());
    }
  }
}
```

Highlighted are the specific lines for the attribute. The attribute's name is "format", so the setter method is `setFormat()`. A data member format is declared to keep the value set by this attribute. Later on, it will be shown that this setter method allows for the date tag to be used as follows:

```
<ex:date format="format value"/>
```

This is beneficial because the attribute format is where the custom tag gets the desired format for the current date/time. If you are familiar with the `java.text.SimpleDateFormat` class, then you should easily recognize the class takes a `java.util.Date` object and a specified format, and produces a pretty-much formatted string.

```
SimpleDateFormat sdf =
   new SimpleDateFormat(format);
out.println(sdf.format(new Date()));
```

This is exactly what the code in the `doTag()` method is doing, and the `format` variable is being used to define the format. A user of the date tag will be able to choose any of the formatting options available with the `SimpleDateFormat` object.

The second part of using a static attribute is declaring it in the custom tag's TLD. Attributes are declared in a TLD by adding an `attribute` child element to a tag's entry. The `attribute` element in turn requires a few more child elements to describe the attribute. The JSP specification defines the following possible child elements for the `attribute` element:

- **name:** The `name` element defines the name of an attribute. Each attribute name must be unique for a particular tag.

- **required:** The `required` element tells the container if the page author must supply a value for this attribute; as this is optional, the container supplies a default value if the element is missing. This default value is `false`.

- **rtexprvalue:** The `rtexprvalue` element is used to declare if a runtime expression value for a tag attribute is valid. It is possible that a static value might be required so that a `TagLibraryValidator` object can properly verify the JSP. `TagLibraryValidator` objects are covered later in this chapter.

- **type:** The `type` element defines the Java class-type of this attribute. By default `String` is assumed, but a custom tag attribute may be of any Java class-type.

- **description:** The container does not use the description element either at page translation or runtime. It is simply there for the tag author to give the page author examples of how to use the tag.

- **fragment:** The `fragment` element is used to declare if this attribute value should be treated as a `JspFragment`.

Only the `name` element is required to define an attribute, but depending on how the attribute is being used, you may need to include some of the optional attribute child elements.

To finish the `FormatDateTag.java` example, a declaration needs to be added for the `format` attribute. Listing 7-9 includes the entry in `example.tld`.

Listing 7-9 Adding a Simple Attribute Entry in a TLD

```
<tag>
  <name>date</name>
  <tag-class>com.jspbook.FormatDateTag</tag-class>
  <body-content>empty</body-content>
  <attribute>
    <name>format</name>
  </attribute>
</tag>
```

In the preceding listing, the highlighted lines of code are the ones responsible for declaring the attribute. Make sure the complete entry is in WEB-INF/example.tld and the custom tag will finally be ready for use. Try out the custom tag by creating a JSP that uses it. Listing 7-10 is such a JSP.

Listing 7-10 FormatDateTagTest.jsp

```
<%@ taglib prefix="ex" uri="http://www.jspbook.com/example" %>
<html>
  <head>
    <title>A Custom Tag Example</title>
  </head>
  <body>
    The current date is <ex:date format="dd/MM/yyyy" />.
  </body>
</html>
```

The format attribute is the same one defined by the TLD and coded in FormatDateTag.java. The value specified in the format attribute is used as the formatting for time-stamp generated by the date tag. This can be verified by revisiting FormatDateTagTest.jsp. Compile FormatDateTag.java and reload the jspbook Web Application to have the TLD and tag handler changes take effect and then visit http://127.0.0.1/jspbook/FormatDateTagTest.jsp. The result is an HTML page with a date formatted as specified in the format attribute. Figure 7-4 shows a browser rendering of the results.

The formatting of the time-stamp can also easily be changed in the future by changing the value of the format attribute. This process is very easy and can be done without changing the TLD or tag handler class. If for instance the tag was being used in the United States, the format attribute would likely be "MM/dd/yyyy". If the tag was being used in the United Kingdom, the format attribute would likely be "dd/MM/yyyy". The values are allowed to be anything the java.text.SimpleDateFormat class supports.

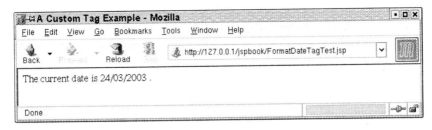

Figure 7-4 FormatDateTagTest.jsp with the New Time-Stamp Formatting

As many static attributes may be used with a tag as are needed. The only requirement is that each attribute has an entry in the corresponding TLD and that a setter method exists for the attribute in the custom tag's class. One other thing to note is that static attributes can be marked as required. If a "required" attribute is missing from the tag entered on the JSP, the page will not compile.

Dynamic Attributes

Coding in setter methods and adding entries in a TLD can become tedious for custom tag developers. In some cases there may even be a need to use a custom tag that does not have a predefined set of valid attributes. In both of these cases a JSP developer can use dynamic attributes. A great example of this is a tag within a tag library that emulates an HTML element. HTML elements may have many attributes that such a tag would simply want to echo to the output stream. Writing such a tag using static attributes would be difficult, but using dynamic attributes would be trivial. Dynamic attributes are not required to be individually declared in a TLD, but a TLD must reference the tag and define that dynamic attributes are valid to use with it.

Coding a custom tag that uses dynamic attributes is slightly different from one that uses static attributes. Instead of requiring a setter method of each attribute, dynamic attributes are all handled by the `javax.servlet.jsp.tagext.DynamicAttributes` interface. This interface defines one method:

```
setDynamicAttribute(String uri, String localName, Object value)
```

The `setDynamicAttribute()` method takes three parameters. The first parameter specifies the URI of the attribute, or null if the default URI is being used. The second parameter is the name of the attribute. The third parameter is the value of the attribute.

A custom tag that supports dynamic attributes must implement the DynamicAttributes interface. All dynamic attributes used with the tag are presented to the tag via the setDynamicAttribute() method and it is up to the custom tag to deal with the attributes appropriately.

As an example, Listing 7-11 includes a simple tag that allows for dynamic attributes and lists any dynamic attributes used with it.

Listing 7-11 DynamicAttributeTag.java

```
package com.jspbook;

import javax.servlet.jsp.tagext.*;
import javax.servlet.jsp.*;
import java.util.*;
import java.io.IOException;

public class DynamicAttributeTag
    extends SimpleTagSupport implements DynamicAttributes {
  protected Hashtable map = new Hashtable();

  public void setDynamicAttribute(String uri, String name,
     Object value) throws JspException{
    map.put(name, value);
  }

  public void doTag() throws JspException, IOException {
    JspWriter out = jspContext.getOut();
    for (Enumeration keys = map.keys();
        keys.hasMoreElements();) {
      Object key = keys.nextElement();
      Object value = map.get(key);
      out.print("<b>Attribute:</b><br>");
      out.print("name: " + key.toString() + "<br>");
      out.print("value: " + value.toString() + "<br>");
    }
  }
}
```

The preceding code illustrates how the DynamicAttributes interface can be implemented. The setDynamicAttribute() method is added to the tag's code and is used to handle dynamic attributes.

```
  public void setDynamicAttribute(String uri, String name,
     Object value) throws JspException{
```

```
    map.put(name, value);
}
```

In Listing 7-11 all of the dynamic attributes are saved in a `java.util.`
`Hashtable` object. Next, the `doTag()` method iterates through all the collected
values and displays information about them.

```
for (Enumeration keys = map.keys();
     keys.hasMoreElements();) {
  Object key = keys.nextElement();
  Object value = map.get(key);
  out.print("<b>Attribute:</b><br>");
  out.print("name: " + key.toString() + "<br>");
  out.print("value: " + value.toString() + "<br>");
}
```

In most situations the values passed by the `setDynamicAttribute()` method
would be applied to a further use, such as the `format` attribute in Listing 7-8.
Additionally, individual setter methods can be coded into the custom tag's code
to be delegated to by the `setDynamicAttribute()` method. Attribute validation
can also be added to the `setDynamicAttribute()` method. If attribute information is invalid at runtime, the `doDynamicAttribute()` method can throw an
instance of `JspException`.

Like static attributes, a custom tag that uses dynamic attributes must be
declared via a TLD; however, the entry need only include the `dynamic-`
`attributes` element as a child element of `tag` instead of numerous child
`attribute` elements. The entry for Listing 7-11 would be:

```
<tag>
  <name>dynamicAttribute</name>
  <tag-class>com.jspbook.DynamicAttributeTag</tag-class>
  <dynamic-attributes>true</dynamic-attributes>
</tag>
```

Save this entry in `/WEB-INF/example.tld` and save `DynamicAttribute`
`Tag.java` in the `/WEB-INF/classes/com/jspbook` directory of the jspbook Web
Application. Compile the code and reload the application. The new tag is then
ready for use. Try out the custom tag with the JSP in Listing 7-12.

Listing 7-12 DynamicAttributeTagTest.jsp

```
<%@ taglib uri="http://www.jspbook.com/example" prefix="ex"%>
<html>
  <head>
    <title>A test of DynamicAttributeTag.java</title>
```

```
  </head>
  <body>
    <ex:dynamicAttribute name="test" value="a value"/>
  </body>
</html>
```

Save `DynamicAttributeTagTest.jsp` in the base directory of the jspbook Web Application and browse to `http://127.0.0.1/DynamicAttributeTagTest.jsp`. A page appears listing all of the attributes that were set for the `Dynamic Attribute` tag. Try editing the page to add or remove attributes and see how the results change. Figure 7-5 provides a browser rendering of Listing 7-12.

The important point here is that custom tags may have attributes defined. The attributes can be either static or dynamic; mix and use the functionality as it best fits your project. Keep in mind when coding a tag that implements the `DynamicAttributes` interface, you can still code in setter methods for individual attributes in case you decide to later use static attributes.

Runtime Attribute Values

By default attribute values are calculated at page translation time and are required to be hard coded strings. In all the previous examples custom tag attributes have been static name/value pairs—for example, `name="value"` or `format="MM/dd/yyyy"`. This is not a limitation of custom tags. Runtime `string` and non-string objects can be used as custom tag attributes when needed. We shall first take a look at using runtime `string` objects as the value for a tag attribute.

When using a runtime `string` object instead of a static string value, the `rtexprvalue` element must be set to `true` for the corresponding attribute declaration in the tag's TLD. This is the only change that is required for both the TLD

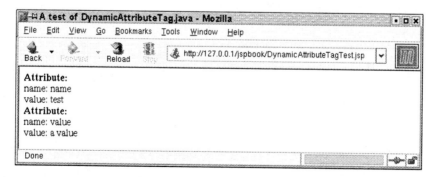

Figure 7-5 Browser Rendering of the Results of DynamicAttributeTagTest.jsp

and the tag handler, assuming that the code was already designed for a static string value. Continuing with the date tag example, a runtime value can be used for the format attribute to dynamically set a format of a generated date. This combined with the HTTP accept-language header allows the JSP to guess and set the date formatting based on a client's locale[7].

For the runtime value example, two things are required. First, the TLD needs to be updated to allow for the format attribute to be a runtime value. The change is small and highlighted in Listing 7-13.

Listing 7-13 Allowing for a Runtime Attribute via a TLD

```
<tag>
  <name>date</name>
  <tag-class>com.jspbook.FormatDateTag</tag-class>
  <body-content>empty</body-content>
  <attribute>
    <name>format</name>
    <rtexprvalue>true</rtexprvalue>
  </attribute>
</tag>
```

The change in FormatDateTagTest.jsp is significant, not because of the TLD change but because of the HTTP header data mining. Save FormatDateTagTest.jsp as FormatDateLocaleTest.jsp and add the following changes in Listing 7-14.

Listing 7-14 FormatDateLocaleTest.jsp

```
<%
  String format = "yyyy/MM/dd";
  request.setAttribute("format", format);
  String language = request.getHeader("accept-language");
  if (language != null) {
    if (language.indexOf("en-us") != -1 ||
        language.indexOf("en-US") != -1 ||
        language.indexOf("EN-US") != -1) {
      format = "MM/dd/yyyy";
    }
    else if (
        language.indexOf("en-uk") != -1 ||
        language.indexOf("en-UK") != -1 ||
```

---

7. The locale header was mentioned in Chapter 2 with HTTP headers. Chapter 12 continues on with further discussion of mining locale information from HTTP headers.

```
         language.indexOf("EN-UK") != -1) {
         format = "dd/MM/yyyy";
    }
  }
%>
```

```
<%@ taglib prefix="ex" uri="http://www.jspbook.com/example" %>
<html>
  <head>
    <title>A test of FormatDateTag.java</title>
  </head>
  <body>
    The date is <ex:date format="${format}" />.
  </body>
</html>
```

The preceding code now uses a simple scriptlet to populate a scripting variable `format` for use as the `format` attribute of the `date` tag. The end effect is that the `format` attribute is dynamically set to try and match the locale of a client. By default the original format "yyyy/MM/dd" is used, but if the scriptlet can detect a UK client, the appropriate formatting is used. Figure 7-6 shows a browser rendering of a client visiting from the United States.

In some cases it might be helpful to pass in a non-String object as a tag attribute. Should this be the case a few changes are required when declaring and coding in support for the attributes. In a TLD the `type` element needs to be used along with a value specifying the Java class of the object. Take for instance the following code assuming it is a line from a JSP.

```
<foo:example date='<%= new Date() %>'/>
```

By default this code throws a translation exception. When an expression is used to set the value of a custom tag's attribute, it does not automatically call the `toString()` method of that object. Instead, the object itself is used when calling the set method of the appropriate tag handler. In order to verify the tag handler is expecting the proper class, in this case `java.util.Date` not `java.lang.String`, the `type` element needs to be declared in the TLD with the appropriate type as a value. In this particular case the TLD entry would be the following:

```
<tag>
  <name>date</name>
  <tag-class>foo.Bar</tag-class>
  <body-content>empty</body-content>
  <attribute>
```

```
    <name>date</name>
    <rtexprvalue>true</rtexprvalue>
    <type>java.util.Date</type>
  </attribute>
</tag>
```

Do not worry about adding this entry into `example.tld`. Understanding and being able to use `String` attributes are far more important.

Body Evaluation and Iteration

So far this chapter has explained how to use the `SimpleTag` interface to create custom tags that can access the current `JspContext` object and that can take advantage of attributes. Quite a lot can be accomplished with just the mentioned functionality; however, simple tags can be used for much more. A very important aspect of the `doTag()` method is that it can optionally evaluate the body content of its corresponding tag in a JSP. The `setJspBody()` method of the `SimpleTag` interface is always called before invoking the `doTag()` method; this sets the value of the `SimpleTagSupport`'s `jspBody` variable. This variable is of type `JspFragment` and can be invoked, sending the data to a specified writer. This means a simple tag can optionally invoke the JSP fragment, which represents its body content, any number of times.

Recall the `HelloSimpleTag.java` example, Listing 7-6. In `HelloSimpleTag.java` the message "Hello World!" is directly sent to the current `JspWriter` object.

```
JspWriter out = jspContext.getout();
out.println("Hello World!");
```

The same functionality can be accomplished by placing the message "Hello World!" in the body of the custom tag and having the `doTag()` method evaluate

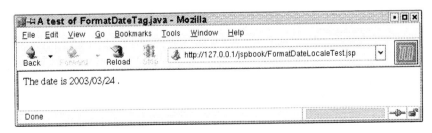

Figure 7-6 Browser Rendering of FormatDateLocaleTest.jsp for a US Client

the body. For example, Listing 7-15 shows the change in `HelloSimpleTagTest.jsp`.

Listing 7-15 BodySimpleTagTest.jsp

```
<%@ taglib prefix="ex" uri="http://www.jspbook.com/example"%>
<html>
  <head>
    <title>A test of BodySimpleTag.java</title>
  </head>
  <body>
    <ex:body>
      Hello World!
    </ex:body>
  </body>
</html>
```

Now instead of using an empty body, the tag includes the message as its body content. In turn, the tag's code needs to be updated to evaluate the body instead of directly using "Hello World!". Listing 7-16 is the new simple tag's code.

Listing 7-16 BodySimpleTag.java

```
package com.jspbook;

import javax.servlet.jsp.tagext.SimpleTagSupport;
import java.io.IOException;
import javax.servlet.jsp.*;

public class BodySimpleTag extends SimpleTagSupport {

  public void doTag() throws JspException, IOException {
    // null means 'send the output to JspContext.getOut()'
    jspBody.invoke(null);
  }
}
```

Before trying out the new tag, add an entry in `example.tld`.

```
<tag>
  <name>body</name>
  <tag-class>com.jspbook.BodySimpleTag</tag-class>
  <body-content>JSP</body-content>
</tag>
```

Compile the tag's code and reload the jspbook Web Application. The example is now ready to be used. Execute Listing 7-16 by browsing to `http://127.0.0.1/jspbook/BodySimpleTagTest.jsp`. The result is identical to Figure 7-5, but this time the content comes from the body of the custom tag. Try changing the body content and see how the changes appear in the result. Now, if you were authoring HTML, it may appear to be silly to even bother using a tag such as `BodySimpleTag.java`. Why not simply write the message in text? Do not miss the point of this example. A layer of abstraction has been placed between the content and the JSP. The custom tag determines what should be done with the JSP fragment and can optionally include, ignore, or do any other prelude or post-processing effects of the content.

It is easy to think of good examples of body-manipulating tags. Conditional or iteration tags, both of which were shown last chapter, are excellent examples. A simple tag does not have to evaluate its body. Based on an attribute value, the custom tag could either include or ignore the JSP fragment of body content:

```
public void doTag() {
    JspWriter out = jspContext.getout();
    if (attributeValue == true) {
        jspFragment.invoke(out, null);
    }
}
```

Even more helpful, the body content might be a template that is to be applied to an array of values.

```
public void doTag() {
    String[] values = {"one", "two", "three"};
    for(int i=0; i<values.length;i++) {
        HashMap map = new HashMap();
        map.put("value", values[i]);
        jspFragment.invoke(null);
    }
}
```

The point to understand is that simple tags can optionally evaluate their body any number of times. Another helpful feature is that the text produced by the body can be buffered to any `java.io.Writer` object. A `JspWriter` object works, but you could just as easily buffer the content for further manipulation using something such as a `java.io.CharArrayBuffer`.

.tag Files

The JSP specification strives to define helpful functionality for all levels of developers. Custom tags have been notoriously known as one of the most complex features of JSP. While true, custom tags are only difficult if you do not know Java. To a Java developer, you, being able to connect simple markup to pure Java classes should be bliss. JSP provides a front end for simple and rapid creation of content. `SimpleTag` classes powering the JSP provide a direct interface to the flexibility of the Java programming language.

JSP 2.0 introduces `.tag` files. These are a very powerful addition to the JSP specification. What `.tag` files do is remove the need for Java when authoring a custom tag. In many cases this is very helpful. One of the reasons for using JSP and Servlets together is to separate content and logic; and the way this is enforced is by not allowing code onto a JSP and not allowing `out.write()` calls in a Servlet. However, both classic and the new simple tags will typically contain many `out.write()` calls, so all that has happened is the code for producing output has moved from one Java component, the Servlet, to another, the tag! Tag files get around this problem by allowing developers to write tags in JSP. Just like in JSP this power should not be abused—Java code should not be put in tag files; otherwise, exactly the same problems arise as when code is placed in JSP. Instead, "tag" files should be written as a mixture of script and expressions. Tag files and simple tags written in Java are complementary technology. You should use simple tags when you need mostly logic with a little data and tag files when you need tags that act as templates with a large(-ish) amount of text and a small number of expressions.

What Is a .tag File?

A `.tag` file is a JSP source file with some additional directives and standard actions available for use. A complete `.tag` file functions identically to a `Simple Tag` and can be used as a custom tag on another JSP. For example, you can author `HelloSimpleTag.java` (as shown previously in Listing 7-4) by using a `.tag` file. The complete `.tag` file is shown in Listing 7-17.

Listing 7-17   hello.tag

```
Hello World!
```

Quite simple, and, yes it is a complete custom tag! To use this `.tag` file as a custom tag, the only thing required would be to drop the `.tag` file into the Web Application. Like Servlet classes, tags cannot simply be added to the root of the application; instead they live in a subdirectory of WEB-INF called tags or in a subdirectory of the `tags` directory. No TLD, no `tag lib` map; simply drop it in and go.

To use the tag inside a JSP the JSP has to reference the tag. Listing 7-18 shows an example of this. Save this file as `HelloSimpleTagFileTest.jsp` into the root of the jspbook Web Application.

Listing 7-17   HelloSimpleTagFileTest.jsp

```
<%@ taglib prefix="h" tagdir="/WEB-INF/tags" %>
<html>
  <head>
    <title>A test of HelloSimpleTag.java</title>
  </head>
  <body>
    <h:hello/>
  </body>
</html>
```

The preceding code is a simple JSP page that has the hello tag used in its body. Browse to `http://127.0.0.1/jspbook/HelloSimpleTagFileTest.jsp`. The resulting page replaces the hello tag with "Hello World!". Figure 7-3 shows a browser rendering of the results.

Notice that the tag is introduced to the page by the `tagdir` attribute of the `tag` directive. This was introduced in JSP 2.0 to add support for tag files. The `tagdir` directive tells the container where to find the tag file and it must start with `/WEB-INF/tags`.

All tags that are in the same subdirectory of the "tags" directory are defined to be part of the same tag library, so the following contains three tag libraries:

```
WEB-INF/tags/alice.tag
WEB-INF/tags/bob.tag
WEB-INF/tags/support/help.tag
WEB-INF/tags/date/time/date.tag
```

with `alice` and `bob` being in the "tags" tag library, `help` being in the `support` tag library, and `date` being in the `date-time` tag library. Using this information the container builds an implicit TLD for each tag library. The TLD contains the short name for the tag library and a `<tag>` entry for each tag in the directory. The short name is derived from the directory name. If the tag file is in the tags directory, then the short name is simply `tags`; otherwise, the short-name is the directory name with all "/" (or "\" on Windows) replaced with a "-", and with `WEB-INF/tags` removed. So in the above example `WEB-INF/tags/date/time` becomes date-time. Notice that short names are not unique. For example, a developer could also create a directory called WEB-INF/tags/date-time.

Tag files can also be packaged in a JAR file. In this case the .tag files should be placed in the JAR's META-INF/tags directory and a TLD created for them. Just like simple tags, this TLD file defines the tag. JSP 2.0 defines two new elements that are used to define .tag files, <tag-file> and <path>. The <tag-file> element is a child of <taglib> element and is used instead of <tag>. The tag-file element simply contains the name of the tag and its path; within a JAR file the path must start with META-INF/tags. For example:

```
<taglib>
    <!-- ... other elements elided for clarity -->
    <tag-file>
        <name>alice</name>
        <location>META-INF/tags/names</location>
    </tag-file>
</taglib>
```

This would define a tag called alice with the .tag file in the META-INF/tags/name directory of the JAR.

In the preceding examples tags in the WEB-INF/tags directory were not given a TLD file. Instead, it was left up to the container to generate an implicit TLD, whereas tags in a JAR file do have a TLD. However, it is possible to also supply .tag files with a TLD. If you do this, simply reference the TLD on the JSP as you would for a simple tag and then write the TLD using the tag-file element. Why would this be necessary? Two reasons: one is that a layer of indirection is often good—changing the tag location in a single TLD is easier than changing multiple tagdir locations in multiple JSPs. The other reason is that you might want to specify more or just different information than goes in the implicit TLD. However, as will be seen shortly, a better way of specifying a .tag file's TLD information is to use the tag directive introduced in JSP 2.0.

How a container implements support for a tag file is ambiguous. The JSP specification only outlines how the functionality must work, not how it is implemented. In some implementations, where performance is key, a .tag file will be compiled directly in to a SimpleTag class. In cases where performance is not as important, a .tag file might be directly interpreted. Other solutions for supporting a .tag file are also valid.

Coding a .tag File

Before coding a helpful `.tag` file there are some important directives and standard JSP actions to be aware of. The directives are used like the JSP directives in Chapter 3, but they are used to specify all of the information normally contained in a TLD file. The directives available for use in a `.tag` file are the `taglib`, `include`, `tag`, `attribute`, and `variable`. The `taglib` and `include` directives are identical to the JSP directives previously explained. The other directives are only available for use in .tag files and are covered in the upcoming sections. Note that the `.tag` file directives do mimic the elements of a TLD; in most cases the directives are completely analogous to elements you can also define in a TLD.

There are two new standard actions available for use with a `.tag` file: the `doBody` and `invoke` actions. These are covered in a following section.

`<%@ tag %>`

The `tag` directive is to a `.tag` file what the page directive is to a JSP. A `tag` directive is completely optional and can be used to define information about a custom tag. Most of the supplied information is identical to the meta-information supplied by a TLD used with a `SimpleTag` class. The `tag` directive may appear many times in the same `.tag` file, but a translation error arises if any two uses of the `tag` directive define values for the same attribute.

The attributes for the `tag` directive are as follows:

- **display-name:** The `display-name` attribute defines a short name that is intended to be displayed by tools. If no value is specified, then the attribute defaults to the value of the `name` attribute.

- **body-content:** The `body-content` attribute provides information on the content of the body of the tag. Valid values for this attribute are `empty`, `tagdependent`, or `scriptless`. A translation error will result if JSP or any other value is used. The default value is `scriptless`.

- **dynamic-attributes:** The `dynamic-attributes` attribute indicates whether this tag supports additional attributes with dynamic names. If the value is `true`, the generated tag handler must implement the `javax.servlet.jsp.tagext.DynamicAttributes` interface. The possible values for this attribute are `true` and `false`. The default value is `false`. If a `.tag` file specifies this attribute, then the container creates a page scope variable for each dynamic attribute passed in.

- **small-icon:** The `small-icon` attribute defines a relative path, from the tag source file, of an image file containing a small icon that can be used by tools. By default it is assumed no small icon is to be used for the tag.

- **large-icon:** The `large-icon` attribute defines a relative path, from the tag source file, of an image file containing a large icon that can be used by tools. By default it is assumed no large icon is to be used for the tag.

- **description:** The `description` attribute defines an arbitrary string that describes this tag. The default value is to have no description.

- **example:** The `example` attribute defines an arbitrary string that represents an informal description of an example use of this action. The default is to assume no example is available.

- **pageEncoding:** The `pageEncoding` attribute functions identically to the `pageEncoding` attribute in the JSP `page` directive.

- **language:** The `language` attribute functions identically to the `language` attribute of the JSP `page` directive.

- **import:** The `import` attribute functions identically to the `import` attribute of the JSP `page` directive.

- **isELIgnored:** The `isELIgnored` attribute functions same as the `isELIgnored` attribute of the JSP `page` directive. Unlike the `page` directive, there is no `web.xml` configuration element for the `isELIgnored tag` directive attribute.

Use of the `tag` directive is straightforward. In most cases you can completely skip the directive and have everything work perfectly fine—for instance, `hello.tag`, Listing 7-17. In a TLD the only information mandated for a custom tag is a unique action name for the tag and the location of the tag's code. With a `.tag` file the developer specifys neither of these, as they can be implied by the container.

In more complex or robust uses of a `.tag` file it may be necessary to provide additional information about the custom tag. In these cases the appropriate attributes can be used as required.

<%@ attribute %>

The `attribute` directive is analogous to the `attribute` element in a TLD file. Multiple `attribute` directives can be used in the same `.tag` file. The `attribute` directive has the following attributes:

- **name:** The `name` attribute defines a unique name of the attribute being declared. A translation error results if more than one `attribute` directive used in the same `.tag` file has identical values for the `name` attribute. The `name` attribute is required to be defined in any occurrence of the `attribute` directive.

- **required:** The `required` attribute is an optional attribute that determines if the attribute being described is required (`true`) or optional (`false`). By default the value `false` is assumed.

- **fragment:** The `fragment` attribute is an optional attribute that determines if the attribute is a fragment to be evaluated by the tag handler. If the value `true` is specified, the `type` attribute is fixed at `javax.servlet.jsp.tagext.JspFragment` and a translation error will result if the `type` attribute is specified. Additionally, if this attribute is `true`, the `rtexprvalue` attribute is fixed at `true` and a translation error will result if the `rtexprvalue` attribute is specified. If the value of the `fragment` attribute is `false`, then the attribute's value is assumed to be a "normal" value evaluated by the JSP container. The default value is `false`.

- **rtexprvalue:** The `rtexprvalue` is an optional attribute that determines if the attribute's value may be dynamically calculated at runtime via an expression. The default value is `false`.

- **type:** The `type` attribute is an optional attribute that determines the runtime type of the attribute's value. By default the value is assumed to be of type `java.lang.String`.

- **description:** The `description` attribute is an option attribute that can be used to provide a description of the attribute.

Use of the `attribute` directive is analogous to the corresponding entries in a TLD. The only difference is that the values are set via the `attribute` directive. You should be easily able to convert the previous date-formatting simple tag to a `.tag` file. Instead of rehashing that example, let's introduce one of the most helpful features of custom tags: abstracting DHTML. This book constantly hints at a good Server, JSP, and Java design pattern MVC, which is fully covered in a later chapter. The design effectively stops Java- and HTML-savvy developers from haphazardly creating unmaintainable pages with HTML and various snippets of Java code; however, the design pattern does nothing to stop an overly ambitious HTML developer from abusing DHTML—for example, creating equally as confusing HTML pages using a combination of HTML, JavaScript, and Cascading Style Sheets. The solution: abstract DHTML via custom tags.

By using custom tags, .tag files in particular, you can easily abstract DHTML widgets to a few simple tags. Take, for example, the popular, simple DHTML rollover effect. When the mouse moves over an image, the image changes; usually a picture of a button changes to a pressed button. Likewise, when the mouse leaves the picture the image changes back to the original. This effect is nothing more than a small chunk of JavaScript. Listing 7-18 provides an example HTML page with the script.

Listing 7-18 rollover.html

```
<html>
The 'off' image:<img src="button_off.gif"><br>
The 'on' image:<img src="button_on.gif"><br>
The rollover image:<br>
<a href="index.htm" onmouseover="button.src='button_on.gif';"
onmouseout="button.src='button_off.gif';">
<img name="button" src="button_off.gif" border=0></a>
</html>
```

Try out the effect by saving the HTML page in the base directory of the jspbook Web Application. Next, create two images for the rollover; for convenience you can download button_on.gif and button_off.gif from http://www.jspbook.com/images. Save both of these images in the base directory of the jspbook Web Application. Browse to http://127.0.0.1/jspbook/rollover.html to see the effect. Figure 7-7 provides an example.

Figure 7-7 DHTML Rollover Image Effect (Showing the "on" Button)

Note the browser rendering is not completely accurate since this is a dynamic effect. Shown is one state of the button, but as you move the mouse on and off, the image changes from the on image to the off image.

The script works by handling DHTML mouse events. Initially, an image is displayed according to the HTML `img` tag.

```
<img name="button" src="button_off.gif" border=0></a>
```

Any image will do, but for the desired effect it is helpful to use a picture that you have a slightly changed version of—for example, a button clicked on for image one and the same button clicked off for image two.

Next the DHTML mouse events are used to execute some JavaScript whenever the mouse enters or leaves the image.

```
<a href="index.html"
onmouseover="button.src='button_on.gif';"
onmouseout="button.src='button_off.gif';">
```

When the mouse enters the image, the JavaScript for onmouseover is executed and the image is changed from `button_off.gif` to `button_on.gif`. When the mouse leaves the image, the JavaScript for onmouseover is executed and the image is changed from `button_on.gif` to `button_off.gif`. Thus, the overall effect is a changing, or rollover, image.

Understanding the DHTML is not important compared to understanding why it is bad to let overly ambitious HTML developers use it. Embedding an image in HTML requires one tag.

```
<img src="button.gif">
```

Making a rollover version of the image requires several tags.

```
<a href="index.htm" onmouseover="button.src='button_on.gif';"
onmouseout="button.src='button_off.gif';">
<img name="button" src="button_off.gif" border=0></a>
```

Which set of code is more intuitive? Which set will be less confusing to a developer after he or she is hired to manage existing HTML code? The answer is obviously the first choice: the single `img` tag; however, that choice doesn't do the cool rollover effect. The obvious solution is to take advantage of JSP, abstract the HTML image tag altogether and make a `.tag` file that is easy to use but creates DHTML rollover images. Listing 7-19 is an example.

Listing 7-19 rollover.tag

```
<%@ attribute name="link" required="true" %>
```

```
<%@ attribute name="image" required="true" %>
<a href="${link}" onmouseover="${image}.src='${image}_on.gif';"
onmouseout="${image}.src='${image}_off.gif';">
<img name="${image}" src="${image}_off.gif" border="0"></a>
```

Save the preceding code as `rollover.tag` in the `/WEB-INF/tags` directory of the jspbook Web Application. The code creates a custom tag, rollover, that requires two attributes, `link` and `image`. The `link` attribute provides the link if the image is clicked on, and the `image` attribute provides the base name of the rollover images (assumed to be a GIF in this case).

Try out the rollover tag by using it in a JSP. Save Listing 7-20 as `rollover.jsp` in the base directory of the jspbook Web Application.

Listing 7-20   rollover.jsp

```
<%@ taglib prefix="x" tagdir="/WEB-INF/tags"%>
<html>
The 'off' image:<img src="button_off.gif"><br>
The 'on' image:<img src="button_on.gif"><br>
The rollover image:<br>
<x:rollover image="button" link="index.html"/>
</html>
```

Test out the page by browsing to `http://127.0.0.1/jspbook/rollover.jsp`. The results are the same as with the previous HTML example.

Behold the power of custom tags! A JSP developer can abstract anything he or she wants behind a simple tag or, better put, minimize the code required to accomplish a task. Instead of hand-coding something such as DHTML widgets repeatedly for a page, abstract the DHTML with a simple tag. Tag files in particular are good for abstracting DHTML since it is as easy to author the tag as it is to author the DHTML.

The design pattern chapter expands upon the idea of abstracting DHTML via custom tags.

<%@ variable %>

The `variable` directive is analogous to the `variable` element in a TLD. Multiple `variable` directives may be used in the same `.tag` file.

The variable directive has the following attributes:

- **name-given:** The `name-given` attribute defines a scripting variable to be defined in the page invoking this tag. A fatal translation error will also occur if two `variable` directives have the same `name-given`.

- **variable-class:** The `variable-class` attribute is optional and used to define the type of the variable. The default value is `java.lang.String`.
- **scope:** The `scope` attribute optionally defines the scope of the scripting variable defined. Valid values for this attribute are `AT_BEGIN`, `AT_END`, or `NESTED`. The default value is `NESTED`.
- **declare:** The `declare` attribute optionally declares whether the variable is declared or not. The default value is `true`.
- **description:** The `description` attribute can be used to provide an optional description of the variable. By default it is assumed no description is present.

The `variable` directive is helpful for use in all cases where scripting variables are helpful with simple tags. The JSTL is designed around being able to easily take advantage of scoped variables. Instead of requiring Java, it is possible to program solely using custom tags, which is a design pattern promoted by the JSTL (and some developers that prefer using JSP instead of Servlets), but a design pattern that is discouraged by this book.

Previously, scripting variables had been introduced solely by scriptlets and declarations; however, custom tags can also create scripting variables. A scripting variable created by a custom tag is accessible as if it was declared by a scriptlet, meaning it can be used elsewhere on the JSP dependent on how the variable was declared. By default the variable will only exist in the body of the tag (`NESTED` scope), but the scope can be set to `AT_BEGIN` or `AT_END` to have the variable be accessible to the page starting at the beginning custom tag or ending custom tag, respectively.

In general, tag-declared scripting variables are not very helpful on their own. Scripting variables are helpful when combined with other custom tags designed to use the scripting variables. The topic of scripting variables will not be discussed at length; however, for completeness here is an example of the `variable` directive.

You'll recall the code for `PageCounter.jsp` (Listing 3-5 in Chapter 3), the JSP that used a declaration, an expression, and a scriptlet to count the number of times a JSP had been requested for view. The code works, although the JSP has a notable amount of script and does not abstract the logic used to count page views. A superior form of the page can be created by using a simple `.tag` file that sets a scripting variable, as shown in Listing 7-21.

Listing 7-21 PageCounter2.jsp

```
<%@ taglib prefix="x" tagdir="/WEB-INF/tags" %>
<x:count/>
<html>
<head>
<title>PageCounter.jsp</title>
</head>
<body>
This page has been visited <%= pageCount %> times.
</body>
</html>
```

Save the preceding code as `PageCounter2.jsp` in the root directory of the jspbook Web Application. The code is an enhanced version of `PageCounter.jsp`, although instead of using a directive the page relies on a custom tag to keep track of page visits. The code for the custom tag is a `.tag` file that keeps count and sets a scoped variable, `pageCount`, for the JSP to use, as illustrated in Listing 7-22.

Listing 7-22 count.tag

```
<%@ variable name-given="pageCount"
              variable-class="java.lang.Integer"
              scope="AT_BEGIN"%>
<%
  Integer pageCount =
    (Integer)application.getAttribute("pageCount");
  if (pageCount == null) {
    application.setAttribute("pageCount", new Integer(1));
  }
  else {
    pageCount = new Integer(1+pageCount.intValue());
    application.setAttribute("pageCount", pageCount);
  }
%>
```

Save the code as count.tag in the `/WEB-INF/tags` directory of the jspbook Web Application. The `.tag` file uses the `variable` directive to declare a scripting variable named `pageCount` of type `java.lang.Integer`. This variable is what is later used by the JSP. The code after the `variable` directive sets and updates a count variable stashed in application scope. The result of using `count.tag` and `PageCounter2.jsp` is that we now have a simplified JSP and an abstract method of keeping page count. Most anyone, including non-Java developers, can use the count tag, and should the logic powering the counting mechanism be changed, only the code of `count.tag` needs to be updated. All JSP using the `count.tag` will automatically reflect the update.

Test out the code by browsing to `http://127.0.0.1/jspbook/Page Counter2.jsp`. A page will appear and function similar to `PageCounter1.jsp`, Figure 3-5.

<jsp:doBody/>

The `doBody` action is a standard JSP action that is only available for use in `.tag` files. Using the action elsewhere raises an exception. The `doBody` action is used by a `.tag` file to execute the body content defined for the `.tag` file. For example, consider the JSP in Listing 7-23, which uses a custom tag and explicitly defines the body for it:

Listing 7-23   doBodyExample.jsp

```
<%@ taglib prefix="x" tagdir="/WEB-INF/tags" %>
<x:aTag>
  <jsp:body>
    Some body content, ${blah}.
  </jsp:body>
</x:aTag>
```

Assume Listing 7-24 is the custom tag's code.

Listing 7-24   aTag.tag

```
Invoke the body:
<jsp:doBody/>
```

The result of executing `doBodyExample.jsp` is shown in Listing 7-25.

Listing 7-25   Text Generated by doBodyExample.jsp

```
Invoke the body:
    Some body content, .
```

Use of the `doBody` action should be clear; it evaluates the body content of the tag. The `doBody` action can be skipped, used, or used multiple times depending on what the `.tag` file is designed to do.

Cooperating Tags

Simple tags collaborate with children tags by being passed the `JspFragment` object that represents the tag's body. However, simple tags can also collaborate with parent tags by using the `getParent()` method. The `getParent()` method returns an `Object` that represents the tag handler class, which wraps the current tag (null if no parent tags exist). The object can appropriately be typecast into either an instance of `Tag` or `SimpleTag` and be further manipulated.

Classic JSP Tag Handlers

Before JSP 2.0, custom tags were more complex to code and deploy. As mentioned previously in this chapter, the new `SimpleTag` interface can be used as a complete replacement for the older custom tag mechanism. It is recommended you use the `SimpleTag` interface as it is easier to use and generally much more intuitive. The following discussion on classic JSP custom tags (i.e., tags that implement the `Tag` interface) is solely for completeness. It can be skipped but is helpful to read because currently the majority of existing custom tags are built based on them.

A *tag handler* is a Java class that comprises the logic of a custom tag. There are three distinct kinds of tags: "basic" tags, "iteration" tags, and "body" tags. In the tag development model each of these tag types is represented by a Java interface: `javax.servlet.jsp.Tag`, `javax.servlet.jsp.IterationTag`, and `javax.servlet.jsp.BodyTag`, respectively. Each of these tag types has a well-defined set of methods and life cycle that will be fully covered by this chapter.

Basic Tags

A *basic tag* is a tag that implements the `Tag` interface. Basic tags are used to create a tag that never needs to process its body or iterate over its body content. Simple tags are the superclass of all the other custom tag interfaces and are the easiest tags to write and understand.

Tag Life Cycle

The `Tag` interface defines six methods all custom tags must implement. Only three of the methods are related to the tag's life cycle. The methods are `doStartTag()`, `doEndTag()`, and `release()`. The `doStartTag()` method is called when the JSP is being evaluated and the starting element of the custom tag is found. The `doEndTag()` method is the complement and is invoked when the ending element of the custom tag is encountered. Once the `doEndTag()` is finished, the `release()` method is invoked to clean up any resources the tag might have initialized. Figure 7-8 shows a graphical representation of this life cycle.

The life cycle is self-explanatory. A custom tag is encountered and the `doStartTag()` method is invoked. Once the end of the tag is encountered, the

javax.servlet.jsp.tagext.Tag

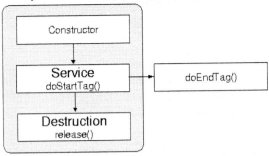

Figure 7-8 Tag Life Cycle

`doEndTag()` method is invoked and the tag is finished. If the tag is an empty element—for example, `<t:someTag/>`, the `doStartTag()` and `doEndTag()`—methods are still invoked in succession. Usually for multiple instances of the custom tag a separate tag handler instance is loaded and used, but a container is free to re-use a tag instance if the set of attributes passed to both tag elements matches. The `release()` method is called after the tag instance is used for the final time.

Imagine the following fictitious JSP that uses the `foo` tag in two different places (Figure 7-9). Each use would typically have a separate instance of the tag handler class corresponding to the `foo` tag. Labeled are the conceptual points where the `doStartTag()` and `doEndTag()` methods are invoked.

Simple tags may have content in between the starting and ending tags, as shown in Figure 7-9, but the tag never gets to process its body content. This

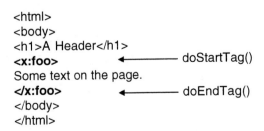

Figure 7-9 JSP Example of the Tag Life Cycle Invocation

means anything that appears as the body of a simple tag cannot be processed by the tag directly, but the contents of the tag may still be processed by the container and any resulting output written to the page's output stream.

Tag Interface

Three of the methods of the `Tag` interface have been briefly mentioned: `doStart Tag()`, `doEndTag()` and `release()`. However, these methods were not fully explained and there are three additional methods included in the `Tag` interface: `getParent()`, `setPageContext()`, and `setParent()`. All six of these methods are important to understand and are summarized as follows.

int doStartTag()

The `doStartTag()` method is invoked when the JSP encounters the starting of the custom tag. This method can be used to either initialize resources needed by the other methods of the tag, or it can perform some logic and choose to either skip evaluation of the tag's body content or skip evaluation of the rest of a JSP. The action a JSP takes after calling the `doStartTag()` method is based on the return value of the method. There are two valid values the `doStartTag()` method can return: `SKIP_BODY` and `EVAL_BODY_INCLUDE`. Both of these values are `final static int` primitives defined by the `Tag` interface. Should the `doStartTag()` method return the `SKIP_BODY` method, the JSP container will skip evaluation of the tag's body content. If the `doStartTag()` method returns `EVAL_BODY_INCLUDE`, the JSP container will evaluate the contents of the tag's body into the current JSP output buffer.

int doEndTag()

The `doEndTag()` method is invoked when the JSP encounters the closing element of a custom tag. This method can be used to perform any logic that needs to be done after the evaluation of the tag's body content but before the tag instance is freed for possible re-use. After calling the `doEndTag()` method, evaluation of the JSP continues as specified by the return value of the method. There are two valid return values for the `doEndTag()` method: `SKIP_PAGE` and `EVAL_PAGE`. Both of these values are `final static int` primitives defined by the `Tag` interface. Should the `doEndTag()` method return the `SKIP_PAGE` value, the current JSP will stop evaluating the current page. If the `doEndTag()` method returns `EVAL_PAGE`, the current JSP will continue to be processed.

void release()

The `release()` method is the final method invoked on a custom tag. The `release()` method is called when the custom tag is no longer going to be used by the JSP container and should release its state. The `release()` method is guaranteed to be invoked at least once before the tag is made available for garbage collection, but multiple `doStartTag()` and `doEndTag()` methods calls may occur before the `release()` method is ever called.

Tag getParent()

The `getParent()` method allows a custom tag to access the closest encapsulating parent custom tag. The tag is returned as the superclass `Tag` but can be typecast accordingly.

void setParent(Tag t)

The `setParent()` method is invoked by the JSP container during runtime to set the correct parent `Tag` object of a particular custom tag. If there is no encapsulating custom tag, `null` is set.

void setPageContext(PageContext p)

The `setPageContext()` method sets the appropriate `PageContext` object for a JSP. The `setPageContext()` method is invoked by the JSP container prior to calling the `doStartTag()` method.

Coding a BasicTag

For most practical purposes the `doStartTag()` and `doEndTag()` methods are all that a developer cares about when implementing a simple tag. The `setPage Context()` and `setParent()` methods are handled by the container, and the `getParent()` and `release()` methods are needed in only a few circumstances.

A simple tag can be coded in a few different ways; however, a developer is rarely required to implement the `Tag` interface from scratch. The JSP API includes the `javax.servlet.jsp.TagSupport` class, which is an adapter class that provides a default implementation of a simple tag. The easiest and most practical method of coding a simple tag is to extend `TagSupport` and override any method that needs customization.

Take, for example, the `foo` tag that has been used in all of this chapter's examples. Listing 7-26 is a simple example of extending the `TagSupport` class to create this previously fictitious tag.

Listing 7-26 FooTag.java

```
package com.jspbook;

import com.jspbook.*;
import javax.servlet.jsp.tagext.*;
```

```java
import javax.servlet.jsp.*;
import java.io.*;

public class FooTag extends TagSupport {

  public int doStartTag() throws JspException {
    JspWriter out = pageContext.getOut();
    try {
      out.println("foo");
    }
    catch (IOException e) {
      throw new JspException(e.getMessage());
    }

    return SKIP_BODY;
  }
}
```

Note the above tag is intended solely for illustration purposes. Listing 7-26 demonstrates a few of the subtle but important points of coding a simple tag. The first thing to notice is the declaration of the custom tag. Instead of implementing all the Tag interface methods by hand, the TagSupport class was extended.

```java
public class FooTag extends TagSupport {
```

By extending TagSupport the complete Tag interface is inherited and the FooTag is a valid tag handler.

Another important part of FooTag.java to notice is that only the method needing customization is actually implemented. Out of the six required methods in the Tag interface only the doStartTag() method is overridden. The convenience of only needing to selectively customize reduces the overall amount of code and makes it easier to understand what the tag handler is doing.

```java
public int doStartTag() throws JspException {
    JspWriter out = pageContext.getOut();
    try {
      out.println("foo");
    }
    catch (IOException e) {
      throw new JspException(e.getMessage());
    }

    return SKIP_BODY;
}
```

Inside the tag handler not much is going on. The `foo` tag is using the `PageContext` object to obtain access to the output stream and print "foo". At the end of the `doStartTag()` method, the `SKIP_BODY` value is returned, indicating that the `doEndTag()` method should not be invoked.

Tag Handler Exception Handling

Tag handlers deal with exceptions differently than JSP. Inside a JSP all of the scripting elements have the benefit of being surrounded by an implicit try-catch block. This often lulls a JSP developer into forgetting Java code does throw exceptions and that they must be handled. A tag handler does not have an implicit try-catch block. All exceptions must be handled explicitly during execution of the tag handler's methods.

`FooTag.java`, Listing 7-26, is a good example of this difference. The `doStartTag()` method is defined to throw a `JspException`, but all other forms of exceptions must be explicitly handled. In the case of a simple `out.println()` call, the possible `java.io.IOException` needs to be caught. The code does this by surrounding everything in a try-catch block and passing any exception out as a `JspException`. The error handling mechanism of the specific JSP is then assumed to handle the problem.

Keep in mind the issue of exception handling when coding tag handlers. This is especially an issue when porting over scripting elements into tag handler code. Often a straight conversion simply does not work because the scripting element relied on the implicit JSP try-catch statement.

TagSupport

The `TagSupport` class is more than a simple implementation of the `Tag` interface. The `TagSupport` object is a full implementation of both the `Tag` and `IterationTag` interfaces along with some other miscellaneous helpful methods. Not all of the methods are worth mentioning right now, but there is one important one to be aware of:

```
static Tag findAncestorWithClass(Tag from, java.lang.Class klass)
```

The `findAncestorWithClass()` method is a superior form of the `getParent()` method provided by the `Tag` interface. If a custom tag relies on cooperating with another custom tag, it needs to be able to easily find the other tag. Calling the `getParent()` method does return the nearest neighboring custom tag, but it might not be the one the tag is expecting to cooperate with. In lieu of always needing to loop through and verify parent class types, the `findAncestorWithClass()` method can be used.

The `TagSupport` helper class is further covered later in the chapter with iteration tags.

Using a Tag Handler and TLD with JSP

So far we have discussed how to build all of the components required for a simple tag but have yet to actually put everything together. It is a helpful exercise to walk through this process and demonstrate a working example of a custom tag built from scratch. So far the only tag we have built in this chapter is the rather unhelpful `foo` tag. If you recall, this tag already has an appropriate TLD entry and is ready to be used. To complement this tag, let us build another slightly more helpful basic tag.

The new tag we are going to build is the `date` tag. The `date` tag is another basic tag handler, and it will be designed to give the current date and time of the server the JSP was executed from. Save Listing 7-27 as `DateTag.java`.

Listing 7-27 DateTag.java

```
package com.jspbook;

import com.jspbook.*;
import javax.servlet.jsp.tagext.*;
import javax.servlet.jsp.*;
import java.util.*;
import java.io.*;

public class DateTag extends TagSupport {

  public int doStartTag() throws JspException {
    JspWriter out = pageContext.getOut();
    try {
      Date date = new Date();
      out.println(date.toString());
    }
    catch (IOException e) {
      throw new JspException(e.getMessage());
    }

    return SKIP_BODY;
  }
}
```

The preceding code greatly resembles `FooTag.java`. It is a simple tag handler that extends `TagSupport` and overrides the `doStartTag()` method. The only difference between the two tags is that `DateTag.java` creates a new `java.util.Date` object and serializes it for a user to see.

The primary reason for creating the `date` tag was so a new tag would need to be added to the example TLD file. This is something that needs to be done each time a tag is added to a tag library so it is helpful to be familiar with the process. You'll recall that the `example.tld` file was previously created and saved in the `/WEB-INF` directory of the jspbook Web Application. Edit this file to now include an entry for the newly created `date` tag as shown in Listing 7-28.

Listing 7-28 DateTag.java Addition to examples.tld

```
<tag>
  <name>date</name>
  <tag-class>com.jspbook.DateTag</tag-class>
  <body-content>empty</body-content>
</tag>
```

Make sure the addition appears as a child of the `taglib` element and either immediately before or after an instance of a `tag` element. Compile both the `FooTag.java` and `DateTag.java` files and reload the jspbook Web Application to reflect the changes.

With both tag handler codes complete and the TLD up to date, the tag library is ready for use in a JSP. Save Listing 7-29 as `TagLibraryExample.jsp` in the root directory of the jspbook Web Application.

Listing 7-29 TagLibraryExample.jsp

```
<%@ taglib prefix="x" uri="http://www.jspbook.com/example" %>
<html>
  <head>
    <title>A Custom Tag Example</title>
  </head>
  <body>
    The date/time is <x:date/>, <x:foo/>!
  </body>
</html>
```

Browse to `http://www.jspbook.com/TagLibraryExample.jsp` to see the results of the custom tags. Figure 7-10 shows the output rendered by a Web browser. Both the `date` and `foo` tags are appropriately executed and appear to the client as some text in an HTML page.

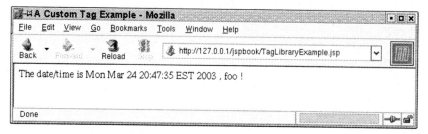

Figure 7-10 Browser Rendering of TagLibraryExample.jsp

The page displayed in Figure 7-10 is the conclusion of this simple walk-though implementation of custom tags. You now know how to create a simple tag, define it in a TLD, and create a JSP that uses the tag. This is a good start to understanding custom tags, but we have yet to see many of the features that make custom tags powerful.

Re-Using Tags

An important and commonly misunderstood point is that a container has the option to cache a tag instance instead of creating a new tag each time a JSP uses a custom tag. This allows containers to create one instance of a tag and re-use it for efficiency reasons when needed. However, there are limitations on the tags that can be re-used. When a tag is first used, it will be initialized by the container. All the properties set in the tag element are passed to the tag; if the tag has optional properties and those properties are not defined on the page, the tag will use default values for those elements. Re-using a tag implies that the container will not need to re-initialize the tag; this has two consequences. First, a tag can only be re-used if it has exactly the same set of attributes as a previous usage. Second, it is vital that a tag instance re-initialize any properties whose values have changed to the state they were in just before `doStartTag()` method was called. In many cases this second criterion is problematic because a container relies on the tag resetting itself when the `doEndTag()` method is invoked. When coding a custom tag that initializes class-wide variables, be sure these variables are reset each time the `doEndTag()` method is invoked.

A simple example of this is `FormattedDateTag.java`, Listing 7-30. `FormattedDateTag.java` declares the class-wide variable `format`. After running through the tag once, the variable might be altered. To prevent this alteration from lingering around if the tag is cached, the `doStartTag()` method should be changed to reset `format` to `null`. The problem was purposely overlooked in previous examples to keep things simple and because it is not really a severe problem. However, to always ensure `FormattedDateTag.java` performs as expected, the following addition needs to be made to the code.

Listing 7-30 FormattedDateTag.java Fixed for Consistency

```java
package com.jspbook;

import javax.servlet.jsp.tagext.*;
import javax.servlet.jsp.*;
import java.util.*;
import java.text.*;
import java.io.*;

public class FormattedDateTag extends TagSupport {
  private String format;

  public void setFormat(String format) {
    this.format = format;
  }

  public int doStartTag() throws JspException {
    JspWriter out = pageContext.getOut();
    try {
      if (format != null) {
        SimpleDateFormat sdf =
          new SimpleDateFormat(format);
        out.println(sdf.format(new Date()));
      }
      else {
        out.println(new Date().toString());
      }
    }
    catch (IOException e) {
      throw new JspException(e.getMessage());
    }
    finally {
      format = null;
    }

    return SKIP_BODY;
  }
}
```

TryCatchFinally Interface

A tag's life cycle is fully defined by the JSP specification. As stated previously, the doStartTag() method is invoked after the tag is fully initialized; between the doStartTag() and doEndTag() method calls, the container assumes that the tag is holding state that must be preserved. After the doEndTag() method, the tag is available for re-use. The release() method is called before the tag is made available for garbage collection. After calling the release() method, the container assumes that the tag has given up all resources including properties, parent references, and so on.

However, it is possible that the doEndTag() method is never called. This happens if the tag throws an exception before the doEndTag() would normally be called. If the tag creates or manages resources and would normally give up those resources in its doEndTag() method, the tag now has a problem! How does the tag release those resources? To guarantee that resources are released even in the case of failure, the tag should implement the TryCatchFinally interface. TryCatchFinally is an interface representation of the try-catch-finally block shown in Chapter 4 and has two methods: doCatch() and doFinally(). These two methods provide identical functionality to the catch and finally clauses available for try statements. An easy way to understand the concept is to assume a custom tag implementing the TryCatchFinally interface always gets translated to a Servlet with the equivalent of the following code:

```
Tag tag = getTagFromSomewhere();
// initialize tag
// ...
// use tag
try {
   tag.doStartTag();
   ..
   tag.doEndTag();
}
catch (Throwable t)
{
   // catch exception
   tag.doCatch(t);
}
finally
{
```

```
    // release usage specific resources
    tag.doFinally();
}

tag.release(); // release long-term resources
```

The preceding code illustrates how a container can use the `TryCatchFinally` interface to provide the equivalent of a try-catch-finally block for a custom tag. Understanding this concept is critical as it is the only way to mimic a try-catch-finally statement that spans across life cycle methods of a custom tag based on the `Tag` interface. It is the responsibility of the tag author to correctly declare and implement the `TryCatchFinally` interface methods in a custom tag.

Cooperating Tags

Among the cardinal rules of programming are keeping your methods short and breaking complex code into reusable components. Supertags should never be written that try to do everything. Each tag should be a self-contained unit that does a single part of a goal. This often means that tags need to cooperate with other tags if they are to work well.

Tags typically cooperate by nesting one tag inside another.

```
<%@taglib prefix="mt" uri="/WEB-INF/mytags.tld" %>
<mt:outerTag>
   <mt:innerTag/>
</mt:outerTag>
```

To cooperate, the `innerTag` needs to get a reference to the `outerTag`. As we saw earlier, when tags are initialized, the container calls the tag's `setParent()` method, passing a reference to the Java object that is the parent. For the outer tag shown in the previous example, the parent would be passed as `null`. However, the inner tag shown previously would be passed a reference to the Java class that implements the `outerTag` tag. The reference passed is of type `Tag`. The inner tag can then call methods on or get data from the parent. To do this, the inner tag would simply cast the reference to the correct type, as shown in Listing 7-31.

Listing 7-31 Fictitious Cooperating Tag Handler

```
public class InnerTag extends TagSupport {
   OuterTag outerTag = null;

   public int doStartTag() throws JspException {
      outerTag = (OuterTag)parent;
```

```
    // invoke any needed methods
    outerTag.fooMethod();
    // do other work here
  }
}
```

Notice that while the inner tag can get a reference to its parent, there is no standard way for the references to be passed the other way. A parent does not get a reference to its children.

In Listing 7-31 the inner tag's `doStartTag()` method defines a variable of type `OuterTag` that is assumed to be the tag handler class of the `outerTag` tag. To use a reference to the outer tag, the inner tag simply casts the parent data member to be an `OuterTag`. But where does the tag get the parent data member from? It's not defined in the tag. Remember that the tag extends `TagSupport` and that `TagSupport` implements `Tag`, which means that `TagSupport` provides an implementation of the `setParent()` method. This implementation simply defines a variable

```
Tag parent;
```

and saves the reference passed to it, the setParent call:

```
public void setParent(Tag t) {
   parent = t;
}
```

While in simple cases Listing 7-31 works perfectly fine, there is a flaw with the code. The child is blindly casting the parent value to the type it should be if one were to assume `innerTag` was always nested directly one level deep from a `outerTag`. But suppose that the tag is nested not one but several levels deep. The following is a perfectly valid JSP:

```
<%@taglib prefix="mt" uri="/WEB-INF/mytags.tld" %>
<%@taglib prefix="yt" uri="/WEB-INF/yourtags.tld" %>
<mt:outerTag>
  <yt:someOtherInnerTag>
    <mt:innerTag/>
  </yt:someOtherInnerTag>
</mt:outerTag>
```

Note that the tag is not only one extra level detached from its parent; its parent is also from a different tag library. Now the inner tag may not know anything about its parent. Not only that, for the inner tag to work it has to get a reference to the `outerTag`, not the random tag stuck in between.

Using only the `Tag` interface to solve this problem is reasonably difficult and requires looping through parent tags and checking each tag handler's type. An alternative is the convenience `findAncestorWithClass()` method provided by `TagSupport`. Recall `TagSupport` provides the following method:

```
static Tag findAncestorWithClass(Tag from, java.lang.Class klass)
```

This method finds a reference to the tag implemented by a given Java class as specified by the `klass` parameter. The container maintains a stack of tags linked by their parent values. Starting at the `from` parameter, this method walks that stack looking for an instance of the right `Class`. Using what was just explained Listing 7-31 would be better coded as shown by Listing 7-32.

Listing 7-32   Better Implementation of Cooperating Tags

```
public class InnerTag extends TagSupport {
  OuterTag outerTag = null;

  public int doStartTag() throws JspException {
    outerTag = (OuterTag)findAncestorWithClass(this,
OuterTag.class);
    if(outerTag != null) {
      // invoke needed methods
      outerTag.callParentMethod();
      // do other work here
    }
  }
}
```

This code works independent of tags nested arbitrarily deep and cases where tags from different tag libraries are mixed.

Mixing New Tags with Classic Tags

Cooperation among classic tags is reasonably simple as all classic tags implement the `Tag` interface. This means that `getParent`, `setParent`, and `findAncestorWith` `Class` can all rely on the fact that the tags they are dealing with are all instances of `javax.servlet.jsp.tagext.Tag`. Cooperation among simple tags is also easy; all simple tags implement the same interface, `javax.servlet.jsp.tagext.SimpleTag`. Problems arise when simple tags and classic tags are mixed. Imagine this scenario:

```
<mt:simpleTag>
    <mt:classicTag/>
```

</mt:simpleTag>

Here, there is a problem. When the container calls the `classicTag`'s `setParent`, it wants to pass a reference to a tag, but the simple tag does not implement `Tag`. To get around this issue, the container instead creates an instance of a `Tag Adapter`. The `TagAdapter` simply wraps a simple tag and exposes it as if it were a tag. The nested `classicTag` could now be coded like this:

```
public class InnerTag extends TagSupport {
    OuterTag outerTag = null;

    public int doStartTag() throws JspException {
        outerTag = (OuterTag)parent.getAdaptee();
        // invoke any needed methods
        outerTag.fooMethod();
        // do other work here
    }
}
```

Notice that the tag now has to call `getAdaptee()`; this method gets a reference to the tag that the adapter is wrapping.

This problem does not arise if the tags were nested like this:

```
<mt:classicTag>
    <mt:simpleTag/>
```

</mt:classicTag>

The simple tag's `setParent()` method takes a reference to a `JspTag` interface. This is a new interface introduced in JSP 2.0 that has no methods. It is simply there to provide a degree of type safety and to support situations such as this. In JSP 2.0 the `Tag` interface extends `JspTag`, so all classic tags extend the `JspTag` interface automatically. The `SimpleTag` interface also extends `Tag` so all simple tags are also instances of `JspTag`.

There is still one problem left to solve. We said previously that simply calling `getParent()` wasn't good enough; a nested tag should really call the `find AncestorWithClass()` method. The `findAncestorWithClass()` method works fine if a classic tag needs to find a reference to another classic tag it is nested inside, but if a classic tag needs to get a reference to an arbitrary simple tag somewhere within the stack of tags, the `findAncestorWithClass()` method will not work because it is typed to return an instance of `Tag` and not an instance of `JspTag`. To fix this problem, `SimpleTagSupport` has its own copy of `find AncestorWithClass` that works correctly.

Given this

```
<mt:simpleTag>
  <yt:someOtherInnerTag>
    <mt:innerTag/>
  </yt:someOtherInnerTag>
</mt:simpleTag>
```

the inner tag should be coded like this:

```
public class InnerTag extends TagSupport {
  MySimpleTag simpleTag = null;

  public int doStartTag() throws JspException {
    simpleTag = ( MySimpleTag
)SimpleTagSupport.findAncestorWithClass(this, OuterTag.class);
    if(simpleTag != null) {
      // invoke needed methods
      simpleTag.callParentMethod();
      // do other work here
    }
  }
}
```

So, if a nested tag is looking for a classic tag ancestor, it should use the `TagSupport.findAncestorWithClass()` method. However, if it's looking for a simple tag ancestor, it should use the `SimpleTagSupport.findAncestorWith Class()` method.

Iteration Tags

Iteration tags are an enhanced version of a simple tag. Iteration tags can do everything a simple tag can with the addition of being able to repeatedly evaluate its body. The reevaluation is managed by introducing a new method in the custom tag life cycle: `doAfterBody()`. The `doAfterBody()` method is invoked after the `doStartTag()` method and before the `doEndTag()` method. The `doAfterBody()` method determines if either the body should be reevaluated, calling `doAfter Body()` again, or if the `doEndTag()` method should be invoked.

With the `doEndTag()` method added to the simple tag life cycle, the iteration tag life cycle now appears in Figure 7-11.

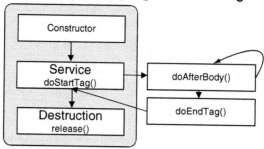

javax.servlet.jsp.tagext.IterationTag

Figure 7-11 Iteration Tag Life Cycle

IterationTag Interface

For a tag handler to be treated as an iteration tag, it must implement the `javax.servlet.jsp.IterationTag` interface. The `IterationTag` interface is a subclass of the `Tag` interface and defines only one new method:

```
public int doAfterBody() throws JspException
```

The `doAfterBody()` method is invoked after the `doStartTag()` method if it returns `EVAL_BODY_INCLUDE`. As illustrated in Figure 7-11 the `doAfterBody()` method can be invoked multiple times depending on the return value of the method. If `doAfterBody()` returns `EVAL_BODY_AGAIN`, then the tag's body is reevaluated and the `doAfterBody()` method is invoked again. If the `doAfterBody()` method returns `SKIP_BODY`, then the `doEndTag()` method is invoked.

While not re-listed, keep in mind all of the simple tag methods are still available to an iteration tag. Converting a simple tag to an iteration tag is as easy as implementing the `IterationTag` interface and coding a `doAfterBody()` method for the tag.

Coding an Iteration Tag

Iteration tags are as easy to code as simple tags. The helper class `TagSupport` implements both the `Tag` and `IterationTag` interfaces. For practical purposes extending `TagSupport` for both simple and iteration tags is of no consequence to a JSP developer. The single method the `IterationTag` interface adds does not interfere with the execution of a simple tag, nor does it add significant overhead to the code. The real difference between coding a simple tag and iteration tag is choosing when you need to have the functionality of the `doAfterBody()` method. If the `doAfterBody()` method is needed, simply code it into a tag handler and have the `doStartTag()` method return `EVAL_BODY_INCLUDE`.

The most helpful use of iteration tags is implied by their name, iteration. By using an iteration tag, redundant chunks of template text can be eliminated in a JSP. The functionality is identical to that of a scriptlet using a `for`, `while`, or `do while` loop. Consider the JSP in Listing 7-33.

Listing 7-33 A JSP with a Few Links

```
<%
  // An array of links
  String[] links = new String[5];
  links[0] = "http://www.jspbook.com";
  links[1] = "http://java.sun.com";
  links[2] = "http://www.jspinsider.com";
  links[3] = "http://www.developmentor.com";
  links[4] = "http://www.aw.com";
%>
<html>
  <head>
    <title>Eliminating Redundancy</title>
  </head>
  <body>
    Some helpful JSP and Servlet links
    <ul>
      <li><a href="<%= links[0] %>"><%= links[0] %>
          </a></li>
      <li><a href="<%= links[1] %>"><%= links[1] %>
          </a></li>
      <li><a href="<%= links[2] %>"><%= links[2] %>
          </a></li>
      <li><a href="<%= links[3] %>"><%= links[3] %>
          </a></li>
      <li><a href="<%= links[4] %>"><%= links[4] %>
          </a></li>
    </ul>
  </body>
</html>
```

Listing 7-33 is illustrating a poor use of JSP. One benefit of the page compared to an HTML equivalent is that it is re-using the array values. This simple re-use allows for each single change to an array value to be reflected in the two later uses on JSP. However, this JSP still contains a lot of redundant markup. Each line of code between the unordered list tag, `<ul>`, is exactly the same as the line above it with the exception of the array slot being accessed. These lines of code should be eliminated in favor of one line of code that is repeatedly used while iterating through the values in the array. This can easily be done with a scriptlet and either a `for`, `while`, or `do while` loop, as illustrated in Chapter 3, but it can also be done by an iteration tag.

Right now it is up to you to eliminate the markup redundancy using what has been explained about iteration tags. This can be done with the iteration tag in Listing 7-34.

Listing 7-34 LinkIterationTag.java

```
package com.jspbook;

import javax.servlet.jsp.tagext.TagSupport;
import javax.servlet.jsp.JspException;
import javax.servlet.ServletRequest;

public class LinkIterationTag extends TagSupport {
  String[] links;
  int count;

  public int doStartTag() throws JspException {
    // get the array of links
    ServletRequest request = pageContext.getRequest();
    links = (String[])request.getAttribute("links");
    // reset count
    count = 0;

    // set current link
    pageContext.setAttribute("link", links[count]);
    count++;
    return EVAL_BODY_INCLUDE;
  }

  public int doAfterBody() throws JspException {
    if(count < links.length) {
      try {
        pageContext.setAttribute("link", links[count]);
        count++;
      }
      catch (Exception e) {
```

```
        throw new JspException();
    }
    return EVAL_BODY_AGAIN;
  }
  else {
    return SKIP_BODY;
  }
}
}
```

In the preceding code a simple iteration tag is created that relies on a variable bound to request scope named links. The tag takes this variable, treats it as an array of strings, and loops through each object in the array. The looping is done by setting a PageContext variable, link, and evaluating the tag's body. Before using this tag we need to add an appropriate entry in this chapter's example TLD file. Edit example.tld to include the tag definition in Listing 7-35.

Listing 7-35   LinkIterationTag.java Entry in example.tld

```
<tag>
  <name>iterateLinks</name>
  <tag-class>com.jspbook.LinkIterationTag</tag-class>
  <body-content>JSP</body-content>
</tag>
```

Listing 7-36 provides an example of how a JSP might use this tag.

Listing 7-36   LinkIterationTag.jsp

```
<%
  // An array of links
  String[] links = new String[5];
  links[0] = "http://www.jspbook.com";
  links[1] = "http://java.sun.com";
  links[2] = "http://www.jspinsider.com";
  links[3] = "http://www.developmentor.com";
  links[4] = "http://www.aw.com";
  request.setAttribute("links", links);
%>
<%@ taglib prefix="x" uri="http://www.jspbook.com/example" %>
<html>
  <head>
    <title>Eliminating Redundency</title>
  </head>
  <body>
```

```
   Some helpful JSP and Servlet links
   <ul>
   <x:iterateLinks>
     <li><a href="${link}">${link}</a></li>
   </x:iterateLinks>
   </ul>
 </body>
</html>
```

Notice the preceding code now eliminates the redundant markup in the unordered list. Now one set of the markup is used with the link values being placed dynamically during each body evaluation of the `iterateLinks` tag.

Save `LinkIterationTag.java` in the `/WEB-INF/classes/com/jspbook` directory of the jspbook Web Application and save `LinkIterationTag.jsp` in the root directory of the jspbook Web Application. After compiling the tag handler, reload the Web Application and visit `http://127.0.0.1/jspbook/Link IterationTag.jsp`. The new tag handler loops through all of the objects in the array and displays them with the expected markup. Figure 7-12 shows a browser rendering of the output.

In addition to coding and seeing an iteration tag work, there are two more points of interest in Listing 7-36; notice that the array of `String` objects, links, is passed to the custom tag via request scope. However, the link variable is passed from the tag back to the JSP in page scope. Why isn't the page scope used in both of these cases? The code is done in consideration of a practical application of this type of code. The preceding JSP can actually be split into two parts: one page that creates the links array and places it in request scope and a second page that con-

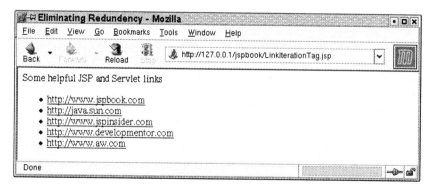

Figure 7-12   Browser Rendering of LinkIterationTag.jsp

tains only the HTML markup and the `iterateLinks` tag. This type of design would cleanly separate the two parts of the page and allow for the second half to be used with any array of links. A degree of separation such as this is very helpful and it is introduced now so that you can start thinking about it before reaching the full discussion of design patterns in Chapter 11. The second point of interest is the use of the `PageContext getAttribute()` method for accessing the appropriate link variable during each evaluation of the `iterateLinks` tag body. For cleaner code this would best be done by either another custom tag or by setting a JavaBean in page scope and using the standard `getProperty` action. In the given example it is used for simplicity.

Body Tags

In this chapter we have so far seen two of the three types of tag handlers: simple tags and iteration tags. The third type of tag handler is a *body tag*. Body tags extend the functionality of an iteration and allow a tag handler to access and manipulate the content contained within its body. Because of this increased functionality-body tags require a more complex life cycle and are more processor, intensive than simple tags and iteration tags.

The body tag life cycle extends the iteration tag life cycle by adding in one new method: `doInitBody()`. The `doInitBody()` method is invoked after the `doStartTag()` method but before the first evaluation of the tag's body content. Figure 7-13 illustrates the body tag life cycle.

BodyTag Interface

A body tag must implement the `BodyTag` interface. The `BodyTag` interface defines the following methods:

- **public int doInitBody():** The `doInitBody()` method is invoked if the `doStartTag()` method returns EVAL_BODY_BUFFERD, a static integer defined by the `BodyTag` interface. The doInitBody() method exists so that a custom body tag can appropriately initialize a `BodyContent` object after it has been set by the JSP container but before evaluation of the tag's body content.
- **public void setBodyContent():** The `setBodyContent()` method is used by the JSP container to set the `BodyContent` object of a body tag before invoking the `doInitBody()` method.

    The `BodyTag` interface also relies on the `BodyContent` object to represent the body content of a custom tag. The `BodyContent` object

javax.servlet.jsp.tagext.BodyTag

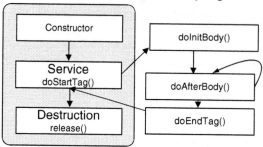

Figure 7-13 Body Tag Life Cycle

is a subclass of `JspWriter` and provides a buffer that a tag handler can locally use to write out content. In addition to the methods provided by `JspWriter`, the `BodyContent` object provides the following methods.

- **void clearBody():** The `clearBody()` method clears the contents of the current `BodyContent` object. This method is helpful should the contents of the `BodyContent` need to be cleared so that new content can be written.

- **void flush():** The `flush()` method is not to be used. It is an override of the `JspWriter` `flush()` method to disable the contents of a `BodyContent` object from being flushed. If the content of a `BodyContent` object needs to be cleared, use the `clearBody()` method. To write the contents of a `BodyContent` object to the current JSP output stream, use the `writeOut()` method and pass in the appropriate `JspWriter` object.

- **JspWriter getEnclosingWriter():** The `getEnclosingWriter()` method returns the `JspWriter` object used to construct the `BodyContent` tag.

- **java.io.Reader getReader():** The `getReader()` method returns the content of this `BodyContent` object as a `Reader` object. This method is helpful when the contents of the `BodyContent` object are to be used for another process such as a transformation.

- **String getString():** The `getString()` method returns the content of the `BodyContent` objects buffer as a `String`.

- **void writeOut(java.io.Writer out):** The `writeOut()` method writes the contents of the `BodyContent` objects buffer to the given `Writer` object.

Coding a Body Tag

The `TagSupport` object previously used when coding simple and iteration tags does not implement the `BodyTag` interface. The `BodyTag` interface adds a noticeable amount of overhead in comparison to a basic simple or iteration tag. Managing a `BodyContent` object is something that a tag does not require unless it wishes to access its body. For this reason the JSP API provides a separate extension of the `TagSupport` object for authoring a body tag, `BodyTagSupport`. The `BodyTagSupport` object is a subclass of `TagSupport` and provides all of the methods required by the `Tag`, `IterationTag`, and `BodyTag` interface.

In addition to all the methods of the `BodyTag` interface, `BodyTagSupport` provides two extra methods:

- **BodyContent getBodyContent():** The `getBodyContent()` method returns the current `BodyContent` object for a body tag, extending the `BodyTag`.
- **JspWriter getPreviousOut():** The `getPreviousOut()` method returns the `JspWriter` object that surrounds the current body tag.

Similar to other tags, body tags can have two types of content in their body: static text or JSP. However, with body tags it is a slightly more important issue to have the correct type of body content for the tag. Since a body tag has access to its body, there is the possibility that the tag might be expecting to interpret the content verbatim, not after the JSP container evaluates it. This is especially important in cases where the body tag might be being used to interpret a JSP-like code that would be munged by the JSP container.

Body tags are rarely used in practice. The functionality they provide is helpful, but it is not functionality that tends to follow good coding practices popular design patterns use. There are a few use cases, some of which are implemented by the JSTL, where a body tag is being used to evaluate code contained within its body. Specifically, it is not uncommon to see a set of custom tags that can process an embedded chunk of XML or SQL. In these cases the tags exist but are rarely used because a different design that does not rely on the tags can better implement the same functionality.

Nested Body Tag Ambiguities

Body tags introduce a few ambiguities with what we understand so far about JSP. The problem arises because of the `BodyContent` buffer a body tag uses to handle content. A `BodyContent` object acts as the `JspWriter` for content in a body tag's content. What happens when a nested tag calls the `pageContext` `getOut()` method? The `getOut()` method returns the `JspWriter` object stored by the `PageContext` object representing the JSP. This is normally the `JspWriter` object, which is associated with sending output to a buffer that eventually flushes directly to a client. However, calling this method directly from a tag embedded within a body tag intuitively seems to break the system. Content of a body tag should be sent to the `BodyContent` of the appropriate body tag. It should not sidestep this process and directly access the main JSP's output stream. An important point to understand is that nested tags in this scenario do not break the system. When a body tag obtains a `BodyContent` object, it does it by calling the `pushBody()` method of `PageContext`. This method saves the existing `JspWriter` and creates a new one that is then associated with the JSP's `PageContext` object as the current output stream. The end result is that nested tags within a body tag always receive the `JspWriter` associated with the parent body tag and therefore work as expected.

Tag Scripting Variables

A custom tag has the ability to define scripting variables for use with the scripting elements. This functionality is not commonly used because it tends to go against commonly agreed-upon, good JSP design patterns. Custom tags are best used to eliminate the amount of scripting elements that appear on a JSP. Using a custom tag to create a few scripting variables only encourages more scripting elements to be used. This is a bad practice and leads to unmaintainable code. For this reason, in general, this entire section is not recommended for use. It is included solely for completeness and so that you as a reader can identify code that attempts to use the functionality.

There are two methods by which a JSP developer can declare scripting variables via a custom tag. The first solution is by means of a Tag Extra Information (TEI) class. Originally this class was designed as the only method to declare JSP scripting variables and validate tag attribute values at translation time. TEI classes were superceded in JSP 1.2 by the combination of TLD elements to declare scripting variables and TagLibraryValidator (TLV) classes. These two methods are covered in the following sections, and TagLibraryValidator classes are covered later in the chapter.

TLD-Declared Scripting Variables

Scripting variables can be declared by the TLD by using the `variable` child element of the `tag` element. The variable element in turn has a few children elements that describe the scripting variable that is being declared. The children elements are as follows:

- **name-given:** The `name-given` element defines the name given for the scripting variable. The name must be unique among the names of other scripting variables in the same scope.
- **name-from-attribute:** The `name-from-attribute` element specifies the name of an attribute whose translation-time value will give the name of the variable. Either the `name-given` or `name-from-attribute` is required.
- **variable-class:** The `variable-class` element specifies the class of the variable. The default class is `java.lang.String`, but any Java class is valid.
- **declare:** The `declare` element specifies whether the variable is declared or not. The default value is `true`.
- **scope:** The `scope` element defines the scope of the scripting variable. The scope can either be `AT_BEGIN`, `AT_END`, or `NESTED`. `AT_BEGIN` specifies the variable comes into scope at the beginning of the custom tag. `AT_END` specifies the scripting variable comes into scope and is available after the ending of the custom tag. The `NESTED_VALUE` specifies the variable is only available in the body of the custom tag.

To declare a simple scripting variable, only the `name-given` attribute is required. Take, for example, the example for an iteration tag, Listing 7-34. For simplicity this code used the `PageContext getAttribute()` method via a scriptlet to access an object passed from a tag handler. The best solution would be to abstract access to the attribute behind another custom tag, but another fairly good solution is to have the tag handler declare a few scripting variables. This can easily be done by adding the change to the tag's TLD entry, as shown in Listing 7-37.

Listing 7-37   Declaring Scripting Variables for the iterateLinks Tag

```
<tag>
  <name>iterateLinks</name>
  <tag-class>com.jspbook.LinkIterationTag</tag-class>
```

```
  <body-content>JSP</body-content>
  <variable>
    <name-given>link</name-given>
    <variable-class>String</variable-class>
  </variable>
</tag>
```

Edit `example.tld` to include the preceding declaration. The newly declared variable will then be available for a JSP using the `iterateLinks` tag. Listing 7-38 modifies `LinkIterationTag.jsp` to show how the scripting variable can be used.

Listing 7-38 LinkIterationTagVariable.jsp

```
<%
  // An array of links
  String[] links = new String[5];
  links[0] = "http://www.jspbook.com";
  links[1] = "http://java.sun.com";
  links[2] = "http://www.jspinsider.com";
  links[3] = "http://www.developmentor.com";
  links[4] = "http://www.aw.com";
  request.setAttribute("links", links);
%>
<%@ taglib prefix="x" uri="http://www.jspbook.com/example" %>
<html>
  <head>
    <title>Eliminating Redundency</title>
  </head>
  <body>
    Some helpful JSP and Servlet links
    <ul>
    <x:iterateLinks>
      <li><a href="${link}">${link}</a></li>
    </x:iterateLinks>
    </ul>
  </body>
</html>
```

Notice the only difference between the preceding code and the code for `LinkIterationTag.jsp` is the preceding code can directly reference the link variable instead of using `PageContext getAttribute()`. Since the TLD file declares the link scripting variable, it is valid to use a direct reference to the `link` variable, even though it was not declared previously by a scriptlet.

TagExtraInfo Classes

TagExtraInfo classes are the original method for declaring JSP scripting variables from a tag handler. A TEI class provides the same information as the TLD `variable` element but in a slightly different method. Unlike the TLD `variable` element, a TEI class declares scripting elements from inside a Java class. The TLD is used only to reference the appropriate TEI class.

When creating a TEI class, two things are required: a `javax.servlet.jsp.TagExtraInfo` subclass and a `teiclass` element in the TLD declaration for the tag. The TagExtraInfo subclass is responsible for declaring any scripting variables the tag creates, and the `teiclass` element provides the name of this class. The TEI class itself is responsible for providing a `getVariableInfo()` method that returns an array of `javax.servlet.jsp.tagext.VariableInfo` objects describing all of the scripting variables.

VariableInfo objects are just a Java object representation of the information needed for a scripting element: the name for the script variable, the type of the variable, its availability scope, and whether the page needs to declare the variable. These values correspond to the `name-given` or `name-from-attribute`, `variable-type`, `scope`, and `declare` elements, respectively, of the TLD `variable` element. In code, all of these values are passed via the `VariableInfo` object construct that is illustrated in Listing 7-39.

Listing 7-39 TEI Class for LinkIterationTag.java

```
import javax.servlet.jsp.tagext.*;

public class LinkIterationTEI extends TagExtraInfo {
  public VariableInfo[] getVariableInfo(TagData data) {
    // create a VariableInfo
    VariableInfo info =
      new VariableInfo("link", "String", true,

                       VariableInfo.NESTED );
    VariableInfo[] vi = { info };
    return vi;
  }
}
```

The preceding code is the equivalent to the previous TLD entry for the `iterateLinks` tag, Listing 7-35. If you wish to try the TEI class, save the above code as `LinkIterationTEI.java` in the `/WEB-INF/classes/com/jspbook` directory of the jspbook Web application. Compile `LinkIteration.java` and add Listing 7-40 in `example.tld`.

Listing 7-40 TEI TLD Entry

```
<tag>
  <name>iterateLinks</name>
  <tag-class>com.jspbook.LinkIterationTag</tag-class>
  <teiclass>com.jspbook.LinkIterationTEI</teiclass>
  <body-content>JSP</body-content>
<!--
  <variable>
    <name-given>link</name-given>
    <variable-class>String</variable-class>
  </variable>
-->
  </tag>
...
```

After adding the preceding entry in `example.tld`, reload the jspbook Web Application and visit `http://127.0.0.1/jspbook/LinkIterationTagVariable.jsp`. The same results are displayed as in Figure 7-12, but this time the JSP is using the TEI class instead of the TLD entry to declare the scripting variables.

Tag Library Listeners

A custom tag library may rely on the functionality provided by a Servlet event listener, but we know from Chapter 2 that listener objects need to be registered with `web.xml`. To solve this problem, JSP custom tag developers may deploy listeners via the Tag Library Descriptor.

```
<!ELEMENT taglib (tlib-version, jsp-version, short-name, uri?,
display-name?, small-icon?, large-icon?, description?, validator?,
listener*, tag+) >
```

And a listener element is as follows:

```
<listener>some.package.MyListener</listener>
```

The order in which listeners defined as tags are called is undefined; it is commonly the order in which the container discovers the TLD files.

Validation

Tags may be authored and used by different people. It can be very difficult for the tag author to tell the tag user exactly how to use the tag. For example, a tag's attributes may have to be a specific type or have a specific value range, a given tag may need a certain type of parent, or tags may expect to have specific children.

While the custom action mechanism of JSP has some built-in validation, this is limited in what it can achieve. For example, the page compiler can check that all the "required" attributes are defined and that the user hasn't set any attribute the tag is not expecting. However, the compiler cannot check that the attribute values are of the right type (perhaps the whole page is text) or that the values are in the correct range. This can only be done by the tag author. Since the JSP 1.2 release, a tag author can specify that he or she wants to validate a page. This is done by creating a class that implements `javax.servlet.jsp.tagext.Tag LibraryValidator` and specifying this class's availability through the TLD. This class gives the author a great deal of flexibility during the validation process.

The TagLibraryValidator class looks like this:

```
java.util.Map getInitParameters()
void release()
void setInitParameters(java.util.Map map)
ValidationMessage[] validate(String prefix,
                             String uri,
                             PageData page)
```

To associate the validator with a tag, an entry is added to the TLD:

```
<!ELEMENT taglib (tlib-version, jsp-version, short-name, uri?,
display-name?, small-icon?, large-icon?, description?, validator?,
listener*, tag+) >
```

Notice that a validator is associated with a tag library, not with individual tags within the library. The DTD for the validator element looks like this:

```
<!ELEMENT validator (validator-class, init-param*, description?) >
```

and for the init-param like this:

```
<!ELEMENT init-param (param-name, param-value, description?)>
```

An example TLD would look something like:

```
<taglib>
    <!-- other taglib entries -->
    <validator>
        <validator-class>some.package.TagValidator</validator-class>
```

```
        <init-param>
            <param-name>count</param-name>
            <param-value>1</param-value>
        </init-param>
        <init-param>
            <param-name>language</param-name>
            <param-value>en</param-value>
        </init-param>
    </validator>
<!-- other taglib entries -->
</taglib>
```

The validator is executed once and only once, when the page is first compiled, and validators have a life cycle. The first thing the page compiler does is call the `setInitParameters()` method passing a `java.util.Map` containing the init-params. Once initialized the page compiler calls the `validate` method. Like tags, validators can be cached for re-use. If the validator is to be re-used, the page compiler first determines if the set of init-params are the same as the previous use; if they are, then `validate` is called again. If the init-params have changed, the page compiler calls release and then calls the `setInitParameters()` method, passing the new set, and finally calls `validate`.

The `validate` method is passed the prefix the tag is using, the URI from the `taglib` directive, and a `PageData` object. It is the `PageData` object that gives the validator access to the page. The `PageData` object wraps an `InputStream` through which the validator can read the page in XML format. This view of the page is the JSP 1.2 XML view. The page starts with a `<jsp:root...>` declaration and contains all the page data as XML elements.

The `validate` method will parse the page and check its validation criteria. If the page is valid, the method returns `null`. If the validation fails, the page returns an array of `ValidationMessage` objects. Each `ValidationMessage` object should contain a validation message, and an `id` identifying the element that caused the error. In JSP 1.2 a container when generating an XML view of a page is able to add a `jsp:id` attribute to each element on the page (this is entirely optional). This attribute extends the attribute set the element normally has and is available to the validator class through the `PageData` object's XML view. If this value is there, the validator should use this when reporting validation errors.

Summary

Custom tags provide an incredibly flexible set of functionality to a JSP developer. Every JSP developer should fully understand custom tags before attempting to code a major JSP project. In this chapter we learned the basics of custom tags and established a sound foundation for later chapters to expand upon the concepts learned here and demonstrate custom tag use cases.

Custom tags are broken down into three main categories: simple tags, iteration tags, and body tags. These categories are all enforced by the `Tag`, `Iteration Tag`, and `BodyTag` interfaces, respectively. The different types of tags all extend from the base functionality of simple tags to provide a more robust functionality. Simple tags are nothing more than a simple mechanism to abstract Java code from a JSP into a tag handler class. Iteration tags extend the simple tag to allow for repetitious evaluation of the content body of a custom tag. Body tags extend both simple and iteration tags to allow for a tag that can abstract code, evaluate its body multiple times, and also manipulate its body.

Custom tags don't do all the work themselves. To enhance what a tag is able to do, the JSP specifications allow for custom tags to have attributes, scripting variables, validators, and listeners. All of these enhancements make custom tags a powerful tool for a JSP developer and allow for many things to be done with custom tags.

Chapter 8

Filters

While Servlets and JSPs are extremely powerful and useful, they are not the best method of fulfilling every need of a Web Application developer. Often an application requires that some code is executed whenever a request is sent to any resource within an application, or maybe to a subset of resources. Security is a classic example of this. If an application requires a user to log on, then typically every resource within the application (except the logon page!) would need a security check to run before the resource was executed. Services such as these are often required by an application and most Web servers have a way of providing these. For example, Tomcat has "valves" and Microsoft Internet Information Server has IS API filters. To allow J2EE Web Application developers the ability to offer these services in a container independent fashion, the Servlet 2.3 specification introduced Filters.

This chapter discusses the following topics:

- Introduction to Filters and a look at Servlet Filters.
- The Filter life cycle.
- Coding a simple Filter.
- Filter configuration
- Wrappers; filtering the request and response.
- Two Filters every Web Application should have: cache and compression Filters.
- Using Filters to replace JSP functionality.

This chapter is meant to be read from start to finish, and it is strongly encouraged that you do so because it is a very important chapter. Filters greatly complement JSP, basically replacing Servlets, and you will find lots of Filters being used in later chapters. Especially in Chapter 15, when we create a complete Web Application, there will be several issues resolved by simply deploying a Filter that was either provided in this chapter, the design pattern chapter, or the internationalization chapter (and the same issues can be solved in most any existing Web Application by doing the same thing; Filters can be that generic). You need to understand Servlet Filters.

Introducing Filters

Filters are components that sit between a request and the intended endpoint of that request. The endpoint could be a static or dynamic resource such as an HTML page, JSP, or a Servlet[1]. Filters are able to:

- Read the request data on the way to the endpoint.
- Wrap the request before passing it on.
- Wrap the response before passing it on.
- Manipulate the response data on the way back output.
- Return errors to the client.
- Request dispatch to another resource and ignore the original URL.
- Generate its own response before returning to the client.

This makes Filters very powerful—in fact, so powerful that developers have to be very careful when using them. When using Filters, the developer is much closer to the HTTP protocol than with a Servlet and must understand the protocol in much more detail. For example, when using Servlets, a developer can pretty much ignore the HTTP `content-length` header, but when using Filters and producing data, the Filter writer may have to know the size of the content and set the value of that header.

What Is a Filter?

Physically a Filter is a component that intercepts a request sent to a resource in a Web Application. Filters exist as part of a chain, with the last link in the chain being the requested resource. A Filter can choose to pass the request on, in which case the request will be forwarded to either the next Filter in the Filter chain or, if this is the last Filter in the chain, to the requested resource. The Filter also sees the response before it is returned to the client. Figure 8-1 illustrates the concept.

---

1. Filters also apply to "fictitious" resources. A request that would normally generate a 404 error can pass through a Filter and the same Filter can optionally generate a response for it instead of displaying the error.

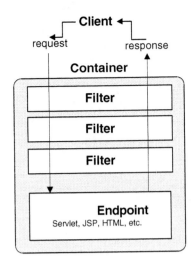

Figure 8-1 Listing Path to Servlet Through Filters

Figure 8-1 shows the code path when Filters are invoked. A client makes a request to a resource, such as a Servlet, JSP, or static file, and the Web Application is configured such that any number of Filters are invoked for the request. Each Filter is invoked in turn, and each Filter passes on the request down the Filter "chain" until the endpoint is executed.

Filters are helpful because they allow a Web developer to cleanly add any number of layers of pre-processing and post-processing to a request and response. The functionality can be mimicked using Servlets and request dispatching, but it is a slightly convoluted approach and requires forwarding all requests through one or more Servlets before reaching the final endpoint. By using Filters it is easy to seamlessly define and apply a Filter to existing Web Application resources.

The Servlet 2.4 specification further extends the utility of Filters. It is now possible to install Filters that get invoked on a `RequestDispatcher` forward or include or that get invoked in the case of an error.

The Filter Life Cycle

The Filter life cycle is conceptually identical to the three-phase Servlet life cycle. A Filter goes through initialization, service, and destruction. The initialization occurs only once, when the Filter is first loaded for use by a Web Application. The service phase of the Filter life cycle is invoked each time the Filter is applied to a request and response. The destruction phase is invoked after a Web Application is completely finished using the Filter and all resources of the Filter need to be properly terminated. Figure 8-2 illustrates the Filter life cycle.

The diagram shown in Figure 8-2 does not need much explanation. Compared to the Servlet life cycle, Figure 2-1, it includes the exact same `init()` and `destroy()` methods matching initialization and destruction phases, respectively. The only difference requiring explanation is the new `doFilter()` method that corresponds to the service phase of the life cycle. The `doFilter()` method is the method invoked by a container when applying a Filter to a `ServletRequest` and `ServletResponse`. Both the request and response are passed as parameters to this method and that is where the Filter is customized to do its specific task.

Coding a Simple Filter

A Filter must implement the `javax.servlet.Filter` interface. This interface defines the life cycle of a Filter and enforces a custom Filter that supports all the needed methods. The Filter interface defines three methods:

- **void init(FilterConfig config) throws ServletException:** The `init()` method is invoked when the container first loads the Filter. This method is used to gather the initialization parameters from the `web.xml` file and to execute any other initialization code placed in the method. It is passed a reference to a `FilterConfig` object that is used to access the initialization data. The method is called once and once only.

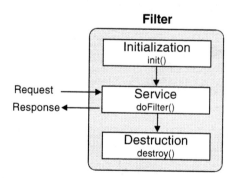

Figure 8-2 The Filter Life Cycle

- **void destroy():** The `destroy()` method is called when the Filter is unloaded from memory. Typically this will be when the application shuts down. The `destroy()` method is best used to properly close any external resources initialized by the Filter.

- **void doFilter(ServletRequest request, ServletResponse response, FilterChain chain) throws IOException, ServletException:** The `doFilter()` method is where all the work is done by a Filter. Three parameters are passed into the method: an instance of a `ServletRequest`, `ServletResponse`, and `FilterChain` object. In the case of an HttpServlet, the `ServletRequest` and `ServletResponse` objects are instances of HttpServletRequest and HttpServletResponse. A Filter needs to typecast them to access methods available only to HttpServletRequest and HttpServletResponse objects, respectively.

  Like the Servlet service methods the doFilter() method may be called by multiple threads simultaneously. Access to non-local variables and resources needs to be done in a thread-safe manner.

The preceding three methods should be fairly intuitive, but there are two new objects introduced: `FilterConfig` and `FilterChain`. The `FilterConfig` object is used for Filter configuration, and the `FilterChain` object represents the current chain of Filters being applied to a request and response. Both of these objects are further explained later in this section.

For all practical purposes a Filter provides the same functionality as a Servlet. The only difference is a Filter enforces a clean separation between each resource in the chain. This is an important concept to understand because it is why Filters are a helpful addition to Servlets, and in some cases a superior form of a Servlet. As an illustration of this point, take for example the Filter in Listing 8-1. It is a Filter generating a simple response to a client—the equivalent of the HelloWorld Servlet seen in Chapter 2.

Listing 8-1 HelloWorldFilter.java

```
package com.jspbook;

import java.io.*;
import javax.servlet.*;
import javax.servlet.http.*;

public class HelloWorldFilter implements Filter{
```

```
public void init(FilterConfig config)
{
}


public void doFilter(ServletRequest req,
                     ServletResponse res,
                     FilterChain filter)
   throws IOException, ServletException {

  HttpServletRequest request = (HttpServletRequest)req;
  HttpServletResponse response = (HttpServletResponse)res;

  response.setContentType("text/html");
  PrintWriter out = response.getWriter();
  out.println("<html>");
  out.println("<head>");
  out.println("<title>Hello World!</title>");
  out.println("</head>");
  out.println("<body>");
  out.println("<h1>Hello World!</h1>");
  out.println("</body>");
  out.println("</html>");

  return;
}


public void destroy()
{
}
}
```

Try out the HelloWorld Filter. Save Listing 8-1 as HelloWorldFilter.java in the /WEB-INF/classes/com/jspbook directory of the jspbook Web Application. Compile the code, but before seeing any results the Filter needs to be deployed with the Web Application. Deployment of a Filter is surprising similar to a Servlet. The only difference is the name of the web.xml elements that are used. Instead of the servlet, servlet-name, and servlet-class elements, the filter, filter-name, and filter-class elements are used. The three new elements provide the same respective functionality, with the only difference being a Filter instead of a Servlet is being loaded and configured. In use it would resemble the entry in Listing 8-2. Add the following code to web.xml in the /WEB-INF directory of the jspbook Web Application.

Listing 8-2 HelloWorldFilter Entry in web.xml

```
<filter>
  <filter-name>HelloWorldFilter</filter-name>
  <filter-class>com.jspbook.HelloWorldFilter</filter-class>
</filter>
<filter-mapping>
  <filter-name>HelloWorldFilter</filter-name>
  <url-pattern>/HelloWorldFilter</url-pattern>
</filter-mapping>
```

Make sure the preceding entry in web.xml occurs before any servlet elements but after the context-param element. Save the changes and reload the jspbook Web Application. Visit http://127.0.0.1/jspbook/HelloWorldFilter to see the newly added Filter in use. Figure 8-3 shows a browser rendering of the results.

It should be clear that a Filter can do exactly what a Servlet can. A "Hello World" example is simple and direct, but do not miss the point: Filters are Servlets with some extra functionality. Any example from Chapter 2 could have been implemented as a Filter. This chapter won't dwell on the point that you can re-create all of the examples in Chapter 2 as Filters. The focus is Filters do a better job than Servlets.

Filter Chains

Filter chains are what make Filters helpful. Listing 8-2 illustrated how a Filter can be used as a Servlet, but this is not what Filters were designed for. Recall the most important method in the Filter interface is the doFilter() method, and it is passed three parameters that are instances of a ServletRequest, Servlet Response, and a FilterChain object. The ServletRequest and ServletResponse

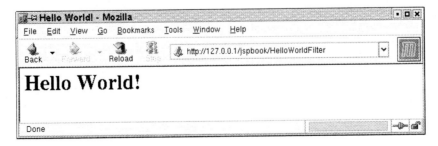

Figure 8-3 Browser Rendering of HelloWorldFilter

objects were covered thoroughly in Chapter 2. They are what allows a Filter to mimic a Servlet, but `FilterChain` is new. The `FilterChain` object represents the possible stack of Filters being executed on a particular request and response. This is where a Filter provides a convenient enhancement over a Servlet.

As illustrated in Figure 8-1 Filters provide a mechanism for cleanly applying layers of functionality to a `ServletRequest` and `ServletResponse`. This is in contrast to the single endpoint a Servlet is designed to be. By using Filters it is easy to divide up functionality into many logical layers and stack them as desired. When using a Servlet this functionality must be done via some clever request dispatching. Figure 8-4 illustrates the concept.

Shown in Figure 8-4 is a mock example of some real-world requirements of a Web Application. Security, efficiency, and content generation are all valid conceptual requirements. In practice how these requirements are implemented varies, but as a Web Application grows, it is difficult to easily manage these requirements unless a clean enforcement of functional separation is used. The separation can be done by both Servlets and Filters, but Filters provide a very direct separation and enforcement layer.

The layered separation Filters provide is due to the `FilterChain` object. A `FilterChain` object represents the chain of Filters a Web Application is configured to use on a particular real or fictitious endpoint. A Filter is passed this object during runtime invocation of the `doFilter()` method because it needs to decide if the Filter should fully handle a request and response or if it should only manipulate the pair and pass them on to the next Filter in the chain. In cases where multiple Filters are applied to the same endpoint, the ordering of Filter

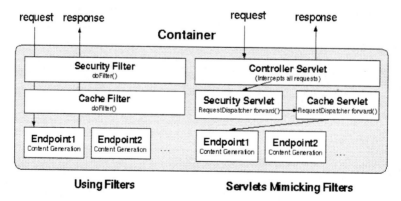

Figure 8-4 Filters Versus Servlets

execution matches the ascending order of `filter-mapping` elements defined in `web.xml`.

As shown with the HelloWorldFilter, Listing 8-1, a Filter can stop execution of subsequent Filters in the chain by simply returning from the `doFilter()` method. This causes the Web Application to return back through any Filters previously executed and to finish sending the response to a client. Should a Filter need to continue executing further links down the chain, then the `FilterChain` object's `doFilter()` method needs to be invoked. The `doFilter()` method of the `FilterChain` object corresponds to the next Filter or the possible endpoint of the chain. By invoking the `doFilter()` method a Filter stops and waits for the next resource in the chain to manipulate the request and response. Upon returning from the `FilterChain.doFilter()` method, the current Filter finishes its own execution.

The concept of a Filter chain is important. It is what distinguishes a Filter from a Servlet. As an example let's start with a Filter that is very commonly used: a link tracking Filter. The Filter will do a very practical task: track the site's traffic. The concept of link tracking is not new; you have already seen a Servlet do the task in Chapter 2. However, the Servlet did not track incoming links and referrals. Filters are well suited for this task since they can seamlessly be applied to all requests. Save Listing 8-3 as `LinkTrackerFilter.java` in the `/WEB-INF/classes/com/jspbook` directory of the jspbook Web Application.

Listing 8-3 LinkTrackerFilter.java

```java
package com.jspbook;

import java.io.*;
import java.util.*;
import javax.servlet.*;
import javax.servlet.http.*;

public class LinkTrackerFilter implements Filter {
  Calendar startDate = Calendar.getInstance();
  static int count = 0;
  public static Hashtable requests = new Hashtable();
  public static Hashtable responses = new Hashtable();
  public static Hashtable referers = new Hashtable();
  FilterConfig fc = null;

  public void doFilter(ServletRequest req, ServletResponse res,
                       FilterChain chain) throws IOException,
```

```
ServletException {
    HttpServletRequest request = (HttpServletRequest) req;
    HttpServletResponse response = (HttpServletResponse) res;

    String uri = request.getRequestURI();
    String path = request.getContextPath();
    String turi = uri.substring(path.length(), uri.length());

    if (turi.startsWith("/redirect")) {
      String url = request.getParameter("url");
      // error check!
      if (url == null || url.equals("")) {
        response.sendRedirect(path);
        return;
      }
      Link l = new Link();
      l.url = url;
      l.count = 1;
      l.lastVisited = Calendar.getInstance().getTimeInMillis();
      if (responses.get(l.url)!=null){
        l = (Link)responses.get(l.url);
        l.count++;
      }
      else {
        responses.put(l.url, l);
      }

      response.sendRedirect(url);
      return;
    }

    if (uri.endsWith(".js") || uri.endsWith(".css") ||
        uri.endsWith(".gif") || uri.endsWith(".png") ||
        uri.endsWith(".jpg")|| uri.endsWith(".jpeg")) {
      chain.doFilter(req, res);
      return;
    }

    {
      // Log request
      Link l = new Link();
      l.url = uri;
      l.count = 1;
```

```
      l.lastVisited = Calendar.getInstance().getTimeInMillis();
      if (requests.get(l.url)!=null){
        l = (Link)requests.get(l.url);
        l.count++;
      }
      else {
        requests.put(l.url, l);
      }
    }

    // log referer
    String referer = request.getHeader("referer");
    if (referer != null && !referer.equals("")) {
      Link l = new Link();
      l.url = referer;
      l.count = 1;
      l.lastVisited = Calendar.getInstance().getTimeInMillis();
      if (referers.get(l.url)!=null){
        l = (Link)referers.get(l.url);
        l.count++;
      }
      else {
        referers.put(l.url, l);
      }
    }

    //log the hit
    count++;
    chain.doFilter(req, res);
}

public void init(FilterConfig filterConfig) {
  this.fc = filterConfig;
}

public void destroy() {
  this.fc = null;
}

// total visitors
public int getCount() {
  return count;
}
```

```
public static Link[] getRequests() {
  Collection c = requests.values();
  Vector v = new Vector(c);
  Collections.sort(v, new LinkComparator());
  return (Link[])v.toArray(new Link[0]);
}

public static Link[] getResponses() {
  Collection c = responses.values();
  Vector v = new Vector(c);
  Collections.sort(v, new LinkComparator());
  return (Link[])v.toArray(new Link[0]);
}

public static Link[] getReferers() {
  Collection c = referers.values();
  Vector v = new Vector(c);
  Collections.sort(v, new LinkComparator());
  return (Link[])v.toArray(new Link[0]);
}

public long getDays() {
  Calendar now = Calendar.getInstance();
  long a = startDate.getTimeInMillis();
  long b = now.getTimeInMillis();
  long between = b-a;

  long days = (between/(1000*60*60*24));
  if (days < 1)
    days = 1;
  return days;
}
}
```

The Filter works by keeping three `Hashtable` objects to track incoming requests, referrals of incoming requests, and outgoing responses.

```
public static Hashtable requests = new Hashtable();
public static Hashtable responses = new Hashtable();
public static Hashtable referers = new Hashtable();
```

Each time the Filter processes a request (which should be every time a request is made), the `Hashtables` are updated accordingly. If a request is sent to the "/redirect" URL, it will be logged in the referral table and the response is redirected.

```java
if (uri.startsWith("/redirect")) {
  String url = request.getParameter("url");
  // error check!
  if (url == null || url.equals("")) {
    response.sendRedirect("/");
    return;
  }
  Link l = new Link();
  l.url = url;
  l.count = 1;
  l.lastVisited = Calendar.getInstance().getTimeInMillis();
  if (responses.get(l.url)!=null){
    l = (Link)responses.get(l.url);
    l.count++;
  }
  else {
    responses.put(l.url, l);
  }

  response.sendRedirect(url);
  return;
}
```

Logging is done via encapsulating the information in a JavaBean that we will create later. The point to see is that the LinkTracker Filter treats the "/redirect" URL specially. If using the LinkTracker Filter with your Web Application, don't have another resource use the "/redirect" URL or else it will never receive a request. All other requests are treated as requests for resources found within the Web Application. The LinkTracker Filter logs the URL the request was trying to reach and the referrer of the request.

```java
{
  // Log request
  Link l = new Link();
  l.url = uri;
  l.count = 1;
  l.lastVisited = Calendar.getInstance().getTimeInMillis();
  if (requests.get(l.url)!=null){
    l = (Link)requests.get(l.url);
    l.count++;
  }
```

```
    else {
      requests.put(l.url, l);
    }
  }

  // log referer
  String referer = request.getHeader("referer");
  if (referer != null && !referer.equals("")) {
    Link l = new Link();
    l.url = referer;
    l.count = 1;
    l.lastVisited = Calendar.getInstance().getTimeInMillis();
    if (referers.get(l.url)!=null){
      l = (Link)referers.get(l.url);
      l.count++;
    }
    else {
      referers.put(l.url, l);
    }
  }
```

The URL is easily obtained using the `HttpServletRequest` object's `getRequestURI()` method.

```
String uri = request.getRequestURI();
```

Referral information is obtained by mining the HTTP `referer` header.

```
String referer = request.getHeader("referer");
    if (referer != null && !referer.equals("")) {
```

Note that the `referer` header is not required to be set, so don't rely on it containing a value. The LinkTracker Filter explicitly checks to make sure the `referer` header is not `null` or an empty string before logging referral information.

Finally, the Filter invokes the all-important `doFilter()` method to allow other Filters, Servlets, and JSP to have a chance at handling the request.

```
chain.doFilter(req, res);
```

The `doFilter()` method is not difficult to use, but it is important to understand why the LinkTracker Filter invoked it and the HelloWorld Filter did not. The HelloWorld Filter was generating the entire response—it had no need to let other Filters, JSP, or Servlets handle the request. In contrast, the LinkTracker Filter is meant to be transparent to the rest of the Web Application; other Filters, Servlets, and JSP shouldn't be affected at all by the link tracking logic. In general, all Filters that are supposed to be transparent—that is, be applied to a whole Web Application and not "break" things, should properly invoke the `doFilter()` method.

Deploy the filter to intercept all requests. Add Listing 8-4 into `web.xml`.

Listing 8-4 LinkTracker Filter Deployment

```
<filter>
  <filter-name>LinkTrackerFilter</filter-name>
  <filter-class>com.jspbook.LinkTrackerFilter</filter-class>
</filter>
<filter-mapping>
  <filter-name>LinkTrackerFilter</filter-name>
  <url-pattern>/*</url-pattern>
</filter-mapping>
```

Before we can test out the LinkTracker Filter, a few more additions are required. The Filter stores information via a JavaBean object. Without the JavaBean, `LinkTrackerFilter.java` won't compile. Listing 8-5 is the required JavaBean.

Listing 8-5 Link.java

```
package com.jspbook;

public class Link {
  protected int count;
  protected String url;
  protected long lastVisited;

  public int getCount() {
    return count;
  }
  public String getUrl() {
    return url;
  }
  public long getLastVisited() {
    return lastVisited;
  }
}
```

Save the preceding code as `Link.java` in the `/WEB-INF/classes/com/jspbook` directory of the jspbook Web Application. There is nothing tricky about the preceding code. The JavaBean provides a read-only method (for code outside the com.jspbook class) to get information about tracked links.

Another requirement for the LinkTracker class is a Comparator class. The Filter provides methods for getting a current list of either the request, referral, or response information. Each method converts the related `Hashtable` into a sorted array. For efficiency the array is sorted using Java's implementation of merge sort via the `Collections` object. In order to do the sorting, an implementation of the Comparator interface is required. Listing 8-6 illustrates the implementation.

Listing 8-6 LinkComparator.java

```
package com.jspbook;

import java.util.*;

public class LinkComparator implements java.util.Comparator {
  public int compare(Object o1, Object o2) {
    Link l1 = (Link)o1;
    Link l2 = (Link)o2;
    return l2.getCount() - l1.getCount();
  }

  public boolean equals(Object o1, Object o2) {
    Link l1 = (Link)o1;
    Link l2 = (Link)o2;
    if (l2.getCount() == l1.getCount()) {
      return true;
    }
    return false;
  }
}
```

Save the preceding code as `LinkComparator.java` in the /WEB-INF/classes/com/jspbook directory of the jspbook Web Application. The code provides two methods, `compare()` and `equals()`, as mandated by the Comparator interface, and provides a method to compare two instances of the Link object. Elaboration on the Comparator interface can be found in the Java documentation for `java.util.Comparator`.

`LinkTracker.java`, `Link.java`, and `LinkComparator.java` are the only classes required for the link tracking Filter, but the Filter is pointless without something to display its statistics. We need to build a Servlet or JSP that displays the link information tracked by the Filter. For simplicity we will use JSP and save

Listing 8-7 as `linktracker.jsp` in the root directory of the jspbook Web Application.

Listing 8-7 linktracker.jsp

```
<%@ page import="com.jspbook.*"%>
<%@ taglib uri="http://java.sun.com/jstl/core_rt" prefix="c" %>
<% Link[] links = LinkTrackerFilter.getRequests();
   Link[] responses = LinkTrackerFilter.getResponses();
   Link[] referers = LinkTrackerFilter.getReferers();
%>
<p class="h1">Requests</p>
<c:forEach var="r" begin="0" items="${requests}">
  <p class="nopad"><a href="${r.url}">${r.url}</a> ${r.count}
${r.lastVisited}</p>
</c:forEach>
<p class="h1">Responses</p>
<c:forEach var="r" begin="0" items="${responses}">
  <p class="nopad"><a href="${r.url}">${r.url}</a> ${r.count}
${r.lastVisited}</p>
</c:forEach>
<p class="h1">Referers</p>
<c:forEach var="r" begin="0" items="${referers}">
  <p class="nopad"><a href="${r.url}">${r.url}</a> ${r.count}
${r.lastVisited}</p>
</c:forEach>
```

The JSP uses three loops to display ordered information about requests, responses, and referrals. Information is obtained from the `getRequests()`, `getResponses()`, and `getReferers()` method, respectively, of the link tracking Filter. The end result is a single HTML page that displays the information tracked by the LinkTracker Filter.

Try out the link tracking Filter by compiling `LinkTracker.java`, `Link.java`, and `LinkComparator.java`, reloading the Web Application, and browsing to `http://127.0.0.1/jspbook/linktracker.jsp`. You will see a page displaying the link tracking statistics. Figure 8-5 provides a browser rendering of the results.

Initially information is sparse; until you make HTTP requests for various resources in the Web Application, there is nothing to track. Try browsing around to various previous code examples. Upon returning to `linktracker.jsp` you will see their information added. Responses are only tracked if links are specially encoded for the link tracking Filter. Links to external resources need to be directed to/redirected (of the jspbook Web Application) with the URL parameter set with

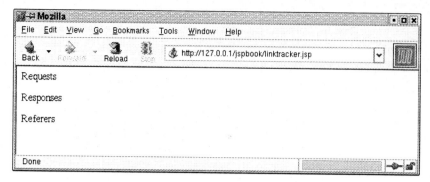

Figure 8-5 Browser Rendering of linktracker.jsp

the outbound URL. For example, the outgoing link "http://google.com" needs to be changed to "/redirect?url=http://google.com". The technique is the same as the one used by the LinkTracker Servlet coded in Listing 2-6 in Chapter 2. If needed, review the Chapter 2 example for a full explanation and how it was used.

So what has been gained by this example? The example illustrates the intended, popular use of Filters: as a component that adds functionality to possibly the entire Web Application but need not affect underlying resources. The doFilter() method is responsible for this, and it is important to realize how powerful the functionality is. Imagine other layered services such as security, caching, or content compression, and you should easily see why Filters are a helpful addition to the Servlet specifications.

Filter Configuration

Filters can be configured in the same method as a Servlet. The Filter web.xml element may contain any number of init-param elements to define custom initialization parameters. Discussion of the init-param and child param-name and param-value elements is skipped because it was already explained in Chapter 2 under Servlet configuration.

Initial parameters defined for a Filter can be accessed via the FilterConfig object passed as a parameter to the init() method. The FilterConfig class has a striking resemblance to the ServletConfig class used with Servlets. The following are the methods provided by FilterConfig:

- **String getFilterName()**: The getFilterName() method returns the name of a Filter as defined in the Filter's web.xml entry.

- **String getInitParameter(String name)**: The `getInitParameter()` method returns the value matched to the name of a given initial parameter name. The parameter's name and value are defined by the `param-name` and `param-value` elements, respectively, in the Filter's `web.xml` entry. If no name match is found, `null` is returned.

- **Enumeration getInitParameterNames()**: The `getInitParameter Names()` method returns a `java.util.Enumeration` object including all of the Filter's initial parameter names. The initial parameter names are the same as the ones defined by the `param-name` elements of the Filter's `web.xml` entry.

- **ServletContext getServletContext()**: The `getServletContext()` method returns the `ServletContext` of the Filter's Web Application.

Filters and Request Dispatching

By default a chain of Filters is only constructed to handle a request made by a client. If a request is dispatched using either the `forward()` or `include()` methods of the `RequestDispatcher` object, Filters are not applied. However, this functionality can be configured via `web.xml`. A `filter-mapping` element may include any number of request `dispatcher` elements to configure how the Filter is applied to requests. The dispatcher element has four possible values: REQUEST, INCLUDE, FORWARD, and ERROR. The different values represent if the Filter should be applied to only client requests, only includes, only forwards, only errors, or any combination of the four.

For example, applying Listing 8-5 to only `RequestDispatcher include()` calls could be accomplished by:

```
<filter>
  <filter-name>LinkTracker</filter-name>
  <filter-class>com.jspbook.LinkTracker</filter-class>
</filter>
<filter-mapping>
  <filter-name>LinkTracker</filter-name>
  <url-pattern>/*</url-pattern>
  <dispatcher>INCLUDE</dispatcher>
</filter-mapping>
```

Note the use of the `dispatcher` element. If the preceding mapping is used, the Filter is no longer applied to incoming client requests, only Request

`Dispatcherinclude()` calls. If the Filter needs to be applied to two or more types of requests, then more `dispatcher` elements can be used:

```
<filter-mapping>
  <filter-name>LinkTracker</filter-name>
  <url-pattern>/*</url-pattern>
  <dispatcher>INCLUDE</dispatcher>
  <dispatcher>REQUEST</dispatcher>
</filter-mapping>
```

Use of the `dispatcher` element is straightforward and helpful if you need to adjust what the Filter is applied to. By default Filters are configured to be ideal for uses such as caching and compression, where an entire page is optionally evaluated or not. You would not want a JSP to evaluate half a page, produce some text, then have an include produce the second half of the page as compressed text because of a Filter. You would want the Filter on the included page to be skipped. By default this is exactly what would happen. However, the opposite might also be desired. A security Filter might need to be applied to all requests, even attempts to include content. In this case the Filter could be configured to do exactly that. The greater point is that Filters can be used with request dispatching; use the functionality if it is needed.

Wrappers

Another very powerful feature of Filters is the ability to optionally wrap a request and/or a response. Wrapping is used to encapsulate a given request or response inside another (customized) one. The benefit of wrapping comes from custom coding a particular wrapping object to manipulate a request or response in a way not normally done. Wrappers are an extremely important part of Filters. There are many uses for this sort of functionality—some of which are demonstrated in this chapter and later in the book.

A side point to note about wrappers is they are not a feature specific to Filters. The functionality and associated classes were introduced with Filters in the Servlet 2.3 specifications, but request and response wrapping can be done by a normal Servlet. Commonly, this fact is ignored, but as the topic is discussed further, keep in mind that the `RequestDispatcher forward()` and `include()` methods can be used with wrappers to do the exact same thing.

Request Wrapping

A request and a response are wrapped differently. A *wrapper* is really just an implementation of the respective object being wrapped. A request wrapper would be an implementation of `ServletRequest`. In the case of an `HttpServlet Request`, the wrapper would be an implementation of `HttpServletRequest`. The Servlet API provides the `ServletRequestWrapper` and `HttpServletRequest Wrapper` classes as wrappers for subclassing. Creating a new custom wrapper can be done by extending the appropriate class and custom coding the desired methods.

In the case of wrapping a request there have been few good uses of the functionality. Pre-processing of request information is normally done to populate objects with information that is later displayed by a Servlet or JSP. In particular, JavaBeans are commonly populated by Filters so the information can easily be shown by a JSP via the `getProperty` standard action or the EL. In this common use case, a request wrapper works, but it is usually easier to populate the JavaBean using a few lines of code and setting it in request scope.

There are a few use cases where request wrapping is absolutely needed. These cases occur whenever the functionality in either the `ServletRequest` or `HttpServletRequest` methods needs to be changed. As an example of one of these use cases, imagine a customization of the `HttpServletRequest` object to provide audit information. Information about the invocation is recorded to a log file each time one of the methods is invoked. Normally this type of auditing would be difficult to accomplish as it would involve editing the source code for the `HttpServletRequest implementation`, but request wrapping easily provides the functionality. The wrapper in Listing 8-8 is a customized version of `HttpServletRequest` that leaves an audit trail of method invocations.

Listing 8-8 Audit Trail Wrapper for HttpServletRequest

```
package com.jspbook;

import java.io.*;
import java.util.logging.*;
import javax.servlet.*;
import javax.servlet.http.*;

class AuditRequestWrapper extends HttpServletRequestWrapper {
  Logger logger;
  public AuditRequestWrapper(Logger logger,
      HttpServletRequest request) {
    super(request);
```

```
      this.logger = logger;
    }

  public String getContentType() {
    String contentType = super.getContentType();
    logger.fine("ContentType[ " + contentType + "]");
    return contentType;
  }

  public int getContentLength() {
    int contentLength = super.getContentLength();
    logger.fine("getContentLength[" + contentLength + "]");
    return contentLength;
  }

  public long getDateHeader(String s) {
    long date =  super.getDateHeader(s);
    logger.fine("getDateHeader[" + s + ": " + date + "]");
    return date;
  }

  public String getHeader(String s) {
    String header = super.getHeader(s);
    logger.fine("getHeader[" + s + ": " + header + "]");
    return header;
  }

  public int getIntHeader(String s) {
    int header = super.getIntHeader(s);
    logger.fine("getIntHeader[" + s + ": " + header + "]");
    return header;
  }

  public String getQueryString() {
    String queryString = super.getQueryString();
    logger.fine("getQueryString[" + queryString + "]");
    return queryString;
  }
  // other methods left out for clarity
}
```

The wrapper is very simple. As shown here it logs calls to certain methods using the `logger` available to the Web Application. Notice that the wrapper has a constructor that takes a `Logger` and an `HttpServletRequest`. This is needed by the wrapper class the Filter uses. Listing 8-9 includes the code for the wrapper.

Listing 8-9 AuditFilter.java

```
package com.jspbook;

import java.io.*;
import java.util.logging.*;
import javax.servlet.*;
import javax.servlet.http.*;

public class AuditFilter implements javax.servlet.Filter {

  public void doFilter(ServletRequest req, ServletResponse res,
      FilterChain chain) throws IOException, ServletException {
    Logger logger = SiteLogger.getLogger();
    AuditRequestWrapper wrappedRequest =
      new AuditRequestWrapper(logger, (HttpServletRequest)req);
    chain.doFilter(wrappedRequest, res);
  }

  public void init(FilterConfig filterConfig) {
    // noop
  }

  public void destroy() {
    // noop
  }
}
```

Notice where the Filter wraps the request. Before calling the `chain.do Filter()` method, the `AuditFilter` wraps the `HttpServletRequest` object with the `AuditRequestWrapper` class.

```
    ...
    Logger logger = SiteLogger.getLogger();
    AuditRequestWrapper wrappedRequest =
      new AuditRequestWrapper(logger, (HttpServletRequest)req);
    chain.doFilter(wrappedRequest, res);
    ...
```

Now subsequent resources, such as JSP or Servlets that use the wrapped request, will leave the audit trail of method invocation information.

Test out the `AuditFilter` by deploying it with the jspbook Web Application. Add the following entry to `web.xml`.

```
<filter>
  <filter-name>AuditFilter</filter-name>
  <filter-class>com.jspbook.AuditFilter</filter-class>
</filter>
<filter-mapping>
  <filter-name>AuditFilter</filter-name>
  <url-pattern>/*</url-pattern>
</filter-mapping>
```

Save the changes to `web.xml`, compile `AuditFilter.java`, `AuditRequestWrapper.java`, and reload the jspbook Web Application for the changes to take effect. Resources in the jspbook Web Application now leave an audit trail of the methods they invoke on the `HttpServletRequest` object.

A direct test of the AuditFilter can be given with a simple JSP. Save Listing 8-10 as `TestAuditFilter.jsp` in the base directory of the jspbook Web Application.

Listing 8-10   TestAuditFilter.jsp

```
<html>
<body>
Testing the Audit Filter.
<%
    request.getContentLength();
    request.getHeader("Host");
%>
</body>
</html>
```

Browse to `http://127.0.0.1/jspbook/TestAuditFilter.jsp` to test the Filter. The output of the JSP does not change. It is a simple line of text, "Testing the Audit Filter". The important point to note is that the API calls the JSP is using are leaving an audit trail[2]. The trail looks something similar to the following.

```
May 15, 2002 3:10:28 PM com.jspbook.AuditRequestWrapper
getQueryString
INFO: getQueryString[null]
```

---

2. The Audit Filter logs at the `FINE` level of the `java.util.logging` package. If the SiteLogger Servlet is configured to ignore `FINE` messages, then you will not see the audit trail. Browse to `http://127.0.0.1/jspbook/SiteLoggerAdmin.jsp?level=ALL` to change the logging level appropriately.

```
May 15, 2002 3:10:28 PM com.jspbook.AuditRequestWrapper
getContentLength
INFO: getContentLength[-1]
May 15, 2002 3:10:28 PM com.jspbook.AuditRequestWrapper getHeader
INFO: getHeader[Host: 127.0.0.1]
```

Notice the JSP calls to the `getContentLength()` method and the `get Header()` methods are logged. However, the Filter also logs a call to the `get QueryString()` method even though it is not explicitly called by the JSP. The `getQueryString()` method must be called by the container. The important thing to realize is that all calls should go through the wrapper classes, even calls made by the container. In other words, the container should not access the underlying request and response objects directly through internal APIs. It should always follow the contract of accessing the objects through the request and response interfaces.

Response Wrapping

Manipulating the response is much more difficult than wrapping the request. The request object is substantially read only, whereas a response contains lots of generated information including the output data. If you want to manipulate the output data, the information needs to either first be captured or a `custom writer` object needs to be used. Either of these changes usually means the HTTP response headers need to be also customized, particularly `Content-Length` and `Content-Type`. Wrapping a response is done in a similar fashion as wrapping a request. The Servlet API includes the `ServletResponseWrapper` and `HttpServlet ResponseWrapper` classes, which can easily be extended and customized.

Along with the complexity of wrapping a response comes a great deal of functionality. Being able to capture and manipulate output content allows a filter to have full authority over what a client sees. This functionality can be put to many good uses, and it is well worth understanding response wrapping.

Compression Filters

Arguably one of the best uses of response wrapping is to provide dynamic compression of content. The idea behind a compression Filter is sending less content to a client means the content downloads faster. This concept is absolutely true; whenever the same information can be sent using less space, it is desirable, especially when dealing with low-bandwidth clients.

Compression works by eliminating redundant information. Most text files are full of redundancy, particularly in the case of markup languages such as

HTML. Compressing a lengthy chunk of HTML or DHTML can result in a size decrease by a factor of six. Compression cannot blindly be applied to all content in a Web Application. Web browsers expect to see information in a format they can understand. Most often a developer simply assumes that every browser can understand HTML sent with the standard encoding. This mindset works, but completely ignores optimizations many Web browsers implement, namely, compression. You'll recall the ShowHeaders Servlet built in Chapter 2 (Listing 2-8). This Servlet dumps a listing of all the HTTP request headers sent by a client. While not used in that example, we can take advantage of them now, specifically the `user-encoding` header. This HTTP header provides a listing of all the encoding formats the client's software understands. If a client lists a compression format here, it means the browser can understand content compressed using the specific format.

Here is a sample listing of the user-encoding header from Chapter 2:

```
accept-encoding: gzip, deflate, compress;q=0.9
```

Notice the listing of the popular GZIP compression algorithm. This algorithm is commonly implemented by current Web browsers and provides an easy method of compressing the output of a lengthy Web page. The Java 2 Standard Edition conveniently includes the `GzipOutputStream` class that is a stream implementation of the compression algorithm. By combining this class with a simple Filter, we can dynamically compress the output of a lengthy Web page. The end result is that a client that supports gzip compression will receive the exact same content as other clients, but will only have to wait a fraction of the time to download it.

A simple compression filter is quite handy to have. The following code is such a Filter. Save Listing 8-11 as `GZIPFilter.java` in the `/WEB-INF/classes/com/jspbook` directory of the jspbook Web Application.

Listing 8-11 GZIPFilter.java

```
package com.jspbook;

import java.io.*;
import javax.servlet.*;
import javax.servlet.http.*;

public class GZIPFilter implements Filter {

  public void doFilter(ServletRequest req, ServletResponse res,
      FilterChain chain) throws IOException, ServletException {
```

```
    if (req instanceof HttpServletRequest) {
      HttpServletRequest request = (HttpServletRequest) req;
      HttpServletResponse response = (HttpServletResponse) res;
      String ae = request.getHeader("accept-encoding");
      if (ae != null && ae.indexOf("gzip") != -1) {
        System.out.println("GZIP supported, compressing.");
        GZIPResponseWrapper wrappedResponse =
          new GZIPResponseWrapper(response);
        chain.doFilter(req, wrappedResponse);
        wrappedResponse.finishResponse();
        return;
      }
      chain.doFilter(req, res);
    }
  }

  public void init(FilterConfig filterConfig) {
    // noop
  }

  public void destroy() {
    // noop
  }
}
```

As mentioned earlier, response manipulating Filters are a bit more difficult to properly code. This occurs because response manipulating Filters need to both capture the original output and also reset HTTP response headers to match the changes. The preceding code for the GZIP Filter illustrates this point. The GZIP Filter by itself does little. In the main `doFilter()` method it checks to see if the client supports GZIP compression.

```
    String ae = request.getHeader("accept-encoding");
    if (ae != null && ae.indexOf("gzip") != -1) {
      GZIPServletResponseWrapper wrappedResponse =
        new GZIPServletResponseWrapper(response);
      chain.doFilter(req, wrappedResponse);
    wrappedResponse.finishResponse();
    return;
```

If so, a `GZIPResponseWrapper` is used. If not, the Filter does nothing. The `GZIPResponseWrapper` is being used to capture the normally generated content to pipe it through a `GZIPOutputStream`. The `GZIPResponseWrapper` class is also a custom-made class. Here is the code for the `GZIPResponseWrapper`. Save Listing

8-12 as `GZIPResponseWrapper.java` in the `/WEB-INF/classes/com/jspbook` directory of the jspbook Web Application.

Listing 8-12 GZIPResponseWrapper

```java
package com.jspbook;

import java.io.*;
import java.util.*;
import javax.servlet.*;
import javax.servlet.http.*;

public class GZIPResponseWrapper extends HttpServletResponseWrapper
{
  protected HttpServletResponse origResponse = null;
  protected ServletOutputStream stream = null;
  protected PrintWriter writer = null;

  public GZIPResponseWrapper(HttpServletResponse response) {
    super(response);
    origResponse = response;
  }

  public ServletOutputStream createOutputStream() throws IOException
{
    return (new GZIPResponseStream(origResponse));
  }

  public void finishResponse() {
    try {
      if (writer != null) {
        writer.close();
      } else {
        if (stream != null) {
          stream.close();
        }
      }
    } catch (IOException e) {}
  }

  public void flushBuffer() throws IOException {
    stream.flush();
  }
```

```java
  public ServletOutputStream getOutputStream() throws IOException {
    if (writer != null) {
      throw new IllegalStateException("getWriter() has already been
called!");
    }

    if (stream == null)
      stream = createOutputStream();
    return (stream);
  }

  public PrintWriter getWriter() throws IOException {
    if (writer != null) {
      return (writer);
    }

    if (stream != null) {
      throw new IllegalStateException("getOutputStream() has already
been called!");
    }

    stream = createOutputStream();
    writer = new PrintWriter(new OutputStreamWriter(stream, "UTF-
8"));
    return (writer);
  }

  public void setContentLength(int length) {}
}
```

The preceding code performs only one important task: use GZIPResponse
Stream instead of ServletOutputStream. The rest of the code is just filler to
ensure the wrapper class uses the GZIPResponseStream with all the HttpServlet
Response methods. The GZIPResponseStream is where all the work is done. In this
class the content that is normally sent directly to a client is instead captured in a
buffer and piped through a GZIPOutputStream. The compressed content is then
sent to a client along with corrections to the appropriate HTTP headers. As with
the GZIPResponseWrapper, the GZIPResponseStream is also a custom class needed
for this example. Here is the code for the GZIPResponseStream class. Save Listing
8-13 as GZIPResponseStream.java in the /WEB-INF/classes/com/jspbook
directory of the jspbook Web Application.

Listing 8-13 GZIPResponseStream.java

```java
package com.jspbook;

import java.io.*;
import java.util.zip.GZIPOutputStream;
import javax.servlet.*;
import javax.servlet.http.*;

public class GZIPResponseStream extends ServletOutputStream {
  protected ByteArrayOutputStream baos = null;
  protected GZIPOutputStream gzipstream = null;
  protected boolean closed = false;
  protected HttpServletResponse response = null;
  protected ServletOutputStream output = null;

  public GZIPResponseStream(HttpServletResponse response) throws
IOException {
    super();
    closed = false;
    this.response = response;
    this.output = response.getOutputStream();
    baos = new ByteArrayOutputStream();
    gzipstream = new GZIPOutputStream(baos);
  }

  public void close() throws IOException {
    if (closed) {
      throw new IOException("This output stream has already been
closed");
    }
    gzipstream.finish();

    byte[] bytes = baos.toByteArray();


    response.addHeader("Content-Length",
                  Integer.toString(bytes.length));
    response.addHeader("Content-Encoding", "gzip");
    output.write(bytes);
    output.flush();
```

```
      output.close();
      closed = true;
    }

  public void flush() throws IOException {
    if (closed) {
      throw new IOException("Cannot flush a closed output stream");
    }
    gzipstream.flush();
  }

  public void write(int b) throws IOException {
    if (closed) {
      throw new IOException("Cannot write to a closed output
stream");
    }
    gzipstream.write((byte)b);
  }

  public void write(byte b[]) throws IOException {
    write(b, 0, b.length);
  }

  public void write(byte b[], int off, int len) throws IOException {
    System.out.println("writing...");
    if (closed) {
      throw new IOException("Cannot write to a closed output
stream");
    }
    gzipstream.write(b, off, len);
  }

  public boolean closed() {
    return (this.closed);
  }

  public void reset() {
    //noop
  }
}
```

The GZIPResponseStream has many important points to understand. The first is what the class is doing. With more complex Filters, a Web developer can completely override the normal functionality found with the Servlet API. In this case the `ServletOutputStream` object is given a major rework. Such a radical change to one of the base classes of Servlets is possible thanks to the custom response wrapper. The change works because the class extends `ServletOutput Stream`.

```
...
public class GZIPResponseStream extends ServletOutputStream {
...
```

The response wrapper, `GZIPServletResponseWrapper`, then takes advantage of Java polymorphism and uses the class as if it were a `ServletOutputStream`.

The next important point is what the `GZIPResponseStream` is doing with information written to it by a JSP, Servlet, or static page. The information is not sent to a client; instead, it is written to a `java.util.zip.GZIPOutputStream` that is buffered locally.

```
...
  public void write(int b) throws IOException {
    ...
    gzipstream.write((byte)b);
  }

  public void write(byte b[]) throws IOException {
    write(b, 0, b.length);
  }

  public void write(byte b[], int off, int len) throws IOException {
    ...
    gzipstream.write(b, off, len);
  }
```

After the entire output is buffered and compressed, the compressed content is then sent directly to the client along with modified HTTP response headers. The `close()` method of the `GZIPResponseStream` is responsible for this as it is guaranteed to be called last and only once for each response.

```
...
  public void close() throws IOException {
    if (closed) {
      throw new IOException("This output stream has already been
closed");
    }
```

```
    gzipstream.finish();
    //get the compressed bytes
    byte[] bytes = baos.toByteArray();

    response.addHeader("Content-Encoding", "gzip");
    output.write(bytes);
    output.flush();
    output.close();
    closed = true;
  }
...
```

The end result is that should a client support GZIP compression, the GZIPFilter automatically compresses content requested by that client. Should compression not be supported, then the normal, uncompressed form of the content is sent. Test out the Filter by deploying it with the jspbook Web Application. Add Listing 8-14 into web.xml to apply the GZIPFilter to all resources in the jspbook Web Application.

Listing 8-14 GZIPFilter web.xml Entry

```
<filter>
  <filter-name>GZIPFilter</filter-name>
  <filter-class>com.jspbook.GZIPFilter</filter-class>
</filter>
<filter-mapping>
  <filter-name>GZIPFilter</filter-name>
  <url-pattern>/*</url-pattern>
</filter-mapping>
```

Save the preceding changes to web.xml, compile GZIPFilter.java, GZIP ResponseWrapper.java, and GZIPResponseStream.java, and reload the jspbook Web Application for the changes to take effect. The Filter can be tested by visiting any of the existing examples made by the jspbook Web Application. Should your browser support compression, the example's output is compressed before being sent. To double-check if your browser does support compression, revisit the ShowHeaders Servlet, http://127.0.0.1/jspbook/ShowHeaders. If the accept-encoding header includes the value gzip, then your browser does.

Unfortunately for the sake of learning, the process of compression on the server-side and decompression on the client-side is done seamlessly to an end user. To see the actual compression yourself, a lower view HTTP is required. Recall in Chapter 2 with the introduction to HTTP, an example used the telnet program to spoof an HTTP request. By doing this, the raw contents of an HTTP request and response can be seen. To see the effect of the `GZIPFilter`, spoof another HTTP request for a resource in the jspbook Web Application. Take, for example, the welcome page, `http://127.0.0.1/jspbook/welcome.html`. Spoof an HTTP request by running telnet on port 80.

```
telnet 127.0.0.1 80
```

After the program loads manually, make the HTTP request.

```
GET /jspbook/welcome.html HTTP/1.0
```

The result is an HTTP response with the contents of the page. Figure 8-6 shows the entire process.

Figure 8-6 is not compressed. This is because the spoofed HTTP request did not include an HTTP header to inform the server it accepts content encoded via GZIP comjjpression. Redo the spoofed request, but this time add the following line to the request.

```
GET /jspbook/welcome.html HTTP/1.0
accept-encoding:gzip;
```

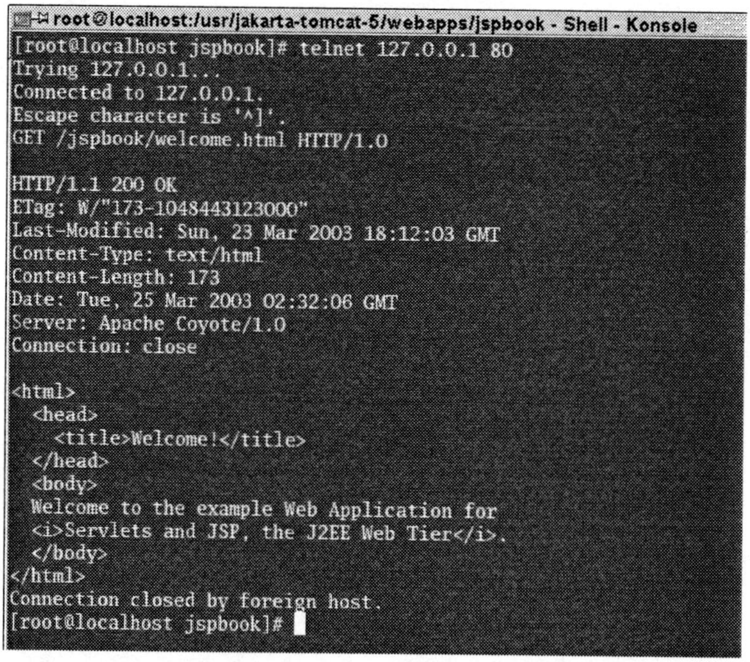

Figure 8-6 Spoofed HTTP Request to welcome.html

Now the response content is compressed. The request and response are shown in Figure 8-7.

The content is gibberish, but compressed gibberish. The important point is that the GZIP compression Filter is working. Should a client accept compressed content, it will be sent. Manually we cannot easily decompress the content, but should a browser be reading this response, it would have little trouble decompressing and rendering the content.

Compression: What Has Been Gained?

The compression Filter is one of the more lengthy examples of this book, but it is also one of the more helpful ones. A compression Filter is a re-usable component that can be applied to just about every Web Application. The strong point of this Filter is that it reduces the amount of information a client must download. The weak point is that it adds extra post-processing to the time it takes to generate the response. In most cases the time it takes to generate a response is dwarfed by the time it takes for a client to download the response. So usually using a plain compression Filter such as the GZIP Filter is always a helpful addition, but for optimum efficiency combine the compression Filter with a cache Filter.

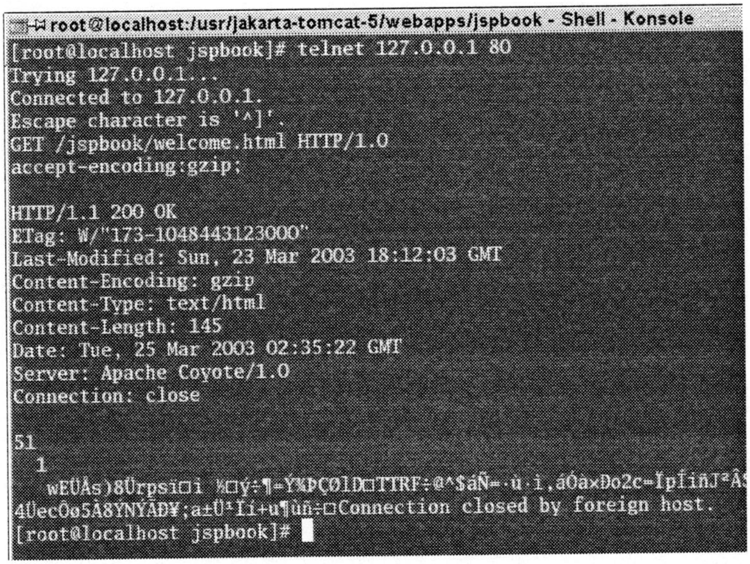

Figure 8-7 Spoofed HTTP Request with Compression to welcome.html

It has been mentioned quite a few times that the GZIP compression algorithm is good because it shrinks the size of the content being sent to a client. Hopefully, you have accepted the usefulness of the compression algorithm, but for clarity let's see just how helpful the compression is. A simple Servlet can show the point. Save Listing 8-15 as `CompressionTest.java` in the `/WEB-INF/classes/com/jspbook` directory of the jspbook Web Application.

Listing 8-15 CompressionTest.java

```java
package com.jspbook;

import java.io.*;
import java.net.*;
import javax.servlet.*;
import javax.servlet.http.*;

public class CompressionTest extends HttpServlet {

  public void doGet(HttpServletRequest request,
                    HttpServletResponse response)
  throws IOException, ServletException {

    response.setContentType("text/html");
    PrintWriter out = response.getWriter();
    out.println("<html>");
    out.println("<head>");
    out.println("<title>Compression Test</title>");
    out.println("</head>");
    out.println("<body>");
    out.println("<h1>Compression Test</h1>");
    out.println("<form>");
    String url = request.getParameter("url");
    if (url != null) {
      out.print("<input size=\"50\" name=\"url\" ");
      out.println("value=\""+url+"\">");
    } else {
      out.println("<input size=\"50\" name=\"url\">");
    }
    out.print("<input type=\"submit\" value=\"Check\">");
    out.println("</form>");
    out.println("URL: "+ url);
    if (url != null) {
      URL noCompress = new URL(url);
      HttpURLConnection huc =
```

```
    (HttpURLConnection)noCompress.openConnection();
huc.setRequestProperty("user-agent","Mozilla(MSIE)");
huc.connect();
ByteArrayOutputStream baos = new ByteArrayOutputStream();
InputStream is = huc.getInputStream();
while(is.read() != -1) {
  baos.write((byte)is.read());
}
byte[] b1 = baos.toByteArray();

URL compress = new URL(url);
HttpURLConnection hucCompress =
    (HttpURLConnection)noCompress.openConnection();
hucCompress.setRequestProperty("accept-encoding","gzip");
hucCompress.setRequestProperty("user-agent","Mozilla(MSIE)");
hucCompress.connect();
ByteArrayOutputStream baosCompress =
  new ByteArrayOutputStream();
InputStream isCompress = hucCompress.getInputStream();
while(isCompress.read() != -1) {
  baosCompress.write((byte)isCompress.read());
}
byte[] b2 = baosCompress.toByteArray();

out.print("<pre>");
out.println("Uncompressed: " + b1.length);
out.println("Compressed: " + b2.length);
out.print("Space saved: "+(b1.length-b2.length)+", or ");
out.println((((b1.length - b2.length)*100)/b1.length)+"%");
out.println("Downstream(2kbps)");
out.println(" No GZIP: "+(float)b1.length/2000+"seconds");
out.println(" GZIP:    "+(float)b2.length/2000+"seconds");
out.println("Downstream(5kbps)");
out.println(" No GZIP: "+(float)b1.length/5000+"seconds");
out.println(" GZIP:    "+(float)b2.length/5000+"seconds");
out.println("Downstream(10kbps)");
out.println(" No GZIP: "+(float)b1.length/10000+"seconds");
out.println(" GZIP:    "+(float)b2.length/10000+"seconds");
out.println("</pre>");
    }
  out.println("</body>");
  out.println("</html>");
  }
}
```

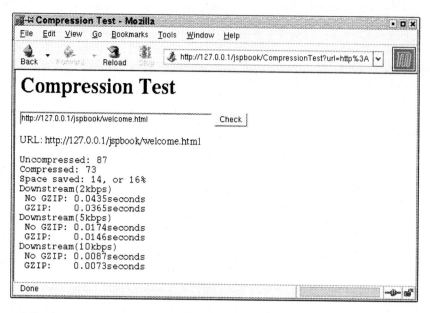

Figure 8-8   CompressionTest Servlet on welcome.html

The preceding code uses a Servlet that uses an HTML page to create a form to query for a URL. After getting a URL, the `java.net.URL` class is used to open a connection up to the URL and receive the response. A second URL is opened up to the same connection and requests a compressed version of the same information. After getting the two, the size of the content is compared and displayed in HTML. Figure 8-8 shows a rendering of the results when testing `http://127.0.0.1/jspbook/welcome.html`.

For `welcome.html` the results are unimpressive. After all this work, the Filter is only saving 16% of the time it takes to download the content. You can try any other example in the jspbook Web Application and you'll see similar results. The 16% hardly seems like it is worth saving. One could argue with really big downloads the 16% is noticeable, but that is not enough justification to Filter content with GZIP compression. The fact is that GZIP is a good algorithm and it can produce up to about 1:6 compression ratio, but the GZIP algorithm approaches this ratio only with highly redundant information or with lots of information so that more redundancy is more likely to occur. All of the examples in the jspbook Web Application are simply too small!

Take into consideration a more realistic example. Consider the main page of JSP Insider, `http://www.jspinsider.com`. This is a fair example of a complex page that has plenty of styled content and some DHTML. Fortunately JSP Insider uses the same GZIP Filter. Try running the compression test Filter on `http://www.jspinsider.com`. Figure 8-9 shows the results.

The results are quite impressive! On a more realistic Web page the compressed content is 79% smaller than the uncompressed. It is about 5 times faster to download the page when using the GZIP Filter.

The lesson learned is the GZIP compression Filter is most helpful when there is a lot of content. For small examples, usually up to 5k, there is really no good reason to compress the content. However, in larger pages, 5k+, the benefit really starts to show.

Cache Filters

Caching is another one of the more helpful uses of response wrapping. The idea behind a cache Filter is to minimize the amount of time it takes to produce a dynamic page. This functionality complements compression Filters and can

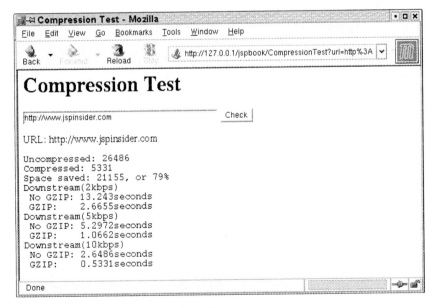

Figure 8-9 CompressionTest Filter on http://www.jspinsider.com

greatly reduce the overhead involved in using dynamic resources such as JSP and Servlets.

A cache Filter works by keeping a copy of a response in memory or on a local disk and re-using it for future requests to the same resource. By doing this the cache Filter can intercept an incoming request, check if the cache for it is valid, and optionally send the cached version of the response. The time benefit comes from using the cache instead of generating the dynamic response. In cases where a Servlet or JSP performs some complex logic or accesses some time-consuming resources, a caching mechanism can greatly increase performance.

The downside to caching is the removal of dynamic generation; some pages cannot be cached. The whole point of using dynamic pages is to create a page on the fly that cannot be done statically. A cache is simply a static version of a page's output. Dynamic pages and caches seem to conflict, but in practice there are plenty of places caching is handy. Consider that not all dynamic pages change each time a client makes a request. Plenty of dynamic pages are only dynamic because they include resources that may possibly change, but are likely not to. One of the most common cases is a dynamic include such as a header or footer. Using a dynamic include is nice, but the end result of the page does not change until one of the includes changes. All of the requests between changes receive the same response. Caching in this case can be very effective as long as the cache is reset occasionally or whenever the includes are changed. The same type of caching can be applied to news pages or listings of links generated by a database.

The point is a good cache Filter is helpful to have because not all dynamic resources need to be generated every time a client makes a request. We have yet to see some good examples in this book to apply a cache filter to, but there will be a few appearing in later chapters. For those examples and to give a concrete example of caching, we are now going to build a simple cache Filter. Save Listing 8-16 as `CacheFilter.java` in the `/WEB-INF/classes/com/jspbook` directory of the jspbook Web Application.

Listing 8-16 CacheFilter.java

```
package com.jspbook;

import java.io.*;
import javax.servlet.*;
import javax.servlet.http.*;
import java.util.*;

public class CacheFilter implements Filter {
```

```java
    ServletContext sc;
    FilterConfig fc;
    long cacheTimeout = Long.MAX_VALUE;

    public void doFilter(ServletRequest req, ServletResponse res,
                         FilterChain chain)
                         throws IOException, ServletException {
      HttpServletRequest request = (HttpServletRequest) req;
      HttpServletResponse response = (HttpServletResponse) res;

      // check if was a resource that shouldn't be cached.
      String r = sc.getRealPath("");
      String path = fc.getInitParameter(request.getRequestURI());
      if (path!= null && path.equals("nocache")) {
        chain.doFilter(request, response);
        return;
      }
      path = r+path;

      // customize to match parameters
      String id = request.getRequestURI()+request.getQueryString();

      // optionally append i18n sensitivity
      String localeSensitive = fc.getInitParameter("locale-
sensitive");
      if (localeSensitive != null) {
        StringWriter ldata = new StringWriter();
        Enumeration locales = request.getLocales();
        while (locales.hasMoreElements()) {
          Locale locale = (Locale)locales.nextElement();
          ldata.write(locale.getISO3Language());
        }
        id = id + ldata.toString();
      }

      File tempDir = (File)sc.getAttribute(
        "javax.servlet.context.tempdir");

      // get possible cache
      String temp = tempDir.getAbsolutePath();
      File file = new File(temp+id);

      // get current resource
      if (path == null) {
```

```java
      path = sc.getRealPath(request.getRequestURI());
    }
    File current = new File(path);

    try {
      long now = Calendar.getInstance().getTimeInMillis();
      //set timestamp check
      if (!file.exists() || (file.exists() &&
          current.lastModified() > file.lastModified()) ||
          cacheTimeout < now - file.lastModified()) {
        String name = file.getAbsolutePath();
        name = name.substring(0,name.lastIndexOf("/"));
        new File(name).mkdirs();
        ByteArrayOutputStream baos = new ByteArrayOutputStream();
        CacheResponseWrapper wrappedResponse =
          new CacheResponseWrapper(response, baos);
        chain.doFilter(req, wrappedResponse);

        FileOutputStream fos = new FileOutputStream(file);
        fos.write(baos.toByteArray());
        fos.flush();
        fos.close();
      }
    } catch (ServletException e) {
      if (!file.exists()) {
        throw new ServletException(e);
      }
    }
    catch (IOException e) {
      if (!file.exists()) {
        throw e;
      }
    }

    FileInputStream fis = new FileInputStream(file);
    String mt = sc.getMimeType(request.getRequestURI());
    response.setContentType(mt);
    ServletOutputStream sos = res.getOutputStream();
    for (int i = fis.read(); i!= -1; i = fis.read()) {
      sos.write((byte)i);
    }
  }
```

```
public void init(FilterConfig filterConfig) {
  this.fc = filterConfig;
  String ct = fc.getInitParameter("cacheTimeout");
  if (ct != null) {
    cacheTimeout = 60*1000*Long.parseLong(ct);
  }
  this.sc = filterConfig.getServletContext();
}

public void destroy() {
  this.sc = null;
  this.fc = null;
}
}
```

The preceding code works by keeping a cache of all resources it is applied to, in the Servlet-defined temporary working directory. If a cache doesn't exist and a response can be cached, the Filter wraps the response and invokes the `doFilter()` method in order to have the container generate a response. Then the Filter both caches the response and sends the content to a client. On subsequent requests for the same resource, the response is used straight from the cache, completely skipping the `doFilter()` method.

Given the preceding description, the Filter's code is easy to understand. First, a check is made to see if a resource should be cached.

```
// check if was a resource that shouldn't be cached.
String path = fc.getInitParameter(request.getRequestURI());
if (path!= null && path.equals("nocache")) {
  chain.doFilter(request, response);
  return;
}
```

By default it is assumed all resources should be cached, but a URL can be ignored by setting an initial parameter of the same name with a value of "nocache". For example, if `/index.jsp` should not be cached, the Filter would have a initial parameter named "/index.jsp" set with the value "nocache".

Should a response be valid for caching, the Filter checks to see if it has already been cached.

```
// customize to match parameters
String id = request.getRequestURI()+request.getQueryString();
```

```
// optionally append i18n sensitivity[3]
...

File tempDir = (File)sc.getAttribute(
  "javax.servlet.context.tempdir");

// get possible cache
String temp = tempDir.getAbsolutePath();
File file = new File(temp+id);

// get current resource
if (path == null) {
  path = sc.getRealPath(request.getRequestURI());
}
File current = new File(path);

try {
  long now = Calendar.getInstance().getTimeInMillis();
  //set timestamp check
  if (!file.exists() || (file.exists() &&
      current.lastModified() > file.lastModified()) ||
      cacheTimeout < now - file.lastModified()) {
```

Two `File` objects are created: one for the possible cache—that is, the saved response in the temporary work directory—and one for the file the container used to generate a response—that is, a JSP. If the cache doesn't exist or the current file has a newer time-stamp, meaning the page has been updated and the cache is invalid, a new cache is made.

```
try {
  long now = Calendar.getInstance().getTimeInMillis();
  //set timestamp check
  if (!file.exists() || (file.exists() &&
      current.lastModified() > file.lastModified()) ||
      cacheTimeout < now - file.lastModified()) {
    String name = file.getAbsolutePath();
    name = name.substring(0,name.lastIndexOf("/"));
    new File(name).mkdirs();
    ByteArrayOutputStream baos = new ByteArrayOutputStream();
```

3. Internationalization (i18N) is covered by a later chapter, but a good cache Filter should check more than just the URL to determine if cached content should be used. In Chapter 15 a proper discussion will address why this is so important.

```
        CacheResponseWrapper wrappedResponse =
            new CacheResponseWrapper(response, baos);
        chain.doFilter(req, wrappedResponse);

        FileOutputStream fos = new FileOutputStream(file);
        fos.write(baos.toByteArray());
        fos.flush();
        fos.close();
    }
}
```

The new cache is made by wrapping the response with a `CacheResponse`
`Wrapper` object, which we will code shortly, that is assumed to take an output
stream and write the contents of a response to it. Ideally, the output stream is a
`ByteArrayOutputStream`, making it possible to buffer a complete response. A
successfully buffered response is then cached as a file in the Temporary Work
directory.

After a new cache is made or the filter decides to use an existing cache, the
cached file is read and sent as the response.

```
FileInputStream fis = new FileInputStream(file);
String mt = sc.getMimeType(request.getRequestURI());
response.setContentType(mt);
ServletOutputStream sos = res.getOutputStream();
for (int i = fis.read(); i!= -1; i = fis.read()) {
    sos.write((byte)i);
}
```

Information about the responses MIME type is taken directly from `web.xml`.
It is assumed a `mime-mapping` element is set for each type of content being
cached. By default Tomcat includes all of the common mappings; however, if you
were to use a non-conventional URL ending, such as ".xhtml" for XHTML, a new
`mime-mapping` element is required in `web.xml`.

```
<mime-mapping>
 <extension>xhtml</extension>
 <mime-type>application/xhtml+xml</mime-type>
</mime-mapping>
```

The end result is that the Filter caches responses and uses its cache to skip the
time required to generate dynamic pages. Cached content is always properly
encoded and sent back identically, as if it was the generated response. However,
one problem still exists. What about pages that slowly change? Pages that can be

cached but need to be updated every once in a while—for example, a news page that is generated by querying a database? It may be fine to cache the page for performance, but the cache should automatically expire every so often in order to refresh the news, regardless if the code for the news page changes or not. The cache Filter also provides this sort of functionality, by allowing a cache time-out value to be specified as an initial parameter. The parameter's name is cacheTimeout, and the value is the number of minutes before a cache should be invalidated.

CacheFilter.java is only part of the complete cache Filter. In order to create cached copies of a response, the response itself needs to be captured. The CacheResponseWrapper class is used by the CacheFilter to capture and cache responses. The code for the CacheResponseWrapper class is very similar to the GZIPResponseWrapper and is as follows. Save Listing 8-17 as CacheResponse Wrapper.java in the /WEB-INF/classes/com/jspbook directory of the jspbook Web Application.

Listing 8-17 CacheResponseWrapper.java

```
package com.jspbook;

import java.io.*;
import javax.servlet.*;
import javax.servlet.http.*;

public class CacheResponseWrapper
    extends HttpServletResponseWrapper {
  protected HttpServletResponse origResponse = null;
  protected ServletOutputStream stream = null;
  protected PrintWriter writer = null;
  protected OutputStream cache = null;

  public CacheResponseWrapper(HttpServletResponse response,
      OutputStream cache) {
    super(response);
    origResponse = response;
    this.cache = cache;
  }

  public ServletOutputStream createOutputStream()
      throws IOException {
    return (new CacheResponseStream(origResponse, cache));
  }
```

```
public void flushBuffer() throws IOException {
  stream.flush();
}

public ServletOutputStream getOutputStream()
    throws IOException {
  if (writer != null) {
    throw new IllegalStateException(
      "getWriter() has already been called!");
  }

  if (stream == null)
    stream = createOutputStream();
  return (stream);
}

public PrintWriter getWriter() throws IOException {
  if (writer != null) {
    return (writer);
  }

  if (stream != null) {
    throw new IllegalStateException(
      "getOutputStream() has already been called!");
  }

  stream = createOutputStream();
  writer = new PrintWriter(new OutputStreamWriter(stream, "UTF-
8"));
  return (writer);
  }
}
```

There is only one important point to note about `CacheResponseWrapper`.
`java`. Instead of a `ServletResponseStream`, the class returns a `CacheResponse`
`Stream`.

```
public ServletOutputStream createOutputStream()
    throws IOException {
  return (new CacheResponseStream(origResponse, cache));
}
```

A clear pattern should be appearing with output-capturing response wrappers.
The wrapper class itself usually has little to do with capturing a response. All of the

logic involved in creating a response is encapsulated by the `ServletOutputStream` class. Custom wrapper objects are commonly just a method of changing the default `ServletOutputStream` returned by a `ServletResponse` to a custom subclass of `ServletOutputStream`. In this case the custom class is `CacheResponseStream`. The important caching code occurs in the `CacheResponseStream` class.

The `CacheResponseStream` class is used by the cache Filter to save a response's content to a given output stream. As the cache Filter uses the class, a `ByteArrayOutputStream` object is used as the output stream and a response is kept as an array of bytes. The cached bytes are then used to save the response as a file and to send the response to the client. The code for the `CacheResponseStream` is as follows. Save Listing 8-18 as `CacheResponseStream.java` in the `/WEB-INF/class/com/jspbook` directory of the jspbook Web Application.

Listing 8-18 CacheResponseStream.java

```
package com.jspbook;

import java.io.*;
import javax.servlet.*;
import javax.servlet.http.*;

public class CacheResponseStream extends ServletOutputStream {
  protected boolean closed = false;
  protected HttpServletResponse response = null;
  protected ServletOutputStream output = null;
  protected OutputStream cache = null;

  public CacheResponseStream(HttpServletResponse response,
      OutputStream cache) throws IOException {
    super();
    closed = false;
    this.response = response;
    this.cache = cache;
  }

  public void close() throws IOException {
    if (closed) {
      throw new IOException(
        "This output stream has already been closed");
    }
```

```
      cache.close();
      closed = true;
  }

  public void flush() throws IOException {
      if (closed) {
        throw new IOException(
          "Cannot flush a closed output stream");
      }
      cache.flush();
  }

  public void write(int b) throws IOException {
      if (closed) {
        throw new IOException(
          "Cannot write to a closed output stream");
      }
      cache.write((byte)b);
  }

  public void write(byte b[]) throws IOException {
      write(b, 0, b.length);
  }

  public void write(byte b[], int off, int len)
      throws IOException {
      if (closed) {
        throw new IOException(
          "Cannot write to a closed output stream");
      }
      cache.write(b, off, len);
  }

  public boolean closed() {
      return (this.closed);
  }

  public void reset() {
      //noop
  }
}
```

There is one important point to note about CacheResponseStream. All of the write methods are overridden to write to a custom OutputStream class, which must be passed as an argument to the class's constructor. By doing this, the `CacheResponseStream` object ensures no content is sent to a client—all content is sent to the provided `OutputStream` object.

With the `CacheFilter`, `CacheResponseWrapper`, and `CacheResponseStream` classes, the cache Filter is ready to be used. Deploy the Filter with the jspbook Web Application by adding Listing 8-19 in `web.xml`. Make sure the second part of this entry appears *after* the mapping for the GZIP Filter.

Listing 8-19 web.xml Entry for the Cache Filter

```
. . .
<filter>
  <filter-name>CacheFilter</filter-name>
  <filter-class>com.jspbook.CacheFilter</filter-class>
</filter>
. . .
<filter-mapping>
  <filter-name>GZIPFilter</filter-name>
  <url-pattern>/*</url-pattern>
</filter-mapping>
<filter-mapping>
  <filter-name>CacheFilter</filter-name>
  <url-pattern>/timemonger.jsp</url-pattern>
  <init-param>
    <param-name>cacheTimeout</param-name>
    <param-value>1</param-value>
  </init-param>
</filter-mapping>
. . .
```

Unlike the GZIP Filter, the cache Filter should not be applied to an entire Web Application. As was previously mentioned, some pages must not be cached because they produce a dynamic output for each client request. This is the reason the `web.xml` entry in Listing 8-18 only maps the cache Filter to `timemonger.jsp`. Currently, `timemonger.jsp` is a fictitious page, but we will soon create it as an example to illustrate the cache Filter in use. Later, discussion will be finished about the cache Filter, explaining how it knows to reset a cache and why it was applied after the GZIP Filter.

The code for `timemonger.jsp` can be anything that consumes time. All dynamic pages will consume time, but it is helpful to have a clear example. For `timemonger.jsp`, we will create a page with a few nested loops that do nothing but consume time as shown in Listing 8-20.

Listing 8-20   timemonger.jsp

```
<html>
  <head>
    <title>Cache Filter Test</title>
  </head>
  <body>
A test of the cache Filter.
<%
 // mock time-consuming code
 for (int i=0;i<100000;i++) {
   for (int j=0;j<1000;j++) {
     //noop
   }
 }
%>
  </body>
</html>
```

You can informally test the page by browsing to `http://127.0.0.1/` `jspbook/timemonger.jsp`. The page takes a few seconds to load, but on subsequent requests you should notice it takes a lot less time. However, an informal test is of little help. The point of a cache Filter is that it provides notable performance increases. We can formally test the page using a simple JSP.

Save Listing 8-21 as `TestCache.jsp` in the root directory of the jspbook Web Application.

Listing 8-21   TestCache.jsp

```
<%@ page import="java.util.*, java.net.*, java.io.*" %>
<%
  String url = request.getParameter("url");
  long[] times = new long[2];
  if (url != null) {
    for (int i=0;i<2;i++) {
      long start = Calendar.getInstance().getTimeInMillis();
      URL u = new URL(url);
      HttpURLConnection huc =
        (HttpURLConnection)u.openConnection();
      huc.setRequestProperty("user-agent","Mozilla(MSIE)");
      huc.connect();
      ByteArrayOutputStream baos = new ByteArrayOutputStream();
      InputStream is = huc.getInputStream();
      while(is.read() != -1) {
```

```
        baos.write((byte)is.read());
      }
      long stop = Calendar.getInstance().getTimeInMillis();
      times[i] = stop-start;
    }
  }
  request.setAttribute("t1", new Long(times[0]));
  request.setAttribute("t2", new Long(times[1]));
  request.setAttribute("url", url);

%><html>
<head>
  <title>Cache Test</title>
</head>
<body>
<h1>Cache Test Page</h1>
Enter a URL to test.
<form method="POST">
<input name="url" size="50">
<input type="submit" value="Check URL">
</form>
 <p><b>Testing: ${url}</b></p>
 Request 1: ${t1} milliseconds<br/>
 Request 2: ${t2} milliseconds<br/>
 Time saved: ${t1-t2} milliseconds<br/>
</body>
</html>
```

The page is a JSP that tests URLs, similar to `TestCompression.jsp`. A connection is opened to a specific URL and the content is requested twice. It is assumed that the server is not currently caching the response to the URL; the first request should take the full time of generating the request. However, the second request is assumed to hit the cache. There is little we can do to ensure that `TestCache.jsp` works as expected for all URLs, but because we know how our cache Filter works and we can control our cache, the test will work for us.

Make sure all of the cache Filter classes are compiled, the `web.xml` modifications are saved, and reload the jspbook Web Application to reflect the changes. Browse to `http://127.0.0.1/jspbook/TestCache.jsp` to start the test. Fill in the form with the URL to `timemonger.jsp`: `http://127.0.0.1/jspbook/time monger.jsp`. Submit the information and a report is presented of the response times. Figure 8-10 provides a browser rendering of the results.

Figure 8-10 Browser Rendering of the Cache Test

The speed difference comes from the cache Filter doing its job. If you look in the temporary work directory Tomcat keeps for the jspbook Web Application, you will notice a new file has appeared, `timemonger.jspnull`. This file is a copy of the HTML generated by `timemonger.jsp`. The cache Filter is saving time by using this file instead of reevaluating `timemonger.jsp` each time a request is made. Note, that `TestCache.jsp` will only work once every minute with the current Filter configuration due to the one-minute cache time-out.

The benefit of a cache Filter should be clear; caching optimizes the amount of time it takes to generate a static, or usually static, response. The cache Filter introduced in this chapter is a helpful Filter to know about and use in a Web Application. The time difference between using a cached copy of content versus a dynamic response by a JSP or Servlet can be quite dramatic. When possible, it is always worth caching dynamically generated responses.

Caching Servlet Responses

The cache Filter we just created caches information based on a URL and by checking if the file that generates that URL is outdated—that is, it checks the time-stamp of the JSP or HTML page. However, the response of a Servlet is cached as easily as the response generated from a JSP or HTML page, but when a Servlet is updated it is difficult to determine based on a URL what `.java` file corresponds to the Servlet. It can be done by parsing `web.xml`, checking the URL mapping element, but this is a task left to you. For simplicity, `CacheFilter.java` uses a manual check. If a URL is mapped to a Servlet, you may ensure that the cache is updated each time the Servlet's code is updated by setting an initial configuration element.

Previously in the chapter, a point was made on how `CacheFilter.java` can be made to not cache particular URLs. An initial parameter of the same name as the URL can be set with the value "nocache". For example, the following configuration would skip caching `index.jsp`.

```
<filter>
  <filter-name>Cache</filter-name>
  <filter-class>com.jspbook.CacheFilter</filter-class>
  <init-param>
    <param-name>/jspbook/index.jsp</param-name>
    <param-value>nocache</param-value>
  </init-param>
</filter>
```

Nothing was noted about what happens if the value is other than "nocache". Any other value is treated as if it is the location of a file in the Web Application that should be time-checked. For example, if the URL `/index.jsp` is generated by a Servlet, `/WEB-INF/classes/com/jspbook/Index.java`, the following mapping would map cache invalidation to that file.

```
<filter>
  <filter-name>Cache</filter-name>
  <filter-class>com.jspbook.CacheFilter</filter-class>
  <init-param>
    <param-name>/index.jsp</param-name>
    <param-value>/WEB-INF/classes/com/jspbook/Index.java</param-value>
  </init-param>
</filter>
```

Using the above mapping, if a change was made to the `Index.java` Servlet (or whatever else the file may be), the cache for `/index.jsp` would be reset. By providing this functionality, it is possible to control caching of both implicitly mapped resources, such as HTML or JSP files, and explicitly mapped resources, such as Servlets and Filters.

Caching and Fault Tolerance

A superb use of caching that is worth mentioning is *fault tolerance*. A cached copy of a response is good for more than simply speeding up a request. Imagine a situation where a Web Application is working perfectly fine with a cache Filter speeding up responses. What happens should a change occur, perhaps a JSP typo or a database failure? Normally an exception is thrown and the user is presented with an error page, as detailed in Chapter 4. However, assuming a cache of the would-be generated response exists, there may be no need to show the error page. Instead show the cache and continue to do so until the resource is fixed—that is, the code typo is corrected or the database comes back online.

The cache Filter we just created tries to be fault tolerant. The code that invokes the `doFilter()` method is surrounded by a try-catch statement.

```
try {
...
    } catch (ServletException e) {
      if (!file.exists()) {
        throw new ServletException(e);
      }
    }
    catch (IOException e) {
      if (!file.exists()) {
        throw e;
      }
    }
```

Should an exception be thrown, the filter optionally re-throws the exception based on if a cache exists or not. If a cache exists, the cache is displayed. When no cache exists, the exception is passed to the Web Application and assumed to be handled by an error page.

The implicit fault-tolerance behavior of `CacheFilter.java` may or may not be what you need, but it is helpful in almost any situation where a cache Filter is helpful. Therefore, bundling the code with the cache Filter is a valid decision. In any case, it is helpful to see that the fault-tolerance mechanism works. Browse to the time-wasting page, `http://127.0.0.1/jspbook/timemonger.jsp`, to ensure a version of it is in the current cache. Next, deliberately introduce an error in the page—make a typo in the code. Browse back to the page and note that instead of an error page, the cached content is displayed.

Filters That Provide JSP-Replacing Functionality

Throughout the book both Servlets and JSPs have been treated as complementary technologies that you should use when building Web Applications. This is true, but in some cases it may be desirable to use another styling language besides JSP. For instance, the standardized XML styling mechanism is the eXtensible Stylesheet Language Transformations (XSLTs). XSLT is popularly used with many XML projects including Java XML projects. Should you be working on a project with a group of XML/XSLT developers, it makes little sense to completely drop XSLT in favor of learning JSP. The better solution would be to stick with XML/XSLT and build a Filter takes care of the transformations.

Such a Filter is not difficult to build and it could easily operate by intercepting requests to all resources of a certain extension—say, `*.xml`. Instead of showing resources ending in XML, the Filter could automatically apply an XSLT stylesheet and return the transformed content. If you are familiar with XSLT, the Filter could additionally do a check to see if the client can do transformations (most current browsers do). If that is the case, then the Filter could simply give the raw XML and XSLT to a client and avoid doing a server-side transformation altogether.

A JSP Replacing Filter will not be demonstrated by this book. It goes against the primary theme, and the topic itself deserves discussing many more unrelated topics for completeness. The important point to take away from this section is that Filters are part of the Servlet specification and are not tied to JSP. Should it be desired to use a JSP replacing technology for style, Filters are an ideal choice for the Web Application implementation.

Summary

Filters are an extremely powerful addition to the Servlet specification. They allow the manipulation of data both before and after the resource has executed and in a method that is cleanly implemented. With that power comes the responsibility of knowing and understanding the HTTP protocol. Filters will be used for many things from data manipulation, through logging and security. Use them, but use them with care!

In this chapter, we didn't introduce many new concepts because a Filter is very much like a Servlet. After explaining the similarities and the few important differences, discussion quickly changed to focus on what Filters are best used for. Link tracking, auditing code, compression, and caching were all demonstrated. The Filters used are all helpful ones to know about, and the code examples can be migrated directly into your Servlet projects.

Look for further uses of Filters in the chapters to come. There are many more great uses that work their way into the chapters that pertain to design pattern, multi-client support, and security.

Chapter 9

Managing State in a Web Application

State is an important concept to be aware of in all types of programming. After all, conventional programming relies on being able to accurately persist what a program has done. Web programming is no different, and there are many important things to be aware of when managing state in a Web Application. In some cases you can get by perfectly fine assuming the state of a Web Application is kept consistent enough to perform adequately. However, a good Web Application programmer needs to understand why state management is an issue and how to always ensure it is done properly. It is the goal of this chapter to clearly define and illustrate how to appropriately manage state in a Web Application.

This chapter discusses the following topics:

- Maintaining session state with HTTP, a stateless protocol.
- The `javax.servlet.http.HttpSession` object and a proper look at session scope.
- Persisting session state.
- Cookies and saving bits of information in the client's browser.
- Initializing session resources.
- State and thread safety.
- The `javax.servlet.SingleThreadModel` interface, which is something that should not be used.

This chapter is intended to be read straight through; however, it is a chapter that is not critical to developing simple JSP-orientated Web Applications. You could skim this chapter and still be able to get your job done although the issues presented and covered by this chapter are critical to Web Applications that **must** work properly. If you plan on making a career out of being a JSP or Servlet developer, you need to read the entire chapter.

HTTP and Session State

HTTP and session state have to do with how a Web Application uses HTTP to maintain the state of a user's session. HTTP is a connected protocol; it goes over TCP[1] and not UDP[2]. When a browser sends a request to a server, the browser establishes a connection, sends an HTTP request, and consumes an HTTP response. If the response is an HTML page, then the client will typically parse the page looking for other tags that require data to be downloaded (such as IMG or applet tags). If there are such tags on the page, then the browser will re-use the same connection to download that data. However, as soon as the page "transaction" is complete, the browser will close the connection. This has a major impact on the way Web Applications work. Most applications maintain data on behalf of a user and need to track users. The data may be a shopping cart or simply user preferences, but as each user request is sent over a different connection, there is no way to link subsequent requests and keep the state.

You may think it would be possible to identify users by their IP address. IP addresses are unique on the network, so why can those not be used? There are many reasons for not using IP addresses. For example, the computer used to author this chapter has an IP address of `192.168.0.2`, this is a "non-routable" IP[3] address. Such an address is used only to identify computers on a local network. The computer is connected through a router. That router has a real routable IP address provided by the ISP it is using. The router uses Network Address Translation (NAT) to the IP address and the connection to the Internet. When the computer browses to a server, the server sees the IP address of the router, not of the PC. Many, many users are connected through routers or proxies of some description. Their IP address never makes it out onto the Internet; instead the IP address of the proxy is sent, so a server trying to use an IP address to uniquely identify a client would end up identifying some group of clients behind a proxy!

---

1. Transmission Control Protocol (TCP) is a "connection-orientated" protocol because the service it provides guarantees information gets to its destination.
2. User Datagram Protocol (UDP) is a "connection-less" protocol because it does not ensure information gets to its destination.
3. The Internet Protocol (IP) distinctly segregates addresses into different categories for use. Non-routable addresses fall into various ranges; one of the ranges starts with `192.168`, which is only valid on internal networks.

The concept that is important to understand can clearly be illustrated by the JSP in Listing 9-1.

Listing 9-1 ShowIPAddress.jsp

```
<html>
<head>
  <title>ShowIPAddress.jsp</title>
</head>
<body>
Remote Address : <%= request.getRemoteAddr()%><br/>
</body>
</html>
```

Save the preceding code as `ShowIPAddress.jsp` in the base directory of the jspbook Web Application. Try out the code to find your IP; browse to `http://127.0.0.1/jspbook/ShowIPAddress.jsp`. The IP address of your local computer is shown. Figure 9-1 shows a browser rendering of the Servlet's output[4].

Now to illustrate the point. Browse the online example of this Servlet running at the book support site, `http://www.jspbook.com/examples/ShowIPAddress.jsp`. There is a good chance that the returned page will display an IP address that is not yours. For example, on the computer used to author this chapter, the example shows an IP address of `194.117.xxx.xxx`, which is a cache server running somewhere inside of an ISP. The point is that a server cannot track users by using their IP address. Something else is needed, and that something has to be provided at either the application or application protocol (HTTP) layer of the stack[5].

Using an ID to Identify Clients

Given the preceding, you should be curious as to how a server identifies a client. Essentially, the client and server code need to exchange some identifier that uniquely identifies this client to this server. Note that this identifier does not uniquely identify this client on the Internet; it is a value that only means something to the server that creates it. This identifier can be exchanged either with or without the client's cooperation.

---

4. If you are using local loopback, 127.0.0.1, this will show up as your IP address when running the example locally. You can check the IP address of your machine (if it has one) using command prompt utilities such as `ifconfig`, on Linux, or `ipconfig`, on Windows.
5. The commonly referenced ISO 7-layer model of the Internet.

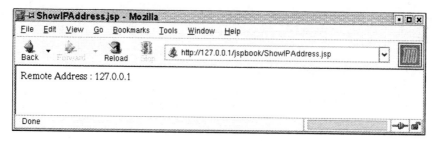

Figure 9-1   Browser Rendering of ShowIPAddress.jsp

There are typically three ways that this ID will be exchanged: as an HTTP header (cookies), as extra data attached to a URL (URL rewriting), or by having each page contain a form and then send the ID as part of the form data (hidden fields). The first two of these mechanisms are supported as part of the Servlet specification, but the third is not. The third option is an application-level way of managing state and will not be discussed further here. Depending on the type of application you are building, there might be an inherent ID mechanism, and not all Web Applications are designed to produce HTML.

javax.servlet.http.HttpSession

The Servlet specification defines a class, HttpSession, and several APIs that allow an application to manage client state, also called session state or conversational state. A Servlet or JSP can create a new HttpSession or get the existing one by invoking the getSession() method. If an instance of HttpSession is created by an application, it will be associated with an ID and will hold the client's data. The generated ID will be sent back to the client either as a Cookie or by using URL re-writing (more on this later).

Information about a client's current session can be obtained at any time. The JSP in Listing 9-2 exposes a client's session for debugging purposes.

Listing 9-2   ShowSession.jsp

```
<html>
<head>
  <title>ShowSession.jsp</title>
</head>
<body>
Session ID : <%= session.getId() %><br>
isNew: <%= session.isNew() %><br>
```

```
</body>
</html>
```

There is one important thing in the preceding code that needs to be explained. There is no call to `HttpServletRequest getSession()`. This is because all JSPs automatically do this in order to establish the implicit `session` object. If the preceding was authored as a Servlet, the `getSession()` call would have to be explicitly coded. This is both a good and bad thing. It is good because the `implicit session` object can be helpful; however, it is bad because if you do not want to have the overhead of sessions, then you need to explicitly declare so in the JSP page directive. In the case of Servlets, sessions are not created until you first call the `HttpServletRequest getSession()` method.

Save the preceding code as `ShowSession.jsp` in the base directory of the jspbook Web Application. Browse to `http://127.0.0.1/jspbook/ShowSession.jsp`. Your unique session ID will be shown. It should resemble Figure 9-2.

The session ID is displayed after "Session ID". Each client a Web Application is keeping track of has one of these unique identification numbers associated with it. The boolean value `isNew` describes if the session was just created, true, or if this is a subsequent request of an existing session.

Session Scope

The `HttpSession` object is a data container. The data stored in the container are private to a given client and will persist until the server destroys the client's session. `HttpSession` has four methods that allow objects to be used with session scope.

- **Object getAttribute(java.lang.String name)**: The `getAttribute()` method returns an object bound to the session with the given

Figure 9-2   Browser Rendering of ShowSession.jsp

name. Usually the object is an instance of a subclass and must be typecast appropriately before use.

- **Enumeration getAttributeNames():** The `getAttributeNames()` method returns a `java.util.Enumeration` object with all of the names of objects bound to the session. In combination with the `getAttribute()` method, this method is helpful in determining what objects are currently bound in session scope.

- **Object removeAttribute(java.lang.String name):** The `removeAttribute()` method removes an object with the given name from session scope and returns it, or `null` is returned if no object is bound with that name.

- **void setAttribute(String name, Object attribute):** The `setAttribute()` method is used to bind an object to the session with the given name. Any object previously bound with the same name is removed.

These methods are used by an application to store data on behalf of a client. The data stored in session scope are held as name/value pairs. The *names* are strings, and the *values* are Java objects.

Session scope is helpful for scoping any object that must be accessed during subsequent requests. For example, if an application manages a shopping cart, the information about the shopping cart needs to somehow be persisted during multiple requests from the client.

The code to persist an object in session scope resembles the following; this would be the code for a fictitious shopping cart object, `ShoppingCart`:

```
ShoppingCart shoppingCart = new ShoppingCart();
HttpSession session = request.getSession();
session.setAttribute("cart", shoppingCart);
```

Subsequent calls to the same Servlet or completely different Servlets can then manipulate the same shopping cart via its session binding.

```
HttpSession session = request.getSession();
ShoppingCart shoppingCart =
  (ShoppingCart)session.getAttribute("cart");
```

From the preceding example it should be clear how to use the `HttpSession` object and why you might want to use it. However, it has been previously mentioned that HTTP is a stateless protocol and that IP cannot be used to accurately track session ID. You should be curious as to how a Web Application successfully keeps track of users. How does the unique ID go back and forth between the sever and client? The mechanism used is one of two things: either Cookies or URL rewriting.

Cookies

Cookies were originally developed by Netscape Communications to solve the problem of keeping session context using HTTP. Cookies consist of a server sending some information, a "cookie", for a client to store locally, and on future requests to that server, the client sends back the cookie information via HTTP headers. Assuming the client's software supports cookies, the whole process requires no user interactions and is an ideal tool for keeping session context.

Cookies are currently standardized by the Internet Engineering Task Force (IETF), `http://www.ietf.org/rfc/rfc2109.txt`, but this does not mean that cookies have absolute support on all Web-savvy software. Due to the nature of cookies they can be used to snoop, to a limited extent[6], on a client's browsing habits. For the most part cookie abuse is not a problem, but because of the issue, most browsers allow cookies to be disabled.

Cookies are name/value pairs that in HTTP are exchanged via two headers: `Set-Cookie` and `Cookie`. `Set-Cookie` goes from the server to the client, and `Cookie` from client to server. The `Set-Cookie` header is sent once, when the session is first established. Cookies have a time-out, and a client keeps a copy of the cookie's value until that time-out expires.

The headers can be seen by spoofing an HTTP request using the same method that was shown in Chapter 2. For example, a spoofed request to Tomcat results in the following content. The `Set-Cookie` header is easily spotted:

```
HTTP/1.1 200 OK
Date: Thu, 30 May 2002 16:48:08 GMT
Transfer-Encoding: chunked
Server: Apache Tomcat/5.0 (HTTP/1.1 Connector)
Set-Cookie:
JSESSIONID=50BAB1DB58D45F833D78D9EC1C5A10C5;Path=/jspbook
...
```

Subsequent requests for content are then responsible for passing the given cookie information back to the server:

```
GET /jspbook/servlet/com.jspbook.SessionState HTTP/1.1
Accept: image/gif, image/x-xbitmap, image/jpeg, image/pjpeg,
```

---

6. See `http://ciac.llnl.gov/ciac/bulletins/i-034.shtml`

```
application/vnd.ms-excel, application/vnd.ms-powerpoint,
application/msword, */*
Accept-Language: en-gb
Accept-Encoding: gzip, deflate
User-Agent: Mozilla/4.0 (compatible; MSIE 6.0; Windows NT 5.1; .NET
CLR 1.0.3705)
Host: localhost:8080 Connection: Keep-Alive
Cookie: JSESSIONID=50BAB1DB58D45F833D78D9EC1C5A10C5
```

Cookies are not designed to only provide session ID; they can be used to share any little "cookie" of information. The Servlet specification defines a cookie that Web Applications should use to convey session ID: JSESSIONID. The value of the cookie follows after the equal sign, =, and is a long hexadecimal string—that is, the session ID. JSESSIONID is a reserved name and you should ensure Servlet and JSP code do not improperly manipulate it.

Besides the simple name/value of a cookie there are extra methods of sending meta-information using the cookie's value. However, understanding the exact method is not important because the Servlet API abstracts away the technical details of a cookie with the javax.servlet.http.Cookie class. Using the Cookie class, you can manipulate all aspects of a cookie using familiar Java methods.

The Cookie object has the following methods:

- **getComment()**: The getComment() method returns the comment describing the purpose of this cookie, or null if the cookie has no comment.

- **getDomain()**: The getDomain() method returns a String object representing the domain name set for this cookie. The domain name defines what hosts the cookie is sent to by the client.

- **getMaxAge()**: The getMaxAge() method returns an int value representing the maximum age of the cookie, specified in seconds. A value of –1 indicates the cookie will persist until browser shutdown.

- **getName()**: The getName() method returns a String object representing the name of the cookie.

- **getPath()**: The getPath() method returns a String object representing the path on the server to which the browser returns this cookie. A path is similar to a Servlet mapping and can narrow a cookie's use to certain URL patterns for a particular domain name.

- **getSecure()**: The getSecure() method returns a boolean value that is true if the browser is sending cookies only over a secure protocol, or false if the browser can send cookies using any protocol. HTTP is an insecure protocol. Secure protocols such as SSL and TLS are discussed in Chapter 10.

- **getValue():** The `getValue()` method returns a `String` object representing the value of the cookie.

- **getVersion():** The `getVersion()` method returns an `int` representing the version of the protocol this cookie complies with.

- **setComment(java.lang.String purpose):** The `setComment()` method is used to specify a comment that describes a cookie's purpose.

- **setDomain(java.lang.String pattern):** The `setDomain()` method specifies the domain within which this cookie should be presented.

- **setMaxAge(int expiry):** The `setMaxAge()` method sets the maximum age of the cookie in seconds.

- **setPath(java.lang.String uri):** The `setPath()` method specifies a path for the cookie to which the client should return the cookie for a particular domain.

- **setSecure(boolean flag):** Indicates to the browser whether the cookie should only be sent using a secure protocol, such as HTTPS or SSL.

- **setValue(java.lang.String newValue):** The `setValue()` method assigns a new value to a cookie after the cookie is created. The default value of a cookie is specified when calling the constructor.

- **setVersion(int v):** The `setVersion()` method sets the version of the cookie protocol this cookie complies with.

Cookies sent from a client's request can be retrieved using the `getCookies()` method of the corresponding `HttpServletRequest` instance. Newly created `Cookie` objects can be sent with a response by calling the `addCookie()` method of the corresponding `HttpServletResponse` instance. A new instance of a `Cookie` object can be created by calling the `Cookie` constructor and providing a cookie name and value as parameters. The only thing you need to worry about is invoking the getter and setter methods of the `Cookie` instance, depending on what you are doing with the cookie.

It is helpful to be familiar with manipulating cookies because they are a powerful tool and something that is used should you like it or not. Being able to read cookies is helpful if you are trying to debug a session or if you are persisting information on the client-side via cookies. Accessing cookies from a request is simple and demonstrated by the JSP in Listing 9-3.

Listing 9-3 ShowCookies.jsp

```
<%@ taglib uri="http://java.sun.com/jstl/core_rt" prefix="c" %>
<html>
<head>
    <title>Cookies Sent By Your Client</title>
</head>
<body>
<h1>Cookies sent by your client</h1>
<c:forEach var="c" begin="0" items="${cookie}">
 Name: <b>${c.value.name}</b><br>
 Value: ${c.value.value}
</c:forEach>
</body>
</html>
```

The JSP uses the JSTL and JSP EL to loop through all of the cookies and display information about each one. Save ShowCookies.jsp in the base directory of the jspbook Web Application. Browse to http://127.0.0.1/jspbook/Show Cookies.jsp at anytime to see what cookies your browser is currently keeping track of. Figure 9-3 shows what the output looks like when rendered by a Web browser.

Figure 9-3 provides a nice insight to what cookies are being used by a Web Application; however, this is not the only use of reading cookie values. The information contained in a cookie can be used for anything.

Depending on the specific browser, the number of cookies a client will keep track of varies, but usually 20 cookies are allowed from a particular domain. Uses of cookies vary depending upon the specific implementation, but it is easy to show how to create, modify, and destroy cookies with another simple Servlet. To extend ShowCookies.jsp, Listing 9-4 is a Servlet that allows cookies to be arbitrarily added, removed, or edited.

Listing 9-4 EditCookies.java

```
package com.jspbook;

import java.util.*;
import java.io.*;
import javax.servlet.*;
import javax.servlet.http.*;

public class EditCookies extends HttpServlet {
```

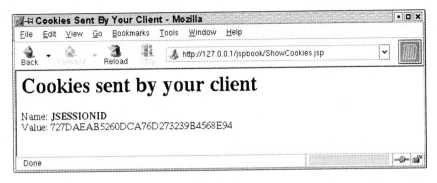

Figure 9-3 Browser Rendering of ShowCookies.jsp

```java
public void doGet(HttpServletRequest request,
                  HttpServletResponse response)
  throws IOException, ServletException {

  response.setContentType("text/html");
  PrintWriter out = response.getWriter();
  Cookie[] cookies = request.getCookies();

  // Get parameters to add/edit a cookie.
  String cookieName = request.getParameter("name");
  String cookieValue = request.getParameter("value");
  if (cookieName != null && !cookieName.equals("")
      && cookieValue != null && !cookieValue.equals("")) {
    Cookie cookie = new Cookie(cookieName, cookieValue);
    response.addCookie(cookie);
    response.sendRedirect("/jspbook/EditCookies");
  }

  // Delete a cookie if requested.
  String cookieToDelete =
    request.getParameter("deleteCookie");
  if (cookieToDelete != null && !cookieToDelete.equals("")) {
    for (int i=0;i<cookies.length;i++) {
      Cookie cookie = cookies[i];
      if(cookie.getName().equals(cookieToDelete)) {
        cookie.setMaxAge(0);
        response.addCookie(cookie);
```

```java
                response.sendRedirect("/jspbook/EditCookies");
            }
        }
    }

    out.println("<html>");
    out.println("<head>");
    out.println("<title>Cookies sent by your client</title>");
    out.println("</head>");
    out.println("<body>");
    out.println("<p>The following cookies were sent:</p>");
    if (cookies == null) {
        out.println("No cookies were sent!<br>");
    }
    else {
        // List the current cookies.
        for (int i=0; i<cookies.length ;i++) {
            Cookie cookie = cookies[i];
            out.println("<h3>Cookie #" +i + "</h3>");
            out.println("<form method=\"post\">");
            out.print("<b>Name</b>: <input name=\"name\" value=\"");
            out.println(cookie.getName()+"\"><br>");
            out.print("<b>Value</b>: <input name=\"value\"");
            out.println(" value=\""+cookie.getValue()+"\"><br>");
            out.print("<input type=\"submit\"");
            out.println(" value=\"Update Cookie\"><br><br>");
            out.println("</form>");
        }
    }
    // A form for creating a new cookie.
    out.println("<h3>Create a New Cookie</h3><br>");
    out.println("<form method=\"post\">");
    out.println("<b>Name</b>: <input name=\"name\"><br>");
    out.println("<b>Value</b>: <input name=\"value\"><br>");
    out.print("<input type=\"submit\"");
    out.println(" value=\"Add Cookie\"><br>");
    out.println("</form>");

    // A form to delete cookies.
    if (cookies!=null) {
        out.println("<h3>Delete a Cookie</h3>");
        out.println("<form method=\"post\">");
        out.println("<select name=\"deleteCookie\">");
        for (int i=0; i<cookies.length ;i++) {
```

```
      Cookie cookie = cookies[i];
      out.print("<option value=\""+cookie.getName()+"\">");
      out.println(cookie.getName()+"</option><br>");
    }
    out.println("</select>");
    out.print("<input type=\"submit\"");
    out.println("value=\"Delete Cookie\"><br>");
    out.println("</form>");
  }
  out.println("</body>");
  out.println("</html>");
}

// Forward all POST requests to the doGet() method.
public void doPost(HttpServletRequest request,
                   HttpServletResponse response)
  throws IOException, ServletException {
    doGet(request, response);
  }
}
```

The Servlet provides a Java version of the code used in ShowCookies.jsp—
that is, using the HttpServletRequest getCookies() method and manipulating
Cookie objects. Additionally, the Servlet makes the cookies available via HTML
forms for easy manipulation, including creation and deletion. Deleted cookies
are not deleted on the server-side; rather the Servlet sets a cookie's life span to be
zero seconds and requests the client to reload the page. To try the Servlet, save the
code as EditCookies.java in the /WEB-INF/classes/com/jspbook directory of
the jspbook Web Application. Compile and deploy the Servlet to the /Edit
Cookies path of the Web Application. After reloaded in the Web Application,
browse to http://127.0.0.1/jspbook/EditCookies to use the Servlet. Figure 9-
4 shows what the Servlet's output looks like when rendered by a Web browser.

Being able to edit cookies is an important skill to have, but do not forget the
original point. Cookies are the primary method of sharing a unique session ID
with a client. The adjective "primary" is used because most of the time cookies do
a great job of seamlessly maintaining session state; however, cookies do not work
all the time. A client can disable support for cookies. Should a Web Application
rely on always keeping session state, this is a problem. The solution is to use an
old URL manipulation trick, URL rewriting.

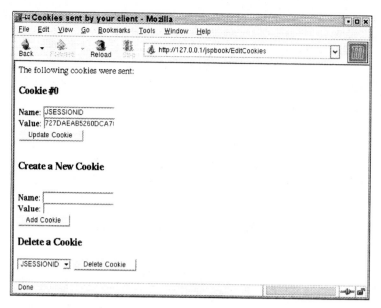

Figure 9-4 Browser Rendering of EditCookies Servlet

Tracking Users via Cookies

A very popular use of cookies is to track how often a user visits your Web site. Most people dislike the notion of a Web site being able to collect this information; however, the vast majority of people are simply unaware it can be done. Because of the default support most browsers provided for cookies, this technique is a good one to know about. The trick to tracking when a user last visited your Web site is to stash a piece of information on their computer with a time-stamp. Each time the user makes a visit, the time-stamp can be checked for, and if it exists, you know exactly when that specific computer last visited your Web site.

The code used to accomplish this is quite simple. Listing 9-5 is an example of a JSP that tracks user visits by using cookies.

Listing 9-5 CookieTracker.jsp

```
<%
  Cookie[] cookies = request.getCookies();
  String timestamp = new java.util.Date().toString();
  Cookie ts = new Cookie("timestamp",timestamp);
  response.addCookie(ts);
  Cookie lastvisit = null;
```

```
    for (int i=0;i<cookies.length;i++) {
      Cookie temp = cookies[i];
      if (temp.getName().equals("timestamp")) {
        lastvisit  = temp;
        break;
      }
    }
    if (lastvisit == null) {
      lastvisit = ts;
    }
    request.setAttribute("lastvisit", lastvisit);
%>
<html>
<head>
<title>Cookie Visitor Tracker</title>
</head>
<body>
You last visited this website: ${lastvisit.value}
</body>
</html>
```

Save the preceding code as `CookieTracker.jsp` in the base directory of the jspbook Web Application. Browse to `http://127.0.0.1/jspbook/Cookie Tracker.jsp` to test out the code. The first time you browse to the page-no timestamp cookie will exist so the last-visit time will be the current time. Wait a few minutes or longer and browse to the page a second time. It will tell you when you last visited! Figure 9-5 shows a browser rendering of the results.

This code will work on any client that supports cookies, which is most every Web browser. While the value of the cookie was read and shown back to the user by `CookieTracker.jsp`, it may not be a good idea to do this to real users. If the information is being kept only for server-side statistics, keep it there. Do not try to amaze users by showing them that you know this information. The feature's "coolness" factor is easily dwarfed by its questionable ethics. Although if you do intend to implement this type of functionality, an easy method of doing so is via a Filter set to intercept all requests to the Web Application.

URL Rewriting

When cookies fail, a container needs to find another method for keeping track of sessions. Most often this is accomplished by using a trick that does not involve anything beyond the basic HTTP protocol. Since a Web Application usually

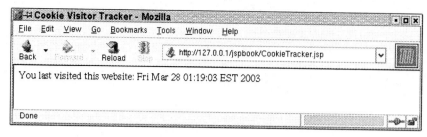

Figure 9-5 Browser Rendering of CookieTracker.jsp

needs to understand HTTP before making a request, this approach is often adequate for providing universal session tracking.

As the name implies, URL rewriting provides an effective way to track sessions with HTTP by rewriting a URL to make a new one. The goal of URL rewriting is to make the original URL contain both itself and a session identification. There is no particular method in which URL rewriting is best done as long as a server is able to correctly parse out information from a rewritten URL. Valid methods include anything from adding parameters to making completely new URLs. A quick example easily shows what a rewritten URL might look like. Assume you were visiting http://www.jspbook.com and the server had assigned you a session identifier of 12345. Some rewritten URLs might resemble the following:

- http://www.jspbook.com?session=12345
- http://www.jspbook.com/session=12345
- http://www.jspbook.com;12345

The downside to URL rewriting is that it involves rewriting every single URL each time a page is generated. If the server sends a link that neglects to include session information, the system breaks when a user follows it because the session ID is lost. While a good implementation would not let this happen, it still means every page has to be dynamically created for different clients. This is very problematic for sites that rely on static pages and caches for good performance. There is no great method of sidestepping this restriction. Unless there is good reason to rewrite URLs, do not bother. Use cookies. Cookies work well and are supported on the vast majority of clients.

As with cookies, the Servlet API makes URL rewriting easy. The HttpServlet Response object provides the following methods for rewriting a URL.

- **encodeURL(java.lang.String url):** The `encodeURL()` method takes as a parameter a URL to encode and returns a String representing the encoded URL. Should no encoding be required, the URL is returned as given.
- **encodeRedirectURL(java.lang.String url):** The `encodeRedirectURL()` method works in the same fashion but encodes the URL for redirection via the HTTP 302 response code.

Using the Servlet API to encode URLs is straightforward. The JSP in Listing 9-6 illustrates using the `encodeURL()` method to encode a session ID with a given URL.

Listing 9-6   EncodeURL.jsp

```
<html>
<head>
<title>Examples of URL encoding</title>
</head>
<body>
A local URL: index.jsp<br>
<%= response.encodeURL("index.jsp") %><br>
<%= response.encodeRedirectURL("index.jsp") %><br>
<br>
A remote URL: http://www.jspbook.com<br>
<%= response.encodeURL("http://www.jspbook.com") %><br>
<%= response.encodeRedirectURL("http://www.jspbook.com") %><br>
<br>
</body>
</html>
```

Save this code as `EncodeURL.jsp` in the base directory of the jspbook Web Application. Disable cookie support on your Web browser and browse to `http://127.0.0.1/jspbook/EncodeURL.jsp`. Look at the source code sent back by Tomcat:

```
<html>
<head>
<title>Examples of URL encoding</title>
</head>
<body>
A local URL: index.jsp<br>
index.jsp;jsessionid=90E613EC5444E9A3441EA8F4725135E1<br>
index.jsp;jsessionid=90E613EC5444E9A3441EA8F4725135E1<br>
<br>
```

```
A remote URL: http://www.jspbook.com<br>
http://www.jspbook.com<br>
http://www.jspbook.com<br>
<br>
</body>
</html>
```

Note that there are two URLs, with one URL being encoded and the other not. The encoding is done by the `HttpServletResponse encodeURL()` method and used to tack on the session ID to a URL. Should the link be clicked on, the server will automatically parse out the ID and use it as needed.

The example just shown directly puts the `encodeURL()` method call in a JSP. Adding java code to a JSP is generally regarded as a bad idea (see the design chapter for more details). The best way to encode URLs on a page is to use tag libraries. If you recall, the JSTL includes the `url` action for doing exactly this. Additionally, custom tag libraries make an ideal mechanism for abstracting all rewriting logic, which means it can be simple to arbitrarily manipulate the logic being used to rewrite URLs. The multi-client support chapter (Chapter 13) discusses this concept further and provides an example.

Initializing Session Resources

Commonly it is helpful to initialize resources once when a session is created so that the resources can be used throughout the session. An excellent example is initializing a database connection, or any remote connection, and using it throughout the entire life span of a session. This is favorable to creating, using, and destroying a remote connection per each request because it takes a notable amount of time to set up remote connections.

There are two methods of initializing session resources. The first method is the more inelegant and relies on checking if the `HttpSession` object is new, by invoking the `isNew()` method, each time the session is accessed.

```
HttpSession session = null;
session = request.getSession(true);
if(session.isNew())
{
  //initialize session resources...
}
```

This method works because it is an explicit call to the `isNew()` method, but it is inelegant because it requires a conditional check. The second, more elegant method is to use the `javax.servlet.http.HttpSessionListener` interface. The

`HttpSessionListener` interface defines two methods that notify a resource if a session is created or destroyed:

- **void sessionCreated(HttpSessionEvent se):** The `sessionCreated()` method is invoked when an `HttpSession` is created.
- **void sessionDestroyed(HttpSessionEvent se):** The `sessionDestroyed()` method is invoked whenever an `HttpSession` is about to be destroyed by the server[7].

Any object that needs to know if a session has been created or destroyed can implement the `HttpSessionListener` interface and be notified accordingly. The `HttpSessionEvent` object only has one method, `getSession()`, which returns the `HttpSession` object that was created or that will be destroyed.

The only tricky part to using the `HttpSessionListener` interface is registering objects that implement it with a Web Application. The interface itself is a commonly used event notification design pattern, well known with other Java API. However, the pattern relies on knowing which objects are registered to receive events. In a Web Application this is done by explicitly declaring session listening objects in `web.xml`. The `listener` element is used to define listener classes, via child `listener-class` elements, as shown in Listing 9-7.

Listing 9-7   Use of web.xml Listener Element

```
<listener>
  <listener-class>com.jspbook.foo.FooListener</listener-class>
</listener>
```

The deployment is straightforward; each listener class is registered by declaring it using the `listener-class` element. The listener class would be a singleton—for instance, a factory object responsible for managing connections—and it would be responsible for managing resources based on the creation and destruction of `HttpSession` objects.

Persisting and Loading Sessions

It can occur that a session needs to be serialized. If a Web Application is distributed on multiple servers, it is likely that each server will not keep a copy of every session being used by the entire Web Application. Instead, sessions will be used when needed and shared with other servers by being serialized and sent

---

7. Note that in the Servlet 2.3 specification this method was defined as being called *after* the session was destroyed.

across a network connection. Another case where sessions will be serialized is when an application needs to persist them while the container is being restarted or the Web Application is reloaded. Whatever the case is, a session can be serialized and reloaded by a Web Application. Should information be in session scope, it needs to be ensured that the information can properly handle being serialized and being reloaded. The `HttpSessionActivationListener` interface is used for this purpose.

The `HttpSessionActivationListener` interface defines two methods:

- **void sessionDidActivate(HttpSessionEvent):** The `sessionDidActivate()` method is invoked immediately after a session is activated or a serialized version of the session was loaded.

- **void sessionWillPassivate(HttpSessionEvent):** The `sessionWillPassivate()` method is invoked just before a session is about to be *passivated*, or serialized. Any object that cannot handle being passivated should be handled appropriately.

Using these two methods, an object can listen for when a session is about to be serialized and act appropriately. For instance, any external resource, such as a URL connection or database connection, will not be serialization-friendly. Instead of attempting to serialize the connection itself, the information needed for the connection should be serialized and the object removed from session scope and closed before the session is passivated. When the session is activated, the serialized information can then be used to re-create the connection.

All containers must support the `java.io.Serialization` interface for objects in session scope. Any object in session scope that implements this interface will be serialized appropriately using the `writeObject()` and `readObject()` methods. Additionally, container vendors may choose to provide special support for serializing other types of objects; however, caution should be taken on relying on this type of functionality because it will limit the Web Application's portability between different containers.

In single-server environments—that is, most every small to medium-sized Web Application—it is usually safe to assume information stored in session scope will not be serialized. The majority of the time, if not all of the time, in these environments, the objects' references are kept in memory by one JVM until the session expires, or is terminated. However, the Servlet specification puts in fair warning that containers in a single-server environment may opt to use multiple JVMs and the `HttpSessionActivationListener` should always be used on objects that are stored in a session, and that themselves reference objects that do not implement the serialization interface. Additionally, static variables should not be relied on for keeping application state[8]: instead, a database should be used. Use the HttpSessionActivationListener interface liberally if you have the time.

Knowing If an Object Is Bound to Session

The Servlet specification provides the HttpSessionBindingListener interface. This interface provides two methods that allow a listener object to know when an object is bound or removed from session:

- **valueBound(HttpSessionBindingEvent event):** The valueBound() method notifies the object that it is being bound to a session and identifies the session.
- **valueUnbound(HttpSessionBindingEvent event):** The valueUnbound() method notifies the object that it is being unbound from a session and identifies the session.

A listener object registered with this interface is notified when an object is either bound or unbound to session scope. The listener is helpful when used to manage resources needed to complement objects in session scope. For example, user information is usually persisted in a database. When a user object is loaded into session scope, it may be necessary to populate it with the correct information; likewise, when the object is unloaded, it may be necessary to update the database with the newest information. The HttpSessionBindingListener interface can be used to create a listener class that loads and persists user information in a database accordingly. The relevant code would be the following:

```
public class UserListener implements HttpSessionBindingListener{
  public void valueBound(HttpSessionBindingEvent e){
    // check for right object type
    if (e.getValue() instanceof foo.User) {
      foo.User user = (foo.User)e.getValue();
      // load user information from database
    }
  }
  public void valueUnbound(HttpSessionBindingEvent e){
    // check for right object type
```

---

8. In this book static variables have been used to maintain state—for example, with the page visit-counting JSP. This practice is improper use of keeping application state, but Tomcat 5 does run in only one JVM on a single-server environment.

```
    if (e.getValue() instanceof foo.User) {
      foo.User user = (foo.User)e.getValue();
      // serialize user information into database
    }
  }
}
  // any other methods
...
```

The methods on this object are called when the object is added to or removed from a session.

Session Time-outs

All HttpSession objects have a finite life. A session either time-outs when it has been inactive for a certain period of time, or a session can also be invalidated by the application. An application can be told to invalidate a session at any time by invoking the HttpSession invalidate() method. If a session is not explicitly invalidated, it will automatically be invalidated after a given period of time. The period of time a session can be idle before it is timed-out can be set via the session-config element and child element session-timeout of web.xml.

```
<session-config>
  <session-timeout>15</session-timeout>
</session-config>
```

By default all sessions time-out after 15 minutes. If an integer value is specified in the body of the session-timeout element, it will be treated as the number of minutes a Web Application should save session information about a client. A negative number or 0 value number means indefinitely.

In addition to being able to directly invoke the invalidate() method of the HttpSession object, there are other methods that can be used to both mine information and manipulate the time-out period of a session:

- **getCreationTime():** The getCreationTime() method returns a long string representing the number of milliseconds since the epoch, midnight January 1, 1970, GMT.

- **getLastAccessedTime():** The getLastAccessedTime() method returns the last time the client sent a request associated with this session, as the number of milliseconds since the epoch, midnight January 1, 1970, GMT, and marked by the time the container received the request.

- **invalidate():** The `invalidate()` method invalidates a session and removes any objects bound to it.
- **isNew():** The `isNew()` method returns a boolean value representing if the session was newly created and the client does not yet know about it.
- **setMaxInactiveInterval(int time):** The `setMaxInactiveInterval()` method can be used to set the amount of time, in seconds, between subsequent requests.

Persistent State

So far this chapter has only discussed the concrete use of sessions and the session API. There is another aspect of session management that has to be discussed: how to manage state in a multi-server(or multi-JVM) environment. Sessions hold user state, and the model that has been discussed up until now is one where the user state is held in memory on a Web server. This leads to a problem when more than one server is being used to handle requests. Either the system will have to ensure that all requests from the same user always go to the same request-processing server or that all of the servers in the system will need to share session information.

The first solution, sending all requests from the same user to the same server, may not be desirable for two main reasons: load balancing and session backup. *Load balancing* is the act where a set of servers handle one large task that an individual server would be unable to cope with by itself—for example, too many HTTP requests to a Web Application. Ideally, load balancing for a Web Application can be done on a per-request basis, each time a request is made to the application; the server that is least burdened handles the request. Figure 9-6 illustrates the concept.

However, keeping session information on one server and forcing all requests to that server ruins this practice. Instead of per-request load balancing, the servers would have to do per-session load balancing. The solution can work, but is usually not favored because it loses the performance benefits of a per-request system. The second problem is, What happens when a server crashes? If state information is only saved in memory on one server and that server crashes, the information is lost. Clearly an unacceptable situation to be in.

The second solution, sharing state information, is the preferred approach. Sharing state information is making session information available to all servers that may need it. Usually, this is accomplished by either one of two ways: session smearing or using a dedicated session database. *Session smearing* is the act of "smearing" a session's state across multiple servers. A dedicated session database

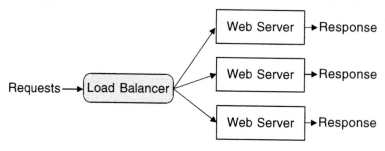

Figure 9-6 Per-Request Load Balancing Using a Server Farm

is just that—a dedicated server that keeps track of sessions and shares the information as needed with other servers. Both session smearing and using a session database are discussed further in the following sections.

Session Smearing

Session smearing is generally a vendor-specific solution. Most containers, especially full J2EE servers, provide some method of seamlessly clustering together many computers to run one Web Application. The Servlet specification defines the `distributable web.xml` element for when this is the case. When the distributable element is used in `web.xml`, it means the Web Application may be distributed across many different servers. It also means that both the session and application scopes become much more difficult to manage. In particular `HttpSession` objects have the possibility of being serialized and shuffled between different servers depending on which server is processing a request related to that session.

The Servlet specification solves this problem by defining a few event listeners and one requirement: objects in session scope *must* implement the `java.io.Serializable` interface (or must be understood by the container to be serializable; see later). Containers that support multi-server environments must support at a minimum the methods of the `Serializable` interface and be able to invoke `writeObject()` and `readObject()` appropriately to persist and load session information. As a developer this gives you the control of overriding these methods and being able to customize what happens as objects are moved between different servers and JVM.

Using the `Serializable` interface does work and generally that is all you need to do in order to successfully have session-scoped objects smear around a multi-server environment. However, the `Serializable` interface does have a few drawbacks including the performance limitations of Java's default object serialization and that serialization works poorly for shuffling around live connections, such as an open URL. The Servlet specification addresses this issue by allowing vendors to optionally implement any other session-persisting functionality they wish. This is both good and bad. Vendor-specific features usually work well but tie a developer to only being able to use that vendor's products. You should avoid vendor-specific container features for Web Application state management if you do not want to be tied to a specific vendor.

Sharing State Information via a Database

Sharing state information via a database is just that: using a centralized server to manage important Web Application state information. The state-sharing server is then the only part of the Web Application that needs fail-safe support. Most databases provide this anyhow, and other servers can rely on the state-sharing server for any information they need. Figure 9-7 provides an illustration of the concept.

A state-sharing database is an appealing solution because it allows a Web Application's developers to have full support over state-persistent functionality. Any code created is not tied to a specific vendor and can be optimized completely for a specific use case. Building a state-sharing database involves more work than using a vendor-made solution, but it is by no means a daunting task. The Servlet API provides a few listener classes that work well as a solution: `ServletRequest Listener` and `HttpSessionListener`.

Both of these classes were previously covered by both this chapter and Chapter 2 with the basics of the Servlet API. The listeners are useful with a state-

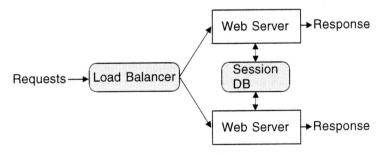

Figure 9-7 Sharing State Using a Dedicated State-Sharing Database

sharing database because they can load and save information based on the creation and destruction events of the listeners. For per-request–style load balancing the `ServletRequestListener` interface is ideal. When a request is created, the interface can access the state-sharing database and populate any needed information. When a request is destroyed, the listener can save any changes to the state-sharing database. For per-session load balancing the `HttpSessionListener` interface is ideal. The loading and saving of state information would be the same as with the `ServletRequestListener` object but done on a per-session basis.

An example of creating and using a state-sharing database will not be provided for two reasons. The first reason is that the functionality is not commonly needed on the average Servlet and JSP-based project. The concepts should be clear and it will be left to you to implement such a system if you need it. Second, is that the functionality can easily slow down a multi-server application and defeat the point of implementing the system in the first place. A central database is almost always the worst-performing piece of software in an application, and as such it is often the most heavily optimized. It is hard to begin building a good state-sharing database without understanding the concepts of Chapter 14, and even then it is difficult to build an optimized one without knowing the specific database being used and the state information that needs to be shared.

State and Thread Safety

Web servers are designed to handle many concurrent users and many concurrent requests from those users. Typically, to handle requests Web servers create many threads, with each thread handling a request. Remember that a given named Servlet is a singleton—that is, there is only one instance of a given named Servlet in memory. This means that when a Web server receives multiple requests for a Servlet, all those requests are dispatched to that Servlet on multiple concurrent threads, which means that Servlets must be written to be thread-safe. This section examines thread safety in Servlets and how to achieve it. There is no getting away from this: Servlets and JSP must be written in a thread-safe manner.

Table 9-1 shows the various "scopes" of data that an application in a Web server will use. Some data are "naturally" thread-safe and no special steps need to be taken to protect access to that data. Some data, however, may be accessed by multiple threads at the same time, and care must be taken when using that data.

In many cases it is obvious what does and does not need protecting. Local variables are thread-safe: a thread has only one stack and local variables live on that stack; only one thread can be touching those variables at any given time. Method parameters are generally safe for the same reason; in particular,

Table 9-1 Scopes of Data in a Web Application

Scope	Naturally Thread-Safe?	Example
Statics	No	```class foo{``` ```private static double d;```
Instance data	No	```class foo{``` ```private double d;```
Method parameters	Yes	```void``` ```doGet(HttpServletRequest``` ```req, HttpServletResponse``` ```resp)```
Local variable	Yes	```void``` ```doGet(HttpServletRequest``` ```req, HttpServletResponse``` ```resp)``` ```{``` ``` double a;```
Session state (HttpSession)	No	```HttpSession sess``` ```= req.getSession();```
Application state (ServletContext)	No	```ServletContext ctx =``` ```getServletContext();```

`HttpServletRequest` and `HttpServletResponse` are guaranteed to be thread-safe. A Web server will either create a new request and response object for each new request, or the server will pool request and response objects. In either case each call is guaranteed to get its own request and response object.

Other objects are also obviously not thread-safe; static data, instance data, session-scoped[9] data, and application-scoped data fall into this category. These objects are worth further discussion because poorly done code that deals with these objects can result in unexpected Web Application behavior. The following sections further explain the relevant issues and how to ensure thread safety.

---

9. It may not be obvious that session state can be accessed from multiple threads concurrently. Surely one client means one session means one thread. However, a given client can send multiple concurrent requests to a server. Each request will have its own thread and each thread can touch the session. How does the client do this? An application may have multiple frames; a client may send a request, cancel the request and the client; and resend the request; a client may have multiple open windows, etc., etc.

Synchronizing

Protecting state in Java is easy in theory but more difficult in practice. Java has built-in support for synchronization with the `synchronized` keyword. This can be used to synchronize entire methods or as a form of "critical section", which protects access to blocks of code. The Java 2 specification defines the official thread synchronization statement and safety mechanisms in section 17, "Threads and Locks". If you are unfamiliar with threads, do take the time to read this section. The Java specifications are available free online at `http://java.sun.com`.

Synchronization is something that should be used minimally in an application. When synchronizing, you are essentially taking a "lock" on a block of code, and locks cause contention. Many threads could be trying to take that lock at the same time. Contention of any sort will harm scalability; contention of threads is no different. Because of this there is one golden rule to remember: Only synchronize what you have to! For example, typically, read access to data often happens far more frequently than write access. It is therefore possible to allow many readers to access data concurrently and so reduce contention. However, only one writer should ever be allowed to access an item of data. Java does not provide native read/write synchronization, but these are not difficult to develop yourself (there are many excellent resources). It may well be worth investing time in defining read locks and write locks to limit the amount of contention you have. Whatever approach an application takes, it is always important to keep lock times at a minimum.

Protecting Servlet State

New Servlet developers often get into trouble with thread safety because they fail to realize that a Servlet container is multi-threaded. One instance of a Servlet will be shared with many concurrent client requests. By default this is exactly what is done, and it makes a simple Servlet a highly scalable piece of code. An easy way to think of this concept is by saying a container only loads one instance of a Servlet into memory, but it calls the service methods each time a client sends a request, regardless if the previous request is finished yet.

As this applies to your code, any variable declared inside a service method[10], such as `doGet()`, will be unique to a specific request. However, any variable defined outside a service method is shared by all requests. This includes all requests by all clients, not just all requests from the same client. For this reason it

---

10. The same issue is present in a JSP. Remember, declaration elements declare code outside of the JSP service method.

is bad practice to declare variables outside the service methods unless there is good reason to do so. This is usually intuitive, but understand that thread safety is part of the reason why. For clarity let's look at a Servlet that is not thread-safe and point out exactly why. For example, look at Listing 9-8, which is the code for the NotThreadSafe Servlet. The goal of this Servlet is to read a few request parameters and display them to a user; however, this would not always happen correctly because the Servlet suffers from poor thread safety.

Listing 9-8   NotThreadSafe.java

```
package com.jspbook;

import java.io.*;
import javax.servlet.*;
import javax.servlet.http.*;

public class NotThreadSafe extends HttpServlet {

    String value1;
    String value2;

    public void doGet(HttpServletRequest request,
                      HttpServletResponse response)
        throws IOException, ServletException {

        response.setContentType("text/html");
        PrintWriter out = response.getWriter();
        out.println("<html>");
        out.println("<head>");
        out.println("<title>NotThreadSafe!</title>");
        out.println("</head>");
        out.println("<body>");
        out.println("The values are:<br>");

        value1 = request.getParameter("value1");
        value2 = request.getParameter("value2");
        out.println("Value 1: "+value1+"<br>");
        out.println("Value 2: "+value2+"<br>");
        out.println("Are they the same as submitted?");
        out.println("</body>");
        out.println("</html>");
    }
}
```

The problem lies in declaring the variables as instance variables rather than local to the doGet() method. What the Servlet is actually doing is showing whatever set of request parameters was last saved in the variables, not necessarily the given client's set of parameters. Yes, it is likely a given client will set the variables and then immediately execute the code that displays the values, but this is not guaranteed. A second request might have changed these values before they are displayed by the NotThreadSafe Servlet. To avoid the problem, the variables would better be declared inside the doGet() method. The ThreadSafe Servlet in Listing 9-9 shows how to fix the code to ensure the correct set of parameter values is always shown.

Listing 9-9 ThreadSafe.java

```
package com.jspbook;

import java.io.*;
import javax.servlet.*;
import javax.servlet.http.*;

public class ThreadSafe extends HttpServlet {

  public void doGet(HttpServletRequest request,
                    HttpServletResponse response)
    throws IOException, ServletException {

    response.setContentType("text/html");
    PrintWriter out = response.getWriter();
    out.println("<html>");
    out.println("<head>");
    out.println("<title>ThreadSafe</title>");
    out.println("</head>");
    out.println("<body>");
    out.println("The values are:<br>");

    String value1 = request.getParameter("value1");
    String value2 = request.getParameter("value2");
    out.println("Value 1: "+value1+"<br>");
    out.println("Value 2: "+value2+"<br>");
    out.println("They are the same as submitted?");
    out.println("</body>");
    out.println("</html>");
  }
}
```

From the simple example above do not think that thread safety equals declaring all variables inside a service method. This is certainly not the case, and there are many good reasons for declaring a variable common to many threads. Examples include anything placed in the session or application scopes as well as some Servlet-specific variables, such as the `Hashtable` used in the LinkTracker Servlet (Listing 2-6 in Chapter 2). Understand that more common than not a variable should be placed inside the appropriate service method. While sometimes inefficient, it usually ensures code is thread-safe.

When a variable needs to be shared by multiple requests, there are methods of ensuring proper synchronization. The easiest method is to simply declare the entire service method as synchronized. Applying the `synchronized` keyword to an entire service method effectively restricts a single Servlet to processing clients' requests one at a time. An example of the `NotThreadSafe` Servlet synchronized in this style is shown in Listing 9-10.

Listing 9-10 SynchronizedNotThreadSafe.java

```
package com.jspbook;

import java.io.*;
import javax.servlet.*;
import javax.servlet.http.*;

public class SynchronizedNotThreadSafe extends HttpServlet {

  String value1;
  String value2;

  public synchronized void doGet(HttpServletRequest request,
                  HttpServletResponse response)
    throws IOException, ServletException {

    response.setContentType("text/html");
    PrintWriter out = response.getWriter();
    out.println("<html>");
    out.println("<head>");
    out.println("<title>NotThreadSafe!</title>");
    out.println("</head>");
    out.println("<body>");
    out.println("The values are:<br>");

    value1 = request.getParameter("value1");
    value2 = request.getParameter("value2");
```

```
    out.println("Value 1: "+value1+"<br>");
    out.println("Value 2: "+value2+"<br>");
    out.println("Are they the same as submitted?");
    out.println("</body>");
    out.println("</html>");
  }
}
```

While proper synchronization is assured, in practice the preceding Servlet would have incredibly poor performance. *Do not do this!* A better approach to take would be using the `synchronized` statement only around the block of code that needs synchronizing. This approach is the preferred method of providing synchronization for objects in the scope of many threads. You should refer to the source code for the LinkTracker Servlet (Listing 2-6) for a good example of using the synchronized statement in this manner.

javax.servlet.SingleThreadModel

The Servlet API contains an interface called `javax.servlet.SingleThread Model`. This is a signature interface (i.e., it has no methods to implement), which, when implemented by a Servlet, marks that Servlet as single-threaded. What does this mean? Typically, a Web server will create a single instance of a Servlet to handle all requests made to that Servlet (remember that it is possible to have multiple instances of the same Servlet, based on the `servlet-name` element in the deployment descriptor), which is one of the reasons why Servlets have to be thread-safe. However, when a Servlet implements `javax.servlet.SingleThread Model`, the container must *only* allow a single thread to call this Servlet instance at any one time. On the surface this seems like a great idea. No more worries about multi-threaded access, as the Servlet is single-threaded. Unfortunately, this is not true.

The `SingleThreadModel` interface introduces issues without solving anything. If you use `SingleThreadModel` you immediately cause scalability problems in your applications. You only allow a single thread through that Servlet at any one time, and the Servlet becomes a bottleneck. Containers are free to create many instances of a `SingleThreadModel` Servlet to ease this problem, but some do not. A bigger issue, though, is that a Servlet that implements `SingleThread Model` still has to care about threads. If a `SingleThreadModel`-implementing Servlet uses either the `ServletContext` or an `HttpSession`, then access to these objects must still be done in a thread-safe way. The `SingleThreadModel` interface only guarantees this instance of the Servlet is single-threaded. It does not stop all the threads in the server, so other Servlets or other instances of the same Servlet could (and will) access `ServletContext` and `HttpSession`. Do not use the `javax.servlet.SingleThreadModel` interface. It comes with a high price for no benefit, and because of the drawbacks, the interface has been deprecated in the Servlet 2.4 specification.

Protecting Session and Application State

Both the `HttpSession` object and the `ServletContext` object are shared resources. The `ServletContext` object can be accessed by many Servlets or JSP at the same time. The `HttpSession` object can be accessed at the same time by two different requests from a client. In uses of both objects proper synchronization should be used.

The simplest solution to providing accurate session and application in state is to always wrap access to the associated object in a synchronized block. Listing 9-11 demonstrates wrapping a session access using a synchronization block.

Listing 9-11 *Synchronizing Session Access*

```
User user = new User();
HttpSession session = request.getSession(true);
synchronized(session) {
   session.setAttribute("user", user);
 // other session access code
}
```

Note that the synchronized block is synchronized using the `session` object itself. This ensures that all access of the `session` object is done in a synchronous manner. Similarly, code that is used to manipulate the `ServletContext` object should include a similar synchronization block as illustrated in Listing 9-12.

Listing 9-12 *Protecting Access to the ServletContext*

```
ServletContext ctx = getServletContext();
synchronized(ctx)
{
  User user = (User) ctx.getAttribute("user");
  // other 'application' access code
}
```

The point to take away from this example is that all access to the `ServletContext` and `HttpSession` objects should be wrapped in an appropriate synchronized block. While a simple practice, it is important to ensure proper state is maintained.

Summary

This chapter introduced some very important and commonly overlooked problems of Servlets and JSP. All Web Applications are expected to maintain state. Where and how that state is maintained is important to understand as a Web developer. Perhaps the most important state-management topic brought up in this chapter was that of the `HttpSession` object. By default HTTP is stateless. Solving this problem are HTTP cookies, but cookies do not always work. For absolute session maintenance, URL rewriting should be used.

State maintenance can be tough, especially in the case of a multi-server environment. In multi-server environments a Web Application is not run on one server by one JVM. Instead, many servers are used to manage running the Web Application in order to handle large volumes of incoming requests. In cases in which a Web Application is marked distributable via `web.xml`, sessions are freely shuffled around a Web Application. Care should be taken to ensure resources in session scope are properly serialized and shared.

The final part of this chapter dealt with the all-important topic of synchronization. Servlets and JSPs are Java code and can have many threads accessing them concurrently. To ensure proper state is maintained, standard Java thread-safety techniques should be employed: Servlets should avoid static and instance variables and JSP should additionally avoid declarations. In all cases where either application or session scope is being accessed, it is important to wrap the relevant code in a synchronized block.

Chapter 10

Security

One of the features of Java is how easily code can be downloaded and composed into a running application. However, such code has the potential to execute critical operations that manipulate sensitive system data, so it is imperative to distinguish code that can be trusted from code that cannot. To this end, the Java security model is based on the origin of the running code. Sensitive operations are allowed or disallowed based on where the classes in the current call stack were loaded from and/or who signed them.

In a distributed system, code representing business operations is hosted on one or more servers. A client request acts as a trigger to execute server code that has the potential to perform critical operations that manipulate sensitive system data. It is important to distinguish requests that can be trusted from those that cannot. The server must enforce security based on who is attempting to run the code, and that means being able to verify the identity of the caller.

Ensuring security gets more complicated when client and server communicate over a public network where servers may be more easily spoofed. The client may also want some guarantee that the server is genuine before accepting or providing certain information. There are questions to be answered. How can the system tell which clients can be trusted? How is it possible to specify which clients can access which functionality? How can the clients tell which servers can be trusted? How can malicious persons be stopped from accessing the system or tampering with requests and responses? How can sensitive data be hidden from prying eyes? All of these are questions of security and are answered in this chapter.

This chapter discusses the following topics:

- What security is.
- Declarative security: securing resources via `web.xml`.
- Programmatic security.

- Encrypting communication: protecting information that is sent between the client and server.
- How secure is secure: a slight tangent on how secure Web Application security really is.

The contents of this chapter are intended to be read straight through. The topic of Web Application security is of great importance. Without it how can you prevent a user from accessing restricted parts of a site? More importantly, think about Web Applications being used for e-commerce; if you are running a business with an online presence, it is imperative to have security in order to protect personal information about clients (e.g., credit card numbers).

What Do We Mean by Security?

There are several terms we have to introduce when talking about security. The first term is *security principal* or principal for short. A principal is one of the parties involved in a communication. It could be a human user or a machine or maybe a piece of software. In the security literature, principals are often given names. Alice and Bob are the two principals trying to communicate; Eve is an eavesdropper listening in on the communication; and Mallory is a malicious attacker trying to change the data being communicated or in someway disrupt the communication. This naming convention will be used by this chapter, and there are many principals that we will introduce.

Security in distributed systems is based on the principals being able to trust each other. Before they can trust each other, principals have to know who they are communicating with—that is, Alice has to be able to know it is Bob on the other end of the communication and vice versa. To do this Alice has to be able to prove that she is talking to Bob. This process is called *Authentication*. In a client/server scenario the server usually wants to authenticate the client. However, there are times when the client wants to authenticate the server—for example, if the client is sending the server credit card details, the client must be able to trust the server. Also, there are occasions where mutual authentication is needed. To authenticate a principal, the principal has to provide a set of credentials. The credentials could be a user name/password pair, a fingerprint, a retinal scan, a certificate, or anything that can uniquely identify the principal. These credentials are then typically passed to a trusted authority (called Trent in security literature) to be checked. Trent could be a database holding the credentials, or it could be a Kerberos server, or some other third party such as a certifying authority—for example, Thwate or Verisign.

Once a principal has been authenticated, the next problem that arises is this: Are they allowed to perform whatever action they have requested? Alice may have proved that she is talking to Bob, but is Bob allowed to perform the requested action? This step is called *authorization*.

When Alice and Bob are exchanging data, attackers may be able to change that data while it is in transit. Alice and Bob may need to know that the data has been changed. There are techniques that can be used to perform this checking. In security this is called *data integrity*.

And finally, suppose that the data exchange between Alice and Bob must be confidential—that is, not only should Mallory not be able to change the data, but Eve should not be able to read it. In this case the data has to be Encrypted. In the world of HTTP the technique used to manage encryption is Transport Layer Security (TLS), formerly known as Secure Sockets Layer (SSL). This is used via the HTTPS protocol that will be examined later.

Declarative Security

Adding security to an application can be a tedious but necessary task, and much of the work is similar regardless of the application being written. Take, for example, the following security operations that all applications share:

- Receives a request.
- Authenticates the caller.
- Checks the caller's authorization.
- Allows or disallows access.

Because of the similarity in the security work different applications have to do, it is possible to abstract security away into a framework. In the case of J2EE, security frameworks are typically not programmatic but are declarative. What does this mean? It means that an application can specify via deployment settings (i.e., web.xml) the level of security that a given resource needs, and that security is provided by the Web Application container. This declarative approach is reasonably flexible and reasonably easy to use. The Servlet specification also allows applications to add "hooks" into the container providing security to allow an application to fine-tune the container's offered security.

An application can also choose to ignore this declarative security entirely and provide its own security. Typically, an application doing this will provide a Filter to handle all requests and will do all the necessary security checks in the Filter. One important thing to realize about security is that all checks should be made as early as possible. For example, an application should not let a request get all the way to the database before deciding the caller is not authorized to use the database. Remember that security is expensive in terms of resources used; therefore, check early and check only as frequently as necessary. For example, once a user has been authenticated, there may be no need to re-authenticate them on every request.

Role-Based Security

The first type of declarative security we will discuss is *role-based* security. In the Servlet world security is based on two things: resources and roles.

- Resources are the things that need protecting.
- Roles are the users authorized to access those resources.

So what is a role? Imagine a public Web site with thousands of individual users, most of whom are unknown to the site's maintainers. Different users will be given different levels of access. For example, there may be a free portion of the site open to all, a portion of the site open to only those who have paid a subscription, and a portion of the site only open to administrators of the site. In theory it would be possible to check every single access to the site based on the user's credentials, so Alice could access all the site, Bob could access the non-subscription part, Joe could access the non-subscription part and the subscription part, and so on and so forth for all the different principals of the site. But for thousands of users, managing individual user access quickly becomes a nightmare. Instead, what happens is that users are assigned to a "role". In this case there may be three roles: non-subscriber, subscriber, and administrator. Each user would be assigned to a role when he or she browses to the site. Each resource in the site is then accessible only to certain roles. Notice that roles and role-names are entirely application-specific; there are no standard roles that all applications can or must use.

The Servlet specification has nothing to say about how users are assigned to roles, in neither the naming scheme you use nor the code used to enforce it. The specification simply says that roles exist and that a container must recognize them. In Tomcat[1] the default mechanism of managing roles is the `tomcat-users.xml` file in the `/conf` directory of your Tomcat installation. The default file looks like this:

```
<tomcat-users>
  <user name="tomcat" password="tomcat" roles="tomcat" />
```

---

1. Remember, the only standard containers must adhere to are the declarative rules in `web.xml`, not the `tomcat-users.xml` file or any other Tomcat mechanism. If you are using a different container, read the container's documentation on defining roles.

```
    <user name="role1"  password="tomcat" roles="role1"  />
    <user name="both"   password="tomcat" roles="tomcat,role1" />
</tomcat-users>
```

This file defines a simple mapping between user name, password, and role. Notice that a given user may have multiple roles, for example, user name="both" is in the `"tomcat"` role and the `"role1"` role. In Tomcat, the areas in which roles are defined are called *realms,* and in particular this XML file-based mechanism is called the memory realm. It is the realm you get by default in your application if you do not change the Tomcat configuration. However, Tomcat ships with other realms, notably the JDBC realm and the JNDI realm. These offer more flexibility for an application. We will come back to realms and configuration in a moment, but first let us take a look at how roles are used in an application.

Role-based security restrictions can be placed on Web Application resources by using the `security-constraint` element in `web.xml`. As an example, add Listing 10-1 to `/web.xml` in the `/WEB-INF` directory of the jspbook Web Application:

Listing 10-1   Security Constraint Entry in web.xml

```
. . .
<web-app>
. . .
    <security-constraint>
        <web-resource-collection>
            <web-resource-name>SecuredBookSite</web-resource-name>
            <url-pattern>/secured/*</url-pattern>
            <http-method>GET</http-method>
            <http-method>POST</http-method>
        </web-resource-collection>
        <auth-constraint>
            <role-name>Reader</role-name>
        </auth-constraint>
    </security-constraint>
    <login-config>
      <auth-method>BASIC</auth-method>
      <realm-name>Read Access</realm-name>
    </login-config>
. . .
```

The preceding entry uses the `<security-constraint>` element to restrict any HTTP GET or POST call to any URL matching `/secured/*`. The `web-resource-name` child element is used to provide an arbitrary name, in this example `SecuredBookSite`:

```
<web-resource-name>SecuredBookSite</web-resource-name>
```

It does not matter what you choose as a name. Later on we will see the name is only used as meta-information. The more important children elements are `url-pattern` and `http-method`. The `url-pattern` element works identically to the `url-pattern` element for a Servlet, JSP, or Filter mapping. The `http-method` element is new, but intuitive to use. It can have a value that matches any of the HTTP methods, and each method specified is checked before use. For instance, in the above example GET and POST were specified:

```
<http-method>GET</http-method>
<http-method>POST</http-method>
```

These two entries would mean any HTTP GET or POST request to a URL matched by `/secured/*` would be subject to the security restriction.

The final part of the `<security-constraint>`, the `auth-constraint` child element, is used to match the security restriction to a defined role. Individual roles are defined by `role-name` elements. In the preceding entry the role `Reader` is given access to the secured resources:

```
<auth-constraint>
    <role-name>Reader</role-name>
</auth-constraint>
```

Last, the `login-config` element is used to describe the basic form of authentication[2].

```
<security-role>
   <role-name>Reader</role-name>
</security-role>
```

The end result is that only users in the role Reader are able to browse to resources under the `/secured` directory of the jspbook Web Application. You can try out the security restriction even without a `/secured` directory or resources in it. Save the security entry and reload the jspbook Web Application. Then try browsing to any URL including the `/security` directory. For instance:

```
http://127.0.0.1/jspbook/secured/SecurityTest
```

Instead of getting a 404 error or seeing a resource (should one exist), you should see a dialog box asking you to log on. Figure 10-1 shows what the log on

---

2. There are multiple types of authentication mechanisms a Web Application offers. Each scheme has a different level of security, and all schemes are discussed later in the chapter.

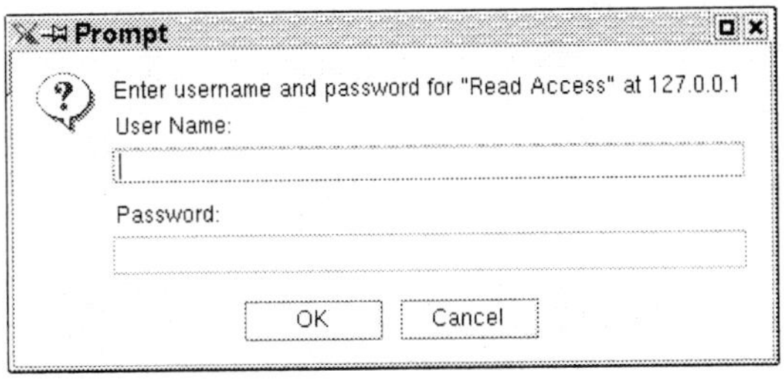

Figure 10-1 Mozilla Log On

box presented by Mozilla looks like. It will be similar regardless of the browser you are using.

Enter anything you like for a user name or password value. Regardless of what you put in, the Web Application will deny you access to the requested resource (even if it does not exist). Click on Cancel to remove the authentication box. Figure 10-2 shows what the typical access denied page looks like.

It should be clear that the /secured virtual directory is now secure to random visitors using HTTP to access the site. If you wish to add users that can see the resource, you need to define them via the container-specific method. As we have

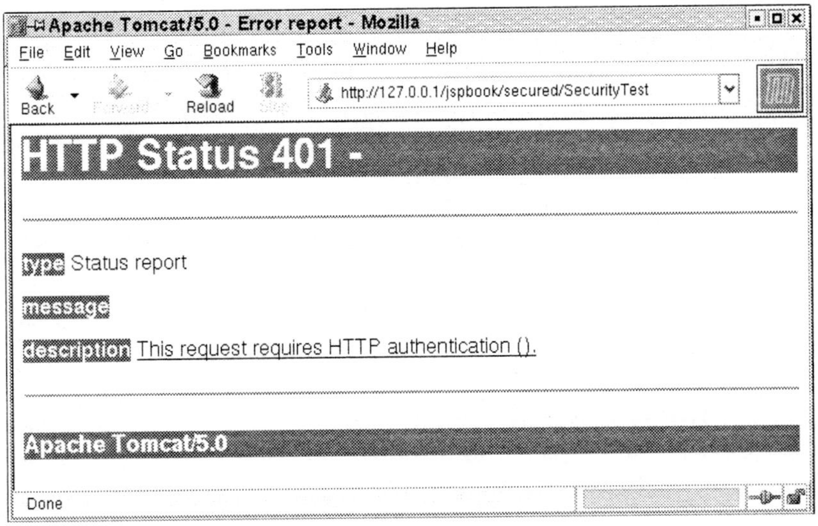

Figure 10-2 Authentication Failure

seen with Tomcat, the `tomcat-users.xml` file works. Add the following entry in this file:

```
<user name="reader" password="reader" roles="Reader" />
```

Reload Tomcat for the memory realm to be updated and try browsing back to the same resource as you did before. This time when the authentication box pops up, enter "reader" as the user name and "reader" as the password, as shown in Figure 10-3.

After submitting the form, the Web Application proceeds to check the user name and password. Should the information be correct, then the resource requested is shown. In the case of a fictitious URL, a 404 page is shown, but should a real resource exist, then it is displayed.

In general, this is how declarative security works with a Web Application. You decide what URL mappings need to be secure and what roles are required, then add the appropriate `security-constraint` entries to `web.xml`.

Configuring Realms

A fair warning: This section is Tomcat-specific. "Realms" are something conceptually similar in just about every container; however, the actual implementation will be slightly different. You cannot apply this specific section to all containers, but you can apply all of the other declarative security that is defined by the Servlet specification.

As just mentioned, Tomcat user definitions are stored as "realms", and Tomcat comes with three realm implementations: a memory realm (the `tomcat-users.xml` file you have just seen), a JDBC realm, and a JNDI realm (see Chapter 15 for more on JDBC and JNDI). Under Tomcat, realms are configured as part of Tomcat's `server.xml` file. A realm can have various scopes: it can be made available for all applications this instance of Tomcat is running, for all applications on a particular virtual host this instance of Tomcat is managing, or simply for a given application. To configure the realm in one of these ways, you simply nest a `<Realm>` element within the appropriate parent element, either within `<Engine>`, `<Host>`, or `<Context>`, respectively. You may think that realms should be specific to an application—that is, a user should separately log onto each application he or she uses. However, many Web sites offer a mechanism called *single-sign-on* where an end user simply logs on once to any given server and that sign-on is shared by all applications on that server. By having a flexible realm configuration, Tomcat is able to offer this ability.

Figure 10-3 Authenticating a User

For all realms the configuration of the `<Realm>` element takes the same form and looks like this:

```
<Realm className="classname" otherAttr1="" otherAttr2="" etc.../>
```

For the memory realm the entry would look like this:

```
<Realm classname="org.apache.catalina.realm.MemoryRealm"
            debug="0"
            digest="MD5"
            pathname="conf/tomcat-users.xml"/>
```

- `debug` specifies the level of logging information produced by the realms: the higher the number the more detail; the default is 0.
- `digest` specifies the name of a security digest algorithm to use so that the passwords can be stored as non-plaintext.
- `pathname` is the absolute or CATALINA_HOME relative path to the .xml file containing the roles. This defaults to `conf/tomcat-users.xml`.

The major problem with the memory realm is that it is static—that is, you cannot dynamically add new users to roles once the application has started. The memory realm should only be used for testing and demonstration purposes (as here), not in real-world applications.

Be aware that Tomcat does not offer any "user management" for any of its realms. It is entirely up to the application to provide mechanisms to add and remove users to and from roles within a realm. Be aware also that the mechanisms defined here are Tomcat-specific. All the Servlet specification requires is that a container provides a mapping between an authenticated user and a role or group of roles. The specification does not say how this mapping is to be made. That is entirely down to the container, and each container will have its own mechanism to do this.

The Big Picture

Figure 10-4 shows the flow of control when a client tries to access a protected resource. Bob (the client) initially makes an HTTP request to Alice (the server). Alice checks the `security-constraint` elements of `web.xml` looking for a `user-data-constraint` element. If the `user-data-constraint` specifies DIGEST or CONFIDENTIAL, Alice will redirect the initial request so that a new request is generated that uses HTTPS. There will be more on this later. When the request arrives, using the correct protocol Alice now checks for a `Web-resource-collection` element within the appropriate `security-constraint` element to see if access to the requested resource is restricted based on the URL and the HTTP method sent in the request. This check can only take place if Bob has already been assigned a set of roles. To assign these roles, Bob has to be authenticated by Alice. So, if Alice has not previously authenticated Bob, then she does so now. How this authentication happens will be discussed shortly. If Bob is not authenticated,

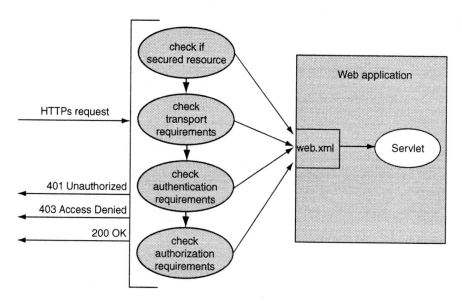

Figure 10-4 Flow of Control for Authentication and Authorization

Alice returns an error. If Bob authenticates, then Alice (not the application) assigns the client to a role. Alice then checks that Bob is authorized to make this call. If Bob is authorized, then the call succeeds; if Bob is not authorized to access this resource, then another, different error is returned by Alice. Note that all of this work is done by the actual Web server (Tomcat, in our examples), not within your application. The application does not get to see the request until all these checks are passed.

HTTP defines a simple challenge/response authentication mechanism that supports two built-in authentication schemes, *basic authentication* and *digest authentication,* each of which verifies that both parties in an exchange know a shared secret password. Basic authentication is defined as part of the HTTP RFC, RFC 2616, while Digest is defined in an adjunct to the main HTTP RFC, RFC 2617. To illustrate the challenge/response mechanism, let us look at the simpler of the two authentication schemes, basic authentication. Authentication is needed if Bob attempts to access a secured resource, perhaps by sending an HTTP request to Alice as shown in Listing 10-2.

Listing 10-2 A Client HTTP Request

```
GET /secureApp/secured/SecurityTest HTTP/1.1
Host: localhost
```

HTTP authentication is based on challenge-response: Alice issues the challenge and Bob must respond with the appropriate credentials. In this case the challenge from Alice takes the form of an HTTP "401 Unauthorized" response with an HTTP "WWW-Authenticate" header as shown in Listing 10-3.

Listing 10-3 The Server Challenge for Basic Authentication

```
HTTP/1.1 401 Unauthorized
WWW-Authenticate: Basic realm="jspbook"
```

The "WWW-Authenticate" header contains the name of the authentication scheme ("Basic") and the security realm ("jspbook"). The security realm tells Bob what set of credentials he should use. Bob's response is to resubmit the request along with an additional HTTP "Authorization" header whose value contains the scheme ("Basic"), the realm ("jspbook"), and the credentials. The credentials are simply a user name and password that have been base-64 encoded. Listing 10-4 illustrates this.

```
GET /secureApp/secured/SecurityTest HTTP/1.1
Host: localhost
Authorization: Basic ZnJlZDp0b21jYXQ=
```

If authentication fails, Alice sends back another "**401 Unauthorized**" response. If authentication succeeds, then Alice will attempt an authorization check. This check determines whether the authenticated caller is allowed access to the resource. If authorization fails—that is, access is not allowed, then the server sends back a "**403 Access denied**" response.

Basic authentication is very limited. The major problem with basic authentication is that the user name and password are essentially sent as plain text. Base-64 encoding is not encryption and is completely reversible by anyone. This means that the user name/password pair is open to be read by Eve or Mallory, who could use it to gain access to any other resource protected by the same user name/password pair. It also means that a malicious server could spoof a service in order to gain a password.

Another problem comes about because of the fact that HTTP is a stateless protocol. Being stateless implies that authentication information must be included with every client request for a secured resource. Once authenticated, Bob will typically cache the credentials for a given subset of server resources (for all resources that share the same URL base perhaps) and will re-issue those credentials, unprompted, with subsequent requests. The problem with this is that it opens up the possibility of "replay" attacks. In a replay attack, a valid request is repeatedly re-sent to the server by an attacker. This is bad if the request represents an operation such as "transfer $100 from account A to account B".

For these reasons it only makes sense to use basic authentication over an already secure link—for example, encrypted and with strong server authentication.

Digest authentication was introduced in HTTP 1.1 and is designed to improve on basic authentication by allowing Bob to prove knowledge of a password without transmitting the password on the wire. Digest authentication also provides more safeguards against replay attacks.

The digest challenge/response mechanism works in a similar way to basic authentication, but the details of the challenge and response are different. This time Alice's challenge looks something like Listing 10-5.

Listing 10-5 The Server Challenge for Digest Authentication

```
HTTP/1.1 401 Unauthorized
WWW-Authenticate: Digest realm="jspbook",
```

```
                       qop="auth",
                       nonce="5fef9f6239b0526151d6eebd12196cdc",
                       opaque="c8202b69f571bdf3ece44c4ce6ee2466"
```

The "WWW-Authenticate" header contains the name of the authentication scheme ("Digest") and the security realm ("jspbook") as before, but digest authentication requires other parameters for the authentication to happen and these are also included in the header. The most interesting parameter is the "nonce", which stands for "number once". The nonce is a number—uniquely generated by the server, meaningful only to the server, and valid only for the current authentication—so the nonce is valid only for a given 401 status code.

Once Bob receives the "401 Unauthorized" he resubmits the HTTP request as in Listing 10-5 with an "Authorization" header whose "response" parameter is the calculated digest. Notice that Bob never sends the password on the wire, but only the digest is transmitted.

A *digest* is a fixed-length encoding of some piece of data. It has the properties that the data cannot be easily deduced from the digest and that two digests are identical for the same data. However, note that two different pieces of data can also produce the same digest, but the chances of randomly selecting two items of data that produce the same digest are very, very small. Bob calculates a digest of the user name, password, realm, nonce, HTTP method, and request URI using a secure digest algorithm. The default digest algorithm used is MD5, although others can be specified. After everything is calculated, a response is sent that resembles Listing 10-6.

Listing 10-6 The Client Resubmits the HTTP Request with Digest Authentication Credentials

```
GET /jspbook/secured/SecurityTest HTTP/1.1
Host: localhost
Authorization: Digest username="reader",
                      realm="jspbook",
                      qop="auth",
                      algorithm="MD5",
                      uri="/jspbook/secured/SecurityTest",

nonce="e60ede51960d0f15dd5b6a9bb715dbd3",
                      nc=00000001,
                      cnonce="d35d64e34652169436cef64df7327f41",

opaque="9da8ed8720b206d71ebce39cf0ca42bd",

response="49f194c2babc4cb28c4e7edc63655a64"
```

When Alice receives this request, she also creates a message digest from the same data used by the client. Alice would have to have received Bob's password using some "out-of-band"[3] technique. Alice then compares the value of the digest she has generated with the digest sent by Bob. If the values are the same, then the credentials are valid, and subject to an authorization check, the caller is allowed access to the requested resource. If the values are different, then authentication fails and the server sends back a "401 Unauthorized" error. If authorization fails, the server sends back a "403 Access Denied" error.

Because the password is never sent in the clear, digest authentication is much safer than basic authentication, but it isn't perfect. For example, the server must hold each user's password in a form suitable for calculating the MD5 digest, and these passwords must be stored securely, because anyone possessing them could masquerade as any valid user. Also, depending on the server's choice of nonce, digest authentication is potentially open to replay attacks. There is nothing stopping Mallory simply taking a copy of the request and re-sending it to Alice with the digest intact. One recommended approach is for the server to compose the nonce from a hash of the resource URL, a resource "ETag" (an ETag is essentially a unique identifier for the requested resource; see the HTTP RFC for more information on ETags), a time-stamp, and a private key known only to the server. This way the server can guard against replay attacks by restricting the re-use of a nonce to the specified resource and limiting the period of the nonce's validity as defined by the time-stamp. That would probably be safe enough for HTTP GET calls, but to completely prevent replay attacks against non-idempotent operations requested by HTTP POST calls, the server would need to refuse to accept a nonce it had seen before. Given that the HTTP protocol is stateless, this is more work for the server. Generally, the safer the nonce, the greater the load on the server, and the more re-authentication is required by the caller[4].

Either basic authentication or digest authentication may be acceptable to a server when securing a resource, in which case the server can send a challenge with multiple "WWW-Authenticate" headers as in Listing 10-7.

---

3. Any method besides sending the password at that moment over the wire. Presumably the shared password is sent in a secure fashion previously, or else it is a moot point to ever assume the digest is providing security.

4. In general, all digital security requires more work to ensure something is secure—that is, of the appropriate difficulty level a malicious principal would have to crack.

Listing 10-7   The Server Challenge for Either Basic or Digest Authentication

```
HTTP/1.1 401 Unauthorized
WWW-Authenticate: Basic realm="jspbook"
WWW-Authenticate: Digest realm="jspbook",
                  qop="auth",
                  nonce="5fef9f6239b0526151d6eebd12196cdc",
                  opaque="c8202b69f571bdf3ece44c4ce6ee2466"
```

Using multiple authentication schemes is not a good idea. The client is at liberty to choose the strongest scheme it understands so there is a possibility that authentication could be downgraded to basic—in other words, the client might not understand digest. This opens up a "man-in-the-middle" attack where Malory (who is malicious, remember) can pretend to be the client, downgrade the authentication scheme, and start acquiring passwords.

There are other techniques not explored here that can be practiced within the scope of the digest authentication scheme by both client and server to minimize the chance of standard "man-in-the-middle" attacks and raise the quality of protection to ensure that both headers and data are safe from tampering. But although digest authentication is somewhat more secure than portrayed here, it is purely designed to be an improvement over the more serious flaws of basic authentication and is not, nor was never intended to be, a means for completely secure communication. Both basic authentication and digest authentication schemes rely on a shared secret. Neither scheme:

- defines how the secret might be exchanged initially,
- allows client and server to be cryptographically assured of each other's identity,
- mandates the use of the secret to guarantee that data exchanged between the two has not been tampered with,
- mandates the use of the secret to encrypt the conversation so that others may not see it.

There are some attacks that can only be prevented by sending HTTP requests and responses over a cryptographically encrypted channel, so that even if bad people can intercept transactions, then they are of no use. The Secure Sockets Layer (SSL), discussed later, addresses all of these concerns.

Configuring Basic or Digest Authentication

In the original example of the declarative web.xml entries, basic authentication was used. This is because basic authentication is the default authentication a Web

Application will use. To change the authentication scheme, the `login-config` element must be used:

```
<login-config>
    <auth-method>BASIC</auth-method>
    <realm-name>Reader</realm-name>
</login-config>
```

This code is an example of the `login-config` element as it was previously used in the chapter. Authentication schemes are configured by setting the `auth-method` child element to be the desired scheme. So far we have seen both basic and digest authentication. These schemes are defined by the `BASIC` and `DIGEST` values, respectively. In the code given, basic authentication is specified. The `realm-name` element provides the name of the security realm.

Custom Form-Based Authentication

Before progressing to HTTPS there is a slight tangent that is well worth discussing. The default authentication box, Figure 10-1, is not mandated. You can build a custom form that will be presented to a user in a much more stylish fashion. The Servlet specification defines this functionality as "Form" authentication.

With HTTP authentication the client application is in control of the user interface that the log in mechanism uses—that is, it is the browser that pops up the dialog box that the user fills in. Giving the `auth-method` setting a value of `FORM` allows the Web Application to define its own login pages so it has control over the look and feel of the login procedure. Listing 10-8 shows how to configure this in the application deployment descriptor.

Listing 10-8 Form-Based Authentication Configuration

```
<web-app>
  . . .
  <login-config>
    <auth-method>FORM</auth-method>
    <form-login-config>
      <form-login-page>/login.jsp</form-login-page>
      <form-error-page>/error.jsp</form-error-page>
    </form-login-config>
  </login-config>
  . . .
</web-app>
```

Note in addition to the `auth-method` element, the `form-login-page` element is used to define the page to use and a custom `error-page`. Use of these elements should be intuitive; `form-login-page` specifies a resource that includes the form and `form-error-page` specifies the error page.

Custom login and error page are free to be any type of resource, for example, Servlet, JSP, HTML, and use any style they prefer. The only restriction is that the login page must direct the request to "`j_security_check`" and provide values for the "`j_username`" and "`j_password`" parameters, such as the example in Listing 10-9.

Listing 10-9 Form-Based Logon Page

```
<html>
<body>
  <form method="POST" action="j_security_check" >
    User Name: <input type="text" name="j_username"><br/>
    Password : <input type="password" name="j_password"><br/>
    <input type="submit" value="Log on">
  </form>
</body>
</html>
```

You can try the preceding page by editing `web.xml` to use the `login-config` element shown in Listing 10-8, saving Listing 10-9 as `login.jsp` in the root directory of the jspbook Web Application, and reloading the Web Application for the changes to take effect. After the application reloads, browse back to `http://localhost/jspbook/secured/SecurityTest`. This time instead of Figure 10-1, the HTML form is displayed. Figure 10-5 provides a browser rendering for the output.

When `FORM` is specified as the `auth-method`, the container still performs the authentication check but not your application. For this reason the Servlet specification defines the value of the form's action as "`j_security_check`" and the names of the user name and password fields as "`j_username`" and "`j_password`". POST must be used as the form method. When the container sees the "`j_security_check`" action, it uses some internal mechanism to authenticate the caller.

If the login succeeds and the caller is authorized to access the secured resource, then the container uses a session-id to identify a login session for the caller from that point on. The container maintains the login session with a cookie containing the session-id. The server sends the cookie back to the client, and as long as the caller presents this cookie with subsequent requests, then the container will know who the caller is.

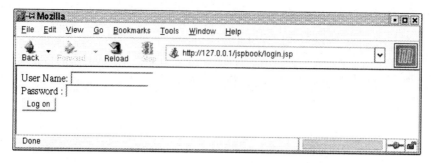

Figure 10-5 Browser Rendering of Custom HTML Authentication Form

If the login succeeds but the calling principal is not allowed access to the requested resource, then the server sends back a "403 Access Denied" response. If the login fails, then the server sends back the page identified by the `form-error-page` setting.

Form-based authentication suffers from the same problems as basic authentication. It is obviously not secure by default as there is no strong authentication of the server and the password is cleared. It is possible to force the form-based login interaction to take place over a secure channel by specifying a transport guarantee for the secured resource, as is later discussed in this chapter. One other issue with form authentication is that because session tracking with form-based authentication and URL rewriting is quite difficult (due to requiring "`j_security_check`"), then, typically, for form-based authentication to work, cookies must be enabled.

Programmatic Security in a Servlet/JSP

All the preceding authentication mechanisms result in one of two things: either the user is not authenticated or he or she is authenticated and assigned membership of one or more roles.

A *role* is just a grouping of authenticated principals, normally defined by some function such as Sales, Marketing, Reader, etc. The means by which principals are placed in roles is entirely vendor-specific and is not covered by the Servlet specification. Once roles have been created and role membership defined, then role-based security constraints can be applied to a Web collection. Access to a resource will be granted if either:

- No authentication scheme is in place.

- The Web collection has no role-based security constraint.
- The caller is in at least one role allowed access.

Otherwise, access is denied.

Role-based security is good because we can keep the access control configuration separate from the Servlet and JSP code. The programmer does not need to write any security-related code at all if they do not want to. But how realistic is this mechanism? Role-based security is a fairly static and inflexible approach: either the caller passes the access check based on role membership or not. If the caller passes, then the resource is returned or the Servlet/JSP code starts executing. If not, a "403 Access Denied" response is sent back to the caller.

However, it may not be possible to work out whether access is allowed until runtime based on questions, such as "What is the caller's credit limit?" In addition it may be that a given resource works very similarly for callers in two different roles. Imagine a request that returns customer details. For salespeople the request might return all the customer information apart from the customer's credit limit, whereas for a manager, the request would return all the information including the credit limit. In this case, if all the application could do was decide whether a call was allowed based on the caller's role, the application would need two separate resources. These resources would be very similar, the only difference being whether the credit limit was included in the output. Duplicating resources is error-prone; if the customer details change, then both resources have to be amended.

To deal with these kinds of scenarios, the application can obtain information about the caller or the caller's role membership at runtime and perform different logic on the basis of what is discovered. The `HttpServletRequest` object provides the following methods, which can be used to mine security information at runtime:

- **String getAuthType():** The `getAuthType()` method returns a `String` object that represents the name of the authentication scheme used to protect the Servlet. While not usually helpful, this can be used to determine how form information was submitted.
- **boolean isUserInRole(java.lang.String role):** The `isUserInRole()` method returns a boolean value: `true` if the user is in the given role or `false` if they are not.
- **String getProtocol():** The `getProtocol()` method returns a `String` object representing the protocol that was used to send the request.

This value can be checked to determine if a secure protocol was used.

- **boolean isSecure():** The `isSecure()` method returns a boolean value representing if the request was made using HTTPS. A value of `true` means it was and the connection is secure. A value of `false` means the request was not.

- **Principle getUserPrinciple():** The `getUserPrinciple()` method returns a `java.security.Principle` object that contains the name of the current authenticated user.

The most helpful of these methods is the `isUserInRole()` method. This method can be used to easily provide programmatic checks to see if a user is in a particular role. For example:

```
void doPost(HttpServletRequest req,
            HttpServletResponse res) {
  if (req.isUserInRole("ManagersRole")) {
    // Do some Manager stuff
  } else if (req.isUserInRole("ReaderRole")) {
    // Do some Sales stuff
  } else {
    throw Exception("User does not have access!");
  }
}
```

There is one problem with using a Servlet to provide programmatic checks such as this. The Servlet is written by a programmer, and the role names are hard coded into the Servlet. The Servlet is deployed by a "deployer", and the names used for the roles by the deployer might not be the same as the names used by the Servlet. To solve this problem, the `security-role-ref` element may be used when defining a Servlet.

The `security-role-ref` element provides a concrete name a Servlet can reference and a configurable name a deployer can optionally change to match whatever role-naming scheme is used. The `security-role-ref` element has two child elements that define this information: `role-name` and `role-link`. The `role-name` element defines the static value a Servlet may reference. The `role-link` value is a role name a deployer can modify as needed. In use, the `security-role-ref` element always resembles Listing 10-10.

Listing 10-10 Example of web.xml security-role-ref Element

```
...
<servlet>
```

```
<servlet-name>FooServlet</servlet-name>
<servlet-class>com.jspbook.FooServlet</servlet-class>
<security-role-ref>
    <!-- role-name is used in the application-->
    <role-name>ReaderRole</role-name>
    <role-link>Reader</role-link>
</security-role-ref>
</servlet>

<security-role>
    <role-name>Reader</role-name>
</security-role>
. . .
```

Note the `security-role-ref` element is used as a child element of the `servlet` element. The reference is only valid for the Servlet it is defined with. Additionally, the `security-role` element has been defined to create a role named "Reader".

```
<security-role>
    <role-name>Reader</role-name>
</security-role>
```

This is required only when doing application-level security and making use of the `security-role-ref` element. The entry is not needed if all the authentication and authorization is managed by the container.

Secure Encrypted Communication

The preceding discussion talked about using security to perform authentication, authorization, and data integrity. However, there are other things that must be done to provide a fully secure conversation between Alice and Bob. The first is encryption. If Bob wants to send private data to Alice—for example, credit card numbers—it had better be encrypted. However, there is no point in encrypting the data if the endpoint Bob is sending the data to is itself not trusted. In other words, before Bob sends private data to Alice, Bob should know that he is talking to Alice; Bob has to authenticate Alice. This is the opposite authentication that was talked about previously where Alice (the server) authenticated Bob (the client). Now, the client has to authenticate the server before sending the data. Modern cryptography allows for both these things to happen.

Cryptography allows data to be encrypted with a key so that it can only be decrypted with a "matching" key. There are two types of key encryption, symmetric key encryption and asymmetric key encryption.

A *symmetric key* represents a shared secret, and the same key is used to both encrypt and decrypt the data. The problem with symmetric key encryption is "key exchange". How do two parties securely exchange a symmetric key? Alice cannot simply send it to Bob because Mallory can see it.

An *asymmetric key* is a key that is split into two parts: the private key and the public key. Either can decrypt data encrypted by the other—that is, data encrypted by the public key only can be decrypted by the private and vice versa. Note that data encrypted by one key can *only* be decrypted with the other key. The private key is truly private. It is only known by a single entity. The public key is truly public and can be known by everyone.

Encrypting data with the public key is useful, as that data can only be decrypted with the private key. That means that no one can read that data except the private key owner. That is, if Bob encrypts data using Alice's public key, only Alice can decrypt that data.

What about encrypting data using a private key? If Alice encrypts data using her private key, anybody can decrypt it with Alice's public key (the key is public and so is available to anybody). This is also extremely useful as it can be used to prove identity. If Alice sends Bob some plain text, and also encrypts that plaintext with her private key and sends the encrypted data, Bob can take the encrypted data and decrypt it with Alice's public key. He can then compare the decrypted data with the plaintext and compare them. If the comparison is equal, then the plain text must have come from the person whose public key Bob has, so Bob "proves" the data has come from Alice. In this case, Alice is said to have "signed" her data, and typically a hash of the data, rather than the data itself, is signed. A question you should be asking at this point is "How does Bob know that he has Alice's key and not somebody else's?" This is where something called *certificates* come in, but we will postpone discussion of certificates for now.

So which do we use, symmetric or asymmetric keys? Asymmetric encryption is fine for encrypting/decrypting a hash but is typically an order of magnitude, or slower than a symmetric key when used for encrypting/decrypting bulk data[5]. So the best bet is for two principals to exchange a symmetric key for data encryption, valid for the lifetime of the interaction between the two principals. But how best to exchange this session key securely so that it cannot be seen and so that both parties really know who they are sharing the key with? The answer

---

5. Using public key private key pairs also has other issues. For example, an attacker will have a copy of the public key; the attacker will also have lots of ciphertext encrypted with the private key. The attacker could also guess some of the plaintext that was encrypted (such as request lines and HTTP headers). The more data an attacker has, the easier it is to break the encryption.

is using asymmetric keys. Not only do asymmetric keys lend themselves toward generating digital signatures but also secure exchange of symmetric keys.

Alice and Bob want to exchange a session key. Alice generates a session key and encrypts it with Bob's public key. She signs the encrypted session key with her private key and sends the signed encrypted session key to Bob. Bob can use Alice's public key to verify the data came from Alice and only Bob can decrypt the session key. Bob now has trust in Alice and the session key. Bob now encrypts the session key with Alice's public key. He signs the encrypted session key with his private key and sends the signed encrypted session key back to Alice. Alice now has trust in Bob and the session key. This assumes, of course, that Alice and Bob have already securely exchanged public keys. Even though public keys can be read and used by anyone, what they cannot do is send public keys to each other on the wire.

If Mallory were to intercept the key exchange, he could just sit in the middle and pretend to be Bob to Alice and Alice to Bob and read all traffic between them. If Alice and Bob knew each other, they could exchange public keys face to face without Mallory being able to get in the middle. If not, they could use a trusted intermediary, Trent (someone they had both securely exchanged keys with in the past). Assume Alice and Bob both trust Trent and have already obtained Trent's public key securely. Also suppose Trent trusts both of them and has already obtained their public keys securely. Trent can put Bob's public key and details in a package called a certificate, sign it, and send it to Alice. She knows it came from Trent and can trust the contents. Likewise, Trent can place Alice's public key in a signed certificate and send it to Bob who knows it came from Trent and has not been tampered with in transit. In fact, Trent could issue Alice and Bob their own certificates, signed by him. This way, for example, Bob could authenticate himself to any other party that also trusted Trent by just sending his certificate (signed by Trent) containing his public key.

Of course, this authentication technique, involving certificate exchange, only works among those parties who trust Trent. Those who have certificates signed by Trudy cannot exchange certificates with those who have certificates signed by Trent, unless, that is, Trudy and Trent both have certificates themselves that are issued and signed by someone they both trust, Todd. This is termed a *certificate chain*. In this case, for Bob to authenticate to Carol (who trusts Trudy) he must pass her both his certificate (signed by Trent) and Trent's certificate (signed by Todd). In this way Carol can verify that Bob is trusted by Trent who is trusted by Todd and that is OK because Trudy (who Carol trusts) is also trusted by Todd. At the top of the tree there must be some single certificate authority (CA) that everyone trusts and who is able to sign their own certificates.

In the real world there is a standard for certificates called X.509, and there are several CAs who are trusted by everyone and whose public keys are well known—for example, Verisign. Certificates issued by Verisign are globally recognized, and Verisign's public key gets distributed with commercial client and server software such as browsers and Web servers. A company could act as its own certificate authority to all of its departments, but those certificates would only be usable within the company, not globally.

So where are we? In order for two parties to authenticate each other they exchange certificates and then they can use asymmetric encryption to exchange a session key securely. From that point on, data can be encrypted or signed using the shared session key. This is essentially what SSL does, although it's a little more complex than that. There are two modes that make sense in SSL. First, mutual authentication where the caller and server exchange certificates so they both know who each other is. Second, server authentication where the server sends a certificate to the caller so the caller knows who the server is. SSL uses a four-way handshake, shown in Figure 10-6, that progressively builds up trust between the two parties.

A vastly simplified explanation follows, involving a client running on behalf of Alice and a server running on behalf of Bob.

- Leg 1: Alice sends a random number and an ordered list of acceptable cipher suites (each cipher-suite indicates the algorithms to be used for data encryption, signatures, etc.) to Bob.

- Leg 2: Bob receives Alice's transmission and sends back a random number of his own (independent of the client-generated random number), the chosen cipher-suite, his certificate, and, optionally, a request for the client's (Alice's) certificate.

- Leg 3: Alice receives Bob's transmission and verifies Bob's certificate. If it is valid, she now has Bob's public key but cannot prove it's him on the other end. If Bob asked her for her certificate, then she sends it. Then she generates another random number (called the *pre-master secret*) and encrypts it with Bob's public key (so only he can read it) and sends that. Next she constructs a signature (using her private key) of all the handshake data that has formed part of the conversation up until this point and sends that. This is sometimes called the certificate verification code. Following that she uses the pre-master secret to generate all the keys required to perform data encryption and provide signatures according to the cipher-suite she negotiated with Bob. She then sends an instruction to say that she is

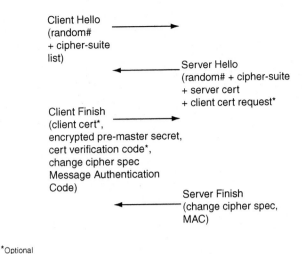

Client Hello
(random#
+ cipher-suite
list)

Server Hello
(random# + cipher-suite
+ server cert
+ client cert request*

Client Finish
(client cert*,
encrypted pre-master secret,
cert verification code*,
change cipher spec
Message Authentication
Code)

Server Finish
(change cipher spec,
MAC)

*Optional

Figure 10-6 Illustration of a Four-Way SSL Handshake

going to start using the negotiated cipher-suite. Finally, she sends a message authentication code (MAC). This is a signature (using the signature generation key from the negotiated cipher-suite) of all the handshake data that has formed part of the conversation up until this point.

- Leg 4: Bob receives Alice's transmission. He verifies her certificate, if she sent it, and if it is valid, he now has Alice's public key but cannot prove it's her on the other end yet. He then decrypts the pre-master secret and uses it to generate all the keys required to perform data encryption and provide signatures according to the cipher-suite he negotiated with Alice. He now has the same set of keys as Alice. This allows Bob to verify the MAC, and if it is OK, then he is sure it is Alice on the other end because the MAC protects the entire conversation so far. Bob now sends an instruction to say that he is also going to start using the negotiated cipher-suite. Finally, he sends a MAC, which is a signature (that uses the signature generation key from the negotiated cipher-suite) of all the handshake data that has formed part of the conversation up until this point.

Alice receives Bob's transmission and uses the negotiated cipher-suite to decrypt it and verify the MAC. If it is OK, then she is sure it is Bob on the other end because only he could have decrypted the pre-master secret used to generate the key used to generate the MAC. They are done. Alice knows she is talking to Bob and Bob may know he is talking to Alice (if he asked her for a certificate). They have exchanged keys used for data encryption and to ensure data integrity.

SSL/TLS is a lot of work! But the work is needed. In cases where it must be ensured, to a best effort, that information is secure and authentic, then you have little choice but to use SSL. The good news is that you do not have to implement the entire SSL protocol before using it with a Web Application. Should your container support SSL, then it is the container vendor's job to implement it. In most popular containers, Tomcat included, SSL support is available. The only thing you need to provide is a certificate from a CA.

Specifying HTTPS

One of the `web.xml` elements that has yet to be explained is the `user-data-constraint` element. The `user-data-constraint` element can be used to specify the level of security a request and response must adhere to. The child element `transport-guarantee` can be used to set a value of either NONE, INTEGRAL, or CONFIDENTIAL. The NONE value is the default and requires no level of security be enforced. The INTEGRAL value specifies that a container must ensure the integrity of information—that is, it has not changed during transit but it might have been read by others. The CONFIDENTIAL value requires that information sent in a request and response is both private and unchanged—for example, SSL.

Use of the `user-data-constraint` element is straightforward. For example, to ensure the protected part of a Web Application is kept completely confidential, the following entry could be used:

```
. . .
 <security-constraint>
   <web-resource-collection>
     <web-resource-name>SecuredBookSite</web-resource-name>
     <url-pattern>/tlssecured/*</url-pattern>
     <http-method>GET</http-method>
     <http-method>POST</http-method>
```

```
  </web-resource-collection>
  <user-data-constraint>
    <transport-guarantee>CONFIDENTIAL</transport-guarantee>
  </user-data-constraint>
</security-constraint>
...
```

Now all resources under the `/tlssecured` virtual folder of a Web Application are completely private, not just difficult to see. If you try this on your PC—for example, browse to `http://127.0.0.1/jspbook/tlssecured/Foo`—instead of HTTP the browser would automatically redirect to a secure port/protocol, for instance, `https://127.0.0.1/jspbook/tlssecured` using port 443. You can try this on your own PC, but there are several things that have to first be done.

- Locate the following entry in `/conf/server.xml` file of your Tomcat installation and make sure the value of `port` is "443", because by default Tomcat uses 8443:

```
<Connector
className="org.apache.catalina.connector.http.HttpConnector"
    port="443" minProcessors="5" maxProcessors="75"
    enableLookups="true"
    acceptCount="10" debug="0" scheme="https" secure="true">
```

- By default the above code is commented out; uncomment it.
- Locate the following entry; also in `server.xml`:

```
<Connector
className="org.apache.catalina.connector.http.HttpConnector"
        port="80" minProcessors="5" maxProcessors="75"
        enableLookups="true" redirectPort="443"
        acceptCount="10" debug="0"
connectionTimeout="60000"/>
```

Make sure that port is set to 80 (as done in Chapter 1) and that redirectPort is set to 443. These values are the default HTTPS and HTTP ports; the values for a default Tomcat install are 8443 and 8080, respectively. The important thing for now is that the value of `redirectPort` in the second entry matches the value of the `port` for the first entry; they are both 443 in the examples shown here.

Once you have uncommented the HTTPS entry, Tomcat is almost ready to listen for HTTPS requests, but to do so, you have to install a security certificate. A certificate is an integral part of HTTPS as will be seen later[6]. Type one of the following to generate a certificate:

- In Windows, execute

```
%JAVA_HOME%\bin\keytool -genkey -alias tomcat -keyalg RSA
```

- In Linux, execute

```
$JAVA_HOME/bin/keytool -genkey -alias tomcat -keyalg RSA
```

Fill in the values that are asked for by keytool. The values may be fictitious as this is a custom certificate made by you, but they will be appearing later. Make sure that both requested passwords are "changeit" (without the quote marks). Figure 10-7 shows a complete execution of the program.

Once that is done a `.keystore` file is generated in your home directory with all the information needed by the certificate. Tomcat needs to know about the certificate you just generated. By default Tomcat looks in the home directory of the user that executed it for the `.keystore` file, which is convenient[7]. Now you can browse to a resource under the `/tlssecured` virtual directory and SSL will be used. For instance, try browsing to `http://127.0.0.1/jspbook/tlssecured/`. The URL is redirected to `https://127.0.0.1/jspbook/tlssecured/` and you are asked for a user name and password. Assuming you put in the correct information the content is displayed same as before, but the complete request and response are thoroughly encrypted (even if it is just a 404 page). Since you created a custom certificate, do not be surprised if your Web browser complains about the certificate's validity. It is a certificate that no third party will verify because you never registered it with a CA. For instance, Mozilla will complain similar to Figure 10-8, but it is fine because the certificate is only being used for an example.

Typically, in HTTPS only the server is authenticated—that is, the server does not care who you are, but a secure connection is still needed. As the discussion of the SSL handshake above shows, HTTPS does allow for mutual authentication.

---

6. If you are using a JDK prior to JDK 1.4, you will need to download and install the Java Secure Sockets Extensions, JSSE. See Sun's Web site at `http://java.sun.com/products/jsse/` for more details.

7. If Tomcat cannot find the `.keystore` file, you need to manually set the location of it using the factory elements keyStore attribute. See `http://jakarta.apache.org/tomcat/tomcat-5.0-doc/ssl-howto.html` for more information.

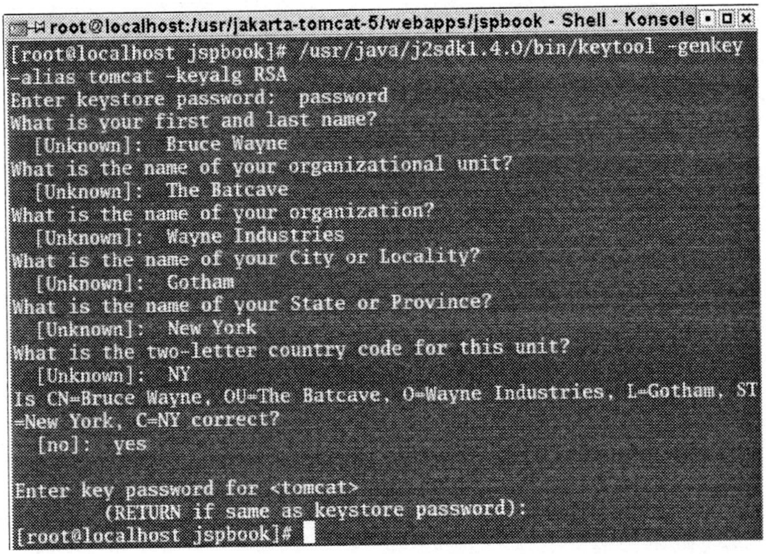

Figure 10-7 Using Java's Keytool to Create a Certificate

In this case where this is needed, the client has to install their certificate in the browser. Additionally, the `auth-method` element must be set to `CLIENT-CERT`.

If a request was made over a secure channel, then the Servlet can find out via `isSecure()`. Additionally, the container associates some of the characteristics of the secure channel with the following request scoped attributes:

- `javax.servlet.request.cipher-suite`: The `javax.servlet.request.cipher-suite` attribute is a `string` object that represents the cipher-suite used by the secure connection.

- `javax.servlet.request.key-size`: The `javax.servlet.request.key-size` attribute is an Integer object representing the size of the key used to encrypt content.

- `java.security.cert.X509Certificate`: The `java.security.cert.X509Certificate` attribute is an array of `java.security.cert.X509Certificate` objects that represent the SSL certificates used with the request.

The attributes can be mined as needed to know more about the security of the connection. For more information about the `X509Certificate` object, consult the Java documentation for the object and the rest of the Java 2 Security API.

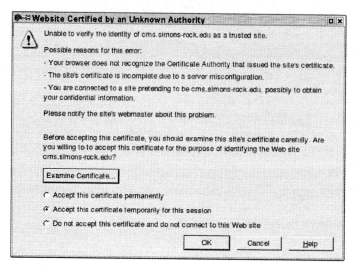

Figure 10-8 Invalid Certificate in Mozilla

How Secure Is Security?

Throughout this whole discussion of security the term "secure" has been used to imply complete security. However, it is important to note that as of yet there have been no absolute foolproof methods of digital encryption. This is not an effort to make you paranoid, but it is a fact that is important to understand as a good developer. For all practical purposes, protocols such as SSL/TLS are agreed to be well beyond what is considered feasible for someone to crack with modern equipment—likely even technology developed in the near future[8]. When using SSL/TLS, the security you can assure users of is well worth placing your bet on.

Why digital encryption is not perfect is worth understanding. In short, all digital information is represented by 1's and 0's, and the only thing encryption does is randomize these 1's and 0's. The randomized 1's and 0's are sent publicly across the Web—and a key is used to privately convert the randomized information back into a meaningful set of 1's and 0's. Hence, when using good cryptography, such as SSL/TLS, your odds of being compromised are directly related to the size of your key.

---

8. It should be noted that it has been proven in theory that quantum computers can break popular encryption, such as SSL/TLS, in small amounts of time; however, as of yet quantum computers do not exist.

Since a key itself is a set of 1's and 0's, basic probability can be used to figure out your odds are as good as 2^x, where x is the length of a key—that is, if the key is one bit long, it is either 1 or 0. If I try both keys, one of the results has to be the correct decrypted information. Likewise, if a key is of length 2, then there are four possibilities, and so on. Being an exponential equation the odds of having your security compromised grow exponentially with key size. In practice the common range of key sizes is usually between 128 bits and 512 bits, equating to 2^{128}, which is $1:34,028,236,692*10^{38}$, and 2^{512}, which is $1:1,340,780,793*10^{154}$. The odds of winning a large lottery are dwarfed by these numbers. Additionally, to convert these figures to processing time, you have to multiply by the time it takes to successfully decrypt using a key and verify if the information is meaningful. Even with extreme parallel processing, these numbers are ridiculously huge.

The point at hand is that security is important and yes a Web Application provides a perfectly good method of implementing it. When developing a "secure" application, it does little good to say it is secure without knowing why it is secure. In this chapter we have covered completely the chore of implementing a "secure" Web Application, and we have also touched on why the application is secure. If you are interested in a complete discussion and dissection of all the acronyms, algorithms, and protocols used by conventional cryptography, it is recommended you read *Cryptography and Network Security, Principles and Practice*, by William Stallings.

Encryption and Compression and Caching

A topic of minor importance but worth mentioning is that of how to properly implement encryption, compression, and caching. In Chapter 8, Filters were introduced and the paradigm was presented that Filters can cleanly be stacked to provide layered functionality (see Figure 8-1). Additionally, the concepts of compression and caching were introduced because they are ideal uses for a Filter. Security and encryption are also ideal for a Filter. If it was not for the fact that most (if not all) containers already implement adequate security, then a security Filter would have made an ideal example for this chapter.

The point to raise is, the three topics, encryption, compression, and caching, are all excellent ways to provide support for in a Web Application; however, you should not haphazardly combine the three. For instance, the point was raised about correctly using compression Filters with caching Filters. A cached copy of compressed content would not work for clients that do not support compression. Be careful not to stack Filters in a method that would create this problem. The same concept applies to encryption. With security introduced by this chapter, the

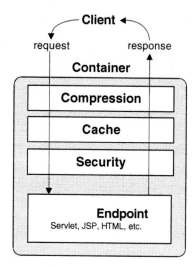

Figure 10-9 Poorly Stacked Filters

topic of encryption has also been introduced and you may desire to use non-standardized encryption for security. Be careful about where encryption is stacked in relation to caching and compression. Do not put encryption behind either a cache or compression layer, as shown in Figure 10-9!

Figure 10-9 is bad because non-symmetric encryption cannot be expected to work if copies of pre-encrypted content are cached. Technologies such as SSL require a lot of processing power and bandwidth because of the security they provide via good encryption. Caching to eliminate this problem is not an option!

Another important point is that the goal of compression is to remove all redundancy content may contain. The goal of encryption is to completely randomize content and eliminate any patterns. Trying to compress encrypted content is futile. Doing so only results in extra, unneeded server-side work.

The correct way to always apply compression and encryption is to compress content, then encrypt the compressed content as shown in Figure 10-10.

Caching can be implemented either before compression, after compression, or at both places. It depends on what you are trying to optimize when using the cache. The concept to take away from this section is that it does matter where and how encryption, compression, and caching are implemented. Thankfully, the security mechanisms defined by the Servlet specification are designed to prevent these problems from ever happening. However, when building custom security

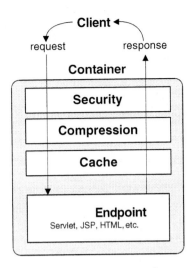

Figure 10-10 Correct Method to Implement Encryption, Compression, and Caching

Filters (or Filter-like functionality if you are using IIS, Apache, etc., to complement a container) be aware of what you are doing!

Summary

Security is important and Web Applications are designed with this in mind. Understanding the basics of cryptography and how it is implemented via Servlets and JSP rounds out your skill-set even further. Instead of creating a site that anyone can freely visit and use, you are now able to clearly define who can see what and how it can be seen. The ability to provide this security is imperative when building Web Applications that contain content or services of a sensitive nature.

Cryptography is complex, but implementing cryptography in a Web Application is designed to be as simple as possible. The Servlet specification clearly defines an interface by which container vendors can implement any form of security. As a developer the only thing that needs to be completely understood is how to configure the Servlet-provided interface. In most cases, this is done via declarative security using `web.xml`. In cases where a finer granularity of control is required, programmatic security can be implemented.

The specific security implementations covered in this chapter ranged from simple to complex. Both HTTP basic and digest authentication were covered along with a Web Application's method of providing custom forms and error pages. In the realm of complex cryptography the SSL/TLS protocol was introduced along with certificates for creating truly secure communications. While none of the specific algorithms available for use with SSL/TLS were covered, it was shown that the security provided is adequate for ensuring "secure" connections.

Chapter 11

Design Patterns

Developers have been building JSP and Servlet Web Applications for a number of years. There are many ways to produce content via Servlets and JSP, but there are only a few ways that are commonly agreed upon as good. Understanding what exists, both good and bad, greatly increases your ability to build a good Web Application. This chapter is an overview of the common design patterns implemented by Web Application developers. In many ways this is one of the most important chapters of this book as it is something you can experiment with only after having a good understanding of the JSP and Servlet specifications.

This chapter discusses the following topics:

- An explanation on why you should use design patterns.
- Discussion of the Model 1 design pattern: naming the way new developers often code.
- Discussion of the Model 2 design pattern: the encouraged method for building a Web Application.
- Discussion of the Model 1½ design pattern: a practical method of doing Model 2.
- Using the Jakarta Struts framework: introducing a very popular Model 2 framework.
- Abstracting DHTML via custom tags.

This chapter is intended to be read through from start to finish, especially since information in this chapter cannot be found in the Servlet and JSP specifications. In many of the previous chapters the information was nothing more than an enhanced description of what you can find in various official J2EE documents. In this chapter realize the value of what is being presented. This is not a chapter where you cut and paste together examples to make a final product. This is a chapter about concepts and how they can be applied using Servlets and JSP.

Why Use a Design Pattern?

There are many reasons why a design pattern is favorable to use. Here is a formal list of the benefits:

- **Reduce Development Time:** A good design pattern helps conceptually to break down a complex system into manageable tasks. This allows developers to individually code parts of the Web Application they are best suited for. It also allows individual components to be built and replaced without harming the existing code base.
- **Reduced Maintenance Time:** The majority of projects involve maintenance of an already existing system. Maintenance can be a nightmare should a system be hacked together when it was initially built. Good design plans ahead to simplify future maintenance concerns.
- **Collaboration:** Not all developers share the same expertise. Often a mixed group of developers is assigned to a task especially in the case of a larger project. A good design can successfully enforce separation of a project's functionality into areas that collaborating developers are most familiar, and ensure separate parts of a project seamlessly fit together.

The importance of having design patterns grows with the size of a project. Rebuilding an existing, working Web Application is never desirable. While rebuilding a small Web Application is feasible, rebuilding a large Web Application is not. Good design ensures a Web Application should never need a complete overhaul.

Common Design Patterns

There are many ways in which to classify design patterns. What is important are the concepts behind the design pattern, not the buzzwords or acronyms. Design concepts hold true to every project and do not date as code does. This chapter focuses on one very important concept: why it is important to logically separate a Web Application's functionality. This concept is the foundation of popular JSP and Servlet design patterns and implies many smaller points of good practice when coding with Java, Servlets, and JSP.

To explain the most commonly used JSP and Servlet design patterns, a common vocabulary is needed. This chapter uses the popular terms of Model 1, Model 2, and Model 1½. The Model 1 and Model 2 design patterns are general classifications of how a Web Application can be structured. Model 1½ is a practical approach at implementing Model 2 concepts using a method, which is quick and can later be ported to a Model 2 design. Both Model 1 and Model 2 are explained further in the following sections. Discussion of Model 1½ is provided after the Model 2 design pattern is covered.

Model 1

Model 1 is used to refer to what is usually the intuitive approach to using JSP and Servlets; a Model 1 architecture is what a new JSP and Servlet developer are likely to build. The concept behind a Model 1 architecture is simple: code functionality wherever the functionality is needed. The approach is very popular because it is both simple and provides instant gratification. Should security be needed, code it in. Should a JSP need information from a database, code in the query.

The concept of a Model 1 architecture should be simple to see. Everything relies on a request going to one resource and the resource returning the correct reply. Figure 11-1 illustrates the concept.

Note in Figure 11-1 the single resource is a JSP or Servlet, not the Web Application. While a Web Application is always responsible for handling a request and response, the issue we are highlighting is *how* the Web Application handles the request and response. In the extreme case of the Model 1 architecture, an entire request and response is handled by a single endpoint such as a JSP or Servlet.

Simple Model 1 Web Site

In code the concept is easy to illustrate. Consider a simple news Web site. The site consists of three different pages: a page about the site, a news page, and a page to

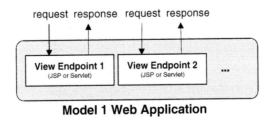

Model 1 Web Application

Figure 11-1   Illustration of the Model 1 Architecture

add news. It is assumed the site only needs to be available in HTML format and users do not have to log on before adding news to the site. Save Listing 11-1 as index.jsp in the /model1 directory of the jspbook Web Application.

Listing 11-1 Model 1 Example of index.jsp

```
<jsp:include page="header.jsp"/>
<%@ page import="
java.io.*,
javax.xml.parsers.*,
org.w3c.dom.*" %>
<%
  ServletContext sc = pageContext.getServletContext();
  String dir = sc.getRealPath("/model1");
  File file = new File(dir+"/news.xml");
  DocumentBuilderFactory dbf =
    DocumentBuilderFactory.newInstance();
  DocumentBuilder db = dbf.newDocumentBuilder();
  Document doc= null;
  if (file.exists()) {
    doc = db.parse(file);
  }
  if (doc != null) {
    NodeList nodes = doc.getElementsByTagName("story");
    for (int i = 0; i < nodes.getLength();i++) {
      Element e = (Element)nodes.item(i);
%>
    <hr>
    <h3><a href="<%= e.getAttribute("link") %>">
    <%= e.getAttribute("title") %></a></h3>
    <%= e.getAttribute("story") %>
<%
    }
  }
%>
<jsp:include page="footer.jsp"/>
```

The page index.jsp is the main page of the site and is responsible for showing all the current news. The important point to note about index.jsp is that the page does not have a form on it but does have some scripting elements. The scripting elements are used to load and read information about the current news. The news is saved in an XML file, news.xml, in the /model1 directory of the jspbook Web Application. We will create the XML file later.

For several reasons a flat file is not a good choice for persisting information; a database management system (DBMS) is the preferred choice as explained later in Chapter 14. The flat file used now is more than adequate to illustrate the important design pattern concepts. Later with the Model 2 design pattern it is shown that the choice of data persistence really does not matter from a JSP or Servlet developer's perspective.

Listing 11-2 is the code for the page to add news. Save Listing 11-2 as addnews.jsp in the /model1 directory of the jspbook Web Application.

Listing 11-2 Model 1 Example of addnews.jsp

```
<jsp:include page="header.jsp"/>
<%@ page import="
java.io.*,
javax.xml.parsers.*,
org.w3c.dom.*,
javax.xml.transform.*,
javax.xml.transform.stream.*,
javax.xml.transform.dom.*" %>
<%
  String title = request.getParameter("title");
  String link = request.getParameter("link");
  String story = request.getParameter("story");
  if (title != null && !title.equals("") &&
      story != null && !story.trim().equals("") &&
      link != null && !link.equals("")) {
    ServletContext sc = pageContext.getServletContext();
    String dir = sc.getRealPath("/model1");
    File file = new File(dir+"/news.xml");
    DocumentBuilderFactory dbf =
      DocumentBuilderFactory.newInstance();
    DocumentBuilder db = dbf.newDocumentBuilder();
    Document doc = null;
    if (file.exists()){
      doc = db.parse(file);
    }
    else {
      doc = db.newDocument();
      Element root = doc.createElement("news");
      doc.appendChild(root);
    }
    Element news = doc.createElement("story");
    news.setAttribute("title",title);
```

```
        news.setAttribute("link",link);
        news.setAttribute("story",story);
        doc.getDocumentElement().appendChild(news);

        TransformerFactory tf = TransformerFactory.newInstance();
        Transformer t = tf.newTransformer();
        DOMSource source = new DOMSource(doc);
        StreamResult result =
            new StreamResult(new FileOutputStream(file));
        t.transform(source, result);
%>

<p align="center">You news has been added!<br>
<a href="index.jsp">Back to main page.</a></p>

<% }
   else {
      if(title == null) {
        title = "";
      }
      if(link == null) {
        link = "";
      }
      if(story == null) {
        story = "";
      }
%>
<h3>Add News</h3>
<p>Fill in all fields to add your news to Foo news.</p>
<form method="post">
 Tile: <input size="50" name="title" value="<%= title%>"><br>
 Link: <input size="50" name="link" value="<%= link%>"><br>
 Story:
    <textarea cols="50" rows="10" name="story">
      <%= story%>
    </textarea>
 <br>
 <input type="submit" value="Add News">
</form>
<% } %>
<jsp:include page="footer.jsp"/>
```

The important points to note about addnews.jsp is that the page includes some scripting elements and a method of soliciting information from a user, an

HTML form. The code itself is nothing spectacular. The page checks to see if form information has been submitted. If so, the information is used to create a news entry. If not, an HTML form is displayed for the user to fill in a news story.

The page with information about the news site is the simplest of the three pages. Save Listing 11-3 as `about.jsp` in the `/model1` directory of the jspbook Web Application.

Listing 11-3 Model 1 Example of about.jsp

```
<jsp:include page="header.jsp"/>
<h2>About</h2>
<p>Foo news is a news resource about Foo. Contact
us at foo@jspbook.com.</p>
<pre>
foo /foo/ 1. interj. Term of disgust. 2. [very common] Used very
   generally as a sample name for absolutely anything, esp. programs
and
   files (esp. scratch files). 3. First on the standard list of
   metasyntactic variables used in syntax examples. See also bar.*
</pre>
*Cited from http://www.jargon.org
<jsp:include page="footer.jsp"/>
```

The important points to note in `about.jsp` are the page does not include scripting elements and it also lacks a method of soliciting feedback from a user. The page consists of only HTML used to display information.

Complementing all three pages is a simple header and footer file. Save Listing 11-4 as `header.jsp` and Listing 11-5 as `footer.jsp`, respectively, in the `/model1` directory of the jspbook Web Application.

Listing 11-4 header.jsp

```
<html>
 <head>
   <title>Foo News - News about Foo, news that matters.</title>
 </head>
 <body>
 <h1>Foo News</h1>
 News about Foo, news that matters.
 <center>
 <a href="about.jsp">About</a>
 <a href="addnews.jsp">Add News</a>
 <a href="index.jsp">View News</a>
 </center>
```

Listing 11-5 footer.jsp

```
<center>
  <small>Copyright &copy; 2002 Foo Bar Inc.</small>
</center>
</body>
</html>
```

What is most important to understand is that all three of the preceding pages work. They have some very deliberate flaws that are discussed later, but they do all work. Test out the pages by browsing to each of them. First, start with about.jsp, http://127.0.0.1/jspbook/model1/about.jsp. Figure 11-2 shows a browser rendering of the results.

The about page always looks the same. The only dynamic action JSP provides for the page is the include action. Besides the two includes the page is just static content. There are many pages similar to this in a real Web Application. They are the pages that can only be done in one way. The only benefit dynamic server-side functionality can provide is to eliminate page redundancies such as a header and footer.

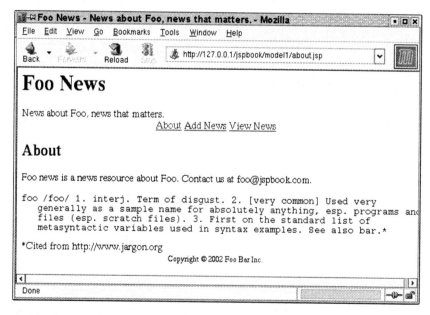

Figure 11-2 Browser Rendering of about.jsp

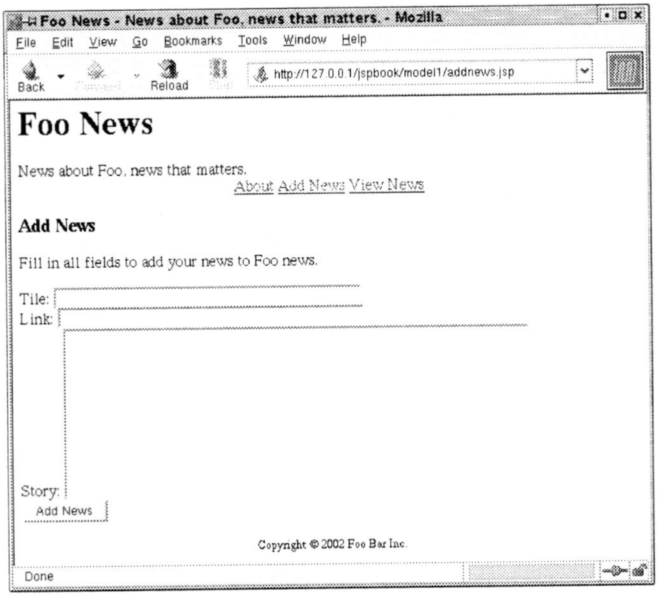

Figure 11-3 Browser Rendering of addnews.jsp

The next page to examine is `addnews.jsp, http://127.0.0.1/jspbook/` `model1/addnews.jsp`. Browse to this page to see what it does. By default the page displays a form that can be filled out to add a news entry. Figure 11-3 shows a browser rendering of the default page.

The page is also the same page that accepts a filled out form. Should a form be filled out with information for a news article and submitted, the page adds the news to `news.xml` and displays a thank-you page. Try out the functionality by filling in all of the fields and submitting the form. Figure 11-4 shows a browser rendering of the results: a thank-you page.

The thank-you page of `addnews.jsp` is a simple confirmation and a link to the main news page.

Finally, try out the main news page, `index.jsp, http://127.0.0.1/jspbook/` `model1/index.jsp`. The news page shows all of the articles recorded in `news.xml`. Each news item is shown sequentially as listed in the file. On the page you should see one news item for each submission done via `addnews.jsp`. Figure 11-5 shows a browser rendering of the results after two pieces of news have been submitted.

It is important to see and understand the entire sample Web site works because this is the initial goal of the Web Application. Should a particular design

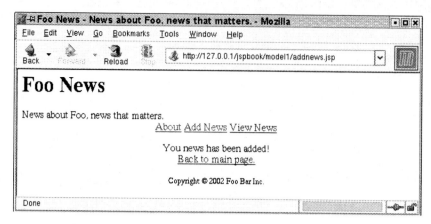

Figure 11-4 Browser Rendering of addnews.jsp Thank-you Page

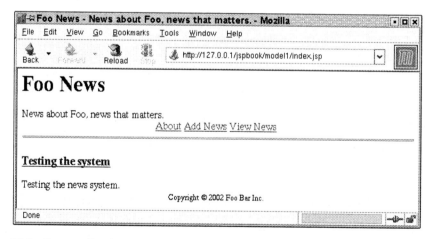

Figure 11-5 Browser Rendering of index.jsp

pattern not work, it would be ridiculous to discuss it. Understand the preceding site does work and it is in what would be considered a Model 1 architecture.

Why Is This Model 1?

Discussion of the Web site's code has initially been avoided because what the code does is not the point of interest in the example. All of the design patterns mentioned in this chapter can be used to make any sort of Web site. Where the code is placed is the emphasis of the chapter. Recall with the introduction of the Model 1 architecture, it was stated the design is classified by each request being mapped to a single endpoint. The endpoint is solely responsible for generating the final response.

What makes the sample application follow a Model 1 architecture is that it directly follows this rule. The diagram of the Web Application is shown in Figure 11-6.

Each request URL goes to exactly one resource in the Web Application. All of the response-generating logic is included in the same resource, and the result is three JSPs with differing levels of complexity. In this example all three pages are specifically chosen to include different types of functionality. Keep in mind that in a more realistic Web Application there are many of the same types of pages. However, for the sake of design discussion consider these three general categories:

- **static page:** A static page is a page easily authored in languages such as HTML. The contents of the page do not change and the best way to author the page is as a single document. The page `about.jsp` is an example of a static type of page. The content generated by `about.jsp` does not rely on any of the advanced features JSP and Servlets offer such as scripting elements.

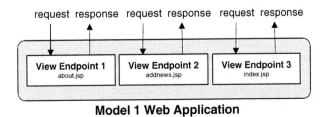

Model 1 Web Application

Figure 11-6 Model 1 Diagram Applied

- **dynamic page:** A dynamic page is one that relies on the dynamic server-side functionality provided by Servlets and JSP. Dynamic pages cannot be authored as a static page because the content generated may be different for each different request. In the sample application, `index.jsp` is an example of a dynamic page. The page's response relies on the embedded scripting elements. Without them the page would not function.
- **dynamic form page:** A dynamic form page is a dynamic page requiring participation from a user. In almost every case this is a page with an HTML form on it. In the example Web Application, `addnews.jsp` is an example of a dynamic page with a form.

All three of the preceding types are important, but the specific names given to the types are not. The names listed are nothing more than self-descriptive terms needed as a point of reference.

The types are important because they are what illustrate the strengths and weaknesses of different design patterns. Static pages are used in all design patterns. Generally, it is desirable to have as many static pages as possible because they are as easy to author as the formatting language being used, usually HTML or XML. Dynamic pages are where different design patterns are important. Where the logic of a dynamic page is placed can greatly impact the ease of which the page is developed and maintained in the future. As illustrated by `about.jsp`, `index.jsp`, and `addnews.jsp` the Model 1 architecture handles all three types of pages by creating a single page for each and adding in dynamic functionality where needed.

Model 1 Weaknesses

There are no great strengths to the Model 1 design pattern, and it is not recommended you use it at all. The only time you should consider using the Model 1 architecture is if you are building a trivial Web Application. Beyond this the only possibly good argument for the architecture is it can be built by developers with limited knowledge and experience in JSP and Servlets. Ease of authoring is commonly a benefit associated with the architecture, but it is simply not true. The Model 1 architecture lacks sufficient benefits to justify a complete section of discussion. Instead, we are going to directly focus on the weaknesses of the architecture as an introduction to the Model 2 design pattern.

There are many weaknesses of the Model 1 design pattern that become apparent on inspection. The design limits development of dynamic pages to developers familiar with JSP and Servlets. The design makes dynamic pages overly complex and cryptic due to excessive amounts of embedded scripts. The design creates pages that are difficult to maintain and makes it hard to collaborate when building the pages. All of these weaknesses are what make the Model 1 design pattern undesirable to use.

The issue of development and maintenance is the most problematic of the Model 1 design pattern. A mixed group of developers is usually involved in construction and maintenance of a Web Application. The Model 1 design pattern directly embeds dynamic code alongside static formatting; this practice requires all developers be familiar with all of the technologies being used. Usually the required technologies include HTML, Java, JSP, and Servlets, but any number of other technologies such as SQL, DHTML, XML, EJB, and XSLT might be present. Requiring all developers are familiar with such a large technology base is problematic because it is hard to ensure every developer has an adequate skill-set to properly manipulate the Web Application, especially in later stages of the project's life cycle when maintenance is required. Lengthy, complex, and usually cryptic JSP and Servlets are hard to edit without breaking existing functionality.

A good example of the complexity introduced by the Model 1 design pattern can be seen in both `index.jsp` and `addnews.jsp`. Compared to `about.jsp`, these pages are hard to digest! You'll recall the following section from `index.jsp` (Listing 11-6).

Listing 11-6 Scripting Elements Used in index.jsp

```
. . .
<%
   ServletContext sc = pageContext.getServletContext();
   String dir = sc.getRealPath("/model1");
   File file = new File(dir+"/news.xml");
   DocumentBuilderFactory dbf =
   DocumentBuilderFactory.newInstance();
   DocumentBuilder db = dbf.newDocumentBuilder();
   Document doc= null;
   if (file.exists()) {
      doc = db.parse(file);
   }
   if (doc != null) {
      NodeList nodes = doc.getElementsByTagName("story");
      for (int i = 0; i < nodes.getLength();i++) {
         Element e = (Element)nodes.item(i);
%>
      <hr>
      <h3><a href="<%= e.getAttribute("link") %>"><%=
```

```
e.getAttribute("title") %></a></h3>
    <%= e.getAttribute("story") %>
<%
    }
  }
%>
```
...

The code is looping through each of the news entries and creating the HTML needed to show them. Complicating this is all of the code required to load and parse the XML file containing news items. The code is needed, but there is no reason the code has to be embedded in a scriptlet. The point here is that the Model 1 design pattern is flawed because it allows a developer to haphazardly insert Java code where they please. There is no separation of the data access code and the code responsible for generating a response. The same flaw is present with the XML-manipulating code in addnews.jsp.

Another good example of haphazardly used scripting elements can be seen in addnews.jsp. The page should really be two separate pages. Instead, both pages are combined into one large JSP with a conditional (Listing 11-7).

Listing 11-7 Condition Scriptlet from addnews.jsp

```
...
<%
  String title = request.getParameter("title");
  String link = request.getParameter("link");
  String story = request.getParameter("story");
  if (title != null && !title.equals("") &&
      story != null && !story.equals("") &&
      link != null && !link.equals("")) {
...
%>


<p align="center">You news has been added!<br>
<a href="index.jsp">Back to main page.</a></p>

<% }
  else {
%>
<h3>Add News</h3>
<p>Fill in all fields to add your news to Foo news.</p>
<form method="post">
Tile: <input size="50" name="title"><br>
```

```
Link: <input size="50" name="link"><br>
Story:<textarea cols="50" rows="10" name="story" /><br>
<input type="submit" value="Add News">
</form>
<% } %>
```

Combining pages is a bad idea because it turns a few relatively simple pages into one complex one. The code is harder to manage, and future attempts to change the page's code have the possibility of breaking any of the other combined pages. In the case of addnews.jsp the troubles caused by combining multiple pages may not be as obvious as it should. Due to the simplicity of the code the combination of pages might seem like a slick JSP trick, but be aware multiple pages should not be combined. Combined pages are common to the Model 1 design pattern, especially when using a form to get feedback from a user and trying to preserve a single endpoint.

Using dynamic pages with forms brings up another good illustration of the mixed logic and formatting the Model 1 design uses. When soliciting information from a user, the information must be validated appropriately. In the case of HTML forms as much validation as possible should be done on the client side to avoid round-trips; however, often the only good place for the validation to go is on the server-side. There is no reason validation logic should be placed with code designed to format output. However, in the Model 1 design pattern this is exactly where the code goes. Review the validation code in addnews.jsp, which was used to ensure a user has entered information (Listing 11-8).

Listing 11-8   Validation Code in addnews.jsp

```
<%
  String title = request.getParameter("title");
  String link = request.getParameter("link");
  String story = request.getParameter("story");
  if (title != null && !title.equals("") &&
      story != null && !story.trim().equals("") &&
      link != null && !link.equals("")) {
...
%>

<p align="center">You news has been added!<br>
<a href="index.jsp">Back to main page.</a></p>

<% }
  else {
```

```
    if(title == null) {
      title = "";
    }
    if(link == null) {
      link = "";
    }
    if(story == null) {
      story = "";
    }
%>
<h3>Add News</h3>
<p>Fill in all fields to add your news to Foo news.</p>
<form method="post">
 Tile: <input size="50" name="title" value="<%= title%>"><br>
 Link: <input size="50" name="link" value="<%= link%>"><br>
 Story:
    <textarea cols="50" rows="10" name="story">
      <%= story%>
    </textarea>
 <br>
 <input type="submit" value="Add News">
</form>
<% } %>
```

The code is as lengthy as the markup needed to create the HTML form! Together, the markup and the validation code are a mess. The page is made overly complex and will not be easy to maintain.

It should begin to be obvious that the flaws of the Model 1 design pattern are due to the JSP scripting elements. JSP scripting elements are a poor interface between the formatting markup and the Java code responsible for generating dynamic content. The result is a cryptic JSP consisting of intermixed markup and Java code. There is no clean separation behind the logically different types of code.

Model 2

The Model 2, also called Model View Control or MVC, design pattern is one that seeks to solve the problems of Model 1. The Model 2 design pattern logically makes sense, works, and is commonly agreed upon as the best method of implementing a Web Application using Servlets and JSP. The Model 2 architecture was popularized in the JSP and Servlet community by the Jakarta Struts Framework, http://jakarta.apache.org/struts. Struts is still a popular Model framework, and it is introduced later in the chapter, but initial examples of the Model 2 design are built from scratch to best illustrate important concepts.

The Model 2 design pattern defines a clean separation of a Web Application's business logic from presentation logic. *Business logic* consists of everything required to get needed runtime information. *Presentation logic* consists of everything needed to format the information into a form a client expects. By separating the two, both parts are kept simple and are more easily manipulated. Model 2 is also called MVC because commonly the separation is termed as creating Model, View, and Control. The *Model component* is a representation of the application's data repository and code involved with reading, writing, and validating information. The *View component* is responsible for interacting with a user. The *Control component* links the other two components and is responsible for providing a proper view to a user and keeping Model current.

As applied to JSP and Servlets, the Model 2 paradigm can be implemented in a few different ways. Almost always the View component is solely done via JSP. JSP provide an excellent method for creating View components for the commonly needed HTML and XML formats. The Model component is usually encapsulated as a set of JavaBeans that are easy to manipulate with JSP, and the Control component is either a Servlet or Filter designed to accept and appropriately direct requests and responses sent by a client. Picture the design implemented as illustrated in Figure 11-7.

There are a few important concepts to understand about the Model 2 design pattern. As illustrated in Figure 11-7 everything is cleanly separated. The clean separation is the most important aspect of the design pattern because it layers the different types of functionality. More important concepts shown by Figure 11-7

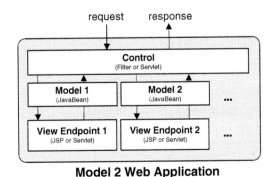

Model 2 Web Application

Figure 11-7 Model 2 Architecture

are the interfaces the different parts of the design use to communicate. Most important are the JavaBeans being used by the View. As is later explained this interface helps to greatly simplify creation and maintenance of the JSP needed to provide the appropriate View. The final important concept to note is how the Control component is implemented. A Filter or Servlet accepting all requests and responses is a very convenient place to implement security, logging, and any other application-wide functionality.

Simple Model 2 Web Site

We are now going to rebuild the simple application used in the Model 1 section to follow a Model 2 architecture. The example is needed to concretely illustrate the concepts of this design pattern. Should you expect to seamlessly extend the example into practical use, there are a few caveats, but these caveats are discussed later and followed by an introduction to a good Model 2 framework for use in real-world applications.

Rebuilding the sample application requires adding in some new classes. A Filter is used as the Control component and a Java bean is required to communicate with the JSP View pages. The resulting application is an example of a Model 2 architecture.

Not all parts of the Model 1 application need to be rebuilt. The static pages header.jsp, footer.jsp, and about.jsp are all the same. Copy these pages from the /jspbook/model1 directory over to the /jspbook/model2 directory. In general, static pages are as efficient as they can be in regard to the Model 1 versus Model 2 designs. The difference between the patterns pivots about dynamic functionality. Also copy news.xml from the /jspbook/model1 directory over to the /jspbook/model2 directory. This keeps example news entries used in the Model 1 example.

The most complex part of the new design is the Filter used as the Control component. The Filter is designed to intercept all requests and execute implicit Java classes that are assumed to contain the Model 2 logic. Save Listing 11-9 as ControlFilter.java in the /WEB-INF/classes/com/jspbook directory of the jspbook Web Application. Discussion of how the Filter works occurs after the code.

Listing 11-9 ControlFilter.java

```
package com.jspbook;

import java.io.*;
```

```java
import javax.servlet.*;
import javax.servlet.http.*;


public class ControlFilter implements Filter {
  protected FilterConfig config = null;

  public void init(FilterConfig filterConfig) {
    config = filterConfig;
  }

  public void doFilter ( ServletRequest req,
                         ServletResponse res,
                         FilterChain chain )
       throws IOException, ServletException {
    if (!(req instanceof HttpServletRequest)) {
      throw new
        ServletException("Filter requires a HTTP request.");
    }

    // determine name of implicit control component.
    HttpServletRequest request = (HttpServletRequest)req;
    HttpServletResponse response = (HttpServletResponse)res;
    String uri = request.getRequestURI();
    int start = uri.lastIndexOf("/")+1;
    int stop = uri.lastIndexOf(".");
    String name = "default";
    if (start < stop) {
      name = uri.substring(start, stop);
    }
    boolean doFilter = true;

    // try to load and run an implicit MVC control component.
    try {
      Object o =
        Class.forName("com.jspbook."+name).newInstance();
      if (!(o instanceof Control)) {
        throw new ServletException("Class com.jspbook."+name+" does
not implement com.jspbook.Control");
      }

      Control control = (Control)o;
      doFilter = control.doLogic(request, response);
    }
```

```
    catch (ClassNotFoundException e) {
      //ignore
    }
    catch (InstantiationException e) {
      throw new ServletException(e);
    }
    catch (IllegalAccessException e) {
      throw new ServletException(e);
    }

    // do whatever is next
    if (doFilter) {
      chain.doFilter(request, response);
    }
  }

  public void destroy() {
    // noop
  }
}
```

The Filter is designed to accept all requests, check for an implicit Model 2 logic component (based on the URL), and execute the implicit logic component, should it exist. The implicit logic component scheme is simple: the name of the resource being accessed is assumed to be the name of a Model 2 logic component in the com.jspbook package.

```
String uri = request.getRequestURI();
String name =
  uri.substring(uri.lastIndexOf("/")+1, uri.lastIndexOf("."));

try {
  Object o =
    Class.forName("com.jspbook."+name).newInstance();
  if (!(o instanceof Control)) {
    throw new ServletException(
"Class com.jspbook."+name+" does not implement
com.jspbook.Control");
  }

  Control control = (Control)o;
  control.doLogic(request, response);
}
```

For example, if `index.jsp` is being requested, then the Filter checks for the `com.jspbook.index`[1] class. If the class exists, it has a chance to process the request and response before `index.jsp`. The only catch is that Java objects are not inherently designed to do this—we need to make an interface. The Control Filter assumes logic components implement the `Control` interface, which we will next create, so that the object has a method, `doLogic()`, that can be passed the current request and response.

Listing 11-10 is the code for the `Control` interface. Save the code as `Control.java` in the `/WEB-INF/classes/com/jspbook` directory of the jspbook Web Application.

Listing 11-10   Control.java

```
package com.jspbook;

import javax.servlet.http.HttpServletRequest;
import javax.servlet.http.HttpServletResponse;
import java.io.IOException;
import javax.servlet.ServletException;

interface Control {
  public boolean doLogic(HttpServletRequest request,
                   HttpServletResponse response)
                   throws ServletException, IOException;
}
```

The interface is straightforward; a single method is defined: `doLogic()` that has instances of the `HttpServletRequest` and `HttpServletResponse` as arguments. The `doLogic()` method also throws instances of `ServletException` and `IOException` so that Servlet-related exceptions can be passed to the Web Application.

The Control Filter only provides a loose contract for coding Model 2 logic components. We still need to code individual logic components for each of the dynamic resources in the Model 2 Web Application. The first component we will code is for the index page, the Model 1 code that was used previously, which is shown in Listing 11-11.

---

1. The use of a lowercase class name, `index.java` instead of `Index.java`, does go against Java-style guidelines; however, the choice is deliberate in order to ensure that implicit control objects don't conflict with existing classes. The practice is questionable, and you can certainly use a different system, such as proper class names, in a control package.

Listing 11-11 Model 1 index.jsp Scripting Elements

```
<%
  ServletContext sc = pageContext.getServletContext();
  String dir = sc.getRealPath("/model1");
  File file = new File(dir+"/news.xml");
  DocumentBuilderFactory dbf =
    DocumentBuilderFactory.newInstance();
  DocumentBuilder db = dbf.newDocumentBuilder();
  Document doc= null;
  if (file.exists()) {
    doc = db.parse(file);
  }
  if (doc != null) {
    NodeList nodes = doc.getElementsByTagName("story");
    for (int i = 0; i < nodes.getLength();i++) {
      Element e = (Element)nodes.item(i);
%>
    <hr>
    <h3><a href="<%= e.getAttribute("link") %>"><%=
e.getAttribute("title") %></a></h3>
    <%= e.getAttribute("story") %>
<%
    }
  }
%>
```

For the Model 2 version of the index page we are attempting to remove all scripts. Therefore, the script's logic needs to be built into a logic component for use with the Control Filter. We will assume the index page will also be named `index.jsp` in this Web site, meaning its implicit logic component is `index.java`. Save Listing 11-12 as `index.java` in the `/WEB-INF/classes/com/jspbook` directory of the jspbook Web Application.

Listing 11-12 index.java

```
package com.jspbook;

import javax.servlet.http.*;
import javax.servlet.*;
import java.io.*;
import javax.xml.parsers.*;
```

```java
import javax.xml.transform.*;
import javax.xml.transform.stream.*;
import javax.xml.transform.dom.*;
import org.w3c.dom.*;
import org.xml.sax.*;
import java.util.*;

public class index implements Control {
  public boolean doLogic(HttpServletRequest request,
                      HttpServletResponse response)
  throws ServletException, IOException {
    try {
      ServletContext sc =
        request.getSession().getServletContext();

      String dir = sc.getRealPath("/model2");
      File file = new File(dir+"/news.xml");
      DocumentBuilderFactory dbf =
        DocumentBuilderFactory.newInstance();
      DocumentBuilder db = dbf.newDocumentBuilder();
      Document doc= null;
      if (file.exists()) {
        doc = db.parse(file);
      }
      if (doc != null) {
        NodeList nodes = doc.getElementsByTagName("story");
        Properties[] ads = new Properties[nodes.getLength()];
        for (int i = 0; i < nodes.getLength();i++) {
          Element e = (Element)nodes.item(i);
          ads[i] = new Properties();
          ads[i].setProperty("link", e.getAttribute("link"));
          ads[i].setProperty(
              "title", e.getAttribute("title"));
          ads[i].setProperty(
              "story", e.getAttribute("story"));
        }
        request.setAttribute("news", ads);
      }
    } catch(SAXException e) {
      throw new ServletException(e.getMessage());
    }
```

```
    catch (ParserConfigurationException e) {
      throw new ServletException(e.getMessage());
    }
    return true;
  }
}
```

The only major difference between the code in Listing 11-10 and Listing 11-11 is the Model 2 version does not send output directly to a client. Instead, the values for each of the news items are stored in a `java.util.Properties` object:

```
Properties[] ads = new Properties[nodes.getLength()];
for (int i = 0; i < nodes.getLength();i++) {
  Element e = (Element)nodes.item(i);
  ads[i] = new Properties();
  ads[i].setProperty("link", e.getAttribute("link"));
  ads[i].setProperty(
    "title", e.getAttribute("title"));
  ads[i].setProperty(
    "story", e.getAttribute("story"));
}
```

All of the news items are placed in one array that is then put in request scope.

```
request.setAttribute("news", ads);
```

By using the request-scoped variable we have created an interface for the presentation JSP to use. Instead of relying on a script, the JSP can now be done purely with markup if we use the JSTL and JSP EL. The new code for `index.jsp` is as follows. Save Listing 11-13 as `index.jsp` in the `model2` directory of the jspbook Web Application.

Listing 11-13   Model 2 index.jsp

```
<%@ taglib uri="http://java.sun.com/jstl/core_rt" prefix="c" %>
<jsp:include page="header.jsp"/>
<c:forEach var="story" begin="0" items="${news}">
  <hr>
  <h3>
    <a href="${story.link}">${story.title}</a>
  </h3>
  ${story.story}
</c:forEach>
<jsp:include page="footer.jsp"/>
```

The code is simple compared to Listing 11-1! The difference is important to see because index.jsp has now become trivial to maintain. Editing the page is as simple as editing an HTML page. Thanks to the JSP standard actions, the expression language, and the JSTL, no scripting elements are required.

The page still produces the same results as you saw previously in Figure 11-5. Try it out by compiling ControlFilter.java and deploying the Filter to accept all requests to the Model 2 application. Listing 11-14 is the entry needed for web.xml.

Listing 11-14   web.xml Entry for ControlFilter.java

```
<filter>
  <filter-name>ControlFilter</filter-name>
  <filter-class>com.jspbook.ControlFilter</filter-class>
</filter>
<filter-mapping>
  <filter-name>ControlFilter</filter-name>
  <url-pattern>/model2/*</url-pattern>
</filter-mapping>
```

After deploying the Filter, reload the jspbook Web Application. Next copy news.xml and header.jsp and footer.jsp from the /model1 directory into the /model2 directory and browse to http://127.0.0.1/jspbook/model2/ index.jsp. The results are the same as Figure 11-5. The benefit is the two simplified components, index.java and index.jsp, compared to one overly complex JSP.

The new code for adding news also benefits from the Model 2 architecture in the same ways as the index page. Instead of one overly complex JSP, such as Listing 11-2, we will create a simple logic component and a simple JSP. Here is the logic for the Control component. Save Listing 11-15 as addnews.java in the /WEB-INF/classes/com/jspbook directory of the jspbook Web Application.

Listing 11-15   addnews.java

```
package com.jspbook;

import javax.servlet.http.*;
import javax.servlet.*;
import java.io.*;
import javax.xml.parsers.*;
import javax.xml.transform.*;
import javax.xml.transform.stream.*;
import javax.xml.transform.dom.*;
```

```java
import org.w3c.dom.*;
import org.xml.sax.*;
import java.util.*;

public class addnews implements Control {
  public boolean doLogic(HttpServletRequest request,
                         HttpServletResponse response)
  throws ServletException, IOException {
    ServletContext sc =
      request.getSession().getServletContext();
    try {
      String title = request.getParameter("title");
      String link = request.getParameter("link");
      String story = request.getParameter("story");
      if (title != null && !title.equals("") &&
          story != null && !story.trim().equals("") &&
          link != null && !link.equals("")) {
        String dir = sc.getRealPath("/model2");
        File file = new File(dir+"/news.xml");
        DocumentBuilderFactory dbf =
          DocumentBuilderFactory.newInstance();
        DocumentBuilder db = dbf.newDocumentBuilder();
        Document doc = null;
        if (file.exists()) {
          doc = db.parse(file);
        } else {
          doc = db.newDocument();
          Element root = doc.createElement("news");
          doc.appendChild(root);
        }
        Element news = doc.createElement("story");
        news.setAttribute("title",title);
        news.setAttribute("link",link);
        news.setAttribute("story",story);
        doc.getDocumentElement().appendChild(news);

        TransformerFactory tf =
          TransformerFactory.newInstance();
        Transformer t = tf.newTransformer();
        DOMSource source = new DOMSource(doc);
        StreamResult result =
          new StreamResult(new FileOutputStream(file));
        t.transform(source, result);
        sc.getRequestDispatcher(
```

```
                    "/model2/addnews_thanks.jsp").forward(request,
                                                           response);
      } else {
        Properties an = new Properties();
        an.setProperty("title", title);
        an.setProperty("link", link);
        an.setProperty("story", story);
        request.setAttribute("form",an);
      }
    } catch (TransformerException e) {
      throw new IOException(e.getMessage());
    }
    catch (SAXException e) {
      throw new ServletException(e.getMessage());
    }
    catch (ParserConfigurationException e) {
      throw new ServletException(e.getMessage());
    }
  return true;
  }
}
```

Compile the code and it is ready for use. No deployment is required because the Control Filter will implicitly check for the class, but we still need to code addnews.jsp. Save Listing 11-16 as addnews.jsp in the model2 directory of the jspbook Web Application.

Listing 11-16   Model 2 Code for addnews.jsp

```
<jsp:include page="header.jsp"/>
<h3>Add News</h3>
<p>Fill in all fields to add your news to Foo news.</p>
<form method="post">
 Tile: <input size="50" name="title" value="${form.title}"><br>
 Link: <input size="50" name="link" value="${form.link}"><br>
 Story:
   <textarea cols="50" rows="10" name="story">
     ${form.story}
   </textarea>
 <br>
 <input type="submit" value="Add News">
</form>
<jsp:include page="footer.jsp"/>
```

The code is simple compared to Listing 11-2. Again, the Model 2 design pattern has turned a complex, code-filled JSP into a simple page of markup. Although, the preceding code is not the complete equivalent of `addnews.jsp` from the Model 1 application. The confirmation page is broken out into its own page. Save Listing 11-17 as `addnews_thanks.jsp`.

Listing 11-17   addnews_thanks.jsp

```
<jsp:include page="header.jsp"/>
<p align="center">You news has been added!<br>
<a href="index.jsp">Back to main page.</a></p>
<jsp:include page="footer.jsp"/>
```

With the new `addnews.jsp` and `addnews_thanks.jsp`, the complex `addnews.jsp` page from the Model 1 example is now two simple pages. Each page can easily be edited by a developer with HTML experience and an understanding of the JSTL actions and the JSP EL.

Try out `addnews.jsp` by browsing to `http://127.0.0.1/jspbook/model2/addnews.jsp`. The result is the same as in Figure 11-3. The functionality is also the same. The input from the page is properly validated and optionally kept should one of the form fields be blank.

Why Is This Model 2?

This is a Model 2 application because it strongly enforces the separation of business logic from presentation. Let's review the application. The application has been split into a controller with several models and views. The Filter is acting as the controller. When it receives a request, the Filter initializes an appropriate model then forwards control to the view, which in this case is a JSP. Before forwarding control, the controller stores needed information in request scope. The view JSP then extracts the data from the model and uses it to create the presentation data, the HTML.

Do not think of this application as Model 2 because we have named something Model, View, and Control. The important thing to see is at no point in this application does business logic mix with presentation—that is, no scripting elements are used and no HTML is produced by the Filter or logic components. Instead, View components contain only HTML markup and the dynamic data to show. Model and Control components are used to abstract out all the code responsible for generating the dynamic data.

The example Model 2 application is separated into a few components. We have one main Filter that accepts all request and pre-processes all responses,

`ControlFilter.java`. In addition to the Filter there are five very simple JSP: `header.jsp`, `footer.jsp`, `about.jsp`, `addnews.jsp`, and `index.jsp`. The pages communicate with the Filter via request-scoped variables. Compared to our original Model 2 diagram, Figure 11-6, the code fits in as shown in Figure 11-8.

The illustration shows the clean separation of presentation and business logic. There is a stark difference between Figure 11-7 and the equivalent diagram for the Model 1 example, Figure 11-6. In the Model 1 example all requests were sent directly to one endpoint. In the Model 2 example all requests are first passed through the Control Filter, optionally executing Model logic, and then sent to the appropriate View. The end result is a few simple, manageable Model 2 components compared to the three complex Model 1 JSP. This is typical of the MVC architecture. Instead of a few hard-to-maintain components, several easy-to-maintain components are created, and that is exactly why it is desirable to use the Model 2 design pattern.

Model 2 Strengths

The primary benefit of the Model 2 architecture is a clean separation of business logic and presentation. This is clearly illustrated by the changes seen in `index.jsp`, Listing 11-1 to Listing 11-13, and `addnews.jsp`, Listing 11-2 to Listing 11-16, and Listing 11-17. The pages are clean, even elegant, compared to the Model 1 versions. Maintenance is as simple as editing HTML. Consider also that the code in any of the View components cannot possibly disrupt the Model code. This is important because it is a problem that plagues the Model 1 design pattern. Making a simple typo fix in a Model 1 page can result in accidentally changing code that affects the entire application. In the Model 2 design pattern

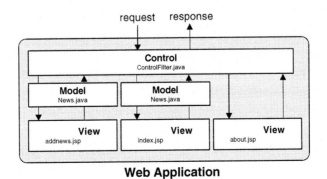

Figure 11-8 Model 2 Illustration of Example Application

this can be made impossible. The request-scoped variables used to pass View information only contain the needed View information. The View page has no idea where the information came from nor does it care. Take a look at `index.jsp`, `addnews.jsp`, and `about.jsp` for the Model 2 example, and you can see the worst thing the page is possible of is creating some bad HTML.

The clean separation of logic and presentation also benefits the Model components. At no time do the View pages care about how the information is obtained. Should the Model use a database, flat file, or anything else, it does not matter. This point alone makes the Model 2 design pattern far superior to Model 1. A proper level of abstraction is always between the View and Model components. A Model 2 application can freely change the underlying data model of a Web Application as much as is needed with no danger of disrupting View components. As long as the interface between the two, the request-scoped variables, are correctly used, the JSP View pages work.

Another minor but helpful strength of the Model 2 design pattern comes from the Control component. The Control component provides a perfect place to manipulate all requests and responses going through the Web Application. It is a convenient place for security, logging, error handling, and anything else a Filter is commonly used for. In some cases, such as error handling, the Control component is arguably better. The Control component can use native Java try-catch-finally statements instead of relying on an error passed via request parameters or as an HTTP error code.

Overall, the Model 2 architecture has many benefits when compared to Model 1. The benefits all come from clean separation of logic and presentation. This separation is not unlike the object-orientated programming concepts on which Java is based. By breaking a Web Application down into logical components, it is much easier to build and maintain the entire thing.

Model 2 Weaknesses

The Model 2 architecture has no significant weakness compared to the advantages it provides for a Web Application. The only arguable weakness is developers following the design pattern must be trained in how it works, but this is a weakness common to any good programming technique.

Potentially arguable weaknesses of the Model 2 design pattern include development time and runtime performance. By sheer numbers a Model 2 application is designed to have more components than a Model 1 application. If the logic is followed that more components means a longer development time, then it is a possible weakness. However, more components in the Model 2 case does not mean longer development time. The components are all encapsulation of logical parts of the application. The result is a bunch of simple components, which can more easily be created and maintained compared to overly complex Model 1 endpoints. The possible argument of the Model 2 architecture performing worse at runtime is also not true. Performance is always dependent on a case-by-case basis, and in all cases the time it takes to populate and pass a request parameter is dwarfed by the time it takes to send a response to a client, so it is the round-trip time that is typically the largest in many applications.

Caveats of This Example

As previously mentioned there are a few caveats with the Model 2 example application. The concepts covered are sound; the code is weak for the Model and Control components. What is provided in our implementation is close to the bare minimum required to get the job done, which is usually all you care for anyhow. However, as is presented later in the chapter, there are several enhancements possible for a Model 2 framework.

Good Model 2 Implementation

Separation of business from presentation logic is the difference between the Model 2 and Model 1 design patterns. What was shown previously in this chapter is how to build upon the strengths of JSP: keeping a clean and easy to author syntax and minimizing the amount of non-presentation logic embedded in the code. The topic left for discussion is how to best implement all of the business logic outside of embedding it in a JSP. Before Filters were introduced, it was common to combine this logic in the Control component of a Model 2 Web Application. With Filters the choice is now between combining logic in a MVC Control component or as additional Filters.

In almost all cases Filters are the best method of implementing code that should be applied to a given set of requests or responses. This type of code includes security, form validation, caching, and compression. The reason Filters are the best method is because the Filter chain has a very strict separation of components. The Filter chain is invoked link by link with each link tied by a contract consisting of the `doFilter()` method. The strict separation allows for multiple specialized Filter components to be built and layered accordingly. The resulting chain can then be an ideal implementation of good object-oriented functionality that is reusable for future projects.

The trick to implementing a good modular Model 2 Web Application is understanding where code should go and why. The current Model 2 design we have is not a good, complete picture of a Web Application. Figure 11-7 should be redrawn as Figure 11-9.

Figure 11-9 adds in one more important and practical parts to our Model 2 design: reusable layered functionality. This functionality comes in the form of Filters because they are a standard component for J2EE Web Applications. The same effect can be achieved with a pluggable component scheme and a good Model 2 Control implementation, but the pluggable components would only be helpful in combination with the same Control component. Filters can be universally helpful regardless of the Web Application.

The important point to understand is why Figure 11-9 adds in the additional layer to our Model 2 design. Think of a request coming to a Web Application. Understanding how Filters work, it is clear an appropriate Filter chain will be constructed by the Web Application to handle the particular request. The chain can consist of zero to many links and eventually results in an endpoint. If you think of the chain hanging vertically, it should be easy to relate it to a stack, much like the OSI or DOD Internet models[2]. Figure 11-10 illustrates our Model 2 stack.

The stack has two layers: business logic and a presentation logic endpoint. The layers are the exact same thing described by any Model 2 design discussion. The business logic layer handles all of the business logic needed by the presentation logic layer. The presentation logic layer is then given only the information

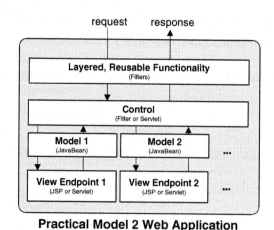

Practical Model 2 Web Application

Figure 11-9 Good, Complete Picture of a Web Application

---

2. International Standards Organization 7-layer stack, or Department of Defense 4-layer equivalent.

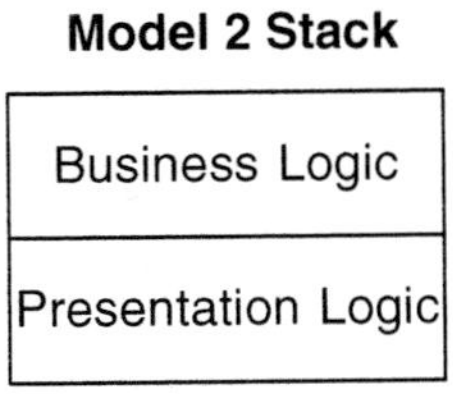

Model 2 Stack

Business Logic
Presentation Logic

Figure 11-10 Model 2 Stack

it needs to create a response. As we previously saw, this method of stacking functionality is good because it makes creating and maintaining a Web Application easier than the Model 1 approach. The question now is, How do we improve this Model 2 stack keeping in mind Servlets and JSP are the tools being used to build it?

There is one great improvement we can make to this Model 2 stack: factor out the reusable business logic into higher layers. This results in moving reusable logic out of the business logic layer and into new, higher level of the stack. This higher level is a place where code can be placed that does not care about the particular endpoint of the stack. It only cares about manipulating a request or response. The new, improved Model 2 stack is as shown in Figure 11-11.

Note the new top level of the stack, reusable Filters. This top level is a place to put code that can be re-used across many Web Applications and is helpful regardless of specific endpoints. It is a separation of business logic specific to a particular endpoint and business logic universal to all endpoints. We want to do this because it further modularizes code and makes building new Web Applications simpler.

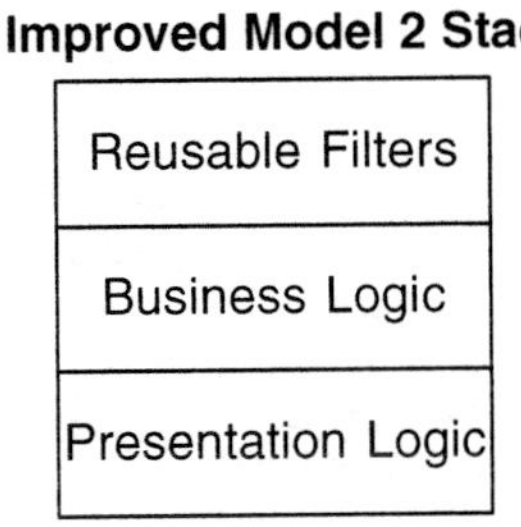

Improved Model 2 Stack

Reusable Filters
Business Logic
Presentation Logic

Figure 11-11 Improved Model 2 Stack

The idea of what we are doing with the improved Model 2 stack can clearly be shown with the existing code examples. Consider the Model 2 application built in this chapter. The code factored out from the scripting elements in the Model 1 application what always had to do with a particular endpoint. For this reason all of this code would naturally go into the business logic stack of the improved Model 2 design. However, consider some realistic needs of the application. What if users were required to be logged into some part of the Web Application, or if caching or compression was desired for the responses? Where would this code go? In a purely conceptual Model 2 application it would go with all the other business logic. However, practically the code would best be implemented as a Filter as demonstrated in Chapter 8. The reason should be clear: by keeping the code in a Filter, it is easier to re-use the Filter in future Web Applications. If the code was coded with the other business logic for a particular endpoint, then it could not be re-used in a future Web Application. Therefore, the code for security, cache, or compression would best be placed in the reusable Filter layer of the improved Model 2 design.

Understanding Model 2 is important. It can save a lot of time in both developing and maintaining a Web Application; however, understanding how to best practically implement a Model 2 application with Servlets and JSP allows you to further optimize the benefits of the design pattern. In all cases try to use a Model 2 design when creating a Web Application. When possible think about how physically you are implementing the Model 2 application. In many cases it is possible to take advantage of Filters to create components applicable to any application.

Jakarta Struts

The Struts Framework is often called "The Framework" for developing Model 2 Web Applications with Servlets and JSP. The Struts framework originated from the Apache Jakarta project, `http://jakarta.apache.org`, alongside Tomcat. Thanks to the dedication and support of many Jakarta developers, Struts quickly became a good framework for developing Model 2 Web Applications.

Struts is still a good framework to use for building Model 2 Web Applications. The Struts framework provides a project with a generic Control Servlet, a supporting tag library for creating forms, and other features such as internationalization support. The Struts framework comes with a full set of user and developer documentation, and Struts has one of the most active user communities around. For all of these reasons Struts is an excellent framework to both understand and use as a Servlet and JSP developer. To finish our discussion on design patterns, we will take a look at the Struts framework and some tips for using the framework to get a project off to a quick start.

Installing Struts

The Struts framework is available in both binary and source code distributions under the Apache Software Foundation license. The project can be used free for both commercial and non-commercial projects, but if you are unfamiliar with the Apache license, be sure to take the time to read and understand it. The Apache group has supported the development of some fantastic software, and the least you can do is spend the time to properly understand the page-long license.

Struts is being covered in this chapter because it is a helpful framework for developing Model 2 Web Applications. Leaving off discussion with a few simple Model 2 examples is no way to get you started on a real-world project. For the Struts discussion you will need to download the latest release of Struts. The specific version used by this book is the binary release of Struts 1.0.2. The release can be downloaded at `http://jakarta.apache.org/struts`. If you do not have this code, download it now.

What Is in Struts 1.0.2?

Included with Struts 1.0.2 are quite a few things including: Struts, documentation, examples, and a quick start Web Application. The Struts download explains all of this in its included documentation and the online version of the same. There is no point in this book providing a rehash of all of this excellent documentation, especially when the material covered here has the potential to be outdated by new releases of Struts. Instead, this chapter provides only a quick overview of Struts in an attempt to complement the documentation. You are wholeheartedly recommended to read the official, current documentation if you would like to use Struts with a project outside the scope of this book.

The only thing this chapter can do better than the Struts' documentation is give an objective view of Struts 1.0.2 functionality and explain how it works with all of the other concepts we have covered in this book. This is the approach that will be taken, but first you need to understand what comes with the Struts download.

Decompress the binary installation of Struts into a convenient directory. The following files are present:

- **lib/struts.jar:** This JAR file contains all of the Java classes included in Struts. It is available so existing Web Applications can take advantage of Struts.

- **lib/struts*.tld:** All of the `.tld` files in the `/lib` directory are the Tag Library Descriptor files for the Struts custom tag libraries. When installing Struts for use with an existing Web Application, these files are needed to describe the Struts tag libraries.

- **webapps/struts-blank.war:** The `struts-blank.war` file is a simple, empty Web Application with all of the Struts resources installed and configured for use. When starting a new Web Application from scratch, this file is an excellent way to have Struts pre-installed.

- **webapps/struts-documentation.war:** The `struts-documentation.war` file includes all of the Struts documentation. The documentation includes generated Java API documentation and user and developer guides. All of the documentation in `struts-documentation.war` can be found online at `http://jakarta.apache.org/struts`. The WAR file is just a convenient method for keeping a local copy of the Struts documentation.

- **webapps/struts-example.war:** The `struts-example.war` file is an example Web Application built using Struts. The application includes a full walk-through along with source code.

- **webapps/struts-exercise-taglib.war:** The `struts-exercise-taglib.war` is a Web Application containing test pages for the various custom tags supported by Struts. The WAR is primarily intended for Struts developers but may also be useful as simple examples of the usage of various Struts tags.

- **webapps/struts-template.war:** The `struts-template.war` file is a Web Application that introduces and demonstrates the Struts template tags.

- **webapps/struts-upload.war:** The `struts-upload.war` file is a Web Application demonstrating how to upload files using the Struts framework.

In this chapter only a few of the included Struts files are examined. Installation of Struts with an existing and a new application are covered along with using the Struts controller Servlet. The example application, documentation, template, and tag library WAR files are not covered.

Creating a New Struts Web Application

Creating a new Struts-based Web Application from scratch is simple. The `struts-blank.war` file is a WAR that automatically deploys an empty Web

Application with Struts pre-installed. Simply deploy the WAR file with a container to have a Web Application ready to go with Struts already installed. With Tomcat the Web Application can be deployed by copying `struts-blank.war` to the `/webapps` directory of Tomcat. Restart Tomcat and the WAR file is deployed to a sub-directory of the same name. Rename the WAR file before deploying the Web Application to get a custom-named directory.

After deploying the `struts-blank.war` file, the Web Application is ready to go. For the later examples of this chapter an example application is required. Copy `struts-blank.war` to the `/webapps` directory of your Tomcat installation. Restart Tomcat and the application is deployed. Browse to `http://127.0.0.1/struts-blank` to test if the new Web Application is correctly installed. If it is, the screen that is shown in Figure 11-12 should be displayed.

You now have a Struts-ready Web Application. As an example of how to use Struts we will re-implement the example Model 2 application with the Struts framework. Not all parts of the application need to be rebuilt. The JSP View pages can remain exactly as they are. Copy `header.jsp`, `footer.jsp`, `index.jsp`, `about.jsp`, `news.xml`, and `addnews.jsp` from the `/webapps/jspbook/model2` directory to the `/webapps/struts-blank` directory of your Tomcat installation. For the View pages the JSTL is required. Copy over `jstl.jar` and `standard.jar` from the `/webapps/jspbook/WEB-INF/lib` directory to the `/webapps/struts-blank/WEB-INF/lib` directory of your Tomcat installation. The `News` JavaBean previously created is also re-used in the Struts version of the application. Copy `News.java` from the jspbook Web Application to the `/WEB-INF/classes/com/jspbook` directory of the struts-blank Web Application.

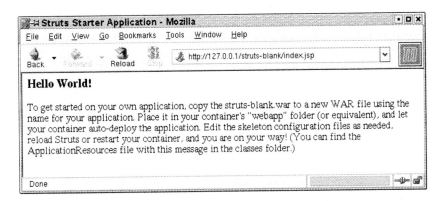

Figure 11-12   Deployment of Struts Blank Web Application

The Vew components are the only ones that seamlessly work with the new Struts-based Web Application. In the next few sections we will rebuild the Model and Control components to take advantage of Struts.

Installing Struts with an Existing Web Application

A Web Application can start using Struts at any time by installing and configuring the needed Struts resources. Compared to using the `struts-blank.war` file, manually installing Struts is slightly more difficult. Complete instructions for installation of Struts with an existing Web Application can be found in the Struts User Guide.

Struts Control Servlet

The core of the Struts framework is the pre-built Control Servlet. The Control Servlet is a configurable Model 2 Control component that allows for pluggable Model components and easy interaction with forms. We can take advantage of the Struts Control Servlet to provide a robust mechanism for the Model components of our Model 2 application. Recall this was the largest caveat of the previous Model 2 example. Struts provides a more appealing alternative to hard coding Model logic into `ControlFilter.java`.

Struts was built around the JSP 1.1 and Servlet 2.2 specifications. What this means is Struts does not currently take advantage of Filter functionality. Instead, the Struts framework relies on all requests ending with a fictitious extension, usually `.do`[3]. The control Servlet intercepts all requests with the fictitious extension and forwards them to the appropriate JSP or Servlet. The specific configuration for the Struts Control Servlet is an entry in `web.xml`, the same as any other Servlet. The `struts-blank.war` file automatically has the Servlet deployed. If you look in `web.xml` of the struts-blank Web Application, you should find the code in Listing 11-18.

Listing 11-18 Default Struts web.xml Entry

```
. . .
  <servlet>
    <servlet-name>action</servlet-name>
    <servlet-class>org.apache.struts.action.ActionServlet</servlet-
```

---

3. The `.do` extension is commonly used because it is what the Struts examples use, but any extension can be used.

```
class>
...
  </servlet>

  <servlet-mapping>
    <servlet-name>action</servlet-name>
    <url-pattern>*.do</url-pattern>
  </servlet-mapping>
...
```

The Struts Control Servlet intercepts all requests ending in .do. Cut out from the preceding entry are the specific initialization parameters for the Control Servlet. All of these parameters are explained further by the Struts documentation. The default entry for the Control Servlet suffices for most situations including this example.

An important point to understand about the Control Servlet is how it differs from the previous Model 2 example's Filter. With the Filter, requests could go directly to a concrete endpoint—for example, the URL for index.jsp is http://127.0.0.1/struts-blank/index.jsp. With the Struts Redirection Servlet all requests need to go to the fictitious .do endpoint. While the fictitious endpoint can be redirected to any concrete endpoint, the difference is usually just exchanging .jsp for .do—for example, a request to index.jsp would be done in Struts by requesting http://127.0.0.1/struts-blank/index.do. The difference is minor and only due to how Struts implements the Model 2 Control component.

There are pros and cons to implementing a Model 2 design with a Control component as either a Servlet or Filter. The general consensus is a Filter is the best approach. Seamlessly and cleanly stacking layers of Filters on top of a concrete endpoint is usually much more intuitive and requires less configuration. However, using the Struts approach is helpful because it keeps a layer of abstraction between all requests and the endpoints they link to. The abstraction is helpful in situations where the underlying endpoints need to change. However, the abstraction creates the classic Struts problem of ensuring potentially malicious users do not try to directly browse .jsp files instead of abstract .do mappings[4].

---

4. Silly or not, the solution to this problem is usually to move all JSP source code to a subdirectory of /WEB-INF. By doing this no direct requests to the JSP can be made by outside clients, but internal Servlet redirection still works.

Actions

The great part about using Struts is taking advantage of the pre-built Model 2 Control component. With this part of the Model 2 application automatically installed and ready to go, the only thing we need to worry about is creating Model and View components. In Struts, Model components are referred to as *Actions*. The Control Servlet allows for a subclass of `org.apache.struts.action.Action` to encapsulate the business logic required for a particular request. An `Action` class in Struts is analogous to the hard-coded business logic used in `ControlFilter.java`.

Struts' Actions are a good reason to use the Struts controller versus the simple `ControlFilter.java` used previously in this chapter. By using Struts' Action classes all of the business logic associated with a particular View page is completely encapsulated in one class. This allows for Action classes to be easily plugged in for use and debugged should something go wrong. It also prevents the controller component from becoming bloated with all of the Model code. `ControlFilter.java` would quickly bloat with code should it be implemented in a real Web Application. An approach such as the `Action` classes Struts uses is clearly a better option.

Using Action Classes

Using an `Action` class requires two things: a subclass of `Action` used to encapsulate all of the business logic for a given request, and an entry to the Struts configuration file to allow Struts to associate a given request or set of requests with a given action.

The `Action` class acts as a base class for Java classes. A new Struts `action` class needs to extend `org.apache.struts.action.Action` and override the `perform()` method. The `perform()` method is invoked by the Control Servlet before forwarding a request to a View page. By encapsulating business logic in the `perform()` method, it is guaranteed to be executed before the request reaches the appropriate View.

The `perform()` method looks like this:

```
ActionMapping perform(ActionMapping am, ActionForm form,
HttpServletRequest request, HttpServletResponse response)
```

The `perform()` method is passed the same parameters as the Servlet service methods with additional parameters of a Struts `org.apache.struts.action.ActionMapping` class and an `org.apache.struts.action.ActionForm` class. The `ActionMapping` class is a representation of the configuration mapping

Struts used to determine the appropriate `Action` class. The `ActionForm` class is an optional class that may be used to represent an HTML form-based request. Returned from the `perform()` method is an instance of `org.apache.action.ActionForward` providing information about what the Control Servlet should next do with a request. If `null` is returned, it is assumed the request and response are completely handled by the current `Action` class.

The skeleton of a custom `Action` class is always the same. Extend `Action` and override the `perform()` method. Listing 11-19 shows how the skeleton class would look in code.

Listing 11-19   BlankAction.java

```java
package com.jspbook;

import java.io.*;
import javax.servlet.*;
import javax.servlet.http.*;
import org.apache.struts.action.*;

public final class BlankAction extends Action {

  public ActionForward perform(ActionMapping mapping,
                               ActionForm form,
                               HttpServletRequest request,
                               HttpServletResponse response)
  throws IOException, ServletException {

    //handle request and response...

    return null;

  }
}
```

The preceding class is an example of a custom `Action` class that does nothing. A more practical implementation of the class would involve placing business logic where the comment is. Because the `perform()` method's parameters include the current `HttpServletRequest` and `HttpServletResponse`, the same business logic a JSP or Servlet would use can be used. Take for instance the code used in `ControlFilter.java` for the `index.jsp`. The same code authored as a Struts `Action` is as follows. Save Listing 11-20 as `IndexAction.java` in the `/WEB-INF/classes/com/jspbook` directory of the struts-blank Web Application.

Listing 11-20 IndexAction.java

```java
package com.jspbook;

import java.io.*;
import javax.xml.parsers.*;
import org.w3c.dom.*;
import org.xml.sax.*;
import javax.servlet.*;
import javax.servlet.http.*;
import org.apache.struts.action.*;
import java.util.*;

public final class IndexAction extends Action {

  public ActionForward perform(ActionMapping mapping,
                               ActionForm form,
                               HttpServletRequest request,
                               HttpServletResponse response)
  throws IOException, ServletException {


    ServletContext sc = getServlet().getServletContext();

    try {
      String dir = sc.getRealPath("/");
      File file = new File(dir+"/news.xml");
      DocumentBuilderFactory dbf =
        DocumentBuilderFactory.newInstance();
      DocumentBuilder db = dbf.newDocumentBuilder();
      Document doc= null;
      if (file.exists()) {
        doc = db.parse(file);
      }
      if (doc != null) {
        NodeList nodes = doc.getElementsByTagName("story");
        Properties[] ads = new Properties[nodes.getLength()];
        for (int i = 0; i < nodes.getLength();i++) {
          Element e = (Element)nodes.item(i);

          ads[i] = new Properties();
          ads[i].setProperty("link", e.getAttribute("link"));
          ads[i].setProperty("title", e.getAttribute("title"));
          ads[i].setProperty("story", e.getAttribute("story"));
```

```
      }
      request.setAttribute("news", ads);
    }
  } catch(SAXException e) {
    throw new ServletException(e.getMessage());
  }
  catch (ParserConfigurationException e) {
    throw new ServletException(e.getMessage());
  }

  // Forward control to the specified success URI
  return (mapping.findForward("success"));
  }
}
```

The preceding code has two changes from the code used in `ControlFilter.java` for `index.jsp`. The first change is how the class accesses the Web Application's `ServletContext` object. The second change is the object returned by the `perform()` method.

The `Action` class is not an instance of a `Servlet` or `Filter`. With all of the previous examples in this book we have used either the `ServletConfig` or `FilterConfig` objects to access the Web Application's `ServletContext`. In `ControlFilter.java` the `ServletContext` object is required in order to find the correct location of `news.xml`.

```
...
  ServletContext sc = fc.getServletContext();
...
      String dir = sc.getRealPath("/model2");
      File file = new File(dir+"/news.xml");
...
```

In `IndexAction.java` the `ServletContext` object is accessed slightly differently. Instead of getting a reference from a configuration object, the `get Servlet()` method is used to reference the Control Servlet, which in turn provides the `getServletContext()` method.

```
...
  ServletContext sc = getServlet().getServletContext();
...
    String dir = sc.getRealPath("/");
    File file = new File(dir+"/news.xml");
...
```

The change is due to a difference in how subclasses of `Action` access the appropriate `ServletContext`.

The second change is much more important and is heavily related to the Struts configuration file. Note `IndexAction.java` returns an instance of `ActionForward` retrieved from the `ActionMapping` parameter passed to the `perform()` method.

```
. . .
    public ActionForward perform(ActionMapping mapping,
                                 ActionForm form,
                                 HttpServletRequest request,
                                 HttpServletResponse response)
    throws IOException, ServletException {
    . . .
        return (mapping.findForward("success"));
    . . .
```

The returned object is telling the Control Servlet the business logic has successfully completed and the View resource identified as "success" should now handle the request and response. In `BlankAction.java` a `null` value is returned. The `null` value informs the Control Servlet the response is finished, which is the same as skipping the optional invocation of `FilterChain doFilter()` in a Filter's `doFilter()` method. By returning an `ActionForward` object, the `Action` class is doing the equivalent of invoking the `FilterChain.doFilter()` method.

Unlike a Filter chain, the resources invoked by the Struts Control Filter are dependent on the Struts configuration file. The Struts configuration file is an XML configuration file that is used in a similar fashion as `web.xml`. By default the Struts configuration file is `struts-config.xml` located in the `/WEB-INF` directory. The Struts configuration file contains four different root elements for the different functionality Struts provides:

- **data-sources:** The `data-sources` element is used to define zero to many `data-source` child elements, which define data sources. A *data source* is a JDBC 2.0 Standard Extension data source object. Data source objects defined by the Struts configuration file are made available as a `ServletContext` attribute (i.e., application scope bean). Data sources are a convenient and modular way to interface with commonly used data repositories. The functionality is not relevant to this chapter, but is covered further in Chapter 14.

- **form-beans:** The `form-beans` element is used to define zero to many `form-bean` children elements, which each define Struts' form bean. A *form bean* is a JavaBean representation of an HTML form. HTML forms are commonly used by Web Applications, and Struts has specialized support for them. Full coverage of Struts' form beans can be found in the documentation included with Struts.

- **global-forwards:** The `global-forward` element is used to define zero to many `global-forward` children elements, which each define a Struts global forward. A *global forward* is a Struts-wide method of mapping an abstract URL to a real endpoint in the Web Application. Global forwards are helpful to a Struts developer, but the functionality is not relevant to this chapter. Further coverage of Struts' global forwards is found in the documentation that is included with Struts.

- **action-mappings:** The `action-mappings` element is used to define zero to many `action-mapping` child elements, which each define an action mapping. An *action mapping* is a mapping between an `Action` class and an abstract Struts URL. The mapping also defines possible endpoints for the `Action` class to forward to.

Right now we are only interested in using the Struts configuration file to define some action mappings. Edit `struts-config.xml` file in the Struts blank Web Application to include the code in Listing 11-21.

Listing 11-21 An Action Mapping for the Struts Configuration File

```
...
  <action-mappings>
    <action
      path="/index"
      type="com.jspbook.IndexAction">
      <forward name="success" path="/index.jsp"/>
    </action>
...
  </action-mappings>
...
```

This entry adds an action mapping for the `/index` URL (i.e., `index.do`) and the custom `IndexAction` class. The `path` attribute defines the abstract URL, and the `type` attribute defines the custom action class to use. Additionally, the forward sub-element is used to define an action forward named "success" that goes to `index.jsp`.

All parts of Listing 11-21 should be intuitive to understand. The entry associates `IndexAction.java` with `index.do`. Additionally, a View page is defined for "success", indicating `index.jsp` is a possible endpoint to use after invoking the `perform()` method of `IndexAction.java`. Recall in `IndexAction.java` the `Action Forward` object identified by "success" is always returned at the end of the `perform()` method. The `ActionForward` object is nothing more than an object representation of the `forward` element in the `action mapping`.

With the preceding entry in `struts-config.xml` and the newly made `action` class, Struts is ready to show the index page of the example Model 2 application. Before trying the code, be sure to compile `IndexAction.java` and copy over the relevant files (`index.jsp`, `news.xml`, `header.jsp`, and `footer.jsp`) to the struts-blank Web Application. Reload the struts-blank Web Application for the changes to take effect. Browse to `http://127.0.0.1/struts-blank/index.do` to see the newly made `action mapping`. Figure 11-13 shows a browser rendering of the results.

Additional `action-mapping` elements can be added to the `struts-config` file for any number of actions. A complete reference for the `action-mapping` element and the `forward` sub-element can be found with the Struts documentation in the Struts User Guide. The important functionality to understand is that Struts provides a convenient method to encapsulate and implement Model logic. This nicely complements the JSP view components we have previously seen and makes Struts a helpful framework to use.

Another action is required for the Model logic corresponding to `addnews.jsp`. The Struts action is very similar to `IndexAction.java`, but it encapsulates the Model code for `addnews.jsp`. Save Listing 11-22 as `AddNews Action.java`.

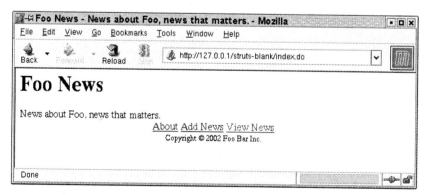

Figure 11-13   Browser Rendering of index.do

Listing 11-22   AddNewsAction.java

```java
package com.jspbook;

import java.io.*;
import javax.xml.parsers.*;
import org.w3c.dom.*;
import org.xml.sax.*;
import javax.xml.transform.*;
import javax.xml.transform.stream.*;
import javax.xml.transform.dom.*;

import javax.servlet.*;
import javax.servlet.http.*;
import org.apache.struts.action.*;

public final class AddNewsAction extends Action {

  public ActionForward perform(ActionMapping mapping,
                               ActionForm form,
                               HttpServletRequest request,
                               HttpServletResponse response)
  throws IOException, ServletException {

    ServletContext sc = getServlet().getServletContext();

    try {
      String title = request.getParameter("title");
      String link = request.getParameter("link");
      String story = request.getParameter("story");
      if (title == null || title.equals("") ||
          story == null || story.trim().equals("") ||
          link == null || link.equals("")) {
        News an = new News();
        an.setTitle(title);
        an.setLink(link);
        an.setStory(story);
        request.setAttribute("form",an);

        return (mapping.findForward("failure"));
      }

      String dir = sc.getRealPath("/");
      File file = new File(dir+"/news.xml");
```

```
DocumentBuilderFactory dbf =
    DocumentBuilderFactory.newInstance();
DocumentBuilder db = dbf.newDocumentBuilder();
Document doc = null;
if (file.exists()) {
    doc = db.parse(file);
} else {
    doc = db.newDocument();
    Element root = doc.createElement("news");
    doc.appendChild(root);
}
Element news = doc.createElement("story");
news.setAttribute("title",title);
news.setAttribute("link",link);
news.setAttribute("story",story);
doc.getDocumentElement().appendChild(news);

TransformerFactory tf =
    TransformerFactory.newInstance();
Transformer t = tf.newTransformer();
DOMSource source = new DOMSource(doc);
StreamResult result =
    new StreamResult(new FileOutputStream(file));
t.transform(source, result);

return (mapping.findForward("success"));
} catch (TransformerException e) {
    throw new IOException(e.getMessage());
}
catch (SAXException e) {
    throw new ServletException(e.getMessage());
}
catch (ParserConfigurationException e) {
    throw new ServletException(e.getMessage());
}
}
}
}
```

The preceding code is a Struts action that encapsulates all of the business logic needed for addnews.jsp. There are two major changes between this code and the code previously used with ControlFilter.java. The Struts action returns two different ActionForward objects depending if the information sub-

mitted by a user is valid. If the information is valid, the `ActionForward` object is
returned corresponding to "success".

```
return (mapping.findForward("success"));
```

Should the validation fail, an `ActionForward` object is returned corresponding to "failure".

```
...
    String title = request.getParameter("title");
    String link = request.getParameter("link");
    String story = request.getParameter("story");
    if (title == null || title.equals("") ||
        story == null || story.trim().equals("") ||
        link == null || link.equals("")) {
      News an = new News();
      an.setTitle(title);
      an.setLink(link);
      an.setStory(story);
      request.setAttribute("form",an);

      return (mapping.findForward("failure"));
    }
...
```

The "success" and "failure" mappings provide a method of choosing between
the two responses possible for the form. If valid information is given, a new entry
is created in `news.xml` and a successful transaction is made. If bad information is
given, the transaction is a failure. The "success" and "failure" mappings are just
self-named mappings for the two respective outcomes of validating the form
information. The endpoint associated with "success" and "failure" is declared in
`struts-config.xml` as follows. Edit `struts-config.xml` in the `/WEB-INF`
directory of the struts-blank Web Application to include the code in Listing 11-23.

Listing 11-23 Action Mapping for addnews.jsp

```
...
  <action-mappings>
    <action
      path="/index"
      type="com.jspbook.IndexAction">
      <forward name="success" path="/index.jsp"/>
    </action>
```

```
<action
  path="/addnews"
  type="com.jspbook.AddNewsAction">
  <forward name="success" path="/addnews_thanks.jsp"/>
  <forward name="failure" path="/addnews.jsp"/>
</action>
...
  </action-mappings>
...
```

The two endpoints are the same ones used in `ControlFilter.java`; `addnews_thanks.jsp` for "success" and `addnews.jsp` for "failure".

With the new entry in `struts-config.xml` the page for adding news is ready to be used. Before trying out the page, compile `AddNewsAction.java` and reload the struts-blank Web Application for the changes to take effect. After reloading the Web Application, browse to `http://127.0.0.1/struts-blank/addnews.do`. The new action is used and `addnews.jsp` displays an HTML form. Figure 11-14 shows a browser rendering of the results.

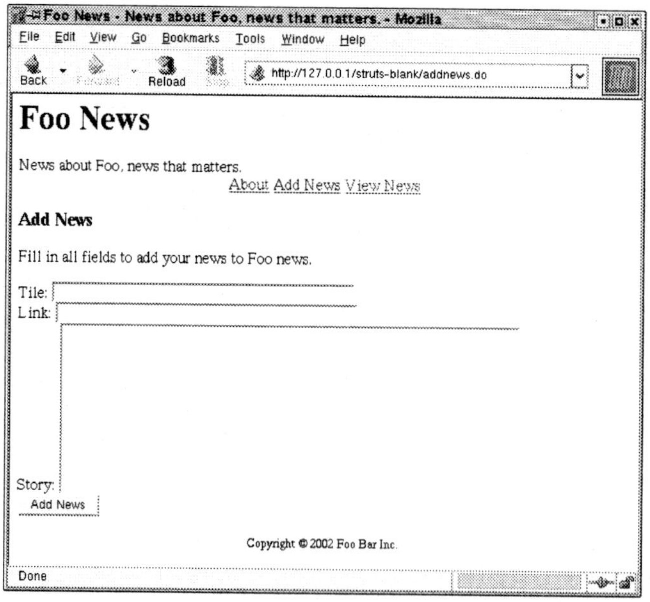

Figure 11-14 Browser Rendering of addnews.do

The page functions the same as it did in the other example applications. If a user correctly fills out the form, a news entry is added to `news.xml` and the confirmation page is shown. Should a user leave any of the form fields blank, the form is redisplayed with all of the previously filled values included.

Using Struts

The Jakarta Struts framework is designed to do many things, but the most helpful thing the framework provides is a pre-built Control component and a method to encapsulate business logic. With the about, index, and add-news pages we have seen how Struts can be used to create a Model 2 Web Application.

Actions are the only Struts functionality we are going to cover in this chapter, but any experienced Struts user will be quick to point out that Actions are not the only things Struts provides. Struts does in fact have much more functionality, including a few tag libraries and an enhanced version of JavaBeans for working with HTML forms. These extra features of Struts are not covered for a few reasons. First, they are not relevant to this chapter. The reason Struts was introduced was to show a good implementation of a system that allowed for modular Model components to complement View components. That is exactly what was covered in this chapter. The second reason the extra Struts functionalities are not fully covered is because they are quickly becoming dated. Many of the most helpful features of Struts such as logic and iteration tags have been officially implemented in the JSTL. Both solutions work, but this book recommends learning the standardized JSTL. Finally, the framework is nice, but there are many ways to implement what some of the "helpful" features are trying to do. Apply the concepts presented in this book and your good judgment to find the best solution for you.

Struts is a great choice for cleanly modularizing Model, View, and Control components. When building a Model 2 Web Application for production use, keep Struts in mind. It is a good way to get a quick start implementing a Model 2 design pattern.

Model 1½

So far two design patterns have been presented: Model 1 and Model 2. We would strongly recommend that you use the Model 2 design pattern when possible, but as you will quickly find, the Model 2 design pattern initially takes a while to become familiar with. Building various different components and then assembling them together can be tedious. It can also slow down the time it takes to test changes. In other words, if you change a JSP, it is recompiled and redeployed automatically; if you change a Java class, you need to compile and deploy it manually. If you are used to building lots of JSP and few Java classes, you will likely agree that JSP is much quicker to develop with. However, if you are used to developing Java classes and have a nice build tool, such as Ant, you will be able to build Model 2 applications just as quickly as Model 1.

Why Model 1½ is brought up in this chapter is because it is a very practical technique for rapidly develop Model 2(ish) code. If you dislike using a build tool, or are in a situation where no build tool is available, Model 1½ is a great way to rapidly develop a Model 2–like page, only using JSP. Then later on the Model 2–like code can easily be changed to be a clean JSP and business logic encapsulated by a Java class. Another tangential reason that Model 1½ is introduced is that it is how the majority of this book's JSP examples are demonstrated. If an example used earlier in the book is helpful, it should be easy for you to port into a Model 2 application.

How the Model 1½ design pattern is implemented is simple. First, develop a JSP as if it were going to be part of a Model 2 Web Application—that is, only responsible for the display logic. Next, create one scriptlet at the head of the JSP that encapsulates all the business logic. For instance:

```
<%
  String foo = "Hello World";
  request.setAttribute("foo",foo);
%>
<html>
 Today's message is ${foo}.
</html>
```

While simplistic, you should get the point. The first part of the page handles all the business logic relating to the JSP: directives and bits of Java code for loading JavaBeans or other scoped variables.

```
<%
  String foo = "Hello World";
  request.setAttribute("foo",foo);
%>
```

Note that leaving the variables in implicit page scope is bad because a Model 2 Control component will not share page scope with the JSP. Always using either request scope, session scope, or application scope ensures the variables will be in a proper scope for either a Model 1 or Model 2 JSP.

The second part of the JSP is all of the presentation logic—that is, exactly what the JSP would have if it was being used in a Model 2 Web Application.

```
<html>
 Today's message is ${foo}.
</html>
```

In practice the Model 1½ design pattern works as follows. Use JSP to quickly develop possibly volatile code. Once the code is adequately tested, port all the business logic into a separate Java class and delete it from the JSP. By doing this, development time can be kept efficient, due to the JSP, and future maintenance can be kept efficient due to a modular Java class. The only slight disadvantage to the Model 1½ approach is that a Java class will not have the implicit JSP variables available for use. This can be solved easily by either naming the respective class variables identically to the JSP implicit variables or by doing a search and replace.

Weaknesses of Model 1½

In general Model 1½ is a helpful concept to be aware of. Being an overzealous Model 2 developer can make life difficult and can result in alienating non–Model 2 developers. Model 1½ is an illustration that the concepts of Model 2 can be applied in a Model 1 environment, thus providing a nice gray area of functionality between Model 1 and Model 2 design patterns. However, the Model 1½ design pattern is not perfect and is not a replacement for Model 2. Model 1½ still allows for the serious Model 1 flaws that Model 2 was designed to eliminate. By allowing scripting elements in a JSP, all of the Model 1 weaknesses are present in Model 1½. With Model 2 it is practical to add the `scripting-invalid` JSP 2.0 configuration element[5], to ensure no scripting elements are present when a JSP is being translated by a container. With Model 1½ it is not. Unless you are developing alone, or with a very benevolent group of developers, is it unwise to assume a Model 1½ design is really working.

Another significant weakness of the Model 1½ design pattern is that it does not ensure appropriate error handling. One of the nice advantages of Model 2 is that the business logic can take full advantage of Java try-catch blocks, and a compiler will enforce that checked errors are handled appropriately. Because of the implicit try-catch block, which scriptlets have—for example,

```
try {
<% //scriptlet code %>
}
catch (Exception e) {//JSP error handling}
```

---

5. You can create a custom Tag Library Validator class in JSP versions prior to 2.0.

There is no similar enforcement that Model 1½ code provides appropriate error handling. Porting Model 1½ code to a Model 2 design is tedious if the code was implemented assuming JSP error handling exists.

Abstracting DHTML via Custom Tags

In the tag library chapter the point was brought up that custom tags are excellent for abstracting DHTML. In general, a good way to think of custom tags is as being good for abstracting repetitive, messy parts of a JSP. Applying this to HTML and XHTML, DHTML is a great candidate for abstraction. A good Model 2 design can ensure Java code does not needlessly mix with HTML and complicate a page; however, the usual Model 2 design does little to ensure the HTML itself is not messy. HTML by itself is simple and straightforward to use and maintain, but by itself HTML does little. In order to spice up HTML, complementary technologies such as the Document Object Model (DOM), JavaScript, JScript, and Cascading Style Sheets (CSS), collectively referred to as Dynamic HTML (DHTML), are used. What is usually considered a "good" HTML page often contains an undecipherable mix of all the HTML complementing technologies.

The bonus to a DHTML page is that it can be styled nicely and contain dynamic functionality, such as a drop-down menu or a rollover image. The drawback to a DHTML page is that it is often a disaster to maintain; a complex page using HTML, DOM, JavaScript, and CSS usually isn't simplified much by removing Java snippets—in other words, the Model 2 design pattern doesn't fix everything. An excellent way to complement a Web Application that takes advantage of DHTML is to abstract any complex DHTML widget via custom tags.

Why Abstract DHTML with Custom Tags?

The primary benefits to abstracting DHTML via custom tags is that complex DHTML widgets can be reduced to a few custom actions. For example, recall the rollover example in the custom tag chapter. A single custom action is all that is needed to author a DHTML rollover image. The bare minimum information is required: the image's name and link; the rest of the DHTML details are taken care of by the custom tag. This example easily demonstrates how a custom action can effectively eliminate a chunk of DHTML that would otherwise complicate the HTML page. Additionally, the DHTML code is now consolidated in one place. Imagine a page that uses multiple rollover effects, perhaps a menu with ten items. Instead of coding the DHTML for several rollover effects and needing to re-code each instance if a change to the DHTML is needed, a single tag file encapsulates the entire DHTML widget.

Using custom actions also reduces the knowledge content developers must have in order to build JSP presentation pages. It is much easier to let one good DHTML developer create complex widgets and have several HTML developers create content. The HTML developers can additionally use the widgets when needed by taking advantage of the simple custom actions. When it comes time to maintain the Web Application, this scheme pays off. Instead of several complex HTML pages, there will be several simpler pages and a few abstracted DHTML widgets.

Coding DHTML Widget Custom Actions

The hardest part of abstracting DHTML widgets is knowing how to author the DHTML. Tag files were presented earlier in this book and provide an intuitive approach for authoring DHTML. The overall tact is to reduce a DHTML widget to its most generic form. Listing 11-24 provides the code you can use as the generic widget. Save it as a .tag file (or a few .tag files) and then deploy the tag for use with a Web Application. An excellent example is the rollover effect that was covered in the tag library chapter. You'll recall Listing 7-18 in Chapter 7, which was the code for rollover.html. It contained the DHTML for a single image rollover effect.

Listing 11-24   DHTML for an Image Rollover

```
<a href="index.html" onmouseover="button.src='button_on.gif';"
onmouseout="button.src='button_off.gif';">
<img name="button" src="button_off.gif" border="0"></a>
```

This code is a specific instance of the DHTML needed for a rollover image. JavaScript is used to change the picture depending on if the mouse is hovering over the image or not. The specific images being used are button_on.gif and button_off.gif.

In order to make Listing 11-24 generic, remove any specific names or values and replace them with a variable. The generic form of Listing 11-25 is illustrated by rollover.tag that you saw previously in Listing 7-18 in Chapter 7.

Listing 11-25   rollover.tag (Redisplayed for Convenience)

```
<%@ attribute name="link" required="true" %>
<%@ attribute name="image" required="true" %>
<a href="${link}" onmouseover="${image}.src='${image}_on.gif';"
```

```
onmouseout="${image}.src='${image}_off.gif';">
<img name="${image}" src="${image}_off.gif" border="0"></a>
```

Note the specific values for the link and image are replaced with variables. The strategy is to have the values replaced at runtime for specific uses of the widget; the custom tag somehow has to provide the specific values, likely by using attributes. In the case of `rollover.tag` this is exactly how the job is accomplished: the `image` attribute provides the base name of the image, and the `link` attribute provides the link.

In general, the technique of abstracting DHTML widgets with custom tags is straightforward and helpful. Use the design pattern to ensure HTML pages are not unnecessarily complicated by DHTML.

Summary

Design patterns can greatly simplify the process of building and maintaining a Web Application. With JSP and Servlets there are two prominent design patterns: Model 1 and Model 2. For all practical purposes Model 1 is not a real design pattern; it is more a name for how most Web Applications are intuitively built. JSP and Servlets are not best used by combining both presentation logic and business logic in the same endpoint. This practice creates unmaintainable code and ignores the strengths of JSP and Servlets. A popular and proved solution to the problem is self-enforcing a clean separation of the business logic and presentation logic. The Model 2 design pattern advocates such a separation and is superior compared to the Model 1 design pattern when developing a Web Application.

Understanding and implementing the Model 2 design pattern are two different things. A flexible Model 2 framework can go a long way toward enforcing a good Model 2 implementation. In this chapter the Struts framework was presented as a practical solution for a modular Model 2 framework. Combining Struts components with JSP and the JSTL, a Model 2 Web Application of any size can be built.

Chapter 12

Internationalization

$\mathbf{T}$he World Wide Web is not truly world-compatible. Most Web sites and the technology used to build them are designed for western European languages—primarily English. This is not a limitation of the Web; it is a restriction developers either choose or are unable to build beyond. The issue of internationalization support is being able to provide a Web site that can produce content in a number of different languages. In this chapter the focus is how to successfully build an internationalized Web Application.

Internationalization, commonly abbreviated as i18n because it starts with an I, ends with an N, and has 18 letters in between, is an important concept to understand. Ideally, this chapter is for developers responsible for Web Applications that are either non-English or for a Web Application that must simultaneously support multiple languages. While it is certainly possible today you personally will not have to build a non-English Web site, in the future you almost certainly will. The concepts are important to understand for a good Servlet and JSP developer, and the implementation techniques used to internationalize an application can be applied to other things. Even if you are developing an English-only Web site, i18n development is something you should still be aware of as a developer. Take, for instance, multiple versions of the same language, such as differences between British and American English. British readers dislike seeing common English words such as colour[1] being spelled incorrectly and the use of the letter "z" where an "s" should be used, such as familiarise rather than familiarize[2].

---

1. Of course, this is written by the British half of the authoring team; the U.S. half insists that colour is spelled color.
2. In the eigthteenth century Noah Webster published the first authoritative American English dictionary that is largely credited for the current spelling differences.

Content Encoding

Blatantly put, the World Wide Web is heavily tied to, if not built around, western European languages. This attachment is likely due to the early origins of the Web[3] that sprouted from Europe and then grew in the United States and European countries. However, what is important to know as a developer is that the default character encoding of HTTP is ISO-8859-1, also called Latin-1. The encoding contains byte-to-character mappings for the characters most commonly used by the western European languages such as English, Spanish, French, Italian, and German. Additionally, HTML provides convenient escape sequences for the ISO-8859-1 character set.

Using characters outside of the ISO-8859-1 by default ends up as gibberish in ISO-8859-1–based applications. This is an experience far too many novice Web developers have and it is easy to understand why. Non–ISO-8859-1 characters treated as ISO-8859-1 characters creates, gibberish; take for instance some Japanese text obtained from Yahoo! Japan, `http://www.yahoo.co.jp`, which is shown in Figure 12-1.

Treating the content as if it were in the ISO-8859-1 encoding results in Figure 12-2.

The point to understand is that text is meaningless without the proper encoding. When developing an i18n Web Application, you need to be careful to use the proper encoding, not just the default. A full list of character encodings and associated RFC documents can be found at `http://www.iana.org/assignments/character-sets`.

ISO-8859-1

As a Web developer you need to be familiar with ISO-8859-1. Not just the keys on your keyboard, but all of the characters HTTP supports by default. Should you be building a Web site that only needs languages supported by ISO-8859-1, then it makes sense to use the standard. English, Spanish, Danish, Dutch, French, Italian, German, and other ISO-8859-1 language–supporting Web sites have this luxury.

The only problem that occurs when developing using ISO-8859-1 is that most keyboards are specialized for a particular language. As an English developer it is easy to to create most of a Spanish Web site, but the common English key-

---

3. Tim Berners Lee defined HTTP and started the World Wide Web at CERN (Conseil European pour la Recherche Nucleaire), the European Organization for Nuclear Research in 1989 and released it into the wild in 1991. See `http://www.w3.org/People/Berners-Lee/` for more details.

Figure 12-1   Yahoo! Japan

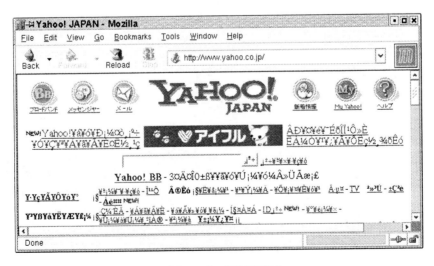

Figure 12-2   Yahoo! Japan Rendered Assuming ISO-8859-1

board does not include certain Spanish characters such as the tilde (ñ). In order to create this character, there are two good options. The first is to use a text editor capable of inserting particular characters not found on your keyboard. As long as the document is encoded as ISO-8859-1, there is no issue displaying the text in a browser. The second option is to use a character entity. HTML 2.0 introduced this functionality. Considering HTML is in version 4 now, it is fairly safe to assume the vast majority of HTML clients support character entities.

An HTML character entity allows any ISO-8859-1 character to be typed using a series of ASCII characters. The series starts with an ampersand, &, ends with a semi-colon, ;, and includes a unique set of characters between. Usually the characters are an abbreviated form of the desired character's proper name. For example, ampersand can only be properly authored using one of these sequences. The sequence for ampersand is `&amp;`. When rendered by a Web browser, the characters `&amp;` are not directly shown; instead, only the & character is.

Knowing how to make an ampersand is not too helpful, but knowing the character entities for all the ISO-8859-1 characters is. Complete references are at `http://www.w3.org/TR/REC-html40/sgml/entities.html` and `http://www.htmlhelp.com/reference/html40/entities/`. By using these characters, it is possible for developers of a specific ISO-8859-1 language to create any of the other default languages supported. For example, Listing 12-1 is the Spanish equivalent of the `HelloWorld.jsp`, authored by using only ASCII.

Listing 12-1 HolaMundo.jsp

```
<html>
<head>
<title>&iexcl;Hola Mundo!</title>
</head>
<body>
En Espa&ntilde;ol:<br>
<h1>&iexcl;Hola Mundo!</h1>
</body>
</html>
```

The same text could also be sent from a Servlet. The characters outputted should all be familiar; it is how a browser renders the characters that is interesting. Figure 12-3 shows a browser rendering of the output from `HolaMundo.jsp`.

The named character entities as just illustrated do not represent all of the ISO-8859-1 characters. Uncommon characters must be referenced using the

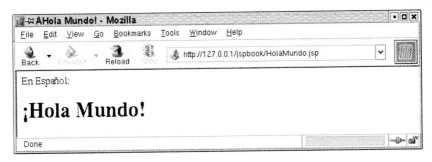

Figure 12-3 Browser Rendering of HolaMundo.jsp

numerical entity. The difference is inserting a pound sign[4], #, and a numerical value. Conveniently, the numerical values correspond to the Unicode escapes for characters, which is explained later in this chapter.

Unicode

A universal character set does exist. The trouble with ISO-8859-1 is that it cannot be easily extended because it uses only 8 bits, meaning 2^8, or 256 possible characters. Many languages, such as Japanese or Chinese, require thousands of characters and symbols. The solution to this problem is to expand the number of bits used to store information. The Unicode Worldwide Character Standard does just that and uses two bytes, 2^{16}, or 65,536 possibilities, and provides support for the principal written languages of the Americas, Europe, the Middle East, Africa, India, Asia, and Pacifica.

The Unicode standard can be found at http://www.unicode.org. Recall that Java uses Unicode as its default character encoding and can convert between Unicode and the encodings summarized by the J2SDK 1.4 documentation, http://java.sun.com/j2se/1.4/docs/guide/intl/encoding.doc.html. The current version of Unicode that Java supports can always be found by referencing the java.lang.Character class. Java 1.4 supports Unicode 3.0. Additionally, the core Java i18n classes provide a helpful mechanism for developers building i18n Java applications. Later in the chapter a few of these classes are used. If you are unfamiliar with the Java i18n classes, refer to Sun's Java internationalization documentation, http://java.sun.com/j2se/1.4/docs/guide/intl/index.html.

---

4. As an internationalization footnote this character (#) is called a *hash* in the United Kingdom (see http://www.theregister.co.uk/content/28/26042.html for an amusing discussion of this character).

Thanks to Java's excellent support for Unicode and translation to other prominent character encodings, it is possible for a Servlet- and JSP-based Web Application to have robust support for i18n content.

UTF-8 and UCS-2

In most cases the best method of generating a page is to put it in the specific encoding of a client. However, in cases where multiple languages must appear on the same page, Unicode should be used. There are two common ways to use Unicode, UCS-2 and UTF-8. Universal Character Set 2-byte form (UCS-2) encodes Unicode characters in their natural format: two bytes per character. UCS Transform Format, 8-bit form (UTF-8), encodes Unicode characters using a varying number of bytes depending on the character set. UTF-8 is more commonly used because it can encode the US-ASCII character set with just one byte per character. For this reason, UTF-8 use on the World Wide Web is much more common than UCS-2.

Most modern applications, specifically Web browsers, have full support for UTF-8. When coding a multi-lingual Web page, it is the de facto standard to use UTF-8 encoding. More information about UTF-8 can be found with RFC 2279, `http://www.ietf.org/rfc/rfc2279.txt`.

Working with Non-ISO-8859-1 Encoding

While the standard encoding is commonly used, clients are never forced to use it, nor are you. By default a Web application assumes information sent with an HTTP request is encoded using ISO-8859-1. Should it not, then it is assumed extra information is sent to determine the correct content encoding. The encoding information is made available through the `HttpServletRequest.getContentEncoding()` method.

Provided a client is using a different encoding, the information is usually specified in the `content-type` header. For example, plaintext information encoded using UTF-8 should have a content header of `text/plain; charset=UTF-8`. First, the header specifies the MIME types, as it should, but afterward, a semi-colon follows with encoding information. This encoding information is what is used to determine the type of encoding that has been applied to content. In the case that either the server or client botches this header, then there is little that can be done.

Most of the time invoking a method such as `getParameter()` returns a properly encoded `string` object. In rare cases the encoding may get incorrectly decoded and gibberish results. To avoid the problem, the decoding of posted information can be manually changed with a few simple lines of code:

```
String value = request.getParameter("param");
value = new String(value.getBytes(),
request.getCharacterEncoding());
```

Alternatively, if you know precisely the encoding that is to be used, it can always be set by replacing the call. For example, forcing UTF-8 would be the following:

```
String value = request.getParameter("param");
value = new String(value.getBytes(), "UTF-8");
```

Assuming an encoding is not recommended for general use because it creates the same problem that previously existed, content encoded differently improperly decodes. However, if the encoding must be set manually, it can be done using the preceding snippet of code.

When sending content to a client, a non-default encoding may be specified by manipulating the content-type header in a similar fashion. Directly invoke the setContentType() method with encoding information appended to the MIME type. However, when doing this, be sure to send content to a client using the specified encoding. Do not set the content-type header to be text/html; charset=Shift_JIS, Japanese, and then send content encoded as the default ISO-8859-1. Either use the ServletResponse setLocale() method to automatically set the content-type header and handle the output, or manually set the content-type header and ensure the content is sent using the appropriate encoding. With a Servlet this can be done by invoking setContentType() and then manually creating a PrintWriter from a ServletOutputStream. For instance a UTF-8 PrintWriter would be as follows:

```
response.setContentType("text/html; charset=UTF-8");
ServletOutputStream sos = response.getOutputStream();
PrintWriter out =
  new PrintWriter(new OutputStreamWriter(sos,"UTF-8"), true);
response.setLocale("","");
out.println("<html>"); // output content as normal
```

Other encodings are done in the same fashion, but by switching UTF-8 to the particular format. When using a JSP the output format can be set by the page directive's pageEncoding and contentType attributes. The meaning of these attributes is slightly dependent on if one, both, or none is used. The attributes are summarized in Table 12-1, which are taken from section 4.1 of the JSP 2.0 spec-ification.

Where

<defaultType> is "text/html" for JSP Pages in standard syntax, or "text/xml" for JSP Documents in XML syntax.

<contentType charset> value is the charset portion of <contentType> if specified, or defaults to <defaultEncoding> if not specified.

<defaultInputEncoding> is "ISO-8859-1" for JSP Pages in standard syntax, or "UTF-8" or "UTF-16" for JSP Documents in XML syntax (depending on the type detected as per the rules in the XML speci-fication). Note that in the case of include directives the default input encoding is derived from the initial page, not from any of the included pages.

Unicode Escapes

Unicode escapes are a method of creating Unicode characters by using ASCII characters, which is very convenient because it allows English developers to insert Unicode characters in Java code. A Unicode escape in Java starts with \u and is followed by four characters describing the hexadecimal value of the Unicode character. For example, the character ñ can be represented by the Unicode escape \u00F1.

What Unicode escapes mean for Servlets and JSP is that code can be authored that takes full advantage of Unicode. A HelloWorld Servlet in the true spirit of saying hello to the world would need to take advantage of Unicode. Listing 12-2 is an example of a Servlet that uses Unicode to send a "HelloWorld" in many dif-ferent languages. Translations are courtesy of the babel fish, `http://babel.altavista.com`.

Listing 12-2 i18nHelloWorld.java

```
package com.jspbook;

import java.io.*;
import javax.servlet.*;
import javax.servlet.http.*;

public class i18nHelloWorld extends HttpServlet {

  public void doGet(HttpServletRequest request,
                    HttpServletResponse response)
```

```
  throws IOException, ServletException {
    response.setContentType("text/html; charset=UTF-8");
    ServletOutputStream sos = response.getOutputStream();
    PrintWriter out =
      new PrintWriter(new OutputStreamWriter(sos,"UTF-8"),
                      true);
    out.println("<html>");
    out.println("<head>");
    out.println("<title>i18n Hello World!</title>");
    out.println("</head>");
    out.println("<body>");
    // Chinese
    out.println("<h1>\u4f60\u597d\u4e16\u754c!</h1>");
    out.println("<h1>Hello World!</h1>"); // English
    out.println("<h1>Bonjour Monde!</h1>"); // French
    out.println("<h1>Hallo Welt!</h1>"); // German
    out.println("<h1>Ciao Mondo!</h1>"); // Italian

out.println("<h1>\u3053\u3093\u306b\u3061\u306f\u4e16\u754c!</h1>");
//Japanese
    out.println("<h1>\uc5ec\ubcf4\uc138\uc694 \uc138\uacc4
!</h1>"); // Korean
    out.println("<h1>\u00a1Hola Mundo!</h1>");// Spanish
    out.println("</body>");
    out.println("</html>");
  }
}
```

Table 12-1   pageEncoding and contentType Attribute Meaning

pageEncoding Page Directive Attribute (<encoding>)	contentType Page Directive Attribute (<contentType)	Input JSP Source Encoding	Output Content Type
specified	specified	<encoding>	<contentType>
specified	not specified	<encoding>	"<defaultType>;charset=<encoding>"
not specified	specified	<contentType charset>	<contentType>
not specified	not specified	<defaultInput Encoding>	"<defaultType>charset=<default InputEncoding>"

When executed, the Servlet displays a series of hellos, each in a different language. The rendered page is shown in Figure 12-4. In order to properly see the page, your Web browser must fully support UTF-8.

In `i18nHelloWorld.java` Unicode escapes are used to author the Unicode characters not found in ASCII. Keep in mind Java source file can also be authored directly as Unicode, which is what most non-ASCII developers do. Using only ASCII and escape characters is tedious. Alternatively, most modern Java compiles provide a command line option of compiling Java source files in just about any encoding. For instance Sun's javac, bundled with the J2SDK 1.4, allows for the `encoding` flag to specify a Java source file's encoding; the list of supported encodings is extensive.

Unicode, and other encodings, can also be used with JSP. As shown in Table 12-1 of the JSP specifications, the encoding attribute can be used to specify a

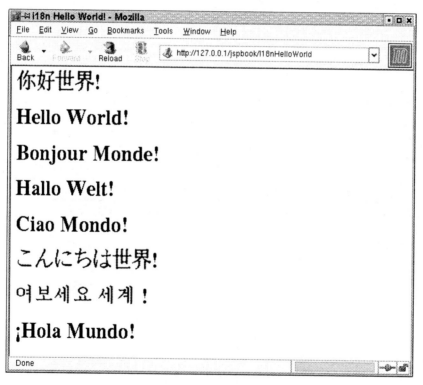

Figure 12-4 Browser Rendering of i18nHelloWorld.java Output

non-default input encoding. For instance, the JSP in Listing 12-3 demonstrates an equivalent of `i18nHelloWorld.java` as a JSP.

Listing 12-3 i18nHelloWorld.jsp

```
<%@ page pageEncoding="utf-8"%><html>
<head>
<title>i18n Hello World!</title>
</head>
<body>
<h1>好世界!</h1>
<h1>Hello World!</h1>
<h1>Bonjour Monde!</h1>
<h1>Hallo Welt!</h1>
<h1>Ciao Mondo!</h1>
<h1>こんにちは世界!</h1>
<h1>여보세요 세계!</h1>
<h1>¡Hola Mundo!</h1>
</body>
</html>
```

The page is encoded in UTF-8 and the `pageEncoding` attribute ensures the JSP is parsed correctly and sent to a client with the correct encoding. If you are typing in this page, be sure to use a UTF-8-capable editor.

i18n Implementation Techniques

Non-standard character encodings allow most any language to be used with Servlets and JSP, but implementing a multi-lingual Web Application is a chore itself. The problem i18n presents a Web developer is how to store and format more than one version of content. With all of the previous examples of this book it has been assumed the Web Application was being built to show one format in one language. This assumption simplified examples by allowing content and formatting to be hard coded in the same Servlet or JSP. With i18n the assumption is no longer valid.

Providing support for multiple versions of the same content can be done in many different ways. Outlined in this chapter are two different methods that are widely used and considered most practical. The first method involves a simple but brute force approach at solving the problem: make a separate page for each language. The second method is a more elegant but complex approach: abstract the content out from the formatting. Either of these two approaches works, and both are suited for different needs. However, the suggestion for building an optimal Web Application is to take the second approach.

Another approach to providing i18n support that is not covered by this chapter is to translate completed Web pages on the fly. A simple Filter and a good set of translation APIs would allow for this; however, there is no good, standard Java translation API available.

Language Detection

All i18n implementation techniques rely on a Web Application being able to detect what type of language a user prefers. Understanding how to properly detect a user's language is critical because without it you are left to guess what type of content is desired. Guessing is no better than showing one language to all users. For all of the i18n implementation techniques it is assumed the appropriate language is detectable.

There are three good methods of detecting the language a client prefers:

- **Inquire:** Use an HTML form to ask what language a user would prefer. This method is not the most elegant but it does work.
- **HTTP accept-language and accept-charset headers:** A Web browser can identify a user's preferred language(s) and encoding(s) by setting the HTTP `accept-language` and `accept-charset` headers, respectively. The value of these headers includes the two-letter language codes the client supports and the encoding formats supported.
- **URL Encoding:** Language preference can be encoded in a URL. The URL may lead to a real page with the correct language or lead to a fictitious resource that is intercepted by an i18n component.

Inquiring

Asking a user via an HTML form is something with which you should be familiar. Reading form parameters was covered in Chapter 2. The only difficult part of using this technique is how to appropriately show the form. If the form is only in one language, then it will not be understood by users of different languages. The solution is to use a form with options in all of the languages supported. The complete form can be translated, or alternative methods of communicating the meaning can be used such as pictures. A popular approach is to use a form with pictures of various countrie's flags.

HTTP Accept-Language and Accept-Charset Headers

Inquiring what type of language a user prefers is not the most elegant method to determine what language to use. It is a guaranteed method of getting the job done, but should a user already provide this information, then it is not necessary to ask. The HTTP `accept-language` and `accept-charset` headers are a method available for a user to specify a preferred language. A better solution to determining a user's preferred language is to first check the `user-language` header and rely on inquiry as a fall-back mechanism.

Mining information from the `accept-language` and `accept-charset` headers is straightforward. To determine a user's preferred language, invoke the `HttpServletRequest getHeader()` method with `"accept-language"` as the parameter:

```
String preferredLanguage = request.getHeader("accept-language");
```

You can check if your browser is sending this information by visiting the ShowHeaders Servlet from Chapter 2, Listing 2-8. An example of what the header usually contains for an English user is the following:

```
en-us, en;q=0.50
```

The two-letter language code for English is `en`; the `-us` is an optional two-letter country code. In addition to the country code preference, information can be included by appending a *q-value*. The q-value determines the preference for language it follows. By convention the languages are listed in order of preference; however, in cases where multiple languages are supported, the q-values are a clear method of indicating which one a user would prefer.

The `accept-charset` header, not to be confused with `accept-encoding`, is mined in the same fashion as the `accept-language` header:

```
String preferredCharset = request.getHeader("accept-charset");
```

The information sent by this browser is another comma-separated list of encodings with option q-values. Should your browser be sending this information, it is also shown by the ShowHeaders Servlet. Usually, the value of this header is similar to the following:

```
ISO-8859-1, utf-8;q=0.66, *;q=0.66
```

An asterisk symbolizes any character encoding. It is a polite method of informing a server to send whatever it can should the preferred encodings not be supported.

Note that the HTTP specifications do not mandate use of the `accept-language` or `accept-charset` headers. While they are commonly provided, it is not guaranteed. For this reason if it is critical to always have a method of language detection, then an HTML form should be relied on as a fall-back mechanism.

Once information has successfully been obtained about preferred languages, it can be used in a variety of different ways. A simple conditional check works, but more commonly Java's built-in support, resource bundles, are used. These techniques are discussed further with the specific implementation techniques.

Persisting Language Information and URL Encoding

Another direct, custom method of determining a user's language preferences is to use URL encoding. Information about a preferred language can be easily encoded in either a real or fictitious URL. For instance, should copies of language-specific content be stored in different directories, the directories can be named according to the two-digit language codes. Language detection can then be achieved by checking to see if a URL includes a particular language code.

```
String url = request.getRequestURI();
if (url.indexOf("/en/") != -1) {...}
```

Likewise, language information can be encoded in a fictitious URL, such as appending a two-letter language code to the end of a real URL or using the same method just described. As explained later in the chapter, there is good reason not to want to keep multiple copies of formatted content. A fictitious URL can be created with the intention of leading to a real language-specific–producing JSP or Servlet.

Language-encoded URLs are a popular approach to avoid reliance on the `accept-language` and `accept-charset` headers. Many popular Web sites—for example, Yahoo!—have registered domain names with extensions for different languages such as `http://www.yahoo.com` for English and `http://www.yahoo.co.jp` for Japanese. The domain names work well for users to bookmark or remember when visiting the site's default main page.

A user's language preferences only need to be detected once, similar to session information. Should a session be used, the preferences can set in session scope and be re-used on subsequent visits. If session context is not being maintained, then URL encoding can be used to persist a user's language preferences. Alternatively, if cookies are supported, the information can be kept using a cookie.

Multiple Pages

The first and usually most rapid method of developing an i18n Web Application is to create multiple copies of all the content. Each copy is translated into a desired language, and the user is directed to the correct copy appropriately. While this approach causes problems with maintenance, it is intuitive to implement and well suited for small projects.

In essence, the strategy is to make a copy of the Web Application for each language. Content in one language refers to other content in that language. A common naming scheme keeps different translations of the content separate. For instance, `welcome.html`, Listing 1-3 in Chapter 1, is a simple example of a Web page with some English content.

```
<html>
  <head>
    <title>Welcome!</title>
  </head>
  <body>
  Welcome to the example Web Application for
  <i>Servlets and JSP the J2EE Web Tier</i>.
  </body>
</html>
```

Following the multiple copy design, a valid naming scheme would be to give all English pages a name, then subsequently translate the pages and insert the language's three-character code followed by a "-" before the English name. For instance, the French version of `welcome.html` would be saved as `welcome-fra.html` and would include the code in Listing 12-4.

Listing 12-4 welcome-fra.html French Translation of welcome.html

```
<html>
  <head>
    <title>Bienvenue!</title>
  </head>
  <body>
  Bienvenue à la demande d'enchaînement d'exemple de
  <i>Servlets and JSP the J2EE Web Tier</i>.
  </body>
</html>
```

If the page required dynamic content, then the code would be inserted and it would be saved as a JSP. The point to see is that the implementation works by providing pre-translated versions of entire Web pages on the server-side. The technique works well with Servlet Filters because a single Filter can seamlessly intercept all requests to a resource, say, `welcome.html`—and attempt to localize to say— `welcome-fra.html`, depending on the preferred language of the client. The overall effect is that all requests can be sent to a single page, such as `welcome.html`, but responses will be appropriately localized if the server has a translated version of the content. To illustrate the technique, Listing 12-5 includes such a Filter.

Listing 12-5 Simplei18nFilter.java

```java
package com.jspbook;

import java.io.*;
import java.util.*;
import javax.servlet.*;
import javax.servlet.http.*;

public class Simplei18nFilter implements Filter {
  protected static FilterConfig config = null;

  public void init(FilterConfig filterConfig) {
    config = filterConfig;
  }

  public void destroy() {
    config = null;
  }

  public void doFilter(ServletRequest req,
                       ServletResponse res,
                       FilterChain chain)
  throws IOException, ServletException {
    if (res instanceof HttpServletResponse) {
      HttpServletRequest request = (HttpServletRequest)req;
      HttpServletResponse response = (HttpServletResponse)res;

      String uri = request.getRequestURI();
      if (uri.endsWith("/")) {
        chain.doFilter(request, response);
        return;
      }
      String path = request.getContextPath();
      uri = uri.substring(path.length(), uri.length());
      uri = getLanguage(uri, request);
      ServletContext sc = config.getServletContext();
```

```
      sc.getRequestDispatcher(uri).forward(request, response);
   }
}

public static String getLanguage(String uri,
                                 HttpServletRequest request) {
   ServletContext sc = config.getServletContext();
   Enumeration enum = request.getLocales();
   String postfix =
     uri.substring(uri.lastIndexOf("."), uri.length());
   String temp = uri.substring(0,uri.length()-postfix.length());
   while(enum.hasMoreElements()) {
     Locale l = (Locale)enum.nextElement();
     String lang = l.getISO3Language();
     String file = sc.getRealPath(temp+"-"+lang+postfix);
     System.out.println("Trying: "+file);
     File f = new File(file);
     if (f.exists()) {
       return temp+"-"+lang+postfix;
     }
   }
   return uri;
  }
}
```

The code works by intercepting a request and attempting to forward it to the most localized version of content.

```
String uri = request.getRequestURI();
String path = request.getContextPath();
uri = uri.substring(path.length(), uri.length());
uri = getLanguage(uri, request);
ServletContext sc = config.getServletContext();
sc.getRequestDispatcher(uri).forward(request, response);
```

The getLanguage() method is responsible for determining the most localized language.

```
Enumeration enum = request.getLocales();
String postfix =
  uri.substring(uri.lastIndexOf("."), uri.length());
String temp = uri.substring(0,uri.length()-postfix.length());
while(enum.hasMoreElements()) {
  Locale l = (Locale)enum.nextElement();
  String lang = l.getISO3Language();
```

```
      String file = sc.getRealPath(temp+"-"+lang+postfix);
      System.out.println("Trying: "+file);
      File f = new File(file);
      if (f.exists()) {
        return temp+"-"+lang+postfix;
      }
    }
  }
  return uri;
}
```

It code checks for files named identically to the base file, such as `welcome.html`, but with the appropriate language, such as `welcome-fra.html`, to match a client's preferred language. Preferences are obtained by invoking the `HttpServlet Request` object's `getLocales()` method, and the files are checked using the `ServletContext getRealPath()` method. If no localized version is found, the file with the base name is returned.

Save Listing 12-5 as `Simplei18nFilter.java` in the `/WEB-INF/classes/com/jspbook` directory of the jspbook Web Application. Deploy the Filter to intercept all requests to `welcome.html`, save `welcome-fra.html` in the base directory of the jspbook Web Application, and reload Tomcat for the changes to take effect. Browse to `http://127.0.0.1/jspbook/welcome.html` to see the localized page. Assuming you have English set to be the preferred language, Figure 12-5 is displayed.

If you have another language set as preferred and a localized version of the page in that language exists on the server, the localized version of the content is displayed. For example, since we also have `welcome-fra.html` in the same directory as `welcome.html`, if you set your browser's preferred language to be French, Figure 12-6 is shown.

Note that the requested URL is still `http://127.0.0.1/jspbook/welcome.html`, but the content of `welcome-fra.html` is returned. This is because the Filter is appropriately localizing the content on the server-side; to the client it appears as if `welcome.html` is authored in their preferred language. This is incredibly helpful because it means a Web Application does not have to code language localized links to go to appropriate language localized pages. For example, in every page linking to the welcome page, regardless of language, the link is `welcome.html`. Compared to manually coding in `welcome-fra.html`, `welcome-jpn.html`, and so on, based on the language, this is much easier. Supporting a new language is always as easy as authoring new pages and naming them appropriately so that the Simple i18n Filter uses them. Plus the Filter is designed to use UTF-8 encoding, which means it supports any language Unicode supports.

Figure 12-5 English Version of welcome.html

Using pre-translated copies of entire Web pages works well for small Web Applications that are not likely to change. A "small Web Application" should be interpreted to mean anything that is not burdensome for your translation method to be used with. This technique for providing i18n support can quickly become a problem with pages that constantly change. Each time a change is made, it must be replicated to all of the translated pages. In regard to content there is little that can be done to prevent this, but there is no reason that changes to a page's formatting should require a change. By consolidating format information into one template page and abstracting the content out of the page, the problem can be minimized. This is the suggested approach for developing complex i18n Web applications, and it is covered in the next section.

Content Abstraction

Implementing an i18n Web application that can grow and change involves abstracting content. Following the Model 2 design pattern, the process is easy to

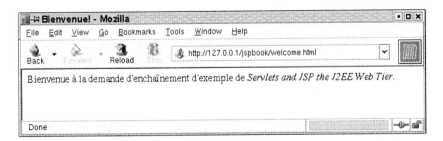

Figure 12-6 French Version of welcome.html

implement. With previous examples it was assumed content is only needed in one language. Only the dynamic parts of the page were generated on the fly; the static content was coded in along with formatting code. In a multi-lingual Web Application, content needs to be abstracted since it is no longer always in the same language.

For example, `welcome.html` is the page that welcomes a user to the Web Application that was shown previously in Figure 1-12 in Chapter 1. You'll recall the code for `welcome.html` is the following:

```
<html>
  <head>
    <title>Welcome!</title>
  </head>
  <body>
  Welcome to the example Web Application for
  <i>Servlets and JSP the J2EE Web Tier</i>.
  </body>
</html>
```

For an internationalized application this page does little good since it is only in English. Abstracting the content from this page allows it to be i18n-friendly. The code in Listing 12-6 is a dynamic version of the page that would allow for any number of languages to be used[5].

Listing 12-6 welcome.jsp

```
<html>
  <head>
    <title>${content.title}</title>
  </head>
  <body>
  ${content.welcome}
  </body>
</html>
```

The only static part of the page is the formatting that is perfectly fine assuming HTML is the only thing being produced. In cases where different formats are required, a multi-client design, as discussed in Chapter 13, should be used. The point of Listing 12-6 is that the title and welcome message are actually identifiers. These identifiers reference the actual text to be displayed. That text

---

5. Assuming the correct encoding is used.

can be changed at runtime to custom-tailor the page to a particular language. Assuming a Model 2 design is being used, a control component would be responsible for populating an object, such as a JavaBean, with the correct title and welcome message for the page, and then passing the object via request scope.

If the user preferred English, the resulting welcome page could be similar to Figure 12-7. Or equally as flexible, if the user preferred French, the resulting welcome page could be similar to Figure 12-8.

The only difficult part to implementing this type of content abstraction is determining the correct language in order to populate the values to display. This logic can be done in many different ways, but the Java API conveniently provides resource bundles.

Resource Bundles

A *resource bundle* is the default J2EE method of determining and preparing locale specific content for a user. A resource bundle is represented by the `java.util.ResourceBundle` object. The object provides a set of static methods that take a base name and `Locale` object and return a resource bundle populated with appropriate values. The values come from searching through provided property files and determining which best matches the requested `Locale`. Resource bundles work very well in practice and are the de facto method of providing i18n content support.

Resource bundles are the i18n mechanism that you are encouraged to use. As so, we need to be more familiar with how they function. The first thing needed to use a resource bundle is a `Locale` object describing a user's locale. Using the `Locale`, the resource bundle loads an appropriate resource file to obtain resource, specific information. The appropriate resource file is determined by using a combination of a *base name* and locale information. The base name determines the

Figure 12-7   welcome.jsp in English, Rendered by a Web Browser

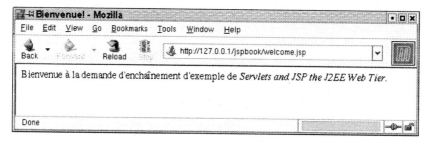

Figure 12-8 welcome.jsp in French, Rendered by a Web Browser

starting name of the file. Locale-specific files are determined by appending an "_" along with the locale's appropriate two-digit country code[6]. For instance, a base name for the welcome page's resource bundle might be `welcome`. The English resource bundle would be named `welcome_en`, because `en` is the two-digit language code for English. The resource bundle for French would be `welcome_fr`, `fr` being the two-digit code for French. The naming scheme continues for all of the languages used. The scheme also extends to cover dialects. For example, as we have already discussed, U.S. English is different from U.K. English, and Canadian French is different from French French is different from Swiss French. To encode these differences, the name of the resource bundle also contains another two-letter encoding for the country. This means you could have `welcome_fr_CH` or `welcome_fr_FR`. And to extend it even further, there is also a "variant" value to specify vendor-specific information. The algorithm used to load resource bundles goes from most- to least-specific value. That is, if an application asks for a "Swiss French" locale (`fr_CH`) and it does not exist, but a more general French locale does, then the existing resource bundle for the French (`fr`) locale is loaded.

Information in a resource bundle property file is specified by name/value pairs. Each line of a property file contains a name followed by a value with an equal sign separating them. The format is designed to be simple and works well for storing small amounts of information. For example, the property file that is needed to produce the same English output that was shown previously in Figure 12-7 would be Listing 12-7.

---

6. The API documentation for `java.util.Locale` provides a reference to all the two-letter language codes.

Listing 12-7 welcome_en.properties (English property File for the Resource Bundle Used in welcome.jsp)

```
title=Welcome!
welcome=Welcome to the example Web Application for <i>Servlets and
JSP the J2EE Web Tier</i>.
```

Note the second line only wraps to fit on this book page. In the property file there is no line return after the word "and". To use this property file, it needs to be in the current class path of the Web Application—that is, the `/WEB-INF/classes` folder or any sub-folder thereof.

To use the newly made property file with `welcome.jsp`, two more components are required. Following a true Model 2 design, the logic that loads the resource bundle needs to be abstracted out of the JSP and a JavaBean used as an interface to pass values. The JavaBean in Listing 12-8 is straightforward.

Listing 12-8 Welcome.java

```java
package com.jspbook;

public class Welcome {
  protected String title = null;
  protected String welcome = null;

  public String getTitle() {
    return title;
  }
  public void setTitle(String title) {
    this.title = title;
  }

  public String getWelcome() {
    return welcome;
  }
  public void setWelcome(String welcome) {
    this.welcome = welcome;
  }
}
```

Appropriate getter and setter methods are all the JavaBean is used for. It is a facade for the real logic responsible for loading the correct i18n content.

The code responsible for loading the i18n values is of interest. Using the `Locale` object obtained from an `HttpServletRequest`, a resource bundle is initialized with the correct i18n content.

```
Locale locale = request.getLocale();
ResourceBundle  rb = ResourceBundle.getBundle("welcome", locale);
```

Only two lines of code are required because the `ResourceBundle` object encapsulates all of the code responsible for determining an appropriate property file and parsing name/value pairs. Use this code with the page's JavaBean to make a complete working example as shown in Listing 12-9.

Listing 12-9 welcome.jsp (Model 1½ Style to Load and Use Dynamic i18n Values)

```
<%@ page import="java.util.*, com.jspbook.*"%>
<%
  Locale locale = request.getLocale();
  ResourceBundle  rb = ResourceBundle.getBundle("welcome", locale);
  Welcome content = new Welcome();
  content.setTitle(rb.getString("title"));
  content.setWelcome(rb.getString("welcome"));
  request.setAttribute("content", content);
%>
<%@ taglib uri="http://java.sun.com/jstl/core" prefix="c" %>
<html>
  <head>
    <title>${content.title}</title>
  </head>
  <body>
  ${content.welcome}
  </body>
</html>
```

Note the code is included with the JSP in a Model 1½ design. This is for simplicity in the example. With a Model 2 design the highlighted code at the start of the page would be removed and placed in a control component.

The complete example can now be executed. Assuming you are an English developer, or that your Web browser sets the `accept-language` header to prefer English, Figure 12-7 is shown when browsing to `welcome.jsp`.

Support for new languages is as easy as adding new property files to the class path. For instance, the property file that is needed for French content is shown in Listing 12-10.

Listing 12-10 welcome_fr.properties

```
title=Bienvenue!
welcome=Bienvenue à la demande d'enchaînement d'exemple de
<i>Servlets and JSP the J2EE Web Tier</i>.
```

Be sure to save `welcome_fr.properties` in the class path of your Web Application, such as `/WEB-INF/classes` directory. Now, should a French developer browse to the site, the content returned is in French. The end result is the same as was shown in Figure 12-8. The example can go on and on with as many different languages as you can build property files for.

The code used with `welcome.jsp` illustrates why using a resource bundle is encouraged for i18n. Another custom solution, such as using a database for content, would work, but it complicates the logic needed for storing and retrieving i18n content. A resource bundle is simple and allows i18n developers to continuously create and modify property files for required i18n locales. Another good point should be raised about using Model 2 with i18n pages. Using the approach shown with Listing 12-9, the content is not limited to coming from a resource bundle. Should resource bundles not be adequate or a different mechanism already exists, the needed code can be exchanged for the resource bundle code.

JSTL i18n Message Tags

As an alternative to following a strict Model 2 design pattern for i18n content, the JSTL provides a set of i18n tags. A specific sub-set of the JSTL i18n tags is the message tags that mimic the functionality illustrated with `welcome.jsp`. The advantage of using the JSTL message tags is that they remove the need for a JavaBean and control component. Instead, the JSP encapsulates all of the logic required to load a resource bundle and retrieves properties from it. The disadvantage of the JSTL message tags is that they limit a JSP developer to only using resource bundles.

It is suggested you follow a strict Model 2 approach as previously described in this chapter. It keeps a proper level of abstraction between the JSP and i18n content generation and is suited for complex and growing Web Applications. However, understanding the JSTL approach is helpful because it allows for i18n applications to be developed rapidly with only a minor drawback.

There are three different JSTL message tags and use of each tag is straightforward; however, only two tags are currently of interest:

- **Bundle:** The bundle tag loads a resource bundle and places it in context for the other JSTL i18n tags to use. The tag has two attributes, `basename` and `prefix`. The `basename` attribute is the `basename` of a property file—for example, "`welcome`" as was used with `welcome.jsp`. The prefix attribute allows for a prefix to automatically be appended to a property key. Prefix values are helpful to ensure no two property names are the same—for example, in `welcome_en.properties` the keys `"title"` and `"welcome"` were used. The prefix `com.jspbook` could be appended to each to create a more unique name.

- **Message:** The message tag relies on an existing resource bundle and extracts messages from the bundle. The message tag requires the `key` attribute that specifies the key of the property message to be retrieved. The message tag also provides attributes for exporting the value to a scoped context variable and/or from a given resource bundle. Complete documentation for the message tag can be found in the JSTL specification.

The third tag is the param tag, which helps simplify generation of dynamic i18n messages at runtime. The topic is discussed further later on in this chapter.

Use of the bundle and message tags is designed to be very similar to what was done with `welcome.jsp`. The differences are that the Model 1½ code is replaced by the bundle tag, and use of the out tag is replaced by the message tag. For example, the JSP in Listing 12-11 provides the same functionality as `welcome.jsp`, provided that resource bundles are always used.

Listing 12-11   jstl_welcome.jsp, the JSTL Version of welcome.jsp

```
<%@ taglib uri="http://java.sun.com/jstl/fmt" prefix="fmt"%>
<fmt:bundle basename="welcome">
<html>
  <head>
    <title><fmt:message key="title"/></title>
  </head>
  <body>
  <fmt:message key="welcome"/>
  </body>
</html>
</fmt:bundle>
```

The preceding code is the complete JSP. Browsing to `jstl_welcome.jsp` results in identical output, depending on your locale, as shown with the examples for `welcome.jsp`.

The benefits of using the JSTL i18n message tags should be clear; they are easy—even easy enough to allow for non-Java programmers to happily use them. However, you should not use the JSTL tags just to avoid the Java code required by a Model 2 design pattern. The JSTL tags are great for rapid development of simple i18n Web Applications. When it is known that resource bundles are always to be used and there is minimal validation logic required of information retrieved, then the JSTL tags are a great fit for developing the application.

Number and Date Formatting

The last important i18n topic is formatting dates and numbers correctly to a specific locale. Different languages and locales use different formats for dates and numbers. For instance, the European and American styles of formatting a date are different. The American standard is to use the month, followed by day, followed by year. The European standard is to use the day, followed by month, followed by year. Both show the same information. The only difference is in how the information is presented.

Number and date formatting is an important topic because it is something that can be done accurately at runtime. Based on one universal representation—core set of Java objects—the specific number or date required by a locale can be generated on the fly. The functionality is analogous to building an application in one language and being able to accurately translate from that language into any other automatically. You know already that no good, standardized language-translation framework exists, but the Java API does provide such a framework for number and date formatting.

The Java API provides the `java.text.Format` class as a base class for creating i18n-friendly content generators. By itself `Format` is not very helpful, but the Java API provides a number of other classes that extend Format to create locale-specific content generators. Out of all the classes that exist, the ones we are interested in are `java.text.DateFormat`, `java.text.NumberFormat`, and `java.text.MessageFormat`. The `DateFormat` and `NumberFormat` classes format dates and numbers, respectively, to locale-specific formats. The `MessageFormat` class combines the functionality of the two classes and parses token strings, inserting localized numbers and dates appropriately.

Understanding the standard Java formatting classes is important because the concept they are built around is important. By representing numbers and dates in a universal fashion, it is possible to build a translation framework from the format to a desired different format. Using such a framework is helpful because it greatly simplifies the amount of effort required each time a date or number needs to be generated at runtime. The existing Java i18n framework is helpful because it works well and is extensible. As a Java developer it makes little sense to develop a completely different i18n framework when a working one already exists.

i18n Numbers and Dates at Runtime

Before showing some examples of using the Java format classes, it is important to understand when it is helpful to use them. The approach promoted for use earlier involved consolidating, formatting, and abstracting content into property files. The techniques explained now are for use when generating runtime number and date values. Numbers and dates that are static should still be abstracted into property files.

For instance, an i18n currency exchange page would need to generate dates and numbers at runtime. Imagine the site produced today's current date and a list of currency values. When rendered in English by a Web browser, it would resemble Figure 12-9.

Assume the service is completely realtime and the date and numbers are generated on the fly. All of the date and number information in Figure 12-9 would need to be dynamic, and if used in an i18n-friendly site, it should also use the Java formatting classes. The code for the page in Model 1 style would resemble Listing 12-12.

Listing 12-12   Model 1 i18n_exchange.jsp

```
<%@ page import="java.util.*, java.text.*"%>
<%
 MessageFormat usdf =
   new MessageFormat("{0,number,currency}", Locale.US);
 MessageFormat gbpf =
   new MessageFormat("{0,number,currency}", Locale.UK);
```

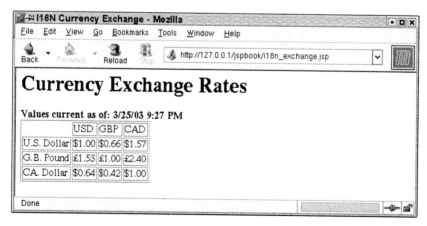

Figure 12-9   Browser Rendering of i18n_exchange.jsp

```
MessageFormat cadf =
  new MessageFormat("{0,number,currency}", Locale.CANADA);

double usd = 1;
double gbp = .65505;
double cad = 1.5716;
String usdusd = usdf.format(new Object[]{new Double(usd)});
String usdgbp = usdf.format(new Object[]{new Double(gbp)});
String usdcad = usdf.format(new Object[]{new Double(cad)});
String gbpusd = gbpf.format(new Object[]{new Double(usd/gbp)});
String gbpgbp = gbpf.format(new Object[]{new Double(1)});
String gbpcad = gbpf.format(new Object[]{new Double(cad/gbp)});
String cadusd = cadf.format(new Object[]{new Double(usd/cad)});
String cadgbp = cadf.format(new Object[]{new Double(gbp/cad)});
String cadcad = cadf.format(new Object[]{new Double(1)});

%>
<html>
<head>
  <title>i18n Currency Exchange</title>
</head>
<body>
  <h1>Currency Exchange Rates</h1>
  <b>Values current as of:
    <%= DateFormat.getInstance().format(new Date()) %><b>
 <table border="1">
  <tr>
   <td></td><td>USD</td><td>GBP</td><td>CAD</td>
  </tr>
  <tr>
   <td>U.S. Dollar</td><td><%= usdusd %></td>
   <td><%= usdgbp %></td><td><%= usdcad %></td>
  </tr>
  <tr>
   <td>G.B. Pound</td><td><%= gbpusd %></td>
   <td><%= gbpgbp %></td><td><%= gbpcad %></td>
  </tr>
  <tr>
   <td>CA. Dollar</td><td><%= cadusd %></td>
   <td><%= cadgbp %></td><td><%= cadcad %></td>
  </tr>
```

```
    </table>
  </body>
</html>⁷
```

Note all of the dates and numbers start as Java either a `java.util.Date` object or as double primitives. From there the information is passed through the `MessageFormat` and `DateFormat` objects to produce the locale-specific format. The information for the numbers is static for simplicity; in a real application it would be mined from a realtime database.

Listing 12-12 is a good example of when it is helpful to take advantage of the Java formatting classes. In contrast, here is an example of when they are not very helpful. Imagine a Web page that included a story, articles, or any other static information that included numbers and dates, for instance, the output illustrated by Figure 12-10.

An i18n-friendly application producing the output seen in Figure 12-10 should still follow the recommended i18n approach shown earlier in this chapter: abstract the content and consolidate the formatting. The code required to produce Figure 12-10 would be similar to Listing 12-13.

Listing 12-13 i18n_static.jsp

```jsp
<%@ page import="java.util.*, java.text.*"%>
<%
 ResourceBundle rb = ResourceBundle.getBundle("i18nstatic");
 MessageFormat mf =
```

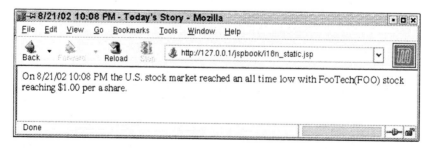

Figure 12-10 Browser Rendering of i18n_static.jsp

---

7. The extensive use of classic JSP expressions is purposely done for this example. Creating the variables, setting the variables in request scope, then using the JSP EL to access them would add a lot of unneeded code (just in this particular example).

```
  new MessageFormat("{0,number,currency}");
Double doub = new Double(rb.getString("price"));
String price = mf.format(new Object[]{doub});
request.setAttribute("price", price);
Locale locale = request.getLocale();
DateFormat df = DateFormat.getInstance();
Date d = df.parse(rb.getString("date"));
String date = DateFormat.getInstance().format(d);
request.setAttribute("date", date);
%>
<%@ taglib uri="http://java.sun.com/jstl/core" prefix="c" %>
<html>
  <head>
    <title><%= date %> - Today's Story</title>
  </head>
  <body>
On <c:out value="${date}"/> the U.S. stock market reached an
all time low with FooTech(FOO) stock reaching
<c:out value="${price}"/> per a share.
  </body>
</html>
```

Like the earlier examples of the i18n hello world pages, Listing 12-13 requires property files for the resource bundle to load. The English property file would be the code in Listing 12-14.

Listing 12-14 English i18n_static Property File

```
date=8/21/02 10:08 PM
price=1
```

Property files for other languages would be similar but with content in the appropriate language. The reason the `DateFormat` and `MessageFormat` classes should not be used in Listing 12-13 is because they are not needed! The dates and numbers are static. Generating them at runtime consumes time and processing power and complicates code.

Using DateFormat, NumberFormat, and MessageFormat

Using the Java formatting classes is straightforward. The number and date representations used by these classes are the same objects and primitives commonly used with Java. Dates are represented by instances of the `java.util.Date` object, and numbers are represented by `long` and `double` primitives. You should already be familiar with these objects and primitives. To use the formatting classes, the only things required are a `Date`, long or double, and a `Locale` object describing the user's locale.

The formatting classes work well with a Servlet or JSP because of the `HttpServletRequest getLocale()` method. As Listing 12-13 demonstrated, the methods of `DateFormat` and `NumberFormat` are intuitive to use.

```
Locale locale = request.getLocale();
DateFormat df = DateFormat.getInstance();
Date d = df.parse(rb.getString("date"));
String date = DateFormat.getInstance().format(d);
```

First, a `Locale` object is obtained by invoking the `getLocale()` method of the request. This step is always required unless a custom method is being used to identify what language a user prefers. After initializing an appropriate `Locale` object the formatting class is initialized with the locale and passed the date or number to format. The returned value is a `String` object describing the date or number in the appropriate locale.

Both `DateFormat` and `NumberFormat` work as described above. Each object provides a `getInstance()` method that takes a `Locale` object as a parameter and returns an initialized instance of either `DateFormat` or `NumberFormat`. After an instance of the needed object is obtained, then the `format()` method is available to provide locale-specific string representations of either dates or numbers.

Formatting Messages Using MessageFormat

The `MessageFormat` class is a combination of the `DateFormat` and `NumberFormat` classes. A complete string with special tokens embedded in it can be formatted by the `MessageFormat` object into a locale-specific representation. The `MessageFormat` object does not translate text from one language into another; it only concatenates language-specific strings together with dynamic values.

It is helpful to use the `MessageFormat` class to avoid situations where using a resource bundle and a property file becomes tedious. Any page that contains a lot of dynamic and static content can be problematic to abstract via a property file. For instance, a page is designed to be custom-tailored to a specific user and to their locale. The English output of the page for a user named "foo" is shown in Figure 12-11.

The code for this page is problematic because of all the dynamic information being used. Recall with `welcome.jsp` the property file needed to contain key/value pairs: title and welcome. Figure 12-11 looks similar but because of the dynamic information, many more key/value pairs are required. The user's name, current date, and money information cannot be stored in a property file. Instead,

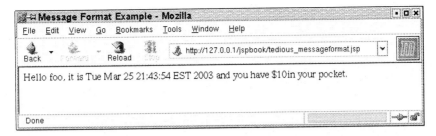

Figure 12-11 Browser Rendering of messageformat.jsp in English

the content must be broken up into smaller sections that can be stored in the property files. A property file describing these static sections would resemble Listing 12-15.

Listing 12-15 Property File for tedious_messageformat.jsp

```
message1=Hello
message2=, it is
message3= and you have $
message4= in your pocket.
```

The tedious part of using a property file for `tedious_messageformat.jsp` is that it requires a complex endpoint. Imagine a JSP designed to use Listing 12-15, and it would resemble Listing 12-16.

Listing 12-16 tedious_messageformat.jsp

```
<%@ page import="java.util.*"%>
<%
  Locale locale = request.getLocale();
  ResourceBundle  rb =
    ResourceBundle.getBundle("tedious_messageformat", locale);
  request.setAttribute("message1", rb.getString("message1"));
  request.setAttribute("message2", rb.getString("message2"));
  request.setAttribute("message3", rb.getString("message3"));
  request.setAttribute("message4", rb.getString("message4"));

  String name = "foo";
  Date date = new Date();
  Integer integer = new Integer(10);
  request.setAttribute("name", name);
  request.setAttribute("date", date);
```

```
    request.setAttribute("integer", integer);
%>
<%@ taglib uri="http://java.sun.com/jstl/core" prefix="c" %>
<html>
  <head>
    <title>Message Format Example</title>
  </head>
  <body>
  ${message1}${name}${message2}${date}
  ${message3}${integer}${message4}
  </body>
</html>
```

The preceding code illustrates when using simple property files and resource bundles, or the equivalent functionality, breaks down. The more dynamic bits of information in a page, the more complex the system becomes. The paragraph of content in the page needs to be broken into many different small chunks, each loaded and passed to the JSP View page. A common solution to the problem is to represent dynamic information with tokens, such as the format `MessageFormat` uses.

The `MessageFormat` class allows for pages such as `tedious_message format.jsp` to still be represented with a few strings, similar to `welcome.jsp`. This is accomplished by escaping dynamic information with tokens. The specific format is fully specified by the Java documentation for `java.text.Message Format`, but the basic format is to pass a string and a token of Java objects into a format method. The string contains a set of numbered tokens such as `{0}`, `{1}`, and `{2}`. Each token is replaced by the corresponding item in the array passed to the format method. For instance, the following code

```
String string = "Hello {0}, good {1}.";
Object[] objects = {"foo", "morning"};
String result = MessageFormat.format(string, objects);
```

ends up with the string result having the value `"Hello foo, good morning"`.

In addition to simple token replacement, the `MessageFormat` object also has direct support for the `DateFormat` and `NumberFormat` classes. A token can include additional information besides the entry number of the array of objects passed to the `format()` method. Date, time, and number options are available as defined in the API documentation for `java.text.MessageFormat`; reference the API documentation for specific information.

The method of specifying locale-specific numbers, times, or dates as tokens requires adding some extra information between the token's { and }. The index number of the array item is still the first argument. Optionally, additional information can be appended after the array index number with comma delimiters. The first argument added can specify if the token is a number, date, or time and further information can detail more information about the token. For instance, the following code

```
String string = "Hello {0}, it is {1,date} and you have {2, number,
currency} in your pocket.";
Object[] objects = {"foo", new Date(), new Integer(10)};
String result = MessageFormat.format(string, objects);
```

results in a string saying the equivalent of, "Hello foo, it is July 31, 2002 and you have $10.00 in your pocket", but formatted to your default locale and with the current date. The code is beneficial because the same array of objects can be passed to the equivalent string but translated in any language. For example, the English property file would have the same string shown in Listing 12-17 as a value to a key.

Listing 12-17 messageformat.properties

```
message=Hello {0}, it is {1,date} and you have {2, number, currency}
in your pocket.
```

Furthermore, a French property file would have the translated string that is the same as the earlier examples of using resource bundles, as shown in Listing 12-18.

Listing 12-18 messageformat_fr.properties

```
message=Bonjour {0}, c''est {1, date} et vous avez {2, number,
currency} dans votre poche.
```

Note the tokens are left verbatim because they are already in the format `MessageFormat` is expecting. The point to see with the two property files is that by using an object like `MessageFormat`, it is possible to avoid the tedious use of property files as illustrated in Listing 12-19. The i18n content with correctly formatted, dynamic numbers and dates is reduced to a few entries in a property file.

Listing 12-19 messageformat.jsp (Model 1½ Style)

```
<%@ page import="java.text.*, java.util.*"%>
<%
```

```
    Locale locale = request.getLocale();
    ResourceBundle rb =
      ResourceBundle.getBundle("messageformat", locale);
    Object[] objects = {"foo", new Date(), new Integer(10) };
    MessageFormat mf =
      new MessageFormat(rb.getString("message"), locale);
    String result = mf.format(objects);
    request.setAttribute("result", result);
%>
<%@ taglib uri="http://java.sun.com/jstl/core" prefix="c" %>
<html>
  <head>
    <title>Message Format Example</title>
  </head>
  <body>
  ${result}
  </body>
</html>
```

Before trying out the preceding code, save `messageformat.jsp` in the base directory of the jspbook Web Application and save `messageformat.properties` and `messageformat_fr.properties` in the `/WEB-INF/classes/` directory. Reload Tomcat for the changes to take effect and browse to `http://127.0.0.1/jspbook/` `messageformat.jsp`. Assuming your browser's language preference is English, Figure 12-12 displays an example. If your browser's language preference is set to French, Figure 12-13 would appear.

Understand why it is helpful to use an object such as `MessageFormat` to simplify handling dynamic i18n content. Numbers and dates can automatically be

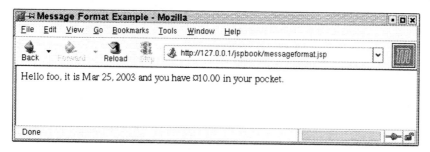

Figure 12-12 English Example of messageformat.jsp

Figure 12-13 French Example of messageformat.jsp

accurately translated on the fly. Abstracting this functionality into a set of objects saves the time and effort needed when coding the equivalent into an i18n application. The Java format classes do exist and work well, especially with the Java i18n framework and the Servlet API.

JSTL Number and Date Formatting Tags

The JSTL includes a complete set of i18n number and date formatting tags. The tags themselves are modeled directly off the `DateFormat`, `MessageFormat`, and `NumberFormat` classes and are straightforward to use. The benefit of using the JSTL i18n tags versus the Model 1½ code examples seen previously in this chapter, or a full-fledged Model 2 implementation, is that no extra code is required to load the appropriate resource bundle and populate request-scoped objects. However, the drawback to using the JSTL i18n tags is that you are always relying on resource bundles to satisfy your internationalization needs, which is a fairly good assumption since resource bundles are about as good of a solution as you will find.

JSTL Message Tag with Parameters

For completeness it is worth mentioning that the JSTL message tag, introduced earlier in this chapter, does use the `MessageFormat` object and so the JSTL resource bundle tags still work well when building a simple i18n Web application based off resource bundles. The third JSTL resource bundle tag not mentioned earlier is the `param` tag. The `param` tag allows for objects to be defined that are subsequently passed as an array of objects to the `MessageFormat` object's `format()` method. The order of items in the array is identical to the order `param` tags.

The `param` tag works as a child to the message tag. As you saw in Listing 12-8 previously, it was shown the message tag can reference a key of a loaded resource bundle. Should the value corresponding to this key be a string with `Message Format` tokens, then the tokens need `param` tags to define the corresponding objects. For example, Listing 12-20 is a modification of Listing 12-8, which uses only the JSTL to accomplish the same functionality.

Listing 12-20   jstl_messageformat.jsp

```
<%@ taglib uri="http://java.sun.com/jstl/fmt" prefix="fmt"%>
<fmt:bundle basename="messageformat">
<html>
  <head>
    <title></title>
  </head>
  <body>
  <%
    java.util.Date date = new java.util.Date();
    request.setAttribute("date", date);
  %>
  <fmt:message key="message">
    <fmt:param value="foo"/>
    <fmt:param value="${date}"/>
    <fmt:param value="${10}"/>
  </fmt:message>
  </body>
</html>
</fmt:bundle>
```

The `param` action is straightforward to use and sets the values needed by `MessageFormat`.

Summary

Internationalization is a serious issue when developing Web Applications that are truly for the global community. Building a successful i18n Web site revolves around three main issues: abstracting content, understanding content encoding, and formating numbers and dates to be locale-specific.

By abstracting content, more than one type of language can be used with an internationally friendly format. For instance, HTML formatting is the same regardless of language. Only the content embedded within the formatting is language-specific. By abstracting out this content, the same formatting can be repeatedly re-used with all of the languages the page is designed for. In this chapter two specific types of content abstraction were given: Model 2 and via the JSTL i18n message tags.

Content encoding is another critical issue to understand when developing an i18n-friendly Web Application. Core Web technologies, such as HTTP and HTML were built for use with the western European languages—ISO-8859-1 encoding. However, the world consists of more than just the western European countries. Unicode does exist and is starting to solve the problem, but for now it is important to ensure content generated in a non-ISO-8859-1 encoding is correctly sent and retrieved from a client.

The final issue covered in this chapter is how to format numbers and dates to locale-specific formats. In many cases the information for numbers and dates is identical in different languages but formatted differently. In these cases there isn't any need to keep completely separate copies of the content for different languages. The same content can be re-used with the correct formatting applied.

Chapter 13

Multi-Client Support

The goal of most Web sites is to build something everyone can see; there are many different types of software used to visit Web pages. When building static Web sites, there is no option apart from building something that everyone hopefully can see. Dynamic Web sites alleviate this problem by allowing content to be generated at runtime, specific to a particular client. By taking advantage of dynamic functionality, it is possible to build something everyone can correctly see.

The term "multi-client" means that there are multiple different types of clients visiting a Web site. Most commonly, developers only think of a Web site as HTML and assume a client is using some software that can view HTML. However, this practice does not always work because HTML is not the only technology used on the Web, and even if it were, there are still problems to be addressed. First, consider the fact that there are different versions of HTML. This alone implies that software exists with varying support for the different versions of HTML. Coding for full backwards-compatibility with HTML 1.0 is not very helpful because it prevents taking advantage of the current HTML features. The only good options are to try and support all of the different versions of HTML or to selectively support a version of HTML the majority of users are able to use.

Now consider all of the other technologies besides HTML. Many technologies exist to complement HTML, technologies such as Cascading Style Sheets, ECMAScript, and the Document Object Model, and many technologies exist that can replace HTML such as XHTML, XML, MS Word, and Adobe's Portable Document Format (PDF). Choosing only to support basic HTML greatly limits the type of content JSP can deliver to users. Likewise, choosing only to support formats such as MS Word limits the number of users able to be served. What this chapter is about is using Servlets and JSP in a fashion that allows tailoring to multiple different types of clients.

This chapter discusses the following topics:

- Who this chapter is for: multi-client design is nice, but not usually a necessity.
- Separating format from content.
- Templates: quick and dirty multi-client support.
- Transformations: robust but harder to implement multi-client support.
- Solving common multi-client problems: making an abstract interface, client detection, and URL encoding.
- Producing non-text formats.

Similar to the other chapters, this chapter is intended to be read straight through; however, this chapter is not critical to developing Servlet- and JSP-based projects, nor do you need the material to understand the rest of the book. What is presented in this chapter is how to make one set of content produce several formats, such as HTML, XHTML, PDF, and so on. Besides being able to produce more than one format, several helpful programming techniques arise from the concepts presented by this chapter and are explained for use. In general, this chapter covers a topic that is currently becoming popular in the world of Servlets and JSP, but is not commonly considered a necessity. Read this chapter if you want to learn more about the trend of abstracting presentation logic.

Who Should Read This Chapter

Before continuing further it is important to understand who this chapter is aimed at helping. In general, a good multi-client design is beneficial for any Web site. The reasons are the same as designing a Web site with international issues in mind. The functionality provided does not hinder anything previously developed; it only expands how easily the site can grow to support future clients. In the case of internationalization, a Web site can more easily grow to support different languages. With multi-client design, a Web site can more easily grow to support different content formats.

How a multi-client design works is the same as the suggested approach to internationalization: add a proper layer of abstraction to the logic required for the functionality. The only drawback to adding a layer of abstraction is that some extra time and effort are required when initially designing the application. The goal of this chapter is to clearly explain and expedite the process of designing a multi-client-compatible Web site. This is done by explaining commonly used techniques and by providing examples. However, this does not mean every single Web Application should be designed multi-client-compatible. If a project has the luxury of only requiring one specific format, then by all means only build that format. For the majority of projects that do not have this luxury, a good multi-client design is a necessity.

Separating Format from Content

A multi-client design relies on separating formatting logic from the content generation. By separating out formatting logic it is possible to abstract that logic behind a common interface. The common interface can then be used freely while the formatting it produces is specialized as needed. As applied to Servlets and JSP, separating format from content and then abstracting formatting can be a very easy process, especially when following a Model 2 design.

Recall with Model 2 the emphasis is on removing all business logic from presentation logic. In practice this means breaking a Web Application into two parts. One part handles all business logic, such as querying a database, logging, or validating information, and creates the dynamic content required for a presentation component. The presentation component is then the second part of the Web Application; it takes the dynamic content, formats it along with static content, and produces a response for a client. When implemented as suggested, the business logic is coded in either a Servlet or Filter, and the presentation logic is a JSP. Communicating between the two components is a custom Java object, usually a JavaBean.

The Model 2 design pattern is important for multi-client design because it eliminates any redundancy of business logic. Presentation logic is completely handled by a JSP—for example, the HTML formatting applied to dynamic content. Separating out formatting logic is then trivial and can be done in a few different ways, specifically, either templates or transformation. The point is illustrated in Listing 13-1.

Listing 13-1 A Model 2 Presentation JSP

```
<html>
<head>
  <title>Model 2 Multi-Client Example</title>
</head>
<body>
<image src="logo.png">
<h1>Welcome ${user.name} to the example!</h1>
<p>This webpage is an example of the type of page you'd see from a
```

```
Model 2 Web Application. No business logic on the page!
</body>
</html>
```

Highlighted in Listing 13-1 is the formatting. The important point is that all of this formatting is the responsibility of the JSP. Dynamic information generated by the business logic is not assuming anything about the formatting: it is only providing the correct user name for the JSP to display. The JSP is responsible for taking all content, both static and dynamic, and formatting it correctly for a client to see.

This is helpful because it means a different format can be applied with minimal effort. For example, imagine the Web site is current with technology trends and provides content in both HTML and XHTML formats. Listing 13-1 formats the content into HTML; formatting into XHTML only requires one more additional JSP. Listing 13-2 is an example of the XHTML formatting JSP.

Listing 13-2 An XHTML Model 2 Presentation JSP

```
<html>
<head>
  <title>Model 2 Multi-Client Example</title>
</head>
<body>
<img src="logo.png"/>
<h1>Welcome ${user.name} to the example!</h1>
<p>This webpage is an example of the type of page you'd see from a
Model 2 Web Application. No business logic on the page!</p>
</body>
</html>
```

Note the two formats chosen in this case are similar. This is on purpose to keep the example simple. It is important to see that Listing 13-1 is not valid XHTML; it is HTML. The corrections to make it valid XHTML are minor: a `</p>` and an ending `/` for the `img` tag; however, the end result a client sees is a page in a distinctly different format. How the application would work is by detecting which type of format a client needs and using the correct JSP. Should it be an HTML client, then the business logic is performed and the response presented by Listing 13-1. Should the client request XHTML, the business logic is performed, and the response is presented by Listing 13-2. Either case the same business logic is executed. Also, future formats can be added by creating new JSP.

In essence, this is exactly what multi-client formatting is all about: isolating formatting logic and abstracting it. However, there are some important issues to consider when implementing a multi-client design. The code that is shown in Listing 13-1 and Listing 13-2, respectively, only works for text-based formatting and if the content is in one language. These are not limitations of Servlets or JSP; they are only limitations of how the example was implemented. In the rest of the chapter we will show how a proper multi-client implementation can allow for any binary format, including non-text. We will also explain how a good multi-client design complements a good internationalization design, meaning i18n-compatible sites available in multiple formats!

Implementing Multi-Client Support

There are a few techniques commonly used to provide multi-client support. Many approaches work, but it is desirable to have a multi-client design that supports the following:

- **Eliminates redundancy:** If something is only needed once, only use it once. Both static text and non-formatting-related code fall into this category. A good solution should not require multiple copies of the same code. If multiple copies of text or code exist, maintenance becomes more difficult because a change to one of the copies requires a change to all. This is the primary reason why a Model 2 design provides a good place to implement multi-client support. Should a JSP embed business logic, such as a user login check, each JSP presentation page would need to have a copy of the code. A simple change to one of the pages would require a change to all of the pages.

  A good multi-client design eliminates all redundancy. Relevant code, formatting, and text should appear only once.

- **Cleanly extensible:** The reason for implementing a multi-client design is to allow for more than one type of content formatting. Restricting to a set number of formats is no better than restricting to the original single format. A good multi-client design provides a framework for implementing any type of formatting that might be required both now and in the future. Formats should also be cleanly separate from each other. Manipulating one format should not affect others.

- **Easy to use:** A good multi-client design should be easy to use. JSP is a powerful tool because it is simple. The markup associated with a JSP is easier to understand than Java code, especially by developers unfamiliar with Java. Moving away from the simplicity of JSP defeats the purpose of using the technology, as with Servlets.

Supporting all of these features is certainly possible with Servlets and JSP. In practice a good multi-client design is just a specific implementation of a good Model 2 design. As mentioned previously the Model 2 pattern provides a method of consolidating business logic and keeping it separate from presentation code. This is good because with multi-client support the emphasis is on specializing presentation code. Therefore, by starting with a Model 2 design, half of the Web application is already finished. What is left is customizing the presentation code to produce multiple formats. There are two methods of accomplishing this: templates and transformations.

Templates

The term *template* refers to creating a JSP formatting template that content is pushed through. Creating support for a new format can then be accomplished by creating a new template. In practice this approach requires building a set of JSP for each format required. Figure 13-1 shows what the high-level design looks like.

An important point to note in Figure 13-1 is there are multiple possible JSP endpoints to a request. The different endpoints generate the equivalent pages but in different formats. The number of endpoints is the number of formats desired. Because of the extra endpoints a slight modification needs to be made to the Filter or Servlet responsible for business logic. Instead of always assuming a single endpoint, the Control component needs to selectively forward to the JSP responsible for the specific format.

The code for selectively forwarding can easily be done by using a fictitious URL and some browser client-detection code. For instance, a Filter can be used to intercept all requests to the Web Application. Requests for the fictitious URL ending with .html are forwarded to an HTML-formatting JSP; requests for the fictitious URL ending with .xhtml are forwarded to an XHTML-formatting JSP. As long as the JSP template pages follow a common naming scheme, the solution is simple to implement. Consider a Web site using Listing 13-1 and Listing 13-2 for different formatting and a Filter to encapsulate all business logic. The code for the Filter is provided in Listing 13-3.

Listing 13-3 MCTemplateFilter.java

```
package com.jspbook;

import java.io.*;
import java.util.*;
```

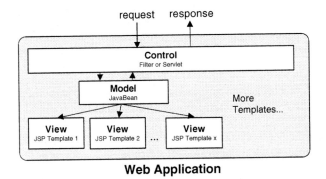

Figure 13-1 Multi-Client Support via Templates

```java
import javax.servlet.*;
import javax.servlet.http.*;

public class MCTemplateFilter implements Filter {
  FilterConfig fc = null;

  public void doFilter(ServletRequest req,
                       ServletResponse res,
    FilterChain chain) throws IOException, ServletException {

    HttpServletRequest request = (HttpServletRequest) req;
    String uri = request.getRequestURI();
    String client = "HTML";
    if (uri.endsWith("xhtml")) {
      client = "XHTML";
    }

    // business logic...
    HashMap user = new HashMap();
    user.put("name", "Bruce");
    request.setAttribute("user", user);

    ServletContext sc = fc.getServletContext();
    sc.getRequestDispatcher("/mc/MCexample"+client+".jsp").
      forward(request, res);

  }
```

```
public void init(FilterConfig filterConfig) {
  fc = filterConfig;
}

public void destroy() {
  fc = null;
}
}
```

Save Listing 13-3 as `MCTemplateFilter.java` in the `/WEB-INF/classes/com/jspbook` directory of the jspbook Web Application. Save Listing 13-1 and Listing 13-2 as `MCexampleHTML.jsp` and `MCexampleXHTML.jsp`, respectively, in the `/mc` directory of the jspbook Web Application. The Filter is designed to intercept a request and direct it to either the HTML or XHTML template depending on the ending of the URL.

```
String uri = request.getRequestURI();
String client = "HTML";
if (uri.endsWith("xhtml")) {
  client = "XHTML";
}
```

By default the client variable is set to HTML, meaning the HTML version of the page will be shown. Should the URL end with ".xhtml", then the XHTML version of the page is shown. Later in the Filter, in lieu of invoking `chain.doFilter()`, the request is forwarded to the correct JSP.

```
ServletContext sc = fc.getServletContext();
sc.getRequestDispatcher("/mc/MCexample"+client+".jsp").

    forward(request, res);
```

The correct JSP is determined by using the begining of the page name, `"MCexample"`, appending either HTML or XHTML, and finally ".jsp".

Try out the code example by deploying `MCTemplateFilter.java` to filter all requests to the `/mc` directory.

```
<filter>
  <filter-name>MCTemplateFilter</filter-name>
  <filter-class>com.jspbook.MCTemplateFilter</filter-class>
</filter>
<filter-mapping>
  <filter-name>MCTemplateFilter</filter-name>
  <url-pattern>/mc/*</url-pattern>
</filter-mapping>
```

After deploying the Filter, reload the jspbook Web Application and browse to `http://127.0.0.1/jspbook/mc/MCexample.html`. The page shown is the HTML version, `MCexampleHTML.jsp`. Listing 13-4 is the code generated for the response.

Listing 13-4   Response from MCexampleHTML.jsp

```
<html>
<head>
  <title>Model 2 Multi-Client Example</title>
</head>
<body>
<img src="logo.png">
<h1>Welcome Bruce to the example!</h1>
<p>This webpage is an example of the type of page you'd see from
a Model 2 Web Application. No business logic on the page!
</body>
</html>
```

The response is the HTML version of the page. Next, try browsing to `http://127.0.0.1/jspbook/mc/MCexample.xhtml`. The response returned this time is the XHTML version of the page. Listing 13-5 shows the code returned in the response.

Listing 13-5   Response Generated by MCexampleXHTML.jsp

```
<html>
<head>
  <title>Model 2 Multi-Client Example</title>
</head>
<body>
<img src="logo.png"/>
<h1>Welcome Bruce to the example!</h1>
<p>This webpage is an example of the type of page you'd see from
a Model 2 Web Application. No business logic on the page!</p>
</body>
</html>
```

This time the code is returned in XHTML format; note that browser renderings of the results are not used because they would look identical. The example illustrates how a template system can be created for a Web site. Formats are detected by the URL extension and one main Filter intercepts all requests and directs them to the proper resource.

The preceding example can be expanded to create a Filter that detects more than just HTML and XHTML support. In the request headers a client sends is the `user-agent` field. This header contains information about the software a client is using to visit a site. The `user-agent` header can be mined to determine if the client is using Mozilla, Internet Explorer, Netscape, or any other popular Web browser and custom-tailor a page specifically to that browser. For instance, if a user is using Internet Explorer, a Web page can be custom-tailored to take advantage of MS-specific Windows features. Likewise, if a client is using Mozilla, the response can take advantage of XUL[1]. Any number of formats can be supported. All that is required is a set of JSP templates to produce the correct format.

Benefits and Drawbacks of Templates

The benefit of templates is that they are easy to and intuitive to create, especially for markup language formats. JSP already excels at producing these formats, and most authors know how to use JSP to make them. The drawback to using a template is each format requires a new JSP. The JSP clutter a Web Application, but more importantly multiple copies tempt a developer to put redundant content in the templates. For instance, in Listing 13-1 and Listing 13-2 only part of the content is dynamic, the name of the user. The rest of the content on the page is copied directly, leaving two copies of the same information. Should the HTML template be changed, the same changes would need to be applied to the XHTML template.

Solving the problem of redundant content on templates requires some work. The solution is to treat all text as if it is dynamic and pull the content from one central location. Static content is then consolidated into one place and more easily maintained. Template pages end up looking like the examples from the internationalization chapter. Listing 13-6 shows what Listing 13-1 might look like should the page be authored in this fashion.

Listing 13-6   Consolidated Content

```
<html>
<head>
  <title>${content.title}</title>
</head>
<body>
<img src="logo.png">
<h1>${content.welcome}</h1>
```

---

1. XUL is an HTML replacement technology designed by the Mozilla developers (http://www.mozilla.org). The technology is similar to HTML, but uses XML and JavaScript to create a much more robust development tool.

```
<p>${content.intro}
</body>
</html>
```

Notice how all of the content, both static and dynamic, has been replaced with JSP expressions. The expressions display dynamic values from a scoped object named `content`; assume the values correspond to the text needed for the title of the page, the welcome message, and the introduction.

By consolidating code, as shown in Listing 13-6, the problem of redundant content is eliminated. All content can be stored in one central location and passed to JSP View components as needed. This solution also allows for easy integration of multiple languages for internationalization purposes.

There is only one major fault to using templates for multi-client support: fitting content to a template. A problem arises when content does not fit a template. In contrived examples the content always has nice places to fit between the formatting, such as Listing 13-6. In practice there are cases where formatting does not fit. For example, consider the following HTML paragraph.

```
<p>this is a paragraph authored in HTML.
```

Abstracted to a template it could be reduced to the following:

```
<p>${paragraph}
```

The problem arises should formatting need to be embedded in the paragraph such as a link in the middle of the text:

```
<p>this is a paragraph with a <a href="foo.html">link</a> in it.
```

Abstracting to a template as previously done no longer works for non-HTML formats. The link would literally appear as "`<a href="foo.html">link</a>`" in the middle of a PDF or MS Word document. This problem is the bane of using templates as a full multi-client solution. Templates still work if the problem is purposely avoided, but a truly robust multi-client design requires a full transformation from an intermediate format into the final format.

Transformations

A *transformation* is a more complex but more robust multi-client solution compared to templates. The difference between a template and a transformation is the transformation uses an interface, or pseudo-format, to cleanly abstract the final format. When a client requests a particular format, the pseudo-format, along with content, is transformed into the final result. A commonly used trans-

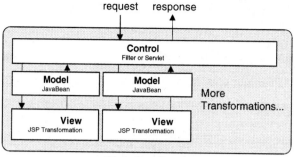

request   response

Control
Filter or Servlet

Model
JavaBean

Model
JavaBean

More
Transformations...

View
JSP Transformation

View
JSP Transformation

Web Application

Figure 13-2   Transformations

formation is to represent a document using Java objects, then to write output streams that rely on the Java objects as input. The Java objects are the abstract interface, and the output stream performs the transformations. Figure 13-2 illustrates the concept as applied to a Model 2 Web Application.

Note that Figure 13-2 only has a single endpoint instead of the many required by templates. With transformations only one endpoint is required because the endpoint is the content with pseudo-formatting. The actual transformation into the final format is done elsewhere.

Transformations are an ideal solution to multi-client design because of the clean abstraction they provide for formatting. Consider the one serious flaw with templates: making content fit to the template. With transformations this is not an issue because the pseudo-format can freely be used. For instance, consider the following transformation JSP:

```
<%@ taglib uri="transformation tags..." prefix="t"%>
<t:h1>A Title</t:h1>
<t:p>Some paragraph with information.</t:p>
```

Note no static formatting is used; all formatting is done via custom tags. The JSP transforms by using the custom tags. If the preceding code was being converted into HTML, the custom tags would output the equivalent HTML formatting, likewise for XHTML or any other format.

Recall the problem with templates was formatting that appears in content. In the case of transformations this is not a problem because all formatting is part of the multi-client interface. For instance, the equivalent of the problematic template would be the following as a transformation JSP:

```
<%@ taglib uri="transformation tags..." prefix="t"%>
<t:h1>A Title</t:h1>
<t:p>Some paragraph with a <t:link url="foo.html">link</t:link> in
it.</t:p>
```

The link is in the same place, but note it is a custom tag. Like the other custom tags, the link tag would be responsible for generating the correct formatting at runtime. Since the link is not static HTML, there is no issue of it conflicting with non-HTML formats.

Implementing Transformations

There are a few good existing approaches to implementing transformations with Servlets and JSP. The common approaches are to use JSP custom tags to abstract all formatting or to use JSP to produce a standard format and have a Filter transform the result. Here are some techniques and frameworks to be aware of:

- **FOP:** Formatting Objects Processor (FOP) is a framework designed to take XSL Formatting Objects, `http://www.w3.org/TR/2001/REC-xsl-20011015/`, and convert them into a number of different output formats. The framework primarily supports PDF, but has partial support for many other formats. The idea behind FOP is great, but not related at all to Servlets and JSP. However, since the framework is authored in Java, it is easy to use JSP to produce XSL-FO and have a Filter execute FOP on the response. More information can be found on FOP at `http://xml.apache.org/fop`.

- **Cocoon:** Cocoon is a framework built by the Apache Jakarta community and is designed to pipeline XML information through templates and/or transformations. The framework allows for JSP as a starting point, but is really more of a JSP alternative. What Cocoon does is take a starting XML document and apply a number of XSLT transformations to it. Cocoon also supports FOP for transformations on XSL-FO. Further information can be found about Cocoon at `http://xml.apache.org/cocoon/index.html`.

- **Multi-Client Tags:** The Multi-Client Tags framework is an attempt at making the simplest possible multi-client interface. The project is centered around a simple HTML-like set of custom tags and Cascading Style Sheets. The project is simple to learn (literally takes five minutes) and generates HTML, XHTML, PDF, and printer-friendly formats. Further information about the Multi-Client Tags (MCT) can be found at `http://www.jspinsider.com/jspkit/mct/`.

Transformations are the best method of providing multi-client support. As so, it is worth examining further to see how transformations can be implemented with Servlets and JSP. For further examples in this chapter we will be using the Multi-Client Tags project from JSP Insider, `http://www.jspinsider.com`. This project is ideal for demonstration as it is geared to be simple and intuitive for a JSP developer. It is also open source and under a liberal license.

Installing the Multi-Client Tags

Before continuing further you will need to download the JSP Insider Multi-Client Tags for later examples in this chapter. Download the example WAR from `http://www.jspinsider.com/jspkit/mct/ji-mct.war`. Deploy the WAR by placing it in the `/webapps` directory of your Tomcat installation and reloading Tomcat. The WAR automatically deploys itself to the `/webapps/ji-mct` directory of Tomcat.

The example Web Application is much like the Struts WAR file used in Chapter 12. When starting from scratch, the MCT WAR is ideal because it pre-installs all of the needed components and configuration files for the framework. However, should you need to install the MCT with an existing Web Application, consult the installation documentation at `http://www.jspinsider.com/jspkit/mct/`.

Solving Multi-Client Problems

Implementing multi-client support revolves around finding good solutions to multi-client problems. In the following sections the common multi-client problems are outlined and solved with an example base of the MCT. The common problems consist of defining a good interface for transformations, detecting client types, and providing non-text formats.

Creating a Multi-Client Interface

A multi-client interface is the intermediate format to which all of the other formats are derived from. It is important to have a robust interface defined in order not to restrict what type of formats the interface can be used to define. It is also important for the interface to be easy to use or else multi-client support becomes a hassle to implement. For our interface we will re-use the simple interface defined by the Multi-Client Tags.

The Multi-Client Tags are modeled directly after HTML and include a few tags that allow for text, tables, links, and images to be defined on a page. The tags are as follows:

- **page:** The page tag is used to represent the common header and footer of a page. All other MCT tags must be used as child elements of this tag. Only one instance of the page tag is allowed to appear per page.

- **p:** The paragraph tag, p, is used identically at the HTML paragraph tag. Text that is surrounded by the tag automatically has line breaks inserted. The tag is a convenient method of applying styles to specific chunks of text.

- **c:** The character tag, c, is used like the HTML span tag. Text surrounded by the tag has the tag's style applied to it. The character tag differs from the paragraph tag in that it does not insert a line break before and after the text it styles.

- **link:** The link tag provides a method of embedding links, should they be supported, in a document. In formats such as HTML the link tag acts identically to an anchor tag.

- **image:** The image tag provides a method of embedding external images into a document. In the case of HTML this is identical to the image, img, tag. In other formats, such as PDF, an image is embedded in a best effort attempt to match.

- **table:** The table tag is analogous to the HTML table tag. This tag allows for structured formatting in a document by means of segmenting a page into rows and columns.

- **tr:** The tr tag is analogous to the HTML table row tag, tr. The tag must be used as a child tag of a table and defines rows of that table.

- **tc:** The tc tag is analogous to the HTML table division tag, td. The tag must be used as a child tag of a table row and defines divisions of that row.

Most of the MCT tags are fairly intuitive and work identically to the HTML equivalents. This is because the tags primarily generate HTML, and most JSP developers are already very familiar with HTML. However, what is important is that this interface is able to support all the features needed. For instance, these tags allow for text, links, images, and tables. For most practical purposes this is perfectly fine; however, should more functionality be required, additional tags would need to be made.

Complementing all of the tags are attributes and styling rules in compliance with Cascading Style Sheets (CSS). CSS is a technology defined by the W3C to style HTML elements. The same HTML CSS rules apply to MCT tags. Together, the small set of custom tags and CSS rules provide an adequate multi-client interface for the most common needs of a Web site.

The MCT interface is intuitive to use for anyone with HTML experience. In most respects it is exactly like authoring an HTML-producing JSP, but the tags on the page need to be MCT markup. Take, for example, the following JSP. Save Listing 13-7 as `HelloWorld.jsp` in the base directory of the `/ji-mct` Web Application.

Listing 13-7 Multi-Client-Compatible HelloWorld

```
<page>
<p style="font-size:20pt; color:blue;">HelloWorld!</p>
</page>
```

The page is a "Hello World" equivalent to the first Servlet and JSP examples of this book. The difference is this example is using a set of multi-client custom tags. At runtime the tags dynamically generate the appropriate format a client desires to view. Try browsing to `http://127.0.0.1/ji-mct/HelloWorld.html` to see the HTML version. Likewise, an XHTML, PDF, or text format of the same content can be viewed by browsing to the same URL but with a `.xhtml`, `.pdf`, or `.txt` extension, respectively. Figure 13-3 shows a browser rendering of the HTML version using a Web browser.

The XHTML version of `HelloWorld.jsp` renders the same as Figure 13-3; you can check the source code to see the difference. The PDF version requires special software to view the format but also looks alike. Figure 13-4 shows the PDF version rendered by Adobe's browser PDF viewer plug-in, `http://www.adobe.com`.

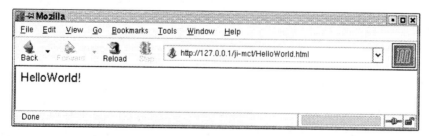

Figure 13-3 Browser Rendering of HelloWorld.jsp

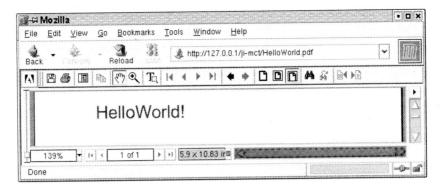

Figure 13-4 PDF Plug-in Rendering of HelloWorld.jsp

Note that PDF is a print-quality format. The multi-client "Hello World" can be printed picture perfect as it appears in Figure 13-4, although the functionality is more helpful when a tutorial or article is authored via multi-client tags. The text format is a simple form that almost everyone can view. Figure 13-5 shows a browser rendering of HelloWorld.jsp as rendered in text.

All of these formats work and only one simple JSP is producing them! The URL extensions are fictitious and managed by a Filter that intercepts requests to the Web Application. Eventually, everything is directed to HelloWorld.jsp. The power of using a good multi-client framework should now be obvious. With a simple custom tag interface it is possible to easily create pages available in many different formats. This allows for seamless support of proprietary formats, old software, and printer-friendly content.

Figure 13-5 Text Rendering of HelloWorld.jsp

Transformations

A good interface is only half of a multi-client framework. The code behind the interface needs to be able to support multiple formats and do a good job of it. The magic of the MCT framework comes from a transformer class that pipes MCT content through different handler classes, as shown in Listing 13-8.

Listing 13-8 Multi-Client Version of a "Hello World" Page

```
<page>
<p style="font-size:20pt; color:blue;">HelloWorld!</p>
</page>
```

Listing 13-9 shows the desired HTML output.

Listing 13-9 HTML Output from the Multi-Client "Hello World" Page

```
<html>
<p style="color:blue;font-size:20pt;">HelloWorld!</p>
</html>
```

Note the content in both cases is the same; the text does not change. Only the formatting before and after bits of content needs to be changed. In the case text markup, it is simple enough to implement this functionality via Java.

```
// before content
out.write("<html>");
out.write(content);
// after content
out.write("</html>");
```

The trick is being able to parse the MCT content and know when a starting tag, ending tag, or content is present. Given what you know about the MCT syntax, it should seem simple enough to start coding such a parser; however, the parser is a component that can be expected to come with the MCT framework. The MCT framework comes with such a parser. The parser only expects MCT developers code "handler" classes—Java code that takes events, such as tag start and tag stop—to generate the appropriate markup.

After seeing one MCT handler class, it is intuitive how they work and how you could code new ones. Listing 13-10 is the code for the MCT's default HTML handler—that is, the class that converts MCT syntax to HTML markup.

Listing 13-10 HtmlHandler.java

```java
package com.jspinsider.jspkit.mct;

public class HtmlHandler extends AbstractHandler {
  public void startTag(int uri, Attributes attributes)
    throws Exception {
    switch (uri) {
      case P: {
        write("<p"+style.getInline()+">");
        break;
      }
      case C: {
        write("<span"+style.getInline()+">");
        break;
      }
      case PAGE: {
        if (!includes) {
          write("<html"+style.getInline()+">");
        }
        break;
      }
      case IMAGE: {
        String u = (String)attributes.get("uri");
        if (u == null)
          break;
        if (u.startsWith("file:"))
          u = u.substring(5,u.length());
        write("<img src=\""+u+"\""+style.getInline());
        String align = style.getProperty("align");
        if (align != null) {
          write(" align=\""+align+"\"");
        }
        write(">");
        break;
      }
      case LINK: {
        String u = (String)attributes.get("uri");
        startLink(u);
        break;
      }
      case TABLE: {
        write("<table"+style.getInline()+">");
        break;
```

```
      }
      case TR: {
        write("<tr"+style.getInline()+">");
        break;
      }
      case TC: {
        write("<td"+style.getInline()+">");
        break;
      }
      default: {
        break;
      }
    }
  }

  protected void startLink(String u) throws Exception {
    MultiClientConfig mcc = MultiClientFilter.getConfig();
    String localRedirect = "";
    String prefix = ".html";
    if (u.indexOf(".") != -1) {
      prefix = "";
    }
    String href = u+prefix;

    // get the link rewriter
    try {
      Object o = Class.forName(mcc.getProperty(
"com.jspinsider.jspkit.mct.MultiClientRewriter")).newInstance();
      if (!(o instanceof MultiClientRewriter)) {
        throw new Exception(
        "Class does not implement MultiClientRewriter.");
      }

      MultiClientRewriter mcr = (MultiClientRewriter)o;
      href = mcr.rewrite(href);
    }
    catch (ClassNotFoundException e) {
      //ignore
    }
    catch (InstantiationException e) {
      // noop
    }
```

```
    catch (IllegalAccessException e) {
      // noop
    }
    write("<a href=\""+href+"\""+style.getInline()+">");
}

public void endTag(int uri) throws Exception {
  switch (uri) {
    case P: {
      write("</p>");
      break;
    }
    case C: {
      write("</span>");
      break;
    }
    case PAGE: {
      if (!includes) {
        write("</html>");
      }
      break;
    }
    case IMAGE: {
      //noop
      break;
    }
    case LINK: {
      write("</a>");
      break;
    }
    case TABLE: {
      write("</table>");
      break;
    }
    case TR: {
      write("</tr>");
      break;
    }
    case TC: {
      write("</td>");
      break;
    }
```

```
      default: {
        break;
      }
    }
  }
}
```

There are several important parts of the `HtmlHandler` class. First, the class extends the `com.jspinsider.jspkit.mct.AbstractHandler` class. The `AbstractHandler` class provides everything the parser needs: a method for writing content, a method for firing a start tag event, and a method for firing an end tag event.

```
package com.jspinsider.jspkit.mct;

public class HtmlHandler extends AbstractHandler {
  public void startTag(int uri, Attributes attributes)
    throws Exception {
  ...
  }

  public void endTag(int uri) throws Exception {
  ...
  }
}
```

The content writing method is implicitly implemented by the `AbstractHandler` class. The method can be overridden, but it will be left as an exercise you can try on your own. More important are the `startTag()` and `endTag()` methods, highlighted in the preceding code snippet. The `startTag()` method is fired each time a new MCT tag is parsed. The `endTag()` method is fired when an ending tag is parsed. The arguments for each method include an integer value that specifies which MCT tag was parsed.

Examine the `startTag()` method more closely to see how the functionality is expected for use.

```
  public void startTag(int uri, Attributes attributes)
    throws Exception {
    switch (uri) {
      case P: {
        write("<p"+style.getInline()+">");
        break;
      }
      case C: {
```

```
      write("<span"+style.getInline()+">");
      break;
  }
  case PAGE: {
    if (!includes) {
      write("<html"+style.getInline()+">");
    }
    break;
  }
...
```

The integer value, `uri`, is used by a switch statement. Each of the different cases appropriately translates the MCT syntax into the appropriate output format. For example, the `P` case, the static integer defined for the `p` tag (paragraph), generates HTML markup for a paragraph.

```
case P: {
  write("<p"+style.getInline()+">");
  break;
}
```

Likewise, in the `endTag()` method the switch case for `P`, a paragraph, generates the complementary HTML.

```
public void endTag(int uri) throws Exception {
  switch (uri) {
    case P: {
      write("</p>");
      break;
    }
...
```

Together the `startTag()` and `endTag()` methods can be used to generate formatting. In the case of the `startTag()` method, an object representing the tag's attributes is also passed.

The `HtmlHandler` class is not the only handler that comes with the MCT framework. All of the default-supported formats have a handler class and you can find the source code in the `com.jspinsider.jspkit.mct` package of the Multi-Client Tags framework. Bringing all of the handler classes together is a Servlet Filter. The Filter handles HTTP requests, generates MCT syntax by forwarding requests to JSP, and pipes MCT syntax through handler classes. The complete code can be found in the `com.jspinsider.jspkit.mct` class; however, the snippet in Listing 13-11 enables you to see what the Filter is doing.

Listing 13-11 Snippet of MCT Servlet Filter

```
       // Get the response (i.e., MCT synatx)
       CacheResponseWrapper crw =
  new CacheResponseWrapper((HttpServletResponse)response, buffer);
       sc.getRequestDispatcher(
         getURI(request)).forward(request, crw);
       // get byte array representing content
       byte[] content = buffer.toByteArray();
```

```
       // Make SAX Handler
       SAXParserFactory spf =
         SAXParserFactory.newInstance();
       SAXParser sp = spf.newSAXParser();
```

```
       // wrap appropriately for the client
       switch (client.getType()) {
         ...
         case MultiClient.HTML : {
           HtmlHandler h = new HtmlHandler();
           h.setOutputStream(out);
           sp.parse(new ByteArrayInputStream(content), h);
           h.flush();
           break;
         }
```

The Filter first buffers the content of a JSP, assumed to be in MCT syntax.

```
       CacheResponseWrapper crw =
         new CacheResponseWrapper(
           (HttpServletResponse)response, buffer);
       sc.getRequestDispatcher(
         getURI(request)).forward(request, crw);
       // get byte array representing content
       byte[] content = buffer.toByteArray();
```

The technique is identical to the cache Filter coded in Chapter 8. The response is wrapped and a custom Servlet `OutputStream` is used to buffer the response.

Next, a parser is created and the content is parsed using an MCT handler class.

```
SAXParserFactory spf =
    SAXParserFactory.newInstance();
SAXParser sp = spf.newSAXParser();

// wrap appropriately for the client
switch (client.getType()) {
    ...
    case MultiClient.HTML : {
        HtmlHandler h = new HtmlHandler();
        h.setOutputStream(out);
        sp.parse(new ByteArrayInputStream(content), h);
        h.flush();
        break;
    }
```

The HTML case is illustrated by the preceding code. The previously buffered response is parsed by a SAXParser class (a Java API XML parser) and handled by the HtmlHandler class. The output stream for the handler is set to be the response to a client—meaning the HTML content is sent as the response to the request. The end result is that JSP content, assumed to generate MCT syntax, gets piped selectively through a handler class and the result is displayed to a client.

The important point is that multi-client syntax, MCT syntax in this case, is transformed to a format a client wants. From our perspective, it doesn't really matter how this is done as long as it gets done correctly—which is what the MCT framework is doing. However, it is helpful to have a good idea of how the internals of the MCT framework work. If you want to extend or implement your own multi-client framework, it is a good place to start.

With the MCT framework installed, you are set to start coding pages. All of the material covered in the previous chapters can be used; however, now instead of assuming HTML syntax, use MCT syntax. There is little point in rehashing all of the previous chapters with an MCT syntax example; it will be up to you to play around with the new functionality[2]. However, it should be clear as to why a multi-client framework is helpful. The only thing content developers, traditionally HTML developers, need to care about is coding to the multi-client interface—that is, the MCT tags. By doing this, your Web Application seamlessly supports HTML, XHTML, PDF, and any other format you can code a transformer for.

---

2. In Chapter 15 a complete Web Application is built. The Web Application uses the MCT for multi-client support and is a great place to look for code examples.

Detecting Client Types

A multi-client design is great for supporting the latest and greatest formats and keeping support for other required formats. Initially, the multi-client design can be designed to support a possibly bland, but required, technology. Later on, new specialized formats can be added as desired. The trick to making a multi-client design stretches beyond knowing how to generate many different formats. With more than one format the problem arises of how to appropriately detect which format a client wants or which format a client should be given.

As illustrated previously in Listing 13-3, there is one very direct method of ensuring a multi-client design generates the appropriate format. Simply encode URLs to be distinctly different for different formats. The method illustrated was to change the extension of a URL based on the type of format desired—that is, `.html` generates HTML, `.pdf` generates PDF and so on. Distinct URLs work, but they have two serious drawbacks. First, for formats such as HTML and XHTML, there are many embedded links that lead to other documents. When using distinct URLs, each of these links must be encoded during runtime to specify the correct format. This issue is a slight hassle but is not to hard too solve; it is discussed later in this chapter with URL rewriting. The second more serious issue is how to distinguish between two slightly different implementations of the same format, for example, the notorious Microsoft Internet Explorer and the early Netscape Navigator, version 4.x and earlier. Both of these Web browsers support HTML, but they each have unique support for Dynamic HTML. Should your multi-client design support DHTML, it is imperative to be able to distinguish which specific style of HTML and client-side scripts should be sent back.

Here are the best methods for detecting what type of format a Web Application user would prefer:

- **Asking:** Usually the least elegant solution, a simple HTML form can be used to inquire what type of format the client would prefer. The information can then be stored in session context for later access.

- **HTTP user-agent header:** The HTTP `user-agent` header is an HTTP header client software can use to describe itself. In practice this header is almost always accurately populated. Many non-mainstream software packages even allow for a client to falsely populate this value assuming it is put to use by a server. By doing this, the software can purposely request it be allowed to see content a server might normally withhold.

- **HTTP accept and accept-encoding header:** The `accept-encoding` header was previously explained with the GZIP compression Filter example in Chapter 6. The header is very helpful for determining the special formats that a client can accept. In practice most of the formats are irrelevant to a multi-client design; a specific Filter such as the GZIP Filter is better suited for handling these types of formats. More helpful for a multi-client design is the HTTP `accept` header. This header lists all of the MIME types a client can accept. Web browsers in particular tend to accept many different types of formats, all of which are normally listed by this header.

For further discussion the HTTP `user-agent` and `accept` headers are going to be more closely examined. Creating an HTML form and using session context is something you should already be very familiar with.

Recall that in Chapter 2 a Servlet was built that demonstrated how to access the HTTP request headers sent by a client. This Servlet is deployed with the `jspbook` Web Application and can be viewed by browsing to `http://127.0.0.1/jspbook/ShowHeaders`. Figure 13-6 shows what a browser rendering of the results looks like.

Notice both of the HTTP headers we are interested in appear. They are sent by a client same as all of the other HTTP request headers. Accessing them is nothing new; understanding them is. Focus on the `user-agent` header. Here is a sample one as shown in Figure 13-6.

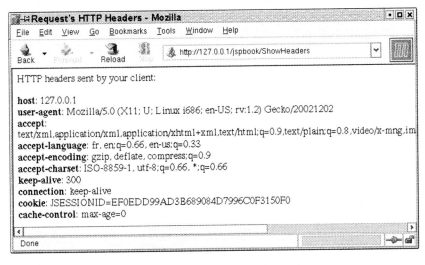

Figure 13-6 Browser Rendering of ShowHeaders Servlet

```
Mozilla/5.0 (X11; U; Linux i686; en-US; rv:1.0.0) Gecko/20021202
```

This is about average for the amount of information you can expect to find in this header. Included is a single text identification for the Web browser followed by optional, more specific information about the platform running the software. The software ID is what is usually most helpful: it can distinguish between browsers such as Netscape 4.x, Internet Explorer, and Mozilla. The preceding browser ID is `Mozilla/5.0`. This identification is for the new Mozilla Web browser, also the core of Netscape 6.x. The first part of the ID references Mozilla as the browser, and the last part claims the browser is version 5.0 of Mozilla. Early versions of Navigator use this ID also, but have the version number changed. This version number is how you can determine if the browser is an early Netscape 4.x or less browser or a version of the rebuilt Mozilla-based browser.

Alternatively, this is what a `user-agent` header sent by Internet Explorer looks like.

```
Mozilla/4.0 (compatible; MSIE 6.0; Windows NT 5.0; Q312461)
```

Note the confusing "Mozilla/4.0" identification. Why Microsoft does this is unclear, but is rumored to be related to the early browser wars with Netscape. What is unique about the IE identification is the later specified "`MSIE 6.0`". This is how Netscape, Mozilla, and IE can all be distinguished from the server-side. The three browsers make up the vast majority of software used by people browsing the World Wide Web.

The other information in the HTTP `user-agent` header is more granular and can be used to understand more about the specific computer. For instance, the Mozilla header identified the client's computer was running Linux on an Intel Pentium 3 using the X11 windowing system to render Mozilla. The Internet Explorer header additionally claimed the client's computer was running Windows NT 5.0, I.E. Windows 2000, and had patch Q312461 applied to it. Usually the platform identification information is not very helpful, but it can affect format rendering. If your multi-client design is based around mining platform information from the `user-agent` header, consult the documentation for particular Web browsers of interest. There you can find specific details on the meaning of extraneous headers.

The `accept` header is much more direct to use than the `user-agent` header. The header lists in order of preference all of the MIME types it can accept. From Figure 13-6 the example header is the following:

```
text/xml,application/xml,application/xhtml+xml,text/html;q=0.9,text/
plain;q=0.8,video/x-mng,image/png,image/jpeg,image/gif;q=0.2,
text/css,*/*;q=0.1
```

MIME types were introduced in Chapter 2. Each MIME type is a unique identifier to a type of content. For example, `text/xml` is the MIME type for XML. Likewise, `text/html` is the MIME type for HTML. Use of the `accept` header is as easy as parsing the string and trying to match the first header with a format your multi-client design supports. In some cases, such as HTML, it may be desirable to also parse the `user-agent` header to see exactly what client software is being used.

Some good examples of mining format preferences using the preceding methods can be found in the multi-client framework. The `com.jspinsider.jspkit.mct.ClientTable` class encapsulates all of the code the framework uses to take an instance of `HttpServletRequest` and determine what format to generate. Consult this class for some code examples.

Printer-Friendly Formats

A very common feature of a Web site is to offer two versions of its content: normal and printer-friendly. The difference between the two is the printer-friendly version is designed for a user to print and read on a piece of paper. A printer-friendly format is nice to have for a few reasons. The primary reason is because most users do not care about advertisements or fancy graphics; they only want the content. Another reason is that many sites are designed to provide print-quality articles, tutorials, or other information online. Whatever the reason is, a good multi-client design is a great method for seamlessly adding printer-friendly formatting to a page.

Keep in mind a multi-client design does not need to produce radically different formats. A good use of a multi-client design is to produce two of the same formats, one in normal and one in printer-friendly form—for instance, via HTML. Such support can be accomplished by adding in completely different APIs for each format, similar to the MCT frameworks handler classes, or by a simple educated decision on how a Web site is made. For instance, most Web sites are completely printer-friendly except for a few banners or navigation included on each page. Ignoring the includes is easy to code and instantly turns a page into a printer-friendly format.

The concept should be clear, but if you are interested in seeing a multi-client framework produce a printer-friendly format, look to the MCT. This framework provides explicit support for both HTML and XHTML printer-friendly formats. Support also allows different header and footer pages to be used.

URL Rewriting

A subtle but very beneficial effect of using JSP custom tags for transformations is the abstraction of link generation. By following the pattern suggested earlier in this chapter, the interface for generating a link is a custom tag, equivalent of the HTML `anchor` tag.

```
<link uri="URL">link text</link>
```

In the MCT framework the `anchor` tag is renamed the `link` tag, but the tag does the same work. The "URL" is specified as an attribute to the `link` tag. By doing this, the value of the URL can be manipulated before being converted to an output format. This allows for session information, parameter encoding, and other custom URL encodings to be used.

Recall the discussion in Chapter 9 about how session context is maintained. By default cookies are used and usually work perfectly fine. However, cookie support is not mandatory. HTTP is a stateless protocol and a client can disable cookie support. If keeping session context is critical, all local links must be encoded to contain session context, e.g., a link to `/index.html` would be encoded as `/index.html;jsessionid=ID#`. The specific session ID is only available at runtime. The encoding must be done by invoking the `HttpSession Response` `encodeURL()` method. In the case of HTML, an encoded `anchor` tag would look similar to the following:

```
<a href="<%= response.encodeURL("URL") %>">link text</a>
```

Or alternatively the JSTL `url` tag may be used as explained in Chapter 6. In either case the syntax is awkward. In a purely cosmetic sense a multi-client `link` tag is both easier to author and read without sacrificing functionality. The awkward `encodeURL()` call can be moved into the handler's code using code that is similar to the following:

```
public void setHref(String rawUrl) {
  HttpServletResponse response = pageContext.getResponse();
  this.url = response.encodeURL(rawUrl);
}
```

More importantly the encoding of the URL is completely abstracted. For instance, imagine the `encodeURL()` method or the JSTL `url` action has been used on all of the local links in a Web Application. Session context is ensured, but what if the application needs to start tracking use of remote links, perhaps as illustrated by both the link tracking Servlet in Chapter 2 and the link-tracking Filter in Chapter 8. The change would require another encoding of the URL, meaning all of the links would have to be changed! The more links, the more tedious and time-consuming the task is. By using a multi-client `link` tag, the change and any future changes are consolidated to one tag handler. This makes it simple to support custom URL-encoding logic needed by any format.

URL Rewriting Using the MCT Framework

Knowledge of URL rewriting is important thing. Complementing the preceding discussion is a concrete example using the MCT framework. One of the good features of the MCT is the support for URL rewriting, and it is important to understand how the functionality works. You'll recall the preceding discussion pointed out that the benefit of using a multi-client interface allowed for easy URL rewriting. Listing 13-12 shows an example of a JSP.

Listing 13-12 A JSP with a Few Hyperlinks

```
<page>
<p>Some Links:</p>
<p>
<link uri="http://www.jspbook.com">Book Support Site</link>,
<link uri="helloworld.html">helloworld.html</link>,
<link uri="helloworld.xhtml">helloworld.xhtml</link>,
<link uri="helloworld.pdf">helloworld.pdf</link>,
<link uri="helloworld.pdf">helloworld.rtf</link>
</p>
</page>
```

The JSP contains a set of links (uses of the MCT `link` action). Save the preceding Listing 13-12 as `links.jsp` in the base directory of the `ji_mct` Web Application. By default the JSP in Listing 13-13 produces an HTML page.

Listing 13-13 Source Listing Produced by links.jsp

```
<html>
<p>Some Links:</p>
<p>
<a href="http://www.jspbook.com">Book Support Site</a>,
<a href="helloworld.html">helloworld.html</a>,
<a href="helloworld.xhtml">helloworld.xhtml</a>,
```

```
<a href="helloworld.pdf">helloworld.pdf</a>,
<a href="helloworld.rtf">helloworld.rtf</a>
</p>
</html>
```

You can test this out for yourself by browsing to `http://127.0.0.1/ji_mct/links.html`. Each of the hyperlinks has an `href` value as expected, the same information specified in the MCT `link` tag. However, imagine you needed all of the links to be encoded to support a particular feature of the Web Application, perhaps to be compatible with a link tracking system as illustrated in Chapter 2[3]. Now, each of the links would need to be rewritten to use the system. Assuming we use the LinkTracker Servlet from Chapter 2, Listing 13-14 shows the new source code.

Listing 13-14 LinkTracker enListingd Page

```
<html>
<p>Some Links:</p>
<p>
<a href="http://www.jspbook.com">Book Support Site</a>,
<a href="/LinkTracker?url=helloworld.html">helloworld.html</a>,
<a href="/LinkTracker?url=helloworld.xhtml">helloworld.xhtml</a>,
<a href="/LinkTracker?url=helloworld.pdf">helloworld.pdf</a>,
<a href="/LinkTracker?url=helloworld.rtf">helloworld.rtf</a>
</p>
</html>
```

The change is that links are encoded to have `/LinkTracker?url=` appended before them in order to use the LinkTracker Servlet. The preceding code shows what a raw conversion of un-encoded links would be; however, it is a poor choice for a few different reasons.

Primarily, the above code is undesirable because it locks the JSP into using the LinkTracker Servlet. If a new, better link-tracker system is implemented, it may require that all the links be encoded again. Doing each encoding by hand is tedious and leaves room for error. Imagine having to encode all of the different links used by a medium-sized Web Application. Additionally, the preceding code is undesirable because it makes simple, intuitive links into something that is neither simple nor intuitive. A developer unfamiliar with the LinkTracker Servlet would be baffled as to why all of the links are encoded.

---

3. `LinkTracker.java`, but another common encoding would be to include session information as explained in Chapter 9.

The preceding problems can be solved by abstracting link encoding using the a multi-client design and a `link` action. With the MCT, the `link` action is already used, as shown previously in Listing 13-12. Changing how the `link` action behaves could be done by editing the source code for the tag; however, the framework knows URL encoding is a helpful feature, and it provides explicit support for it through the `com.jspinsider.jspkit.mct.MultiClientRewriter` interface. A class implementing this interface can be created and defined as an initial parameter for the MCT framework to use. For example, save Listing 13-15 as `ExampleRewriter.java` in the `/WEB-INF/classes/com/jspbook` directory of the `ji_mct` Web Application.

Listing 13-15 ExampleRewriter.java

```
package com.jspbook;

import com.jspinsider.jspkit.mct.MultiClientRewriter;

public class ExampleRewriter implements MultiClientRewriter {

  public String rewrite(String url) {
    url = "/LinkTracker?url="+url;
    return url;
  }
}
```

The codes implements the one method of the `MultiClientRewriter` interface: public String rewrite(String url). The method takes a URL as a parameter and returns a new URL as the rewritten version.

```
url = "/LinkTracker?url="+url;
return url;
```

When used with the MCT framework, this class will filter all `uri` attribute values of the link action and generate properly encoded links, hence, encoding all of the links properly. Try out the class by compiling it and specifying it for use. Edit `web.xml` in the `/WEB-INF` directory of the `ji_mct` Web Application to include Listing 13-16.

Listing 13-16 Using ExampleRewriter with the MCT Framework

```
...
  <filter>
    <filter-name>MultiClientFilter</filter-name>
    <filter-class>
```

```
          com.jspinsider.jspkit.mct.MultiClientFilter
      </filter-class>
      <init-param>
         <param-name>
            com.jspinsider.jspkit.mct.MultiClientRewriter
         </param-name>
         <param-value>com.jspbook.ExampleRewriter</param-value>
      </init-param>
   </filter>
...
```

Reload the `ji_mct` Web Application and browse back to `http://127.0.0.1/ji_mct/links.html`. This time instead of seeing Listing 13-12, the properly encoded links are present as in Listing 13-13. All of the link encoding has been consolidated to the one link-rewriting class!

The preceding illustration of URL rewriting is an excellent example of how URL rewriting should be done in a Web Application. Links can still be authored using the simple, intuitive approach HTML offers, and functionality, such as link tracking, or even session tracking, can be encoded as needed. Should the encoding the links use need to be changed, one class can be edited and all of the Web Application's links will reflect the change. All of this is possible thanks to a good multi-client design.

Non-Text Formats

Non-text formats are easy to produce using Servlets or Filters, as illustrated in the Dynamic Image Servlet, Listing 2-5 in Chapter 2; however, the simplicity of using JSP and custom tags for multi-client design comes at a very obvious drawback. JSP is not designed to produce non-text formats, such as PDF, MS Word documents, or images. The problem is directly related to the `JspWriter` object. It is assumed you are always sending text from a JSP. Getting around this design feature is difficult, even futile, using only JSP. However, getting around the issue is simple using a Servlet or Filter. Both of these classes can directly obtain a `ServletOutputStream`.

Generating a non-text format is tough compared to markup languages. Most non-text formats do not have an intuitive format that can be appropriately represented by the simple `startTag()` and `endTag()` scheme promoted earlier in this chapter, nor do non-text formats usually adhere to representing content as text. A great benefit to non-text formats is they can completely optimize or alter the encoding of text, which usually they do. For these reasons it is not prudent to attempt to understand everything about non-text formats, especially ones with closed documentation. The better alternative is to turn to pre-built Java libraries which accomplish the task.

Finding and using Java APIs for specialized formats is a task up to you. Servlet Filters provide a method of sending arbitrary binary content to a client. You need to find APIs that can generate the desired format. Using the MCT as an example, PDF support is implemented by using the FOP project, http://xml.apache.org/fop/index.html. Previously, we examined how the MCT Filter uses the `HtmlHandler` in order to better understand how text formatting is produced; examining how the Filter generates PDFs sheds light on how a binary format can be produced, as shown in Listing 13-17.

Listing 13-17 PDF Generation Snippet of the MCT Filter

```
case MultiClient.PDF : {
  response.setContentType("application/pdf");

  // FO format
  FOHandler h = new FOHandler();
  ByteArrayOutputStream baos =
    new ByteArrayOutputStream();
  h.setOutputStream(baos);
  sp.parse(new ByteArrayInputStream(content), h);
  h.flush();

  // use FOP
  Driver driver = new Driver(new InputSource(
    new ByteArrayInputStream(baos.toByteArray())),
                             out);
  driver.setRenderer(Driver.RENDER_PDF);
  driver.run();

  break;
}
```

PDF is produced by using the FOP framework's PDF driver. It just so happens the FOP framework requires XML FO syntax, which is text, as its interface. The Filter uses the `FOHandler` to produce XML FO from the MCT syntax.

```
// FO format
FOHandler h = new FOHandler();
ByteArrayOutputStream baos =
  new ByteArrayOutputStream();
```

```
h.setOutputStream(baos);
sp.parse(new ByteArrayInputStream(content), h);
h.flush();
```

The XML FO is then piped to the FOP framework's driver.

```
// use FOP
Driver driver = new Driver(new InputSource(
    new ByteArrayInputStream(baos.toByteArray())),
                            out);
driver.setRenderer(Driver.RENDER_PDF);
driver.run();
```

The FOP framework uses the response as an output stream, sending PDF content to the client. Note also that the statement explicitly sets the response content type to be `"application/pdf"`, which is the MIME type for PDF.

If you are interested in exactly how the FOP project generates PDFs from XML FO—in other words, if you want to know how to make PDFs from scratch, take a look at the FOP project's code. For all practical purposes, there is no point in understanding it as long as the FOP project correctly generates PDFs. What we care most about is having a Java interface for producing the binary format. Once we have Java, we have a method of using it, namely Servlets and JSP.

Summary

Multi-client design enables a Servlet and JSP developer to create truly robust, dynamic Web Applications. Many simple Web sites require only one format of content, HTML. However, designing around only HTML inherently limits what a Web Application is able to do. By abstracting formatting logic, similar to abstracting content with i18n applications, it is possible to use any number of different formats on the same content. A Web site can support basic HTML, modern XHTML, and any other format desired.

By abstracting formatting logic with a multi-client design, a few benefits are readily available to a developer. Developing many versions of the same format is easily possible. For instance, both regular HTML and printer-friendly HTML can be seamlessly supported. URL rewriting is also one of the inherent benefits to a multi-client design. An abstraction of representing links between content provides an ideal place to put custom logic for encoding session state, i18n information, or any other miscellaneous information such as link tracking.

Most commonly Servlets and JSP are thought only to be good for generating dynamic Web pages with text content; however, this is not true. While it is more intuitive to generate purely text, it is certainly possible to generate non-text formats. In order to generate any binary format, a Servlet or Filter must be used, similar to the dynamic picture Servlet in Chapter 2. By complementing the Servlet or Filter with custom tags, it is possible to allow JSP to also produce any binary format.

Chapter 14

Database Connectivity

Why have a chapter about database connectivity in a book on Servlets and JSP? Databases are widely used in business today. Just about every real-world application will use databases in some form or another. The advertised mindset in J2EE is to build an application that uses an EJB[1] layer to hide database connectivity. In practice this can work, but it is often more problematic than it is helpful. In this book we are taking the approach that you should not have to use EJB and that instead you should know more about database connectivity. By taking this approach, you will be able to build complete Web Applications without having to worry about a slew of other J2EE specifications. However, if one day you decide those other specifications are needed, you will be more than prepared for them. In this chapter we will briefly introduce databases and SQL, but the focus will be on JDBC and successfully using Java to manipulate a database. You will be expected to pick up a good book on SQL if you want to be a database guru.

This chapter discusses the following topics:

- What a database, relational database, and SQL are.
- CRUD (Creating, Reading, Updating, and Deleting database tables).
- JDBC (Java Database Connectivity).
- **javax.sql.DataSource:** an abstract method for obtaining a reference to a database.
- **java.sql.Connection:** Java representation of a database connection.
- **java.sql.Statement:** Executing queries against a database.
- **java.sql.ResultSet:** Obtaining results of a database query.

---

1. Enterprise JavaBeans (EJB) is a J2EE method of abstracting database access and cooperation between multiple computers in a server-side Web farm. EJB is discussed further in Chapter 15.

- Optimally using JDBC.
- JDBC Web Application design patterns.

This chapter is intended to be read straight through; however, if you are already familiar with SQL and JDBC, there is no harm in skipping this chapter. At best, it is a decent introduction to JDBC, nothing more. Embedding JDBC code in Servlets and JSP is no different than embedding other Java code in Servlets and JSPs.

What Is a Database?

Put simply a *database* is an organized collection of data. There are many forms this collection can take: an XML DOM, a flat file, object stores, or relational data. Different types of databases work better for different uses, but all databases exist to organize a collection of data. The most popular type of database is the "relational"[2]. Relational databases were first conceived by Dr. Edgar F. Codd (an IBM researcher) in 1969, and since then have become the dominant form of database. Much like HttpServlets to Servlets, whenever the term database is mentioned, it nearly always means a relational database, and it is likely that you will have to use a relational database in your day-to-day work.

Data in a relational database is held in tables; a table consists of rows and columns. Figure 14-1 shows a visual representation of such a table.

The columns in this table are labeled EMPLOYEE_NO, FIRST_NAME, LAST_NAME, and SOFTWAREITEM. The order that the data is listed in the

EMPLOYEE_NO	FIRST_NAME	LAST_NAME	SOFTWAREITEM
1001	Fred	Wesley	8001
1002	Sarah	Smith	null
1003	Rachel	Axelrod	null
1004	Alice	Bennet	8013
1005	Michael	Sinclair	null
1006	Louis	Smith	8013

Figure 14-1 A Database Table

---

2. Relational databases are loosely based around the mathematics of sets. In practice the purity of the mathematics has been altered for performance and practical use, but if you have previously studied sets you should recognize the concepts.

table is completely unimportant. Each column defines a field and each row is a record. In a well-designed database each column will contain only one value. Each table will have one column known as the primary key column; the *primary key* will uniquely identify the record (i.e., it uniquely identifies the row of data). For instance, in Figure 14-1 EMPLOYEE_NO uniquely identifies each person, since the other information might not be unique.

Each table can have more than one type of key. As just mentioned, each table will have a primary key to be used as a unique identifier; each table could also have foreign keys. A *foreign key* is a reference to a different table's primary key and is used to establish a relationship between tables. Figure 14-2 shows an example of this.

Here, there are two tables, EMPLOYEE and SOFTWARE. The EMPLOYEE table has a primary key field called EMPLOYEE_NO, and the SOFTWARE table has a primary key field called SOFTWARE_ITEM. The EMPLOYEE table also has a foreign key field, SOFTWARE_ITEM. The connection between the SOFTWARE_ ITEM columns in both tables defines the relationship between the tables. There are three types of relationships that can be defined:

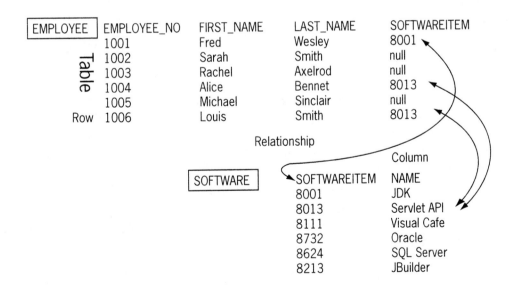

Figure 14-2 Database Relationships

- **one-to-one:** In a one-to-one relationship, a record in one table refers to exactly one record in another table, and the foreign key refers to exactly one primary key.

- **one-to-many:** In a one-to-many relationship, a record in one table refers to many records in another table, but a single record in the second table refers to exactly one record in the primary table (the tables in Figure 14-2 show a one-to-many relationship).

- **many-to-many:** In a many-to-many relationship, many records in one table can refer to many records in another table. Since primary keys must be unique, a many-to-many relationship cannot be established directly. Instead, this relationship is achieved typically by having a linking table, providing two one-to-many relationships.

The types of relationships are important for various reasons, and there are several theories about the best method of creating and referencing tables. In practice the topic is very important as it has a direct impact on how efficiently data stored in a relational database is managed and maintained. However, full discussion of the topic is outside the scope of this text. Before going out and designing a set of tables for real-world use, it is strongly suggested you read through *Database Systems: A Practical Approach to Design, Implementation, and Management*, 3/e by Thomas Connolly and Carolyn Begg.

SQL

The language used to manage and manipulate data in a relational database is Structured Query Language, better known as SQL. SQL is simple to learn but difficult to master. We will spend a little time using SQL to help learn the basics, but full coverage is deferred to the previously suggested text. To learn SQL it helps to have a relational database. There are many, many databases available from all sorts of vendors such as Oracle, IBM, and Microsoft. There are even a few excellent, free open-source databases such as MySQL and PostgreSQL. For the examples in the book we are going to use hsqldb (formerly Hypersonic SQL). This is an open source, pure Java database that is ideal for this book's use because it is free, coded in Java, and simple to download and install. While hsqldb is fantastic for learning and testing SQL, it is not good for most real-world situations. The simplicity of the DB comes at the cost of performance and lack of advanced features.

Installing hsqldb

You do need to download and install a copy of hsqldb for this chapter's examples. If you have access to an existing relational database, it will also work, but it is suggested you use hsqldb to avoid any nuances. Download the latest copy of hsqldb at `http://hsqldb.sourceforge.net`. Version 1.7 is used by this book's examples, available directly at `http://prdownloads.sourceforge.net/hsqldb/hsqldb_1_7_0.zip`.

    Installation of hsqldb is simple. Decompress the ZIP file and place `hsqldb.jar` in the `/commons/lib` directory of your Tomcat installation[3]. The installation is then complete.

Making a Database

Primarily, for reasons just mentioned, this chapter will focus on using SQL for database manipulation, but SQL is also used for creating a database from scratch. SQL statements can be used to create tables, put restrictions on those tables, and most anything else you would think to do when creating a data repository. To not get sidetracked into describing good database design and the SQL needed to create said database, a pre-made SQL script is provided. In practice a database is only created once; the majority of work is done by populating the database with information and using the database to further manipulate the information.

    For simplicity the database creation will be encapsulated by a JSP. This is admittedly one of the worst ways to accomplish this task, but it is familiar and will suffice. Save Listing 14-1 as `CreateDatabase.jsp` in the root directory of the jspbook Web Application.

Listing 14-1 CreateDatabase.jsp

```
<%@ page import="java.io.*,java.sql.*" %>
<%
  // keep code portable
  File tempDir =
(File)application.getAttribute("javax.servlet.context.tempdir");
  String dbDir = tempDir.getAbsolutePath();
  String url = "jdbc:hsqldb:" + dbDir+"/jspbook";
  String user      = "sa"; // hsqldb default
  String password  = ""; // hsqldb default
```

---

3. The `/common/lib` directory makes the API available to both Tomcat and all of the Web Applications it is running. You can put `hsqldb.jar` in the `/WEB-INF/lib` directory, but later examples will not work because they rely on Tomcat's having access to the API.

```
// load JDBC driver - BAD! Use DataSource.
Class.forName("org.hsqldb.jdbcDriver");
Connection conn =
  DriverManager.getConnection(url, user, password);
try {
  Statement statement = conn.createStatement();
  String link = ""; // create LINK table
  link += "CREATE TABLE LINK(";
  link += "  URL VARCHAR(128) PRIMARY KEY,";
  link += "  TITLE VARCHAR(128),";
  link += "  DESCRIPTION VARCHAR(256)";
  link += ")";
  statement.executeQuery(link);
  String uri = ""; // create URI table
  uri += "CREATE TABLE URI(";
  uri += "  URI VARCHAR(40),";
  uri += "  URL VARCHAR(128),";
  uri += "  PRIMARY KEY(URI, URL)";
  uri += ")";
  statement.executeQuery(uri);
}
finally {
  conn.close();
}
%>
<html>
  <head>
    <title>JSP Book Sample Database Creation</title>
  </head>
  <body>
  The Database has been successfully created.
  </body>
</html>
```

Do not worry about understanding the preceding database code. The idea behind the JSP is simple: browse to `CreateDatabase.jsp` and the database is created. The database is serialized in the Servlet-defined temporary directory and is not guaranteed to persist between restarts of a container. If persistence is desired, change the value of `dbDir` to be any other directory, perhaps `/WEB-INF` of the jspbook Web Application. The current scheme relies on `CreateDatabase.jsp` to be executed each time the database needs to be created, which should only be once for the following examples.

Use `CreateDatabase.jsp` to create the example database. Browse to `http://127.0.0.1/jspbook/CreateDatabase.jsp`. After the database is created, a page is returned that confirms the creation. Do not run `CreateDatabase.jsp` repeatedly or SQL-related exceptions will be thrown because the database tables have already been created.

The actual database created by `CreateDatabase.jsp` is a practical example of a database that can be used to manage links for a Web site. Two tables are created: `LINK` and `URI`. The link table holds information about a link, including columns for a title, url, and description. The `URI` table holds a collection of unique identifiers that describe groups of links. There are two columns in the uri table, url and uri. The url column matches a url from the link table. The uri column defines an identifier for a group of links. Later on we will populate these tables with some links and see how to use the database with Servlets and JSP.

CRUD

CRUD is the SQL-related acronym used to describe data manipulation. CRUD comes from the four basic types of data manipulation: Create, Read, Update, and Delete. *Create* creates information in a database table. *Read* retrieves existing information for display. *Delete* removes rows from a table, and *Update* changes existing information. Commonly when dealing with SQL and a database, you will hear people talking about "CRUD statements"; this is the SQL needed to accomplish one of the CRUD operations.

There are four main SQL statements that are analogous to the CRUD operations but named differently. The SQL statements are SELECT, INSERT, DELETE, and UPDATE. The following sections lay down the fundamental concepts of these statements but by no means provide comprehensive coverage.

INSERT

The SQL INSERT statement is an implementation of the "C" from CRUD, or Create. By using insert statements, new rows of information can be placed in an existing database table. Information added by using an INSERT statement must comply with the database's data integrity[4] rules or else an error will occur. In the case of Java database connectivity, often an exception is raised when invalid information is used with an INSERT statement.

---

4. SQL provides a robust mechanism for defining rules that tables must follow. Common examples are unique values for primary keys and restrictions on the size of values being placed in a database. The job of appropriately creating these rules is usually left to the database administrator.

The basic structure of an INSERT statement is as follows:

```
INSERT INTO table-name VALUES(value1, value2, value3)
```

where the value of the correct table is used for `table-name` and all of the values needed for a row are specified between the parens following VALUES. The values must be valid SQL types and need to be delimited by commas.

In the tables previously created by `CreateDatabase.jsp`, the data integrity rules are simple. All values are *strings*, meaning they are a string literal surrounded by single quotes. The LINK table has three columns: url, title, and description. The sizes of the strings can be up to 128, 128, and 256 characters, respectively. The url string must be unique from all others in the table. The URI table has two columns: uri and url. The sizes of the columns are up to 40 and 128 characters, respectively. Together, the combination of the uri and url columns must be unique from all others in the table. With these simple rules in mind you should be able to imagine the SQL INSERT statements needed to put some values in the database. Try the statements out; the JSP in Listing 14-2 provides a simple form for executing SQL statements against the database.

Listing 14-2 ArbitrarySQL.jsp

```
<%@ page import="java.io.*,java.sql.*" %>
<%
  // keep code portable
  File tempDir =
(File)application.getAttribute("javax.servlet.context.tempdir");
  String dbDir = tempDir.getAbsolutePath();
  String url = "jdbc:hsqldb:" + dbDir+"/jspbook";
  String user      = "sa"; // hsqldb default
  String password  = ""; // hsqldb default
  Statement sStatement  = null;
  Connection cConnection = null;
  // load JDBC driver - BAD! Use DataSource.
  Class.forName("org.hsqldb.jdbcDriver");

  cConnection = DriverManager.getConnection(url, user, password);
  try {
    sStatement  = cConnection.createStatement();

%>
<html>
  <head>
    <title>JSP Book Sample Database Creation</title>
```

```
    </head>
    <body>
<% // poor form, Model 1
    String query = request.getParameter("query");
    if (query != null && !query.equals("")) {
      out.println("<h2>Results of query:</h2>");
      out.println(query);
      ResultSet rs = sStatement.executeQuery(query);
      ResultSetMetaData rsmd = rs.getMetaData();
      out.print("<table border=\"1\"><tr>");
      for (int i=0; i<rsmd.getColumnCount();i++) {
        out.println("<td>"+rsmd.getColumnName(i+1)+"</td>");
      }
      out.print("</tr>");
      while (rs.next()) { // show results
        out.println("<tr>");
        for (int i=0; i<rsmd.getColumnCount();i++) {
          out.println("<td>"+rs.getString(i+1)+"</td>");
        }
        out.println("</tr>");
      }
      out.print("</table>");
      cConnection.close();
    }
%>
      <h2>New Query</h2>
      <form method="POST">
        Query: <textarea name="query" cols="65"></textarea><br>
        <input type="submit">
      </form>
<%
    }
    catch (Exception e) {
      out.println("<h2>Problem with Query</h2>");
      out.print(e.getMessage());
    }
    finally {
      cConnection.close();
    }
%>
    </body>
</html>
```

Save Listing 14-2 as `ArbitrarySQL.jsp` in the base directory of the jspbook Web Application. Don't worry exactly what it does right now; it will be explained later in pertinent sections. The page provides a simple form that allows statements to be done on the database and shows any information returned by the database. Browse to `http://127.0.0.1/jspbook/ArbitrarySQL.jsp` to test it out. Figure 14-3 provides a browser rendering of the results.

Add a value to the `link` table by executing the appropriate SQL INSERT statement. For example, the `'Book Support Site'` would be:

```
INSERT INTO LINK VALUES(
  'http://www.jspbook.com',
  'Book Support Site',
  'The book support site for Servlets and JSP; the J2EE Web Tier');
```

The line need not be broken; it is only so that it fits in this text. Type in the preceding `insert` statement and click on the Submit Query button. The statement is executed on the database and the results are displayed. Figure 14-4 shows a browser rendering of the results.

Notice that it appears as if nothing happened, but that is because the INSERT statement does not read information from the database. It only adds information. To read information, the SELECT statement needs to be used.

SELECT

The SQL SELECT statement is analogous to the CRUD letter "R", or Read. A SELECT statement queries a database for information and the database returns a

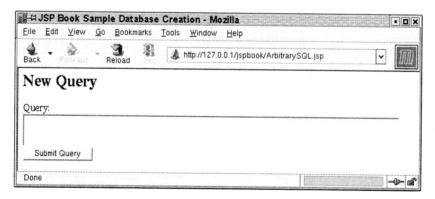

Figure 14-3 Browser Rendering of ArbitrarySQL.jsp

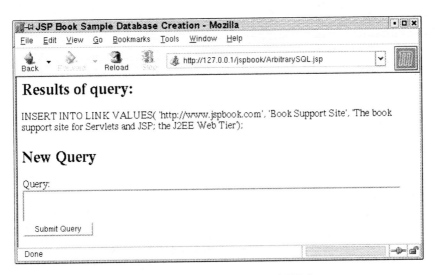

Figure 14-4 Browser Rendering of Results after the INSERT Statement

set of rows describing the desired information. The SQL SELECT statement is often called the "workhorse" of SQL because in practice it is usually used far more than the other CRUD statements. The basic format of the SELECT statement is as follows:

```
SELECT columns FROM table-name WHERE condition(s)
```

SQL SELECT statements start with SELECT, followed by desired columns to display, and a FROM clause that determines the table(s) to use when generating the result. Optionally, a WHERE clause can be used to define a set of conditions that must be met. Multiple conditions can be used and are joined by using the AND or OR keyword. The conditions result in one boolean statement, determined following the same rules as conditions combined by and, &&, or or, | |, in Java.

The columns to show can be specified in a few different ways. We will only look at the simplest two options including the * symbol and a comma-delimited list of column names. The * *symbol* is used to mean show all columns. For instance, to show all the entries in the link table, the following SELECT statement can be used.

```
SELECT * FROM LINK
```

Try executing the statement using ArbitrarySQL.jsp. The result will be a listing of the entire LINK table or all the entries you have added using INSERT statements. Figure 14-5 shows a browser rendering of the results when only one row is in the LINK table.

Only one row is shown because only one is in the database. If you have previously added more rows, then multiple rows will be displayed, with all column values showing.

A more selective set of values can be retrieved by listing the specific columns which are needed. For instance, try executing the following SELECT statement:

```
SELECT URL, TITLE FROM LINK
```

This time only the url and title information are returned. Figure 14-6 shows a browser rendering of the results returned from ArbitrarySQL.jsp.

In both of the preceding examples, all of the rows of the table were shown. If only selected rows are wanted, then the WHERE clause can be used to request specific rows. For example, the following statement would only select the link for the book support site:

```
SELECT * FROM LINK WHERE url = 'http://www.jspbook.com'
```

Try the statement out using ArbitrarySQL.jsp and see that only the one row is returned regardless of the number of rows the LINK table has. In general, SQL

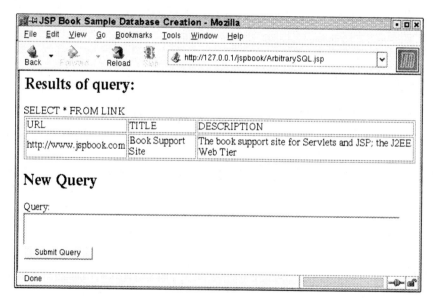

Figure 14-5   Browser Rendering of a Row in the LINK Table

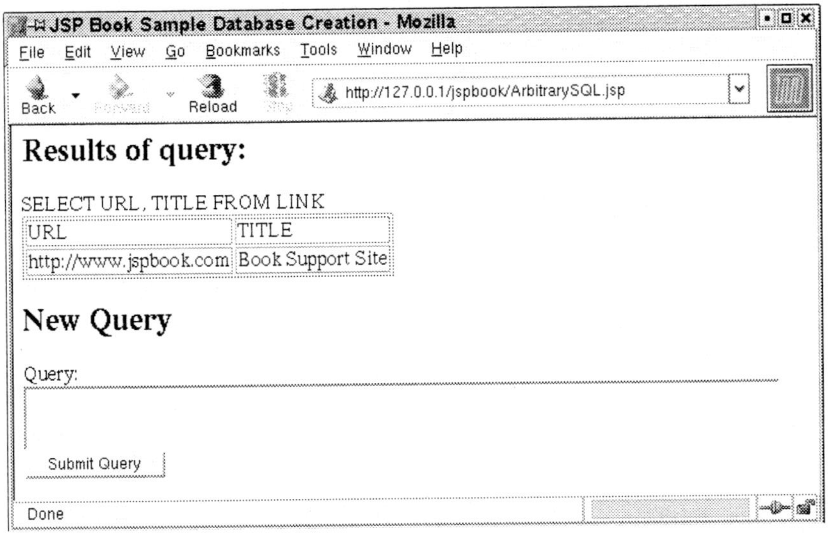

Figure 14-6 Browser Rendering of Columns Returned from the LINK Table

has many operators besides equal, =. Included are operators for less than, <, greater than, >, and similar to, LIKE. Some more uses will be shown throughout the chapter, but the full set of operators is left outside the scope of this book. What is important to understand is that SELECT statements can selectively return any number of columns or rows. Which set of information is returned is up to you and how the SELECT statement is constructed.

So far a lot can be accomplished using the SQL INSERT and SELECT statements. The database can be populated with information, and queries can be made to return sets of that information. Rounding out this functionality are the UPDATE and DELETE statements that do exactly what the CRUD words with the same name imply.

UPDATE

The SQL UPDATE statement updates existing rows in a table, compared to the INSERT, which adds completely new rows. The basic format of the UPDATE statement is as follows:

```
UDPATE table-name SET column-value(s) WHERE condition(s)
```

Where the `table-name` value is replaced with the name of a table, the `column-value(s)` are a comma-delimited set of values for columns of that table, and an optional WHERE clause selects specific rows that are to be updated. For example, the book support site entry can be changed by executing the following statement:

```
UPDATE LINK SET title = 'Superb Book Support Site'
  WHERE url = 'http://www.jspbook.com'
```

Try the statement using `ArbitrarySQL.jsp` and follow it up with a SELECT statement to list the contents of the database. The row describing the book support site will now have the new title, as illustrated in Figure 14-7.

Not illustrated in the shown UPDATE statement is that multiple column values can be specified at the same time using commas to delimit them. However, be aware that any changes made by an UPDATE statement are subject to the data integrity rules of the database. For instance, the unique primary-key values cannot be changed by an UPDATE statement. Likewise, any other restrictions might prevent column values from being changed. Be sure you understand the data integrity rules of a database before trying to execute arbitrary UPDATE statements.

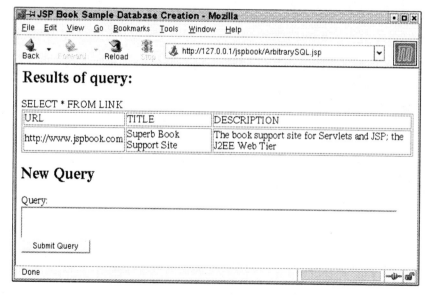

Figure 14-7 Updated Title for the Book Support Site's Entry in the LINK Table

DELETE

The final SQL CRUD statement is DELETE. The SQL DELETE statement is used to delete a select number of rows from a table(s). The basic syntax of the SQL DELETE statement is as follows:

```
DELETE FROM table-name WHERE condition(s)
```

The table-name is the table to delete information from, and a WHERE clause specifies rows that are to be deleted. Only complete rows can be deleted.

The SQL That Was Skipped

It was previously mentioned that SQL is easy to learn but hard to master. This statement is very true. The basics of SQL are simple to learn and can be taught in a few minutes, but understanding everything you can do with SQL and how it works is not as easy. In fact, many highly paid SQL gurus are employed with the sole task of managing a database. Mastering SQL is outside the scope of this book and rightly so. What has been covered is enough so that you can perform enough SQL to get by. In no way is it a complete tutorial.

There is a lot of SQL and database-related information that was skipped by this chapter. It is important that you realize this and seriously consider reading a good database/SQL book. Combined with this text, it will enable you to build some truly impressive Web Applications. Using only what this chapter covers, it is very likely you will be unable to build a good database. You will be able to execute just about any CRUD operation or transaction[5] on it you like, but you will be lacking the theory and techniques needed to ensure the integrity of your database. Do not take the topic lightly. If you want to act as both Web tier developer and database administrator, learn them both!

JDBC

All DBMSs provide mechanisms for performing I/O against the database. However, most DBMS I/O mechanisms are proprietary. If a proper layer of abstraction is not present between the database-specific I/O operations and a project's code, the project is confined to the database it is built around. In Java

---

5. A *transaction* is a series of related SQL statements that must be part of an atomic unit—that is, all the statements pass or all the statements fail. Transactions are introduced later in the chapter with JDBC.

the popular solution to this issue is to use the standardized JDBC API. JDBC is Java's universal data access strategy. It allows data stored in different databases to be accessed using a common Java API. JDBC defines a set of abstract interfaces that a database provider implements as a piece of code called a *JDBC driver*. A database client chooses an appropriate driver and uses the interfaces to access the underlying database.

In all of the preceding code in this chapter, JDBC is what was used to communicate with hsqldb. In general, Java applications that use a database almost always use JDBC to communicate with it. By learning JDBC you will be able to successfully integrate a database with your Servlet- and JSP-based Web tier.

There are a few key classes and interfaces you need to be aware of in order to use JDBC:

- **javax.sql.DataSource:** A `DataSource` interface is the JDBC method of obtaining connections to a database.
- **java.sql.Connection:** The `Connection` object represents a physical connection with a database. The communication between the database and the `Connection` object is governed by an underlying JDBC driver.
- **java.sql.Statement:** The `Statement` interface provides a method for a Java developer to execute SQL statements on a database. The results are returned as a `java.sql.ResultSet` object.
- **java.sql.ResultSet:** The `ResultSet` object represents the results of an SQL statement. Primarily the object is only used with SQL `SELECT` statements.

All of the preceeding objects are covered further in the following sections. Additionally, there are many more JDBC objects that can be used to optimally perform database operations. These objects will be discussed where relevant but largely left as second priority to the preceding key classes.

javax.sql.DataSource

The `DataSource` interface is the preferred method of obtaining a connection to a database. The `DataSource` object provides the `getConnection()` method that can be used to obtain a connection to a database. As a Java developer, using the `DataSource` interface is ideal because it completely abstracts any vendor-specific information that might be attached to creating a database connection. When combined with another Java technology, JNDI, `DataSource` objects also provide a convenient method of consolidating how connections are obtained to a database. This is important because it makes it theoretically[6] possible to completely switch databases without causing problems to your existing code.

`DataSource` objects have not always been the method of obtaining a JDBC connection. Early versions of JDBC relied on an object called a `DriverManager` to manually load and return connection objects. The code for doing so can be found in both `CreateDatabase.jsp` and `ArbitrarySQL.jsp`. It is as follows:

```
String url = "jdbc:hsqldb:" + dbDir+"/jspbook";
String user     = "sa"; // hsqldb default
String password = ""; // hsqldb default
Class.forName("org.hsqldb.jdbcDriver");
Connection conn =
    DriverManager.getConnection(url, user, password);
```

The code can be broken down into a few simple parts. First, a JDBC URL is created that specifies the name and location of the database along with the appropriate user/password information. All of this information is used by the JDBC driver to connect to the database. The second part of the code loads an instance of the appropriate JDBC driver:

```
Class.forName("org.hsqldb.jdbcDriver");
```

In the preceding code the `org.hsqldb.jdbcDriver` is loaded because it is the JDBC driver that the hsqldb project uses. The line of code might seem pointless, but it is needed for the later `DriverManager getConnection()` method call.

```
Connection conn =
    DriverManager.getConnection(url, user, password);
```

The `DriverManager` object internally manages JDBC drivers and given the JDBC url tries to return the appropriate driver. Assuming a valid JDBC url is used and the JDBC driver has been loaded by the class loader—the `Class.forName()` call—a connection to the database is opened.

As previously illustrated, a connection to a database can be obtained without using a `DataSource` object, but there are a few things that are very undesirable about using the previously shown method. A minor problem is the fact that supposedly vendor-neutral code is suddenly vendor-specific due to the

---

6. In practice there are several vendor-specific "features" that might not allow a seamless transition between different databases, but that is an issue that needs to be addressed on a case-by-case basis. When using basic SQL, as in this chapter, it is a safe assumption that the code can easily be moved to any database.

`Class.forName()` call. The problem can be avoided with a creative placement of the call, but the best way to ensure the class loader has the appropriate class is to do as the preceding code illustrates. Another very significant problem with the code is that `DriverManager` is not an interface but a class. This matters because vendors cannot easily optimize use of the `DriverManager`. There are many excellent JDBC techniques that can result in huge performance increases, but using the `DriverManager` thwarts integrating these techniques with the basic JDBC objects.

A `DataSource` object solves all of the problems with the classic JDBC code. Because `DataSource` is an interface, vendors can code a `DataSource` object any way they choose, including using optimizations. Additionally, `DataSource` objects can conveniently be managed by containers so that the multiple calls to `Class.forName()` and the loading of user/password and JDBC url information are consolidated.

Configuring a DataSource for Use on Tomcat

The reason `DataSource` objects were not used with `ArbitrarySQL.jsp` and `CreateDatabase.jsp` is because the `DataSource` needs to be configured for use with Tomcat[7]. The configuration is simple but was delayed all the same. Add Listing 14-3 to the `server.xml` file located in the `/conf` directory of your Tomcat installation. Make sure the entry is a child of the `Context` element that defines the jspbook Web Application.

Listing 14-3   Tomcat server.xml DataSource Configuration for the jspbook Web Application

```
...
<Context path="/jspbook" docBase="jspbook" debug="0">
  <Resource name="jdbc/jspbook"
    auth="Container"
    type="javax.sql.DataSource"/>
  <ResourceParams name="jdbc/jspbook">
    <parameter>
      <name>username</name>
      <value>sa</value>
    </parameter>
    <parameter>
      <name>password</name>
      <value></value>
    </parameter>
```

---

7. `DataSource` configuration is done in a container-dependent method. If you are not using Tomcat, consult the documentation for your specific container.

```
    <parameter>
      <name>driverClassName</name>
      <value>org.hsqldb.jdbcDriver</value>
    </parameter>
    <parameter>
      <name>url</name>
      <value>JDBC url</value>
    </parameter>
  </ResourceParams>
</Context>
. . .
```

Information about the specific elements can be found in the Tomcat documentation; however, it should be easy to understand what the entry is doing. A `DataSource` object is being registered as a resource. Included is all of the information needed for the JDBC driver: user name, password, and connection `url`. Note that the highlighted code does not include the specific value for the `url` parameter. This is because the value will change depending on where the hsqldb is being kept. Choose a place on your computer where the database should be serialized: a good candidate is either the temporary directory provided by your container or somewhere under the `/WEB-INF` directory of the jspbook Web Application. For simplicity, choose the name `jspbookdb` under the `/WEB-INF` directory of the jspbook Web Application. For example, if Tomcat was installed to `/usr/jakarta-tomcat-5`, then the value would be the following(the URL must always start with `jdbc:hsqldb:`):

```
. . .
    </parameter>
    <parameter>
      <name>url</name>
      <value>jdbc:hsqldb:/usr/jakarta-tomcat-5/webapps/jspbook/WEB-
INF/jspbookdb</value>
    </parameter>
  </ResourceParams>
</Context>
. . .
```

This entry would serialize the hsqldb contents in a few text files that started with `jspbookdb` and were located under the `/WEB-INF` directory of the jspbook Web Application. It does not matter where exactly you choose to save the database; choose a location and all the upcoming examples will automatically use it.

Upgrading CreateDatabase.jsp and ArbitrarySQL.jsp

Both `CreateDatabase.jsp` and `ArbitrarySQL.jsp` are going to be helpful in the upcoming examples. Change both of the examples by removing the following lines:

```
// keep code portable
File tempDir =
  (File)application.getAttribute("javax.servlet.context.tempdir");
String dbDir = tempDir.getAbsolutePath();
String url = "jdbc:hsqldb:" + dbDir+"/jspbook";
String user      = "sa"; // hsqldb default
String password  = ""; // hsqldb default
// load JDBC driver - BAD! Use DataSource.
Class.forName("org.hsqldb.jdbcDriver");
Connection conn =
    DriverManager.getConnection(url, user, password);
```

Replace with the following:

```
InitialContext ctx = new javax.naming.InitialContext();
DataSource ds =
  (javax.sql.DataSource)ctx.
    lookup("java:comp/env/jdbc/jspbook");
Connection conn = ds.getConnection();
```

Additionally, import the `javax.sql` and `javax.naming` packages in the page directive. Save the new code as `CreateDatabaseDataSource.jsp` and `Arbitrary SQLDataSource.jsp`, respectively, as to distinguish from the old code. For completeness, Listings 14-4 and 14-5 include the code for each of the pages, respectively.

Listing 14-4 CreateDatabaseDataSource.jsp

```
<%@ page import="java.io.*,java.sql.*, javax.naming.*, javax.sql.*"
%>
<%
  InitialContext ctx = new InitialContext();
  DataSource ds =
    (DataSource)ctx.lookup("java:comp/env/jdbc/jspbook");
  Connection conn = ds.getConnection();
  try {
    Statement statement = conn.createStatement();
    String link = ""; // create LINK table
    link += "CREATE TABLE LINK(";
    link += "  URL VARCHAR(128) PRIMARY KEY,";
```

```
    link += "  TITLE VARCHAR(128),";
    link += "  DESCRIPTION VARCHAR(256)";
    link += ")";
    statement.executeQuery(link);
    String uri = ""; // create URI table
    uri += "CREATE TABLE URI(";
    uri += "  URI VARCHAR(40),";
    uri += "  URL VARCHAR(128),";
    uri += "  PRIMARY KEY(URI, URL)";
    uri += ")";
    statement.executeQuery(uri);
  }
  finally {
    conn.close();
  }
%>
<html>
  <head>
    <title>JSP Book Sample Database Creation</title>
  </head>
  <body>
  The Database has been successfully created.
  </body>
</html>
```

Listing 14-5 ArbitrarySQLDataSource.jsp

```
<%@ page import="java.io.*,java.sql.*, javax.sql.*, javax.naming.*"
%>
<%
  InitialContext ctx = new InitialContext();
  DataSource ds =
    (DataSource)ctx.lookup("java:comp/env/jdbc/jspbook");
  Connection conn = ds.getConnection();
  try {
    Statement statement  = conn.createStatement();
%>
<html>
  <head>
    <title>JSP Book Sample Database Creation</title>
  </head>
  <body>
<% // poor form, Model 1
  String query = request.getParameter("query");
```

```java
    if (query != null && !query.equals("")) {
      out.println("<h2>Results of query:</h2>");
      out.println(query);
      ResultSet rs = statement.executeQuery(query);
      ResultSetMetaData rsmd = rs.getMetaData();
      out.print("<table border=\"1\"><tr>");
      for (int i=0; i<rsmd.getColumnCount();i++) {
        out.println("<td>"+rsmd.getColumnName(i+1)+"</td>");
      }
      out.print("</tr>");
      while (rs.next()) { // show results
        out.print("<tr>");
        for (int i=0; i<rsmd.getColumnCount();i++) {
          out.println("<td>"+rs.getString(i+1)+"</td>");
        }
        out.print("</tr>");
      }
      out.print("</td></table>");
      //conn.close();
    }
%>

    <h2>New Query</h2>
    <form method="POST">
      Query: <textarea name="query" cols="65"></textarea><br>
      <input type="submit">
    </form>
<%
  }
  catch (Exception e) {
    out.println("<h2>Problem with Query</h2>");
    out.print(e.getMessage());
  }
  finally {
    conn.close();
  }
%>
  </body>
</html>
```

Save Listing 14-4 as `CreateDatabaseDataSource.jsp` in the root directory of the jspbook Web Application. Save Listing 14-5 as `ArbitrarySQLDataSource.jsp` in the root directory of the jspbook Web Application.

DataSources and JNDI

The Java Naming Directory Interface (JNDI) is the Java standard for providing access to a *directory*. A directory is a centralized location for obtaining access to a resource used by Java Applications. A good way to think of JNDI is like a phone book with phone numbers. If you wish to call a friend, you can look in the phone book under the friend's name for their number. With JNDI you can look in the directory using a unique string to find a needed object. The directory is very important because it potentially provides a place that any Java application can look up a resource and obtain it for use, even applications that are running in a different JVM, including those running on different servers.

The underlying mechanisms that JNDI uses will not be discussed. On a single server, JNDI can be considered a roundabout method of calling, a factory method, to obtain a class. In a multi-server environment, JNDI provides an abstraction to a directory that may be responsible for indexing objects for use with multiple applications running on different JVMs and computers. Should the case arise where you are building a multi-server Web Application, then you can take the time to look further into taking advantage of JNDI.

For our purposes, use of JNDI is very straightforward. First, an instance of a JNDI context is obtained. Next, the JNDI context is used to look up the needed `DataSource` object:

```
InitialContext ctx = new InitialContext();
DataSource ds =
  (DataSource)ctx.lookup("java:comp/env/jdbc/jspbook");
```

The `DataSource` is identified by the unique string, `"java:comp/env/jdbc/jspbook"`, which was previously defined by the entry added to Tomcat's `server.xml`:

```
. . .
  <ResourceParams name="jdbc/jspbook">
. . .
```

The `java:comp/env/` that comes before the name is a standard defined by JNDI. The important thing here is that by using JNDI we are able to obtain access to a `DataSource` object. In doing so we do not have to care about anything besides an arbitrary name being used to index the `DataSource` object. Once the `DataSource` object is obtained, we can then use it to establish a connection with the database.

java.sql.Connection and java.sql.Statement

JDBC connections are represented by the `java.sql.Connection` object. This object can be used for a number of things including obtaining a `java.sql.Statement` object. The `Statement` object is what puts JDBC into the realm of what you should be familiar with. Once a `Statement` object has been obtained, it can be used to execute SQL queries on the database.

The `Statement` object provides a number of methods for executing SQL queries. The mostly straightforward and most commonly used method is `Statement execute()`. The `execute()` method takes as an argument a `String` object describing an SQL query and returns a result from the database. For example, if you look at the code for `ArbitrarySQLDataSource.jsp`, it should be clear how the JSP is executing familiar SQL statements:

```
. . .
    InitialContext ctx = new InitialContext();
    DataSource ds =
      (DataSource)ctx.lookup("java:comp/env/jdbc/jspbook");
    Connection conn = ds.getConnection();
    try {
      statement  = conn.createStatement();
. . .
    String query = request.getParameter("query");
. . .
      ResultSet rs = statement.executeQuery(query);
. . .
```

First, a `DataSource` is obtained, which is then used to get a `Connection` object. Once the `Connection` object has been retrieved, it is used to obtain a `Statement` object that in turn executes SQL statements. The request parameter named `"query"` is the value of the form's text area in `ArbitrarySQLDataSource.jsp`: it is nothing more than an SQL statement, such as SELECT * FROM LINK.

Manage Connections Carefully

Database connections are a valuable resource, especially when the database is on a dedicated server that is shared potentially by multiple computers. There are a few reasons why database connections are so valuable. Most important is the fact that a database connection does not automatically close when an exception is thrown in your program. It stays open and eventually times-out, at which point the database closes the connection. In all of the code examples in this chapter, you will notice that `Connection` objects are always closed using a finally clause. This is important because database servers can only keep so many connections open. If too many connections are left open, the database may perform poorly or be unavailable for use completely. To ensure this does not happen, it is important to always make sure to properly close database connections. The same argument also holds for JDBC statements. A JDBC version 2 driver must close any open statements when a connection is closed. However, JDBC version 3 drivers (which is currently what most drivers are) do not have to do this; in JDBC 3, closing a connection automatically closes any related statements. Therefore, it is important that you call 'close' on any open statements just before you close any connections. Notice as well the odd usage: both `statement.close()` and `connection.close()` are marked as throwing an SQLException. This means the the close methods in the finally block must themselves be wrapped in a try-catch clause. About all that can be done in the try-catch, though, is for the exception to be logged.

Managing database connections in practice is straightforward. Simply make sure the call to the `Connection` object's `close()` method is always in a finally clause. If no try statement exists, it will be a reminder you need to make one.

SQL Transactions

So far our look at JDBC has appeared to involve an extra step. It appears that the `Connection` object's only purpose is to provide a means of obtaining a `Statement` object. While partly true, there is another very important thing the `Connection` object is in charge of: *SQL transactions*. An SQL transaction is a set of SQL statements that must be executed at an atomic unit. Either they all work or they all fail. This is important because there are many times when actions on a database must be regulated. For instance, imagine a Web site created for a bank. The site provides account services, meaning people can withdraw and deposit money using this system. Think about the actions needed when one person gives a sum of money to another:

- Bank withdraws money from person A.
- Back deposits money into person B's account.

Now imagine that person B does not exist. What happens? The money is taken out of person A's account but goes nowhere. Letting it simply disappear would surely aggravate the bank's users. Instead, the problem should be detected and the money put back in person A's account. In summary, this is what SQL transactions are all about, and there are many situations where transactions are needed.

Previously, we had only been executing one SQL statement on the database and looking to see what happened. With SQL transactions, the process is slightly different. The `Connection` object controls if SQL statements are committed, or made official. The following methods are provided:

- **boolean getAutoCommit():** The `getAutoCommit()` method returns a boolean value representing if SQL statements are automatically committed to the database. If `true`, then each statement sent using this connection is automatically committed to the database and cannot be undone. If false, then statements are not committed until the `commit()` method is invoked.

- **void setAutoCommit(boolean commit):** The `setAutoCommit()` method sets if SQL statements are automatically committed or not. If true, statements are committed automatically. If false, the `commit()` method must be explicitly used to commit statements.

- **void commit():** The `commit()` method is used to explicitly commit a set of SQL statements.

- **void rollback():** The `rollback()` method provides a way to undo all of the SQL statements executed since the last `commit()` call. A database is responsible for logging and correctly undoing SQL statements when a rollback is done.

At this level SQL transactions are very easy to use because the database is responsible for keeping track of statements and rolling them back if needed. Previously, it had been assumed that SQL statements are automatically committed to the database, that is, a statement is executed and that changes can instantly be seen. Should an SQL transaction be needed only a slight modification needs to be made. For example, here is the code which would do a transaction of inserting three links in the LINK table of the jspbook database.

```
conn.setAutoCommit(false);
try {
  statement.execute("INSERT INTO LINK VALUES('foo','foo','foo')");
  statement.execute("INSERT INTO LINK VALUES('bar','bar','bar')");
  statement.execute("INSERT INTO LINK VALUES('baz','baz','baz')");
  conn.commit();
}
```

```
catch (Exception e) {
  conn.rollback();
}
```

Obviously, the values being put into the LINK table are bogus, but that is not the point of this example. Unless auto-commit is set to false, the database will use a transaction for each executed statement. To use a transaction for a group of statements, the connection must first be put into non-auto-commit mode. Next, a try block is used to encapsulate all of the statements, including an explicit call to commit the changes. Should something go wrong, a catch clause is used to handle the exception and roll back any statements. By doing this, it is always ensured that the SQL transaction will either successfully occur or appear to never have happened.

Database Meta-Data

Another feature of the Connection object is to provide *meta-data*, data about the database it is connected to. The focus of this chapter has been on being able to safely execute SQL statements. However, what if you had no clue about what was in the database? How would you know which tables existed and what information they contained? This information can be obtained by using the java.sql.DatabaseMetaData object. A DatabaseMetaData object can be obtained by invoking the Connection object's getMetaData() method. The DatabaseMetaData object itself provides a robust set of methods of determining information about a database's tables, schema used on those tables, and all sorts of other meta-data about the database. Consult the JavaDocs for complete information on all of the meta-data methods available.

As a Web tier developer, the DatabaseMetaData object is of limited use. If you were not responsible for creating the database, then usually pertinent information about a database is provided to you; otherwise, there would be no way to accomplish your work. It is rare a project keeps around a tutorial on the database being used, but usually there is either the database administrator or a copy of the SQL used to create the database; either of these can be used to discover what is available.

The DatabaseMetaData object will not be given further coverage by this book. Be aware it exists, but do not be surprised if you never have to use it as a Web tier developer.

java.sql.ResultSet

The java.sql.ResultSet interface is used to describe the results of an SQL statement that has successfully been executed on a database. Information requested by an SQL query is always in the form of a table, so in essence the `ResultSet` object is just a representation of a table of information. An instance of a `ResultSet` object is returned each time a `Statement` object executes a query on a database. Information is then obtained from the `ResultSet` on a per row basis using a cursor to keep track of which row is currently being read:

- **boolean next():** The `next()` method requests the `ResultSet` move to the next row in the table of returned information.
- **boolean first():** The `first()` method moves the cursor to the first row of the `ResultSet`. A boolean value is returned: `true` if there is a first row or `false` if there are no rows. If the `ResultSet` for any reason cannot move the cursor back to the first row, then an `SQLException` is raised.
- **boolean last():** The `last()` method moves the cursor to the last row of the `ResultSet`. A boolean value is returned: `true` if there is a last row or `false` if there are no rows in the result. If the `ResultSet` for any reason cannot move the cursor to the last row, then an `SQLException` is raised.
- **boolean previous():** The `previous()` method moves a cursor to the previous row in the `ResultSet`. A boolean value is returned: `true` if the cursor is on a valid row or `false` if the cursor is off the `ResultSet`.

The `next()` method is the most commonly used. This is because there are different types of `ResultSet` objects. All `ResultSet` objects allow for reading through rows using the `next()` method, but many instances of `ResultSet` will not allow for jumping the cursor around using `first()`, `last()`, `previous()`, or any other non-forward method. To determine what functionality is available with the result set, the `getType()` method can be used and matched to a set of self-describing static `int` values defined by the `ResultSet` interface.

Generally, figuring out if you can scroll both forwards and backwards through a `ResultSet` object is too much work compared to doing an iteration using only the `next()` method. In code the iteration is simple, as previously illustrated by `ArbitrarySQL.jsp`.

```
    ResultSet rs = statement.executeQuery(query);
...
    while (rs.next()) { // show results
...// read from row here...
    }
```

Once at a desired row in a result set (usually all rows are desired), column information can be obtained by invoking a number of different get methods. In all cases the get method takes as an argument the column to retrieve. The values returned are dependent on the method. For example, a generic getObject() method can be invoked that will return an Object that you can typecast; alternatively, a getString() method can be invoked which returns the value of the column as a String object. In general, a convenient get method exists for all of the different SQL data types.

Applying what we now know about ResultSet objects, it is possible to start building some code that takes advantage of SQL and JDBC. As a first example, let us build a simple JSP that shows the current state of the LINK and URI tables, as illustrated in Listing 14-6.

Listing 14-6 ShowTables.jsp

```
<%@ page
import="java.io.*,java.sql.*,javax.sql.*,javax.naming.InitialContext
" %>
<%
  InitialContext ctx = new InitialContext();
  DataSource ds =
    (DataSource)ctx.lookup("java:comp/env/jdbc/jspbook");
  Connection conn = ds.getConnection();
  try {
    Statement statement  = conn.createStatement();
%>
<html>
  <head>
    <title>Show LINK and URI Tables</title>
  </head>
  <body>
  <h2>Contents of LINK Table</h2>
  <table border="1">
  <tr>
    <td>URL</td>
    <td>Title</td>
    <td>Description</td>
  </tr>
<%
  ResultSet rs = statement.executeQuery("SELECT * FROM LINK");
  while (rs.next()) { // show results
    out.println("<tr>");
    out.println("<td>"+rs.getString("url")+"</td>");
```

```
      out.println("<td>"+rs.getString("title")+"</td>");
      out.println("<td>"+rs.getString("description")+"</td>");
      out.println("</tr>");
    }
%>
  </table>
  <h2>Contents of URI Table</h2>
  <table border="1">
  <tr>
    <td>URI</td>
    <td>URL</td>
  </tr>
<%
  rs = statement.executeQuery("SELECT * FROM URI");
  while (rs.next()) { // show results
    out.println("<tr>");
    out.println("<td>"+rs.getString("uri")+"</td>");
    out.println("<td>"+rs.getString("url")+"</td>");
    out.println("</tr>");
  }
%>
  </table>
<%
  }
  catch (Exception e) {
    out.println("<h2>Problem with Query</h2>");
    out.print(e.getMessage());
  }
  finally {
    conn.close();
  }
%>
  </body>
</html>
```

Save the preceding code as ShowTables.jsp in the root directory of the
jspbook Web Application. Before trying the JSP out, be sure to visit Create
Database DataSource.jsp so that the database is ready. Also, add some information to both of the database tables. Use ArbitrarySQLDataSource.jsp to
execute the following SQL commands:

```
INSERT INTO LINK VALUES('http://www.jspbook.com',
  'Book Support Site', 'The book support site.')
INSERT INTO LINK VALUES('http://www.jspinsider.com', 'JSP Insider',
```

```
'JSP information site.')
INSERT INTO LINK VALUES('http://servlets.com', 'Servlets.com',
 'A information site about Java Servlets.')
INSERT INTO URI VALUES('jsp','http://www.jspbook.com')
INSERT INTO URI VALUES('jsp','http://www.jspinsider.com')
INSERT INTO URI VALUES('servlets','http://servlets.com')
```

With the information in the database, now visit `http://127.0.0.1/jspbook/ShowTables.jsp`. Displayed is a listing of all the entries in each of the tables. Figure 14-8 shows a browser rendering of the results.

The specific entries may vary if you have further manipulated the database. The important point is that `ShowTables.jsp` is listing all of the links in the two tables. This is accomplished by iterating through a `ResultSet` for both the "`SELECT * FROM LINK`" and "`SELECT * FROM URI`" SQL queries. The specific code can be seen in `ShowTables.jsp`—for instance, the information from the `LINK` table is shown using:

```
...
  <h2>Contents of LINK Table</h2>
  <table border="1">
  <tr>
```

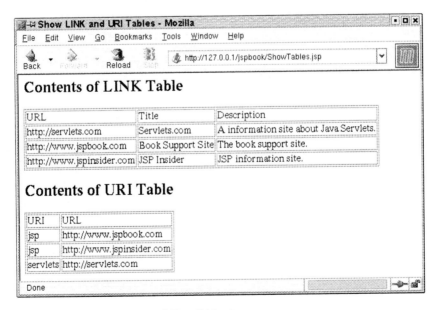

Figure 14-8   Browser Rendering of ShowTables.jsp

```
      <td>URL</td>
      <td>Title</td>
      <td>Description</td>
    </tr>
    <tr>
<%
  ResultSet rs = statement.executeQuery("SELECT * FROM LINK");
  while (rs.next()) { // show results
    out.println("<tr>");
    out.println("<td>"+rs.getString("url")+"</td>");
    out.println("<td>"+rs.getString("title")+"</td>");
    out.println("<td>"+rs.getString("description")+"</td>");
    out.println("</tr>");
  }
%>
    </tr>
    </table>
  . . .
```

The highlighted code is the `Statement` object executing "SELECT * FROM LINK" to obtain a `ResultSet` object. After the query, the result set is iterated through using a `while` loop and the `ResultSet next()` method. Since we know that each of the columns in the `LINK` table is a string, the `getString()` method is called for each column[8,9]. Mixed in with the JDBC code is the HTML required to pretty-print the results in a table. The code for showing the `URI` table is done in a similar fashion.

ResultSet Meta-Data

The `ResultSet` object also provides a method, `getMetaData()`, which returns a `ResultSetMetaData` object, that describes results returned from a database. Like the `DatabaseMetaData` object, the `ResultSetMetaData` object is usually not very helpful to a developer. Assuming you know information about the database being used and you know the SQL command being executed, then you know what to expect in the results.

---

8. Note that column indexes start from one, not zero. Additionally, the `ResultSet` object starts before the first row of the results, so invoking `next()` in the `while` loop will not skip the first row.
9. Note also that the JDBC specification only guarantees "left-to-right", "top-to-bottom" access of a ResultSet. This means that to guarantee that your code works, you must access rows only using the `next()` method, and you must access columns in the order they are retrieved from the database.

What the `ResultSetMetaData` object is good for is mining information about columns. A good example of the functionality can be seen in `ArbitrarySQLData Source.jsp`. Recall that although the JSP allows for arbitrary queries to be made, it does not restrict to queries on a specific table or tables like `ShowTables.jsp` does. The functionality was accomplished by using a `ResultSetMetaData` object as follows:

```
. . .
    ResultSet rs = statement.executeQuery(query);
    ResultSetMetaData rsmd = rs.getMetaData();
. . .
    while (rs.next()) { // show results
      for (int i=0; i<rsmd.getColumnCount();i++) {
        out.println("<td>"+rs.getString(i+1)+"</td>");
      }
    }
. . .
```

The first part of the code should be familiar: an SQL query is being made to obtain a `ResultSet`. Next, a `while` loop is used to iterate through all of the rows in the `ResultSet`. However, instead of hard coding in the get calls for the column values, as done in `ShowTables.jsp`, a `ResultSetMetaData` object is used to get a column count. The count is obtained by calling the `getColumnCount()` method, and the value is used to create a `for` loop that iterates over each of the columns.

The only shortcoming of the code that is used in `ArbitrarySQLDataSource. jsp` is the assumption that the value of each column is a string. SQL has many data types and this will not always be true. For the `LINK` and `URI` tables it is, but in a more robust version of an arbitrary SQL page, the `ResultSetMetaData` object should be used to determine the appropriate type of each column. The `getColumnType()` method can be used in conjunction with the values defined in `java.sql.Types` to achieve this functionality.

Multiple Results

Some statements are complex enough to produce multiple results. Usually these statements are due to JDBC optimization techniques or batch operations being executed on a database. Whatever the case may be, it is possible for multiple `ResultSet` objects to be returned from a database query. In these cases special functionality of the `Statement` interface must be used:

- **boolean getMoreResults():** The `getMoreResults()` method moves to the next set of results for an executed statement. The new results can be obtained by executing the `getResultSet()` method of the `Statement` interface. The `getMoreResults()` method returns a boolean value: `true` if another set of results exists or `false` if not.

- **boolean getMoreResults(int current):** The `getMoreResults()` method moves to the next set of results and performs a specified action on the current set of results. The action is determined by using different self-named static integer values of the `Statement` interface: `CLOSE_ALL_RESULTS`, `CLOSE_CURRENT_RESULT`, or `KEEP_CURRENT_RESULT`.

A single SQL statement will never result in multiple results. Do not worry about needing to handle multiple results unless a special JDBC operation is being executed that results in them. In that case, code accordingly using the `getMoreResults()` and `getResultSet()` methods appropriately.

A Simple JDBC-Based Application

By now all of the basics of SQL and JDBC have been covered. Each of the topics deserves a book in itself to fully cover them; however, with what this chapter has introduced, you should have a good understanding of the fundamental concepts of SQL and JDBC. It is about time that these concepts were put to practical use. The current `LINK` and `URI` tables are designed for use as a Web site's link management system. We shall now build such a system as an exercise of applying SQL and JDBC to JSP and Servlets.

The basic ideal behind the system is easy to grasp. Most Web sites in some form provide a number to links to other resources on the World Wide Web. The links could be to other pages on the same site or to completely different Web sites. What this application does is use the `LINK` and `URI` tables to manage a collection of links and group them by a common index. Refresh your memory on the entries in the `LINK` and `URI` tables; browse to `ShowTables.jsp`. Excluding any additional links you might have added, the links should be present in the `LINK` table that is shown in Figure 14-9. The `URI` table should include the information that is shown in Figure 14-10.

If the links are not there, go back to and execute the SQL statements provided previously in `ResultSet` interface discussion. If you have not yet noticed, there is a pattern between the `LINK` and `URI` tables. The `LINK` table provides raw information about a link: a URL, a title, and a description. The `URI` table provides indexes for types of links and relates them to the `LINK` table using the unique URL

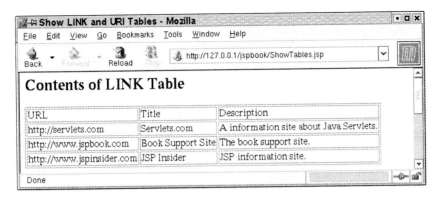

Figure 14-9 Links in the LINK Table

or the foreign key[10]. For example, the URI table contains two rows that have jsp as the value of the URI column. Each of those rows also has a URL that can be used to reference a link in the LINK table. The end result is that a query can be done on the URI table to find all links that are indexed by jsp, or, as is meant, are about JSP topics. The SQL query would be the following:

```
SELECT l.url, l.title, l.description FROM LINK l, URI u WHERE u.url
= l.url AND u.uri = 'jsp'
```

Figure 14-10 Indexes in the URI Table

---

10. A *foreign key* is a value in one database table that references a primary key in another table. Because primary keys are guaranteed to be unique, foreign keys are the method for relating database tables.

The preceding SQL statement uses a "join" of two tables to find the appropriate LINK entries that are indexed by jsp. The query could have been accomplished using multiple, simple SELECT statements, but the preceding is the proper way to do the query[11]. The LINK table, associated with l, and the URI table, associated with u, are combined into one big table. The larger table is then evaluated to find entries where the URLs match and the uri value is 'jsp'.

Try the preceding query using ArbitrarySQLDataSource.jsp. The results are as expected: a list of links about JSP. Excluded is the obviously non-JSP site, http://servlets.com. Figure 14-11 shows a browser rendering of the results.

Making Use of the URI and LINK Tables

Given that you know how to add, remove, and edit entries in both the LINK and URI tables, the SQL statement demonstrated at the end of the last section is all that is needed to use the link management system. Instead of showing the links using ArbitrarySQLDataSource.jsp, create a custom Servlet or JSP that displays

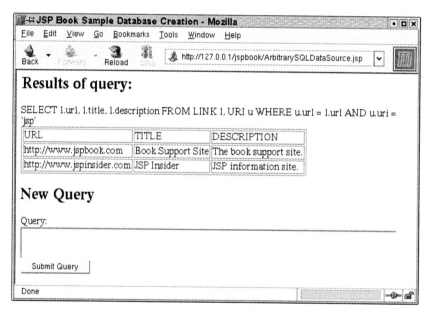

Figure 14-11 Browser Rendering of Returned JSP-Related Links

---

11. The join is a good example of an SQL skill that it is very useful or even necessary to have, but it is not covered in this chapter.

links based on an index. For example, Listing 14-7 is a page that prints out a pretty list of links in HTML.

Listing 14-7 ShowLinks.jsp

```jsp
<%@ page import="java.io.*,java.sql.*, javax.sql.*, javax.naming.*,
java.util.*" %>
<%
  InitialContext ctx = new InitialContext();
  DataSource ds =
    (DataSource)ctx.lookup("java:comp/env/jdbc/jspbook");
  Connection conn = ds.getConnection();
  LinkedList links = new LinkedList();
  request.setAttribute("links", links);
  try {
    Statement statement  = conn.createStatement();
    String uri = request.getParameter("uri");
    if (uri != null && !uri.equals("")) {
      ResultSet rs = statement.executeQuery("SELECT l.url, l.title,
l.description FROM LINK l, URI u WHERE l.url = u.url AND u.uri =
'"+uri+"'");
      while (rs.next()) { // show results
        Hashtable map = new Hashtable();
        map.put("url", rs.getString(1));
        map.put("title", rs.getString(2));
        map.put("description", rs.getString(3));
        links.add(map);
      }
    }
  }
  finally {
    conn.close();
  }
%>
<html>
  <head>
    <title>JSP Book Sample Database Creation</title>
  </head>
  <body>
<%@ taglib uri="http://java.sun.com/jstl/core" prefix="c" %>
<c:forEach var="link" begin="0" items="${links}">
    <h3 style="margin-bottom:2px;">
      <a href="${link.url}">${link.title}</a>
    </h3>
```

```
    ${link.description}
  </c:forEach>
  </body>
</html>
```

The page relies on a request parameter name `uri` that is expected to match a `uri` in the `URI` table. If so, a list of links is displayed for all links that match the `URI`. Try the page out to view JSP-related links; browse to `http://127.0.0.1/jspbook/ShowLinks.jsp?uri=jsp`. An HTML page appears with all the JSP-related links. Figure 14-12 shows the results.

The page works equally as well to show the other types of links that have been indexed, Servlet links. Try browsing to `http://127.0.0.1/jspbook/ShowLinks.jsp?uri=servlets`. This time the page shows all of the Servlet-related links. Figure 14-13 is a browser rendering of the results.

In general the link viewing page can be used to show any type of links that are indexed in the `URI` table. The only information that needs to be changed is the `uri` value passed as a parameter. Links are taken straight from the database and formatted nicely for display.

Why Put Links in a Database?

`ShowLinks.jsp` is, initially, not incredibly impressive. Sure it works with a database to display links, but just because it uses JDBC does not make it good. What makes storing links in a database helpful is that they can very easily be managed. `ShowLinks.jsp` is just a small example of how helpful database-managed information is. For example, Show Links is a consolidated template for showing any collection of links a site may use. Compared to keeping around mul-

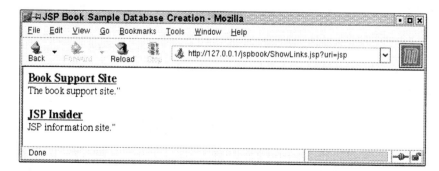

Figure 14-12 ShowLinks.jsp Showing JSP-Related Links

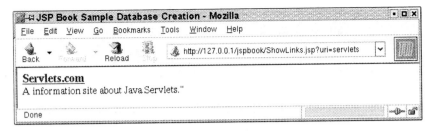

Figure 14-13 Browser Rendering of Servlet-Related Links

tiple pages filled with various links, the advantage is huge. Just imagine how easy it would be to change the style that ShowLinks.jsp displays links compared to changing a few dozen HTML(ish) pages.

Styling is not the only reason for consolidating links. The Web is constantly changing. Links to other Web sites often go bad, resulting in aggravated users. By consolidating links in a database, it becomes incredibly easy to take care of bad links on your Web site. A complete list of links can be obtained by looking at the LINK table. To complement ShowLinks.jsp, another utility can be built that looks through the LINK table and tests each link to see if it is still valid. If it is not, then the link can be removed. When run on a regular basis, this would ensure that users are not left with a collection of bad links. Thanks to the J2SE, building such a link-checker is quite easy, assuming you have a database. Listing 14-8 is an example.

Listing 14-8 LinkChecker.jsp

```
<%@ page import="java.io.*,java.sql.*, javax.sql.*, javax.naming.*,
java.util.*, java.net.*" %>
<%
  InitialContext ctx = new InitialContext();
  DataSource ds =
    (DataSource)ctx.lookup("java:comp/env/jdbc/jspbook");
  Connection conn = ds.getConnection();
  LinkedList deleted = new LinkedList();
  try {
    Statement statement  = conn.createStatement();
    ResultSet rs =
      statement.executeQuery("SELECT * FROM LINK");
    while (rs.next()) { // show results
      String url = rs.getString(1);
```

```
      URL u = new URL(url);
      boolean failed = false;
      try {
        HttpURLConnection huc =
          (HttpURLConnection)u.openConnection();
        int responseCode = huc.getResponseCode();
        if (responseCode >= 400 && responseCode < 500) {
          failed = true;
        }
        huc.disconnect();
      }
      catch (UnknownHostException e) {
        failed = true;
      }
      catch (UnknownServiceException e) {
        failed = true;
      }
      if (failed) {
        statement.execute("DELETE FROM LINK WHERE url = '"+url+"'");
        deleted.add(url);
      }
    }
  }
  finally {
    conn.close();
  }
%>
<html>
  <head>
    <title>Link Checker</title>
  </head>
  <body>
  <h2>Links Deleted</h2>
<% while(deleted.size() > 0) {
    String deletedUrl = (String)deleted.remove(0); %>
    <%= deletedUrl %><br>
<% } %>
  <%@ taglib uri="http://java.sun.com/jstl/core_rt" prefix="c" %>
  <c:forEach var="link" begin="0" items="${links}">
    <hr>
    <h3>
      <a href="${link.url}">${link.title}</a>
    </h3>
    ${link.description}
```

```
    </c:forEach>
    </body>
</html>
```

The code uses the `java.net.URL` and `java.net.URLConnection` classes to try and open a connection to each link in the LINK table.

```
ResultSet rs = statement.executeQuery("SELECT * FROM LINK");
while (rs.next()) { // show results
  String url = rs.getString(1);
  URL u = new URL(url);
  boolean failed = false;
  try {
    HttpURLConnection huc =
       (HttpURLConnection)u.openConnection();
```

If the connection can be opened, the HTTP response code is obtained and checked. If it is in the 400's, then the link is considered bad and a boolean delete flag, `failed`, is set to `true`. Likewise, if the connection cannot be opened—that is, an exception is thrown—then the delete flag is set to `true`.

```
      int responseCode = huc.getResponseCode();
      if (responseCode >= 400 && responseCode < 500) {
        failed = true;
      }
      huc.close();
    }
  catch (UnknownHostException e) {
    failed = true;
  }
  catch (UnknownServiceException e) {
    failed = true;
  }
```

Finally, if the delete flag is set, an SQL DELETE statement is used to remove the link. Because of the database integrity rules, this also deletes any related entries in the URI table.

```
  if (failed) {
    statement.execute("DELETE FROM LINK WHERE url = '"+url+"'");
    deleted.add(url);
  }
```

The end result is that all links in the LINK table that are not valid are removed. Try out `LinkChecker.jsp` by browsing to `http://127.0.0.1/jspbook/`

`LinkChecker.jsp`. You may wish to use `ArbitrarySQLDataSource.jsp` to add in a few bogus links in order to see them removed. Any links that `LinkChecker.jsp` removes are displayed in an HTML page. Figure 14-14 shows what a browser rendering looks like after removing some bad links.

Overall, there are many other uses the `LINK` and `URI` tables can be put to. Some more good uses would be building a simple page for people to submit links from, perhaps, an online guest book of sorts, or building a voting system that could keep track of a link's popularity and display collections of links based on the information. The link tracking is easy to do, as demonstrated in Chapter 2, and with the link information in a database, it is easy to access and change it. The point is that there are many things that a database full of links can be used for. Without JDBC and the database, accomplishing the same functionality would be difficult and involve spending the time to code an ad hoc solution.

In general, consolidating information into a database-like system is a very good thing. By keeping everything in one central place, it is easier to manage the information on the whole. After all, that is the idea behind databases and it is the reason databases have such widespread adoption in programming. The demonstrated link management system is an excellent example of the type of functionality JDBC and databases can add to a Web Application. Use it!

Using JDBC Optimally

Much like SQL, there is a lot more to JDBC than can be fully covered in a single chapter. However, what this chapter has explained of JDBC so far details most everything that is needed to successfully use JDBC in an application. What has

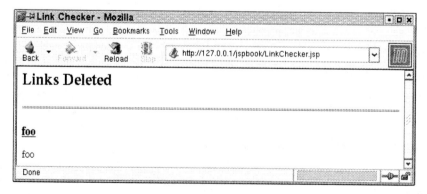

Figure 14-14   A Few Bad Links Removed by LinkChecker.jsp

yet to be covered is some of the more complex uses of JDBC which usually relate directly to a more complex use of a DBMS. In this section of the chapter some of the more complex concepts of JDBC and DBMS will be introduced. When possible, concrete examples are provided, but much of the functionality is related directly to the specific database being used and the JDBC implementation provided. It would be futile for this book to try and cover all the possible databases or guess which database you will be using for future projects. For these reasons there will be several sections where an important concept is introduced but not demonstrated. Instead, you are directed to consult the documentation for whatever particular DBMS and JDBC implementation is being used.

Connection Pooling

The classic staple technique to increasing JDBC performance is to use connection pooling. *Connection pooling* involves optimizing the time required to establish a connection with a database. In most practical situations a database is being run on a completely separate server somewhere else in the world, commonly on the local network. In these cases the time it takes to create a connection with the server is notably time-consuming. Therefore, the idea is to open up a pool of connections, initially taking up time, then constantly re-use those connections and never spend time establishing new connections. The technique works quite well and pivots around keeping a pool of enough connections to handle all of your application's needs but not wastefully opening too many connections for the pool.

"Classic" was used to describe connection pooling because now the practice is commonly handled automatically by `DataSource` implementations. Along with being able to specify JDBC url, user-name, and password information for a `DataSource`, most implementations allow for extra features such as the amount of connections to pool. A database administrator can then specify the amount of desired connections to pool and allow the `DataSource` to seamlessly optimize connection management. Because of the commonality of connection pooling, it is recommended you consult the documentation for the JDBC drivers being used on your specific project. Connection pooling at the `DataSource` level is ideal because it requires no extra effort on your part.

If the database you decide to use does not provide connection pooling, you can still do it the classic way. The best technique is to create a custom `DataSource` object and a `Connection` object that wrap your vendor-specific ones. The custom `DataSource` is used to pool connections. For example, it initially opens up *x* connections from a vendor's `DataSource`. When calls to the `getConnection()` method are made, it provides a connection from the pool instead of requesting a new connection from the vendor's `DataSource`. The custom `Connection` object needs to wrap the vendor's `Connection` object and override the `close()` method. Instead of closing the connection the wrapper should return the still-open `Connection` to the pool. The end result is your custom `DataSource` object juggles around a fixed number of open connections, never spending time opening up new connections.

Pooling resources is a great performance concept to be aware of, and it can be applied to many things besides database connections. Custom tags are a good example; just look at the life cycle. It is appealing to provide a clever example in this chapter of a `DataSource` pooling `Connection` objects, but many good, free implementations of connection pooling code exist. Also, as mentioned, most JDBC vendors already have connection pooling rolled into their products. For these reasons you will be left to consult your vendor's JDBC documentation, and if no connection pooling is implemented, consult the following links:

- **Jakarta Commons DBCP:**
  `http://jakarta.apache.org/commons/dbcp.html`: The Database Connection Pooling (DBCP) project is part of Jakarta's Commons and is designed to pool JDBC connections. The JDBC project happens to also be the listing that Tomcat uses to pool database connections. Being under the liberal Apache license, the listing is great to both learn from and use.

- **Jakarta Commons Pool:**
  `http://jakarta.apache.org/commons/pool.html`: The Jakarta Commons Pool project is a general-purpose set of APIs used to pool any type of object (not that all objects should be pooled). The API is the foundation of the DBCP project. Being under the Apache license, the listing is great to both learn from and use.

Optimized Statements

Execution of SQL statements is often the slowest part of database interaction. Opening and closing connections is manageable, but a poorly done SQL statement can dramatically slow a database down. The first step to ensuring an SQL statement performs well is by optimizing the statement itself. This involves structuring the SQL in such a fashion that it optimizes the joining of tables and checking of conditions. Optimizing SQL can be very complex and is outside the scope of this book. What is covered by this book are the different types of JDBC `Statement` interfaces that can be used.

In this chapter only the `Statement` interface has been used. This interface is suited for providing completely ad hoc queries on a database, but it is not designed to allow a database to easily optimize those statements. Two other `Statement` interfaces are available that can be used for this purpose. The interfaces are `java.sql.PreparedStatement` and `java.sql.CallableStatement`.

Prepared Statements

The `PreparedStatement` interface extends `Statement` and provides support for pre-compiled, parameterized statements with input parameters. A vendor-specific `PreparedStatement` implementing object can be obtained by invoking a factory method on the `Connection` interface: `prepareStatement()`. There are several different versions of the `prepareStatement()` method, each with a specific purpose. Only the most basic one will be covered by this text, although conceptually all of the methods are similar.

In `PreparedStatement prepareStatement(String sql)`, the `prepareStatement()` method takes as an argument a parameterized SQL statement and returns a `PreparedStatement` object. The SQL statement passed to the `prepareStatement()` method is then optimized for repeated use, requiring the `PreparedStatement` to fill in needed parameters.

In use, a `PreparedStatement` is much like a `Statement` but with the SQL provided when the statement is obtained. Instead of the no-argument `getStatement()` method, now there is the `prepareStatement()` method that relies on the SQL beforehand. For example, a simple query to obtain all of the entries in the LINK table would be done as follows:

```
PreparedStatement ps =
    connection.prepareStatement("SELECT * FROM LINK");
ResultSet = ps.execute();
```

Optimization occurs by letting the database see the statement before it needs to be executed. By doing this the database is free to compile the statement into an optimal form that can later be used. For single-use ad-hoc statements this optimization is obviously not very helpful. A database can already optimize SQL statements before using them when the `Statement` interface is used. Where the `PreparedStatement` interface is helpful is when multiple queries are going to be done using the same statement or a similar statement. For instance, if the preceding code executed the prepared statement multiple times, it would likely be notably faster than using a `Statement` object to do the same.

Where the `PreparedStatement` interface comes in really handy is when it is used in the parameterized form. The initial SQL statement used in the `prepareStatment()` call does not have to be complete. Parameters can be replaced by a question mark, `?`, and replaced later before executing the statement. What this does is allow the database to optimize the SQL statement and used the optimized statement for different parameters. For example, in `ShowLinks.jsp` it is always known what the basic SQL statement is:

```
SELECT l.url, l.title, l.description FROM LINK l, URI u
    WHERE u.url = l.url AND u.uri = ?
```

The only unknown parameter is what `uri` should be used, or what category of links should be shown. The better way to code `ShowLinks.jsp` would be to use a `PreparedStatement` instead of `Statement` and specify the preceding SQL. At runtime the JSP would then no longer have to obtain a new statement each time it was making a query. Instead, the changing parameter could be applied and a database-optimized statement used. Parameters are specified by calling an appropriate set method on the `PreparedStatement` object. The set methods are much like the get methods on the `ResultSet` object. To set a string, the `Prepared Statement setString()` method is used. Different set methods are available for all the SQL data types. Like the `ResultSet` get methods, the set methods also require an index number of which parameter is being set. For the SQL just shown, there is only one parameter:

```
String uri = request.getParameter("uri");
PreparedStatement ps =
    connection.prepareStatement("SELECT l.url, l.title, l.description
                                 FROM LINK l, URI u
                                 WHERE u.url = l.url AND u.uri = ?");
ps.setString(1, uri);
ResultSet = ps.execute();
```

In cases where multiple question marks were used in the prepared SQL statement, then multiple set methods would need to be called to set each of the parameters.

We have not provided a complete example of using `PreparedStatement` here; however, `PreparedStatements` should be used wherever possible to maximize your database performance. The usage model for `PreparedStatement` is exactly the same as for a statement:

```
Get a Connection;
Create a PreparedStatement;
Use the PreparedStatement;
Close the PreparedStatement;
Close the Connection;
```

The strong point of PreparedStatements is to allow the database to optimize the statement being executed, typically by creating what is called an *execution plan*. However, databases will throw away that execution plan when the statement is closed. When you look at the previous usage pattern, you will realize that each time you use a PreparedStatement, the database works to create an execution plan and then throws the plan away as soon as the statement is closed, so it appears that using a PreparedStatement actually hurts rather than improves performance. As a footnote to this, never keep statements or connections open longer than is absolutely necessary. Connections and Statements both use database resources: those resources should be given back as soon as possible to allow the database to be as efficient as possible. In the case of Servlets, connections and statements must not outlive a single HTTP round-trip (a request/ response pair). To allow developers to get the improved performance of using a PreparedStatement and not violate the rules of having to close statements after each request, many database pooling implementations also pool Prepared Statements. This means that in the same way that database connections are put back into the pool when closed, so will preparedstatements. Notice that connections and statements are being kept open longer than a single request, but the pool will only keep a limited number open (specified by the database administrator).

Stored Procedures

The CallableStatement interface extends PreparedStatement and is used to execute statements programmed natively into the database. A performance increase comes from the code not needing to be compiled at all by the database. Instead, a programmer can code the procedure natively on the database, taking advantage of any database-specific API, and compile the procedure so that it is ready for use. Stored procedures are very database-specific but are also the most optimal method of performing database queries. Effectively, they sidestep the need for SQL.

A CallableStatement is obtained by calling the callableStatement() method of a Connection object. Like a PreparedStatement a parameterized statement needs to be provided when calling the callableStatement() method. Unlike a PreparedStatement the parameterized statement is not usually in SQL. JDBC uses the XOpen escape clause ({? = call procedure_ name(?, ?)}) to provide a vendor-neutral method of calling prepared statements; however, many vendors also allow a vendor-specific statement to be used. After obtaining a CallableStatement object, a JDBC developer needs to provide the proper parameters to satisfy the prepared statement. This is done using the same set methods of PreparedStatement. The results of executing a CallableStatement can be obtained by invoking ResultSet-like get methods or by using the functionality inherited from the Statement interface.

Due to the nature of stored procedures, they will not be discussed further. It is very likely that when building a high-performance database-based system that stored procedures will be how statements are executed. However, stored procedures are always vendor-specific. You will have to consult the specific documentation for your favorite database to see what level of support stored procedures have and how you can take advantage of them[12].

Database Administrators Are Expected to Know a Lot

Tech books can be expensive and tedious to read. This is exactly why this chapter was added to this book, and it is why you have yet to be directed to pick up a good JDBC book. In practice, what you have learned in this chapter should be more than enough to avoid needing a learn-JDBC book. You should be able to get by just fine working with a database and incorporating JDBC with your Servlets and JSPs. However, should you be a developer who for whatever reason is also the acting database administrator, seriously consider finding extra help. The SQL book suggested earlier in this chapter is a fantastic start, but it also helps to know a lot about the database that you will be using. If the database you choose to use comes with excellent documentation, then the issue is solved. If it does not, or you are using a very robust (likely also extra-complex) database, such as the pricey Microsoft, Oracle, or IBM line of products, look into a good book that covers JDBC and that database.

JDBC Web Application Design Patterns

SQL and JDBC are powerful skills to add to your skill-set and can greatly enhance a Web Application; however, like all things there are both good and bad ways to implement the functionality. Sadly, this chapter has shown bad implementation after bad implementation of good SQL and JDBC concepts. In an

---

12. A slight tangent: there do exist some excellent free, open source databases that can easily satisfy most real-world applications. Most notably is the popular MySQL database. However, MySQL is well known for its lack of uber-optimal features such as stored procedures. As of the writing of this book, there are currently no free extra-high-performance databases. If there were, it would have been promoted for use with JDBC and all Web Applications.

attempt to rectify this misdeed, a proper attempt to discuss implementing database-functionality is provided.

First off, this section is only discussing JDBC implementation. Installing a database and figuring out the SQL to use against it should be completely independent of your Servlet and JSP code. As so, this discussion of JDBC design patterns does apply to all databases and is helpful for use in any Web Application. Regardless of which database/JDBC product you are using, both open source and commercial alike, you should read this part of the chapter as a guide to how to code JDBC functionality into your Servlets and JSPs.

There are three roughly distinct methods of coding JDBC functionality into a Web Application: Model 1, Model 2, and using Data Access Objects (DAO). The first two methods should be self-explanatory given the previous chapter on design patterns. Both approaches assume a differing number of the Web Application developers know JDBC. In the case of the Model 1 approach, it is assumed that the Servlet and JSP developers know JDBC. A Model 1 implementation freely intermixes JDBC code where it is needed in a JSP or Servlet, much like all the examples in this chapter. The design is intuitive but suffers from all of the problems of the Model 1 design pattern. The Model 2 approach assumes only the "Model" developer needs to know JDBC. Recall the Model 2 design is based around abstracting out where and how information comes to a JSP or Servlet, commonly just a JSP. Instead, the focus is to restrict a JSP or Servlet to only worrying about presentation logic: all other code is placed in separate, complementary components.

For most Web Applications and collaborative projects involving Web Applications, the Model 2 design pattern will be the best method of implementing JDBC with Servlets and JSP. Fewer people will be required to understand JDBC, and the code will be safely abstracted into Model components. However, there are certain situations where it must be guaranteed that JDBC functionality will be used responsibly. Usually this situation is identifiable by the people in charge of the database, not wanting developers to have the ability to use ad hoc queries on a database. The reason being, a few malicious, or just poorly done, queries can trash the all-important data repository.

In cases where JDBC functionality needs to absolutely be used responsibly, there are two good options. The first is to find a very good database administrator who will go to the trouble of securing the database against any problematic

---

13. A *view* is what a user is able to see and access in a database. Views can be completely fictitious or derived from other parts of a database.

queries. This can be done using SQL to specify appropriate data-integrity rules, user permissions, and database views[13]. However, finding such a database administrator can be difficult. An alternative solution is to abstract database access using a DAO design pattern.

Data Access Objects Design Pattern

The Data Access Objects (DAO) design pattern, as applied to Java/JDBC, is to create a set of Java objects that provide the appropriate CRUD actions. The objects are then used as the sole interface for Web Application developers that need to access a database. The design pattern has many benefits. The critical benefit of the design pattern is that database access, including SQL queries, becomes the responsibility of whoever codes the DAO. This means the DAO could log on to the database with administrative privileges which it would not be a problem if they were coded properly. Another advantage of the design pattern is that only the data object coder(s) needs to know JDBC. Web Application developers are exposed to a pure Java interface that can be as basic and/or intuitive as need be. Finally, the design pattern provides true transparency of the database being used. If later on it was desired to switch to a completely different database, only the DAO would need re-coding. The rest of the Web Application would be safe from breaking.

Conceptually, the DAO design pattern is nothing new. It is a logical abstraction of database-specific code. In J2EE the official implementation of the concept is referred to as Enterprise JavaBeans (EJB). EJB can be used as a functional implementation of the DAO design pattern, but many developers, including both of this book's authors, believe that EJB are simply overkill for most every use. The concepts are good, but the EJB learning curve is difficult, and the performance of the technology often suffers because of poor implementation. The preferred approach is to dissect the various components that make up EJB and understand why they are important. From there, implement the concepts as they best fit your particular project. That is the approach promoted by this book, and that is what the last part of this chapter (and part of the next chapter) trys to explain.

Implementing the DAO Design Pattern

If you followed this chapter's previous discussion of CRUD, implementing the DAO design pattern is easy. The important thing to do is create a set of objects that have a `create()`, `update()`, `delete()`, and `read()` method or equivalents thereof. A common practice is simply to put these methods on an associated JavaBean. Listing 14-9, `News.java`, is an example.

Listing 14-9   News.java

```
package com.jspbook;

public class News {
  protected String title = null;
  protected String link = null;
  protected String story = null;

  public String getTitle() { return title; }
  public void setTitle(String title) { this.title = title; }

  public String getLink() { return link; }
  public void setLink(String link) { this.link = link; }

  public String getStory() { return story; }
  public void setStory(String story) { this.story = story; }
}
```

Converting `News.java` into a DAO would be as simple as adding the following methods:

```
package com.jspbook;

public class News {
  protected String title = null;
  protected String link = null;
  protected String story = null;

  public static void create(News[] news) {
    // JDBC code to add news entries in a database
  }
  public static News[] read(String index) {
    // JDBC code to read news entries in a database
  }
  public static void update(News[] news) {
    // JDBC code to update news entries in a database
  }
  public static void delete(News[] news) {
    // JDBC code to remove the given news entries
  }

  public String getTitle() { return title; }
  public void setTitle(String title) { this.title = title; }
  ...
```

The `create()` method takes an array of new `News` objects and serializes them into the database. The `read()` method is given an index string that the database can use to return a select set of `News` objects. The `update()` method takes a modified set of news objects that were previously read from the database and saves the changes to the database. Finally, the `delete()` method takes a set of previously read `News` objects and deletes their entries from the database. For completeness, each of the methods should additionally throw an exception in order to provide feedback if any of the CRUD operations cannot be accomplished.

In general, any JavaBean being used to store information, such as `News.java`, can be modified using the DAO technique described previously. However, there are many ways in which the same functionality can be achieved. The drawback of the previous approach is that each JavaBean being used in your Web Application now has to be cluttered up with the CRUD methods and JDBC code. To avoid this, another popular DAO implementation is to use factory classes to encapsulate all of the CRUD functionality. This approach results in twice as many classes, but overall, the code is simpler in each class. Using factories to implement the DAO design pattern is going to be the approach we will explore further. Keep in mind that at any time you can certainly move the logic the factories are providing into either the JavaBean itself or into any other desired class.

DAO Factories

As a complete example of an implementation of the DAO design pattern, we will now build a simple application that uses the `LINK` and `URI` tables to provide a link management system for a Web site. The functionality will be identical to that which the chapter previously accomplished using `ArbitrarySQLDataSource.jsp` and `ShowLinks.jsp`. The difference will be that the previous JDBC code is now replaced by DAO, and the JSP used will follow the Model 1½ design pattern.

The first piece of code that is needed is a JavaBean that can be used to store information about a link, as shown in Listing 14-10.

Listing 14-10 LinkBean.java

```
package com.jspbook;

public class LinkBean {
  protected String title = null;
  protected String url = null;
  protected String desc = null;
```

```java
public String getTitle() { return title; }
public void setTitle(String title) { this.title = title; }

public String getUrl() { return url; }
public void setUrl(String url) { this.url = url; }

public String getDescription() { return desc; }
public void setDescription(String desc) { this.desc =desc;}
}
```

Save `LinkBean.java` in the `/WEB-INF/classes/com/jspbook` directory of the jspbook Web Application. The code is straightforward; it consists of getter and setter methods for a link's URL, title, and description. There is nothing else that is significant about the preceding code.

The next, more interesting piece of code is a factory class that provides the CRUD methods needed to manipulate database entries that correspond to `LinkBean` objects. Listing 14-11 is an example.

Listing 14-11 LinkFactory.java

```java
package com.jspbook;

import java.util.*;
import javax.naming.*;
import java.sql.*;
import javax.sql.*;

public class LinkFactory {
  public static void create(LinkBean[] links) throws Exception {
    InitialContext ctx = new InitialContext();
    DataSource ds =
      (DataSource)ctx.lookup("java:comp/env/jdbc/jspbook");
    Connection conn = ds.getConnection();
    Statement statement  = conn.createStatement();
    try {
      for (int i=0; i<links.length;i++) {
        LinkBean link = links[i];
        if (link == null) continue;
        if (link.getUrl() == null) {
          throw new Exception("Link #"+i+" has null for url
value!");
        }
        statement.executeQuery("INSERT INTO LINK
VALUES('"+link.getUrl()+"', '"+link.getTitle()+"',
```

```java
'"+link.getDescription()+"')");
      }
    }
    finally {
      statement.close();
      conn.close();
    }
  }


  public static LinkBean[] read(String index) throws Exception {
    String sql = "SELECT * FROM LINK";
    if (index != null) {
      sql = "SELECT l.url, l.title, l.description FROM LINK l, URI u
WHERE l.url = u.url AND u.uri = '"+index+"'";
    }
    InitialContext ctx = new InitialContext();
    DataSource ds =
      (DataSource)ctx.lookup("java:comp/env/jdbc/jspbook");
    Connection conn = ds.getConnection();
    Statement statement  = conn.createStatement();
    LinkedList ll = new LinkedList();
    try {
      ResultSet rs = statement.executeQuery(sql);
      while (rs.next()) { // show results
        LinkBean link = new LinkBean();
        link.setUrl(rs.getString(1));
        link.setTitle(rs.getString(2));
        link.setDescription(rs.getString(3));
        ll.add(link);
      }
      LinkBean[] links = new LinkBean[ll.size()];
      for(int i=0;ll.size() >0;i++) {
        links[i] = (LinkBean)ll.remove(0);
      }
      return links;
    }
    finally {
      conn.close();
    }
  }

  public static void update(LinkBean[] links)
      throws Exception {
    // validate input
```

```java
      if (links == null || links.length == 0) return;
      InitialContext ctx = new InitialContext();
      DataSource ds =
         (DataSource)ctx.lookup("java:comp/env/jdbc/jspbook");
      Connection conn = ds.getConnection();
      Statement statement  = conn.createStatement();
      LinkedList ll = new LinkedList();
      try {
        for (int i=0;i<links.length;i++) {
          LinkBean link = links[i];
          if (link.getUrl() == null) continue;
          statement.executeQuery("UPDATE LINK SET
title='"+link.getTitle()+"', description='"+link.getDescription()+"'
WHERE url='"+link.getUrl()+"'");
        }
      }
      finally {
        conn.close();
      }
  }

  public static void delete(LinkBean[] links)
      throws Exception {
      // validate input
      if (links == null || links.length == 0) return;
      InitialContext ctx = new InitialContext();
      DataSource ds =
         (DataSource)ctx.lookup("java:comp/env/jdbc/jspbook");
      Connection conn = ds.getConnection();
      Statement statement  = conn.createStatement();
      LinkedList ll = new LinkedList();
      try {
        for (int i=0;i<links.length;i++) {
          LinkBean link = links[i];
          if (link.getUrl() == null) continue;
          statement.executeQuery("DELETE FROM LINK WHERE
url='"+link.getUrl()+"'");
        }
      }
      finally {
        conn.close();
      }
    }
}
```

Save the preceding code as `LinkFactory.java` in the `/WEB-INF/classes/`
`com/jspbook` directory of the jspbook Web Application. It is important to see that
the preceding code is encapsulating all of the JDBC the Web Application needs.
The self-describing methods `create()`, `read()`, `update()`, and `delete()` use only
the `LinkBean` object as an interface. Thus developers do not need to know anything about the database; the only thing needed is an understanding of the
`LinkFactory` class.

The code for `LinkFactory.java` is relatively lengthy compared to other code
examples in this chapter, but none of the code is new. Each of the CRUD methods
is responsible for executing the SQL needed to manipulate the database, and
information is interfaced by using the `LinkBean` object. For example, the `read()`
method takes an index string and returns an array of `LinkBean` objects. First, an
index is passed to the method and a connection is opened to the database:

```
public static Link[] read(String index) throws Exception {
  // validate input
  if (index == null) return new LinkBean[0];
  InitialContext ctx = new InitialContext();
  DataSource ds =
    (DataSource)ctx.lookup("java:comp/env/jdbc/jspbook");
  Connection conn = ds.getConnection();
```

Next, an SQL statement is used to query the appropriate links:

```
Statement statement  = conn.createStatement();
LinkedList ll = new LinkedList();
try {
  ResultSet rs =
    statement.executeQuery("SELECT l.url, l.title, l.description
      FROM LINK l, URI u
      WHERE l.url = u.url AND u.uri = '"+index+"'");
```

Finally, the `ResultSet` is iterated through to create an array of `Link` objects.

```
while (rs.next()) { // show results
  LinkBean link = new LinkBean();
  link.setUrl(rs.getString(1));
  link.setTitle(rs.getString(2));
  link.setDescription(rs.getString(3));
  ll.add(link);
}
LinkBean[] links = new LinkBean[ll.size()];
for(int i=0;ll.size() >0;i++) {
```

```
    links[i] = (LinkBean)ll.remove(0);
  }
  return links;
```

The other CRUD methods work in a similar fashion. Either an array of
`LinkBean` objects is taken and used to generate queries on the database, or the
database is queried to produce a collection of `Link` objects. In all cases a Servlet
and JSP developer is left only with `LinkBean` objects and needs to know nothing
about JDBC. The code for `LinkFactory.java` is just one example of a factory
class providing DAO functionality. If there were multiple types of JavaBeans for
the site used, then a factory would need to be built for each one.

Using the `LinkFactory` in a Servlet or JSP should be intuitive. For example,
the equivalent of `ShowLinks.jsp` would be Listing 14-12.

Listing 14-12 DAOShowLinks.jsp

```
<%@ page import="com.jspbook.*" %>
<%
  String uri = request.getParameter("uri");
  LinkBean[] links = LinkFactory.read(uri);
  request.setAttribute("links", links);
%>
<html>
  <head>
    <title>JSP Book Sample Database Creation</title>
  </head>
  <body>
  <%@ taglib uri="http://java.sun.com/jstl/core_rt" prefix="c" %>
  <c:forEach var="link" begin="0" items="${links}">
    <h3 style="margin-bottom:0px;">
      <a href="${link.url}">${link.title}</a>
    </h3>
    ${link.description}
  </c:forEach>
  </body>
</html>
```

Note the differences in the code between `ShowLinks.jsp` and `DAOShowLinks.`
`jsp`. The preceding code is both clean and simple in comparison. At no time does
the JSP developer have to worry about JDBC, SQL, a database, or anything unrelated to the `LinkBean` and `LinkFactory` objects. Due to this abstraction, there is
no issue with the JSP developer's executing poor queries, nor is there a problem
with any future changes to the database.

LinkChecker.jsp is another good example to use with the `LinkBean` and `LinkFactory` classes. Instead of mixing the JSP and JDBC code, a much cleaner page can be developed using DAO and Model 1½ as shown in Listing 14-13.

Listing 14-13 DAOLinkChecker.jsp

```
<%@ page import="com.jspbook.*, java.net.*, java.util.*" %>
<%
  LinkBean[] links = LinkFactory.read(null);
  for (int i=0;i<links.length;i++) {
    LinkBean link = links[i];
    String url = link.getUrl();
    LinkedList deleted = new LinkedList();
    request.setAttribute("deleted", deleted);
    boolean failed = false;
    try {
      URL u = new URL(url);
      HttpURLConnection huc =
        (HttpURLConnection)u.openConnection();
      int responseCode = huc.getResponseCode();
      if (responseCode >= 400 && responseCode < 500) {
        failed = true;
      }
    }
    catch (UnknownHostException e) {
      failed = true;
    }
    catch (UnknownServiceException e) {
      failed = true;
    }
    catch (MalformedURLException e) {
      failed = true;
    }
    if (failed) {
      LinkFactory.delete(new LinkBean[] {link});
      deleted.add(url);
    }
  }
%>
<html>
  <head>
    <title>Link Checker</title>
  </head>
  <body>
```

```
    <h2>Links Deleted</h2>
    <%@ taglib uri="http://java.sun.com/jstl/core_rt" prefix="c" %>
    <c:forEach var="link" begin="0" items="${deleted}">
      ${link}<br>
    </c:forEach>
    </body>
</html>
```

Save the preceding code as `DAOLinkChecker.jsp`. If you like, try the code out by browsing to `http://127.0.0.1/jspbook/DAOLinkChecker.jsp`. The results are the same as if `LinkChecker.jsp` was used. The important thing to see about the preceding code is not what it does, but how it goes about doing it. The code is again simplified by removing all of the JDBC code with a few calls to the CRUD methods of the `LinkFactory`. The JSP developer is able to easily take advantage of a database but does not have to worry about JDBC, SQL, or anything besides `LinkBean` and `LinkFactory`.

Given the preceding two examples it should be clear how the DAO design pattern can be implemented to abstract JDBC logic. The `create()` and `update()` methods of the `LinkFactory` class were not shown in an example, but conceptually the functionality should be very clear. As an exercise, try building a JSP or Servlet that adds or updates links using the `Link` and `LinkFactory` objects.

Summary

This chapter has been a broad overview of Java database connectivity and how to implement a database for use with Servlets and JSP. Databases are the de facto standard for consolidating a Web site's important information, and rightly so. Introduced in this chapter were the topics of SQL, JDBC, and methods of incorporating database connectivity code with your Web Application. All of the topics could be expanded into a book themselves, especially SQL and JDBC, but what was covered by this chapter should be sufficient to get you well on your way with Java database connectivity.

What was sparingly covered in this chapter was the topic of SQL. Instead of attempting a full crash course on SQL, only the fundamental concepts were introduced. It is likely that when working on a database-driven project, a SQL-savvy database administrator will be around to handle SQL woes. However, should you wish to take on the roll of both Web tier developer and database administrator, a good SQL book was suggested.

The final part of this chapter dealt with optimal uses of JDBC and practical implementations of JDBC logic with Servlets and JSPs. In the case of optimal uses the important concepts of connection pooling, prepared statements, and stored procedures were introduced. In the practical implementation discussion, it was explained where JDBC code fits in when using either a Model 1 or Model 2 design, and in special cases where complete abstraction of database functionality is needed, the Data Access Objects (DAO) design pattern was introduced for use.

The next chapter concludes this book. You have previously learned everything this book has to teach about Servlets and JSPs, and you have completed the all-important database connectivity tangent. In the last chapter we will make a quick review of the entire book and discuss a few of the other technologies in J2EE and why you might want to consider using them.

Chapter 15

Building a Complete Web Application

This is it—the last chapter! So far you have learned about coding Servlets, JavaServer Pages, JavaBeans, custom tags, and Filters. Rounding out these skills several popular design patterns such as Model 2, Model 1½, multi-client design, and internationalization have been included. Finally, several practical topics such as error handling, security, and database access have been discussed so that you can truly create a complete Web Application using Servlets and JSP. However, there still exists one sole deficiency in this book's content. At no time has a real, complete Web Application been built. Each chapter focused entirely on a single subject. Several times chapters relied on previous chapters' material, but the chapters have never been combined into what you are really trying to do: build a complete Web Application.

The final chapter of this book is going to provide a review of the entire book's material as it should best be done: by building a complete Web Application. When writing a book it is easy to claim "in practice you will need to use this" or to create a contrived example to illustrate a good point. This book has done both, and rightly so because for educational purposes, that is often the best method of introducing a good concept. However, readers of this book are assumed to be paid professionals or those working on becoming such—generally people who need to be able to build a complete Web Application. Following up on such an assumption, it is now time to demonstrate exactly what this book is all about: building a complete Web Application using Servlets and JSP. At each possible point while building the Web Application, a complete discussion is provided on what is being built, which is essentially a review of the content in the various chapters that constitute this book.

This chapter discusses the following topics:

- Designing a Web Application.
- Distributing the workload; dividing up who does what.
- Implementing database support; creating a database and using JDBC.
- Implementing Business Logic; Filters and the Model 2 design pattern.
- Implementing Presentation Logic; JSP, Multi-Client Design, and Internationalization.
- Finishing up the site: security, error handling, link tracking, caching, and compression.

The topics should be no surprise. Everything is a logical part of a Web Application, and everything is a topic that has been covered in detail by this book. At every part of this chapter, discussion will be provided on why each part of the Web Application is being built as it is, but discussion will not replace having read the earlier chapters of this book—it is assumed you have read the book in its entirety. Do read this chapter straight through. It provides several tips and techniques for building a complete Web Application.

Designing a Web Application

All Web Applications, usually projects in general, start from the same point: design. Somewhere someone is responsible for determining what a Web Application needs to do, possibly also how it should be done. Depending on what type of Web Application you are building and your place of employment, there are several different ways a Web Application is designed. Commonly, designs are created by either a single arbiter (i.e., you want to build a Web Application), a project manager with feedback from a development team (i.e., a small group of developers is responsible for building a Web Application), or from a completely separate group of *thinkers*[1] who provide a complete blueprint to the developers of a Web Application (i.e., you or your team must build a given Web Application's blueprint). The most personally rewarding of the three is likely the first, building

---

1. This is meant both as good and bad; however, it almost always implies a tedious project lies ahead. Comics, such as Dilbert (http://dilbert.com), thrive off the imbroglios of corporations, who are responsible for the vast majority of large-scale Web Applications, that let one group design independently of the development team.

a complete Web Application by yourself. This chapter will design and implement a Web Application from this viewpoint, but the design will be done as if the workload of implementing the Web Application should be done by several independent groups of people. This strategy will do two things: you will be responsible for building an entire Web Application, and you will gain some insight on how the task of building a Web Application can be split into smaller independent tasks.

Serious effort has been put into using the phrase "a complete Web Application" rather than "a real Web Application" in this chapter. What we will design is a "real" Web Application, meaning something really in use—the complete code for a Web site you have likely seen on the Internet. This chapter covers the design and implementation of the book support site, http://www.jspbook. com[2]. However, "a real Web Application" is misleading because it implies all of the previous chapters are educational fluff when they are not. The phrase "a complete Web Application" is used because that is exactly what this chapter makes: a complete Web Application that re-uses real concepts and real code from previous chapters.

The basic outline of the site design is to satisfy the following criteria:

- Create a book support site for this book including a news page, a page detailing book information (and purchase information), an errata page, FAQ, a reader feedback page, a page providing the book's code and, when possible, functional examples of the code, and a promotional page with sample chapters and publicity photos.

- Support commonly used Web browsers—namely, it must be authored in HTML.

- Support translated versions of its content so that readers of different languages can view the site in their desired language.

- Provide an administrative front so that non-SQL developers and non-Java developers can manage relevant parts of the Web Application.

The preceding outline identifies the basic criteria a Web Application would initially have, but it still needs more details about the content of the site's pages. A more practical developer (such as us in this case) would also mandate the following criteria:

---

2. Surely, not all Web Applications are alike; however, good effort is made in demonstrating how code in this book can be adapted for use in any real Web Application.

- A proper layer of data abstraction; use a database so the project is easier maintained in the future.
- A proper layer of code abstraction; make it so a non-Java developer can still make styled content; also ensure the code of the Web Application is easily maintained in the future.
- Track user information; track requests and responses and provide realtime viewing of site hits, site referrals, popular pages, what user-agent (i.e., browser) is most commonly used, and what language is most commonly requested.
- Properly handle all errors; don't ever show a user a cryptic stack trace generated by Tomcat.
- Keep sensitive information sensitive; use a Web Application's security mechanisms to ensure users can only access what they are supposed to access.
- Put an Easter egg in the application[3].

This chapter implements the preceding list of criteria and provides an example at `http://www.jspbook.com`. Often the preceding criteria are exactly what you would expect from good initial Web Application design. The design is purposely made slightly more complex, especially with the i18n requirements, than what you will likely have to build if employed as an average Web developer; however, all the requirements are reasonable if you are employed as a good Web developer.

Physical Implementation

Web Application design typically goes in two phases: logical design and physical design. A *logical design* is a rough description[4] of what the application must support. A *physical design* describes is how the logical requirements are to be implemented, in our case with Servlets and JSP. A good developer should be able to implement a proper physical design, regardless of who made it. The following is the summarized physical implementation of the book support site. Greater detail is left for discussion later in the chapter.

---

3. We're joking, but in the case of the book support site, one is added for fun—exactly as if we were underpaid, overworked, slightly creative Web developers.
4. This book's discussion of logical and physical design is either grossly deficient (traditional business person's opinion) or more than is required (traditional engineer's opinion). The greater point is that the design is adequate for the project at hand, which is illustrated by the rest of this

The database to use is hsqldb, the database from Chapter 14, and the database is connected to use JDBC via a `DataSource` object. No database-specific optimizations are to be used so that another SQL-compliant database may be used in the future.

The Web Application must follow a simple Model 2 design. A Filter will encapsulate all of the Java code required to connect to the database and populate request-scoped variables. JSP will be used to present the request-scoped variables and any other static information in the appropriate format.

Conceptually, an idea of the site's layout should be forming. Figure 15-1 provides a conceptual view of the site's physical components.

Intuitively, the physical design is stating that each logical goal is going to be accomplished using material this book has previously covered. The specifics of the physical design are expanded upon in the following sections.

Create a Web Application for the Book Support Site

The first step to building any new Web Application is creating it in your container. Start the book support site by making a new directory in the `/webapps` directory of your Tomcat. Create the `jspbook_site` directory in the `/webapps` directory of your Tomcat installation. Next, add the default directories, `jspbook_site/WEB-INF`, `jspbook_site/WEB-INF/lib`, and `jspbook_site/WEB-INF/classes`, and create a blank `web.xml` file[5]. Finally, create a new XML file, required by Tomcat, describing the new Web Application. Save the following file as `jspbook_site.xml` in the `/webapps` directory of Tomcat.

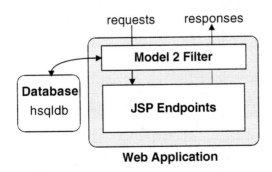

Figure 15-1   Conceptual View of Initial Physical Design of the Web Application

---

5. Listing 1-1 in Chapter 1 is an example of a blank `web.xml` file. We are now repeating the steps required to create a Web Application using Tomcat—exactly what was covered in Chapter 1.

```
<Context path="/jspbook_site" docBase="jspbook_site"
        debug="0" privileged="true">
</Context>
```

With everything created, the `/webapps` directory should include the following entries:

```
webapps/jspbook_site.xml
webapps/jspbook_site
webapps/jspbook_site/WEB-INF
webapps/jspbook_site/WEB-INF/web.xml
webapps/jspbook_site/WEB-INF/lib
webapps/jspbook_site/WEB-INF/classes
```

Distributing the Workload: Dividing Up Who Does What

There are three distinct parts to this project: database work, Java programming, and presentation. The database work consists of creating the Web Application's database and providing a JDBC connection (or some other form of Java connection). The Java programming consists of all the Java code that is to be placed in the Model 2 logic components—the code that uses the database to populate request-scoped variables. The presentation logic consists of creating pages that display request-scoped information and any static information. These three divisions can be logically found in almost all Model 2-based projects, and it is usually a good idea to divide labor according to them. Why? Because each division has a clearly defined interface, and each part requires different skills.

Take for example any project that involves more than one developer. Each developer will have a different set of skills, and it will be desirable to have everyone working at the same time. However, it is important that when matching skills and assigning work that developers do not interfere with each other. An HTML-savvy, Java-deficient developer should be allowed nowhere near the database or Java code. Likewise, a Java or SQL guru with no sense of style should not edit the appearance of the site's user interface. However, each developer should be able to fully work on his or her part of the project and know their work will not hinder the other developers. The greater point here is: it is always desirable to enforce a division of labor for efficiency. It is also important to truly enforce a division of labor—if a developer should not be able to do something, make it so he or she can't. The concept is nothing new; it is prevalent in object-oriented programming and Java. However, it is helpful to realize the concept needs to be applied to Web Applications, which are usually a combination of Java, SQL, and HTML.

A good method of enforcing division of the work required to build a Web Application is to use JDBC and request-scoped variables as strict interfaces. The database developer(s) will be responsible for everything to do with the database, ending at the JDBC driver. The Java developer(s) will be responsible for everything to do with accessing a pre-defined database and populating pre-defined request-scoped variables. The presentation developer will be responsible for everything that has to do with formatting request-scoped variables via the JSP EL, JSTL actions, and markup such as HTML. Enforcement of the divisions is done via the JDBC driver, (i.e., only SQL calls can communicate with the database), and by disallowing JSP scripting: JSP can only read request-scoped variables via the EL and standard actions.

Practical Use of Web Application Labor Division

For practical use the division of labor described by this chapter works well, primarily because of its strict interfaces. The bane of maintaining a project is having to deal with what is considered *spaghetti code*, sloppy code that tends to work but appears as gibberish—hence, not even the original coder can easily edit it, let alone someone inheriting the code. Scripts that mix database calls, Java, and HTML are almost always spaghetti code. It is the same issue that was discussed in length in the design pattern chapter. However, eliminating spaghetti code is not the only benefit of dividing labor as described. Keeping a strict interface means you can easily determine what exactly needs to be fixed. In our case the fix can be narrowed down to either a database table, a Java class, or a JSP—all of which are relatively simple compared to the entire Web Application.

It should be easy to realize why the method of dividing a Web Application's labor as described by this chapter works; the method is exactly what has been preached by the last few chapters. The design pattern chapter discussed the Model 2 design pattern, including JSP and logic components, and the database chapter discussed both simple SQL and using JDBC. However, examples are surely the best method of bringing everything together, which is exactly why this chapter builds the book support site. In the following three sections each division of labor is covered in depth, as it would be applied to the book support site. You will benefit from seeing how each section is done, and much of the code can be directly recycled for use in other Web Applications.

Implementing Database Support: Creating a Database and Using JDBC

The first division of labor we will discuss is the site's database. This section entails the task of creating the site's database and providing a JDBC method (i.e., `DataSource` object) for access to the database. In this chapter's previous discussion of the site's database and its logical design, little was covered. Now, a complete physical design is created, and that physical design will be implemented by our database of choice, hsqldb.

Database Physical Design

As mentioned in Chapter 14, to create a relational database, SQL is used. Little was discussed on the actual SQL required and how to ensure the information kept in a database is kept as it should be—in other words, ensuring data integrity. This topic does merit a book of its own. If you wish to be a true database administrator, read the suggested book and learn a popular database. In almost every case where a database is being used, a proper database administrator is expected to implement it, so as a Java, Servlet, and JSP developer, this is likely not you.

This chapter will not assume you are a database administrator, but we will discuss what is required and provide the exact syntax for it. So if you do wish to learn about relational databases or already understand relational databases, you do have all of the important information for the book support site's database right here.

Logically, the site's database needs to keep track of all the dynamic information we are going to use. In the case of the book support site there are a few places it makes sense to use a database: errata, news items, FAQ, and user feedback. Each of these places is a dynamic part of the site—users will be able to read the current list and suggest additions. Additionally, the site's administrator will want to be able to edit the information. In order to keep track of errata, FAQ, feedback, and news, the database will have four tables. Each table will keep track of content, via a time-stamp, and a flag will keep track if the content is visible or not. Figure 15-2 provides a conceptual view of the database tables.

The idea of the preceding four tables is that each can be queried for a current list, validated list, of related information. For example, if a current list of news items is desired, the news table can be queried for the latest few news items that have been validated for showing. The information each row of the table contains describes the unique identifier of the news entry, which also happens to be a time-stamp, and if the item has been validated by an administrator.

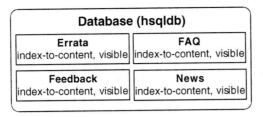

Database (hsqldb)	
Errata index-to-content, visible	**FAQ** index-to-content, visible
Feedback index-to-content, visible	**News** index-to-content, visible

Figure 15-2   Database Tables

The content that is displayed to a visitor of the Web site is not contained in the database because of internationalization requirements. Instead of managing the information in a database, it will be arranged in a simple file structure. The file structure is straightforward and extensible: the default language (English) content is authored in an arbitrarily named JSP. Other languages are also in a JSP, named the same, but with "-" and the three-digit[6] language code appended. For example, if a page of content, index.jsp, was created, the French alternative page (if it exists) would be index-fra.jsp: encoding issues are assumed to be handled appropriately. More on the internationalization support is discussed later when the actual content is being built.

Database Creation SQL

Before providing the SQL required to create the Web Application's database, we need to install a database. The hsqldb is going to be re-used because it works and was covered by Chapter 14. The hsqldb JAR file is not required to be re-installed because it was previously placed in the /common/lib directory of your Tomcat installation, which is shared by all Web Applications[7]. The installation requirement is a new resource deployment for the jspbook_site Web

---

6. ISO 639-2 (ftp://dkuug.dk/i18n/iso-639-2.txt) lists the standardized three-digit language codes. The java.util.Locale object provides the getISO3Language() method that provides the three-digit country codes.

7. It is still a bad idea to place all JAR files in this directory instead of /WEB-INF/lib of a specific Web Application. JAR files in /WEB-INF/lib are included in a WAR, and the functionality they provide is portable, meaning you can re-use it with any Web Application. However, code in the /common/lib directory of Tomcat needs to be manually copied from container to container; the only reason hsqldb.jar was placed in the /common/lib directory is because we are using Tomcat to deploy the JDBC DataSource, as discussed in Chapter 14.

Application. Edit `jspbook_site.xml` in the `/webapps` directory of Tomcat to match Listing 15-1.

Listing 15-1 DataSource Configuration for the Book Support Site

```
<Context path="/jspbook_site" docBase="jspbook_site"
        debug="0" privileged="true">
  <Resource name="jdbc/jspbook_site"
    auth="Container"
    type="javax.sql.DataSource"/>
  <ResourceParams name="jdbc/jspbook_site">
    <parameter>
      <name>username</name>
      <value>sa</value>
    </parameter>
    <parameter>
      <name>password</name>
      <value></value>
    </parameter>
    <parameter>
      <name>driverClassName</name>
      <value>org.hsqldb.jdbcDriver</value>
    </parameter>
    <parameter>
      <name>url</name>
      <value>jdbc:hsqldb:/usr/jakarta-tomcat-
5/webapps/jspbook_site/WEB-INF/jspbookdb[8]</value>
    </parameter>
  </ResourceParams>
</Context>
```

The preceding code initializes a `DataSource` object that the Java developer can use to obtain JDBC connections to the hsqldb database. Additionally, Tomcat automatically pools connections for performance enhancement.

Reload the `jspbook_site` Web Application to have the changes take effect. Once the Web Application reloads, the `DataSource` object can be used. Copy `ArbitrarySQLDataSource.jsp` (Listing 14-5 in Chapter 14) and save it in the `admin` directory of the `jspbook_site` Web Application. Edit the following lines to use the `jspbook_site` database:

---

8. Note this value needs to be changed to somewhere on your computer, and preferably in the `jspbook_site` Web Application.

```
<%@ page import="java.io.*,java.sql.*, javax.sql.*, javax.naming.*"
%>
<%
  InitialContext ctx = new InitialContext();
  DataSource ds =
    (DataSource)ctx.lookup("java:comp/env/jdbc/jspbook_site");
  Connection conn = ds.getConnection();
  try {
...
```

With the preceding change, `ArbitrarySQLDataSource.jsp` now works with the book support site's database. SQL statements can be executed, and they will be reflected appropriately.

The following lines of code in Listing 15-2 will create the database tables for the book support site as described earlier in the chapter.

Listing 15-2 Database Creation Listing

```
CREATE TABLE NEWS (
  TS BIGINT PRIMARY KEY,
  VISIBLE BIT
)
CREATE TABLE FAQ (
  TS BIGINT PRIMARY KEY,
  VISIBLE BIT
)
CREATE TABLE FEEDBACK (
  TS BIGINT PRIMARY KEY,
  VISIBLE BIT
)
CREATE TABLE ERRATA (
  TS BIGINT PRIMARY KEY,
  VISIBLE BIT
)
```

Execute the above code using `ArbitrarySQLDataSource.jsp`. Figure 15-3 shows a browser rendering of the results.

With the tables created and the `DataSource` object available, the database work is done.

Interfacing without SQL

A side note is worth mentioning before jumping straight to coding the site's logic components. It is assumed that the Java developers, who are responsible for inter-

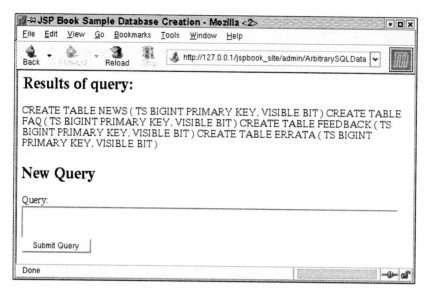

Figure 15-3 Browser Rendering of Database Creation

facing with the database, understand SQL. Given a `DataSource` object, a Java developer has a method of executing SQL statements, CRUD actions, which is a great solution, assuming the Java developers know SQL. However, should SQL be a skill only found with the database developer, the Java developers will need an alternative interface. Recall the Data Access Object design pattern mentioned in Chapter 14. If required, a Java–JDBC developer can build a set of objects that abstract the SQL calls using a simple set of Java objects.

The idea is, if your Java developers don't know SQL, don't use SQL as an interface. Instead, use a set of Data Access Objects and a strict interface can still be maintained.

Implementing Business Logic: Filters and the Model 2 Design Pattern

With a database in place, the next step of the Web Application is to build Model 2 logic components that interface with the database and populate request-scoped variables. The book support Web site was logically modeled earlier in the chapter. The site itself is not complex and does not merit a complex Model 2 scheme. For the site's Model 2 design we will re-use the simple Model 2 Filter from Chapter 11. Recall the Filter relies on implicit logic components named after the URL being accessed. If the logic component exists for a particular URL, it is loaded and used before the contents of the URL are displayed.

Copy the simple Model 2 Filter, Listing 11-9 in Chapter 11, and the required interface, Listing 11-10 also in Chapter 11, and save in the /WEB-INF/classes/com/jspbook directory of the jspbook_site Web Application. Deploy the Filter to intercept all requests to the Web Application as shown in Listing 15-3.

Listing 15-3 Updated web.xml

```
<web-app xmlns="http://java.sun.com/xml/ns/j2ee" version="2.4">

  <filter>
    <filter-name>ControlFilter</filter-name>
    <filter-class>com.jspbook.ControlFilter</filter-class>
  </filter>
  <filter-mapping>
    <filter-name>ControlFilter</filter-name>
    <url-pattern>*.jsp</url-pattern>
  </filter-mapping>

</web-app>
```

Reload the Web Application to have the changes take effect. The Model 2 Filter now attempts to load and execute implicit logic components each time a request is made.

For internationalization support, the site will rely on the i18n Filter created in Chapter 12. The Filter takes a request and attempts to localize the resource—for example, the Filter interprets a request from a client who prefers French for index.jsp to mean look for index-fra.jsp first, and if it is not found, fall back on the English version, index.jsp. The process is similar for all other languages with English always being the default. This decision makes i18n support as easy as translating a page and saving it with the appropriate country code. Deploy the Simplei18nFilter to intercept all requests to the JSP book site Web Application. Listing 15-4 shows the updated web.xml.

Listing 15-4 Updated web.xml

```
<web-app xmlns="http://java.sun.com/xml/ns/j2ee" version="2.4">

  <filter>
    <filter-name>ControlFilter</filter-name>
```

```
    <filter-class>com.jspbook.ControlFilter</filter-class>
  </filter>

  <filter>
    <filter-name>Simplei18nFilter</filter-name>
    <filter-class>com.jspbook.Simplei18nFilter</filter-class>
  </filter>

  <filter-mapping>
    <filter-name>ControlFilter</filter-name>
    <url-pattern>*.jsp</url-pattern>
  </filter-mapping>

  <filter-mapping>
    <filter-name>Simplei18nFilter</filter-name>
    <url-pattern>*.jsp</url-pattern>
  </filter-mapping>

</web-app>
```

By deploying the two Filters, we have added support for the Model 2 design pattern and an extendable method of adding internationalized content to the Web Application. This process was near trivial thanks to Filters and the previous chapters of this book. Note it is important how the two Filters are deployed; the implicit Model 2 Filter needs to intercept requests before the i18n Filter. If not, the implicit Model 2 Filter will be searching for implicit `control` objects named `index_en` and the like, which is not what we desire. There is no reason for this Web Application to have multiple versions of the Control components for specific languages.

Coding Model 2 Logic Classes and Populating Request-Scoped Variables

The Model 2 Filter and the Simplei18nFilter are key parts of the Web Application, but they are not parts that need be cared about by the site's Java developers. Once the Filters are deployed, they should never need to be changed. The majority of the work is placed on creating Model 2 `Logic` classes and JSP content pages. Following the division of labor suggested earlier in the chapter, currently we are now playing the role of the Java–JDBC developers. What now needs to be implemented is a set of Model 2 logic components that interface with the database and populate request-scoped variables.

Recall that the index page, errata page, FAQ page, and feedback page obviously need logic components. The components are required to query the database for current news, errata, feedback, or FAQs, respectively, and populate request-scoped variables for the JSP developers to use. The following sections individually discuss the logic components.

An Abstract Logic Component

Because we are using the Control Filter discussed in Chapter 11, we know that all logic components must implement the `doLogic()` method of the Logic interface. A fine solution would be to start each logic component from scratch as done in Chapter 11; however, an easier solution exists if you consider the interfaces the book support site uses. Several of the dynamic logic components are doing the same thing: querying a named database table and populating a request-scoped variable of the same name. The only thing that changes between these logic components is the name of the database table queried and the name of the request-scoped variables.

Due to the similarity shared by the site's database-to-request-scoped variable interface, we can consolidate the logic components' code into one abstract component and take advantage of Java polymorphism to support specific instances of the interface. Listing 15-5 includes the code for the abstract interface class.

Listing 15-5 AbstractContent.java

```
package com.jspbook;

import javax.servlet.http.*;
import javax.servlet.*;
import java.io.*;
import java.util.*;
import java.sql.*;
import javax.sql.*;
import javax.naming.*;
import java.text.*;

public abstract class AbstractContent implements Control {
   public abstract boolean doLogic(HttpServletRequest request,
                       HttpServletResponse response)
   throws ServletException, IOException;

   public boolean doLogic(HttpServletRequest request,
                       HttpServletResponse response,
                       String table)
                   throws ServletException, IOException {
```

```
LinkedList content = new LinkedList();
request.setAttribute(table, content);

try {
  InitialContext ctx = new InitialContext();
  DataSource ds =
   (DataSource)ctx.
     lookup("java:comp/env/jdbc/jspbook_site");
  Connection conn = ds.getConnection();
  try {
    Statement statement  = conn.createStatement();
    ResultSet rs =
      statement.executeQuery("select * from "+table+" where
visible=true");
    ResultSetMetaData rsmd = rs.getMetaData();
    while (rs.next()) { // show results
      long l = rs.getLong(1);
      Timestamp ts = new Timestamp(l);
      SimpleDateFormat sdf =
        new SimpleDateFormat("EEE, MMM d, yyyy HH:mm:ss z");
      java.util.Date d = new java.util.Date(l);
      String con =
        "<p class=\"date\">"+sdf.format(d)+"</p>";
      String u=
        "/WEB-INF/"+table+"/"+new Long(l).toString()+".jsp";

      // fix this...
      StringWriter sw = new StringWriter();
      String file =
        request.getSession().getServletContext()
        .getRealPath(Simplei18nFilter.getLanguage(u,
                                          request));
      FileInputStream fis = new FileInputStream(file);
      int i = 0;
      while ((i = fis.read()) != -1) {
        sw.write(i);
      }

      con += new String(sw.toString());
      content.add(con);
    }
  } catch (Exception e) {
    throw new ServletException(e);
  } finally {
```

```
      conn.close();
    }
  } catch (SQLException e) {
    throw new ServletException(e);
  }
  catch (NamingException e) {
    throw new ServletException(e);
  }
  return true;
  }
}
```

Save the preceding listing as `AbstractContent.java` in the `/WEB-INF/`
`classes/com/jspbook` directory of the `jspbook_site` Web Application. It is
important to see how the listing is abstracting the process of querying a database
and populating a request-scoped variable. Two methods are used: a `doLogic()`
method, as required by the `Control` interface,

```
public void doLogic(HttpServletRequest request,
                    HttpServletResponse response)
                throws ServletException, IOException {
  //noop
  }
```

and another `doLogic()` method that includes an extra parameter, a String for the
table's name.

```
public void doLogic(HttpServletRequest request,
                    HttpServletResponse response, String table)
                throws ServletException, IOException {
...
```

Note the code for the `Control` interface's `doLogic()` method is empty: by
default nothing is done if the listing is used by the Control Filter. In contrast, the
`doLogic()` method with the extra parameter contains code that queries the site's
database and populates a request-scoped variable. Both the table queried and the
request-scoped variable's name are dynamically set by the extra parameter.

```
public void doLogic(HttpServletRequest request,
                    HttpServletResponse response, String table)
                throws ServletException, IOException {
  LinkedList content = new LinkedList();
  request.setAttribute(table, content);
```

```
try {
    InitialContext ctx = new InitialContext();
    DataSource ds =

(DataSource)ctx.lookup("java:comp/env/jdbc/jspbook_site");
    Connection conn = ds.getConnection();
    try {
        Statement statement  = conn.createStatement();
        ResultSet rs =
            statement.executeQuery("select * from "+table);
...
```

It is assumed a Control component will extend the `AbstractContent` class and override the `doLogic()` method to query the correct database and populate an appropriately named request-scoped variable. For example, the code for the news page would override the `doLogic()` method as follows.

```
public boolean doLogic(HttpServletRequest request,
                       HttpServletResponse response)
                       throws ServletException, IOException {
    doLogic(request, response, "news");
    return true;
}
```

The complete code for the index logic component is provided later in the chapter; however, it should be clear how the `AbstractContent` class is used. By passing in `"news"` as the dynamic value, `"news"` will be used as the table's name— that is, query the news table in the database, and `"news"` will be used as the request-scoped variable's name. The functionality is helpful because the news, errata, feedback, and FAQ pages will all recycle the same code. Instead of coding four classes that resemble `AbstractContent.java`, we will simply change the name of the dynamically passed value to either "news", "errata", "feedback", or "faq".

Logic Component for index.jsp

The index page of the book support site is being used to display current news. Information about current news articles is maintained by the News table of the Web Application's database. The logic component for `index.jsp` needs to query the database for current news, via JDBC, and populate an array of news items that are placed in request scope.

It is intended that the request-scoped variables are accessed using the JSTL and the JSP expression language. Therefore, no specific component, such as a News object, is required to represent each news item. The interface is as follows:

a request-scoped variable, news, is an array of `string` objects. Each String represents the language localized content for a news item. The interface is intended to be used as demonstrated by the following example JSP code:

```
<%@ taglib uri="http://java.sun.com/jstl/core_rt" prefix="c" %>
<c:forEach var="n" begin="0" items="${news}">
  ${n}
</c:forEach>
```

It is important to note that no scripting is required. This is important because scripting will be disabled. JSP developers—that is, the content developers—should not be able to embed arbitrary Java code in JSP.

The logic component itself is simple, thanks to the `AbstractContent` class (Listing 15-6).

Listing 15-6 index.java

```
package com.jspbook;

import javax.servlet.http.*;
import javax.servlet.*;
import java.io.*;

public class index extends AbstractContent {
   public boolean doLogic(HttpServletRequest request,
                    HttpServletResponse response)
                throws ServletException, IOException {
     doLogic(request, response, "news");
      return true;
   }
}
```

Save the preceding code as `index.java` in the /WEB-INF/classes/com/jspbook directory of the jspbook_site Web Application. The code re-uses the code for querying the site's database and populating a request-scoped variable by overriding the `doLogic()` method.

```
     doLogic(request, response, "news");
```

As the highlighted code shows, the value, `"news"`, is passed so that the News table is used and a request-scouped variable named news is created.

Thanks to the simple Model 2 Filter we previously installed, the task of deploying Model 2 logic components is trivial. By saving the code in the /WEB-INF/classes/com/jspbook directory, the logic component is ready for use. No configuration files need updating because the Control Filter automatically checks for the logic component each time `index.jsp` (or fictitious deviants thereof) is requested.

Logic Components for Adding and Editing News

In order to make the site more user-friendly for the administrators, a non-technical method is required for adding and editing news items; a technical method currently exists, such as manually creating content files and editing the database via `ArbitrarySQL.jsp`. The non-technical method will be a set of HTML forms that allow relevant information to be added, edited, or deleted. For the set of HTML forms (which we will create shortly), a set of logic components is needed. Save Listing 15-7 as `addnews.java` in the `/WEB-INF/classes/com/jspbook` directory of the `jspbook_site` Web Application.

Listing 15-7 addnews.java

```
package com.jspbook;

import javax.servlet.http.*;
import javax.servlet.*;
import java.io.*;
import java.sql.*;
import javax.sql.*;
import java.util.*;
import javax.naming.*;

public class addnews implements Control {
  public boolean doLogic(HttpServletRequest request,
                    HttpServletResponse response)
  throws ServletException, IOException {

    String title = request.getParameter("title");
    String link = request.getParameter("link");
    String text = request.getParameter("text");

    // check values are not null
    if (title == null || link == null || text == null) {
      return true;
    }
```

```
   try {
     InitialContext ctx = new InitialContext();
     DataSource ds =
   (DataSource)ctx.lookup("java:comp/env/jdbc/jspbook_site");
     Connection conn = ds.getConnection();
     try {
       Statement statement = conn.createStatement();

       ServletContext sc =
         request.getSession().getServletContext();
       String dir = sc.getRealPath("/WEB-INF/news");
       new File(dir).mkdirs();
       long l = Calendar.getInstance().getTimeInMillis();

       // write out news item
       FileWriter fw = new FileWriter(dir+"/"+l+".jsp");
       fw.write("<p class=\"title\"><a href=\"");
       fw.write(link+"\">"+title+"</a></p>");
       fw.write("<p class=\"content\">");
       fw.write(text);
       fw.write("</p>");
       fw.flush();
       fw.close();
       // add entry in db
       statement.executeQuery("insert into news values ("+l+",0)");
       response.sendRedirect("index.jsp");

     } catch (Exception e) {
       throw new ServletException(e);
     } finally {
       conn.close();
     }
   } catch (SQLException e) {
     throw new ServletException(e);
   }
   catch (NamingException e) {
     throw new ServletException(e);
   }
   return false;
  }
}
```

The preceding code adds entries, via JDBC and SQL, to the News table of the site's database. It is assumed an HTML form will post three parameters: the title of the news item, the link for the news item, and the news item itself. The first thing this logic component does is check for these three parameters.

```
String title = request.getParameter("title");
String link = request.getParameter("link");
String text = request.getParameter("text");

// check values are not null
if (title == null || link == null || text == null) {
  return;
}
```

Should the check fail, the logic component does nothing—the request proceeds through, presumably back to the HTML form. If the check passes, the information is saved to a content file in the /WEB-INF/news directory.

```
ServletContext sc =
    request.getSession().getServletContext();
String dir = sc.getRealPath("/WEB-INF/news");
new File(dir).mkdirs();
long l = Calendar.getInstance().getTimeInMillis();

FileWriter fw = new FileWriter(dir+"/"+l+".jsp");
fw.write("<p class=\"title\"><a href=\"");
fw.write(link+"\">"+title+"</a></p>");
fw.write("<p class=\"content\">");
fw.write(text);
fw.write("</p>");
fw.flush();
fw.close();
```

Note the name of the file is a time-stamp—that is, a long value—which represents today's date and time. The same time-stamp value is then used to create a new entry in the News table of the site's database.

```
statement.executeQuery("insert into news values ("+l+",0)");
response.sendRedirect("index.jsp");
```

A standard SQL insert statement is used to add the entry. By default the news item is not set to be visible, meaning it won't appear on the Web site until something else sets the visible flag to true. Later, we will see how this is beneficial for several reasons, including letting anonymous people add news items. After the SQL statement is executed, the response is then redirected back to an index page, which is assumed to be index.jsp.

In order for the `addnews` logic component to work, two complementary HTML forms are required. Save Listing 15-8 as `addnews.jsp` in the `/admin` directory of the `jspbook_site` Web Application.

Listing 15-8 addnews.jsp

```html
<html>
<h2>Add News</h2>
<form method="POST">
  Title: <input name="title"><br>
  Link: <input name="link"><br>
  Text: <textarea name="text"></textarea><br>
  <input type="submit" value="Submit">
</form>
</html>
```

The form's code is standard HTML and contains no surprises. Fields are provided for the title, link, and text of the news item. Note that the form's name is `addnews.jsp`, which means it will implicitly use the `addnews.java` logic component.

The second form required is the generic index page, `index.jsp`. We already created an index page for the Web site, but we have yet to create an index page for the administrative pages—that is, everything in the `/admin` directory. Save Listing 15-9 as `index.jsp` in the `/admin` directory of the `jspbook_site` Web Application.

Listing 15-9 index.jsp

```html
<html>
<h2>Add</h2>
<a href="addnews.jsp">Add News</a><br>
<a href="addfaq.jsp">Add FAQ</a><br>
<a href="adderrata.jsp">Add Errata</a><br>
<a href="addfeedback.jsp">Add Feedback</a><br>

<h2>Edit</h2>
<a href="edit.jsp?table=news">Edit News</a><br>
<a href="edit.jsp?table=faq">Edit FAQ</a><br>
<a href="edit.jsp?table=errata">Edit Errata</a><br>
<a href="edit.jsp?table=feedback">Edit Feedback</a><br>

<h2><a href="ArbitrarySQL.jsp">SQL Interface to DB</a></h2>
<br>
```

```
<a href="../index.jsp">Return to Index.</a>
</html>
```

Again, there is nothing tricky on this page; it is all standard HTML. There are several links, including some that currently don't exist. Don't worry about the non-existent links; the pages will be added later in the chapter. Overall, the page is not meant to be anything but a convenience for administrators.

You can now add news entries to the Web Application. Be sure to save and compile the new code and reload the `jspbook_site` Web Application for the changes to take effect. After the Web Application reloads, browse to `http://127.0.0.1/admin/addnews.jsp`. The HTML form appears and you can type in information about a new news item. Figure 15-4 provides a browser rendering of the results.

Fill out the form and click on the "Add News" button to submit the information. Once submitted, the information is added to the database; however, currently, we don't have an easy way to see the information. You can use `ArbitrarySQL.jsp` to execute `"select * from news"` for quick verification, but we will now create a more user-friendly interface for future use.

Another HTML form and logic component are required for editing existing news items. Similar to `AbstractContent.java`, we can consolidate the code required for the news, errata, FAQ, and feedback pages, which is exactly what we will do. Save Listing 15-10 as `edit.java` in the `/WEB-INF/classes/com/jspbook` directory of the `jspbook_site` Web Application.

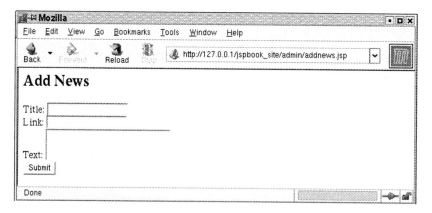

Figure 15-4   Browser Rendering of addnews.jsp

Listing 15-10 edit.java

```java
package com.jspbook;

import javax.servlet.http.*;
import javax.servlet.*;
import java.io.*;
import java.util.*;
import java.sql.*;
import javax.sql.*;
import javax.naming.*;
import java.text.*;

public class edit implements Control {
  public boolean doLogic(HttpServletRequest request,
                         HttpServletResponse response)
  throws ServletException, IOException {

    // filter random requests
    String table = request.getParameter("table");
    if (table == null) {
      response.sendRedirect("index.jsp");
      return false;
    }
    else if(!table.equals("faq") && !table.equals("news") &&
            !table.equals("errata") && !table.equals("feedback")){
      response.sendRedirect("index.jsp");
      return false;
    }

    try {
      InitialContext ctx = new InitialContext();
      DataSource ds =
    (DataSource)ctx.lookup("java:comp/env/jdbc/jspbook_site");
      Connection conn = ds.getConnection();
      try {
        Statement statement  = conn.createStatement();

        ResultSet rs =
          statement.executeQuery("select * from "+table);
        LinkedList dates = new LinkedList();
        LinkedList longs = new LinkedList();
        LinkedList visibles = new LinkedList();
        LinkedList texts = new LinkedList();
        while (rs.next()) {
```

```
      long l = rs.getLong(1);
      longs.add(new Long(l).toString());
      Timestamp ts = new Timestamp(l);
      SimpleDateFormat sdf =
    new SimpleDateFormat("EEE, MMM d, yyyy HH:mm:ss z");
      java.util.Date d = new java.util.Date(l);
      dates.add(sdf.format(d));

      if (rs.getBoolean(2)) {
        visibles.add("checked");
      } else {
        visibles.add("");
      }

      ServletContext sc =
        request.getSession().getServletContext();
      String f = sc.getRealPath(
        "/WEB-INF/"+table+"/"+String.valueOf(l)+".jsp");

      StringWriter sw = new StringWriter();
      FileReader fr = new FileReader(f);
      for (int i=fr.read();i!=-1;i=fr.read()) {
        sw.write(i);
      }
      texts.add(sw.toString());

    }
    request.setAttribute("dates",
      dates.toArray(new String [0]));
    request.setAttribute("longs",
      longs.toArray(new String [0]));
    request.setAttribute("visibles",
      visibles.toArray(new String [0]));
    request.setAttribute("texts",
     texts.toArray(new String [0]));
  } catch (Exception e) {
    throw new ServletException(e);
  } finally {
    conn.close();
  }
} catch (SQLException e) {
  throw new ServletException(e);
}
catch (NamingException e) {
```

```
      throw new ServletException(e);
   }
   return true;
 }
}
```

The preceding code relies on one parameter, "table", to be posted from an HTML form.

```
String table = request.getParameter("table");
if (table == null) {
  response.sendRedirect("index.jsp");
}
else if(!table.equals("faq") && !table.equals("news") &&
        !table.equals("errata") && !table.equals("feedback")){
  response.sendRedirect("index.jsp");
}
```

The parameter is used to select which table is being edited—for example, if the value `"news"` is provided, the News table will be displayed. Some validation code is also used to ensure that either the FAQ, news, errata, or feedback is selected. If a bad value for the table parameter is provided the request is forwarded back to the default index page.

Note the links from `index.jsp` in the `/admin` directory already provide correct values for the four different database tables.

```
<a href="edit.jsp?table=news">Edit News</a><br>
<a href="edit.jsp?table=faq">Edit FAQ</a><br>
<a href="edit.jsp?table=errata">Edit Errata</a><br>
<a href="edit.jsp?table=feedback">Edit Feedback</a><br>
```

Compile `edit.java` and reload the `jspbook_site` Web Application for the changes to take effect. Next, save Listing 15-11 as `edit.jsp` in the `/admin` directory of the `jspbook_site` Web Application.

Listing 15-11   edit.jsp

```
<html>
<h2>Edit</h2>
<form action="update.jsp" method="POST">
  <input type="submit" value="Update"><br>
  <input type="hidden" name="table" value="<%=
request.getParameter("table")%>">
  <% String[] dates = (String[])request.getAttribute("dates");
     String[] longs = (String[])request.getAttribute("longs");
```

```
String[] visibles = (String[])request.getAttribute("visibles");
String[] texts = (String[])request.getAttribute("texts");
for (int i=0;i<dates.length;i++) { %>
  <h3><%= dates[i]%></h3>
  Visible: <input name="visible<%=i%>"
                  type="checkbox" <%= visibles[i] %>>
  Delete: <input name="delete<%=i%>" type="checkbox"><br>
  <input name="date<%=i%>" type="hidden"
         value="<%= longs[i]%>"><br>
  News Item: <textarea cols="80" rows="4"
                  name="text<%=i%>"><%=texts[i]%></textarea><br>
<% } %>
<input type="submit" value="Update">
</form>
</html>
```

Now, you can try the editing code. Try out the new functionality by clicking on any of the edit links found at the admin index, `http://127.0.0.1/jsp-booksite/admin/index.jsp`. Click on edit news, `http://127.0.0.1/jsp-booksite/admin/edit.jsp?table=news`, to see the entry you recently added to the News table; all the other tables should still be blank. Figure 15-5 provides a browser rendering of what the results look like.

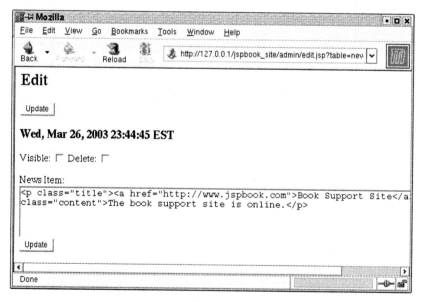

Figure 15-5 Browser Rendering of the Results

All of the important information is available. You can see the entry's time-stamp, toggle the entry (to see if visible or not), delete the entry, or edit the actual content's code. Do not try and edit anything as no logic component exists for that yet. This part of the administrative tools is only for listing information about the news, FAQ, feedback, and errata tables.

In order to have edited information saved back into the database, another logic component is required. Save Listing 15-12 as `update.java` in the `/WEB-INF/classes/com/jspbook` directory of the `jspbook_site` Web Application.

Listing 15-12   update.java

```
package com.jspbook;

import javax.servlet.http.*;
import javax.servlet.*;
import java.io.*;
import java.util.*;
import java.sql.*;
import javax.sql.*;
import javax.naming.*;
import java.text.*;

public class update implements Control {
  public boolean doLogic(HttpServletRequest request,
                      HttpServletResponse response)
  throws ServletException, IOException {

    // filter random requests
    String table = request.getParameter("table");
    if (table == null) {
      response.sendRedirect("index.jsp");
    }
    else if(!table.equals("faq") && !table.equals("news") &&
          !table.equals("errata") &&
          !table.equals("feedback")){
      response.sendRedirect("index.jsp");
      return false;
    }

    try {
      InitialContext ctx = new InitialContext();
      DataSource ds =
    (DataSource)ctx.lookup("java:comp/env/jdbc/jspbook_site");
```

```java
Connection conn = ds.getConnection();
try {
  Statement statement  = conn.createStatement();

  // loop through all posted items
  for (int i=0; request.getParameter("date"+i)!=null;
                                                  i++) {
    // get variables we care about
    String date = request.getParameter("date"+i);
    String text = request.getParameter("text"+i);
    String visible = request.getParameter("visible"+i);

    // optionally delete
    String delete = request.getParameter("delete"+i);
    if (delete != null && !delete.equals("")) {
      ServletContext sc =
        request.getSession().getServletContext();
      String f =
        sc.getRealPath("/WEB-INF/news/"+date+".jsp");
      new File(f).delete();
      statement.executeQuery(
        "delete from "+table+" where ts="+date);
      continue;
    }

    ServletContext sc =
      request.getSession().getServletContext();
    String dir = sc.getRealPath("/WEB-INF/news");

    // write out news item
    FileWriter fw =
      new FileWriter(dir+"/"+date+".jsp");
    fw.write(text);
    fw.flush();
    fw.close();

    if (visible != null && visible.equals("on")) {
      visible = "1";
    } else {
      visible = "0";
    }
    statement.executeQuery(
     "update " + table + " set visible=" + visible +
     " where ts="+date);
```

```
        }
        response.sendRedirect("index.jsp");
      } catch (Exception e) {
        throw new ServletException(e);
      } finally {
        conn.close();
      }
    } catch (SQLException e) {
      throw new ServletException(e);
    }
    catch (NamingException e) {
      throw new ServletException(e);
    }
    return false;
  }
}
```

Like `edit.java`, the preceding logic component works for all the database tables. When we code the logic components for the FAQ, feedback, and errata pages will be the task almost trivial.

Compile `update.java` and reload the Web Application for the changes to take effect. With the update component in place, a user-friendly method exists for adding and editing news; however, for good measure, save Listing 15-13 as `update.jsp` in the `/admin` directory of the `jspbook_site` Web Application.

Listing 15-13   update.jsp

```
<html>
Update Complete.
</html>
```

The preceding code is silly but required due to a nuance of Tomcat. When `edit.jsp` submits information, it submits the information to `update.jsp` (which is intentionally fictitious). By doing this, we can put update logic in `update.java` and listing logic in `edit.java`, making both all the simpler. However, some containers, namely Tomcat, are not happy making a request to a fake resource, even if the resource is never really reached. By creating `update.jsp`, we ensure the Web Application won't complain about using a fake resource.

Test out the new logic components and HTML forms. You should be able to add news items, edit news items, and delete news items using only the HTML forms. Later on, we will build the presentation page for users, which will display all of the currently visible news items in a pretty HTML or XHTML format.

Logic Component for faq.jsp

The FAQ page is designed to show a list of frequently asked questions along with answers. Information about individual questions is kept in the FAQ table. The logic component for `faq.jsp` needs to query the FAQ table and include the localized version of current FAQ. In general, the code for the FAQ logic component is similar to `index.java`, but for the FAQ table.

Save Listing 15-14 as `faq.java` in the `/WEB-INF/classes/com/jspbook` directory of the `jspbook_site` Web Application.

Listing 15-14 faq.java

```
package com.jspbook;

import javax.servlet.http.*;
import javax.servlet.*;
import java.io.*;

public class faq extends AbstractContent {
  public boolean doLogic(HttpServletRequest request,
                   HttpServletResponse response)
                   throws ServletException, IOException {
    return doLogic(request, response, "faq");
  }
}
```

The changes from `index.java` are trivial but required.

```
doLogic(request, response, "faq");
```

Note that the value `"faq"` is passed instead of `"news"`, the FAQ table of the database is queried, and the FAQ request-scope variable is populated.

Deployment of `faq.java` is identical to `index.java`. The Control Filter implicitly checks the `/WEB-INF/classes/com/jspbook` directory for the class. No extra configuration is required.

Logic Components for Adding and Editing FAQ

The additional logic components for adding and editing FAQ are simple. We are going to rely on `edit.java` and `update.java` for editing existing values. The only new component is one that adds entries to the FAQ database table. Like `addnews.java`, the FAQ addition logic component will rely on an HTML form posting information. The required information is everything that a FAQ logically needs: a question and an answer. Save Listing 15-15 as `addfaq.java`.

Listing 15-15 addfaq.java

```java
package com.jspbook;

import javax.servlet.http.*;
import javax.servlet.*;
import java.io.*;
import java.sql.*;
import javax.sql.*;
import java.util.*;
import javax.naming.*;

public class addfaq implements Control {
  public boolean doLogic(HttpServletRequest request,
                         HttpServletResponse response)
  throws ServletException, IOException {

    String question = request.getParameter("question");
    String answer = request.getParameter("answer");
    // check values are not null
    if (question == null || answer == null) {
      return true;
    }

    try {
      InitialContext ctx = new InitialContext();
      DataSource ds =
    (DataSource)ctx.lookup("java:comp/env/jdbc/jspbook_site");
      Connection conn = ds.getConnection();
      try {
        Statement statement  = conn.createStatement();

        ServletContext sc =
          request.getSession().getServletContext();
        String dir = sc.getRealPath("/WEB-INF/faq");
        new File(dir).mkdirs();
        long l = Calendar.getInstance().getTimeInMillis();

        // write out news item
        FileWriter fw = new FileWriter(dir+"/"+l+".jsp");
        fw.write("<p class=\"title\">"+question+"</p>");
        fw.write("<p class=\"news-content\">");
        fw.write(answer);
        fw.write("</p>");
```

```
        fw.flush();
        fw.close();
        // add entry in db
        statement.executeQuery(
          "insert into faq values ("+1+",0)");
        response.sendRedirect("index.jsp");
      } catch (Exception e) {
        throw new ServletException(e);
      } finally {
        conn.close();
      }
    } catch (SQLException e) {
      throw new ServletException(e);
    }
    catch (NamingException e) {
      throw new ServletException(e);
    }
    return false;
  }
}
```

Given that we examined the code for addnews.java, the code for addfaq.
java is trivial. First, the two required pieces of information are checked for: the
question and the answer.

```
String question = request.getParameter("question");
String answer = request.getParameter("answer");

if (question == null || answer == null) {
  return;
}
```

The information is analogous to the title, link, and text of a news item: if the
question and answer are not present, the logic component does nothing. If the
information is posted correctly, it is saved in a content file and an entry is inserted
into the FAQ table of the site's database.

```
FileWriter fw = new FileWriter(dir+"/"+1+".jsp");
fw.write("<p class=\"title\">"+question+"</p>");
fw.write("<p class=\"content\">");
fw.write(answer);
fw.write("</p>");
fw.flush();
fw.close();
```

```
statement.executeQuery(
    "insert into faq values ("+1+",0)");
```

Finally, the request is directed back to the default index page.

```
response.sendRedirect("index.jsp");
```

Before trying the new logic component, a complementary HTML form is required. Save Listing 15-16 as `addfaq.jsp` in the `/admin` directory of the `jspbook_site` Web Application.

Listing 15-16   addfaq.jsp

```
<html>
<h2>Add FAQ</h2>
<form method="POST">
  Question: <textarea name="question"></textarea><br>
  Answer: <textarea name="answer"></textarea><br>
  <input type="submit" value="Add FAQ">
</form>
</html>
```

There is nothing interesting about the preceding form; it is a standard HTML form with fields for the question and answer. Try out the functionality by compiling `addfaq.java` and reloading the `jspbook_site` Web Application for the changes to take effect. After reloading, browse to `http://127.0.0.1/jspbook site/admin/addfaq.jsp`. Figure 15-6 provides a browser rendering of the results.

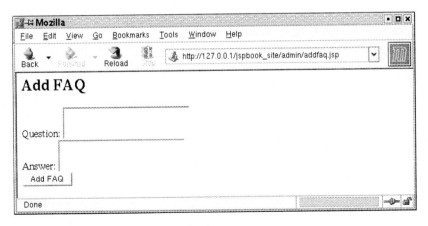

Figure 15-6   Browser Rendering of addfaq.jsp

Fill the form in with information and click the Add FAQ button. The form's content will then be added to the FAQ table of the site's database. You can verify the new logic component works by next trying to edit the table's content, `http://127.0.0.1/jspbook_site/edit.jsp?table=faq`. The entry you just added should be displayed and be editable. Figure 15-7 provides a browser rendering of what the results should look similar to.

We now have a more user-friendly method of adding, editing, and deleting FAQ from the Web Application. As with the news page, FAQ can always be added via `ArbitrarySQLDataSource.jsp` and manually authoring content pages—but that is relatively difficult compared to a few simple HTML forms. Before we move on, take note of how much less work we had to do in order to add and edit FAQ entries compared to news entries; much less new code was required for adding and editing FAQ. Thanks go directly to the generic `edit.java` and `update.java` logic components. By re-using them, we had nothing more to do but create a method of adding FAQ into the database.

In general, it is easy to make lots of simple logic components; however, lots of simple logic components still take time to make. Always think ahead and determine what can be consolidated using standard, good Object-Oriented Programming (OOP). For example, we could have made three logic components

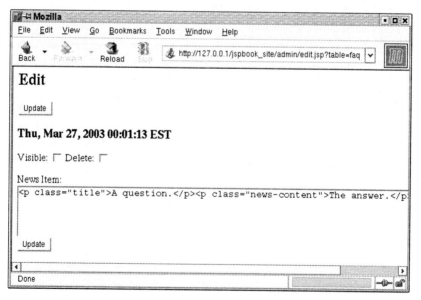

Figure 15-7   Browser Rendering of the Edited FAQ Entries

for each dynamic page, such as `addfaq.java`, `editfaq.java`, and `updatefaq.java`, instead of only `addfaq.java` and re-using `edit.java` and `update.java`. In the end we would have had to code 12 logic components (assuming 3 for each: news, FAQ, feedback, and errata) instead of 6. Certainly, in some cases you will need to code lots of logic components, but always try to code as few as possible; more code always equals more work, in both creating and maintaining.

Logic Components for the Feedback and Errata Pages

Excluded are the logic components of the feedback and errata pages; the code can safely be omitted for brevity since it is nothing but a slight edit of the previous pages. Given the news and FAQ pages, it should be obvious how the logic components for the feedback and errata pages are created. If it is not, the complete code for the entire Web Application can be obtained from `http://www.jspbook.com`.

Dealing with Overly Complex Logic Components

Usually logic components are simple, straightforward classes, much like all of the logic components for the book support site. However, it is certainly possible that an overly complex component is required—basically, anything that seems too large to place in a single Java class. In cases such as this, do not forget you are using Java. Nothing stops you from building a set of classes that the single logic class uses. The technique is also helpful for more things than reducing a single class's size. For example, multiple `logic` classes may benefit from sharing the same `abstract` class, perhaps with generic functions for validating request parameters, or good object-oriented practices may dictate similar code that is used by all `logic` classes be placed in a single helper class.

The point to remember is that when coding with Java, use Java. Don't feel restricted to using a single class for things such as Model 2 logic components just because other examples do so.

Implementing Presentation Logic: JSP, Multi-Client Design, and Internationalization

So far we have built the database and several logic components. The final part of the Web Application is to build a series of display components that generate an HTML page for the user's browser. Each display component is a simple JSP that provides some static content and displays information set in request-scoped variables. JSPs already provide a mechanism for authoring content in all the well-known languages, as covered in Chapter 12, and JSPs also provide a method, the JSP EL, easily accessing request-scoped objects.

It is assumed that the JSTL and JSP expression language are familiar topics. If you do not remember these, consult the appropriate chapter; a complete review will not be provided. The JSTL is covered in Chapter 6, and the JSP EL is covered in Chapter 5.

Building a Simple Presentation Page

In the simplest case a JSP presentation page is nothing more than HTML used to mark up some content. In the most complex case, some of the dynamic features of JSP are used to customize the HTML on the fly. In all cases even the most complex presentation page of this Web Application will contain near-trivial code; this is as expected and due to good Model 2 use. Listing 15-17 is an example of one of the most complex presentation pages, the main page of the site, the news page.

Listing 15-17 index.jsp

```
<p style="padding-left:15px;">Welcome to the official book support
site for <i>Servlets and JSP; the J2EE Web Tier</i>. This site was
created and is maintained by the authors of the book in order to aid
readers. Here you can find out the latest book related news, find
answers to questions people commonly ask about the book, errata, the
book's Listing, and sample chapters of the book's material.</p>
<p class="h1">News</p>
<%@ taglib uri="http://java.sun.com/jstl/core_rt" prefix="c" %>
<c:forEach var="n" begin="0" items="${news}">${n}</c:forEach>
<p><a href="addnews.jsp">Suggest a news item</a>.</p>
```

Save the preceding code as `index.jsp` in the root directory of the `jspbook_site` Web Application, and copy the `jstl.jar` and `standard.jar` from the jspbook Web Application to the `jspbook_site` Web Application's `/WEB-INF/lib` directory. The entire code is straightforward. The paragraph of text is nothing more than that. After the introduction, the news items are displayed. Assuming the request-scoped variables are set correctly, which is the Java programmer's job, the JSTL iteration tag loops through the array of news items and displays each one.

```
<c:forEach var="n" begin="0" items="${news}">${n}</c:forEach>
```

Overall, the code for `index.jsp` is quite basic—which is exactly the way it should be. Someone developing or maintaining content should not care about anything but the content. Styling content, checking for spelling mistakes, and editing grammar are all valid issues, but coding around scriptlets is not. By keeping the presentation logic simple, like we are doing, one of the most volatile parts of the site is easy to maintain.

However, the presentation coder's job is not restricted only to coding pages such as `index.jsp`. If you actually browse to `index.jsp`, as it currently is, you will notice the content is bland. Browse to `http://127.0.0.1/jspbook_site/index.jsp`. Figure 15-8 shows an example browser rendering of the output.

Certainly the content is presented in HTML format, but it is not very appealing. Another part of the presentation coder's job is to style content. This book is minimally concerned with style issues, but it is not difficult to spend a second to make the book support site look decent.

Creating MCT Headers and Footers

The first element of style we shall add to the book support site are a header and footer, something that will go on all pages and give a consistent look to pages. It will also provide an easy method to implement a navigation bar and link a Cascading Style Sheet. The code itself is of little interest: there is nothing more than HTML; however, how we implement use of the header and footer is of slight interest. First, we will get the code for the header and footer out of the way, and then we will discuss how to use the `web.xml` JSP configuration elements to make them work properly .

Save Listing 15-18 as `prelude.jsp` in the base directory of the `jspbook_site` Web Application.

Figure 15-8 Browser Rendering of the Unstyled index.jsp

Listing 15-18   prelude.jsp

```
<html>
 <head>
   <title>Servlets and JSP the J2EE Web Tier
        - Jayson Falkner and Kevin Jones</title>
   <link rel="StyleSheet" type="text/css" href="style.css"/>
 </head>
<body style="margin:0px;padding:0px;font-family:helvetica;">
<table width="100%" cellpadding="0" cellspacing="0">
  <tr>
    <td height="78" style="background-color:#788dad;
                           border-width:2px;
                           border-style:solid;
                           border-color:black;
                           padding:0px;
                           margin:0px;" valign="bottom">
    <img src="http://www.jspbook.com/images/title.jpg"
      align="left" valign="bottom">
    <img src="http://www.jspbook.com/images/gnome1.jpg"
      align="right">
    </td>
  </tr>
  <tr>
    <td height="15" style="color:white;
                           background-color:#444444;
                           border-width:2px;
                           border-style:solid;
                           border-top-width:0px;
                           border-color:black;" align="center">
    <a style="color:white;"
      href="http://www.jspbook.com/about.jsp">About the Book</a>
  - <a style="color:white;"
      href="http://www.jspbook.com/code.jsp">Code</a>
  - <a style="color:white;"
      href="http://www.jspbook.com/errata.jsp">Errata</a>
  - <a style="color:white;"
      href="http://www.jspbook.com/faq.jsp">FAQ</a>
  - <a style="color:white;"
      href="http://www.jspbook.com/freechapters.jsp">
      Free Chapters</a>
  - <a style="color:white;"
      href="http://www.jspbook.com/index.jsp">News</a>
  - <a style="color:white;"
```

```
       href="http://www.jspbook.com/feedback.jsp">
       Reader's Feedback</a>
    </td>
    </tr>
</table>
```

Save Listing 15-19 as `coda.jsp` in the base directory of the `jspbook_site` Web Application.

Listing 15-19   coda.jsp

```
<br/>
<p align="center">Contact <a href="jayson@jspinsider.com">Support
  </a> for questions or comments.</p>
<p align="center" style="font-size:8pt;">
  Copyright &copy; 2003 Jayson Falkner</p>
  </body>
</html>
```

The header, `prelude.jsp`, and the footer, `coda.jsp`, contain nothing more than HTML. As mentioned before, the relevant part is not in the code but in how we will use it. In order to have the code displayed on all of the pages of the Web site, we will use the `include-prelude` and `include-coda` JSP configuration elements of `web.xml`. Recall in Chapter 3 these elements were introduced. Because Web Applications commonly have the same code included before and after the content of a page, a standard mechanism was created for simplifying the task. Listing 15-20 is the entry for `web.xml`.

Listing 15-20   Updated web.xml for Using Site-Wide Header and Footer

```
  . . .
  <jsp-config>
    <jsp-property-group>
      <url-pattern>*.jsp</url-pattern>
      <include-prelude>/prelude.jsp</include-prelude>
      <include-coda>/coda.jsp</include-coda>
    </jsp-property-group>
  </jsp-config>
  . . .
```

Reload the `jspbook_site` Web Application for the changes to take effect. With the new configuration, every page will automatically include the contents of `prelude.jsp` at the start and `coda.jsp` at the end; this functionality is identical to manually using JSPs to include a header and footer on each page, but with much less code.

Now, when `index.jsp` is rendered as HTML, the implicit header and footer are included. Try browsing to `http://127.0.0.1/jspbook_site/index.jsp` to see the change. Figure 15-9 provides a browser rendering of the results.

The site now looks much more professional. Standard HTML can do all sorts of things, including many spiffy things, and the site is showing a little more style. Note that if you do not have an Internet connection, the images will not appear because they were sneaked in by using absolute URLs.

```
<img src="http://www.jspbook.com/images/title.jpg"
    align="left" valign="bottom">
<img src="http://www.jspbook.com/images/gnome1.jpg"
    align="right">
```

This book is not about graphic design, rightly so, and it is assumed if you want to include graphics on your pages, you would independently create them. Both the title graphic and gnome image are graphics previously created and uploaded to the online version of the book support site.

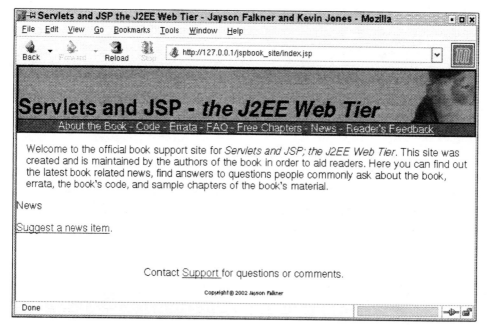

Figure 15-9 Browser Rendering of index.jsp

Adding Some More Style, Cascading Style Sheets

Rarely do professionally done Web sites rely on the default styles of Web browsers. The majority of sites choose fonts and colors that the majority of people find user-friendly and easy to read. The book support site is intended to be a professional site and we shall style the content as one. Cascading Style Sheets (CSS) is the standard method of styling HTML; CSS offers far more style control than pure HTML. A simple style sheet can add a lot to the site's appearance; save Listing 15-21 as `style.css` in the base directory of the `jspbook_site` Web Application.

Listing 15-21   style.css

```css
.h1 {
  padding-left:15px;
  font-size:20pt;
  font-weight:bold;
}
.h2 {
  padding-left:13px;
  font-size:18pt;
  font-weight:bold;
}
p {
  padding-left:15px;
}
link {
  font-style:none;
  color:blue;
  text-decoration:none;
}
.code {
  font-style:italic;
}
.nopad {
  margin-bottom:0px;
  padding-bottom:0px;
  margin-top:0px;
  padding-top:0px;
}
.date {
  padding-left:5px;
  font-size:18pt;
  text-decoration:underline;
```

```
}
.title {
  padding-left:10px;
  font-family:times;
  font-size:16pt;
  font-weight:bold;
}
.content {
  padding-left:10px;
  padding-right:10px;
}
```

The style sheet defines several generic styles for the site's presentation pages. By default, all of the content in the `jspbook_site` Web Application will be styled in a font that is different from the default, often thought of or simply taken to be more professional, but more importantly it is also a font that is commonly preferred to the standard Times New Roman. Browse back to `http://127.0.0.1/jspbooksite/index.jsp` to see the new styles applied. Figure 15-10 provides a browser rendering of the results.

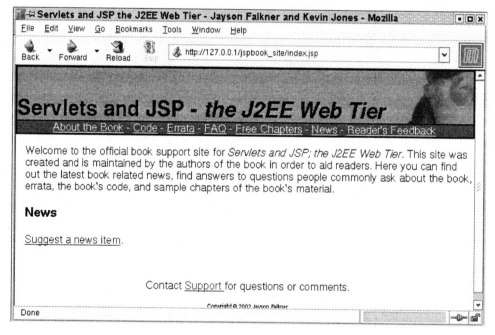

Figure 15-10 Browser Rendering of the Styled index.jsp

In general, styles can be added to `style.css`, and they will be applied to all of the content in the book support site. This functionality won't be needed for this site, but it is generally helpful to have when developing a Web Application.

Letting a User Suggest News

Previously, we created a system for administrators to submit and edit news items; however, it is helpful to also allow users the ability to submit news. Less work on site administrators is always a good thing, especially if the same effect is achieved. The `addnews.java` logic component can easily be re-used in a user page—in other words, one not in the `/admin` directory. By doing so a user can submit news, and the administrators will only have to worry about validating the news.

Creating a page that a user can submit news from is straightforward. Like all the other presentation pages, we will create a JSP. Save Listing 15-22 as `addnews.jsp` in the root directory of the `jspbook_site` Web Application.

Listing 15-22 addnews.jsp

```
<p class="h1">Suggest News</p>
<p>Completely fill out the following form to suggest a news item.
 Note, all news must be filterd by an administrator before it is
 posted on the site. Do not expect a news item that was just
 submitted to instantly appear.</p>
<form method="POST" action="addnews.jsp">
<table>
  <tr>
    <td>Title:</td><td><input name="title" size="50"/></td>
  </tr>
  <tr>
    <td>Link:</td><td><input name="link" size="50"/></td>
  </tr>
  <tr>
    <td>Text:</td>
    <td><textarea name="text" cols="60" rows="8"></textarea>
    </td>
  </tr>
</table>
  <input type="submit" value="Suggest News"/>
</form>
```

The page is similar to the previous `addnews.jsp`, placed in the `/admin` directory. Verify the page works by visiting `http://127.0.0.1/jspbook_site/ addnews.jsp`. Figure 15-11 provides a browser rendering of the results.

Now users and administrators alike can submit news; however, only administrators can edit news items and decide what items are publicly displayed. Test the page out by filling out the form and submitting the information. The `addnews.java` logic component we created earlier handles this new page and adds the entry to the site's database. Try to edit the news entries, `http://127.0.0.1/jspbook_site/admin/edit.jsp?table=news`, and you will find the new entry—note also it is by default not visible.

Creating the Other Presentation Pages

With `index.jsp` we have finished the tedious part of building a presentation page: creating the headers, footers, and styles. For the other presentation pages we

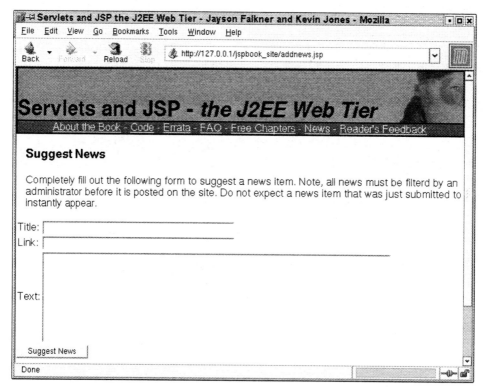

Figure 15-11 Browser Rendering of addnews.jsp

need only author a document that accurately describes the page. For static pages, such as the about page, there will be nothing but a few paragraphs of text. For dynamic pages, such as the FAQ, feedback, and errata pages, there will be paragraphs of static text and some code that displays request-scoped variables—much like index.jsp.

For completeness two more examples are provided of JSP view pages: one more dynamic page and one static page. However, given the code for index.jsp it should be obvious how these pages are to be created. Nothing new or interesting is introduced by the code; static pages are nothing more than HTML markup and some content. Dynamic pages are similar to index.jsp but with different static text.

Coding the About the Book Page

The about page is nothing more than a description of the book *Servlets and JSP: The J2EE Web Tier*. In many ways it is a summarized version of this book's preface; as Listing 15-23 shows, there is nothing suspect about this page at all. Do not worry about spending time reading through all the markup; the text is easier to read when rendered as HTML.

Listing 15-23 about.jsp

```
<p class="h1">About the Book</p>
<p><i>Servlets and JSP the J2EE Web
 Tier</i> is a book authored by Jayson Falkner and Kevin Jones
 about the latest in Servlets and JSP. The current version of
 the book covers Servlets 2.4, JSP 2.0, and the JSTL 1.0.
 Both Jayson and Kevin helped directly make the
 specifications and are proud to publish one of the first
 books covering technologies. Servlets and JSP the J2EE
 Web Tier is comprehensive and covers everything you need to
 know about building Java Web Applications.</p>

<p class="h2">Who Is This Book For?</p>
<p>Servlets and JSP the J2EE Web Tier is designed for
 developers of all levels. The book assumes a reader is
 familiar with HTML and the basics of Java. The book begins
 by covering how to install a Servlet/JSP environment and
 what is in the JSP 2.0, Servlet 2.4, and JSTL 1.0
 specifications. After discussion of the raw technologies, the
```

book focuses on practical uses of them. The later chapters of
the book cover topics such as state management, design
patterns, internationalization support, multi-client design, and
Java database connectivity. At all possible places Jayson
and Kevin try to share the millions of little things, both
in the specs and not, that they have learned from being
long-time Servlet and JSP developers.</p>

<p>If you are a new user, this book is for you. It starts from
the basics and covers everything up to the most advanced
topics. If you are an experienced developer, this book
provides a reference for the Servlet 2.4, JSP 2.0, and JSTL
specifications and a good discussion of advanced design
patterns and problem-solving techniques. If you are in
management, you are advised to buy multiple copies: this
is a book that will be permanently borrowed by
employees.</p>

<p class="h2">Book Specs</p>
<p class="nopad">Title: Servlets and JSP the J2EE Web Tier</p>
<p class="nopad">Published: 2003 Addison Wesley</p>
<p class="nopad">Pages:</p>
<p class="nopad">ISBN:</p>

<p>Table of Contents:</p>
<p class="nopad">Preface</p>
<p class="nopad">1 - Setting Up a Servlet and JSP Environment</p>
<p class="nopad">2 - Java Servlets</p>
<p class="nopad">3- JavaServer Pages</p>
<p class="nopad">4- Exception Handling</p>
<p class="nopad">5- JavaBeans</p>
<p class="nopad">6 - Custom Tag Libraries</p>
<p class="nopad">7 - JavaServer Pages Standard Tag Library</p>
<p class="nopad">8 - Filters</p>
<p class="nopad">9 - Managing State in a Web Application</p>
<p class="nopad">10 - Security</p>
<p class="nopad">11 - Design Patterns</p>
<p class="nopad">12 - Internationalization</p>
<p class="nopad">13 - Multi-Client Support</p>
<p class="nopad">14 - Database Connectivity</p>
<p class="nopad">15 - Building a Complete Web Application</p>

```
<p>What Other People Have Said About the Book</p>
<p>This site is authored by the authors of the book. While we
 try to be benevolent, there is something to be gained from
 third-party feedback. Here is an unbiased list of all the
 reviews we have found.</p>

<p class="nopad">
 <a href="http://www.jspbook.com/feedback.jsp">
  Feedback sent to the book support site</a></p>
<p class="nopad">
  <a href=" ">Amazon.com Reviews</a></p>
<p class="nopad">
  <a href=" ">Barnes and Nobles Reviews</a></p>

<p class="h2">Jayson Falkner</p>
<p>Jayson's bio here.</p>

<p class="h2">Kevin Jones</p>
<p>Kevin's bio here.</p>
```

Save the preceding code as `about.jsp` in the root directory of the
`jspbook_site` Web Application. You can verify the preceding page, as lengthy as
it is, as nothing more than pure HTML markup; no dynamic JSP actions or JSP
expressions are used. As a result there is little discussion about the page unless we
wish to critique its use of the English language. For completeness, Figure 15-12 is
a browser rendering of the page. Browse to `http://127.0.0.1/jspbook_site/`
`about.jsp` to see this locally.

If you want to, you can read through the description. Due to this description
being this book's preface, you will likely find it repetitive, but for new visitors to
the book support site, `http://www.jspbook.com/`, the description is the type of
information they should be interested in.

Coding the Other Static Pages: Free Chapters Page and Code Page

The free chapters page of the site is another purely static page. The page explains
that portions of this book are available for free and how the free portions may be
obtained. If you are interested in the source code, it is available at `http://`
`www.jspbook.com`. The code page contains links to all the code mentioned in this
text which can be found by visiting the book support site. Similar to the other
static pages, it contains nothing but HTML markup; however, you may obtain the
source code at the book support site.

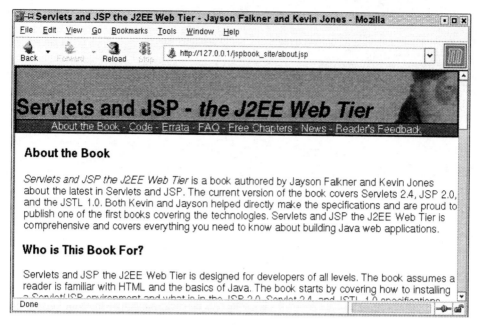

Figure 15-12 Browser Rendering of about.jsp

Errata Page

The errata page contains a list of the latest errata for the book. Being that erratum may possibly be added at any given time, this page cannot do with purely static content. Instead, a current list of errata is assumed to be maintained by the ERRATA table in the site's database. Each time the errata page is viewed, the current list of errata, as provided by the database, is displayed.

Coding the errata page is conceptually identical to the index page. Some static content is required along with the JSTL iteration tag and a JSP expression for displaying the errata, which are dynamically populated in request scope. The code for obtaining the current errata and populating request-scoped objects is of no concern. It is assumed the Java developer(s) (us, in this case) previously coded a Model 2 component for this purpose (which we did earlier in this chapter). The code for errata.jsp is as follows. Save Listing 15-24 as errata.jsp in the root directory of the jspbook_site Web Application.

Listing 15-24 errata.jsp

```
<p class="h1">Errata</p>
<p style="padding-left:15px;"><i>Servlets and JSP the J2EE Web
```

```
Tier</i> is not perfect, nor are the authors. We made our best
attempt at getting the book done right the first time, and we are
already trying to improve the book for the 2nd edition. If you think
something could be improved for the next edition of the book, please
<a href="mailto:jayson@jspinsider.com">let us know</a>. Formal
errata for the 1st edition are listed on this page. You may formally
suggest the edition of a new erratum. <a
href="adderrata.jsp">here</a>.</p>
<%@ taglib uri="http://java.sun.com/jstl/core_rt" prefix="c" %>
<c:forEach var="e" begin="0" items="${errata}">${e}</c:forEach>
```

Of interest in the preceding code is the way in which the request-scoped
interface is used.

```
<c:forEach var="e" begin="0" items="${errata}">${e}</c:forEach>
```

As with `index.jsp` the JSTL iteration tag is combined with a JSP expression.
Except for the specific syntax change from using the "news" request-scoped
object to using the "errata" request-scoped object, nothing merits technical discussion; the bulk of the code is simple styled content.

Letting Users Suggest Errata

As with the news items, it is beneficial to allow users to suggest errata. Providing
an email address for the book's authors, as each page does in the footer, is a fine
solution, but it is a hassle compared to a simple HTML form—especially if the
submitter wishes to remain anonymous. In order to allow users to easily suggest
errata we will re-use the `adderrata.java` logic component and create an
`adderrata.jsp` user page.

Save Listing 15-25 as `adderrata.jsp` in the root directory of the `jspbook_
site` Web Application.

Listing 15-25   adderrata.jsp

```
<p class="h1">Suggest Erratum</p>
<p>You may suggest an erratum by filling out the following form.
Please completely list the fix, including where the fix is
required (i.e., page number, figure, or code). Note that
suggested erratum are not official until verified by one of the
book's authors. Do not expect suggested erratum to appear
instantly on the book's errata page.</p>
```

```
<form method="POST" action="adderrata.jsp">
  <p><textarea cols="60" rows="5" name="errata"></textarea></p>
  <input type="submit" value="Suggest Errata"/>
</form>
```

Now, users can submit errata, anonymously or not, via `adderrata.jsp`. Test the page out by browsing to `http://127.0.0.1/jspbook_site/adderrata.jsp`. Figure 15-13 provides a browser rendering of the results.

Verify the page works by filling out the form and submitting the information. Next, edit the errata, `http://127.0.0.1/jspbook_site/admin/edit.jsp?table=errata`, to see the new entry. It should be no surprise that the page works since we are not changing the HTML form nor the `adderrata` logic component, just the style of the page.

Coding the Other Dynamic Pages: FAQ Pages and Feedback Pages

The other dynamic pages of the site, the FAQ pages and the feedback pages, are similar to both the index and errata pages. One page contains a description along

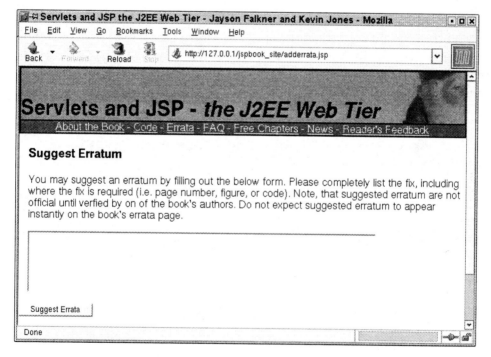

Figure 15-13   Browser Rendering of adderrata.jsp

with the JSTL iteration tag and a JSP EL expression to display dynamic content. The other pages are HTML forms that allow users to submit new content to the site. Nothing merits discussion of these pages as the code is nearly identical to the previous dynamic pages in this chapter. If you wish, the source code may be obtained from `http://www.jspbook.com`.

Localized Content

Up until now it has been assumed that English is the only language supported by the book support site. However, we did create a generic system for allowing language-specific versions of content to be authored. English is only assumed as the default language. If sometime in the future, translated versions of the book support site's content are available, the content can be placed in the Application for use. In order to be recognized, the translated content must start with the same name as the default content but end with "-" followed by the standard three-letter language code.

We shall look at a few pages of localized content. One example will be using a language that works with default HTTP encoding—say, French—and another example that uses a language that requires a different encoding—say, Japanese. Together, the two examples will demonstrate how most any language-specific content can be added to the book support site—the greater point is that relying on ISO-8859-1, HTTP standard encoding, does not always work, but if using a more universal encoding, such as UTF-8, you are set for most practical purposes.

En Francais

Consider first that the Web site must support French. People fluent in French would likely enjoy a French version of the site's content, and our framework certainly supports French text. The method to authoring French content is to append "-fra", the three-letter language code for French, to the end of the default content pages. For example, the index page is saved as `index.jsp`. To create a French version of the index page, save Listing 15-26 as `index-fra.jsp`.

Listing 15-26 index-fra.jsp

```
<p style="padding-left:15px;">Bienvenue pour à l'emplacement
officiel de soutien de livre <i>Servlets and JSP; the J2EE Web
Tier</i>. Cet emplacement a été créé et est maintenu par les auteurs
du livre afin d'aider des lecteurs.  Voici que vous pouvez découvrir
```

```
les nouvelles reliées le dernier par livre, les réponses de
trouvaille aux personnes de questions s'enquièrent généralement du
livre, des errata, du code du livre, et des chapitres d'échantillon
du matériel du livre. </p>
<p class="h1">News</p>
<%@ taglib uri="http://java.sun.com/jstl/core_rt" prefix="c" %>
<c:forEach var="n" begin="0" items="${news}">${n}</c:forEach>
```

Save the preceding code as `index-fra.jsp` in the root directory of the
`jsbpook_site` Web Application. Note there is nothing tricky besides using
French instead of English. Since French characters are easily authored using ISO-
8859-1 encoding, the JSP was authored with no special page encoding directives.
To see the French version of the page, set your Web browser's preference to be
French and browse to `http://127.0.0.1/index.jsp`[9]. The Web Application is
relying on the HTTP language accept-language header to be set, which is com-
monly what Web browsers do when providing language preference information.
To configure Mozilla to specify it prefers French content, go to the Edit —>
Preferences —> Languages menu and add French as the first choice. Figure 15-
14 provides a rendering of the menu.

With the language preference set, browse to `http://127.0.0.1/jsp
booksite/index.jsp`. Instead of the default English content, the French content
is now shown, as is illustrated in Figure 15-15.

The important point here is that our system of integrating localized content
works: we added French content and it is available to those who specify they preferred French. Now the site simultaneously supports both an English and French
version of the index page; however, a slight glitch still exists with the French
version: the header and footer are both still in English. Changing these is as
almost as easy (the implicit header and footer do not use our i18n Filter, but that
is easily fixed) as translating the header and footer files into French and saving
the information in the correct JSP.

Due to the implicit prelude and coda, we cannot rely on the Simplei18n Filter
to correctly translate implicitly included files. The includes are statically done (as
explained in Chapter 2) and will not provide a chance for the Filter to manipulate
them. The fix is to make `coda.jsp` and `prelude.jsp` dynamically include internationalized text on their own. An easy method of accomplishing this is using the
JSTL message tags demonstrated in Chapter 12.

---

9. The standard three-letter language code is strictly for internal use, via request dispatching, by the
Web Application. To the outside world, the URLs for content are the same regardless of the language
being shown.

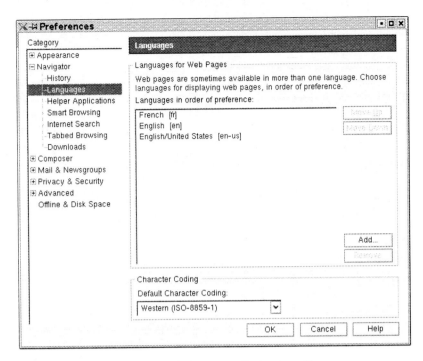

Figure 15-14 Screenshot of the Mozilla Language Preferences Menu

Save Listing 15-27 as the new `prelude.jsp` in the base directory of the `jspbook_site` Web Application

Listing 15-27 prelude.jsp (updated version)

```
<%@ taglib uri="http://java.sun.com/jstl/fmt" prefix="fmt"%>
<fmt:bundle basename="prelude">
<html>
 <head>
   <title><fmt:message key="title"/></title>
   <link rel="StyleSheet" type="text/css" href="style.css"/>
 </head>
 <body style="margin:0px;padding:0px;font-family:helvetica;">
 <table width="100%" cellpadding="0" cellspacing="0">
   <tr>
     <td height="78" style="background-color:#788dad;
                            border-width:2px;
                            border-style:solid;
```

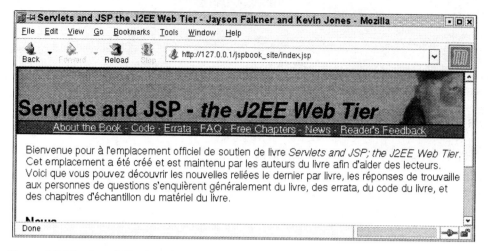

Figure 15-15   French Version of the Index Page

```
                                    border-color:black;
                                    padding:0px;
                                    margin:0px;" valign="bottom">

    <img src="http://www.jspbook.com/images/title.jpg"
      align="left" valign="bottom">
    <img src="http://www.jspbook.com/images/gnome1.jpg"
      align="right" valign="bottom">
   </td>
  </tr>
  <tr>
   <td height="15" style="color:white;
                                    background-color:#444444;
                                    border-width:2px;
                                    border-style:solid;
                                    border-top-width:0px;
                                    border-color:black;" align="center">
    <a style="color:white;"
      href="http://www.jspbook.com/about.jsp"><fmt:message
key="about"/></a>
    - <a style="color:white;"
      href="http://www.jspbook.com/code.jsp"><fmt:message
key="code"/></a>
    - <a style="color:white;"
      href="http://www.jspbook.com/errata.jsp"><fmt:message
key="errata"/></a>
```

```
  - <a style="color:white;"
     href="http://www.jspbook.com/faq.jsp"><fmt:message
key="faq"/></a>
  - <a style="color:white;"
     href="http://www.jspbook.com/freechapters.jsp">
     <fmt:message key="freechapters"/></a>
  - <a style="color:white;"
     href="http://www.jspbook.com/index.jsp"><fmt:message
key="news"/></a>
  - <a style="color:white;"
     href="http://www.jspbook.com/feedback.jsp">
     <fmt:message key="feedback"/></a>
  </td>
  </tr>
 </table>
</fmt:bundle>
```

Save Listing 15-28 as the updated `coda.jsp` in the base directory of `jspbook_site` Web Application.

Listing 15-28   coda.jsp (Updated to Use i18n Tags)

```
<%@ taglib uri="http://java.sun.com/jstl/fmt" prefix="fmtc"%>
<fmtc:bundle basename="coda">
<br/>
<p align="center"><fmtc:message key="contact"/></p>
<p align="center" style="font-size:8pt;">
  <fmtc:message key="copyright"/></p>
  </body>
</html>
</fmtc:bundle>
```

The new files rely on resource bundles in order to display the appropriate content. Now localizing the prelude and coda is as easy as creating the appropriate property files in the `/WEB-INF/classes` directory. For example, Listing 15-29 provides the French property files.

Listing 15-29   prelude_fr.properties

```
title=Servlets and JSP the J2EE Web Tier - Jayson Falkner and Kevin
Jones
about=Au sujet du livre
code=Code
errata=Errata
faq=Questions Fréquemment Posées
```

```
freechapters=Chapitres Libres
news=Nouvelles
feedback=La Rétroaction Du Lecteur
```

Listing 15-30 provides the coda.

Listing 15-30   coda_fr.properties

```
contact=Soutien de contact des questions ou des commentaires.
copyright=Copyright &copy; 2003 Jayson Falkner
```

Save the two property files in the `/WEB-INF/classes` directory of the `jspbook_site` Web Application and reload Tomcat to ensure the changes are reflected. The localized header and footer will now be used when French or any other language is preferred. Browse back to `http://127.0.0.1/jspbook_site/index.jsp` with the browser's preference still set to French. Now the entire page appears completely in French. Figure 15-16 provides a browser rendering of the results.

The localized content for the prelude and coda are appropriately placed. In general this is now true for all languages; new localized property files can be added, and they will be used appropriately.

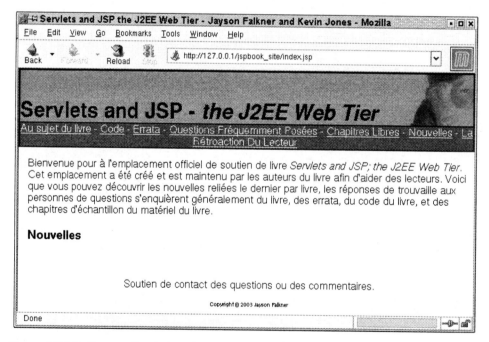

Figure 15-16   Browser Rendering of French Content with Header and Footer

For brevity the rest of the content pages will not be translated into French by this chapter. Instead we will focus on the other issue relating to internationalized content: using non-default encoding.

日本語 (in Japanese)

The general idea of translating content to Japanese is the same as translating content to French: each page needs to be translated and saved with the appropriate extension. However, unlike the French content, authoring Japanese text using JSPs is slightly more difficult. Instead of relying on the default encoding, we must inform the container that the JSP will be using a special encoding and that the JSP requires a special output encoding. Additionally, authoring Japanese text requires a text editor that is capable of producing Japanese characters. If you do not have such a text editor, it will be difficult to author the content in this section so it is suggested that you download the examples from `http://www.jspbook.com`.

In order to author a document in Japanese an encoding must be used that supports Japanese characters. For all of the examples in this section `UTF-8` encoding is used. It does not matter what text editor you use as long as it is capable of saving in `UTF-8`. Assuming you are using a `UTF-8`-producing text editor, type Listing 15-31.

Listing 15-31   index-jpn.jsp

```
<p style="padding-left:15px;">公式のブックエンドの場所への歓迎のための <c
style="font-style:italic;">Servlets and JSP; the J2EE Web Tier</c>.読者を助ける
ためにこの場所は本の著者によって作成され，維持される。ここにあなたは
質問人々への発見の答えは本の材料の本尋ねる，誤り，本のコード，及びサン
ブル章について一般に最も
遅い本関連ニュースを見つけることができる。</p>
<p klass="h1"> ニュース </p>
<%@ taglib uri="http://java.sun.com/jstl/core_rt" prefix="c" %>
<c:forEach var="n" begin="0" items="${news}">${n}</c:forEach>
```

Save the preceding code as `index-jpn.jsp` in the root directory of the `jspbook_site` Web Application. The code is a Japanese translated version of the content contained in `index.jsp`. Similar to the French version of the page, the primary difference is that the content is no longer English; however, unlike the other two versions of `index.jsp`, `index-jpn.jsp` must use a different content encoding. We could explicitly declare the encoding via a JSP directive:

```
<%@ page pageEncoding="utf-8"%>
```

However, the preferred method is to use the JSP configuration elements of `web.xml` to configure all JSP. This saves the effort of putting a JSP directive on each page, and since it is safe to assume Unicode will suffice for i18n content in the foreseeable future, it is a generally fine solution. Listing 15-32 is the updated `web.xml` to dictate the use of `UTF-8`.

Listing 15-32   web.xml Configured for UTF-8

```
...
<jsp-config>
  <jsp-property-group>
    <url-pattern>*.jsp</url-pattern>
    <include-prelude>/prelude.jsp</include-prelude>
    <include-coda>/coda.jsp</include-coda>
    <page-encoding>UTF-8</page-encoding>
  </jsp-property-group>
</jsp-config>
...
```

In order to flush out the Japanese example, an appropriately translated set of property files is required. Here are the Japanese property files for the prelude and coda; save Listing 25-33 as `prelude_ja.properties` in the `/WEB-INF/classes` directory of the `jspbook_site` Web Application.

Listing 15-33   prelude_ja.properties

```
title=Servlets and JSP the J2EE Web Tier - Jayson Falkner and Kevin
Jones
about=\u672c\u306b\u3064\u3044\u3066
code=\u30b3\u30fc\u30c9
errata=\u8aa4\u308a
faq=\u983b\u7e41\u306b\u5c0b\u306d\u3089\u308c\u305f\u8cea\u554f
freechapters=\u81ea\u7531\u306a\u7ae0
news=\u81ea\u7531\u306a\u7ae0
feedback=\u30cb\u30e5\u30fc\u30b9
```

Save Listing 15-34 as `coda_ja.properties` in the `/WEB-INF/classes` folder of the `jspbook_site` Web Application.

Listing 15-34   coda_ja.properties

```
contact=\u8cea\u554f\u307e\u305f\u306f\u30b3\u30e1\u30f3\u30c8\u306e
\u305f\u3081\u306e\u63a5\u89e6\u30b5\u30dd\u30fc\u30c8\u3002
copyright=Copyright &copy; 2003 Jayson Falkner
```

Note the contents of the property files are completely authored in ISO-8859-1 encoding. Unicode characters are escaped appropriately. This is different from our content pages, such as `index-jpa.jsp`, which was authored directly via UTF-8. Normally, authoring directly in UTF-8 encoding is easier (assuming you are working with a plaintext editor) than manually writing Unicode escape sequences; however, property files require the escape sequences to be used.

Test out the Japanese version of the pages by setting your browser's language preference to Japanese and browsing to `http://127.0.0.1/jspbook_site/index.jsp`. Figure 15-17 provides a browser rendering of the results.

For brevity the rest of the book support site will not be translated to Japanese by this chapter. There is nothing relevant to show; the code for displaying request-scoped variables and specifying encoding is exactly the same. The point to understand is that content in any language may be authored and used by the Web Application. Normally, this is problematic because the default encoding, ISO-8859-1, only supports certain languages, but by using Unicode, UTF-8 encoding, it is possible to support most any language.

Finishing the Site

Before moving on, there are a few bits and pieces of the site that need to be addressed. The bulk of the site consists of the custom components previously

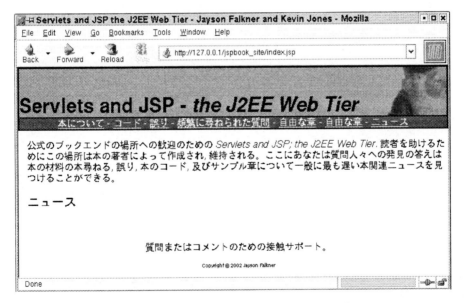

Figure 15-17 Browser Rendering of the Japanese-Translated Index Page

addressed by this chapter. All of the custom components required coding from scratch. Now we shall address several complementary components that were demonstrated in previous chapters. All the components will be relatively simple to implement; instead of coding from scratch, we will simply deploy previously explained code listings.

The list of things to implement is as follows: site-wide error handling, security, link tracking, caching, compression, and the site's hidden Easter egg. Each of the components was completely covered in previous chapters, but each component is briefly rehashed in the following sections as it is installed for use with the book support site.

Site-Wide Error Handling

All of the code previously provided for the book support site uses proper error handling; however, an error can still be thrown (although it probably never will) by the Web Application. Should this happen, the container will have to handle the error. Normally, as with Tomcat, a stack trace is printed and displayed in a developer-friendly fashion, meaning a cryptic page is shown to a user. To prevent this from happening, we need to create a Web Application error page. You'll recall in Chapter 4 that this topic was discussed at length. The error page needs to be nothing more than a simple JSP or Servlet that is registered via web.xml.

Listing 15-35 shows a simple error page.

Listing 15-35   error.jsp

```
<p class="h1">Oops!</p>
<p>An error has occurred. Information about the problem has been
logged and will be handled by administrators as soon as possible. If
you would like to send further information, please contact <a
href="mailto:support@jspbook.com">support</a>.</p>
```

The page doesn't do anything fancy. It apologetically informs a user that the site has failed to function correctly. Additionally, an email address is provided in case the user wishes to communicate further about the problem.

Save error.jsp in the root directory of the jspbook_site Web Application. Deploy the page as the site's default error page by adding Listing 15-36 to web.xml.

Listing 15-36   Setting error.jsp as the Site's Default Error Page

```
<error-page>
  <exception-type>java.lang.Throwable</exception-type>
```

```
<location>/error.jsp</location>
</error-page>
```

Reload the Web Application for the changes to take effect. Now we have a fail-safe counter to Tomcat's displaying a cryptic stack trace to use. Although it should never happen, plan for the worst. You can test the page by browsing `http://127.0.0.1/jspbook_site/error.jsp`. The page provides a polite error message and is rendered with the site's implicit header and footer. Figure 15-18 provides a browser rendering of the results in English.

Note also that the Model 2 and i18n Filters are applied to this page. A localized error page can be added by creating a localized version of `error.jsp`.

Logging Errors

Chapter 4 devoted a large section of its text to error handling, and it would be a shame to neglect the concepts for the book support site's Web Application. Logging could have been more extensively used to provide information about any of the book's code, such as database queries, but it was omitted for simplicity. Now logging cannot be omitted. The error page handles important information; we must be able to keep track of what goes wrong with the Web Application so

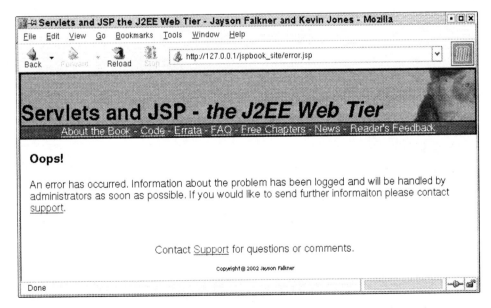

Figure 15-18 Browser Rendering of the Polite Error Page

that administrators can attempt to correct the problem. To handle error logging, we shall re-use the `SiteLogger` code (Listing 4-24 in Chapter 4).

Deploy the `SiteLogger` listener, save, and compile Listing 4-23 and Listing 4-24 in the `WEB-INF/classes/com/jspbook` directory for the `jspbook_site` Web Application. The listener takes care of creating a `Logger` class that the error page can use at any time to log information. Listing 15-37 is required to deploy the `logger`.

Listing 15-37   web.xml Update for Deploying the SiteLogger Class

```
...
  <listener>
    <listener-class>com.jspbook.SiteLogger</listener-class>
  </listener>
...
```

The Web Application will need to be reloaded for the changes to take effect, but before reloading it copy the classes required for the `SiteLogger` listener to the `jspbook_site` Web Application.

With the `logger` deployed, we can now take advantage of it to log any information about site errors. The Java code for doing this can be nicely encapsulated by a Model 2 component. Listing 15-38 is the error page's implicit Model 2 component.

Listing 15-38   error.java

```
package com.jspbook;

import javax.servlet.http.*;
import javax.servlet.*;
import java.io.*;
import java.util.logging.*;

public class error implements Control {
  public boolean doLogic(HttpServletRequest request,
                         HttpServletResponse response)
  throws ServletException, IOException {

    // get logger
    Logger logger = com.jspbook.SiteLogger.getLogger();
    // get exception
    Exception e =
      (Exception)request.
        getAttribute("javax.servlet.jsp.jspException");
```

```
    //log the stack trace
    if (e != null) {
      StringWriter message = new StringWriter();
      e.printStackTrace(new PrintWriter(message));
      logger.severe(message.toString());
    }
    return true;
  }
}
```

Save the preceding code as `error.java` in the `/WEB-INF/classes/com/jspbook` directory of the `jspbook_site` Web Application. Compile the code and reload the Web Application for the changes to take effect. Now the Web Application both appropriately handles errors and saves information for administrators in the `/WEB-INF/log.txt` file. If you have forgotten how the `SiteLogger` class works, revisit Chapter 4.

Adding Security

Chapter 10 went to great lengths explaining the basics of security and why you should use it. The greater point to take away from Chapter 10 is if only certain people should be able to access part of a Web site, ensure only those people have access. Never assume users are too dumb to use administrative tools (like `ArbitrarySQLDataSource.jsp`), and never think the administrative portion of the site is safe because you don't provide a link to it.

Various levels of security exist for a Web Application: simple unencrypted user name and password combinations, hashed user name and password schemes, and finally completely secure communication via SSL/TLS. Each type of security is simple to implement and can be done by configuring `web.xml`. For the book support site we need to make sure only administrators have access to the edit pages. Configure `web.xml` to restrict access to any URL beginning with `/admin` (Listing 15-39); this will ensure regular users cannot use the administrative tools[10].

Listing 15-39 Securing the /admin Directory

```
...
<security-constraint>
    <web-resource-collection>
```

---

10. You'll recall security is always an arms race. Current security schemes don't guarantee absolute security, although the protection is very difficult—reasonable enough to call impossible—to break.

```
    <web-resource-name>Protected Area</web-resource-name>
    <url-pattern>/admin/*</url-pattern>
  </web-resource-collection>
  <auth-constraint>
    <role-name>jspbook_admin</role-name>
  </auth-constraint>
</security-constraint>

<login-config>
  <auth-method>BASIC</auth-method>
  <realm-name>Edit Access</realm-name>
</login-config>
...
```

Add the preceding code to `web.xml` in the `WEB-INF` directory of the `jspbook_site` Web Application and reload the Web Application for the changes to take effect. Now the `/admin` directory requires a user name and password for access. Test the security by browsing to `http://127.0.0.1/jspbook_site/admin/index.jsp`. Figure 15-19 provides a browser rendering of the security box.

You'll recall the user name and password information need to be provided only once per session; once you correctly type in the user name and password, the HTTP protocol takes care of remembering you did so. The particular user name and password we are using are the same as configured in Chapter 10 (Listing 15-40).

Listing 15-40   Tomcat's XML Configured Security Domain

```
<?xml version='1.0' encoding='utf-8'?>
<tomcat-users>
  <role rolename="jspbook_admin"/>
  <user username="username"
```

Figure 15-19   Security Prompt for Accessing Resources in the /admin Directory

```
         password="password" roles="jspbook_admin"/>
</tomcat-users>
```

By adding Listing 15-40 we are done providing security for the Web Application. In general, security is this easily added unless you are trying to use a more complex security scheme, such as various different security levels for users, or when using SSL/TLS to protect sensitive HTTP traffic such as personal information and credit card numbers. Revisit Chapter 10 if you have forgotten how to use the more complex security mechanisms.

Link Tracking

Most Web Applications care about tracking hits, referrers, and outbound traffic. This functionality can easily be implemented via either a Servlet or a Filter. In Chapter 2 and Chapter 8 we saw examples of a link tracking Servlet and a link tracking Filter. For the book support site, we will re-use the link tracking Filter demonstrated in Chapter 8. Copy the code for the Filter (Listing 8-3, Listing 8-5, and Listing 8-6 from Chapter 8), and save it in the /WEB-INF/classes/com/jspbook directory of the jspbook_site Web Application. Deploy the LinkTracker Filter to intercept all requests (Listing 15-41).

Listing 15-41   Deployment of the LinkTracker Filter

```
. . .
  <filter>
    <filter-name>LinkTrackerFilter</filter-name>
    <filter-class>com.jspbook.LinkTrackerFilter</filter-class>
  </filter>
  <filter-mapping>
    <filter-name>LinkTrackerFilter</filter-name>
    <url-pattern>/*</url-pattern>
  </filter-mapping>
. . .
```

The important note for this deployment is that the LinkTracker Filter takes effect before the SimpleI18nFilter. The internationalization Filter does not chain requests through anything else down the Filter chain. With the Filters deployed, the Web Application conceptually looks like Figure 15-20.

Now we have three different Filters stacked to provide various functionality. Links are tracked, Model 2 logic components are executed, and internationalized multi-client content is properly handled. At the end of the Filter chain are presentation JSPs responsible for generating content.

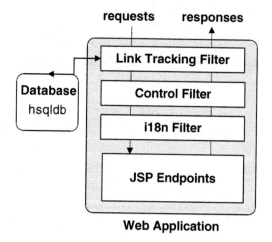

requests   responses

Link Tracking Filter

Control Filter

Database
hsqldb

i18n Filter

JSP Endpoints

Web Application

Figure 15-20 Updated Version of the Web Application

Without a complementary JSP, the link tracking Filter is pointless. The Filter will track links, but there will be no method of seeing the information. Save Listing 15-42 as `linktracker.jsp` in order to see the link tracking information.

Listing 15-42 linktracker.jsp

```
<%@ taglib uri="http://java.sun.com/jstl/core_rt" prefix="c" %>
<p class="h1">Requests</p>
<c:forEach var="r" begin="0" items="${requests}">
  <p class="nopad"><a href="${r.url}">${r.url}</a> ${r.count}
${r.lastVisited}</p>
</c:forEach>
<p class="h1">Responses</p>
<c:forEach var="r" begin="0" items="${responses}">
  <p class="nopad"><a href="${r.url}">${r.url}</a> ${r.count}
${r.lastVisited}</p>
</c:forEach>
<p class="h1">Referrers</p>
<c:forEach var="r" begin="0" items="${referrers}">
  <p class="nopad"><a href="${r.url}">${r.url}</a> ${r.count}
${r.lastVisited}</p>
</c:forEach>
```

The preceding code is a JSP that iterates through three arrays of `Link` objects, assumed to be loaded in request scope. In order for the page to work correctly, we need to add a Model 2 logic component that uses the LinkTracker class's `getRequests()`, `getResponses()`, and `getReferrers()` methods to populate request-scoped variables. Save Listing 15-43 as `linktracker.java` in the /WEB-INF/classes/com/jspbook directory of the `jspbook_site` Web Application.

Listing 15-43   linktracker.java

```
package com.jspbook;

import javax.servlet.http.*;
import javax.servlet.*;
import java.io.*;

public class linktracker implements Control {
    public boolean doLogic(HttpServletRequest request,
                        HttpServletResponse response)
    throws ServletException, IOException {

      Link[] requests = LinkTrackerFilter.getRequests();
      request.setAttribute("requests", requests);
      Link[] responses = LinkTrackerFilter.getResponses();
      request.setAttribute("responses", responses);
      Link[] referrers = LinkTrackerFilter.getReferrers();
      request.setAttribute("referrers", referrers);

      return true;
    }
}
```

Now `linktracker.jsp` can be used to see the statistics tracked by the LinkTracker Filter. Browse to `http://127.0.0.1/jspbook_site/linktracker.html` to see a summary of the tracked information. Figure 15-21 provides a browser rendering of the results.

With the Filter installed as is, it will successfully track incoming requests and referral information; however, outgoing requests are more difficult to track. Recall that the method of tracking an outgoing request is to send it back to your local site, record the outbound URL, and use an HTTP client-side redirection. The LinkTracker Filter provides the code for recording and redirecting requests, but it relies on all of the links in the Web Application being encoded to use it.

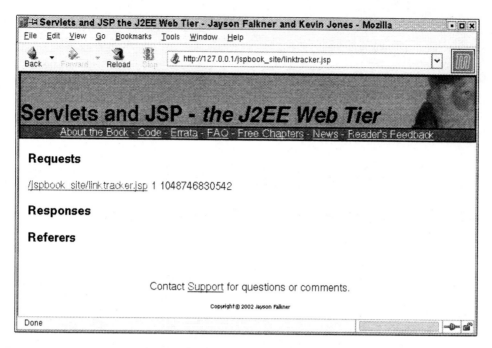

Figure 15-21 Browser Rendering of linktracker.jsp

The encoding scheme for links is simple: each link must go to `/linktracker` and contain an HTTP parameter named "`url`" that provides the outbound URL. The difficult part about encoding links is that each and every link in the Web Application must be encoded. Doing this task by hand is tedious and not recommended for large Web Applications; however, we have little choice but to do it for the book support site. A quick search and replace, using your favorite text editor, does the job. Recall that in the multi-client chapter a much better scheme was suggested for encoding links: abstract all links (similar to what the JSTL url tag does). Then the links can be encoded at runtime by the abstraction, likely a custom tag.

After changing the links to use the link tracking Filter, note the links to external references are now encoded to be local. For example, the link to Tomcat, normally `http://jakarta.apache.org/tomcat`, is changed to `redirect?url=http://jakarta.apache.org/tomcat`. If you click on the link, it still appears to go directly to the Tomcat Web site, but it really goes back to the book support site, records the outbound URL, and then finally redirects to Tomcat's homepage.

Verify the outbound traffic tracking works by revisiting `http://127.0.0.1/jspbook_site/linktracker.jsp`—note the outbound link now appears in the tracked statistics. Figure 15-22 provides a browser rendering of the results.

The site's link tracking functionality is now complete. The LinkTracker Filter is an excellent modular component that is easy to add to most any site. The only tricky part is encoding all outbound links (if you want to track them), but the Multi-Client framework made this task trivial.

Caching and Compression

A final touch to the book support site can make the site notably more efficient and fault-tolerant. Several layers of functionality are abstracted in order to make coding the site simpler. Examples of this functionality include using the MCT for abstracting formatting, querying the database for dynamic information, and using Model 2 logic components instead of embedding code. For most practical purposes, mostly because the book support site will likely never get more than a moderate level of traffic, all of this abstraction doesn't matter; however, the

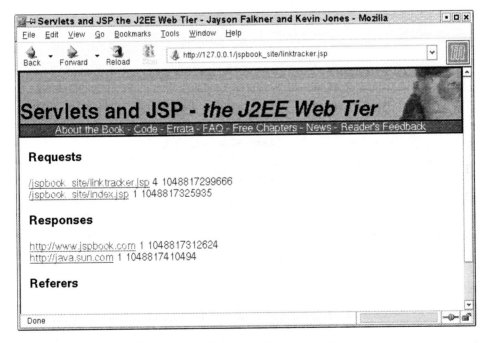

Figure 15-22 Browser Rendering of Statistics on Outbound Links

abstraction does slow things down. In order to eliminate all of the time required to generate a dynamic response, we can cache the response using a Filter, as demonstrated in Chapter 8. The cache can also act as fault tolerance in case for some reason, such as a poorly done code "fix" or the database crashes, a JSP throws an exception. Additionally, for optimal performance we can take advantage of HTTP's compression mechanism, also demonstrated in Chapter 8.

For the book support site we will be able to directly re-use the cache and compression Filters created in Chapter 8. As described in Chapter 8, these two Filters are easily re-used in most every Web Application, which is absolutely true, and make the code quite handy. Once the Filters are applied, the conceptual view of the Web Application will look as in Figure 15-23.

The Filters are applied as they should be: compression first, caching second. Not all HTTP clients support compression so we cannot assume compression should always be used. Deploy the two Filters by adding Listing 15-44 to web.xml.

Listing 15-44 Cache and Compression Filter Deployment

```
<filter>
  <filter-name>Cache</filter-name>
  <filter-class>com.jspbook.CacheFilter</filter-class>
  <init-param>
```

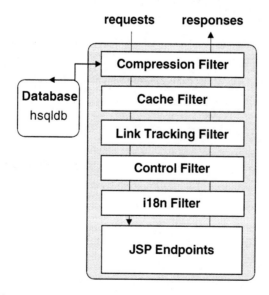

Figure 15-23 Updated Conceptual View of Web Application

```
      <param-name>cacheTimeout</param-name>
      <param-value>1</param-value>
   </init-param>
   <init-param>
      <param-name>locale-sensitive</param-name>
      <param-value>true</param-value>
   </init-param>
</filter>

<filter>
   <filter-name>Compress</filter-name>
   <filter-class>com.jspbook.GZIPFilter</filter-class>
</filter>

<filter-mapping>
   <filter-name>LinkTracker</filter-name>
   <url-pattern>/*</url-pattern>
</filter-mapping>

<filter-mapping>
   <filter-name>Compress</filter-name>
   <url-pattern>*.jsp</url-pattern>
</filter-mapping>

<filter-mapping>
   <filter-name>Cache</filter-name>
   <url-pattern>*.jsp</url-pattern>
</filter-mapping>
```

Next, copy the code for the two Filters and related classes from the `jspbook/WEB-INF/com/jspbook` directory to the `jspbook_site/WEB-INF/com/jspbook` directory (Listings 8-11, 8-12, 8-13, 8-15, 8-16, and 8-17, respectively, from Chapter 8). Finally, reload the Web Application for the two Filters to take effect.

An important point to note is that the cache Filter is still working properly even though we are using localized content. Go ahead and try out the cache Filter by requesting the same resources with different language preferences; you will get the same content as we did previously in the chapter. Recall in Chapter 8 that we based the cache solely off the request URL. This strategy will obviously not work with the Simple i18n Filter; remember the same URL—say, `index.jsp`—may possibly lead to a resource of the same name or a localized resource, such as `index-fra.jsp`. To solve this problem, the cache Filter has the locale-sensitive parameter set.

```
<filter>
 <filter-name>Cache</filter-name>
 <filter-class>com.jspbook.CacheFilter</filter-class>
 <init-param>
   <param-name>cacheTimeout</param-name>
   <param-value>1</param-value>
 </init-param>
 <init-param>
   <param-name>locale-sensitive</param-name>
   <param-value>true</param-value>
 </init-param>
</filter>
```

This parameter was not introduced in Chapter 8 because we had yet to discuss i18n issues, but now the parameter should make sense. You'll recall that the code in the `CacheFilter` class uses the following parameter:

```
// optionally append i18n sensitivity
String localeSensitive = fc.getInitParameter("locale-
sensitive");
 if (localeSensitive != null) {
   StringWriter ldata = new StringWriter();
   Enumeration locales = request.getLocales();
   while (locales.hasMoreElements()) {
     Locale locale = (Locale)locales.nextElement();
     ldata.write(locale.getISO3Language());
   }
   id = id + ldata.toString();
 }
```

The code takes all of the user's preferred languages and uses them to customize the cache. By doing this, the cache is effectively tied to both the URL and the HTTP headers that dictate language preference. Between the two, the cache Filter can successfully cache both non-i18n and i18n content alike, which is exactly what we have it doing. In general, a good cache Filter should allow for several variables to dictate how it manages cached copies of content—for example, the URL and language-preference headers—and allow configuration of these options via initial parameters. This allows the same cache Filter to then be used with most any Web Application by simply configuring a few initial parameters—a helpful Filter indeed.

Don't Cache Always-Dynamic Resources!

There is another huge "gotcha" of using a cache Filter: caching resources that must be dynamic. For simplicity we deployed the cache Filter to intercept all requests to resources ending in .jsp; for practical use this is a mistake. Think of all the resources that must remain dynamic—for instance, the add news component or any of the other components that rely on a client to upload information via an HTML form. If we leave the cache Filter as it is now, all of these resources are broken; the cache Filter occurs before the control Filter.

```
. . .
  <filter-mapping>
    <filter-name>Cache</filter-name>
    <url-pattern>*.jsp</url-pattern>
  </filter-mapping>

  <filter-mapping>
    <filter-name>ControlFilter</filter-name>
    <url-pattern>*.jsp</url-pattern>
  </filter-mapping>
. . .
```

The problem is, when the control logic needs to be executed, it won't. If a cache exists, the cache Filter returns it and prevents any other Filter in the chain from executing. This will prevent the control Filter from ever getting a chance to execute logic components associated with a URL.

What is the solution? Simply putting the cache Filter after the control Filter works, but in a sense defeats the purpose of the cache Filter. Control components can take a relatively long time compared to executing a JSP or Servlet, therefore, it is helpful to cache away this time. There are a few good solutions, which can even be used together if required. The first is to selectively cache only what should be cached. For example, don't deploy the cache Filter to all JSP.

```
  <filter-mapping>
    <filter-name>Cache</filter-name>
    <url-pattern>*.jsp</url-pattern>
  </filter-mapping>
```

Instead, deploy the Filter to only the resources that should always be cached.

```
  <filter-mapping>
    <filter-name>Cache</filter-name>
    <url-pattern>/index.jsp</url-pattern>
  </filter-mapping>
```

```
<filter-mapping>
  <filter-name>Cache</filter-name>
  <url-pattern>/about.jsp</url-pattern>
</filter-mapping>
...
```

This prevents the problem from ever occurring in the first place, but it adds more work when deploying the Filter, especially if there are lots of resources that should be cached by the Web Application.

Another good solution is to deploy the Filter to cache all resources and selectively instruct the Filter to not cache specific resources via initial parameters. Recall the cache Filter from Chapter 8 treats any initial parameter with a name matching a URL to mean "don't cache that URL". This method is excellent for easily deploying the Filter to cache everything, but telling it to ignore one or two things is not so easily done via `filter-mapping` elements.

The final solution is to use two instances of the same Filter in combination with the preceding methods. There are two obvious points that are valid for caching: before execution of the logic component (and implicitly the JSP or Servlet endpoint) or after the logic component but before the endpoint. If the control logic must always be executed—for example, in the case of `addnews.jsp`—you cannot cache before the logic component, but you can cache after it to speed up the time it takes to execute the endpoint (the Servlet or JSP).

If you are trying this chapter's code, it is assumed you will configure the cache Filter to not cache all of the resources that must execute logic components, basically everything in the `/admin` directory or any of the user feedback components. For brevity the modified cache Filter deployment code is not provided, but if you would like to see it, it is available at `http://www.jspbook.com`.

Adding the Egg

A little bit of fun is in order before calling the site complete. As mentioned earlier in the chapter, we are going to put an egg in the book support site. The egg is not malicious, but purely something for fun and an application of techniques learned from previous chapters. For the egg we will add in a page where people are encouraged to upload pictures of the book; this was mentioned in the preface. Given the strange phenomena surrounding yard gnomes and that the cover of this book is a yard gnome, you are encouraged to send in a photo that creatively displays the book or many copies of the book. However, we have yet to provide a method for uploading images. A photo upload page is required.

The egg, like all other components of the site, will be split into a Model 2 logic component and a presentation JSP. The JSP is a simple HTML form for uploading a picture. Save Listing 15-45 as `egg.jsp` in the root directory of the `jspbook_site` Web Application.

Listing 15-45 egg.jsp

```
<p class="h1">Photos of the yard gnome!</p>
<p>You will soon notice pictures appearing in the top right-hand
corner of the Web site. They will be images of people who have read
Servlets and JSP the J2EE Web Tier cleverly placed in the photos.
How did we get them? Simple. Readers sent them in. The rules are
simple. If you have bought and read the book, you can send a photo
in. From then on your photo will randomly appear in the top right-
hand corner of the Web site. It is a silly way of saying thanks for
reading the book.</p>
<p>Why do this? Mainly because it is fun, but in the United States
many people have a tradition of taking a yard gnome with them on
vacations. The gnome then serves as a hidden surprise in all of the
various photos taken during the trip. It can only be guessed as to
how this tradition ever started, but it is likely that normal
vacation photos were just too bland or that many people enjoy being
silly. We figure a normal photo of your workplace is also bland or
that you enjoy being silly. So, send in photos of the gnome.</p>
<p>Note that this is a completely random/arbitrary system. If you
send in a photo of you with the book, we will put it up. Creativity
is encouraged, but if for any reason we do not want to put the photo
up, then it will not be used. This is all in good fun, but it is
important to keep it within the limits of good taste and fun.</p>
<form method="POST" action="upload.jsp" enctype="multipart/form-
data">
  <p>Upload a Picture: <input name="file" type="file"/></p>
  <input type="submit" value="Submit Photo"/>
</form>
<center><image src="${image}"/></center>
```

The page consists of a lot of static text explaining the egg and a simple HTML form. The form is the only thing that merits discussion.

```
<form method="POST" action="upload.jsp" enctype="multipart/form-
data">
<p>Upload a Picture: <input name="file" type="file"/></p>
<input type="submit" value="Submit Photo"/>
</form>
```

The form is almost identical to the HTML form demonstrated in the file upload discussion in Chapter 2. There are three important points: the form is sent to `upload.jsp` (which we'll create later), the form is set to be encoded as `multipart/form-data`, and an input exists for submitting a file. Consult Chapter 2 for further information about the form.

Currently, `upload.jsp` does not exist, but that is where the form is posting its content. The most important reason we have to `upload.jsp` is to create a logic component that can deal with uploaded pictures. The general scheme for handling newly uploaded pictures will be similar to the scheme used for the rest of the site's content. The image will be saved in a special directory (`/images`), and an entry to the site's database will be made with the image set as not visible. It will be assumed that later on a site administrator will verify the image is okay and flag it as visible. Listing 15-46 provides the code for the upload logic component.

Listing 15-46 upload.java

```
package com.jspbook;

import javax.servlet.http.*;
import javax.servlet.*;
import java.io.*;
import java.sql.*;
import javax.sql.*;
import javax.naming.*;
import java.util.Calendar;
import org.apache.commons.fileupload.*;
import java.util.*;

public class upload implements Control {
  public boolean doLogic(HttpServletRequest request,
                         HttpServletResponse response)
  throws ServletException, IOException {
    long ts = Calendar.getInstance().getTimeInMillis();

    ServletContext sc =
      request.getSession().getServletContext();
    String path = sc.getRealPath("/images");
    org.apache.commons.fileupload.FileUpload fu = new
        org.apache.commons.fileupload.FileUpload();
    fu.setSizeMax(-1);
    fu.setRepositoryPath(path);
    try {
      List l = fu.parseRequest(request);
```

```
Iterator i = l.iterator();
while (i.hasNext()) {
  FileItem fi = (FileItem)i.next();
  String postFix = ".unknown";
  String name = fi.getName();
  int lastDot = name.lastIndexOf(".");
  if (lastDot != -1) {
    postFix = fi.getName().
      substring(lastDot, name.length());
  }
  fi.write(path+"/"+ts+postFix);

  // update db
  try {
    InitialContext ctx = new InitialContext();
    DataSource ds =
      (DataSource)ctx.
        lookup("java:comp/env/jdbc/jspbook_site");
    Connection conn = ds.getConnection();
    try {
      Statement statement  = conn.createStatement();
      statement.executeQuery(
       "insert into images values('"+ts+postFix+"', 0)");
    } catch (Exception e) {
      throw new ServletException(e);
    } finally {
      conn.close();
    }
  } catch (SQLException e) {
    throw new ServletException(e);
  }
  catch (NamingException e) {
    throw new ServletException(e);
  }
}
} catch (Exception e) {
  throw new ServletException(e);
}

response.sendRedirect("index.jsp");
return false;
  }
}
```

An `Images` table (which we will soon create) is used to store the names of the images and information about which images are available to show. Later on, this table will be helpful in order to determine which images should be shown by the egg.

Before trying to use the code for `upload.java`, be sure to create the Images table in the site's database. Use `ArbitrarySQLDataSource.jsp` to execute the following SQL statement:

```
CREATE TABLE IMAGES (
   TS VARCHAR PRIMARY KEY,
   VISIBLE BIT
)
```

Before testing the new upload component, ensure Tomcat doesn't throw an exception due to lacking `upload.jsp`. Save Listing 15-47 as `upload.jsp`—a user should never see it.

Listing 15-47 upload.jsp

```
Upload Complete.
```

Test the file upload page by copying the JAR file for the Jakarta Commons FileUpload API to the `jspbook_site` Web Application's `/WEB-INF/lib` directory, compiling the new code, reloading Tomcat, and browsing to `http://127.0.0.1/jspbook_site/egg.jsp`. Select an image file to upload and click on the Submit Photo button. After the file uploads, the index page should be displayed. You can verify the upload worked by browsing the `/images` directory of the `jspbook_site` Web Application. A new image is there with a time-stamp for a name and the same extension of the uploaded image.

By itself, the egg does little. What good are uploaded images if they are not displayed on the Web site? To complement the egg page, we will modify the header to randomly display uploaded images that have been set as visible. In order to accomplish this, we will create a `.tag` file that replaces the static image with a dynamical image. Recall the header displays an image in the top right-hand corner of the Web page.

```
<img src="images/gnome1.jpg" align="right">
```

Normally, this image is a picture of the gnome from the book's cover, but we are going to replace this image with a randomly selected, image from the images uploaded by book readers. The change in the JSP will be minor; we will create a custom tag to replace the HTML image tag. The custom tag needs to query the site's database, pick a random visible image, and generate the HTML for the image tag.

Here is the code for the dynamic image tag. Save Listing 15-48 as `image.tag` in the `/WEB-INF/tags` directory of the `jspbook_site` Web Application.

Listing 15-48   image.tag

```
<%@ tag
import="java.sql.*,javax.sql.*,javax.naming.*,java.text.*,java.util.
*" %>
<%
  LinkedList ll = new LinkedList();
  try {
    InitialContext ctx = new InitialContext();
    DataSource ds =
     (DataSource)ctx.
       lookup("java:comp/env/jdbc/jspbook_site");
    Connection conn = ds.getConnection();
    try {
      Statement statement  = conn.createStatement();
      ResultSet rs = statement.
     executeQuery("select * from images where visible=true");
      ResultSetMetaData rsmd = rs.getMetaData();
      while (rs.next()) { // show results
         ll.add(rs.getString(1));
      }
    } catch (Exception e) {
      throw new ServletException(e);
    } finally {
      conn.close();
    }
  } catch (SQLException e) {
    throw new ServletException(e);
  }
  catch (NamingException e) {
    throw new ServletException(e);
  }
  String image = (String)ll.get((int)(Math.random()*ll.size()));
  request.setAttribute("image", image);
%>
<a href="egg.jsp"><img src="images/${image}" align="right"
border="0"></a>
```

The code for the tag flushes out the previous definition. A linked list is created and populated with all of the visible images.

```
LinkedList ll = new LinkedList();
...
    Statement statement  = conn.createStatement();
    ResultSet rs = statement.
  executeQuery("select * from images where visible=true");
    ResultSetMetaData rsmd = rs.getMetaData();
    while (rs.next()) { // show results
      ll.add(rs.getString(1));
    }
```

Based on how many images are in the linked list, a random image is chosen. The HTML image tag is generated for that image.

```
String image = (String)ll.get((int)(Math.random()*ll.size()));
request.setAttribute("image", image);
%>
<a href="egg.jsp">
<img src="images/${image}" align="right" border="0"></a>
```

Additionally, the image is wrapped by an anchor tag linking back to the egg page.

Test out the new functionality by replacing the static HTML image tag in `prelude.jsp` with the new dynamic image tag. Listing 15-49 shows what the relevant updated section of `prelude.jsp` should look like.

Listing 15-49 Using image.tag with prelude.jsp

```
...
    <img src="http://www.jspbook.com/images/title.jpg"
      align="left" valign="bottom">
    <%@ taglib tagdir="/WEB-INF/tags" prefix="x"%>
    <x:image/>
    <%-- <img src="http://www.jspbook.com/images/gnome1.jpg"
      align="right" valign="bottom">--%>
...
```

Test out the new functionality by browsing to `http://127.0.0.1/jsp-booksite/index.jsp`. Assuming the cache is not being shown, the page will look identical to the older version, but you can now click on the image to see the egg page.

In order to fully test the egg page, you will need to upload more images and toggle them to be visible (via `ArbitrarySQLDataSource.jsp` or perhaps another database edit page similar to `edit.jsp`). This exercise is left up to you; it should be straight-forward given that we have already done something similar for the news, errata, FAQ, and feedback pages. If you really want to see the tag in action, visit the book support site, `http://www.jspbook.com`. You'll notice the image in the top right-hand corner is constantly changing.

Summary

The book is complete. You have learned all about Web Applications, Servlets, JavaServer Pages, JavaBeans, JSP actions, the JSTL, Filters, security, design patterns, internationalization, and database connectivity. Each of the first 14 chapters dealt individually with these topics. This final chapter provided a comprehensive look at all the previous chapters by building an actual Web Application, which is currently used on the World Wide Web.

You should now be able to go out and build complete Web Applications using Servlets and JSPs. Much of the code in this book can be directly recycled, such as the link tracking, caching, and compression Filters, and all of the concepts can be applied to get your job done. Several of the first few chapters provide complete references for Web Application creation, Servlets, JavaServer Pages, and Filters. The last few chapters provide practical design patterns for getting complex tasks done, including creating multi-lingual content, dividing up logic from presentation, and dividing up a Web Application's workload between multiple developers. Overall, the theme of this book has been understanding Servlets and JSPs and breaking down a Web Application into simple, logical components. Now that you know these things, go do your job.

Index

A

O

OFF log level, 200
One-to-many relationships, 594
One-to-one relationships, 594
Operators
    in expression language, 230
    in SELECT, 603
OPTIONS method, 40
OR operator
    in expression language, 230
    in SELECT, 601
org.apache.struts.action.Action class, 496, 499
org.apache.struts.action.ActionForm class,
        496–497
org.apache.struts.action.ActionMapping class, 496
OS X, installing Tomcat on, 15–17
otherwise tag, 249
out action, 239–240
out implicit object, 154–155
"Out of environment space" error, 14–15
OutputStream class, 53

P

p tag, 567
Packages, 20
page directive, 127–128
page-encoding element, 134
page implicit object, 159
Page scope, 154
page tag, 567
page value in scope, 217
PageContext class, 153–154
pageContext implicit object, 153–154
PageCounter$jsp.java Servlet, 121–125
PageCounter.jsp JSP, 120–121
PageCounter2.jsp JSP, 298
PageData class, 330
pageEncoding attribute
    in page, 129, 519–521
    in tag, 292
pageScope implicit object, 228
paragraph tag, 567
param action, 139–143
param implicit object, 228–229
param-name element, 47, 50
param tag, 252–253, 538
param-value element, 47, 50
Parameters
    in functions, 231
    for HttpServletRequest forms, 67–72
params action, 139–143
paramValues implicit object, 229

Parentheses () in expression language, 231
parseRequest method, 87
Passivated sessions, 408
Passwords
    in digest authentication, 436
    in role-based security, 429–430
Path mapping, 45
PDF format
    FOP framework for, 587–588
    for HelloWorld.jsp, 568–569
Percent signs (%) for scriptlets, 117
perform method
    in Action, 496
    in ActionForward, 500
    in AddNewsAction, 503–504
    in BlankAction, 497
    in IndexAction, 498–499, 502
Performance with logging, 208–210
Persistent state, 411–412
    databases for, 413–414
    session smearing for, 412–413
Persisting language information, 526
Persisting sessions, 407–409
plugin action, 139–143
Plus signs (+) in expression language, 230
Pooling
    in CGI, 3
    connections, 633–634
Populating request-scope variables, 665
Portability, custom tags for, 260
Ports for Tomcat, 17–18
POST requests, 39–40, 428
PostgreSQL, 594
Pound signs (#), 517
Pragma field, 58
Pre-built Control component, 507
prefix attribute, 537–538
prelude_fr.properties file, 707–708
prelude_ja.properties file, 710
prelude.jsp JSP
    for headers and footers, 689–691
    image.tag with, 732
    updated, 705–707
Premaster keys, 446
Prepared statements, 635–637
PreparedStatement interface, 635–637
prepareStatement method, 635–636
Presentation
    for book support site, 687–688
        about page, 697–699
        Cascading Style Sheets for, 693–695
        code page, 699
        errata page, 700–701
        errata suggested by users, 701–702
        FAQ pages and feedback pages, 702–703

webapps directory, 492
webapps/struts-documentation.war file, 492
welcome file, 23–24
welcome_en.properties file, 535
welcome-file-list element, 46
welcome.fr.properties file, 536–537
welcome-fra.html file, 527–528
welcome.html file, 527–528, 530–532
Welcome.java Servlet, 535
welcome.jsp JSP, 532–534, 536–537
when tag, 249
WHERE clause, 601–602
Whitespace
    in directives, 126
    in JSP, 145–147
Widgets, actions for, 511–512
width attribute, 140
Windows
    installing J2SE 1.4 on, 7
    installing Tomcat on, 9
Windows Installation Wizard, 9–14
work directory, 113
Workload distribution, 656–657
Wrappers, 352
    request, 353–357
    response
        cache filters, 371–387
        compression filters, 357–371
write method
    in CacheResponseStream, 381
    in GZIPResponseStream, 363–364
    in PrintWriter, 52

writeObject method
    in Serializable, 412
    in Serialization, 408
writeOut method, 323
WWW-Authenticate headers, 434–437

X

X.509 certificates, 446
X509Certificate class, 451
XHTML
    HelloWorld.jsp in, 568
    Model 2 presentation in, 556–557
XML manipulation in JSTL, 236, 255–256
XML namespaces, 271
XML syntax
    directives in, 164–165
    and JSP, 116–117, 159–165, 271
    rules in, 162
    scripting elements in, 163–164
    template text encapsulation in, 165
XMLComment.jsp JSP, 148–149
XMLFormatter class, 198
XSLT (Extensible Stylesheet Language
            Transformations), 387–388

Z

zip utility, 26